SYLLOGE OF COINS
OF THE BRITISH ISLES

47

SYLLOGE OF COINS
OF THE BRITISH ISLES

A British Academy Research Project

The British Sylloge project was first promoted in the early 1950s by Christopher Blunt and other members of the British and Royal Numismatic Societies. An informal committee was formed under the chairmanship of Sir Frank Stenton, who in 1956 secured its admission as a Committee of the British Academy. The first volume, on Anglo-Saxon coins in the Fitzwilliam Museum, Cambridge, was published by the British Academy in 1958, since when more than forty-five volumes have appeared.

The aim of the series is to publish detailed and fully illustrated catalogues of coins of the British Isles in British and foreign collections. The volumes range in scope from Ancient British coins to seventeenth-century tokens, with most detailed coverage of the Anglo-Saxon coinage. The collections recorded include those of national, university and provincial museums in Britain and Ireland and of museums in Scandinavia, Germany, Poland, Latvia and the United States of America.

Chairmen of the Sylloge Committee:
Sir Frank Stenton, F.B.A. (1956–66)
Professor Dorothy Whitelock, C.B.E., F.B.A. (1966–79)
Professor H. R. Loyn, F.B.A. (1979–93)
Lord Stewartby, P.C., F.B.A. (1993–)

General Editors:
C. E. Blunt, O.B.E., F.B.A. (1956–87)
Professor M. Dolley, M.R.I.A. (1956–83)
Dr M. A. S. Blackburn (1980–)

The present members of the Sylloge Committee are:
Miss M. M. Archibald
Dr M. A. S. Blackburn (*General Editor and Secretary*)
Professor N. P. Brooks, F.B.A.
Professor P. Grierson, F.B.A.
Dr S. D. Keynes
Professor H. R. Loyn, F.B.A.
C. S. S. Lyon
Dr D. M. Metcalf
H. E. Pagan
Dr Veronica Smart
Lord Stewartby, P.C., F.B.A. (*Chairman*)

A full listing of the series is printed at the end of this volume.

SYLLOGE OF COINS OF THE BRITISH ISLES

47

HERBERT SCHNEIDER COLLECTION

Part I

English Gold Coins and their Imitations

1257–1603

BY

PETER WOODHEAD

LONDON

PUBLISHED BY SPINK & SON LIMITED

1996

© P. WOODHEAD 1996

PUBLISHED BY SPINK & SON LIMITED
LONDON
1996

ISBN 0 907605 66 4

Typeset from the author's discs by Columns Design and Production Services Ltd, Reading
Printed in Great Britain on Fineblade Smooth 130 gsm acid free paper
at the University Press, Cambridge

CONTENTS

LIST OF TABLES AND FIGURES

The English gold coinage, 1257–1603.

HERBERT SCHNEIDER

PREFACE

The Schneider collection is without doubt the largest and most complete collection of English gold coins in private hands. Initially formed by one man with clear collecting policies, coupled to a profound scholarly knowledge of the coins and their economic significance, it provides a detailed and coherent view of the development of the series by reference to the finest possible specimens that could be obtained. It is thus entirely appropriate that the collection should be published in the Sylloge of Coins of the British Isles series.

In the first chapter Douglas Liddell provides us with a personal reminiscence of Herbert Schneider and outlines the history of the formation of the collection and its continuing growth. What Mr Liddell's modesty prevents him from saying is that the credit for the idea of making the Schneider collection the subject of a volume in the Sylloge of Coins of the British Isles series belongs to himself. He first raised it in conversation with Herbert Schneider's sons, Edward and John in 1986. Mr Schneider was already ailing at the time and it was decided that it would be best to explore the possibility a little before raising it with him. With the Schneider family's support Douglas Liddell contacted the late Christopher Blunt, who at that time was general editor of the Sylloge series, and who was warmly encouraging. The matter was then put to Mr Schneider who accepted the suggestion with alacrity. Following a further meeting, at which Mr Schneider, Mr Liddell and Mr Blunt were all present, the idea was formally laid before the Sylloge Committee who at their meeting on 6 November 1986 expressed their formal approval.

At first it was intended that the Sylloge should be prepared by Douglas Liddell himself, but it became evident that his other commitments made this impracticable, and in 1989 the present writer was approached. As work got under way it soon became apparent that there was too much material for a single volume and that, for the English material, two volumes would be required with a break at the end of the reign of Elizabeth I.

To some extent this Sylloge has written itself, as indeed a catalogue of any soundly assembled collection should. Mr Schneider chose the coins for his collection with care and purpose, and in certain series, as may be seen, he evidently aimed to collect by dies. His informative tickets contain many interesting comments and insights and were of the greatest value in preparing the Sylloge. No acknowledgement, then, can be more important than that to Herbert Schneider himself, who created the collection to which the writer has tried to do justice. Thanks are also due to the Schneider family, to Douglas Liddell and to Patrick Finn, who had the confidence to entrust the most rewarding task of preparing this Sylloge to me.

Coins of any sort are, of course, the consequence of economic demand. Guaranteed by the state as to their metal content, their denominations reflecting trading needs, they illuminate and can themselves be illuminated by their economic and historical content. The opportunity to study a collection of English gold coins of this extent and quality has led me to write an introduction in which I try, perhaps rather ambitiously, but I hope with some measure of success, to underline these aspects. After all, gold coins are not just pretty faces; they were very utilitarian objects indeed! In taking this approach I have drawn heavily on, and gladly acknowledge, the published work of others. These may be seen from bibliography (pp. 132–40) but certainly without Christopher Challis's publications on the Tudor mint and the collaborative volume he edited, *A New History of the Royal Mint*, this aspect of the book would have been much weaker.

I count myself especially fortunate to have found nothing but generous co-operation and advice from those who are acknowledged experts on the various series covered in this book. I should particularly like to thank: Peter Mitchell, who took a lot of trouble to help me get the coins of Edward III into the correct order, particularly those of the post-treaty period; Tim Webb Ware, who has been generous with his wide knowledge of medieval gold coins and has allowed me to make use of work on the coinages of Richard II, Richard III and Henry VII which he had spoken about to the British Numismatic Society but which has yet to appear in print; Christopher Challis, who read an early draft of the Introduction and who provided much useful advice on the Tudor period in particular; Joe Bispham, who led me to an understanding that his work on the shillings of Edward VI could be used to help elucidate the gold; and Chris Comber, whose advice on the coinage of Elizabeth I in the light of his recent work with I. D. Brown was most helpful, and who helped me to confirm my own ideas on the coinage of Philip and Mary. There are many others who have helped with tasks, information and advice at various stages. Amongst these I owe thanks to Marion Archibald, Barry Cook, Robin Cooch, Cor de Graaf, G. P. Holloway, Nick Mayhew, Hugh Pagan, May Sinclair, and Peter Spufford. Notwithstanding all this generous help the faults of this book are my responsibility alone.

On the production aspects, I should like to acknowledge the painstaking work of Frank Purvey who photographed the coins directly using the Polaroid process, in many cases taking numerous exposures to ensure the best possible result and match. I owe special thanks to Mark Blackburn, who as general editor of the Sylloge series has been a wise counsellor, and has steered me patiently and courteously past many solecisms guiding me towards producing what is, hopefully, an accurate manuscript on disc for the printer. Finally, but by no means least, I owe thanks to Douglas Saville for all the trouble he has taken to arrange printing and publication.

Peter Woodhead   *September 1995*
Daglingworth

HERBERT SCHNEIDER
AND THE DEVELOPMENT
OF THE COLLECTION

by Douglas Liddell

Herbert Schneider was born on 27 April 1914 at Brunswick in Germany. His father was an opthalmic surgeon who came from an Anglo-Hanoverian family of cotton merchants and industrialists. His mother was Belgian from a prominent Antwerp family with interests in tobacco manufacturing in Manila and Hong Kong. The family was of British nationality and their cotton interests took them continually between Germany, Manchester in England, Riga in Latvia and St Petersburg in Russia.[1]

When Herbert was about 16 years old the family moved to Zurich, being disquieted by the political evolution in Germany in the early nineteen thirties. In Zurich he continued his studies and at that time was much influenced by Professor Meunier, who helped considerably to develop his interest in history. He was much above average intelligence and showed a keen interest in the arts. He already spoke fluent English, French and German: later he added Flemish and some understanding of Spanish and Italian. He was also a keen and talented tennis player.

After completing his studies he went to Antwerp as a partner in the firm of his grandfather, Werner Davidis. He was to spend the whole of his professional career with the Davidis-Ingenohl group, which had trading and petro-chemical interests in Belgium, the Netherlands, Germany and France, and made a considerable contibution to its development. Herbert Schneider became Davidis's closest and most trusted associate and a relationship developed that was a combination father/son, partner and close friend.

Having obtained a thorough knowledge of the business, Herbert came to London to obtain a knowledge of the Stock Market by training with a leading firm of stockbrokers, Williamson, Fawcett and Sterling. It had been originally intended that he should go to Cambridge to read politics, philosophy and economics and he had ambitions to enter journalism, but at the end of his period with Williamson, Fawcett and Sterling, he was summoned back to Antwerp to take charge of the family interests. Again in the family group he was soon given important responsibilities. At that time he was still a bachelor, but in the late 1930s he met Ines Fuhrmann, the daughter of a notable Antwerp wool family, and they were on the point of becoming engaged when war broke out in 1939.

---

[1] Unavoidably this memoir repeats some of the information that was included in my obituaries of Herbert Schneider published in *NCirc* (Liddell 1989a) and *BNJ* (Liddell 1989b).

Herbert immediately volunteered for service in the British army. With his cosmopolitan background and linguistic abilities he was well suited for a number of special services. He was always very reticent in talking about these, but it is known that he was engaged in several undercover operations, some with the Special Operations Executive. After the war he served in Rome and then in Vienna, where he was involved in the restoration of democratic press and broadcasting facilities, and was not demobilised until 1947. He then resumed his responsibilities in the family business and some years later became, in addition, a non-executive director of the merchant banking subsidiary, Kleinworth Benson Europe. He married Ines Fuhrmann in 1947 after an enforced separation of seven years because of the war, and they had three children, Edward (born 1951), John (born 1953) and Isabel (born 1956).

Herbert Schneider continued to live in Antwerp until his death on 6 January 1989 at the age of 74.

The collection

Prompted by his interest in history, Herbert Schneider had started to collect coins as a schoolboy and by the early 1930s he was focusing his interest on medieval gold coins, particularly of the Low Countries, the Hanseatic states and England. One may see in this two strands of his personal interests: the interwoven economic history of those countries, through their textile trade during the middle ages, and the handsome gothic artistry of the gold coins of the period. In 1937 he started to add English milled gold and by 1939 he had already formed a significant collection, which was held in London for safe-keeping during the war.

Following Herbert's demobilisation in 1947 he resumed active collecting and by then English gold had become his first priority, although he retained his interest in coins of the Low Countries and added to it from time to time. At first, and for many years, he limited his collection to the issues of the London and Calais mints; later he added royalist Oxford. During his lifetime very few coins of other provincial mints were added to the collection. He was, above all, interested in currency issues and acquired very few pattern or proof coins.

The early post-war years saw the dispersion of some important collections and Herbert took full advantage of the opportunities offered. Undoubtedly the largest single source was Lockett, but others of importance were Raynes, Ryan, Lingford and Carter, and for milled coins, Hewitt and Le Mare. Later the Hird, Norweb and Beresford-Jones sales made significant contributions. Many of his acquisitions, however, were single items appearing in anonymous sales in Britain or on the Continent, and a review of the list of provenances (pp. 117–25) shows how diverse his sources were.

Most of Herbert's purchases were made from, or through the agency of, Spink and Son Ltd or A. H. Baldwin and Sons Ltd. We first met in 1947, soon after I joined Spink and he and I became close friends, as he also did with Albert Baldwin and Peter Mitchell at Baldwins. He would refer to the two firms collectively as 'Spaldwinks', engaging with both in voluminous and witty correspondence which at times required no little skill to decipher. He was ever a humourous, constant friend.

Herbert Schneider had a keen eye for quality and a very high proportion of the coins are in excellent condition. He would frequently acquire better specimens to replace those that did not meet his high standards, and several collections, public and private, have reason to be grateful for the generousity which he showed in disposing of his duplicates. From the student's point of view there are great advantages in quality, particularly in being able to see what is on the coins with a minimum of ambiguities. This is especially the case when, as in the first volume, one is dealing with medieval coins.

Herbert was a Fellow of the Royal Numismatic Society and, since 1944, a member of the British Numismatic Society of which he had become a Vice-President in 1968. He contributed a number of important papers to the *British Numismatic Journal*, of which his work on the Tower Gold of Charles I published in instalments between 1957 and 1961, his paper on the hammered gold of Charles II published in 1967, and his publication of the Angers hoard in 1968, are perhaps the most important.[2] His publications brought him the award of the Sanford Saltus Gold Medal in 1965. He endowed the British Numismatic Society with a Research Fund in 1967.

Although, by the time of his death, the collection of English gold was the most complete in private hands, it lacked coins of provincial mints as well as a number of rarities which had eluded Herbert over the years, or which had simply never been available for him to acquire. During Herbert's lifetime the collection was placed in the legal ownership of a trust and, after his death, the Schneider family decided that the collection should be kept intact and should continue to be augmented when suitable opportunities occured. There have been some notable additions in the last few years: these have included a number of coins of provincial mints and some rarities including a Richard III angel, a Henry VIII crown of the (single) rose, the unique half-George noble with i.m. lis (a recent detector find), and an Edward VI double-sovereign. Another recent addition has been a group of fifteen Richard II gold rarities from Mr Mygind's collection which makes the Schneider collection, already strong in that reign, now outstandingly so. These, and other less sensational but still important additions, have continued Herbert Schneider's collecting policies. The Schneider family have also extended the scope of the collection into two new fields, Anglo-Gallic gold where they made a strong start by making purchases from the Elias and Beresford-Jones collections; and Anglo-Hanoverian gold, a series particularly appropriate to Herbert Schneider's family background. It is planned that, in due course, these, too, will be published in Sylloge format.

Douglas Liddell   *November 1995*

---

[2]   For a list of Mr Schneider's numismatic publications see Woodhead 1989.

THE ENGLISH GOLD COINAGE 1257–1603

IN the period covered by this volume, gold coins, with their high intrinsic value, would have been little used by ordinary people for day to day purposes. Such people may, indeed, have concentrated their resources into gold for major transactions or for savings purposes, but it would have been the wealthy and powerful who would have used gold for high value purchases, such as personal luxuries, land and buildings, and, no doubt, paying taxes to the Crown. The Crown itself used gold coin for buying supplies in bulk, for political and diplomatic payments, and for donations and benefactions. Documentary money (i.e. bills of exchange), though progressively more used from the thirteenth century onwards, was neither universal nor freely acceptable outside major commercial centres. Gold coin was, above all, used for trade and commerce, particularly where large settlements were involved.

The larger English denominations, nobles, ryals, angels, and sovereigns, are all particularly handsome, broad pieces whose designs reflect the dignity and power of the Crown and underline the contemporary view of its spiritual sanction. As such, they can be appreciated as impressive artefacts of the late medieval and early modern periods. However, they and their fractions are witnesses to more than artistic taste; they are important sources of historical evidence. When studied in conjunction with the surviving documentation, their designs, their nominal value in terms of silver coin, their weights and finenesses, and the proportion of different varieties that survive can all shed light on aspects of the economy, trade, politics and administration of their day.

The extent and high quality of the Schneider collection makes it an ideal source for such interpretive work and the purpose of this introduction is to provide a framework of information to assist the reader to an understanding of the coins in their historical context, and, through references, to help those who are interested towards further study. Each reign is reviewed under the following headings:

Background	– the general historical and economic background.
Issues	– information on the different phases of coinage in the reign.
Mints	– mints in operation during the reign.
Conditions	– principal terms of contracts for each issue (when known).
References	– the more important and current references pertaining to the gold coinage of the reign,
Classification	– the classification(s) used in describing and placing in order the coins in the Sylloge.

Output   – output from each mint, based on contemporary documentary
                                evidence (when available), with notes on sources of bullion
                                and correlation with classification.

It is not possible to present a uniform coverage of all reigns since the majority have
been studied to different degrees in different ways by different scholars. In a few cases,
where there have been no recent studies in depth, an attempt has been made to fill
the gap, at least to the extent of trying to give a reasonable account of the surviving
material.

HENRY III (28 October 1216–16 November 1272)

Background

In the thirteenth century gold coinage was not used as currency in England, or, indeed,
in Europe north of the Alps. Gold carried across the Sahara from west Africa was made
into coin in north Africa and in that part of Spain under Moorish rule or influence. Sicily
and south Italy used a gold coinage resulting from their trade with north Africa. Some
gold moved west and north from the Byzantine empire and the near east. However there
was as yet no demand for gold from any of these sources to be recoined to fit into the
structures of north-west European coinage or moneys of account. During the twelfth
and thirteenth centuries gold was increasingly drawn into the expanding Western
European economies but it was not until the mid-thirteenth century that there was sufficient gold available, and sufficient demand for gold coin for trading purposes, for it to
commence to be struck in central and north Italy. This was in Florence and Genoa
respectively. These were shortly followed by Lucca and, in 1284, by Venice. In
England, it was to be well into the fourteenth century before gold coins would become
an established part of the currency.[1]

Kings always had need for gold, however—large amounts, from time to time, for
foreign enterprises; a steady supply, all the time, to maintain their status and dignity.
The former could include such things as dowries, the purchase of allies and the financ-
ing of wars. The latter might include the purchase of luxurious objects, the giving of
political presents and prestigious alms-giving. Henry III acquired gold for all these ends
and, when circumstances permitted, accumulated large amounts.[2] The gold could take
the physical form of strips or coins. The latter might be besants (Byzantine or Nicean
hyperpera), *oboles* or *dinars de Musc'* (dinars or double dinars of the Almohad rulers
of Spain or north Africa)[3] and, to a lesser degree, other coins including at least a few of
the *augustales* struck for the emperor Frederick II in Sicily in 1231.[4]

---

[1] The summary in this paragraph is largely derived from Spufford 1988, 163–86.
[2] Carpenter 1986 and 1987.
[3] Grierson 1951. Carpenter 1987 notes that they were also sometimes described as *Oboli de Murc'* and attributes those
     to the Almohad, Spanish, city of Murcia (surrendered to the Castilians in 1243).
[4] Among coins transfered from Gascony in 1254. *CPR*, 1247–58, 314.–1–85. Carpenter 1986 and 1987.

Issue

It is not known for sure what prompted Henry III to strike a pure gold coinage in his own name in the late summer of 1257. It seems likely that most of the issue was struck from gold accumulated over a period of time by the king.[5] Carpenter has suggested three possible reasons:[6]

1. Creation of a prestigious coinage for use on a proposed expedition to place his second son, Edmund, on the Sicilian throne. This is perhaps unlikely because Sicilian and south Italian coins, including the *augustales*, were made from $20\frac{1}{2}$ ct gold; it is also evident that the gold pennies were put into circulation in England.
2. Enhancement of value by converting gold reserves into coin of a fixed value in terms of silver. A possible motive for this at the time was Henry's need for finance for a campaign in Wales. This seems to be a more likely reason than the last.
3. Prospect of profit from coinage charges if merchants and traders could be persuaded to bring gold to the mint to be converted into the new coins. If this was so, it seems to have been a wrong view, as events were to show.

Henry seems to have been fascinated by gold,[7] and to the above suggestions may be added the possibility that the news of the new, pure gold coinages of Genoa and Florence and the sight of the splendid *augustales* may have made him feel that instead of having to use foreign coins of varying fineness with, to most inhabitants of England, incomprehensible designs and legends, the time had come for his dignity to be enhanced through the means of a fine national coinage.

Mint

London is the only mint at which we know that the coins were struck and it is highly unlikely that they were produced elsewhere. All extant specimens name as moneyer William of Gloucester, the king's goldsmith, who was effectively in control of the London and Canterbury mints and exchanges between 1257 and 1262.[8]

Conditions

No records are known that give the precise terms under which the coins were struck. The only official record concerning the introduction of the gold penny is a Close Roll entry of a command to the mayor and sheriffs of London dated 16 August 1257 requiring them to proclaim that the gold money of the king should be current in the city, as elsewhere in England, at 20 sterling pennies.[9] In addition to this there is a contemporary

---

[5] Carpenter 1986 and 1987.
[6] Carpenter 1987.
[7] Carpenter 1987.
[8] Mayhew 1992, 116.
[9] *CCR* A.41. Henry III, 88. The Latin text is printed in Evans 1900, which also includes a translation into English.

chronicle[10] which, under 1257, confirms that in that year the king created a gold penny weighing two sterlings and valued at 20 sterlings. The same chronicle later in the same year (November) records a meeting between the king and the mayor and citizens of London at the Exchequer at which they told him:

1. that the coin was harmful, especially to the poor. This, presumably, referred to the cost of converting a gold penny into more convenient, smaller coin.
2. that the wide dispersion of the new coin had led to a drop in the price of gold. This, presumably, was the effect of the release of a large amount of gold, previously hoarded, on to the market.

The king's reply only dealt with the first point. He said that no-one should be compelled to take the coin, but that those who had taken it should be able to exchange it without loss. Alternatively, it could be brought to the king's exchange and exchanged for $19\frac{1}{2}$ pence.

In spite of the statement in the contemporary chronicle, it is a fact that all seven known gold pennies weigh slightly more than two pennyweights (2.893g).[11] One has been pierced and plugged and weighs 2.91 g. The remaining six, including the Schneider specimen, are all sound and average a weight of 2.95 g (this is also the modal weight). The theoretical weight of two sterlings is thus about 2% less.[12] Our source of information that the gold pennies were made of 'pure' gold and weighed two pennyweights is, of course, not an official document and thus may represent a general belief and/or a near approximation. Another possible explanation of the difference could be that the coins were to contain two pennyweights of pure gold plus a small amount of alloy to make them harder.[13]

In the hope of resolving this enigma and with the kind co-operation of the British Museum Department of Scientific Research,[14] it was possible to subject five of the seven known gold pennies[15] to two different forms of non-destructive analysis, using X-Ray fluorescence (XRF) and specific gravity measurements. The full text of the report will be found in Appendix 1 below (pp. 78–9). Its conclusions are:

1. That the fineness of the gold pennies is approximately 0.988 (say, 23ct 3gr.).
2. That that is about 1.2% less fine than could have been obtained at that date by rigorous refining.

---

[10] *Cronica Maiorum et Vicecomitum Londoniarum.*

[11] Weights, illustrations and other particulars of the six specimens then known are very usefully set out in Norweb 1. The weight of the seventh specimen is 2.93 gr.

[12] Sterling short- and long-cross pennies were struck at 242 to the Tower pound of 5,400 grains = 22.31 gr. per coin or 1.446 g. See Mayhew 1992.

[13] A suggestion made by the late Dr J. D. Brand. See Carpenter 1987.

[14] I should like to acknowledge the help of Dr Barrie Cook in arranging this.

[15] These were the three specimens in the British Museum collection, the Schneider specimen (**1**), and the Lockett specimen (lot 1196) that was about to be offered in Spink Auction 97 (lot 1) on 13 May 1993.

3. The results, therefore, cannot confirm that the gold was deliberately debased or that any such action could account for the slightly high weights.

It is of interest to note that the fineness of 0.988 is only a little less (0.7%) than the fineness formally adopted for the English gold coinage in the fourteenth century (0.995) and that there is evidence that suggests that at the latter date the expression 'fine' gold and the fineness of 0.995 meant the same thing.[16] Despite the statement in the chronicle it seems likely that the theoretical weight of the gold pennies was intended to be more than the theoretical weight of two sterlings and that the weights chosen would rightly and reasonably have been the result of a carefully judged assessment of the gold/silver ratio at the date of issue. Undoubtedly a gold/silver ratio in the neighbourhood of 1:10 was usual in the mid-thirteenth century, though with considerable variations from time to time in response to local conditions of supply and demand,[17] see examples in Table 1.

From this it will be seen that the gold pennies were, if anything, undervalued when they were introduced. The revaluation to 24 pence in about 1265 fits in with the appreciation in the value of gold in the second half of the century, already refered to.[18]

TABLE 1. *Gold/silver ratios in the mid-thirteenth century*

Year	Coin	Wt	Fineness	'Pure' gold content	Value in sterlings	Wt of sterlings[3]	'Pure' silver content	Gold/Silver ratio
1244	Obole de Musc'[1]	2.25 g	20½ ct (0.854)	1.92 g	15	21.69 g	20.06 g	1 : 10.45
1245	Obole de Musc'[1]	2.30 g	20½ (0.854)	1.96 g	16	23.14 g	21.40 g	1 : 10.92
1257	Gold penny	2.95 g	0.988[2]	2.91 g	20	28.92 g	26.75 g	1 : 9.19
1265	Gold penny	2.95 g	0.988[2]	2.91 g	24	34.70 g	32.09 g	1 : 11.03

Notes: 1. Weights and finenesses of two examples cited in Grierson 1951.
2. Finenesses from British Museum lab. report see Appendix 1.
3. Sterling short- and long-cross pennies were struck at 242 to the pound of 5,400 gr. = 22.31 gr. per coin or 1.446 g.

References and Classification

The specialised references used for classifying these coins are those of Lawrence[19] who divided the coins into four types (essentially the four different die pairings) and Sir John

---

[16] The statement that the fineness of gold coin should be 23 ct 3½ gr. (0.995 fine) first appears in the indenture of 27 January 1349. The previous indentures of 14 December 1343, 9 July 1344 and 28 July 1346 simply specified 'fine' gold. A comparison of the net receipt and gold/silver ratios for 1346 and 1349 (see Table 2) suggests that, although the 1349 indenture specifies fineness more precisely than before, there was no actual change at that date.

[17] Spufford 1988, 272.

[18] Spufford 1988, 272.

[19] Lawrence 1912.

Evans[20] who listed the (six) specimens known to him and who dealt more fully than Lawrence with the documentary record. Pedigrees of six of the seven known coins are conveniently set out in the Norweb 1 sale catalogue.[21] There is no certain record of any hoard containing gold pennies of Henry III nor, indeed, of any isolated finds. Two of the seven known pieces are reputed to have been acquired in Italy,[22] perhaps a reflection of the use of these coins for religious donations or a consequence of the sale of many of them on the Continent.[23]

Output

Although documentary records exist for output of silver coins at the period,[24] nothing has yet come to light for the gold. There is no evidence as to whether the coins were struck after the year 1257. From the extant specimens we know that at least four different pairs of dies were used. There are records relating to payments made in gold pennies.[25]

EDWARD III (25 January 1327–21 June 1377)

Background

Following the introduction of gold coinages at Florence and Genoa in 1252, the use of fine gold coin began to spread beyond the bounds of Italy and, particularly, into France. The gold coin of Florence, the florin containing 3.54 g of pure gold, in time came to be used as an international trading currency throughout Western Europe. The gold coinages of Genoa and, later, Venice, although they circulated in Italy, had their main external influence at a later date, particularly in the Levant.

In 1290 Philip IV of France introduced his *petit royal d'or* of the same weight and fineness as the florin and in 1296 this was followed by his *masse d'or* (*masse* = the mace held by the king) equal in weight to two florins, but a little less fine. Although at first the circulation was modest, they were the start of a continuous and, eventually abundant, French gold coinage. The earlier *écu d'or* of Louis IX of *c.*1270 had failed just as had the gold penny of Henry III: at those dates there had been insufficient demand for such coins for trading purposes.

It was the discovery and exploitation from about 1320 onwards of the large gold deposits at Kremnica in the (then) Hungarian province of Slovakia that gave a major impetus towards the use of gold currency throughout Western Europe. At first exported

---

[20] Evans 1900.
[21] Norweb 1, lot 122.
[22] Norweb 1, lot 122.
[23] Carpenter 1987, 112, f. 30.
[24] Blunt and Brand 1970.
[25] The numbers struck cannot have been insignificant, see Carpenter 1987, 112, which records transactions involving some thousands of the coins.

to Italy and coined there, from 1328 it was struck into florins in Hungary itself. Gold florins were soon extensively copied in other lands.

The first decade of the fourteenth century saw England with an abundant silver coinage, but after about 1310 output declined and coin became progressively more scarce. The reasons for this were, in the first place, purely national; a consequence of reduced receipts from wool sales due to trading problems with Flanders.[26] In the second place, the early effects of the European silver shortage, that was to worsen progressively and persist to the end of the middle ages, began to make themselves felt.[27] The period starting about 1330 saw a progressive decline in the amount of silver available for coinage relative to demand.[28] New sources of silver were no longer being found and technology had not yet progressed to a stage which permitted further exploitation of old mines.

In a society where coin was still by far the most important form of money, and where the value of coin depended primarily on its precious metal content, the possession of coin was a government's principal means of exerting control and effecting its plans and decisions, including the waging of war. Governments might, if they were fortunate, obtain coin from newly mined metal; most relied, above all, on taxes, duties and occasional levies (loans were usually secured on the future yields of some or all of these). The intrinsic value, the precious metal content, was vital to this system and was closely controlled by each government through its mints. As the want of silver for coins grew throughout Europe, the natural consequence was that governments, acting through their mints, progressively bid more for it. In practice this was done by offering an improved mint price to those who brought silver to the exchange for conversion into the national coin. Up to a point this might be done by reducing mintage charges, but all rulers regarded their mints as a source of profit[29] and, once those charges had been reduced to an acceptable minimum, there was no alternative to reducing the amount of silver in the coinage, either by reduction of weight or of fineness or both.

There was a reluctance to reduce either weight or fineness in England. One consequence was that no one brought silver to be coined. Another was that silver was drawn out of the country[30] in spite of attempts to stop that.[31] A rather half-hearted attempt to meet the problem and to improve the amount of silver coin in circulation was tried in 1335 by slightly reducing both weight and fineness of halfpence and farthings. These circulated alongside the existing, mostly 15–25 year-old silver coinage without driving

[26] Lloyd 1977, 108–14 and T.12.

[27] See Spufford 1988, Ch. 12 for an analysis of developments at this period.

[28] Mayhew 1992, 143; but it must be emphasized that bullion could always be obtained if the right price could be offered.

[29] Munro 1972, 22.

[30] Mate 1978, 127.

[31] In 1279 (Statute of Stepney) and 1335 (SR.I,23).

it out—an indication of the state to which the coin that was left in the country had declined.[32]

The commencement of the Hundred Years War in 1337 exacerbated this situation. The king needed a lot of money, both to pay his armies, and to secure the support of his allies. He obtained this in three ways: through taxation, by effectively pre-empting on the Continent a large part of the silver receipts from the sale of wool,[33] and by borrowing.[34] The first of these is likely, in some degree, to have removed more silver coin from circulation; the second prevented fresh silver being received for coinage purposes; and the third could mean that money was transferred from a Continental lender to a Continental beneficiary without entering England at all, even though repayment of principal and interest had to come from England. There seems little doubt that some of the loss of silver in circulation was replaced by foreign gold and there are records of Continental florins and French gold coins in use for making large payments or for storing wealth.[35] The king's borrowings included huge amounts in gold from Florentine bankers for subventions to allies, as also did similar borrowings by the king of France, and although the initial recipients were outside England, by these means much gold was brought into north-western Europe.[36] Later in the reign English military successes brought some returns for all this expenditure, of which the outstanding example was the ransom of £500,000 agreed for John the Good, the French king, captured at the battle of Poitiers (1359). The recoinage of the gold *francs à cheval*, in which instalments of this were paid, will have brought work to the mint in the 1360s.[37]

In March 1343 a three-year truce was signed with France and attempts could be made to improve the English economy, including the amount and quality of the currency. In doing this the weight of the silver penny was reduced, thus recognising the real value of silver, and a gold coinage was introduced, for which a demand now existed.[38]

Issues

The first two coinages of Edward III's reign were of silver only. The first gold issues were thus part of the third coinage (1344–51). They are characterised by a degree of experimentation during which differing levels of coinage charges and gold/silver ratio

---

[32] Woodhead 1989a. Nine years later, in 1344, the deterioration of the extant silver currency, the greater part of it struck 30 or 40 years before at the rate of 243 pence to the pound, is reflected in the weight chosen for the new coinage of 270 pence to the pound. The indenture specifically directs that the new silver coins should be struck 'at the weight of the sterlings current in the land' (*CCR* 1343–6, 261–2), and currency-type hoards of sterlings deposited in the 1330s and 40s confirm that this was about right.

[33] Lloyd 1977, 144.

[34] Spufford 1988, 277–8.

[35] Mate 1978, 127.

[36] Spufford 1988, 278.

[37] McKisack 1959, 225, says that Edward III received £268,000 on account of the ransoms of the king of France, the king of Scotland and the duke of Burgundy during this period.

[38] The demand for gold coin was above all for large scale trade, particularly that of an external nature.

TABLE 2. *Changes in coinage charges, mint price and gold/silver ratios under Edward III and Richard II (source: data from mint indentures cited in Challis 1992b)*

	Gold coinage					Gold/silver ratios			
Date	Face value to be struck from one Twr lb	Acct. for by Warden	Master moneyer	Total deductions	Net receipt (mint price)	Pure gold value of one Twr lb	Face value from one Twr lb of silver	Pure silver value of one Twr lb	Ratio
	(0.995 fine)					*[(1) ÷ 0.995]*			*[(6) ÷ (8)]*
	(1)	(2)	(3)	(4)	(5)	(6)	(7)	(8)	(9)
	£ s d	£ s d	s d	£ s d	£ s d	£	£	£	
4.12.1343[1]	15 0 0	1 0 0	3 6	1 3 6	13 16 6	15.075	1.050	1.261[2]	1:11.96
9.7.1344[1]	13 3 4	5 0	3 4	8 4	12 15 0	13.233	1.108	1.198	1:11.05
23.6.1345[1]	13 3 4	5 0	2 0	7 0	12 16 4	13.233	1.117	1.208	1:10.95
28.7.1346[1]	14 0 0	10 0	1 8	11 8	13 8 4	14.070	1.125	1.216	1:11.57
27.1.1349	14 0 0	10 6	1 2	11 8	13 8 4	14.070	1.125	1.216	1:11.57
12.1.1350	14 0 0	10 6	1 2	11 8	13 8 4	14.070	1.125	1.216	1:11.57
20.6.1351	15 0 0	7 3	2 0	9 3	14 10 9	15.075	1.250	1.351	1:11.16
28.3.1353	15 0 0	7 3	2 0	9 3	14 10 9	15.075	1.250	1.351	1:11.16
31.5.1355	15 0 0	5 6	1 2	6 8	14 13 4	15.075	1.250	1.351	1:11.16
27.1.1356	15 0 0	5 6	1 2	6 8	14 13 4	15.075	1.250	1.351	1:11.16
1.11.1356	15 0 0	5 6	1 2	6 8	14 13 4	15.075	1.250	1.351	1:11.16
3.3.1361	15 0 0	3 4	1 8	5 0	14 15 0	15.075	1.250	1.351	1:11.16
20.6.1361	15 0 0	3 6	1 6	5 0	14 15 0	15.075	1.250	1.351	1:11.16
11.2.1363	15 0 0	3 6	1 6	5 0	14 15 0	15.075	1.250	1.351	1:11.16
1.3.1363[3]	15 0 0	3 6	1 6	5 0	14 15 0	15.075	1.250	1.351	1:11.16
20.5.1371[3]	15 0 0	3 6	1 6	5 0	14 15 0	15.075	1.250	1.351	1:11.16
20.5.1372[3]	15 0 0	4 0	1 0	5 0	14 15 0	15.075	1.250	1.351	1:11.16
9.10.1394	15 0 0	3 6	1 6	5 0	14 15 0	15.075	1.250	1.351	1:11.16
9.7.1395	15 0 0	3 6	1 6	5 0	14 15 0	15.075	1.250	1.351	1:11.16

Notes: 1. These indentures do not specify the exact fineness of the gold; they simply say, 'fine gold'. The 1349 indenture is the first to specify 23 ct $3\frac{1}{2}$ gr. (0.995) gold. For the purposes of this table it is assumed that the earlier issues are of the same fineness.
2. Based on the indenture of 6.7.1335 for halfpence. There were probably no pence.
3. These indentures relate to the Calais mint.

were tried (Table 2). For the gold, therefore, Edward III's third coinage can be divided into three periods:

1. an initial period from January to July 1344 during which double leopards, valued at 6s 0d, weighing 108 gr. (6.998 g) and equivalent to two Florentine florins, were struck together with their halves and quarters.
2. a second period from July 1344 to July 1346 when nobles valued at 6s 8d and weighing $136\frac{3}{4}$ gr. (8.861 g) were ordered, together with their halves and quarters.[39]
3. a third period from July 1346 to June 1351 when nobles valued at 6s 8d and weighing $128\frac{1}{2}$ gr. (8.327 g) were struck together with their halves and quarters.

[39] No halves are known today.

With the introduction of the fourth coinage in July 1351 a further reduction in the weight of the noble of 6s 8d was made to 120 gr. (7.776 g), and this, with its half and quarter, was to remain unchanged for the rest of the reign.

Mints

Edward III's gold coinage was initiated at the London mint which remained in operation throughout the reign. It was joined by Calais in February 1363. Calais had been in English hands since 1347 and, shortly after that date, had produced coins in the name of Edward III to French standards.[40] However, the town acquired a new importance when the wool staple was established there on 1 March 1363, following its withdrawal from Bruges in the autumn of the previous year.[41] In anticipation of this Calais was reopened in February 1363 to operate as an English royal mint. There the Continental gold and silver received in exchange for English wool was recoined into English coinage denominations, and thence found its way into circulation in England.

Both the royal and archiepiscopal mints functioned in York during this reign, but only silver coins were struck there.

Conditions

1. Third coinage, first period

The first gold coinage of Edward III was ordered in accordance with an indenture made with George Kirkyn, Lote Nicholyn and others dated 14 December 1343.[42] This provided for a fine gold coin weighing 108 gr. (6.998 g) equivalent to two florins of Florence (the double leopard) to be current for 6s 0d sterling, together with its half and quarter.

The double leopard, with its design of the king enthroned, clearly drew its inspiration from Philip IV's *masse d'or* of which it was notionally the equivalent. Its half, the leopard, took its name from its obverse design. The half leopard was called a helm, like the leopard, from its obverse design.

Although the accounts show that a considerable volume of these coins was struck initially (Table 3),[43] it was realised already by June 1344 that the coinage was a failure. The two obvious reasons for this were, first, the exceptionally high coinage charges of 23s 6d on each pound weight of metal coined—3s 6d for the master moneyers and 20s 0d to be accounted for by the warden—and, second, the gold/silver ratio which was nearly 1:12.0. This overvalued gold in terms of silver and, as events were to show, a ratio of about 1:11.2 would have been more appropriate (see below). Another possible

[40] Woodhead 1979.
[41] Rymer, 1816–30, vol. III, part II.
[42] Challis 1992, 701, citing *CCR* 1343–6, 261–2.
[43] It is possible that all or some of this output could have been gold held in the treasury and used for 'pump priming'.

Double leopard, leopard and helm 1:1 (photograph by courtesy of the British Museum)

contributory reason for their failure, at least for domestic use, would have been the inconvenience of the values chosen within the system of English money of account; 6s 0d could neither be divided exactly into the mark (13s 4d) nor the pound (20s 0d). In any case, this problem was overcome in future issues.

Very few coins of this issue have survived, and there are none in the Schneider collection. Two double leopards are known, both found in the bed of the River Tyne in 1857, 3 leopards and 2 helms, and all are in institutions.[44]

2. Third coinage, second period

On 9 July 1344 a new indenture was made with Percival de Porche for a revised fine gold coinage.[45] The principal coin was explicitly called a gold noble which was to weigh $136\frac{3}{4}$ gr. (8.861 g) and to be current for 6s 8d. Coinage charges were drastically reduced to 8s 4d—3s 4d to the master-worker and 5s 0d to be accounted for by the warden. The new weight gave a gold/silver ratio of about 1:11.0. Unlike the double leopard, the noble was designed to fit conveniently into the English monetary system being, at 80 pence, equal to half a mark and one third of a pound. Half and quarter nobles were to be made as well, although none of the former are known today.

3. Third coinage, third period

A new indenture providing for further alterations to the standard was made with Lote Nicholyn, George Cleckyn and others on 28 July 1346.[46] The weight of the noble was

---

[44] There are two of each of the three denominations in the BM and, in addition, one leopard in the Ashmolean Museum, Oxford.

[45] Challis 1992b, 701, citing *CCR* 1343–6, 456–7 and 583–4.

[46] Challis 1992b, 701–2, citing *CCR* 1346–9, 39 and 143; PRO. C54/180 m.23d.

reduced to $128\frac{1}{2}$ gr. (8.327 g); the fineness and value remained as before. The gold/silver ratio was now 1:11.6. Coinage charges were increased to 11s 8d, of which 1s 2d was for the master-workers and 10s 6d was to be accounted for by the warden.

Coinage standards remained unchanged until the major revisions of 1351, although two further indentures dealing with gold coins were made with different masters prior to that date. The first of these, that of 27 January 1349, for the first time defined the fineness of the gold as 23 ct $3\frac{1}{2}$ gr. (0.995) and there was a small change in the allocation of coinage charges as between the masters and the warden.[47]

4. Fourth coinage

The fourth coinage provided for changes to both the gold and the silver and established standards that were to remain unaltered until at least 1408 (see below, pp. 20–2).

The indenture was made on 20 July 1351 with Henry de Brisele and John de Cicestria,[48] and, so far as the gold was concerned, provided for nobles of 6s 8d weighing 120 gr. (7.776 g), together with their fractions. Initially, the master-workers received 2s 0d per pound weight and the warden accounted for 7s 3d, but these two figures were progressively decreased in a series of new indentures with successive masters[49] (see Table 2). In terms of weight and nominal value this coinage was exactly proportionate to the original leopard coinage, since in both cases £15 face value was struck from one pound weight of gold. However, the reductions in coinage charges meant that people taking gold to the mint now got much more of it back, and with the reduction in the weight of the silver coins the gold/silver ratio now became 1:11.16 exactly, a ratio that remained unchanged until at least 1408.

References and Classification

The most recent study of the double leopards, their halves and quarters is that of Sir John Evans published in 1900.[50] The subsequent gold issues between 1344 and 1351 are dealt with by Potter.[51] From 1351 the classification evolved by Lawrence[52] remains the basis of that used today. Prompted by the then recent Clarke-Thornhill bequest to the British Museum, Lawrence's original four papers were brought together in a book, with a supplement and corrigenda prepared by Derek Allen.[53] Subsequently, additional notes were published by Whitton.[54] In 1964 Potter continued his study of the early issues to the end of the reign.[55] Summaries embodying the work of all these scholars,

---

[47] Challis 1992b, 702–3.
[48] Challis 1992b, 703, citing *CCR* 1329–54, 379–81; PRO. C.54/189 m.15d.
[49] Challis 1992b, 703–6.
[50] Evans 1900.
[51] Potter 1963.
[52] Lawrence 1926–33.
[53] Lawrence 1937.
[54] Whitton 1944.
[55] Potter 1964.

in abbreviated form, are included in the catalogues of North[56] and Seaby.[57] Mitchell's catalogue of the Doubleday collection (which included Lawrence's coins) is a valuable work of reference which contains a number of important insights.[58] An illuminating discussion of the background to the coinages is contained in Mayhew's chapter in *A New History of the Royal Mint.*[59]

The pre-1351 coins are arranged in accordance with Potter. Those after 1351 are arranged in accordance with with the Lawrence classification with other references supplied where helpful. Lawrence divided the post-1351 coins into three main groupings:

1. The Pre-Treaty issue. Those struck between 1 July 1351 and October 1360 including the title of king of France (**2–54**).
2. The Treaty issue. In accordance with the Treaty of Bretigny signed at Calais in October 1360, Edward III surrendered his claim to the crown of France and, accordingly, the title was removed from the coins. In its place the title of lord of Aquitaine was inserted (**55–106**).
3. The Post-Treaty issue. Those struck between 1369 and 1377, a period in which, following the resumption of war between England and France and the consequential ending of the Treaty of Bretigny, the title of king of France was resumed by Edward III. The title of lord of Aquitaine, however, continued to appear on many coins (**107–16**).

Lawrence divided the Pre-Treaty issue into seven main classes (called A to G). The last of these was further divided into eight sub-classes, and there are many mules between classes and sub-classes.

The Treaty issue is divided into two classes. The early varieties, which are essentially a progression from the Pre-Treaty types, use many of the same punches on the dies and for that reason are described as Transitional (or Treaty A) (**55–74**). After a short period, a fount of completely new punches was introduced, and the coins produced from these form the regular Treaty (or Treaty B) series (**75–106**).

With the Post-Treaty issues, apart from the change in obverse legend, the earlier coins are very similar in style to the later Treaty issues and, in fact, the reverses are essentially the same. For this reason Lawrence referred to them as mules although listing them separately (p. 221) and Potter described them as 'Transitional' (p. 316). The later coins show many changes in lettering and style which leads them to be referred to as the true Post-Treaty type.

Output

The correlation between mint output and the various coinages is set out in Table 3.

---

[56] North 1991.
[57] Seaby 1993.
[58] Mitchell 1972.
[59] Mayhew 1992.

TABLE 3. *Output of gold coin from London and Calais mints during the reign of Edward III (source: Crump and Johnson 1913)*

Accounting period	Months (approx.)	Weight coined[1]			Face value (nearest £)[2]	
		lb (Tower)	s	dwt		
LONDON MINT						
THIRD COINAGE, FIRST PERIOD. Leopards of 6s 0d weighing 108 gr., with halves and quarters.						
20.1.1344–10.7.1344	6	2,129	18	$8\frac{1}{4}$	31,949	
THIRD COINAGE, SECOND PERIOD. Nobles of 6s 8d weighing $136\frac{3}{4}$ gr., with halves and quarters.						
10.7.1344–29.9.1344	$2\frac{1}{2}$	560	7	$5\frac{1}{4}$	7,378	
30.9.1344–23.6.1345	9	669	11	4	8,816	
23.6.1345–29.9.1345	3	87	13	3	1,154	
30.9.1345–30.7.1346	10	350	3	$9\frac{1}{4}$	4,611	
THIRD COINAGE, THIRD PERIOD. Nobles of 6s 8d weighing $128\frac{1}{2}$ gr., with halves and quarters.						
30.7.1346–29.9.1346	2	265	5	5	3,714	
30.9.1346–23.11.1346	2	585	10	$0\frac{1}{2}$	8,197	
23.11.1346–29.9.1347	10	2,028	5	$2\frac{1}{4}$	28,396	
30.9.1347–17.5.1348	$7\frac{1}{2}$	1,795	13	$2\frac{3}{4}$	25,139	
17.5.1348–29.9.1348	$4\frac{1}{2}$	1,297	3	$2\frac{3}{4}$	18,160	
30.9.1348–27.1.1349	4	243	1	$9\frac{1}{2}$	3,403	
27.1.1349–2.6.1349	4	549	16	11	7,698	
2.6.1349–12.4.1350	$10\frac{1}{2}$	2,046	1	8	28,645	
12.4.1350–29.9.1350	$5\frac{1}{2}$	546	13	6	7,653	
29.9.1350–24.1.1351	4	49	12	6	695	
24.1.1351–24.6.1351	5	56	15	$6\frac{1}{2}$	795	
FOURTH COINAGE. Nobles of 6s 8d weighing 120 gr., with halves and quarters.						
24.6.1351–25.10.1351	4	6,272	9	$8\frac{3}{8}$	94,087	Pre-treaty period
25.10.1351–4.3.1352	4	1,655	14	$3\frac{1}{4}$	24,836	
4.3.1352–24.6.1352	4	1,704	9	$1\frac{3}{4}$	25,567	
24.6.1352–11.11.1352	$4\frac{1}{2}$	1,480	8	2	22,206	
11.11.1352–6.5.1353	6	407	15	3	6,116	
7.5.1353–24.12.1353	$7\frac{1}{2}$	3,181	13	8	47,725	
24.12.1353–29.9.1354	9	8,300	11	$1\frac{1}{2}$	124,508	
30.9.1354–5.4.1355	6	2,436	9	3	36,547	
5.4.1355–31.5.1355	2	1,036	7	$8\frac{3}{4}$	15,546	
31.5.1355–24.12.1355	7	2,177	3	$5\frac{1}{4}$	32,658	
24.12.1355–6.11.1356	$10\frac{1}{2}$	551	17	11	8,278	
6.11.1356–8.4.1357	5	239	4	8	3,588	
8.4.1357–29.9.1357	$5\frac{1}{2}$	4,910	6	$8\frac{1}{2}$	73,655	
30.9.1357–1.4.1358	6	3,169	13	$9\frac{3}{8}$	47,545	
1.4.1358–29.9.1358	6	4,308	2	$7\frac{7}{8}$	64,622	
30.9.1358–21.4.1359	$6\frac{1}{2}$	2,248	11	$2\frac{5}{8}$	33,728	
21.4.1359–29.9.1359	$5\frac{1}{2}$	4,284	0	$2\frac{3}{4}$	64,260	
30.9.1359–5.4.1360	6	2,029	13	$9\frac{1}{8}$	30,445	
5.4.1360–17.6.1360	$2\frac{1}{2}$	2,164	5	$0\frac{1}{4}$	32,464	

(*Continued*)

TABLE 3. *Continued*

Accounting period	Months (approx.)	Weight coined[1]			Face value (nearest £)[2]	
		lb (Tower)	s	dwt		
29.9.1360–5.3.1361	5	3,222	14	$6\frac{3}{8}$	48,341	Treaty period
6.3.1361–18.6.1361	$3\frac{1}{2}$	5,960	3	3	89,402	
18.6.1361–29.9.1361	$3\frac{1}{2}$	4,675	1	$2\frac{1}{2}$	70,126	
30.9.1361–22.3.1362	6	4,339	1	$3\frac{1}{2}$	65,086	
22.3.1362–29.9.1362	6	4,403	13	$6\frac{3}{4}$	66,055	
30.9.1362–11.2.1363	$4\frac{1}{2}$	736	1	$3\frac{1}{2}$	11,041	
11.2.1363–29.9.1363	$7\frac{1}{2}$	1,780	6	$9\frac{3}{4}$	26,705	
30.9.1363–29.9.1364	12	1,365	16	$9\frac{1}{4}$	20,487	
30.9.1364–29.9.1365	12	1,043	15	$8\frac{3}{4}$	15,657	
30.9.1365–29.9.1366	12	1,101	5	$7\frac{1}{4}$	16,519	
30.9.1366–29.9.1367	12	741	0	$11\frac{1}{2}$	11,116	
30.9.1367–29.9.1368	12	1,680	4	1	25,203	
30.9.1368–29.9.1369	12	4,847	13	$9\frac{3}{4}$	72,715	
30.9.1369–29.9.1370	12	1,480	7	0	22,205	Post-treaty period
30.9.1370–29.9.1371	12	1,029	15	$0\frac{1}{2}$	15,446	
30.9.1371–29.9.1372	12	1,455	1	6	21,826	
30.9.1372–29.9.1373	12	973	2	$3\frac{1}{8}$	14,597	
30.9.1373–29.9.1374	12	642	16	0	9,642	
30.9.1374–29.9.1375	12	694	5	$4\frac{3}{4}$	10,414	
30.9.1375–24.7.1376	10	376	6	6	5,645	
24.7.1376–20.9.1377	14	273	8	$2\frac{1}{4}$	4,101	
CALAIS MINT						
20.2.1363–10.4.1364	$1\frac{1}{2}$	3,528	13	4	52,930	Treaty period
10.4.1364–13.4.1365	12	683	3	$3\frac{3}{4}$	10,247	
13.4.1365–13.4.1366	12	6,387	1	$11\frac{1}{2}$	95,806	
13.4.1366–20.3.1368	23	7,597	6	$7\frac{1}{2}$	113,960	
20.3.1368–27.8.1368	5	606	13	$6\frac{1}{4}$	9,100	
27.8.1368–26.10.1370	26	3,461	10	$5\frac{3}{4}$	51,923	Post-treaty period
26.10.1370–16.10.1371	$11\frac{1}{2}$	1,030	17	$3\frac{1}{2}$	15,463	
16.10.1371–4.11.1373	$24\frac{1}{2}$	4,672	7	9	70,086	
4.11.1373–16.6.1374	$7\frac{1}{2}$	608	10	11	9,128	
16.6.1374–4.11.1374	$4\frac{1}{2}$	123	12	$7\frac{1}{2}$	1,854	
4.11.1374–14.7.1375	$8\frac{1}{2}$	110	4	$7\frac{1}{4}$	1,653	
14.7.1375–4.11.1375	$3\frac{1}{2}$	97	19	0	1,469	
4.11.1375–15.5.1381	$66\frac{1}{2}$	1,984	11	11	29,769	

Notes: 1.   Weights are expressed as pounds Tower (5,400 gr.) = 20 s = 240 dwt.
2.   Face value figures are obtained from weight coined figures as follows:

$$\text{weight coined in lbs} \times \text{no. of coins struck per lb} \times \frac{\text{value of coin in pence}}{240}$$

Example:
20.1.1344–10.7.1344, weight coined 2129 lb 18 s $8\frac{1}{4}$ dwt = 2129.934 lb.

$$2129.934 \times 50 \times \frac{72}{240} = 31,948.95, \ 31,949 \text{ to the nearest £.}$$

RICHARD II (22 June 1377–29 September 1399)

Background

The ongoing war with France led to a continued drain of good money from the country and there was a shortage of bullion for conversion into coin. From 1384 onwards the position was dominated and worsened by what Munro has called 'The war of the Gold "Nobles"'.[60] This started with what was essentially a trade war between Flanders and Brabant in the course of which debasements of the Flemish coinage attracted bullion away from England. At about the same time, between 1383 and 1388, the staple was temporarily removed from Calais to Middleburg because of a French military threat to the former. When the staple was returned to Calais, in an attempt to force gold to the royal mint there, an old regulation of Edward III requiring staple merchants to accept English nobles only in payment for wool was re-imposed. This placed the cost of converting foreign gold to English gold on the buyers of the wool. To thwart this the Flemish mints began to strike gold nobles in imitation of the English, but of slightly less weight and fineness.[61] This was successful to the extent that the inferior Flemish nobles appeared in circulation in England and that there was an even greater shortage of bullion at the English mints.

England fought back with the *Ordonance de la Bullion*, a law requiring all merchants to supply the royal mint with one ounce of gold 'in foreign coin' for each woolsack, 240 woolfells, and half-last of hides that were exported. This was initially successful as the mint output shows (Table 4). In retaliation, Flanders banned the circulation of English nobles in its territory and ordered their confiscation as bullion, thus hoping to force merchants to have them converted in Flemish mints into Flemish nobles. The count of Flanders also strictly banned the export of bullion (i.e. anything other than his slightly inferior nobles) to Calais. Needless to say, it was the merchants who suffered from these measures and relaxations were sought, but before anything had been achieved Richard II had been deposed.

Issues

Richard II's gold coinage is a continuation of that of his predecessor, struck to the same standards, and with no basic changes in design other than that of the name of the monarch on the obverse and the replacement of E with R in the centre of the reverse. Altered dies of Edward III exist and are represented in this collection (**119**, **123**, **124**).

---

[60] Munro 1972, ch.II. The contents of this paragraph are mainly derived from this.
[61] In fact the Flemish nobles were only worth 1d less than the English. See Spufford 1963, 130.

Mints

The London mint operated throughout the reign, but Calais was closed for a short period from January 1384 to January 1387[62] while the staple was at Middleburg.

Conditions

The indentures made with Walter de Barde at the Tower in 1363[63] and with Bardet de Malepilys at Calais in 1372[64] continued into the new reign until 1394. In that year a new indenture for both mints was made with John Wildeman,[65] and in 1395 this was replaced by another in favour of Nanfre Molekyn.[66] In all cases the weight, fineness, value and denominations of the gold remained unaltered. The total gold coinage charges continued at 5s 0d, of which 1s 6d was for the master-worker and 3s 6d to be accounted for by the warden (with the exception of the Calais indenture of 1372 in which the charges were 1s 0d and 4s 0d respectively).[67]

References and Classification

The coins in this collection have been arranged in accordance with the new classification of T. G. Webb Ware, recently described by him in a paper to the British Numismatic Society[68] at which time he circulated a summary of it. It is understood that this will shortly be published in the *British Numismatic Journal*. Prior to Webb Ware's recent work, the latest published study of the gold coinage of Richard II had been that of Walters published in 1904.[69] This had been developed further by Brooke on the basis of four different forms of lettering,[70] and that is the classification followed in North.[71] More recently, in 1960, Potter published a study of the silver coinage[72] and it is known that he and Winstanley had been planning to publish further work on the gold, but this was prevented by their respective deaths (Schneider was evidently aware of their work at the time and no doubt they consulted him, since some of his tickets make enigmatic references to it).

The difficulty in using the Brooke classification according to lettering arises from the apparent confusion of different letter forms on some individual coins, and Webb Ware

---

[62] Challis 1992b, 681.
[63] Challis 1992b, 706, citing *CCR*, 1360–4, 535–6.
[64] Challis 1992b, 706–7, citing PRO. C54/210 m.17d.
[65] Challis 1992b, 707, citing *CCR*, 1392–6, 381–4. Starting with this indenture, the mints of London and Calais were operated under the same master.
[66] Challis 1992b, 707, citing PRO. C54/237 m.28d.
[67] Challis 1992b, 706, citing PRO. C54/210 m.17d.
[68] At the meeting on 28 January 1992. I am grateful to Mr Webb Ware for permitting his new classification to be used in the preparation of this sylloge in advance of the appearance of the printed version and to his kindness and help in applying it to this collection.
[69] Walters 1904.
[70] In *English Coins*, Brooke 1950,
[71] North 1991.
[72] Potter 1958–9.

has demonstrated that there were, in fact, more founts in use than the four that Brooke had perceived. The Webb Ware classification is primarily based on the presence or absence of the king's French title and on various privy marks used. When applied to the nobles, which are the most abundant and continuously issued gold denomination, it demonstrates a rational and satisfactory progression. Half- and quarter-nobles were evidently issued less continuously and, particularly in the case of the half-nobles, in smaller quantities. At the time of writing, Webb Ware has still to finalise his conclusions on these but they have been noted in the catalogue with reference to the nobles, so far as is practicable.

The Webb Ware classification divides the coinage into four main issues, each of which further divides into a number of sub-issues. Since, at the date of writing, this has not been published, with Mr Webb Ware's kind permission, the essential details of the summary circulated at the meeting are set out here:

1. Coins in the style of Edward III with French title

1a. Edward III lettering, lis over sail. London mint only (**120–5**).
1b. New lettering. Annulet over sail (London); quatrefoil over sail (Calais) (**126–43, 157**).

2. Coins with French title omitted

2a. Crude style. Saltire over sail (London); no marks (Calais) (**144–8**).
2b. Robust style. Trefoil over sail (London and Calais) (**149–52**).
2c. Porcine face style. Always HYB instead of HIB. No marks (London and Calais) (**153–6**).

3. Coins with French title resumed

3a. No marks (London and Calais) (**157–70**).
3b. Lis on rudder (London); lion on rudder (Calais) (**171–4**).
3c. Trefoil at shield (London); two pellets at shield (Calais) (**175–81**).

4. Coins in the style of Henry IV's

4a. Escallop on rudder (London only) (**182–5**).
4b. Crescent on rudder (London only) (**186–8**).

As is customary in this sylloge, references to North and Seaby are given in the catalogue. The current editions of those works are, of course, based on the Brooke/Walters classification and are thus inconsistent with the new Webb Ware classification. The references given in the catalogue thus provide a concordance between the old and new classifications so far as any exact equivalence is possible.

TABLE 4. *Output of gold coin from London and Calais mints during the reign of Richard II (sources: Stokes 1929 (London mint), Woodhead 1979 (Calais mint), Munro 1981 (Calais mint))*

Accounting period	Months (approx.)	Weight coined[1]			Face value (nearest £)
		lb (Tower)	oz	dwt	
LONDON MINT					
20.9.1377–29.9.1384	84	2,277	6	$2\frac{1}{2}$	34,163
29.9.1384–29.9.1387	36	2,290	18	$0\frac{3}{4}$	34,373
19.1.1388–29.9.1389	$20\frac{1}{2}$	1,824	7	$5\frac{3}{4}$	27,370
29.9.1389–29.9.1390	12	1,626	15	3	24,409
29.9.1390–29.9.1391	12	1,535	7	9	23,034
29.9.1391–9.12.1392	$14\frac{1}{2}$	1,694	13	$5\frac{1}{2}$	25,427
9.12.1392–29.9.1393	$9\frac{1}{2}$	869	0	23	13,036
29.9.1393–29.9.1395	24	1,807	3	4	27,106
29.9.1395–29.9.1396	12	536	14	3	8,058
29.9.1396–29.9.1398	24	2,290	0	18	34,351
29.9.1398–15.10.1399	$12\frac{1}{2}$	1,109	0	$12\frac{1}{2}$	16,636
CALAIS MINT					
4.11.1375–15.5.1381	$66\frac{1}{2}$	1,984	11s	11	29,769
15.5.1381–7.1.1384	32	5	19s	10	90
7.1.1384–17.1.1387	36	MINT INOPERATIVE			
17.1.1387–17.1.1390	36				32,537
17.1.1390–17.1.1393	36				6,618
17.1.1393–17.1.1394	12				22,184
17.1.1394–17.10.1395	21				19,680
17.10.1395–18.10.1397	24				10,564
18.10.1397–25.8.1399	22				363

Note: 1. Weights are expressed are pounds Tower (5,400 gr.) = 12 oz = 240 dwt except that the entries for Calais for 4.11.1375–7.1.1384 are expressed as pounds Tower (5,400 gr.) = 20 shillings = 240 dwt.

Output

Output is set out in Table 4. The London accounts show that production was small during the first ten years of the reign and, although it increased somewhat in later years, it was never large. The Calais figures point to a more erratic output which must, in some measure, reflect the flows of silver and gold between England and the Continent as the relative market values of the two metals fluctuated.[73]

[73] See Glossary p. 91 below.

HENRY IV (30 September 1399–20 March 1413)

Background

The new king, insecure because of the manner in which he had usurped the crown, was anxious to obtain the support of the merchants, and so he procured the withdrawal of the *Ordonnance de la Bullion*. However, at first there was no reciprocal concession from Flanders. Imitation nobles continued to be minted there, and the ban on the circulation of English nobles continued in force. Eventually, in 1400, after persistent pressure from Flemish weavers whose trade was suffering as a result of difficulty of access to the Calais staple, the count of Flanders agreed to let English nobles circulate again and within the next two years the output of Flemish nobles died out.

However, the proportion of inferior Flemish nobles in circulation in England is said to have accounted for as much as a quarter of England's gold circulation. To have converted them to English coin at the current mint price would have involved their holders in serious loss and, despite the efforts of Parliament to force metal to the mint, little came. In the end, Parliament was forced to overcome its reluctance and to accept that it was not immune to the consequences of the changing international values of bullion. Accordingly a debasement was decided upon for both gold and silver, and this effectively took place from Easter 1412 (but see p. 21 below). It was immediately successful and for the remainder of the reign output continued at a high level (see Table 5).

Issues

Until 1408, and probably until 1412, the weight standard for the nobles remained at the old figure, 120 gr. to the noble of 6s 8d. From Easter 1412 the weight of the noble was reduced to 108 gr., value and fineness remaining unaltered.

Mints

Initially, both London and Calais continued to account for the gold output, with production at the latter mint petering out in 1404. London kept on at a low level until at least 1408 (the accounts are missing for the period 30 September 1408 to 29 November 1411), but after the weight reduction of 1412 it struck large volumes of gold for the rest of the reign. Calais remained closed until well into the next reign.

Conditions

The indenture with Nanfre Molekyn made under Richard II continued until he was replaced as master by Walter Merewe whose indenture is dated 1 July 1402. The new terms were the same as before, that is to say that the noble of 6s 8d was to be struck at a weight of 120gr. (7.776 g) and a fineness of 23ct $3\frac{1}{2}$ gr. (0.995 fine), together with its half and quarter. Coinage charges remained at 5s 0d—1s 6d for the master-worker and 3s 6d to be accounted for by the warden.[74]

---

[74] Challis 1992b, 707, citing *CCR* 1399–1402, 579–82.

The indenture with the next master, Richard Garner, who was appointed in February 1409,[75] is only known from an undated contemporary copy in the possession of the Society of Antiquaries. It provides for a reduction in the weight of the gold, but this was probably never acted upon (see below for a discussion of this).

The reduction in the weight of the noble to 108 gr. (6.998 g) with effect from Easter 1412 was approved by Parliament[76] and is not marked by a new indenture. The conditions which applied may very well have been those set out to Henry V's first master, Lewis John, on 14 April 1413.[77] Those included an allowance for loss of weight on recoinage of old coin. At the same time as the 1412 reduction in weight of the gold, a reduction was made in the weight of the silver coin, although this was proportionately not so great. In consequence the gold/silver ratio changed to 1:10.33 (see Table 7).

References and Classification

The most recent and authoritative analysis of the heavy coinage is that of Christopher Blunt[78] published in *BNJ* 1941–4, as extended and augmented by the same author in 1967.[79] The light coinage has not been extensively dealt with since Walters' paper of 1905[80] and much new material has come to light since then. Brooke's *English Coins* preceeded Blunt's work, but North presents a simplified version of the latter in *English Hammered Coins*.

Blunt's 1967 paper discusses what happened between Michaelmas 1408 and November 1411 for which period the accounts are missing. Professor Reddaway had recently published the undated and apparently unenrolled indenture with Richard Garner,[81] which may have been prepared shortly after his appointment in February 1409. This provides for a weight reduction, in the case of the noble, to 112.5 gr., suggesting that Henry IV's coinage might have passed through three weight stages and not, as had been thought, only two. Blunt reviewed the coins of Henry IV known at that date and came to the conclusion that there were no specimens whose weight and condition could allow them confidently to be attributed to a 112.5 gr. issue, although one quarter-noble, possibly clipped (Ryan lot 26), might just qualify. This remains true today.

It is quite possible that this indenture for an intermediate weight coinage was never acted upon or, indeed, that it was never formalised. If the rate remained at 120 gr. until Easter 1412, it is distinctly likely that little or no gold would have been struck. If a rate of 112.5 gr. had been put into effect in 1409, then a rise in output might certainly have been expected, even if not to the dramatic extent that the 108 gr. rate was to produce in 1412. There are dangers in arguing from silence, but the absence of coins that clearly

[75] Challis 1992b, 708, citing Blunt 1967.
[76] Mayhew 1992, 172–3, citing *Rot.Parl.*III, 658.
[77] Challis 1992b, 708, citing *CCR* 1413–19, 64–6.
[78] Blunt 1941–4.
[79] Blunt 1967.
[80] Walters 1905.
[81] Reddaway 1967.

relate to the 112.5 gr. rate, and the absence of accounts for the period of time when it may have applied, both suggest, though inconclusively, that the intermediate rate was never effected.

For the purpose of listing all the Henry IV coins in the Schneider collection the Blunt classification of types I to III for the heavy coins has been extended so that it can be applied to all gold denominations and to the light coins. This can be set out as follows:

Heavy coinage

Ia. Four lis in French arms. Crescent on rudder (London); crown vertically on rudder (Calais) (**189–93**).

Ib. Three lis in French arms ✛✦✛. Crescent on rudder (London only) (**194–5**).

Ic. Three lis in French arms ✛✦✛. Crescent on rudder (London) (**196**).

IIa. Three lis in French arms ✛✦✛. Broken annulet stops and lis on rudder (London); saltire stops and crown horizontally on rudder (Calais) (**197**).

IIb. Three lis in French arms ✦✛✦. Crown horizontally on rudder (Calais) (not represented in this collection).

IIIa. Three lis in French arms ✛✦✛. Pellet on rudder, saltire at tail of lion in second quarter (London); saltire on rudder (Calais) (not represented in this collection).

Light coinage

IIc. As IIa of the heavy coinage, but with annulet and slipped trefoil added to the side of the ship and a slipped trefoil in one quarter of the reverse (London) (**198–99**).

IIIb. As IIIa of the heavy coinage, but with annulet and slipped trefoil added to the side of the ship and a slipped trefoil in one quarter of the reverse (London) (**200**).

IV. Again and henceforth three lis in French arms ✛✦✛. Nothing on rudder. Slipped trefoil, or annulet and slipped trefoil on side of ship. Still with crennelated fore and aft castles, as on previous types (London) (**201–3**).

V. Ship's fore and aft castles not crennelated. Nothing on rudder. Annulet and slipped trefoil, or slipped trefoil and annulet, or trefoil alone on side of ship. Slipped trefoil in one quarter of reverse. Usually pellet to left of h in centre of reverse (**204–12**).

Output

This is set out in Table 5.

TABLE 5. *Output of gold coin from London and Calais mints during the reigns of Henry IV and Henry V (sources: Stokes 1929 (London mint), Woodhead 1979 (Calais mint), Munro 1981 (Calais mint))*

Accounting period	Months (approx.)	Weight coined[1]			Face value (nearest £)
		lb (Tower)	oz	dwt	
LONDON MINT					
14.10.1399–29.9.1402	35½	1,465	13	10½	21,992
30.9.1402–29.9.1403	12	298	12	10	4,486
30.9.1403–24.1.1404	4	97	13	4	1,472
24.1.1404–29.9.1404	8	216	3	6½	3,244
30.9.1404–29.9.1405	12	221	7	2	3,324
30.9.1405–29.9.1406	12	360	10	0½	5,413
30.9.1406–29.9.1407	12	198	15	0¾	2,989
30.9.1407–29.9.1408	12	144	13	1¼	2,176
30.9.1408–28.11.1411	38	ACCOUNTS MISSING			
29.11.1411–29.11.1412	12	8,992	3	10	149,876
29.11.1412–29.9.1413	10	8,329	7	0	138,829
30.9.1413–29.9.1417	48	18,810	6	3	313,515
30.9.1417–31.3.1419	18	2,864	18	4	47,760
31.3.1419–31.8.1420	17	2,447	12	1	40,801
31.8.1420–30.9.1420	1	151	5	0	2,524
30.9.1420–31.3.1422	18	5,908	5	8	98,476
CALAIS MINT					
25.8.1399–29.9.1401	25				12,745
29.9.1401–30.3.1403	18				2,597
30.3.1403–30.3.1404	12				301
30.3.1404–30.7.1422		MINT CLOSED			

Note: 1.   Weights are expressed are pounds Tower (5,400 gr.) = 12 oz = 240 dwt.

HENRY V (21 March 1413–1 September 1422)

Background

The reign of Henry V was mainly taken up with his successful wars in France, starting with his victory at Agincourt on 25 October 1415 and concluding with the Treaty of Troyes on 21 May 1420 which recognised him as heir to the throne of France.

The effects of the debasement of 1411 continued to be felt well into the new reign but, after 1417, the competitive effects of French debasements caused a rise in the value of gold and a sharp drop in bullion available for coinage in England. By 1421 a full-weight noble was worth more than its face value, and in that year the government agreed to accept worn nobles at 6s 8d for tax payments and to remit seignorage charges on all worn gold brought to the mint before Christmas.[82] As concern at the shortage of

[82] Munro 1972, 173.

coin grew, the English reacted predictably by requiring foreigners to pay the Calais staplers for their wool purchases in English nobles. As a consequence of this, the Calais mint, closed since 1404, was reopened in 1422 and a large output followed (Table 5). There was a significant increase in output at London, too, perhaps the combined effect of all the steps taken.

Issues

The gold coinage of this reign is a continuation of the light coinage of Henry IV and there is no factor which allows a clear-cut distinction to be made between the coinage of the two reigns. Mules from dies attributable to both reigns are known (**214–16**).

Mints

The London mint was in operation throughout the reign. Calais, closed since 1404, reopened in July 1422.

Conditions

The first indenture of the reign was made with Lewis John on 14 April 1413 and provided for nobles of 6s 8d weighing 108 gr., together with their halves and quarters. Fineness continued to be 23ct $3\frac{1}{2}$ gr. Coinage charges were set at 5s 10d, comprising 2s 4d for the master-worker (of which 10d was specifically to compensate for loss of weight) and 3s 6d to be accounted for by the warden.[83] This indenture was modified on 26 July 1421 by removing the allowance for loss of weight and reducing the remedy.[84]

A second indenture, made on 13 February 1422 with Bartholomew Goldbeter, for the London and Calais mints provided for the same coins at the same standards. Coinage charges were set at 1s 6d for the master-worker and 3s 6d to be accounted for by the warden.[85]

References and Classification

Brooke's analysis remains the standard classification.[86] This is mainly based on the lettering founts and the progressive appearance of privy marks. The coins were divided into nine main classes designated by the Roman numerals I–IX. Subsequently, in his *English Coins*,[87] Brooke reduced the number of classes to seven, designated by the letters A to G. It is this simplified classification that is followed in North's *English Hammered Coins*.

---

[83] Challis 1992b, 708, citing *CCR* 1413–19, 64–6.
[84] Challis 1992b, 708, citing *CCR* 1419–22, 204–5.
[85] Challis 1992b, 708–9, citing *CCR* 1419–22, 230–4.
[86] Brooke 1930.
[87] Brooke 1950.

Brooke did not suggest any absolute chronology for his classes, but we now have available more exact information on the reopening of the Calais mint, and thus the introduction of the annulet issue. Both Brooke[88] and Whitton[89] had been influenced by the belief, then held, that Calais did not reopen until early in Henry VI's reign, and they thus regarded the annulet issue as having been introduced at London at that time. Indeed, Brooke speculated that the introduction of Henry V class G might have coincided with the appointment of Richard Goldbeter as master moneyer for both London and Calais in February 1422.[90] In fact, it seems far more likely that Goldbeter's appointment coincided with the introduction of the annulet issue. We have no means of confirming this, but if we take the March 1422 accounts date as that for the end of class G we shall probably not be wrong by more than a month or so.

An attempt by the present writer to arrive at a chronology for the other Henry V classes by comparing the survivors in the Fishpool hoard with mint output has demonstrated the unreliability for this purpose of the hoard's composition for the period appreciably before the deposit date (see Appendix 2, pp. 80–4).

In the catalogue references are given to both the longer and shorter Brooke classifications. In the former case Brooke identified a number of sub-classes designated by lower case letters. Brooke also listed, but did not illustrate, the dies known to him for each variety, and these are indicated in those cases where a positive identity can be made.

Output

This is set out in Table 5.

HENRY VI, First Reign (1 September 1422–4 March 1461)

Background

Henry VI was a nine-month-old infant on his accession, the son of Henry V and Catherine, daughter of Charles VI, king of France. His uncles, the dukes of Bedford and Gloucester, contended for power, and it was only after political manoeuverings that the former was appointed protector of England.

Bedford tried to continue the policies of Henry V. These included the maintenance of an alliance with Burgundy, whose lands included Flanders, the main market for English wool, and whose support was vital for the maintenance of England's position in France. The king of France died very shortly after Henry V, in October 1422. The Treaty of Troyes (1420), made following the Anglo-Burgundian victories, had disinherited the dauphin and instead named Henry V as heir to the kingdom of France. The French

[88] Brooke 1950, 140.
[89] Whitton 1938–41.
[90] Brooke 1950, 139.

throne could, therefore, be claimed in the name of Henry VI, but this was only a reality north of the Loire. The dauphin claimed the throne as Charles VII and maintained a position from his capital at Bourges. The Anglo-Burgundian alliance weakened, both as a result of military adventures by the duke of Gloucester in the Low Countries, and by trade and bullion disputes. At the same time the appearance of Joan of Arc rekindled French national pride. English power in France began its decline which can be said to have started with the relief of Orleans in 1429. In 1435 Burgundy made a separate peace with France and entered the war on their side. By 1453 all French territory had been lost, except Calais.

Bedford had died in 1435 and with him the strongest force for unity in the kingdom. The divisions and uncertainties formed during Henry VI's minority were in no way eased by the weakness of character he showed after he assumed personal rule. Discontent, maintained and fed by the losses in France and the unbridled ambitions of great lords, were among the factors that led to the War of the Roses (commenced 1455) and to Henry's deposition in 1461.

The reopening of the Calais mint in 1422 must be seen in the context of other actions being taken to bring more bullion to the mints. The most obvious of these was a require-ment that aliens should pay for their wool in Calais in English nobles, thus compelling them to take coin in other currencies to the mint there for recoinage. Another action, suggested by Lloyd,[91] is that the Staple Company (acting like a cartel) were tightening the credit extended to alien buyers of wool in order to force them to pay a larger por-tion of the price in bullion sooner, and that this was foreshadowing the imposition of the bullion ordinances of 1429. Evidently these tactics worked, for there was a high output of gold coin at the Calais mint between 1422 and 1424 (Table 6). This increased level of coinage was not to last, however. Debasements in the Burgundian Netherlands and in France south of the Loire drew bullion away from English mints.[92] Furthermore, in order to raise funds the king's council had been undermining the position of the Calais staple by granting licences to merchants to trade direct.[93] Coin was flowing out of the country and it was necessary to renew regulations against this.[94]

In 1429 a series of statutes known as the Calais Staple Partition and Bullion Ordinances were enacted by Parliament. These imposed upon the staple merchants obli-gations to obtain a better price for wool, to sell only for cash in hand, allowing no credit, and to deliver one third of the wool price in bullion to the Calais mint after each sale.[95] The Council agreed not to sell any more licences to merchants permitting them to trade outside the staple. The Partition Ordnance required merchants to divide their receipts, not in proportion to sales, but in proportion to the amount of wool each had brought to

---

[91] Lloyd 1977, 259.
[92] Munro 1972, 76–83.
[93] Lloyd 1977, 260.
[94] Lloyd 1977, 260.
[95] Munro 1972, 84–5.

the staple. This seems to have had the effect of favouring the larger, more established, merchants at the expense of the smaller traders or those whose trade depended on credit. Thus business was concentrated into the hands of a smaller number of larger merchants who were thereby better able collectively to monopolise the trade, fix prices at higher levels and enforce the bullion laws.[96]

The effect of the new regulations was an immediate sharp increase in output from the Calais mint, although this was almost entirely in silver coin.[97] So far as gold was concerned, all that may be said is that the measures may have slightly extended the date until which gold continued to be struck there. The output increase was of short duration; the loss of trade soon offset the short-term cash benefit. The new laws were very offensive and injurious to the Flemish drapery trade which could not finance the requirement for payment in cash, and the consequence for England was a steep decline in wool sales. At the same time the vital alliance with Burgundy was threatened just when England's power in France was starting to decline.

At first the Burgundians sought to retaliate in economic terms. The manufacture of wool into cloth had increased in England, and the value of sales abroad of woven pieces began to exceed that of raw wool in sacks. The Burgundians held that the increase in English cloth exports to the Low Countries was damaging their drapery industries,[98] and they therefore banned its entry from June 1434. However, the peace which Burgundy concluded with France in September 1435 soon led to a state of war between England and Burgundy, including, of course, Flanders. This caused a severe disruption to the wool trade, although it was worse for Flanders than for England which was able to continue to export wool to Holland and Zealand. These states, although part of the Burgundian Netherlands, opposed the war, ignored the ban on trade with England issued by the duke of Burgundy and evaded his attempts to enforce it.[99]

These and other internal commercial and economic pressures eventually forced the duke of Burgundy to seek peace with England, and a treaty was signed on 29 September 1439. The conditions were in England's favour. The Calais Ordinances remained in place, and cloth trade with the Low Countries (except Flanders) was resumed. As might be expected, trade increased,[100] yet in spite of the Ordinances there was no burst of activity at the Calais mint. There are two obvious reasons for this. First, there appears to have been a progressive collapse in the observation of the Ordinances, in which the Crown itself played a leading part. As early as 1435 there had been complaints about licenses being sold to wealthy merchants allowing them to disregard the conditions. In fact, the Ordinances had become unpopular with many merchants as they realised that

---

[96] The statutes were devised by the crown and the Staple Company together. There is at least a suggestion that they were inspired by the larger merchants, often creditors of the crown, in their own interest.
[97] Challis 1992a, 683.
[98] Munro 1972, 104–7.
[99] Lloyd 1972, 114–17.
[100] Munro 1972, 119.

they obstructed trade. In the end the Ordinances fell into such disrepute that they were widely disregarded and, in 1442, they were, in practice, abandoned.[101] The second reason was the great shortage of bullion, both in England and in the Low Countries, part of the general bullion famine that worsened as the century progressed.[102] This was to influence mint-output figures for the rest of the reign.

England continued to strive to extract from the Burgundian Netherlands as much precious metal as it could obtain in exchange for wool or cloth. Burgundy sought by all available means to reduce its loss of bullion in this way. Both were reacting to the gold and silver shortage and to conservative views as to the use of credit. England was disinclined to use debasement. Burgundy, having held its coinage unchanged for twenty years, introduced new, baser gold coin in 1454 and was immediately able to attract a substantial amount of gold to its mints, some, undoubtedly, at the expense of English currency. In England gold was available for coin only in very small amounts until, finally, in 1464, the need for debasement was accepted.

Issues

The coinage of gold at 108 gr. to the noble continued throughout Henry VI's first reign without any change in standards.

Mints

London operated throughout the reign. Calais, which had reopened towards the end of Henry V's reign, in July 1422, continued to strike gold up to August 1431[103] and remained open, striking silver only, until Michaelmas 1440.[104] York, for the first time, struck gold between August 1423 and August 1424.[105]

Conditions

The indenture made with Bartholomew Goldbeter in February 1422 was renewed on 16 February 1423. The conditions remained the same except that the provision for gold and silver coin at London and Calais was extended by the addition of Bristol and York.[106] The mandate for Bristol does not appear to have been exercised. Further indentures were made with successive master-workers, William Rus on 8 September 1431[107] and John Paddesley on 10 July 1434,[108] on exactly the same conditions.

The next indenture, made with Robert Manfeld on 13 December 1445, included some alterations. First, it provided for mints at London and Calais only. Second, the coinage

---

[101] Munro 1972, 124–6.
[102] Spufford 1988, 356–8.
[103] Woodhead 1979.
[104] Woodhead 1979.
[105] Brooke 1932.
[106] Challis 1992b, 709, citing *CCR*, 1422–29, 59–62.
[107] Challis 1992b, 709, citing *CCR*, 1429–35, 173–7.
[108] Challis 1992b, 710, citing *CCR*, 1429–35, 318–22.

charges for gold were increased from 5s 0d to 5s 10d, the additional 10d being for 'depreciation'. Third, the remedy was doubled from $\frac{1}{16}$ to $\frac{1}{8}$ ct per pound weight.[109] The reduction in mints can be explained by the very small amounts of coin then being struck. The 10d for 'depreciation' was an allowance for loss of weight on coin brought to the mint for restriking. Two further indentures, another with Robert Manfeld on 16 December 1451[110] and one with Sir Richard Tunstall on 11 April 1459,[111] are on the same terms as before but with the word 'depreciation' replaced by 'loss of weight'.

References and Classification

Whitton's study of the heavy coinage of Henry VI remains the basis of the classification used today.[112] He elaborated on the already well established division of the coinage into issues determined by characteristic privy marks, the sequence being based on a. study of dies and the punches used in forming the dies. A few years earlier Brooke had proposed a chronology for the series in his *English Coins*.[113] Whitton did not entirely agree with this and proposed an amended chronology.[114]

We now have fuller information on the period of activity of the Calais mint than was available to Brooke and Whitton. In particular, we know now that what can only have been annulet issue dies were issued to Calais on 16 May 1422[115] and that first deliveries of new coin took place there on 20 July 1422.[116] We can be reasonably sure that gold ceased to be struck at Calais in 1431.[117] We can also be reasonably sure that, after a period of decline, silver ceased to be struck at Calais in 1440.[118]

In recent years some large hoards have come to light that were deposited late in, or just after the end of, Henry VI's first reign. Specifically, these are the Fishpool hoard (gold, deposited *c.*1463–4);[119] the Reigate, Broke's Road, hoard (silver and gold, deposited *c.*1460);[120] and the Reigate, Wray Lane, hoard (mostly silver, deposited *c.*1454–5).[121] With this new information at our disposal it is appropriate to review the dates attributed to the different issues, especially as Brooke and Whitton did not entirely agree on these.

This new data is examined in detail in Appendix 2 (pp. 78–84) and, subject to the reservations noted there, some minor amendments to the chronology put forward by Brooke and amended by Whitton are now proposed.

[109] Challis 1992b, 710, citing PRO. E101/306/2 no.6.
[110] Challis 1992b, 710, citing *CCR*, 1447–54, 368–71.
[111] Challis 1992b, 711, citing *CCR*, 1454–61, 384–7.
[112] Whitton 1938–41.
[113] Brooke 1932, 145.
[114] Whitton 1938–41, 406–14.
[115] Woodhead 1979, 189, citing *Proceedings and Ordinances of the Privy Council*, ii, 332.
[116] Woodhead 1979, 189, citing *CPR* 1422–29, 337–40.
[117] Woodhead 1979, 189.
[118] Woodhead 1979, 189.
[119] Archibald 1967.
[120] Information kindly supplied in advance of publication by Dr Barrie Cook.
[121] Archibald 1978.

	New	*Brooke*	*Whitton*
Annulet (**268–304**)	Spring 1422–30	1422–5	1422–7
Rosette-mascle (**305–17**)	1430–1	1425–8	1427–30
Pinecone-mascle (**318–27**)	1431–2	1428–33	1430–4
Leaf-mascle (**328–30**)	1433–6	1433–7	1434–5
Leaf-trefoil (**331–4**)	1436–8	1438	1435–8
Trefoil (**335**)	1439–41	1440	1438–43

There is not, at present, sufficient evidence to justify modifying the provisional, but sketchy, chronology for the period 1441–61 already put forward by Whitton, namely:

Trefoil-pellet
  (no gold coins known)   1443–5

Leaf-pellet
  (**336–7**)   } 1445–54

Unmarked

Cross-pellet   } six gold coins known, all ex Fishpool, all in BM.   } 1454–61

Lis-pellet

Output

This is set out on Table 6.

TABLE 6. *Output of gold coin from London, Calais and York mints during the first reign of Henry VI (sources: Stokes 1929 (London mint), Woodhead 1979 (Calais mint), Brooke 1931 (York mint))*

Accounting period	Months (approx.)	Weight coined			Face value (nearest £)
		lb (Tower)	oz	dwt	
LONDON MINT					
30.3.1422–29.9.1424	30	19,746	11	$0\frac{1}{2}$	329,115
30.9.1424–29.9.1425	12	3,465	12	10	57,767
30.9.1425–20.4.1427	$18\frac{1}{2}$	3,078	4	$12\frac{1}{2}$	51,306
20.4.1427–29.9.1427	$5\frac{1}{2}$	762	$2\frac{1}{2}$	$2\frac{1}{2}$	12,704
30.9.1427–29.9.1428	12	1,691	10	$7\frac{1}{2}$	28,198
30.9.1428–31.3.1430	18	1,528	10	$7\frac{1}{2}$	25,481
31.3.1430–29.9.1431	18	1,300	$11\frac{3}{4}$	$2\frac{1}{2}$	21,683
30.9.1431–29.9.1433	24	1,143	$4\frac{1}{4}$	2	19,056
30.9.1433–26.6.1434	9	477	4	$7\frac{1}{2}$	7,956
26.6.1434–29.9.1434	3	157	6	15	2,626
30.9.1434–24.6.1435	9	300	0	$1\frac{1}{4}$	5,000
24.6.1435–29.9.1436	15	505	7	$6\frac{1}{2}$	8,427
30.9.1436–29.9.1437	12	339	9	5	5,663
30.9.1437–29.9.1438	12	315	1	$2\frac{1}{2}$	5,252
30.9.1438–18.12.1439	$14\frac{1}{2}$	545	7	$13\frac{3}{4}$	9,094
18.12.1439–16.4.1441	16	505	$4\frac{1}{2}$	0	8,423
16.4.1441–29.9.1443	$29\frac{1}{2}$	691	3	$11\frac{1}{4}$	11,522
30.9.1443–29.9.1444	12	243	8	$14\frac{1}{2}$	4,062
30.9.1444–29.9.1445	12	162	0	$3\frac{3}{4}$	2,700
30.9.1445–13.12.1445	$2\frac{1}{2}$	37	8	0	628
13.12.1445–24.6.1447	$18\frac{1}{2}$	$236\frac{1}{2}$	1	$8\frac{3}{4}$	3,944
24.6.1447–24.6.1448	12	87	10	$17\frac{1}{2}$	1,465
24.6.1448–11.10.1449	$15\frac{1}{2}$	204	10	$2\frac{1}{3}$	3,414
11.10.1449–29.9.1450	$11\frac{1}{2}$	357	1	$1\frac{1}{4}$	5,951
30.9.1450–9.4.1452	$18\frac{1}{2}$	415	1	$3\frac{3}{4}$	6,918
9.4.1452–1.4.1453	$11\frac{1}{2}$	262	$0\frac{1}{2}$	0	4,367
1.4.1453–21.4.1454	$12\frac{1}{2}$	123	10	$7\frac{1}{2}$	2,064
21.4.1454–28.3.1456	23	149	6	$0\frac{1}{2}$	2,492
28.3.1456–29.9.1457	18	128	$2\frac{1}{2}$	$7\frac{1}{2}$	2,137
30.9.1457–29.9.1458	12	84	10	0	1,414
30.9.1458–29.9.1459	12	19	5	11	324
30.9.1459–29.9.1460	12	113	2	15	1,887
30.9.1460–15.9.1462	$23\frac{1}{2}$	ACCOUNTS MISSING			
CALAIS MINT					
30.7.1422–30.1.1424	18	3,636			60,612
24.2.1424–24.12.1427	46	2,135			35,590
20.5.1428–2.8.1431	$38\frac{1}{2}$	361			6,018
YORK MINT					
12.8.1423–14.8.1424	12	2,538			42,310

EDWARD IV, First reign (4 March 1461–3 October 1470)

Background

The Yorkist forces entered London on 26 February 1461 and Edward, duke of York, who claimed the throne on the grounds of his descent from Edward III, took oaths as king on 4 March. Henry VI and his queen, with their army, were pursued northwards and defeated near Towton in Yorkshire on 29 March, whence they fled to Scotland. Warwick, the Yorkist earl who had been instrumental in securing the throne for Edward, eventually fell out with him and joined the Lancastrian cause. With French aid he was able to secure the brief restoration of Henry VI in 1470–71.

Output of coin in both metals was small during the first three years of Edward's reign. This was partially the consequence of a decline in the wool trade,[122] but was also due to a combination of the general shortage of coinage metals[123] and the value placed on bullion in England (unchanged since 1412), particularly compared to that in France.[124] Finally, in August 1464, the inevitable was reluctantly accepted, and the decision to devalue the English currency was taken. A large output followed and continued until Henry VI's restoration.

Issues

There were effectively two issues of gold coinage during Edward IV's first reign, the heavy coinage struck between his accession and 6 March 1465 (**338–9**), and the light coinage struck after that date (**340–425**). The noble of 6s 8d was revalued to 8s 4d from 13 August 1464 and any nobles struck between then and 6 March 1465 will have been issued at the higher value, but weights were unchanged and coins struck before and after 13 August 1464 cannot be distinguished from each other with any certainty.[125]

Mints

London, active throughout the reign, was the only mint in the heavy coinage period. To cope with the large amounts of bullion brought in after the devaluation additional mints were opened in July 1465 at Bristol, Coventry and Norwich, at all of which gold was struck. The royal mint at York was also mandated to strike gold at that date. Canterbury struck silver only, but, despite being mentioned in the indentures as a mint, there is no evidence that coins in either metal were struck at Calais.

[122] Spufford 1988, 339–62.
[123] Munro 1972, 165.
[124] Munro 1972, 157.
[125] Blunt and Whitton thought the nobles with i.m. rose might belong to the later period.

Conditions

Sir Richard Tunstall, Henry VI's last master, a courtier and a Lancastrian, was replaced in 1461 by Sir William Hastings, a councillor of Edward IV,[126] although particulars of any indenture with him of that date do not appear to be known.

Sir William Hastings (by then created Lord Hastings) first appears as a party to an indenture for London and Calais dated 13 August 1464.[127] This covers the first stage of the devaluation when the existing nobles were revalued to 8s 4d, an increase of 25% from 6s 8d. The same indenture provided for a reduction in weight of the silver penny from 15gr. to 12gr. This maintained the gold/silver ratio of 1:10.33 which had existed since 1411. The coinage charges for the gold were set at the high figure of 50s 0d per lb of which 2s 4d was for the master-worker (including 10d for 'deficiencies') and 47s 8d was to be accounted for by the warden. Thus, although the face value of the coin struck was increased by 25%, the actual mint price was only increased by 11.9% (see Table 7).

Apparently this was insufficient to attract gold to the mint, for a further indenture was made with Hastings on 6 March 1465, again for London and Calais, that made far reaching changes to the gold coinage.[128] It provided for a further increase of 8% in the value of gold; this would have the effect of valuing a 108 gr. noble at 9s 0d, and, as this would, no doubt, have been an inconvenient figure, the denomination was discontinued and replaced by a 'new' noble called the ryal or 'rose' noble, weighing 120 gr. (7.776 g) and valued at 10s 0d. At the same time a coin to restore the 6s 8d half-mark denomination was introduced, the angel weighing 80 gr. (5.184 g). Half and quarter ryals were struck, but fractions of the angel did not appear until the time of Henry VI's restoration.

These innovations were accompanied by a substantial reduction in the amount to be accounted for by the warden, as compared to the 1464 indenture. This had the effect that, even though the revaluation of gold was 8% the amount received from the mint in exchange for bullion increased by 17%. It is also interesting to note that these changes restored the 1:11.16 gold/silver ratio used between 1351 and 1413 (Table 7)

A large output was stimulated by these changes which led, for short periods, to the use of mints at Bristol, Coventry, Norwich and York to augment the capacity in London. However, output soon fell away again, no doubt affected by more competitive terms offered for gold in the Low Countries in 1466.[129] It was probably in response to this that a further indenture was made with Hastings on 2 March 1469[130] which only varied from the preceeding one by reducing the overall charges. In fact the master-worker's share rose by 2d to 2s 6d, but the amount to be accounted for by the warden fell by 6s 6d to 12s 0d, thus increasing the actual amount received by merchants from the mint by 6s 4d per Tower pound of gold coined. A similar reduction was made in the charges for coining silver.

[126] Challis 1992a, 179.
[127] Challis 1992b, 712, citing *CPR*, 1461–7, 370–1.
[128] Challis 1992b, 713, citing PRO. E101/306/2 no.8.
[129] Munro 1972, 169–71 and graph VI.
[130] Challis 1992b, 713 citing *CPR*, 1467–77, 138–9.

TABLE 7. Changes in coinage charges, mint price and gold/silver ratios during the fifteenth century (source: data from mint indentures cited in Challis 1992b)

Date	Gold coinage					Gold/silver ratios			
	(1) Face value to be struck from one Twr lb	(2) Acct. for by Warden	(3) Master moneyer	(4) Total deductions	(5) Net receipt (mint price)	(6) Pure gold value of one Twr lb	(7) Face value from one Twr lb of silver	(8) Pure silver value of one Twr lb	(9) Ratio
	(0.995 fine)					[(1) ÷ 0.995]			[(6) ÷ (8)]
	(1) £ s d	(2) £ s d	(3) s d	(4) £ s d	(5) £ s d	(6) £	(7) £	(8) £	(9)
1. 7.1402	15 0 0	3 6	1 6	5 0	14 15 0	15.075	1.250	1.351	1:11.16
1409[1]	16 0 0	4 8	2 0	6 8	15 13 4	16.080	1.400	1.514	1:10.62
14. 4.1413	16 13 4	3 6	2 4	5 10	16 7 6	16.750	1.500	1.622	1:10.33
13. 2.1422	16 13 4	3 6	1 6	5 0	16 8 4	16.750	1.500	1.622	1:10.33
16. 2.1423	16 13 4	3 6	1 6	5 0	16 8 4	16.750	1.500	1.622	1:10.33
8. 9.1431	16 13 4	3 6	1 6	5 0	16 8 4	16.750	1.500	1.622	1:10.33
10. 7.1434	16 13 4	3 6	1 6	5 0	16 8 4	16.750	1.500	1.622	1:10.33
13.12.1445	16 13 4	3 6	2 4	5 10	16 7 6	16.750	1.500	1.622	1:10.33
16.12.1451	16 13 4	3 6	2 4	5 10	16 7 6	16.750	1.500	1.622	1:10.33
11. 4.1459	16 13 4	3 6	2 4	5 10	16 7 6	16.750	1.500	1.622	1:10.33
13. 8.1464	20 16 8	2 7 8	2 4	2 10 0	18 6 8	20.938	1.875	2.027	1:10.33
6. 3.1465	22 10 0	18 6	2 4	1 0 10	21 9 2	22.613	1.875	2.027	1:11.16
2. 3.1469	22 10 0	12 0	2 6	14 6	21 15 6	22.613	1.875	2.027	1:11.16
6. 3.1471	22 10 0	8 0	2 6	10 6	21 19 6	22.613	1.875	2.027	1:11.16
23. 2.1472	22 10 0	5 0	2 6	7 6	22 2 6	22.613	1.875	2.027	1:11.16
3. 2.1477	22 10 0	5 0	2 6	7 6	22 2 6	22.613	1.875	2.027	1:11.16
12. 2.1483	22 10 0	5 0	2 6	7 6	22 2 6	22.613	1.875	2.027	1:11.16
20. 7.1483	22 10 0	5 0	2 6	7 6	22 2 6	22.613	1.875	2.027	1:11.16
4.11.1485	22 10 0	5 0	2 6	7 6	22 2 6	22.613	1.875	2.027	1:11.16
20.11.1492	22 10 0	8	1 10	2 6	22 7 6	22.613	1.875	2.027	1:11.16
22.11.1505	22 10 0	8	1 10	2 6	22 7 6	22.613	1.875	2.027	1:11.16
6. 8.1509	22 10 0	8	1 10	2 6	22 7 6	22.613	1.875	2.027	1:11.16

Note: 1. Indenture probably not executed.

It is interesting to observe the changing levels of the amount to be accounted for by the warden during this reign (Table 7). Since what mattered most to those taking gold to the mint was how much they got back, the adjustments can be seen as a means of responding to market conditions without the need to make frequent adjustments to the weight or nominal value of the coin, while, at the same time, when circumstances allowed, making considerable profit for the Crown.

References and Classification

The general reference for the coinage of Edward IV's first reign, Henry VI's restoration and Edward IV's second reign is Blunt and Whitton's series of papers.[131] Webb Ware has published a partial die study covering the same periods and taking advantage of the very considerable amount of new material that had come to light in the intervening 40 years.[132] In particular this deals with the ryals of types V and VI and with the angels, and references to this are given in the catalogue wherever appropriate. In fact, Mr Webb Ware was not able to illustrate in his paper all the dies he had recorded, and where examples of these occur in the Schneider collection he has kindly provided the relevant die numbers so that the number of illustrated examples of dies identified by him is here increased.

In cataloguing the coins an attempt has been made to place each denomination in chronological sequence. This has been done by ordering them in accordance with the main Blunt and Whitton types and, within those, by the Webb Ware obverse die number. The varieties recorded by Blunt and Whitton within each of their types are recorded where appropriate, but, since these are not necessarily listed by them in chronological order, they do not always appear in the published sequence.

Output

This is set out in Table 8,

---

[131] Blunt and Whitton 1945–8.
[132] Webb Ware 1985.

TABLE 8. *Output of gold coin from Edward IV to Richard III, inclusive (sources: Challis 1992, pp. 194 and 197, Stokes 1929)*

Accounting period	Months (approx.)	Weight coined			Face value (nearest £)	
		lb (Tower)	oz	dwt		
LONDON MINT						
30.9.1460–15.9.1462	23½	ACCOUNTS MISSING				Edward IV, first reign
15.9.1462–1.9.1464	23½	293	5	5	4,891	
1.9.1464–29.9.1466	25	12,389	11	10	278,774	
30.9.1466–25.10.1468	25	ACCOUNTS MISSING				
26.10.1468–29.9.1469	11	2,044	6	0	46,001	
30.9.1469–29.9.1470	12	2,289	5	0	51,512	
30.9.1470–13.4.1471	6½	ACCOUNTS MISSING				Henry VI, restored.
1.5.1471–29.9.1471	5	880	4	0	19,807	Edward IV, second reign
30.9.1471–29.9.1472	12	2,153	1	0	48,444	
30.9.1472–29.9.1473	12	1,679	0	0	37,778	
30.9.1473–29.9.1474	12	1,538	1	0	34,607	
30.9.1474–29.9.1475	12	1,315	2	0	29,591	
30.9.1475–5.5.1476	7	451	10	0	10,166	
6.5.1476–29.9.1477	17	1,802	3	0	40,551	
30.9.1477–29.9.1478	12	1,121	1	0	25,224	
30.9.1478–13.9.1479	11½	1,047	5	0	23,567	
14.9.1479–29.9.1480	12½	1,387	8	0	31,222	
30.9.1480–29.9.1481	12	794	0	0	17,865	
30.9.1481–29.9.1482	12	768	0	0	17,280	
30.9.1482– .12.1482	3	97	1	0	2,184	
.2.1483– .4.1483	3	141	8	0	3,188	
.5.1483– .6.1483	2	49	10	0	1,121	Edward V
.7.1483– .9.1483	3	178	0	0	4,005	Richard III
30.9.1483–29.9.1484	12	735	1	0	16,539	
30.9.1484–29.9.1485	12	388	6	0	8,741	
BRISTOL MINT						
.7.1465–29.9.1469	c.50	ACCOUNTS MISSING				
30.9.1469–29.9.1470	12	142	3	0	3,201	
30.9.1470–30.4.1471	7	ACCOUNTS MISSING				
1.5.1471–23.7.1472	14	117	3	0	2,638	
COVENTRY MINT						
.7.1465– .9.1465	c.2	ACCOUNTS MISSING				
NORWICH MINT						
.7.1465– .9.1465	c.2	ACCOUNTS MISSING				
YORK MINT						
.7.1465–29.9.1469	c.50	ACCOUNTS MISSING				
30.9.1469–29.9.1470	12	88	0	0	1,980	
30.9.1470–13.4.1471	6½	ACCOUNTS MISSING				
14.4.1471–29.9.1471	5½	54	7	10	1,229	

HENRY VI, Restored (3 October 1470–11 April 1471)

Background

Following the Earl of Warwick's defection from the Yorkist to the Lancastrian camp in September 1470 and Edward IV's flight to the Low Countries, Henry VI was placed back on the throne. His restoration was of short duration: by the spring of 1471 Edward had gathered an army, landed in Yorkshire and he entered London on 10 April. Following the battles of Barnet, at which Warwick was killed, and Tewkesbury, Edward returned to London as undisputed king on 21 May.

Mints

London functioned throughout the reign. The existence of coins shows that Bristol was operative also, while a record of profit from coining gold and silver coins at the York mint between Christmas 1470 and Easter 1471 indicates that there was production there too.[133] Unfortunately, there are no accounts for the period from the two provincial mints. The Bristol coins have the characteristic B in the waves beneath the ship (**446**). No coins with an E in the same location relating to York have yet come to light, although it is just possible that a closely die linked group marked with a lis may be from that mint (see below).

Issues

The only gold struck during this reign was in the form of angels and half-angels. There are no ryals. There was just one issue during the reign at the same standard as that introduced by Edward IV.

Conditions

The only indenture recorded for this reign was made towards its end, on 6 March 1471, with Sir Richard Tunstall,[134] who had been Henry's master-moneyer at his deposition in 1461. This provided for coinage to the same standards as previously, but once again there was a reduction in charges. The master-workers share remained at 2s 6d, but the amount to be accounted for by the warden was again reduced by 4s 0d to 8s 0d.

There can be little doubt that Tunstall was in charge from the date of Henry's restoration as it is highly unlikely that Lord Hastings, a prominent Yorkist, would have remained master. This view is supported by the record of the wardenship being taken over by one of Warwick's close supporters, Sir John Langstruther, together with John Delves, upon Edward's deposition.[135] It seems to have been fairly common at this period for indentures to be prepared to confirm existing arrangements.

---

[133] Stokes 1929, 56 (30 in the reprint).
[134] Challis 1992b, 717, citing PRO. C54/312.
[135] Challis 1992a, 181.

References and Classification

Webb Ware's die study[136] draws on and updates that of Allen.[137] The latter had previously been updated by Blunt and Whitton.[138] All three references are used in the catalogue, as appropriate.

Webb Ware's work on dies[139] has shown that the 'Lis group' have the characteristics of a separate mint. These have customarily been included with the London coins (obverse dies G and H) and their name arises from the fact that two of the three reverse dies associated with them (m, m' and n) have a lis in the legend. They form a closely interlinked group which does not link in with other dies attributed to London, which themselves are closely interlinked. The examples of these coins in the Schneider collection have been grouped separately (**447–50**). Whether they are the product of a separate 'officina' at London, or were struck there in a self contained period of time, or whether they represent the 'missing' output of the York mint, is unknown at present. In regard to this last possibility, it is perhaps worth noting that a somewhat similar group of Edward IV half-ryal dies with lis in the waves (**389–90, 392**) do have at least one die-link into the regular London series (**389**).

Output

Unfortunately London accounts for this short reign seem not to have survived. This is also the case for Bristol and York, although in the latter instance there is a record of £7 9s profit being made on the coinage of gold and silver between Christmas 1470 and Easter 1471.[140]

EDWARD IV, Restored (11 April 1471–9 April 1483)

Background

The Lancastrian defeats in 1471 were comprehensive, and Edward's position was never seriously threatened from that quarter again, although struggles with France and Scotland meant that the reign was by no means peaceful. Edward IV now emerged as a strong ruler ever seeking to control the turbulent nobility and to strengthen the finances of the Crown. He favoured merchants and engaged in trade himself.

The return to firm rule and to a relatively stable political situation favoured commerce.[141] The bullion and trade difficulties with the Burgundian Netherlands had largely disappeared once Charles the Bold became duke (1467).[142] The continuing

---

[136] Webb Ware 1985.
[137] Allen 1937.
[138] Blunt and Whitton 1945–8.
[139] Webb Ware 1985.
[140] Stokes 1929, 56.
[141] Munro 1972, 172, T.II.
[142] Lloyd 1977, 281.

favourable terms offered by the mint ensured that there was a steady output of gold coin during most of the reign. A slow downward trend in output reflects a gradual loss of competitiveness once the possible reductions in seignorage had been used up; but the extreme edge had been taken off the European bullion famine following the exploitation from the 1460s of silver ore at Schwaz in the Tirol and at Schneeberg in Saxony.[143]

Issues

Only angels and half-angels were struck in gold, and all at the standards introduced in 1465 (80 gr. to the angel of 6s 8d). There were, apparently, no ryals struck even though they continued to be provided for in the indentures.

Mints

There was continuous output from London. Bristol closed in August 1472, and a few coins have survived from the tiny output recorded for that mint (Table 8). York closed in September 1471, but no coins have yet come to light that can be attributed to the few months following Edward's restoration.[144]

Conditions

Lord Hastings resumed his position as master-moneyer on Edward's restoration. The first indenture, for London and Calais, is dated 23 February 1472,[145] although the only respect in which its terms differed from the previous indenture, the charges, had applied from 14 April 1471, five days after the restoration. This change to the charges was a reduction of the amount to be accounted for by the warden to 5s 0d compared to the figure of 8s 0d established under Henry in March 1471 (Table 7). A further indenture, again with Hastings, on the same terms was made on 3 February 1477.[146] It varied from the previous one by introducing regulations as to the use of trial plates.[147]

A final indenture was made towards the end of Edward's reign with Hastings' successor as master, Bartholomew Reed, on 12 February 1483.[148] This, for the first time in the fifteenth century, omits any reference to the Calais mint. Apart from this, the material conditions are the same as before.

---

[143] Spufford 1988, ch.16.
[144] Edward gained control of York in March during his advance towards London.
[145] Challis 1992b, 714, citing PRO. E101/306/2 no. 10; printed *CPR*, 1467–77, 313–15.
[146] Challis 1992b, 715, citing *CPR*, 1476–85, 20–1.
[147] Challis 1992a, 185.
[148] Challis 1992b, 715–16, citing PRO.C66/550: *CPR*, 1476–85, 340–1.

References and Classification

As with Edward IV's first reign and Henry VI's restoration, the coins are classified according to the main types described by Blunt and Whitton.[149] Webb Ware's recent work incorporates a die analysis,[150] and his numeration is used to place the coins in chronological order within the Blunt and Whitton types. Webb Ware has also put forward an absolute chronology which has been incorporated in Table 8.

Output

A full record exists and is incorporated in Table 8.

EDWARD V (9 April 1483–deposed 25 June 1483)

Immediately upon succeeding, Edward V, the twelve-year-old son of Edward IV, became the object of intrigue between, on the one hand, the family of the late king's queen, Elizabeth Woodville, and her brother, Lord Rivers; and on the other hand, the late king's brother, Richard, duke of Gloucester. Gloucester, acting quickly, captured Edward, arrested Rivers and got himself appointed Protector of the Realm. By the start of June the king and his brother, Richard were in the Tower, and it was being put about that Edward IV's children were not rightful successors to the throne and that Gloucester's own claim was better. Dissent was treated ruthlessly; one notable victim was Lord Hastings who, as well as being Chamberlain of the Royal Household and Lieutenant of Calais, continued to be active in mint affairs at the time.[151] He was summarily arrested at a Council meeting and executed on 13 June. On 25 June a packed convention drew up a petition asking Gloucester to assume the crown, which he did the next day.

Edward V and his brother are believed to have died in the Tower sometime between July and September 1483.

Issues

The attribution of coins to this reign has been the subject of much discussion (see below). Whatever coinage was struck during the two and a half months was to the same standards as those introduced under Edward IV in 1465.

Mints

Only the mint of London was active in this reign.

---

[149] Blunt and Whitton 1945–8.
[150] Webb Ware 1985.
[151] Possibly acting as master-moneyer. Stokes 1929, 58.

References and Classification

That coins were struck during the reign of this king is clear from the accounts (Table 8). The issue as to which coins these were has engaged the attention of numismatists since Montagu wrote in the *Numismatic Chronicle* in 1895.[152] Until recently the conclusions reached by Blunt[153] and supported by Whitton,[154] that coins reading ЄDW∧RD and with the obverse initial mark boars' head were the only ones likely to have been struck in that reign were generally accepted.

In 1987, in a paper on the coinage of Richard III read to the British Numismatic Society,[155] Mr Webb Ware presented a compelling argument based on a study of the dies and related to surviving accounts, that necessitates a review of this position. Since, at the time of writing, Mr Webb Ware's conclusions have not yet been published, it is necessary to summarise them here:

1. Coins of Blunt and Whitton (BW) type XXII, with i.m. sun and rose 1[156] and made from a batch of dies reading ЄDW∧RD DЄI GR∧, a reading carried on from earlier types (**469**), began to be struck under the indenture with Bartholomew Reed of 12 February 1483. These, therefore, are of Edward IV (Feb.–April 1483, 141lb 8oz of gold struck).

2. Coins of the same type and with the same initial mark but from a second batch of dies with the later form of reading ЄDW∧RD DI GR∧ (**482**) were probably struck under the direction of Lord Hastings acting without indenture but by mandate of the Lord Treasurer.[157] These are thus attributable to Edward V and possibly were struck before June 13 in view of Hasting's dramatic disgrace and execution on that date (May-June 1483. 49lb 10oz of gold struck).

3. Coins reading RIɊ∧RD DI GR∧ with initial mark sun and rose 1 (one die known) were probably struck prior to Robert Brackenbury's indenture of 20 July 1483. These are thus Richard III's first type. There is no example in the Schneider collection.

4. Following Brackenbury's appointment coins were struck using existing dies— those reading ЄDW∧RD DI GR∧ referred to in 2 above and that reading RIɊ∧RD DI GR∧ referred to in 3 above—on which the sun and rose 1 i.m. on the obverse has been overstruck with the boar's head i.m. (**483–7**). As the coinage progressed new dies were made reading RIɊ∧RD DI GR∧ and with the boar's head i.m. (**488–93**). These are Richard III's second type.

[152] Montagu 1895.
[153] Blunt 1934–7.
[154] Whitton 1941–4.
[155] On 23 June 1987.
[156] The three versions of the sun and rose and the two versions of the boar's head initial marks are illustrated in Winstanley 1941–4, 182, and North 1991, 97.
[157] Stokes 1929, 58 (p. 32 in the reprint). It is not clear what happened to Bartholomew Reed at this period. He had possibly been a deputy or protege of Hastings while the latter was in favour. The entry quoted by Stokes clearly suggests that Hastings was in charge during at least part of the Protectorate. Reed reappears in the reign of Henry VII as a master-worker.

5. From about June 1484[158] the sun and rose i.m. was readopted using two new punches, sun and rose 2 and 3, and these continued in use into the reign of Henry VII (on the gold sun and rose 3 was not introduced until the reign of Henry VII). Gold coins using sun and rose 2 are of Richard III's third type (**494–8**).

The effect of these new conclusions is to transfer the coins that Blunt attributed to Edward V to Richard III (**483**) and to advance a coin formerly attributed to Edward IV to Edward V (**482**). The Schneider collection also contains a coin of BW type XXII with i.m. sun and rose 1 that is of the earlier Edward IV type reading ЄDWΛRD DЄI GRΛ (**469**).

Output
See Table 8.

RICHARD III (26 June 1483–22 August 1485)

Background

Richard's ruthless seizure of the crown had left a core of bitter opposition. When the rumour spread that the princes in the tower were dead, support moved towards Henry Tudor, earl of Richmond, whose paternal grandmother, Catherine of Valois had been the wife of Henry V and daughter of Charles VI of France, and whose mother was great-granddaughter of John of Gaunt. Henry had found asylum in Brittany and with aid from the king of France was able to land a small force at Milford Haven on 7 August 1485. Marching eastwards he gained adherents all the time, and the decisive battle took place at Bosworth in Leicestershire on 22 August 1485. Richard was killed and Henry was crowned on the battlefield. The War of the Roses had ended.

Political instability had been no help to trade, and mint output for both gold and silver, was low during Richard's reign. However, so far as gold coin was concerned, probably a more significant factor in reducing production in England was the increasing value placed on that metal in terms of silver, especially in France.[159]

Issues

The standards instituted in 1465 continued during this reign. The only gold denominations struck continued to be the angels and their halves.

Mints

The only mint in operation in Richard's reign for the striking of gold was London.

---

[158] This date is estimated by Mr Webb Ware based on the relative proportions of dies and output,
[159] Spufford 1988, 370.

Conditions

An indenture was made on 20 July 1483 with Robert Brackenbury[160] who had been Richard's ducal treasurer.[161] The conditions for the coinage and the charges were the same as before. Calais was once again named in the indenture as a mint, even though there is no evidence that any coins were struck there after 1440.

References and Classification

The latest published study of the coinage of this reign is that of Winstanley.[162] However, Mr Webb Ware's new and, as yet, unpublished die-study takes matters a lot further.[163] His conclusions, which outline a coherent development from Edward IV's last type are summarised above (under Edward V). They divide Richard's coinage into three main types, and he has kindly allowed his work to be used in arranging the coins in this collection. References to his die numbers as well as to the varieties noted by Winstanley are therefore included in the catalogue.

Output

This is set out in Table 8, with cross-references added to the chronology proposed by Webb Ware.

HENRY VII (22 August 1485–21 April 1509)

Background

Although Henry VII's reign was by no means peaceful—he had to suppress two rebellions, those of Lambert Simnel and Perkin Warbeck—he progressively created stability and saw that the road to political strength lay through the accumulation of wealth. Thus he was always interested in creating good conditions for trade, as with the comprehensive agreement, the *Magnus Intercursus*, made with the Burgundians in 1496 whereby much was done to remove obstacles to trade between England and the Low Countries. Ramsay has shown that the customs records point to 'a period of unspectacular progress for the first two-thirds of the reign followed by a marked boom which persisted into the reign of Henry VIII'.[164] Henry also tried to extract good financial results from diplomatic and military ventures. Thus, when it became apparent that his intervention to prevent France from annexing Brittany[165] could not succeed, he agreed under the Treaty of Etaples to withdraw his forces in return for a substantial payment from France. This,

---

[160] Challis 1992b, 716, citing PRO. E101/306/2 no. 13; *CPR*, 1476–85, 463–4.
[161] Challis 1992a, 180.
[162] Winstanley 1941–4.
[163] Paper read to the British Numismatic Society on 23 June 1987.
[164] Ramsey 1953–4.
[165] Brittany had sheltered Henry during the Yorkist period and there was concern about the control over the entrance to the English Channel that France would gain.

when consolidated with other sums due, amounted to about £150,000 in English money, to be paid off at the rate of approximately £5,000 per year in gold.[166] Further money came from abroad in 1501 when the first half of Catherine of Aragon's dowry of £50,000 was paid over on the occasion of her marriage to the king's eldest son, Arthur. All these receipts are likely to have been converted to English coin at the mint.

No less a cause for minting activity will have been the king's large diplomatic expenditures, including advances of £226,000 made to secure the friendship of the emperor Maximilian, his son Philip, duke of Burgundy and his grandson Charles (future king of Spain and Emperor). Other stimuli to mint production will have been the reduction of coinage charges from 1 March 1489[167] and the vigorous attempts made to eliminate clipped money from circulation and to replace it with full-weight coin during the years 1504–6.[168] While trade was probably the most important consideration, all these elements will have contributed to the substantial growth in mint activity, which applied to the silver as much as to the gold, in the years after 1500 (see Table 9).

Issues

There were no changes to the standards of weight and fineness, nor to the related values of coins issued in this reign, but there were important innovations. In fact, the period was one of development in many aspects of the coinage as a whole. Those in the silver included the introduction of sovereign-type pence, the experiments with portcullis and sovereign-type groats that were not proceeded with, the appearance of testoons and groats with profile portrait busts, and the general adoption of the arched 'imperial' crown.[169] With the gold, the major innovation took place in 1489 with the introduction of the sovereign of 20s 0d. Shortly after this, probably in 1492, the ryal made a brief reappearance.[170] Both these denominations used the arched crown from the outset. Finally, from 1493, on the angel St Michael and the dragon were represented in a more 'humanistic' style. St Michael, who had been dressed solely in feathers came, after a short transition, to be dressed in armour, and the dragon acquired a less ferocious character.

The sovereigns were struck under a separate commission and at times employ initial marks not used on the other gold coins (cross fitchée, dragon, lis). The variety employing the first of these, the cross fitchée, has been associated with the siege of Boulogne or the subsequent Peace of Etaples, because it also displays French symbols in its design and thus can be seen as a celebration of what was presented as a considerable coup on Henry's part. A few sovereigns of double or even triple weight are known. They were

---

[166] Challis 1978, 187.
[167] Thereby increasing the amounts received back from the mint by those taking bullion. See Challis 1992a, 196 and T. 10.
[168] Challis 1992a, 207.
[169] Grierson 1964.
[170] Perhaps struck for the French expedition of 1492; Challis 1978, 52.

struck from regular dies and must be regarded as special issues perhaps for use as diplomatic presents. Certainly the normal sovereigns were used in this way. Challis records four instances in 1502 and 1506 from the book of payments of John Heron, treasurer of the Chamber.[171]

Mints

Gold coins were struck at the London mint only. This was probably in operation continuously throughout the reign, although the absence of accounts for a five year period from Michaelmas 1489 to Michaelmas 1494 makes it impossible to be absolutely sure of this.

Conditions

Richard III's last master, Robert Brakenbury, had died at Bosworth,[172] and Henry's first indenture was with Sir Giles Daubeney and Bartholomew Reed, both of whom had served Edward IV. Indeed, Reed had been Edward IV's last master, appointed in 1483. The new indenture was dated 4 November 1485,[173] and in respect of gold coin it provided for a ryal of 10s 0d weighing 120 gr. (7.776 g), together with its half and quarter, and an angel of 6s 8d weighing 80 gr. (5.184 g), together with its half. In all cases fineness continued at 23 ct $3\frac{1}{2}$ gr. (0.995 fine). In fact, no ryals or their fractions are known that were struck under this indenture. Mintage charges were set at 2s 6d for the master-worker and 5s 0d to be accounted for by the warden, the same as had applied since 1472.

The next development was a special instruction issued on 1 March 1489[174] reducing mintage charges by 5s 0d. Challis interprets this as anticipating the indenture of 1492 in which the master-worker's fee was reduced to 1s 10d and the amount to be accounted for by the warden, to 8d.[175] This was perhaps a response to the small amount of gold being brought to the mint, but, if so, it does not seem to have led to any dramatic increase in output during the seven months to Michaelmas 1489 (see Table 9). Unfortunately, there are no accounts for the five years from Michaelmas 1489 to Michaelmas 1494 since, very exceptionally, the warden was excused from rendering any.[176] This may have been because the mint was entering a period of experimentation during which new denominations and designs were tried out. Little record of this has survived.

---

[171] Challis 1990.
[172] Challis 1992a, 207.
[173] Challis 1992b, 717, citing PRO. C66/562.
[174] Challis 1978, 46, citing PRO. E159/271, Rec. Mich. 2.
[175] Challis 1992a, T. 10.
[176] Challis 1978, 46.

The first step towards the introduction of new coinage designs is found in a mandate to William Stafford, the warden, dated 28 March 1489 which calls for the manufacture of dies of the 'sovereign' type for both gold and silver coin.[177] The order for the introduction of the gold sovereign was given in a commission dated 28 October 1489[178] issued to the same two master-workers and providing for the production of sovereigns of 20s 0d weighing 240 gr. (15.552 g). Fineness remained as before. The commission specified that two sovereigns were to made from every pound weight of gold struck, that is, in terms of face value, £2 out of every £22 10s 0d. There were no instructions as to mintage charges.

In 1492 Sir Giles Daubeney surrendered his appointment and John Shaw was appointed joint master with Bartholomew Reed. This was the occasion for a new indenture dated 20 November 1492[179] which provided for exactly the same coins to the same standards as the indenture of 1485. It contained no mention of sovereigns, although there can be no doubt that they were struck from time to time throughout the rest of the reign. The reduced coinage charges introduced on 1 March 1489 were included in the new indenture. It was under this indenture that the only ryals known for the reign were struck. The last indenture for the reign was made on 22 November 1505 with new joint masters, Robert Fenrother and William Rede.[180] In all material respects the terms were the same as those of 1492.

References and Classification

The classification of the coinage of Henry VII used today is essentially that set forth by Potter and Winstanley (PW),[181] which, in turn, had built on the work of Brooke,[182] Lawrence,[183] Carlyon-Britton,[184] and others.

PW followed Brooke by dividing the coinage into five consecutive types. Within some types they define a number of groups and, in some cases, individual dies are listed and described. In its application to the gold coinage there is some unevenness, essentially because the classification is based on the more abundant and continuously struck groats. Later amendments to the PW classification applicable to the gold coinage are Schneider's proposal that the i.m. rose angels should be treated as an early variant of type II rather than as a variety of type I,[185] and Grierson's proposal, mainly on typo-

---

[177] Metcalf 1976, xxvii citing *CPR*, 4 H.VII, 265.
[178] Challis 1992b, 717 citing *CPR*, 1485–94, 319. On the distinction between an indenture and a commission see Challis 1978, 22–3, or Challis 1992b, 699.
[179] Challis 1992b, 718, citing PRO. C66/574, m. 1–2.
[180] Challis 1992b, 718, citing CCR, 1500–9, no. 556.
[181] Potter and Winstanley 1960–3. The gold coins are dealt with in *BNJ* 1963 but references are made to lettering in the earlier volumes.
[182] Brooke 1950.
[183] Lawrence 1918.
[184] Carlyon-Britton 1925–6.
[185] Schneider 1974.

logical grounds, that the sovereigns of type II (with i.m. cinquefoil) should precede those of type I (with i.m. cross fitchée).[186] Additionally, Stewart was been able to demonstrate[187] that changes were needed to the absolute chronology proposed by Potter,[188] and, building on this, Metcalf has put forward a fully revised chronology in *SCBI* 23.[189] To avoid confusion the PW order has been retained here, but the amendments are noted in the catalogue. Cross-references to *SCBI* 23 are also given whenever possible.

For fuller information on the historical, administrative and economic background to the coinage of this reign, as with the other Tudor reigns, reference should be made to Challis, *The Tudor Coinage*.[190]

Output

Mint output figures, set out in Table 9, are quoted from Challis[191] and superseded those earlier published by Stokes[192] and Craig.[193] It should be noted, however, that to aid comparison with later Tudor issues Challis gives[194] weights in Troy pounds of 5760 grains, whereas in Table 9 the weights are given in Tower pounds of 5400 grains, as used by the mint until 1526.

HENRY VIII (22 April 1509–28 January 1547)

Background

The trade boom that had started in Henry VII's later years continued well into the new reign,[195] and must have accounted for a substantial proportion of the fairly steady output of gold coin during the first ten years of the reign (Table 10a). This will have been supplemented by the success of Henry's early ventures. Thus in the peace settlement with France of 1514, England was left in possession of Tournai and the pension from France, already payable under Henry VII's Treaty of Etaples, was amalgamated with a new indemnity giving a total to be paid of about £217,000.[196] When Tournai was sold back to the French in 1516 for about £16,000, that sum was added to the principal and further additions were secured until the annual payment in some years reached over £40,000, until all were ended in 1534.[197]

---

[186] Grierson 1964.
[187] Stewart 1974.
[188] Potter and Winstanley 1960–3. Chapter IX in *BNJ* 1963 on the subject of absolute chronology is, however, in the name of Potter, alone.
[189] Metcalf 1976, xxxvi–xxxix.
[190] Challis 1978.
[191] Challis 1978.
[192] Stokes 1929.
[193] Craig 1953.
[194] Challis 1978, 307, and Challis 1992b, 684–5.
[195] Ramsay 1953–4.
[196] Challis 1978.
[197] Challis 1978.

TABLE 9. *Output of gold coin during the reign of Henry VII showing approximate correlation with initial marks and Potter and Winstanley (PW) types (sources: Challis 1978 (with weights changed from Troy to Tower) and Metcalf 1976)*

Accounting period	*Months (approx.)*	*Weight coined*		*Face value (nearest £)*	*Initial marks*			
		lbs (Tower)	*oz*		*Angels and Half Angels*	*PW*	*Sovereigns and Ryal*	*PW*
LONDON MINT								
2.11.1485–29.9.1486	11	472	2	10,624	To summer 1487: sun and rose,	I		
30.9.1486–29.9.1487	12	345	0	7,763	lis and rose. Summer 1487 to			
30.9.1487–29.9.1488	12	403	$7\frac{1}{2}$	9,082	Feb. 1488: rose. Feb. 1488 to	II		
30.9.1488–29.9.1489	12	238	3	5,361	Spring 1489: no mark. Spring			
30.9.1489–29.9.1490	12				1489 to spring 1493: cinquefoil.		October 1489 to spring	II
30.9.1490–29.9.1491	12						1493(?): cinquefoil.	
30.9.1491–29.9.1492	12	NO ACCOUNTS MADE						
30.9.1492–29.9.1493	12				Spring 1493 to autumn 1495:	III	Late 1492(?) to spring	I
30.9.1493–29.9.1494	12				escallop.		1493(?): cross fitchée	
30.9.1494–29.9.1495	12	1,056	$2\frac{1}{2}$	23,764			Spring 1493 to autumn	III
30.9.1495–29.9.1496	12	586	$3\frac{3}{4}$	13,192	Autumn 1495 to Michaelmas	III	1495: dragon.	
30.9.1496–29.9.1497	12	764	$11\frac{1}{4}$	17,211	1498: pansy.			
30.9.1497–29.9.1498	12	868	$2\frac{1}{8}$	19,534				
30.9.1498–29.9.1499	12	1,020	$5\frac{3}{8}$	22,096	Michaelmas 1498 to Michaelmas			
30.9.1499–29.9.1500	12	805	$0\frac{1}{4}$	18,133	1499: lis-issuant-from-rose.		Lis/dragon	IV
30.9.1500–29.9.1501	12	1,109	$6\frac{1}{8}$	24,964	Michaelmas 1499 to Michaelas			
30.9.1501–29.9.1502	12	1,314	$2\frac{5}{8}$	29,570	1502: anchor.			
30.9.1502–29.9.1503	12	1,272	$1\frac{1}{8}$	28,622	Michaelmas 1502 to spring 1504:	IV		
30.9.1503–29.9.1504	12	1,612	$6\frac{3}{8}$	36,282	greyhound's head.			
30.9.1504–29.9.1505	12	2,112	$1\frac{5}{8}$	47,523	Spring 1504 to Nov. 1505 (?):	V		
30.9.1505–29.9.1506	12	4,246	$9\frac{5}{8}$	95,553	cross-crosslet.		Lis/cross-crosslet	V
30.9.1506–29.9.1507	12	3,804	$9\frac{5}{8}$	85,608	November 1505(?) to April			
30.9.1507–29.9.1508	12	5,452	$11\frac{3}{4}$	122,692	1509: pheon.		Lis/pheon	V
30.9.1508–29.9.1509	12	5,300	$0\frac{1}{2}$	119,251				

After 1520 gold output dropped, although this was partially offset by an increase in that of silver. Nevertheless, the aggregate value of money being struck declined. Cardinal Wolsey was commissioned in 1526 to adjust English coin to bring it into equivalence with Continental specie,[198] so for an understanding of what was happening that is the direction in which we should first look.

England's most important trading partner continued to be the Low Countries, now part of the Hapsburg empire. Apart from this, the major economy which was of most concern to England was that of France. Both had recently made adjustments to their currencies. France had debased both gold and silver by about 11–12% in 1519. As a result French mints were in a position to offer an improved mint price. However, this did not lead to any marked increase in output,[199] and there was no significant change to the gold/silver ratio until 1521, when silver alone was debased by a further 4.2%.[200] In the Low Countries, where a dual standard gold currency existed, silver was debased by 4.4% in 1520, but the finer gold not at all. The baser gold, however, was debased by 3.1%.[201] The increase in the value of silver in terms of fine gold drew in supplies of the latter and the consequences of this can be seen from the sharp increase in output of fine gold coins, *reals* and *demi-reals*, following 1520.[202] The gold florins, which had been debased almost as much as the silver, were perhaps aimed more at trade with the other florin-using states along the Rhine. There can be little doubt that steps taken in the Low Countries in 1520 accounted in a large measure for the drop in output in English gold and its partial replacement by an increased output of silver after 1520.

As can be seen from Table 10 the initial English response of August 1526, by making silver cheap in terms of gold, would at once attract large quantities of the former metal. The subsequent adjustment of November 1526 reversed the position. Also, by debasing further the value of the coinage in both metals, it permitted an improved mint price which was evidently sufficient to achieve a reasonable flow of both.

It is no surprise, therefore, that after 1526 the Engish accounts show a marked increase in the output of silver coin. What is less readily explained is the large but short-term increase in the output of gold after 1526. One probable explanation is the conversion of 23 ct $3\frac{1}{2}$ gr. coin into 22 ct coin, although the advantage of doing this is not fully evident.[203]

Other factors are likely to have affected this picture. There was an ineffective campaign against France in 1522–3 at a cost estimated at £400,000.[204] Forced loans and heavy taxes were imposed to pay for this and for other diplomatic expenses. While

---

[198] Challis 1992

[199] Spooner 1972, 124–6, also graph 30B.

[200] Duplessy 1989, 6. The price paid by the mint for silver had been raised for the express purpose of issuing testoons and represented an increase of about 6.0% on the 1519 price for coining douzains. See Spooner 1972, 126.

[201] Van Gelder and Hoc 1960. The statement on p. 75 of that work, that no debasement took place in the 1520s, can be shown to be wrong from the figures they quote for the gold and silver content of individual denominations.

[202] Van Gelder and Hoc 1960, 77.

[203] Challis 1978

[204] Mackie 1962, 303.

TABLE 10. *Changes in coinage charges, mint price and gold/silver ratios during the sixteenth century (source: data from mint indentures and proclamations cited in Challis 1976 and 1992b)*

Columns (1)–(5) = Gold coinage; columns (6)–(9) = Gold/silver ratios.

Date	Fineness (1) ct, gr. (1.000)	Face value to be struck from one Troy lb (2) £ s d	Total deductions (3) £ s d	Net receipt (mint price) (2)−(3) (4) £ s d	Pure gold value of one Troy lb (5) £	Silver fineness (6) oz dwt (1.000)	Face value struck from one Troy lb of silver alloy (7) £	Pure silver value of one Troy lb (8) £	Ratio (5) ÷ (8) (9)
6. 8.1509[1]	23 3½ (0.995)	24 0 0	2 6	23 17 6	24.121	11 2 (0.925)	2.000	2.162	1:11.16
22. 8.1526	23 3½ (0.995)	26 8 0	2 6	26 5 6	26.533	11 2 (0.925)	2.000	2.162	1:12.23
5.11.1526	23 3½ (0.995)	27 0 0	2 6	26 17 6	27.136	11 2 (0.925)	2.250	2.432	1:11.16
	22 0 (0.917)	25 2 6	2 6	25 0 0	27.399	11 2 (0.925)	2.250	2.432	1:11.27
6. 4.1533	23 3½ (0.995)	27 0 0	2 9	26 17 3	27.136	11 2 (0.925)	2.250	2.432	1:11.16
	22 0 (0.917)	25 2 6	3 0	24 19 6	27.399	11 2 (0.925)	2.250	2.432	1:11.27
16. 5.1542	23 0 (0.958)	28 16 0	1 4 0	27 12 0	30.063	9 2 (0.758)	2.400	3.166	1: 9.50[2]
27. 3.1545	22 0 (0.917)	30 0 0	2 5 0	27 15 0	32.715	6 0 (0.500)	2.400	4.800	1: 6.82
1. 4.1546	20 0 (0.833)	30 0 0	4 5 0	25 15 0	36.014	4 0 (0.333)	2.400	7.207	1: 4.50
.10.1546	20 0 (0.833)	30 0 0	4 0 0	26 0 0	36.014	4 0 (0.333)	2.400	7.207	1: 4.50
5. 4.1547	20 0 (0.833)	30 0 0	1 10 0	28 10 0	36.014	4 0 (0.333)	2.400	7.207	1: 4.50
16. 2.1548	20 0 (0.833)	30 0 0	1 0 0	29 0 0	36.014	4 0 (0.333)	2.400	7.207	1: 4.50
24. 1.1549	22 0 (0.917)	34 0 0	1 0 0	33 0 0	37.077	8 0 (0.667)	4.800	7.196	1: 5.15
18.12.1550	23 3½ (0.995)	28 16 0	2 9	28 13 3	28.945	—	—	—	—
5.10.1551	23 3½ (0.995)	36 0 0	2 9	35 17 3	36.181	11 1 (0.921)	3.000	3.257	1:11.11
	22 0 (0.917)	33 0 0	3 0	32 17 0	35.987	11 1 (0.921)	3.000	3.257	1:11.05
20. 8.1553	23 3½ (0.995)	36 0 0	4 0	35 16 0	36.181	11 0 (0.917)	3.000	3.272	1:11.06
5. 8.1557	23 3½ (0.995)	36 0 0	4 0	35 16 0	36.181	11 0 (0.917)	3.000	3.272	1:11.06
31.12.1558	23 3½ (0.995)	36 0 0	4 0	35 16 0	36.181	11 0 (0.917)	3.000	3.272	1:11.06
	22 0 (0.917)	33 0 0	4 0	32 16 0	35.987	11 0 (0.917)	3.000	3.272	1:11.00
8.11.1560	23 3½ (0.995)	36 0 0	5 0	35 15 0	36.181	11 2 (0.925)	3.000	3.243	1:11.16
	22 0 (0.917)	33 0 0	4 0	32 16 0	35.987	11 2 (0.925)	3.000	3.243	1:11.10
19. 4.1572	23 3½ (0.995)	36 0 0	4 0	35 16 0	36.181	11 2 (0.925)	3.000	3.243	1:11.16
15. 9.1578	23 3¼ (0.992)	36 1 10½	7 9	35 14 1½	36.378	11 1 (0.921)	3.013	3.272	1:11.12
28. 8.1582	23 3¼ (0.992)	36 1 10½	7 9	35 14 1½	36.378	11 1 (0.921)	3.013	3.272	1:11.12
30. 1.1583	23 3½ (0.995)	36 0 0	6 0	35 14 0	36.181	11 2 (0.925)	3.000	3.243	1:11.16
10. 6.1593	22 0 (0.917)	33 0 0	7 0	32 13 0	35.987	11 2 (0.925)	3.000	3.243	1:11.10
29. 7.1601	23 3½ (0.995)	36 10 0	10 0	36 0 0	36.683	11 2 (0.925)	3.100	3.351	1:10.95
	22 0 (0.917)	33 10 0	10 0	33 0 0	36.532	11 2 (0.925)	3.100	3.351	1:10.90

Notes:
1. In this table the Tower lb (5,400 gr.), in use until 1526, has been converted to the Troy lb (5,760 gr.) so that figures are comparable.
2. The extremely low ratios between gold and silver of the debasement period reflects the fact that silver was much more debased than gold. Thus silver in coin was much overvalued by comparison with gold in coin.

these, of course, could have been a cause of mint activity rather than otherwise (converting plate into coin, for example), the whole venture was a drain on the wealth of the country, it interrupted trade, and, when England and France were at war, French pensions would not be paid.

An account of the dramatic political events of the 1530s arising from Henry's desire for a male heir, but which, in turn, led to the rupture with Rome and the English Reformation, is outside the scope of this book, but these events had their effect on the coinage.

Substantial quantities of gold and silver found their way to the mint between 1536 and 1540 from the treasuries of dissolved monasteries and from the embellishments of shrines that had been places of pilgrimage. It has been estimated that from 1537 at least £50,000, and possibly a good deal more, came from this source.[205] This wealth was soon consumed and pressure for further funds to forward the king's policies continued.

It was at this time that the plan to make money by manipulating the coinage was conceived. Possibly the idea had grown out of a successful but modest experiment with the Irish coinage in 1536.[206] However, what was now planned was a major clandestine debasement of the national coinage for the express purpose of making large profits for the Crown.

It must be emphasized that this was quite a different matter from the long-established general aim that the mint should operate profitably on the basis of appropriate mintage charges being made. What was now sought were gains of quite a vastly greater order which were to be obtained by making baser coin to exchange for finer without the recipient being aware of the debasement. In other words the state was planning to carry out a fraud.

The first, secret, step in 1542 provided for slightly debased coin to be made and stored, while at the same time the mint continued to produce coin at the publicly declared standard. The bullion for the debased coin was supplied from the king's own resources plus such small purchases as the master workers could make without giving rise to suspicion as to their purpose. £15,595 of gold and £52,927 of silver coin had been made in this way and stored in the Tower by March 1544.

Meanwhile, in 1543, war had broken out with Scotland and France acting in alliance. It was to last until 1546 and it has been calculated that its cost amounted to the huge figure of £2.2 million,[207] much in excess of the yield of regular and exceptional taxes and loans available at the period.[208]

---

[205] Challis 1978
[206] Challis 1978
[207] Mackie 1962, 410, quoting Dietz.
[208] Mackie 1962, 410–11.

There had thus arisen a need for money that was even more acute than usual. It was seen that for the maximum potential profits of the debasement scheme to be realised, the volume of bullion coined had to be as large as possible, in any case much larger than the amount of bullion that had been provided from the discreet sources so far used. To do this it was necessary to be able to buy bullion on the open market offering the advantageous mint price that debasement made possible. It was also seen that the success of the fraud depended on the fact that as much coin as possible should be disposed of before the reduced fineness was discovered and, to this end, that the mint should be able to produce large quantities of coin quickly. It was also clear that the profits of the scheme should go to the Crown and not to benefit mint officials (as would have been the case in the system where the master worker was an independent contractor who received a fixed sum relating to every pound struck).

Steps to meet all these requirements were taken in spring 1544. The advantageous mint price attracted large amounts of silver and gold to the mint, but soon the deception was realised and to continue to attract bullion the process had to be repeated, each step involving reductions in precious metal content. Inevitably, by Henry's death, in 1547, the coinage was sadly debased and internationally discredited. Although a separate figure cannot be deduced for Henry's reign, it has been estimated that the net profit from minting operations between 1542 and 1551 amounted to approximately £1.27 million.[209]

The end of the war with Scotland and France in 1546 left England in possession of Boulogne and with substantial financial promises from France, and, although these were small in relation to the cost of the war, they were of some advantage in the next reign.

Issues

The coinage of this reign is customarily divided into three periods. These can best be understood in relation to the indentures and commissions that were issued and which are set out under Conditions, below.

Mints

During the first two periods gold coins were struck at the Tower mint in London only. Following the reorganisation in 1544 the Tower mint was split into two production units, Tower I and Tower II, both of which struck gold. In addition, from 1545, gold was struck at the Southwark mint and, from 1546, at Bristol.

Conditions

First Period, 1509–26

The first coinage indenture of the reign, made on 6 August 1509 with William Blount,[210] is essentially a repeat of the last indenture issued under Henry VII. In

---

[209] Challis 1992a, 240.
[210] Challis 1992b, 718–19 citing PRO. C54/377, m.16d.

relation to gold, provision was made for ryals of 10s 0d weighing 120 gr. (7.776 g), together with halves and quarters, and angels of 6s 8d weighing 80 gr. (5.184 g), together with their halves. Fineness remained unchanged at 23 ct 3½ gr. (0.995 fine). There were no changes in coinage charges. The great bulk of the gold coinage issued under this indenture consisted of angels and half-angels. A single specimen of the ryal survives which is in the British Museum,[211] and no fractions of it have yet been found. Sovereigns were struck in small quantities. Since they were not included in the indenture they were presumably ordered under a separate commission.[212]

Second Period, 1526–44

As a consequence of the lack of bullion arriving at the mint, a commission was issued to Cardinal Wolsey on 24 June 1526 authorising him to make whatever adjustments were needed to bring English coin into parity with the principal Continental currencies.[213] The resulting changes came in two steps:

1. On 22 August 1526
   (a) all existing denominations were increased in value by one tenth. Thus the sovereign became 22s 0d, the ryal 11s 0d and the angel 7s 4d.
   (b) a new denomination, the crown of the rose, 'of the fineness, weight and goodness' of the French 'crown of the sun' was introduced. The French *ecu d'or au soleil* current at that date (since July 1519) had a nominal weight of 53 gr. (3.434 g), a fineness of 23 ct (0.958 fine) and passed for 4s 6d in England.
2. On 5 November 1526
   (a) the value of existing denominations was again increased to bring the total increase, including that of 22 August 1526, to one eighth. Thus the sovereign became 22s 6d, the ryal 11s 3d, and the angel 7s 6d.
   (b) a new coin, the george noble, valued at 6s 8d and to weigh 71.1gr. (4.607 g) was introduced together with its half. Fineness was to be 23 ct 3½ gr. Evidently this was intended to meet the demand for a half-mark coin previously supplied by the angel.
   (c) the crown of the rose was abandoned, but in its place a new coin, the crown of the double rose valued at 5s 0d was introduced. This had a nominal weight of 57.3 gr. (3.713 g) and was struck at the reduced fineness of 22 ct. A half-crown was also introduced.

It will be seen that, at least in theory, all existing gold coins remained in circulation and, indeed, continued to be struck at the same weight and fineness as before. It was purely their nominal value that was increased. Of the new coins, the george noble was

---

[211] This was condemned as false by Brooke and Whitton. Subsequently it has been rehabilitated in Kent 1963.
[212] But there seems to be no trace of any such document.
[213] Challis 1992b, 720, citing *LP*, iv, no. 2338; *Tudor Royal Proclamations*, nos. 111–12.

apparently not struck in very large quantities nor for any long period.[214] It is rare and its half, rarer still, is only known from two specimens, one in the British Museum and the Schneider specimen (**577**), a recent find. The crown of the rose presumably was only struck between August and November 1526 and today is recorded from three specimens of which one is in the Schneider collection (**575**).[215] The crown of the double rose brought a major innovation, the introduction of 'crown', as opposed to 'fine' or 'angel' gold. The specification of crown gold denominations as well as those of fine gold continued until the indenture of 1670. Since then, 22 ct has been the standard fineness for British gold coin up to the present day.

The changes made on 5 November 1526 were repeated in an indenture made with new master workers, Ralph Rowlett and Martin Bowes, on 6 April 1533.[216] This is the first indenture to include provision for sovereigns alongside the other denominations. Gold coinage charges were also increased to give mintage charges on angel gold of 2s 9d divided between the master workers, 1s 6d, the moneyers, 7d, and to be accounted for by the warden, 8d. The mintage charges on crown gold were 3s 0d, divided 1s 7d, 9d, and 8d respectively. In comparing these charges with those made previously, it should be remembered that they relate to pounds weight struck, and that as, since 1526, they no longer refer to pounds Tower, but to the heavier pound Troy, the total mintage charge on angel gold had only risen by 1d.[217]

Third Period, 1544–7

The next major change was ordered in an indenture dated 28 May 1544,[218] and this marked the first public step into the period of progressive debasement. The effect was greatest in regard to silver coins which were to be reduced in fineness from 11 oz 2 dwt (0.925 fine) to 9 oz (0.750 fine). For the fine gold the reduction was a comparatively small one, from 23 ct 3$\frac{1}{3}$ gr. (0.995 fine) to 23 ct (0.958 fine). The 1544 indenture had been preceded by another on the same terms dated 16 May 1542,[219] which had not been made public. It was under this earlier, clandestine, indenture that debased coins were struck, and not put into circulation, but held in the Tower.[220] Until 1544 coins were still being struck for public use in accordance with the indenture of 1533.

---

[214] See Kent 1981 for a discussion of the likely extent of the period of issue of george nobles.
[215] The others are in the British Museum and in the collection of the American Numismatic Society.
[216] Challis 1992b, 720, citing PRO. E159/313, Rec. Mich. 46.
[217] For fine, angel, gold the new charge of 2s 9d compares to 2s 6d $\times \dfrac{5760 \text{ grains}}{5400 \text{ grains}}$ = 2s 8d.
[218] Challis 1992b, 721, citing PRO. E101/302/27.
[219] Challis 1992b, 721, citing PRO. E101/306/2.
[220] Challis 1992a, 228–9, also Challis 1967.
[221] Challis 1992a, 230–1.

The indenture of 1542 included provision for coinage charges of 2s 8d for the master workers and 8d for the moneyers. The wardens share remained at 8d, but an additional 20s 0d was reserved for the Crown. In 1544 the management structure of the mint was revised whereby the master moneyer ceased to exist as an independent contractor and his functions were exercised by a salaried crown employee, the under-treasurer.[221] The functions of the warden came to be exercised by the head of the mint, the high treasurer. The costs of production and administration and the profit were covered in a single coinage charge. In the May 1544 indenture this was the same as the 1542 indenture total, 24s 0d.[222] During the period when the mint was operating under its two quite distinct indentures, it was by far and away more concerned with producing the debased gold of 23ct according to the 1542 indenture rather than with the fine issues under the earlier indenture of 1533. Other changes made in the 1542 and 1544 indentures were the restoration of the value of the sovereign to 20s 0d with a corresponding reduction in its weight from 240 gr. to 200 gr., and the introduction of two new denominations, the half-sovereign and the quarter-angel.

The steps of progressive debasement that followed the indenture of 1544 are recorded in a series of indentures and commissions between that date and the end of the reign:

1. 27 March 1545. An indenture for Tower I and Tower II to coin gold at 22 ct (0.917 fine). The weight of the sovereign was reduced from 200 gr. (12.960 g) to 192 gr. (12.441 g) and of the crown from 50 gr. (3.240 g) to 48 gr. (3.110 g), with their fractions pro-rata.[223] Coinage charges were 50s 0d to the pound Troy.[224]

2. 6 September 1545. A commission for Southwark to coin gold at 22 ct (0.917 fine).[225] Coinage charges were initially 50s 0d, reducing to 39s 0d on 1 January 1546.[226]

3. 1 April 1546. Indentures for Tower I, Tower II, Southwark and Bristol to coin gold at 20ct (0.833 fine).[227] Coinage charges were initially 90s 0d, reducing to 80s 0d on 1 October 1546.[228]

References and Classification

The standard reference used for the coinage of Henry VIII is Whitton's series of papers collectively entitled 'The coinages of Henry VIII and Edward VI in Henry's name'.[229]

---

[222] Challis 1967, T.10.
[223] Challis 1992b, 721, citing PRO. E101/302/27.
[224] Challis 1967, T.10.
[225] Challis 1992b, 722, citing PRO. E101/331. Rec.Trin.41.
[226] Challis 1967, T.10.
[227] Challis 1992b, 722–3, citing PRO. E101/302/27 (Tower I and Tower II), PRO. E101/302/30 (Bristol), PRO. E159/331. Rec.Trin.41 (Southwark).
[228] Challis 1967, T.10.
[229] Whitton 1949–51.

TABLE 11A. *Output of gold coin during Henry VIII's first coinage period, 1509–26. All coins were struck in 23 ct 3½ gr. gold and at the rate of £22.10s.0d face value per Tower pound weight of gold (source: Challis 1978, with weights changed from Troy to Tower)*

Accounting period	Months	Weight coined lbs (Tower)	Weight coined oz	Face value £	Initial marks	Denominations struck Sov.	Ryal	Ang	½ Ang
30.9.1509–29.9.1510	12	3,073	$5\frac{5}{8}$	69,153	Castle			x	x
30.9.1510–29.9.1511	12	2,243	$10\frac{7}{8}$	50,488	Castle			x	x
30.9.1511–29.9.1512	12	1,196	$8\frac{1}{2}$	26,926	Castle			x	x
30.9.1512–29.9.1513	12	3,250	$11\frac{3}{4}$	73,147	Castle?			x	x
30.9.1513–29.9.1514	12	1,419	$6\frac{5}{8}$	31,940	Portcullis?			x	x
30.9.1514–29.9.1515	12	1,866	$1\frac{1}{8}$	41,988	Portcullis			x	x
30.9.1515–29.9.1516	12	2,379	$0\frac{3}{4}$	53,529	Portcullis	SEE		x	x
30.9.1516–29.9.1517	12	ACCOUNTS MISSING		45,894	Portcullis	NOTE 1		x	x
30.9.1517–29.9.1518	12	2,039	$8\frac{3}{4}$	45,894	Portcullis			x	x
30.9.1518–29.9.1519	12	2,441	4	54,930	Portcullis			x	x
30.9.1519–29.9.1520	12	1,612	$4\frac{3}{4}$	36,279	Portcullis			x	x
30.9.1520–29.9.1521	12	1,203	$5\frac{5}{8}$	27,078	Portcullis			x	x
30.9.1521–29.9.1522	12	652	$9\frac{1}{4}$	14,687	Portcullis			x	x
30.9.1522–29.9.1523	12	406	$3\frac{1}{4}$	9,141	Portcullis			x	x
30.9.1523–29.9.1526	36	ACCOUNTS MISSING			Portcullis			x	x

Note 1. The dates at which sovereigns and ryals were struck is not known. All of this period have i.m. portcullis.

TABLE 11B. *Output of gold coin during Henry VIII's second and third coinage periods, 1526–47 (source for accounts: Challis 1978)*

Accounting period	*Months*	*Fineness*		*Weight coined*[1]		*Value/lb (Troy)*			*Face value*	*Initial marks*		*Denominations struck*									
												Fine gold							*Crown G.*		*23 ct.*
		ct	*gr.*	*lbs (Troy)*	*oz*	*£*	*s*	*d*	*£*	*Fine G.*	*Crown G.*	*Sov.*	*½ sov.*	*Ang.*	*½ Ang*	*¼ Ang*	*Geo. N*	*½ GN*	*CDR*	*½ CDR*	*CR*[2]
30.9.1526–29.9.1527	12	22	0	4.857	1⅞	25	2	6	122,036		rose								x	x	
		23	0	?		24	9	0½	?												x?
		23	3½	?[3]		27	0	0	?	rose							x	x			
30.9.1527–29.9.1528	12	22	0	1,231	0¾	25	2	6	30,930		rose								x	x	
		23	3½	?		27	0	0	?	rose							x	x			
30.9.1528–29.9.1529	12	22	0	533	2	25	2	6	13,396		rose								x	x	
		23	3½	?		27	0	0	?	rose							x	x			
30.9.1529–29.9.1530	12	22	0	394	5½	25	2	6	9,911		lis								x	x	
		23	3½	?		27	0	0	?	lis							?	x			
30.9.1530–29.9.1531	12	22	0	320	3	25	2	6	8,046		lis								x	x	
30.9.1531–28.2.1533	17	ACCOUNTS MISSING																			
1.3.1533–30.10.1534	20	22	0	1,087	0⅙	25	2	6	27,311		arrow								x	x	
1.11.1534–29.9.1536	23	ACCOUNTS MISSING																			
30.9.1536–29.9.1537	12	22	0	1,011	0⅚	25	2	6	25,403		arrow								x	x	
		23	3½	31	5⅙	27	0	0	849	sunburst		x		x							
30.9.1537–31.5.1540	32	22	0	3,113	2	25	2	6	78,218		arrow								x	x	
1.6.1540–29.9.1540	4	ACCOUNTS MISSING																			
30.9.1540–29.9.1541	12	22	0	432	7	25	2	6	10,869		arrow								x	x	
		23	3½	28	10	27	0	0	849	lis		x		x	x						
30.9.1541–29.9.1542	12	ACCOUNTS MISSING																			
30.9.1542–29.9.1543	12	22	0	275	6	25	2	6	6,922		arrow/ pheon								x	x	
30.9.1543–31.3.1544	6	22	0	181	9	25	2	6	4,566		pheon								x	x	
		23	3½	31	6	27	0	0	851	lis/ arrow		x		x	x						
DEBASED COINAGE																					
1.7.1542–31.3.1544	21	23	0	541	6	28	16	0	15,595	lis		x	x	x	x	x					
1.6.1544–31.3.1545	10	23	0	5,751	6	28	16	0	165,931	lis		x	x	x	x	x					
1.4.1545–31.3.1546	12	22	0	12,435	11¾	30	0	0	372,179	lis/⊙	⊙	x	x						x	x	
1.4.1546–31.3.1547	12	20	0	8,772	2	30	0	0	263,165	{⊙ S,E,WS	{⊙ S,E,WS	x	x						x	x	

Notes
1. From 1526 weights are recorded in Troy pounds (5,760 gr.) instead of Tower pounds (5,400 gr.).
2. The crown of the (single) rose was introduced in August 1526 and abandoned in November of the same year. We have no means of knowing whether any production fell into the accounting year 30.9.1526–29.9.1527.
3. According to Challis 1971, 125, £20,157 in 23 ct 3½ gr. gold coin was made between 1526 and 1544. The surviving records only account for £2,509 of this, leaving £18,648 to be accounted for. This may have been struck during the periods for which the accounts are missing. It certainly includes the george nobles, i.m. rose, and the recent discovery of a half-george noble with i.m. lis (**577**) suggests that these fine gold coins were struck over a period of several years, even if in small quantities and not recorded in the extant accounts.

Subsequently, additions and corrections were published by Schneider[230] and considerable progress in clarifying the sequence of the initial marks in the second coinage was made by Potter.[231] The documentary evidence for the coinage had been published by Symonds[232] and this aspect has been extended and re-interpreted by Challis.[233]

One of the difficulties in dating coins of this reign arises from lack of evidence for the dates of the introduction of the various initial marks. This is particularly a problem for the first period (1509–26); the second period has been substantially clarified by Potter,[234] and the shorter, third, period is provided with more markers resulting from the progressive debasements and the opening of the Southwark and Bristol mints. One thing that has been clearly demonstrated is that, in the second period, a different series of initial marks was used for the fine and crown gold respectively.

Output

An attempt has been made in Tables 11A and B to correlate mint output figures, data on initial marks in use, and denominations issued at different dates, using the information now available. While this is certainly not complete and must, in our present state of knowledge, leave some questions unanswered, it is intended to give an overall view of the evolution of the gold coinages in this reign. In interpreting weights expressed other than in grains, it must always be remembered that from 1526 the Tower pound of 5,400 grains (349.914 g) was abandoned in favour of the Troy pound of 5,760 grains (373.242 g).

EDWARD VI (28 January 1547–6 July 1553)

Background

The debasements of the last years of Henry VIII's reign were the result of his 'great necessity' for money to pay for his costly foreign enterprises. Those costs did not cease at his death, and at the start of the new reign the short-term increase in mint output resulting from the previous step of debasement was starting to fall away. Had not the the mint price been improved in 1547 and again in 1548 by a reduction in coinage charges it would have fallen more than it did.[235] The new administration was all too aware of the chaos and loss of confidence in English coinage that had resulted from the policies of the previous reign, and although they wished to restore the coinage, making what was to be an abortive start in June 1547,[236] continuing heavy expenditure made this impossible.

[230] Schneider 1952–4.
[231] Potter 1955–7.
[232] Symonds 1913.
[233] Challis 1967 and Challis 1978.
[234] Potter 1955–7.
[235] For the mint price improvement in 1547, see Challis 1978, 96. The improvement in 1548 was effected by reducing coinage charges from 30s 0d to 20s 0d, see below.
[236] Challis 1978, 96.

Early in 1550 peace was concluded with France, and the largest item of military expense, Boulogne, was surrendered in return for a payment from the French of 400,000 ecus (about £90,000). Against this improving financial background steps could be taken to return towards a fine gold coinage.

Issues

Edward VI's coinage is conventionally divided into three periods. The first was essentially a continuation of the types and standards of Henry VIII's last coinage. The second, starting in January 1549, was an attempt to improve the appearance of the coinage by raising its fineness and introducing new designs (though weight reductions exactly offset the improved fineness in the case of silver and, in the case of gold, the fine gold content was actually slightly diminished[237]). The third, starting in December 1550, was a restoration of the coinage to pre-1542 standards of weight and fineness, although with increased nominal values resulting from the inflationary effects of the policies of the previous eight years.

Mints

The two London mints, Tower I and Tower II, the Southwark mint and the mint at Bristol all continued to strike gold into the reign of Edward VI. Additionally, in January 1549, both gold and silver were ordered to be struck at the newly opened mint at Durham House, Strand. Durham House had probably already closed by the end of 1549. Bristol had ceased production by October 1549 and was officially closed on Lady Day 1550. Southwark closed in August 1551, and, finally, Tower II closed in the spring of 1552, leaving Tower I as the sole mint in England.[238]

Conditions

First Period, 5 April 1547–24 January 1549

This covers two coinages. The first was ordered under indentures for Tower I, Tower II and Southwark dated 5 April 1547.[239] The second was ordered under indentures for the same three mints dated 16 February 1548.[240] Both sets of indentures called for coinages of the same standards and values, which were also the same as those of the last coinage of Henry VIII. The difference lay with the coinage charges, which in the 1547 indentures were 30s 0d (a steep drop from the October 1546 figure of 80s 0d) and in 1548 were again decreased to 20s 0d. The greater part of the coinage of this period was deliberately struck in the name of Henry VIII, almost as if to distance the new king from such

---

[237] Challis 1978, 98.
[238] Challis 1978, 111.
[239] Challis 1992b, 723–4, citing PRO. E101/306/3 (Tower I and Tower II); PRO.E101/306/3 (Southwark).
[240] Challis 1992b, 724–5, citing PRO. E351/2078 (Tower I and Tower II), PRO. E101/306/3 (Southwark).

base ill-reputed coins. A few dies were made with Edward VI's name instead of that of his father, and it is clear from initial marks and punctuation that they came early in the period, though, perhaps not at the very beginning since they are not the dies found muled with those of Henry VIII. Types were the same as the last coinage of Henry VIII, except that all the half-sovereigns, even when in Henry's name, use the seated, unbearded, image of Edward.

Second Period, 24 January 1549–18 December 1550

This also covers two coinages. The first was struck according to commissions issued on 24 January 1549 to Tower I and Southwark.[241] Durham House was added to these in a commission of 29 January 1549.[242] These provided for the fineness of the gold coinage to be restored to 22 ct, but the weight was reduced to 169.4 gr. (10.977g) for the sovereign of 20s 0d and the other denominations pro-rata. Coinage charges were set at 20s 0d to the pound weight of gold.[243] The second coinage was ordered in commissions dated 12 April 1549[244] to the same mints[245] and called for exactly the same conditions, so far as the gold was concerned, but reduced the fineness of the silver. The net effect of the changes was to reduce the amount of pure gold contained in any coin of any given value[246] and thus to allow yet more attractive terms for buying gold to be offered. The sovereign retained the facing, seated, king design, but on all other denominations a new, more 'modern' profile portrait was introduced. On earlier coins this was uncrowned: later a crown was added.

Third Period, 18 December 1550–6 July 1553

This period yet again covers two coinages, the first of which was very small in volume, the second resulted in the re-establishment of pre-1542 standards on a lasting basis. The two coinages can be placed together in one period because their weight and fineness was the same: it was the values attributed to them that varied.

The first coinage was ordered in a commission to the Southwark mint on 18 December 1550,[247] which authorised the striking of a gold coinage of 23 ct 3½ gr. (0.995 fine) at a weight of 240 gr. (15.552g) to the sovereign of 24s 0d. The denominations ordered were sovereign, ryal (12s 0d), angel (8s 0d) and half-angel. Coinage charges were 2s 9d per Troy pound. The values attributed to the coins were evidently

---

[241] Challis 1992b, 725–6, citing PRO. E351/2078 (Tower I), PRO. E159/331, Rec.Trin.41 (Southwark).
[242] Challis 1992b, 726, citing *CPR*, 1548–9, 303–4.
[243] Challis 1967, T.10.
[244] Challis 1992b, 726, citing PRO. E351/2078 (Tower I), PRO. E159/331, Rec.Trin.41 (Southwark).
[245] However, gold coin also seems to have been struck at Tower II (i.m. grapple and i.m. martlet).
[246] A First Period sovereign would ideally contain:
      $20/24 \times 192.0 = 160.0$ gr. of pure gold.
    A Second Period sovereign would ideally contain:
      $22/24 \times 169.4 = 155.3$ gr. of pure gold.
[247] Challis 1992b, 727, citing *CPR*, 1549–51, 345.

too low and only £2,778 face value was struck.[248] Indeed, it is possible that this amount was made up of small sums for the king's use while on progress,[249] and this suggestion is supported by the survival of two double-weight sovereigns, one in the Schneider collection (**700**)—no doubt made for use as diplomatic or political gifts. This must be the coinage that used the initial mark 'ostrich head'.[250] The commission for its issue was addressed first to Sir Edward Peckham and this seems to have been a period when punning initial marks were popular.[251]

The second coinage was ordered under a commission to Tower I and II dated 5 October 1551.[252] This authorised the striking of gold at the same standards of weight and fineness as the previous order but valued at 30s 0d to the sovereign. The denominations ordered were sovereign, angel (10s 0d) and half-angel. In addition, the commission provided for 22 ct, crown gold, coins to be struck at the weight of 174.6 gr. (11.314 g) to the sovereign of 20s 0d. It will be noted that this is heavier than the 22 ct coins of the Second Period and that they contain marginally more gold than the sovereigns of the First Period.[253] The denominations ordered in crown gold were sovereign, half-sovereign, crown (5s 0d), and half-crown. Coinage charges per Troy pound weight were 2s 9d for fine gold and 3s 0d for crown gold.

The fine gold denominations of this period employed the traditional sovereign and angel designs. The crown gold denominations used a new design of a half length figure of the king in profile, holding a sceptre in his right hand and a sword in his left. All the coins reintroduced Gothic lettering, perhaps to emphasize the idea of a return to the 'good old standards'.[254] The Schneider collection provides evidence that when Southwark mint closed in August 1551 at least one angel die was transfered to the Tower and the 'ostrich head' initial mark was overstruck with the 'tun' initial mark (**686**).

References and Classification

There is no single study of the coinage for the whole of Edward's reign. Morrieson undertook the task for the silver coinage,[255] but his work is now superseded and there is no equivalent for the gold. We therefore look to separate references for the three coinage periods.

---

[248] See Table 11.

[249] Challis 1978, 105.

[250] A bird's head anyway. Ostriches cannot have been very widely known in sixteenth-century England.

[251] Other examples are Bowes (a bow), Egerton (a tun) and, more doubtfully, for Vaughan (perhaps a Seymour protege) a grapple (sea moor).

[252] Challis 1992b, 727, citing BL, Additional MS, 18, 759, fo.69.

[253] Compare with n. 246.
          $22/24 \times 174.6 = 160.5$ gr. of pure gold.

[254] Foreigners had become suspicious of English coins and only wanted payment in the older types, see Challis 1978, 173–4.

[255] Morrieson 1916.

The standard work for the First Period continues to be Whitton's 'The coinages of Henry VIII and Edward VI in Henry's name'.[256] For the Second Period we have Potter's paper,'The coinage of Edward VI in his own name'.[257] There is no recent scholarly study of the Third Period and, although a number of varieties are recorded by Kenyon,[258] the arrangement generally followed is that used by North[259] who follows Brooke.[260] Particular aspects of the reign are addressed by Bispham (the base shillings),[261] Challis (mints, officials and moneyers),[262] and Symonds (documentary evidence),[263] though the latter is now largely superseded by the work of Challis.[264]

Initial Marks

The correct attribution of coins to the Tower I, Tower II and Southwark mints by means of their initial marks is yet to be fully resolved.[265] Bispham's work on the shillings[266] has made some progress possible with the gold. Die production was centralised at the Tower,[267] and Bispham has demonstrated that dies first intended for one mint could have their marks altered to meet the need of another mint. This is confirmed for the gold coinage by specimens in the Schneider collection (**665, 689**). Bispham has also demonstrated that, as a result of muling between obverse and reverse dies, a convincing series of marks can be shown for each mint. Potter's observation that some marks are more abundant than others and that, in all probability, the more uncommon ones were used contemporaneously with the common ones and, for some reason, had a secondary character, remains true.

[256] Whitton 1949–51.
[257] Potter 1962.
[258] Kenyon 1884.
[259] North 1991.
[260] Brooke 1950.
[261] Bispham 1985.
[262] Challis 1975.
[263] Symonds 1915.
[264] Challis 1978.
[265] Of the two other mints that struck gold, Bristol presents no problem because the only gold coins known of that mint for this reign are the First Period sovereigns with the initial mark WS (William Sharington, who ceased to be under-treasurer there on 25 December 1548); Durham House, during its brief existence, used the initial mark bow (John Bowes, under-treasurer).
[266] Bispham 1985.
[267] Challis 1975.

For the gold, then, we can now attribute the initial marks as follows:

Mint and Period	*I.m.*	*Notes*
Tower I		
First Period		
(5.4.1547–24.1.1549)	Arrow	Found muled with pellet-in-annulet (Henry VIII); Sir Martin Bowes, under-treasurer, to 29.9. 1550.
	Lis	Found muled with arrow.
Second Period		
(24.1.1549–18.12.1550)	Arrow	
	Swan	Found muled with arrow.
Third Period		
(18.12.1550–6.7.1553)	Y	Sir John York, under-treasurer, 29.
9.1551–25.3.1552.		
	Tun	Thomas Egerton, under-treasurer, 25.3.1552–25.12.1555.
Tower II		
First Period		
(5.4.1547–24.1.1549)	K	Thomas Knight, under-treasurer, 25.3.1545–Feb. 1548.
	Grapple	Stephen Vaughan, under-treasurer, 25.3.1544–25.12.1549.
	Martlet	
Second Period		
(24.1.1549–18.12.1550)	Grapple	As above.
	Martlet	
Third Period		
(18.12.1550–6.7.1553)	No identifiable mark. The commission of 5 October 1551 joins Tower II with Tower I.	
Southwark		
First Period		
(5.4.1547–24.1.1549)	E	
	S	

(*Continued*)

Mint and Period	I.m.	Notes
Second Period (24.1.1549–18.12.1550)	Lis	
	Y	Sir John York, under-treasurer, 25.3.1545–23.9.1551 (see above, Tower I).
Third Period (18.12.1547-Aug. 1551)	'Ostrich Head'	23 ct 3½gr. gold only. Commission to Sir Edmund Peckham, high treasurer and others, 18.12.1550

Uncertain Attribution

First Period (5.4.1547–24.1.1549)	Lis florencée ('lis with feelers')	used on the First Period sovereign. Probably Tower I where on other denominations a lis is securely attributable through being muled with arrow.
Second Period (24.1.1549–18.12.1550)	6	A very rare mark. Found with rosette stops.

The Schneider collection contains one coin each bearing these marks of uncertain attribution (**642**, **671**). They are provisionally included with the Tower I coins in the catalogue.

Output

The total output of gold coin from all mints except Durham House[268] is set out in Table 13. The face value totals for each accounting period (column 5) correspond with the figures given by Challis.[269] These exclude the output from Tower II after 31 December 1548, for which no records survive. However, an estimate of Tower II output can be made using the total figures for the First and Second Periods given in a contemporary document published by Challis and Harrison.[270] This is included in Table 13 to give an adjusted total figure. Table 12 shows the outputs from individual mints when these were open. The totals correspond with the adjusted totals in Table 13. In both Tables 12 and 13 the correlation between output and initial marks is given, so far as this is known. Table 13 also shows the denominations issued in each period.

---

[268] No records exist for the output of Durham House. A contemporary estimate gives £80,000 total for both gold and silver. See Challis and Harrison 1975.

[269] Challis 1978 and Challis 1992b.

[270] Challis and Harrison 1975.

TABLE 12. *Production of gold from Tower I, Tower II, Southwark and Bristol, 1.6.1544–30.6.1551*[1]

	Tower I		Tower II		Southwark		Bristol		Totals[2]
Dates	£ s d	Dates	£ s d	Dates	£ s d	Dates	£ s d	£ s d	

INDENTURE OF 13 MAY 1544, 23 ct, struck at £28 6s 0d per Troy lb.
Undertreasurer Sir Martin Bowes (i.m. lis)

1.6.1544–31.3.1545	165,931 4 0						–	165,931 4 0

INDENTURE OF 27 MARCH 1545, 22 ct, struck at £30 0s 0d per Troy lb.
Tower I: Undertreasurer Sir Martin Bowes (i.m. lis, ☉)
Tower II: Undertreasurer Thomas Knight
Southwark: Undertreasurer Sir John York (i.m. S)

1.4.1545–31.12.1545	142,485 0 0	1.7.1545–	39,526 17 6	15.9.1545–31.12.1545	20,627 10 0		–	
1.1.1546–31.3.1546	63,600 0 0	31.3.1546	29,800 0 0	1.1.1546–31.3.1546	76,140 0 0		–	372,179 7 6[3]

INDENTURE OF 1 APRIL 1546, 20 ct, struck at £30 0s 0d per Troy lb.
Tower I: Undertreasurer Sir Martin Bowes (i.m. ☉)
Tower II: Undertreasurer Thomas Knight (i.m. ☉)
Southwark: Undertreasurer Sir John York (i.m. S)
Bristol: Undertreasurer Sir W. Sharington (i.m. WS)

1.4.1546–30.9.1546	82,620 0 0	1.4.1546–	33,000 0 0	1.4.1546–30.9.1546	88,480 0 0	1.5.1546–	6,415 0 0	
1.10.1546–31.12.1546	24,960 0 0	(31.3.1547)	4,470 0 0	1.10.1546–28.2.1547	23,220 0 0	31.3.1547		263,165 0 0

(HENRY VIII DIED, 28 JANUARY 1547)
Tower I: (i.m. arrow, lis)
Tower II: (i.m. K) Undertreasurer Stephen Vaughan (i.m. grapple, martlet)
Southwark: (i.m. E)

1.5.1547–31.12.1547	239,520 0 0	1.4.1547–31.12.1547	18,765 0 0	1.5.1547–31.12.1548	153,285 0 0	17.1.1547–30.9.1547	6,130 0 0	439,467 10 0
		1.1.1548–31.12.1548	21,767 10 0					

702,632 10 0

COMMISSION OF 24 JANUARY 1549, 22 ct, struck at £34 0s 0d per Troy lb.
Tower I: Undertreasurer Sir Martin Bowes (i.m. arrow, swan)
Tower II: Undertreasurer Stephen Vaughan (i.m. grapple, martlet)
Southwark: Undertreasurer Sir John York (i.m. Y, lis)

1.2.1549–31.10.1550	48,246 0 0	early 1549–late 1549	5,678 0 0	1.1.1549–31.12.1550	28,594 0 0		–	82,518 0 0

COMMISSION OF 18 DECEMBER 1550, 23 ct 3½ gr., struck at £28 16s 0d per Troy lb.
Southwark: Undertreasurer Sir John York[5] (i.m. ostrich head)

				1.1.1551–30.6.1551	2,777 14 0			2,777 14 0

Notes:
1. Sources are Challis 1967 and Challis and Harrison, 1973. In the case of Tower II, for which there are no extant accounts for the years 1548 and 1549, the figures given are obtained by deducting the amounts for the other mints from the overall totals.
2. Excluding the small amount from the only other gold issuing mint, Durham House. The total output of that mint in both gold and silver has been estimated at £80,000, see Challis 1992a, 232.
3. £372,200 0s 0d in Challis 1992a, 233. The small discrepancy of £20 12s 6d is discussed in Challis and Harrison 1973.
4. From February 1548.
5. Although Sir John York accounted for the Southwark output between 1.1.1551 and 30.6.1551, the commission is addressed to the treasurer, Sir Edmund Peckham, as well as to York (Challis 1976, 317), and it is at least an entertaining fancy to see the use of the so-called ostrich head initial mark as a punning allusion. There can be no real doubt that the coins with this mark were struck at this mint at the time.

TABLE 13. *Output of gold coin during the reigns of Edward VI, Mary, and Philip and Mary*

Dates	Months (1)	Fineness (2) ct	gr	Wt of coin (3) lb	oz	Value/lb[1] (4) £	s	d	Face value[1] (5) £	s	d	Adjustments (6) £	s	d	Adjusted totals (7) £	s	d	Initial marks Twr I	Twr II	Swk	Br	Fine gold Sov	Ryal	Ang	¼A	22 or 20 ct gold Sov	¼ sov	Cr	½ Cr
EDWARD VI FIRST PERIOD																												
1.4.1547–30.9.1547	6	20	0	7,190	10	30	0	0	215,725	0	0	} 21,767 10 0[2]			439,467	10	0	Arrow / lis	K / grapple / martlet	} E	WS	x				x	x	x	x
1.10.1547–30.9.1548	12	20	0	5,812	6	30	0	0	174,375	0	0																		
1.10.1548–31.12.1548	2	20	0	920	0	30	0	0	27,600	0	0																		
TOTAL	20			13,923	4				417,700	0	0	21,767	10	0	439,467	10	0												
SECOND PERIOD																												
1.1.1549–30.9.1549	9	22	0	1,237	7	34	0	0	42,078	0	0	} 5,678 0 0						Arrow / 6 / Swan	grapple / martlet }	Y / lis						x		x	x
1.10.1549–31.12.1550	15	22	0	1,022	5	34	0	0	34,762	0	0																		
TOTAL	24			2,250	0				76,840	0	0	5,678	0	0	82,518	0	0												
THIRD PERIOD																												
1.1.1551–30.6.1551	6	23	3½	96	5⅜	28	16	0	2,777	14	0									Ostrich head									
1.10.1551–31.3.1552	6	23 / 22	3½ / 0	small / 109	0	36 / 33	0	0	— / 3,597	0	0	small[3]							Y "										
1.4.1552– .7.1553	15	23 / 22	3½ / 0	small / ACCOUNTS MISSING		36	0	0	—			small 17,556	0	0					Tun "										
TOTAL	27								6,374	0	0	over 17,556	0	0	over 23,930	14	0					x	x	x		x		x	x
MARY and PHILIP and MARY																												
20.8.1553–24.12.1553	4	23	3½			36	0	0	ACCTS MISSING									P'gran											
25.12.1553–24.12.1554	12	23	3½	613	0	36	0	0	22,068	0	0							Castle & sun											
25.12.1554–24.12.1555	12	23	3½	1,025	0	36	0	0	36,900	0	0																		
25.12.1555– .7.1556	7	23	3½			36	0	0	ACCTS MISSING																				
.7.1556–31.12.1558	29	23	3½			36	0	0	ACCTS MISSING			19,676	10	0[4]				lis											
TOTAL	64								58,968	0	0	19,676	10	0	over 78,634	10	0					x	x	x	x	x		x	x

Notes:
1. From Challis 1978.
2. The figures in Challis 1978 exclude Tower II output after 31.12.1548 because no accounts survive. A reasonably accurate total (excluding Durham House) is available from Challis and Harrison 1973. The Tower II figures may be deduced by subtracting the output of other mints from the total figures.
3. That there was a small output of fine gold between 1.10.1551 and July 1553 is strongly suggested by the coins (i.m. Y and tun) and such was provided for in the indenture. There is no record of it, however, from the surviving accounts; the 'contemporary estimate' (Challis and Harrison 1973) must include it.
4. The 'contemporary estimate' (Challis and Harrison 1973) states that £78,634 10s 0d of fine gold was struck at £36 0s 0d per lb Troy between 1.10.1551 and July 1556. Subtracting the figures in the accounts for 25.12.1553 to 24.12.1554 we are left with £19,676 10s 0d. This must be divided between the Edward VI output from 1.10.1551 to July 1553 and the periods between 20.8.1553 to 24.12.1553 and 25.12.1555 and July 1556.

MARY, alone (19 July 1553–25 July 1554);
with PHILIP (25 July 1554–17 November 1558)

Background

It is not possible to point to any one principal source of the gold that was struck into coin in this reign. Trade, particularly with the Low Countries, prospered at this period, with London shipping 135,000 pieces of unfinished cloth in 1554 compared to 50,000 around 1500,[271] and this is likely to have been one important source. Some of the gold struck may have been recoinage of base gold coin of the previous two reigns into a form that would make it more acceptable for external trade and diplomatic payments. Evidence for this may be the reappearance of ryals as well as the relatively large numbers of sovereigns that survive, and this may be associated with the events leading up to and following Mary's marriage. Some precious metal came from Spain with Philip, although what evidence there is points to this as being silver. Nevertheless there is a record of £50,000 worth of that being conveyed to the mint[272] and, no doubt, if required, some could have been used to buy gold. Finally, a very small amount of gold came from the recoinage of church plate that was in the pipeline before Mary put a stop to it.[273]

Issues

All the coins of this reign were struck to the same standards, and they fall broadly into two issues, those struck in the name of Mary alone and those in the name of both monarchs. Output appears to fall into two periods, 1553–5 and 1557–8. In the case of the gold coins, those issued in the first period are in the name of Mary alone and those in the second period in the name of Philip and Mary. This is not the case with the silver coins which were issued in the name of Philip and Mary from 1554 onwards.

Mint

The only mint in operation during the reign was that in the Tower of London.

Conditions

The first indenture of Mary's reign was made on 20 August 1553[274] with Thomas Egerton, under-treasurer, and others. So far as gold was concerned this provided for sovereigns of 30s 0d weighing 240 gr. (15.552 g), ryals of 15s 0d weighing 120 gr. (7.776 g), angels of 10s 0d weighing 80gr. (5.184 g) and half-angels. All were to be

---

[271] Van Houtte 1977, 178.
[272] Challis 1978, 113.
[273] Challis 1978, 165, gives 192¾ oz. received at the Jewel House at the Tower, but whether all or any went to the mint is not certainly known.
[274] Challis 1992b, 728–9, citing PRO. E101/307/1.

struck in fine gold of 23 ct $3\frac{1}{2}$ gr. (0.995 fine).[275] Coinage charges were set at 4s 0d per Troy pound weight. No coinage in crown gold was foreseen.

Egerton was dismissed from his post in December 1555, and thereafter commissions were issued to Sir Edmund Peckham, the high treasurer. Until June 1557 these commissions were purely for Irish base silver, however, in that month a commission was issued for English groats, and that was followed on 5 August 1557 by a further commission covering a range of gold and silver coins.[276] In respect of the gold this called for angels and their halves to the same weights, fineness and values as the indenture of 1553. Charges remained at 4s 0d per pound.

References and Classification

There is no detailed study of the coinage of the reigns of Mary and Philip and Mary. The coins are summarily listed in the standard works of general reference.[277] Symonds has dealt extensively with the documentary evidence,[278] and Challis has extended and re-interpreted this where necessary.[279] Pending a more detailed study, it is possible to suggest an outline classification with reference to the accounts which record an output of gold in 1554–5 and again in 1557, the indenture of 1553, Egerton's dismissal in 1555, the commission of 1557 and, of course, the coins themselves.

The earliest coins, in the name of Mary alone, appear to be those using the privy mark[280] pomegranate (see **706** and **707** where a sovereign die has been altered by punching the privy mark halved rose and castle over the privy mark pomegranate, showing that the former is later). On the most prolific denomination, the angels, a progression can be seen:

Class 1. Coins with large Gothic lettering and annulet punctuation. Privy mark pomegranate. (**710–22**)

Class 2. Coins with small or mixed Gothic lettering and pellet punctuation. Privy mark pomegranate. (**723–4**)

Class 3. Coins with large Roman lettering and pellet punctuation. Privy mark halved rose and castle. (**725**)

All these are in the name of Mary alone. In all cases the privy mark is placed after the queen's name on the obverse and after ISTVD on the reverse. In the Schneider collection angels of class 1 are found muled with 2, and 2 with 3.

---

[275] This indenture, as well as the commissions of 5 October 1551, 5 August 1557 and 31 December 1558, refer to the gold as being of 23 ct $10\frac{1}{2}$ gr. For this short period an alternative, German, system based on 12 grains to the carat instead of the usual, English, 4 grains to the carat was being used. In this context 23 ct $10\frac{1}{2}$ gr. is the same as 23ct $3\frac{1}{2}$ gr. See Grierson 1963 and Challis 1978, App.I, T.10.

[276] Challis 1992b, 730, citing *CPR*, 1557–8, 194–5.

[277] Brooke 1950, North 1991, Seaby 1993.

[278] Symonds 1911.

[279] Challis 1978.

[280] The term 'privy mark' is used instead of 'initial mark' for coins in the name of Mary alone because the mark appears after the first word of the legend and not in the initial position. The mark returns to the initial position on the coins in the joint names of Philip and Mary.

Class 4. Finally, we have the coins with Philip's name joined to that of Mary. These, too, have Roman lettering, though not so large as on class 3, and pellet punctuation. The privy mark returns to the initial position and is a lis. (**726–8**)

The sovereigns and ryals can be related to the first three classes although, since fewer dies were used, the evolution is less lucid. In the Schneider collection class 1 is represented by two coins dated 1553 and 1554 respectively (**704** and **705**). These both have privy mark pomegranate and annulet stops. The 1554 coin, however, has lettering of mixed size, a feature of class 2, although in other respects it is normal for class 1. The earlier obverse die dated 1553 then reappears with the privy mark altered to halved rose and castle, but muled with a privy mark pomegranate reverse (**706**). The same altered obverse die then appears again with a reverse with privy mark halved rose and castle and with pellct stops, which may be equated to class 2 (**707**). Finally, a new undated obverse die with privy mark halved rose and castle and with pellet stops is used with the same reverse die as the previous piece (**708**). In the catalogue the sovereigns have been grouped together to illustrate these die links.

It is less easy to attribute absolute dates to these evolutions. We have a sovereign with the pomegranate mark dated 1554. The die dated 1553 with the privy mark altered to halved rose and castle must, in spite of the unaltered date, have been used later. We can infer that the undated die was used later still. The accounts tell us that £36,900 of gold was struck between December 1554 and December 1555, but from then to the end of the reign there is no record of what was struck. The angels and half-angels with Philip's name all have the initial mark lis and appear to have no links at all with the coinage in the name of Mary alone. The lis initial mark also appears on sixpences dated 1557 and it seems reasonable to relate coinage with that mark to the commission of that year. If this is correct, it appears that gold coinage in the name of Mary alone continued to be struck at least until the end of 1555.

Philip and Mary married in July 1554. It is surprising that proper recognition of Philip's new position should not have been made on gold coinage struck immediately after the wedding, especially the large, prestigious sovereigns. Certainly, shillings and sixpences dated 1554 were struck in both names from December of that year,[281] but those have no privy mark. Base pence in the names of both rulers, although undated, have the privy mark halved sun and castle, sure evidence that the mark was in use after July 1554.

To sum up then, the evidence available points to the gold coinage in Mary's sole name having been struck between her accession and up to some date after her marriage, probably at least until 1555. Thereafter, probably little or no gold coin was struck until that in the name of Philip and Mary between August 1557 and the end of the reign. It

[281] Symonds 1911, 188.

may be that there was no significant amount of gold available for coinage between 1555 and 1557.[282]

Output

Mint output is set out in Table 12. As with Edward VI there is evidence that more fine gold was struck than is accounted for in the surviving records, and the figures given by Challis,[283] which are set out in column 5, are augmented to give an adjusted total based on the data published by Challis and Harrison.[284]

ELIZABETH I (17 November 1558–24 March 1603)

Background

For most of the second half of the sixteenth century there was a stable mint price and continuous minting activity.[285] It can reasonably be deduced from this that there was an abundance of precious metal in the country.[286] Peace was made with France in 1559 and, in 1564, a useful contribution was received when England renounced her claim to Calais in exchange for a payment of 220,000 crowns (about £70,000).

Most of the coined metal coming to the mint was Spanish.[287] The ultimate source for this will have been the flow of precious metals from the New World into Spain, and some will have permeated other Western European economies as a result of the new wealth being spent so liberally to assert Spanish power in the Low Countries from 1566 onwards.[288] Another source of considerable importance, particularly in the second half of Elizabeth's reign, was the bullion secured as a result of the privateering activities of such men as Sir Francis Drake. Gold and silver seems to have been brought back to England in huge quantities in this way.[289] Certainly, England was able to find resources to support the emerging Dutch Republic in its struggle for independence from Spain forming an alliance with them in 1577, providing financial aid,[290] and sending troops under the earl of Leicester in 1585.

---

[282] Symonds interpreted a statement in a Privy Council letter of September 1556 as implying that the mint was virtually inactive between November 1555 and August 1557 (Symonds 1911, 192). Challis's interpretation is simply that this implies a lack of continuous activity (Challis 1978, 116).

[283] Challis 1978 and Challis 1992b.

[284] Challis and Harrison 1975.

[285] Challis 1978, 281.

[286] Challis 1978, 151–98.

[287] Challis 1978, 193–8.

[288] The central treasury of the Spanish Netherlands received 6,910,000 florins from Spain in 1572–3, and in 1574 the running costs of the Spanish army in Flanders were estimated at 1,200,000 florins per month; see Parker 1977, 162–5. Parker states that these are florins of account valued at 20 patards and rated at approximately 10 to the English pound.

[289] Challis 1978, 190.

[290] For example, £110,000 to the Low Countries between 1577 and 1584; see Challis 1978, 189.

Issues

The gold coinage of Elizabeth I does not run exactly in parallel with the silver and cannot satisfactorily be classified with it. This fact has caused difficulties for compilers of general reference works as, for instance, may be seen by comparing the different treatments in North[291] and Seaby.[292] It was an awareness of this that first stimulated Schneider to propose a separate division of the gold coinage into five groups.[293] This, in turn, drew a response from Comber[294] and then inspired Brown to propose his classification into three main periods of issue.[295] Brown's classification has recently been restated and updated by Brown and Comber,[296] and it is this which has been used as the basis for listing Elizabeth I's coins in the catalogue.

The first issue covers the period from 1558 to 1572 and includes both fine and crown gold coins. It also includes the milled gold coinage of Eloy Mestrelle. The second issue covers the period from 1572 to 1593 and is resticted to fine gold coins. The third issue runs from 1593 to 1603 and again includes the production of both fine and crown gold coins. The second issue includes a minor fluctuation in fineness and the third issue embodies a small reduction in weights after July 1601.

Mints

The only minting of gold in this reign took place at the Tower of London. Tower II, which had been closed in 1552, reappeared at the time of the great recoinage of base silver coin[297] between September 1560 and October 1561. Later references to Tower I in 1601,[298] cannot be assumed to imply the existence of a Tower II, because no separate under-treasurer or master was appointed, as had been the case previously. There is at no time any suggestion that gold was struck other than at the main mint, Tower I, except that, between 1562 and 1572, Eloy Mestrelle operated his screw-press mint as a separate production unit within the Tower.

---

[291] North 1991.

[292] Seaby 1993.

[293] Schneider 1983.

[294] Comber 1983.

[295] Brown 1984.

[296] Brown and Comber 1989.

[297] There was no need to re-coin the base gold because even the basest and lightest coin of the debasement period contained, for all practical purposes, the same amount of pure gold as its counterpart struck under the 1558 indenture. For example:

A half-sovereign of 10s 0d struck according to the indenture of 16 February 1548 contained:

$96 \times 20/24 = 80.00$ grains of pure gold.

A half-pound of 10s 0d struck according to the indenture of 31 December 1558 contained:

$87.25 \times 22/24 = 79.98$ grains of pure gold.

[298] Challis 1992b, 736–7, citing *The Register of Letters* … , ed. Sir G. Birdwood and W. Foster (1893), 13–18.

Conditions

First Issue, 1558–72

This was initiated by a commission dated 31 December 1558 to Sir Edmund Peckham, high-treasurer, and others.[299] It ordered coins in both fine and crown gold. In fine gold of 23 ct 3½ gr. (0.995 fine), it provided for sovereigns of 30s 0d weighing 240 gr. (15.552 g), angels of 10s 0d weighing 80 gr. (5.184 g) and half-angels. In crown gold of 22 ct (0.917 fine), the denominations were to be sovereigns of 20s 0d (henceforth referred to as pounds) weighing 174.5 gr. (11.307 g), half-pounds, crowns and half-crowns. Coinage charges on both standards of fineness were 4s 0d per pound Troy.

This was followed by an indenture dated 8 November 1560 with Thomas Stanley, under-treasurer,[300] which provided for the same coins at the same weights, values and finenesses. In addition, the ryal denomination was reintroduced at a value of 15s 0d and weight of 120gr. (7.776g) in fine gold. The coinage charge was increased to 5s 0d per pound Troy on fine gold but remained at 4s 0d on crown gold.

In spite of being specified, no pounds of 20s 0d (other than patterns) or ryals are known for this issue.

Milled Gold Coinage

This was struck by Eloy Mestrell at the Tower during the period of the first issue and to its standards. No formal mandate for its introduction survives, but there is considerable evidence for the techniques used which has been reviewed by Dr Challis in two of his Presidential Addresses to the British Numismatic Society.[301] The coins are readily recognised by the superior appearance of the finished product, the separate sequence of initial marks (star and lis), the absence of any beaded inner circle and the knurled edge on the later specimens (i.m. lis).

Second Issue, 1572–93

Thomas Stanley, the last under-treasurer, died in 1571, and from 1572 the mint reverted to the pre-1544 system of control through a warden and master-worker.[302] On 19 April 1572 a new indenture was made with John Lonyson, master-worker, which, so far as gold was concerned, provided for fine angels of 10s 0d weighing 80gr. (5.184 g) together with half-angels and quarter-angels.[303] No coins of crown gold were ordered. Charges were set at 4s 0d per pound Troy of which 1s 6d was for the master and 2s 6d was to be accounted for by the warden.[304]

---

[299] Challis 1992b, 731, citing PRO. C66/941, m.19d.
[300] Challis 1992b, 732, citing PRO. E159/342, Rec.Hil.145.
[301] Challis 1989 and 1990.
[302] Challis 1978, 133–5.
[303] Challis 1992b, 733, citing PRO. C54/868.
[304] The warden had to pay the other crown employees, as well as maintain the mint buildings, out of his share; see Challis 1978, 20–1.

This was augmented by a commission dated 1 November 1577 which provided for the addition of sovereigns of 30s 0d and ryals of 15s 0d to the denominations in the 1572 indenture.[305] For the new denominations the total coinage charge was unaltered at 4s 0d, but the master was to receive 3s 6d and the warden was to account for only 6d. This alteration to the allocation of coinage charges was an interim measure partially anticipating the charges that would be laid down by a commission the following year. This new commission was issued on 15 September 1578 to Richard Martin, warden, and John Lonyson, master-worker, ordering angels, half-angels and quarter-angels at the same weight and value as before but with the fineness very slightly reduced to 23 ct $3\frac{1}{4}$ gr. (0.992 fine).[306] Charges were increased to 5s $10\frac{1}{2}$d per pound of which 3s $4\frac{1}{2}$d went to the master and 2s 6d was to be accounted for by the warden. In addition, the master was to receive the half remedies at the assay of $\frac{1}{6}$ ct per pound of gold.

The reduction in fineness, the increased allowance to the master-worker and the allowance to him of half the remedy at assay were all the consequence of an agreement reached following the discovery, resulting from pyx trials, that the master had been using the remedies on both gold and silver to increase his profit. It was established that in doing so he was not in breach of the terms of his indenture, which had been incorrectly drafted, and that, furthermore, he needed the profit in order to operate the mint.[307] Nevertheless, even though he had been cleared of breach of contract, as a result of this episode Lonyson was seen as a man who needed watching, as is evident from the naming of the warden, Richard Martin, as an additional party to the commission, and in the frequent short term renewals to it up to Lonyson's death in 1582.[308]

Richard Martin, in fact, became the next master-worker and is named in the commission of 22 August 1582[309] after Lonyson's death. This is essentially in the same terms as the commission of 15 September 1578. It was evidently issued so that things could be kept running at the mint, and it was replaced by a completely new indenture with Sir Richard Martin (now knighted) on 30 January 1583.[310] This reverted to a gold fineness of 23 ct $3\frac{1}{2}$ gr. and provided for angels with their halves and quarters at the same weights and values as before. Charges were 6s 0d per pound of which 4s 9d went to the master and 1s 3d was to be accounted for by the warden. There was no sharing out of the remedy and things were as they had been before the discovery of Lonyson's activities, except that the master's costs were now more realistically viewed.

---

[305] Challis 1992b, 734, citing PRO. C66/1152, m.25.
[306] Challis 1992b, 734, citing BL.Harleian MS, 698, fo.97r.
[307] See Challis 1978, 135–40, for a fascinating and detailed account of sixteenth-century creative accounting!
[308] Renewals on 27 September 1578 (PRO. C66/1167, m.25), 29 December 1578 (PRO. C66/1181), 25 May 1579 (PRO. C66/1606), 23 December 1579 (PRO. C66/1606), 28 November 1580 (PRO. C66/1606), 3 May 1582 (PRO. C66/1212 and PRO. C66/1210), and 30 May 1582 (PRO. C66/1210).
[309] Challis 1992b, 735, citing PRO. E159/392, Rec.Hil.338.
[310] Challis 1992b, 736, citing PRO. C54/1157.

On 20 April 1584 a commission was issued adding fine sovereigns of 30s 0d (described as double-nobles) and ryals to the indenture of 1583.[311] Charges remained unchanged.

Third Issue, 1593–1603

Initially this issue saw a return to coins of crown gold standard at the same weights as those of the First Issue, and a new, elaborately draped bust was introduced. The indenture of 10 June 1593 with Sir Richard Martin provided for pounds of 20s 0d weighing 174.5 gr. (11.307 g) together with half-pounds, crowns and half-crowns.[312] All were to be struck in gold of 22 ct (0.917 fine). Charges were 7s 0d per Troy pound with 5s 9d going to the master-worker and the balance of 1s 3d to be accounted for by the warden. Evidently the indenture of 1583 was still effective as small quantities of fine gold coins in accordance with it continued to be struck during this issue period.

A new indenture dated 29 July 1601 made with Sir Richard Martin and his son Richard Martin provided for both fine and crown gold denominations of a slightly reduced weight.[313] The fine gold (23 ct 3½ gr., 0.995 fine) denominations were the angel of 10s 0d weighing 78.9 gr. (5.113 g) with its halves and quarters. The crown gold (22 ct, 0.917 fine) denominations were pounds of 20s 0d weighing 171.9 gr. (11.139 g) together with half-pounds, crowns and half-crowns. Charges were 10s 0d per Troy pound on fine gold, of which 4s 9d went to the master and 5s 3d was to be accounted for by the warden. On crown gold charges were also 10s 0d, but 5s 9d went to the master and only 4s 3d was left for the warden to account for.

For the first time in the reign the pound coin was struck as a regular denomination. The small reduction in weight in 1601, which was accompanied by a rather larger weight reduction for the silver coin, was an attempt to adjust for a perceived undervaluation of English coin as compared with that on the Continent. In fact the change in the gold/silver ratio led to an influx of silver and an outflow of gold, and the necessary corrective action was not taken until the next reign.

References and Classification

Earlier studies have largely been superseded by that of Brown and Comber, already referred to.[314] Of the more specialised works, the milled coinage is dealt with by Borden and Brown (the coins),[315] and Challis (the documentary evidence).[316] The portrait punches on both the gold and the silver coins are analysed by Brown and

---

[311] Challis 1992b, 736, citing PRO. C82/143/1416.
[312] Challis 1992b, 736, citing PRO. C54/1457.
[313] Challis 1992b, 737, citing PRO. E101/304/20.
[314] Brown and Comber 1989.
[315] Borden and Brown 1983.
[316] Challis 1978.

Comber[317] and the thrones used on the later sovereigns are studied by Whicher.[318] Whitton's 1949 listing of varieties then known remains useful.[319] As with the other Tudor coinages, the documentary evidence is set out in detail by Symonds,[320] and this is much extended and re-interpreted by Challis.[321]

Output

Although Elizabeth I's gold coins do not bear dates, a regular system of control using pyx trials was operated and records of these allow, in most cases, exact dates to be accorded to initial marks. In addition, estimates of outputs of different denominations have been made using these and survival data.[322] A consolidated view of all this is set out alongside the mint output records in Table 14.

---

[317] Brown and Comber 1988.
[318] Whicher 1938. I am indebted to Mr Comber for pointing out that the date, 1597, in the title of this paper ('Types of throne treatment on the "fine" sovereigns of Elizabeth during the period 1584 to 1597') is probably a typographical error for 1593. There is no evidence that fine sovereigns were minted much later than mid-1593.
[319] Whitton 1949.
[320] Symonds 1916.
[321] Challis 1978, Challis 1992a and Challis 1992b.
[322] Brown and Comber 1989.

TABLE 14. *Output of gold coin during the reign of Elizabeth I showing correlation with initial marks and denominations struck (source: Brown and Comber 1989)*

Accounting period	Amount struck (£) Fine gold	Crown gold	Initial marks	Dates for initial marks	Amount struck for I.M. Fine	Crown	Fine 30s.	10s.	5s.	2s. 6d.	Crown 20s.	10s.	5s.	2s. 6d.
	£	£			£	£								
FIRST ISSUE														
1.1.1559–31.7.1560	23,685	1,951	lis	1.1.1559–31.7.1560	23,685	1,951	x	x	x	–	–	x	x	x
1.12.1560–31.10.1561	6,459	3,812	cross-crosslet		7,145	(106,278)[1]	x	x	x	–	–	x	x	x
1.11.1561–31.10.1562	686	75,133	"	1.11.1561–31.8.1565										
1.11.1563–31.8.1565	–	37,333	"											
1.10.1565–31.3.1566	–	32,634	rose	1.10.1565–31.3.1566	–	32,634	–	–	–	–	(pattern)	x	x	x
1.5.1566–31.1.1567	–	15,373	portcullis	1.5.1566–31.1.1567	–	15,373	–	–	–	–	–	x	x	x
1.2.1567–30.6.1567	–	6,850	lion	1.2.1567–30.6.1567	–	6,850	–	–	–	–	–	x	x	x
1.7.1567–30.4.1569	7,794	32,381	coronet		12,026	(42,671)[1]	x	x	x	x	–	x	x	x
1.5.1569–28.2.1570	–	7,079	"	1.7.1567–28.2.1570										
1.5.1569–30.9.1569	4,232	–	"											
1.3.1570–15.12.1571	–	23,411	castle	1.3.1570–15.12.1571	–	(14,200)[1]	–	–	–	–	–	x	x	x
MILLED COINAGE														
Included in above figures			star	1.1.1561–c.1564	–	(10,000)[1]	–	–	–	–	–	x	x	x
			lis	14.2.1567–1.9.1568	–	(6,000)[1]	–	–	–	–	–	x	x	x

TABLE 14. Continued

Accounting period	Amount struck (£) Fine gold £	Crown gold £	Initial marks	Dates for initial marks	Amount struck for I.M. Fine £	Crown £	Denominations known Fine 30s.	15s.	10s.	5s.	2s. 6d.	Crown 20s.	10s.	5s.	2s. 6d.
SECOND ISSUE															
19.4.1572–30.10.1573	21,022	–	ermine	19.4.1572–30.10.1573	21,022	–	–	–	×	×	×	–	–	–	–
1.11.1573–25.5.1574	8,143	–	acorn	1.11.1573–25.5.1574	8,143	–	–	–	×	×	×	–	–	–	–
29.5.1574–13.7.1578	14,525	–	eglantine	29.5.1574–30.7.1578	14,525	–	–	–	×	×	×	–	–	–	–
1.10.1578–17.5.1580	20,261	–	cross	1.10.1578–17.5.1580	20,261	–	–	–	×	×	×	–	–	–	–
1.6.1580–31.12.1581	33,517	–	long cross	1.6.1580–31.12.1581	33,517	–	–	–	×	×	×	–	–	–	–
23.8.1582–31.1.1583	35,697	–	sword	23.8.1582–31.1.1583	35,697	–	–	–	×	×	×	–	–	–	–
1.2.1583–31.1.1584	41,972	–	bell	1.2.1583–29.11.1583	(34,977)[1]	–	–	–	×	×	×	–	–	–	–
1.2.1584–31.1.1585	37,563	–	gothic Α	1.2.1583–13.2.1585	(44,558)[1]	–	×	×	×	×	×	–	–	–	–
1.2.1585–31.1.1586	33,481	–	} scallop	14.2.1585–30.5.1587	56,562	–	×	×	×	×	×	–	–	–	–
1.2.1586–31.1.1587	20,451	–													
1.2.1587–31.1.1588	7,889	–													
1.2.1588–31.1.1589	24,969	–	} crescent	1.6.1587–31.1.1590(?)	46,973	–	×	×	×	×	×	–	–	–	–
1.2.1589–31.1.1590	16,745	–													
1.2.1590–31.1.1591	12,653	–	} hand	1.2.1590–31.1.1592(?)	40,778	–	×	×	×	×	×	–	–	–	–
1.2.1591–31.1.1592	28,128	–													
1.2.1592–10.6.1593	–	–	tun	1.2.1592–10.6.1593	(12,000)[1]	–	×	×	×	×	×	–	–	–	–
THIRD ISSUE	73,915[2]														
10.6.1593–31.1.1597			tun	10.6.1593–8.5.1594	–	(28,009)[1]	–	–	–	–	–	×	×	×	×
				9.5.1594–13.2.1596	(2,652)[1]	(42,739)[1]	–	–	?	?	?	×	×	×	?
1.2.1597–29.9.1599	14,105	7,290	woolpack	14.2.1596–7.2.1599	(14,167)[1]	(13,981)[1]	–	–	×	×	×	×	×	×	×
1.10.1599–28.7.1601	7,556	33,417	{ 0 key	1.5.1600–20.5.1601	(5,000)[1]	(26,477)[1]	–	–	×	–	–	×	×	–	×
29.7.1601–24.3.1603	1,292	21,737	{ 1	29.7.1601–14.5.1602	(292)[1]	(14,737)[1]	–	–	×	–	–	×	×	×	×
			{ 2	15.5.1602–24.3.1603	(1,000)[1]	(7,000)[1]	–	–	×	–	–	×	×	×	×

Notes: 1. Estimates. See Brown and Comber 1989.
2. The accounting period 1.2.1592 to 31.1.1597 includes, 1. Fine gold of the second issue i.m. tun; 2. Fine and crown gold of the third issue with i.m.'s tun, woolpack and some key.

APPENDIX 1

REPORT ON THE ANALYSIS OF FIVE GOLD PENNIES OF HENRY III BY THE DEPARTMENT OF SCIENTIFIC RESEARCH, THE BRITISH MUSEUM

INTRODUCTION

Henry III gold pennies are consistently heavier than the weight standard of two silver pennies recorded in a contemporary chronicle. It has been suggested that the coins may contain an amount of pure gold consistent with that standard with additional alloy, silver and copper, to bring the weight up to that observed. The coins were therefore analysed to determine their gold content.

ANALYSIS

The five coins analysed included two from private collections and three from the British Museum's collections. In all cases the coins were analysed non-destructively by X-ray fluorescence (XRF). Since this is a surface method of analysis and there may be some surface enrichment of the gold, the results must be regarded as semi-quantitative. The compositions of the three British Museum collection examples were checked by specific gravity (SG) measurements. Unfortunately, similar SG measurements made on the private collection examples are probably unreliable due to a temporary fault in the analytical balance used.

The SG measurements alone cannot be used to determine accurately the gold content because this method is only strictly applicable to binary alloys and the XRF analyses indicate that the coins contain both silver and copper in the alloy as well as gold. However, the XRF analysis can be used to indicate the approximate relative amounts of silver and copper in the alloy and the likely gold content can then be calculated from the SG.

RESULTS

The results, below, show the XRF analyses, the SG where measured, and the calculated gold contents and weights of the coins.

BMRL ref	Coin	XRF Analysis			SG	Calculated % Au	Wt g
		% Au	% Ag	% Cu			
43784R	Spink 18883	99.5	0.3	0.2	–	–	2.95
43785P	Schneider	99.3	0.6	0.1	–	–	2.96
43786Y	BM E2135	99.8	0.2	<0.1	19.23	99.1	2.93
43787W	BM 6238	99.6	0.3	0.1	19.07	98.5	2.92
43788U	BM 1915, 5–7, 571	99.6	0.3	2 1	19.12	98.9	2.89

The precisions of the XRF analyses are $\pm 1-2\%$ for gold and $\pm 20\%$ for silver and copper. The accuracies may be worse than this, however, due to surface enrichment. The precision of the SG measurements are $\pm 0.1\%$.

The average fineness of the British Museum collection coins is therefore about 98.8 $\pm 0.5\%$ gold (allowing for error in the SG measurement and the proportions of silver and copper). The private collection examples, having similar semi-quantitative XRF analyses, are almost certainly of similar fineness. The average weight of the five coins is 2.93g which is slightly higher than the theoretical weight of two silver pennies (2.90g). It should be noted that the current weights of these coins are likely to be lower than their weights at issue because of wear.

DISCUSSION

The discrepancy in weight between the coins and the recorded weight standard is approximately 1% but may originally have been greater. The composition of the coins also indicates that the gold content is lower than, theoretical, pure gold by a margin of approximately 1.2%. However, the purest gold achievable by rigorous refining in the thirteenth century was probably not better than 99.8% pure. Hence the true discrepancy is nearer 1% or less but still close to the weight difference.

The results indicate, therefore, that the fineness of the coins is significantly lower than the fine (purest) gold of the period. They equate, approximately, with a standard of 23ct 3gr. (23 3/4ct) which should have a gold content of 98.96%. However, the analyses do not, of course, clarify whether these small reductions in fineness were deliberate or the result of using rather poorly refined gold.

M. R. Cowell
15 June 1993

APPENDIX 2

DATING OF HENRY VI CLASSES

THIS Appendix considers the dating of the different classes of Henry VI's coinage based on the evidence of the Fishpool hoard (gold), the Reigate, Wray Lane, hoard (silver element), and the Reigate, Brokes Road, hoard (silver element). In the tables below the proportions, by value, of coins in these hoards are compared with the recorded output for London and Calais respectively. Silver and gold outputs have to be looked at separately because the output pattern for the two mints is quite different. The gold contents of the two Reigate hoards have been excluded because they are small.

The results of such comparisons must be treated with caution. Not only are there uncertainties relating to the degree to which a hoard may be regarded as a random sample – whether, for example, a selection of heavier and thus perhaps more recently struck coins has been made – but there are also factors that will affect the make-up of the national currency stock at any particular time. Even in a period which saw stability in standards of weight and fineness, there may have been considerable wastage of coins from circulation, fluctuating in its rate, which would distort the representation of older coins in a hoard.

Four factors, in particular, would contribute to this wastage:

1. Attrition through wear. If it assumed that all the coinage stock is subject to a steady, progressive, rate of wear, then older coins will tend to be removed from it when their weight falls to a level at which they can be no longer used as coin and become bullion.
2. Attrition through loss. A small proportion of the coinage stock is lost to the currency (perhaps by being placed in long term hoards) each year. Older coins have had more chance of being lost, simply by having been around longer.
3. Replacement of older coin by new coin as a result of international gold and silver price fluctuations. For example, when it was advantageous to make payment abroad in English gold coin rather than in silver, the national stock of gold coin would have been reduced regardless of the age of individual coins. When the reverse applied and foreign gold came into the country, that would immediately be converted into new coin. Over a period of years these differing conditions could arise several times, each cycle reducing old coin and adding new.
4. Major political payments, ransoms, dowries, subventions, could at times have significant effects.

Of these factors, 1 and 2 could be expected to apply at a more or less steady rate, while 3 and 4 may have fluctuated considerably, depending on the frequency of each event, the number of cycles and their relative intensity.

The overall effect is that hoard content is liable to be progressively more under-representative the older it is when compared to known mint output. The Fishpool hoard is a case in point. Deposited *c.* 1464, its content of 37 Henry IV and 265 Henry V coins, all over 40 years old at the date of deposit, are liable to give very misleading results if attempts are made to use them to arrive at different dates for the different types. For the coins of Henry VI there is certainly some distortion, too, but the nearer to the deposit date the more accurate the proportions of survivors are likely to be – until amongst the very latest one may find undispersed groups, fresh from the mint, another form of distortion.

Tables A and B compare, for London and Calais respectively, the proportions of coins issued in terms of cumulative face value with the cumulative mint output figures. Tables C and D show the progressive cumulative output figures used in compiling Tables A and B. The proportions of survivors later than 1441 are too small or, in the case of the Reigate, Wray Lane hoard, too unrepresentative to be of use. For the silver the Reigate, Brokes Road hoard should provide better evidence than the Wray Lane because it is a larger sample. For the same reason, the evidence of the Calais mint should be of more value for the early silver, and that of the London mint for the early gold. All or any of the hoards may be unrepresentative because of the factors noted above and, indeed, for a variety of unknowable reasons. However, the evidence of the three hoards taken together and prudently interpreted should reduce the effect of this, although the greatest caution must still be exercised.

With these considerations in mind, and looking at Tables A, B, C, and D, it can be seen that for the annulet issue the largest samples are the London gold and the Calais silver and these combine in suggesting a date for its completion not before 1430. Only the Reigate, Brokes Road, silver disagrees with this, suggesting an earlier date, but this can probably be seen as a peculiarity of that hoard when viewed against the weight of the other evidence.

The low numbers of coins of later issues in the Fishpool hoard (where the chance presence or absence of a single coin could make a material difference) means that after the annulet issue it can only be used to check on the evidence of the other two hoards. In both of those the Calais evidence points to the rosette-mascle issue having lasted only a very short time and being complete before 3rd August 1431. The pinecone-mascle issue is clearly suggested by both hoards to have been completed by about the end of September 1432, although the relatively large number of survivors from the London mint in the Reigate, Wray lane, hoard point to a later date; again against the weight of other evidence.

The later issues, leaf-mascle, leaf trefoil and trefoil, are represented by comparatively few survivors in all three hoards, but of these the Reigate, Brokes Road hoard provides the largest samples which suggest end dates of 1433–4 and 1438–9 for the first two, and, of course, for the trefoil issue, the relatively secure date of 1441 (derived from our knowledge of the date at which output ceased at the Calais mint. These conclusions are summarised on page 30, above.

TABLE A. LONDON MINT. *Comparison of the value of coin in each hoard with output figures*

	Fishpool hoard Gold, dep. c. 1463-4					Reigate, Brokes Road, hoard[1] Silver, dep. c. 1460						Reigate, Wray Lane, hoard[1] Silver, dep. c. 1454-5					
	No. of coins	Face value (£)	% (up to trefoil)	Cum. proportion %	Date of same prop'n in accounts	No. of coins	Face value (pence)	% (up to trefoil)	Cum. face value (pence)	Cum. proportion %	Date of same prop'n in accounts	No. of coins	Face value (pence)	% (up to trefoil)	Cum. face value (pence)	Cum. proportion %	Date of same prop'n in accounts
Annulet	421	124.08	85.2	85.2	1430-31	204	740	35.9	740	35.9	1427	43	172	56.2	172	56.2	1430-31
Rosette-mascle	16	5.00	3.4	88.6	1431-33	48	182	8.8	922	44.7	1428-30	2	8	2.6	180	58.8	1430-31
Pinecone-mascle	37	12.00	8.2	96.8	1437-38	121	452	21.9	1374	66.6	1431-33	17	66	21.6	246	80.4	1438-39
Leaf-mascle	4	1.17	0.9	97.7	1438-39	2	8	0.4	1382	67.0	1433-34	0	0	0	246	80.4	1438-39
Leaf-trefoil	4	2.33	1.6	99.3	1439-41	131	460	22.3	1842	89.3	1438-39		52	14.0	298	94.4	1439-41
Trefoil	3	1.00	0.07	100.0	1439-41	55	220	10.7	2062	100.0	1439-41	2	8	5.6	306	100.0	1439-41

Notes: 1. Only the silver coins in the Brokes Road and Wray Lane hoards are included.

TABLE B. CALAIS MINT. *Comparison of the value of coin in each hoard with output figures*

	Fishpool hoard Gold, dep. c. 1463-4					Reigate, Brokes Road, hoard[1] Silver, dep. c. 1460						Reigate, Wray Lane, hoard[1] Silver, dep. c. 1454-5					
	No. of coins	Face value (£)	% (up to trefoil)	Cum. proportion %	Date of same prop'n in accounts	No. of coins	Face value (pence)	% (up to trefoil)	Cum. face value (pence)	Cum. proportion %	Date of same prop'n in accounts	No. of coins	Face value (pence)	% (up to trefoil)	Cum. face value (pence)	Cum. proportion %	Date of same prop'n in accounts
Annulet	62	19.50	95.1	95.1	1428-31	2,376	8,288	57.6	8,288	57.6	1428-31	433	1632	62.8	1,632	62.8	1428-31
Rosette-mascle	3	1.00	4.9	100.0	1428-31	959	3,531	24.5	11,819	82.1	1428-31	145	562	21.6	2,194	84.4	1428-31
Pinecone-mascle						632	2,397	16.6	14,216	98.7	1431-32	101	402	15.4	2,596	99.8	1436
Leaf-mascle						34	130	0.9	14,346	99.6	1436	2	4	0.2	2,600	100.0	1439-41
Leaf-trefoil						6	24	0.2	14,370	99.8	1436	0	0	0	2,600	100.0	1439-41
Trefoil						7	28	0.2	14,398	100.0	1439-41	0	0	0	2,600	100.0	1439-41

Notes: 1. Only the silver coins in the Brokes Road and Wray Lane hoards are included.

TABLE C. *Cumulative mint output figures for gold*

Period of account	Output in period[1]	Cumulative output	% to 29.9.1460	% to 16.4.1441	% from 16.4.1441 to 29.9.1460
GOLD LONDON	£	£			
1.4.1422–29.9.1424	329,114	329,114	50.4	55.1	
30.9.1424–29.9.1425	57,767	386,881	59.2	64.7	
30.9.1425–20.4.1427	51,306	438,187	67.1	73.3	
20.4.1427–29.9.1427	12,704	450,871	69.0	75.4	
30.9.1427–29.9.1428	28,198	479,089	73.4	80.1	
30.9.1428–31.3.1430	25,481	504,570	77.3	84.4	
1.4.1430–29.9.1431	21,683	526,253	80.6	88.0	
30.9.1431–29.9.1433	19,056	545,309	83.5	91.2	
30.9.1433–29.9.1434	10,582	555,891	85.1	93.0	
30.9.1434–24.6.1435	5,000	560,891	85.9	93.8	
24.6.1435–29.9.1436	8,427	569,318	87.2	95.2	
30.9.1436–29.9.1437	5,663	574,981	88.0	96.2	
30.9.1437–29.9.1438	5,252	580,233	88.9	97.1	
30.9.1438–18.12.1439	9,094	589,327	90.2	98.6	
18.12.1439–16.4.1441	8,423	597,750	91.5	100.0	
16.4.1441–29.9.1443	11,522	609,272	93.3		20.8
30.9.1443–29.9.1444	4,062	613,334	93.9		28.2
30.9.1444–29.9.1445	2,700	616,034	94.3		33.1
30.9.1445–13.12.1445	628	616,662	94.4		34.2
13.12.1445–24.6.1446	3,944	620,606	95.0		41.3
24.6.1446–24.6.1447	1,465	622,071	95.3		44.0
24.6.1447–11.10.1449	3,414	625,485	95.8		50.2
11.10.1449–29.9.1450	5,951	631,436	96.7		60.9
30.9.1450–9.4.1452	6,918	638,354	97.8		73.4
9.4.1452–1.4.1453	4,367	642,721	98.4		81.3
1.4.1453–21.4.1454	2,064	644,785	98.7		85.1
21.4.1454–28.3.1456	2,492	647,277	99.1		89.6
23.3.1456–29.9.1457	2,137	649,414	99.4		93.4
30.9.1457–29.9.1458	1,414	650,828	99.7		96.0
30.9.1458–29.9.1459	324	651,152	99.7		96.6
30.9.1459–29.9.1460	1,887	653,039	100.0		100.0 55,289 = total output from 16.4.1441– 29.9.1460
GOLD CALAIS					
30.7.1422–30.1.1424	60,612	60,612	59.3		
24.2.1424–24.12.1427	35,590	96,202	94.1		
20.5.1428–2.8.1431	6,018	102,220	100.0		

Note: 1. Source, Challis 1992b.

TABLE D. *Cumulative mint output figures for silver*

Period of account	Output in period[1]	Cumulative output	% to 29.9.1460	% to 16.4.1441	% from 16.4.1441 to 29.9.1460
SILVER LONDON	£	£			
1.4.1422–29.9.1424	10,386	10,386	8.2	21.9	
30.9.1424–29.9.1425	2,419	12,805	10.1	27.0	
30.9.1425–20.4.1427	4,054	16,859	13.2	35.6	
20.4.1427–29.9.1427	898	17,757	13.9	37.5	
30.9.1427–29.9.1428	1,746	19,503	15.3	41.2	
30.9.1428–31.3.1430	4,342	23,845	18.7	50.4	
1.4.1430–29.9.1431	4,222	28,067	22.0	59.3	
30.9.1431–29.9.1433	3,493	31,560	24.8	66.7	
30.9.1433–29.9.1434	855	32,415	25.5	68.5	
30.9.1434–24.6.1435	786	33,201	26.1	70.1	
24.6.1435–29.9.1436	546	33,747	26.5	71.3	
30.9.1436–29.9.1437	820	34,567	27.2	73.0	
30.9.1437–29.9.1438	2,216	36,783	28.9	77.7	
30.9.1438–18.12.1439	6,433	43,216	33.9	91.3	
18.12.1439–16.4.1441	4,127	47,343	37.2	100.0	
16.4.1441–29.9.1443	794	48,137	37.8		1.0
30.9.1443–29.9.1444	234	48,371	38.0		1.3
30.9.1444–29.9.1445	311	48,682	38.2		1.7
30.9.1445–13.12.1445	63	48,745	38.3		1.8
13.12.1445–24.6.1446	3,788	52,533	41.3		6.4
24.6.1446–24.6.1447	133	52,666	41.4		6.7
24.6.1447–11.10.1449	1,052	53,718	42.2		8.0
11.10.1449–29.9.1450	6,953	60,671	47.7		16.7
30.9.1450–9.4.1452	16,184	76,855	60.4		36.9
9.4.1452–1.4.1453	6,135	82,990	65.2		44.6
1.4.1453–21.4.1454	5,408	88,390	69.4		51.3
21.4.1454–28.3.1456	8,205	96,603	75.9		61.6
28.3.1456–29.9.1457	9,993	106,596	83.7		74.1
30.9.1457–29.9.1458	5,491	112,087	88.0		81.0
30.9.1458–29.9.1459	4,655	116,742	91.7		86.8
30.9.1459–29.9.1460	10,564	127,306	100.0		100.0 79.963 = total output from 16.4.1441– 29.9.1460
SILVER CALAIS					
1.7.1422–18.9.1422	1,439	1,439		0.5	
31.10.1422–28.9.1423	7,080	8,519		2.9	
22.10.1423–30.1.1424	2,252	10,771		3.7	
25.2.1424–31.1.1428	101,618	112,389		38.8	
28.2.1428–3.8.1431	134,491	246,880		85.3	
31.10.1431–30.9.1432	39,274	286,154		98.9	
10.2.1436–30.3.1436	2,655	288,809		99.8	
1439–40	585	289,394		100.0	

Note: 1. Source, Challis 1992b.

CONTINENTAL IMITATIONS

THE Schneider collection contains three groups of imitations: nobles imitating those of Henry VI, ryals imitating those of Edward IV, and ryals imitating those of Elizabeth I. All available evidence points to all these imitations having been struck in the Low Countries during the sixteenth century.[323] Most are fairly close copies of the English prototype struck in good quality gold. Rarely, they show some indication of the place of striking (**851–4** and **889**). In the case of the imitations of the Elizabethan ryal, there is documentary evidence for the circumstances in which they were struck.[324]

NOBLES IMITATING THOSE OF HENRY VI

No attempt to classify the copies of Henry VI nobles has yet been made. They are mentioned in Ives' paper of 1941[325] and commented on, in passing, in Thompson's paper on the imitation ryals of Edward IV.[326] The specimens in the Serooskerke hoard are described by Van Gelder[327] and some are illustrated in the catalogue of the Schulman sale in which much of the hoard was dispersed.[328]

The great majority take as their model English nobles of the London mint of the annulet issue, no doubt reflecting the fact that those were by far the commonest.[329] There are just a few, represented in this collection by two coins (**837–8**), which are evidently inspired by a different prototype, but it is not always possible to be certain which. In the absence of an established classification it has been thought best to arrange the coins in order of their nearness to a typical annulet noble prototype, grouping those with particular features (such as pellets on the side of the ship), and this arrangement is most conveniently set out in tabular form (Table 15). While this is largely self-explanatory, it is worth noting that, on the obverses, the lis following hƐПRIɑ is soon lost and that, on the reverses, Ihɑ is most commonly rendered as IhƐ. It is also of interest to note the closely die-linked family of imitations having two pellets on the side of the ship (Group 1 on the table). These were strongly represented in the Serooskerke hoard and have some letter punches in common with dies found in Group 2. It seems likely that they represent the output of a single mint in one period.

---

[323] Thompson 1945–8 and Ives 1941 review the evidence for this. The Serooskerke hoard (dep. 1622) is typical of the finds in which they occur.

[324] Thompson 1941.

[325] Ives 1941.

[326] Thompson 1945–8.

[327] Van Gelder 1965–6.

[328] Schulman 1966.

[329] For example, the Fishpool hoard contained 494 nobles of Henry VI of which 320 were London nobles of the annulet issue.

TABLE 15. *Arrangement of imitations of Henry VI nobles*

	Obverses							Reverses						
	Orna-ments	Ropes	After hENRIC	By wrist	Stops	On ship	Nos in catalogue	Initial mark	First word	After IhϾ	In spandrel	Stops	Nos in catalogue	Notes
ENGLISH PROTOTYPE (Annulet issue)	1–1–1	2/1	lis	annulet	trefoil	nothing		lis	IhϾ	cinquefoil	annulet	annulet		
Group 1–2 pellets in ship														
a	1–1–1	2/1	lis	annulet	trefoil	two pellets	826, 827, 828, 829	lis	IhϾ	cinquefoil	annulet	annulet	826, 827, 828, 829	
b	1–1–1	2/1	trefoil	nothing	trefoil	two pellets	830	lis	IhϾ	trefoil	annulet	annulet	830	
Group 2 – nothing in ship														
a	1–1–1	2/1	lis	annulet	trefoil	nothing	831	lis	IhϾ	trefoil	annulet	annulet	831	
b	1–1–1	2/1	trefoil	annulet	trefoil	nothing	832	lis	IhϾ	cinquefoil	annulet	annulet	832	
c	1–1–1	2/1	trefoil	annulet	trefoil	nothing	833	lis	IhϾ	trefoil	annulet	annulet	833	
d	1–1–1	2/1	trefoil	annulet	trefoil	nothing	834, 835	lis	IhϾ	trefoil	annulet	annulet	834, 835	
Group 3 – annulet in ship, trefoil stops on rev.														
a	1–1–1	3/2	trefoil	annulet	trefoil	one annulet	836	lis	IhϾ	trefoil	nothing	trefoil	836	
Group 4 – diverse, inspired by non-annulet prototype														
a	1–11–1	3/2	trefoil	nothing	trefoil	nothing	837	cross	IhϾ	trefoil	nothing	trefoil	837	
b	–11–11	3/2	trefoil	lis	trefoil	nothing	838	cross	IhϾ	trefoil	nothing	trefoil	838	ħ in centre inverted

RYALS IMITATING THOSE OF EDWARD IV

Ryals imitating those of Edward IV were first systematically analysed by Thompson.[330] The Schneider collection contains a very extensive series of them – probably more than Thompson himself saw when compiling his paper—and casts new light on certain aspects of the classification, while confirming its essential correctness. Accordingly, Thompson's arrangement has broadly been followed here.

There are considerably more dies than Thompson envisaged. He described three groups:

Group I. Early Style. These are characterised by having i.m. sun on the obverse and crown or sun on the reverse. They are smaller in diameter than the later imitations (which are rather larger than the English prototype). Other features, such as the size of the rose and the length of the sword are nearer to those on the prototype than on later imitations. There are two coins of this group in the Schneider collection (**839–40**).

Group II. Coins attributable to the Gorinchem (Gorcum) mint (831–76). This attribution is certain because at least one die which uses the same punches as the rest embodies the arms of Arkel in the design (**851–4**). This group, the most numerous, is broken down into:

Class 1 (**841–4**) which is represented by one obverse die and varies from class 2 only in its use of a distinctive punch for the head (designated by Thompson as his head II). Apart from this, the difference between class 1 and class 2 is no greater than that between any two dies in class 2.

Class 2 (**845–55**) uses a slightly different head from that of class 1 (designated by Thompson as his head IIa). Classes 1 and 2 use the same lettering and the king's arm has the same appearance. The form of the lis on the side of the ship is easily distinguished from a new form introduced in class 3.

Class 3a (**856–65**) introduces a new head (Thompson head III) which he describes as having round pellet eyes unlike the previous heads. Actually, examination of coins in fine condition reveals that the eyes, though indeed round, have pupils punched into their centres. What matters, however, is that they are round; earlier eyes are lenticular. Apart from the head and a new form of lis on the side of the ship, other features are the same as on class 2.

Class 3b (**866–7**) has the same head as 3a, but new letters are introduced, clearly exemplified by I and A. Details of the king's right arm are altered. Another feature of this class and the next, not noticed by Thompson but visible on all specimens in this collection, is a small pellet between the tails and the heads of the four lions in the reverse design.

---

[330] Thompson 1945–8.

Class 3c (**868–76**) is purely a punctuation variant of 3b, known to Thompson from one die only but in this collection represented by no less than 7 obverse dies on 9 coins.

Class 3d is described from a single coin illustrated by Montagu in *NC* 1893, pl. III,3. There is no example in this collection.

A resume of the number of coins and dies of group II represented in the Schneider collection is as follows:

	No. of coins	*No. of dies*	
		Obv.	*Rev.*
Class 1	4	1	4
Class 2	11	6	11
Class 3a	9	9	4
Class 3a/3b–c	1	1	0 (in 3c)
Class 3b	2	1	2
Class 3c	9	7	7
	36	25	28

Group III. Coins attributable to the Culemborg mint. These ryals read MO.ORD.FRISIZꓥꟼ.ꓥD.LɛGɛM or similar and have design features which make their attribution unmistakeable. There are no specimens in this collection.

Finally, at the end of his list Thompson describes, but does not embody in his classification, a few coins that do not readily fit into the above three groups. Two of these are distiguished by a very distinctive form of the letter ɛ in the banner on the obverse (Figure 1). The Schneider collection includes no less than nine coins with this feature. All but two are from different dies and these are here accorded a separate group:

Group IV. The Ornate ɛ. Three classes can be distinguished principally from their lettering;

Class 1 (**877–78**) has the ornate ɛ without cross-bar and a Gothic G in the legend. The ampersand is of distinctive form.

Class 2 (**879–81**) has the ornate ɛ with a cross-bar and there is no ampersand. The punch for the letter R is slightly different from that on class 1, but it could be the same punch in a different state.

Class 3 (**882–4**) is characterised by the use of a Roman form of the letter G. There is either no ampersand or else a new one in the form of a meat hook. An entirely new punch is used for the letter R.

At present, it is impossible to say where these pieces were struck, or when. Generally, on grounds of style, they seem late, especially class 3 with its Roman G.

All the coins of Groups I to IV are generally of consistent and full ryal weight and

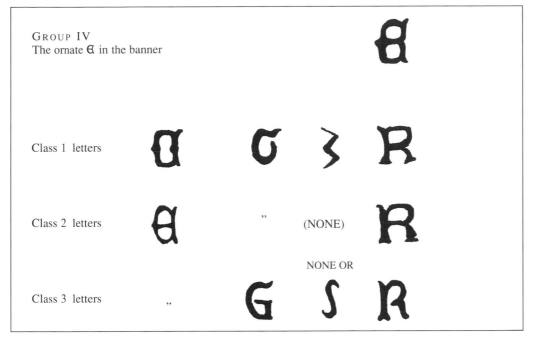

Figure 1. Lettering forms on Group IV (enlarged)

have the appearance of being struck in good gold. They can probably be described as 'official' in the sense of having been struck for trade use by the official mints of small Continental states. No doubt the gold content and the premium for the denomination ensured that this was a profitable way of converting gold, but it was at least done in a controlled manner and with some regard for those who could judge the quality of the coin in which they were paid.

A small group of much cruder imitations is included at the end (**886–8**) which certainly fall into a different category. These may, indeed, not be Continental, although it should be noted that two of them come from the Angers hoard.[331] They are contemporary forgeries.

RYALS IMITATING THOSE OF ELIZABETH I

The popularity in the Low Countries of the fine, high value, ryal of Edward IV had led to its imitation there during the sixteenth century. When England became involved in the struggle of the Low Countries against Spain, and sent an army under the earl of Leicester to help them, this presented an opportunity for the crown to make a modest, but worthwhile, fiscal profit. This was done by converting Spanish gold coin into ryals and double-nobles (in accordance with the commission of 20 April 1584, see p. 74) and

---

[331] Schneider 1968.

sending them to the Netherlands to support Leicester's army. The profit has been estimated at about 4% after the costs of refining and minting.[332]

Not surprisingly those mints in the Netherlands which sought to make profit by imitating the coins of other states, and which had probably been imitating Edward IV ryals, saw the opportunity too. Such a mint, as we have seen, was Gorinchem (Gorcum). Thompson has set out in detail the evidence for the production there of ryals imitating those of Queen Elizabeth.[333] The ryals sent over for the use of Leicester's army were imitated there between 1585 and 1587.[334] A placard issued by Leicester, which Thompson dates to 4 August 1586, denounced Gorinchem as the principal source of imitations and describes two varieties of ryals produced there. One was made in the name of 'Don Anthonie' with the letters ꟿPR ꓥL included in the obverse legend; the other was in the name of 'principis a Summeii' and had the letters ꟿꓥDGPꓥL inserted into the obverse legend.[335]

Thompson identifies 'Don Anthonie' with Don Antonio, Prior of Crato, and claimant to the throne of Portugal. He reads ꟿPR ꓥL as *M(oneta) P(ortugalliae) R(egis) A(d) L(egem)*. The 'principis a Summeii' he identifies with the Principiate of Chimay and particularly with the princess, Marie of Brumeu, who is known to have used the mint at Gorinchem to issue a variety of unauthorised coinages. He reads ꟿꓥDGPꞒꓥL as *M(oneta) A(urea) D(e) G(oricum) P(rincipum) C(himaiensum) A(d) L(egem)*; there is also an additional ꓵ at the end of the reverse legend which has yet to be explained. The Schneider collection contains a specimen of the latter type (**889**).

Challis, expressing a reservation about Thompson's conclusions, has pointed out that, in a letter to Lord Burghley of 18 June 1586, Leicester says that coins issued from Gorinchem being made under licence from the Princess of Chimay carried her print and arms rather than those of Elizabeth.[336] In view of the placard (issued two months later, if Thompson's date is to be relied upon) it would seem that Leicester may have had cause to change his mind.

As well as the imitation ryals which, in the light of the placard, can be attributed with confidence to the Gorinchem mint, there is another group of inter die-linked coins, which are close copies of the English prototype, though of coarser style, and which Thompson firmly attributes to a source in the Netherlands. Whether they are a copy of the English coins made officially for the Leicester administration, a possibility suggested by Thompson, seems unlikely in the light of another statement made in Leicester's 18 June 1586 letter to Burghley.[337] More likely they were a sideline of the Gorinchem mint or even the product of some other unofficial source. The Schneider collection contains one such coin (**890**).

---

[332] Challis 1978, 263–8.
[333] Thompson 1941, see also Ives 1941. In his 1941 paper Thompson refers to the mint as Gorcum and in his 1945–8 paper as Gorinchem. They are, of course, the same place. Gorinchem is the modern name.
[334] Symonds 1916.
[335] Snelling 1763, 20, n.(Z).
[336] Unlikely according to Challis 1978, 266, n. 44.
[337] Challis 1978, 266, n. 44.

GLOSSARY

FINENESS. Theoretical fineness is expressed in accordance with the terms of the coinage indentures in carats (ct) and grains (gr.). Pure gold is 24 carats. One carat = 4 grains.[338] The equivalent fineness in parts per 1000 is also given.

GOLD/SILVER RATIO. Market values of silver and gold could and did vary from time to time in response to supply and demand. Any coinage system including coins in both gold and silver, where the face value was substantially that of the metal they contained, and with a fixed monetary relationship between them, automatically assumed a particular ratio for the value of gold to silver. If the ratio assumed at the outset was wrong, or if the gold/silver ratio determined by the wider market varied, the variance from the market ratio could, at least in theory, make it more or less advantageous to accept payments in one or the other of the metals, or, in an extreme case, to convert coin of one metal into coin of the other.

In practice, mintage charges would make it uneconomic to convert coinage of one metal into coinage of another unless there was a large difference in their values. There were, however, opportunities for those who traded abroad, and, if the value placed on gold at the English mint was too low, only silver would be brought to it, and *vice versa*.[339]

---

[338] Except for a short time in the sixteenth century, see n. 275.

[339] This point may be illustrated by looking at the position in England and Flanders in 1434. In Flanders, according to Van Gelder and Hoc 1960, Philip the Good's new system of 1434 included a gold cavalier d'or containing 3.63 g of 0.992 gold and valued at 24 sols. The major silver coin at that date was the double gros containing 3.40 g of 0.479 fine silver valued at 1 sol. This gives a pure gold/pure silver ratio of 1:10.854 and compares with that in England in the same year of 1:10.327.

If we assume a case where a payment containing 1,000 g in pure gold was made in Flanders, this would be equivalent to $\dfrac{1,000}{3.63 \times 0.992}$ = 277.704 cavaliers d'or. These would be equal to 6,664.896 double gros containing 6,664.896 × 0.479 × 3.40 = 10,854.39 g of pure silver.

In England, 10,854.39 g of pure silver = $\dfrac{10,854.39}{0.925}$ = 11,734.55 g of sterling silver = 33.5353 Tower pounds.

33.5353 Tower pounds would yield 12,072.70 pence at 15 gr. each = £50.303.

£50.303 in gold coin would contain 16,298.146 gr. of 0.995 fine gold (at £16 13s 4d to the Tower lb. of 5,400 gr.). 16,298.146 gr. = 1056 g = 1051 g of pure gold.

Thus it can be seen that there would be an theoretical profit of 1051 – 1000 = 51 g of pure gold worth £2 8s 10d. This would only be the case, however, if there were no coinage or exchanging charges. In such event it would indeed be profitable to receive payments in Flanders in silver, to have the silver recoined into English coin, then to change it into gold. However, even with such costs, if a trader would not be left with any profit on this deal at least a large proportion of those costs would have been absorbed, which would not have been the case had Flemish gold been brought for conversion into English money.

One can see why the main output of the Calais mint at this period was in silver coin. The same reason may underlie the change in the English silver coinage charges made in the next indenture (1445) when an additional 2d was added, thought by Challis (Challis 1992b, 710) to be for the purpose of covering deficiencies in the bullion.

The gold/silver ratio can be expressed in at least three ways, and it is not always clear which method is being used. In its simplest form it is expressed as the ratio between the market price of a unit weight of pure gold and the same weight of pure silver.[340]

For England, where coinage standards enjoyed a comparatively high degree of consistency during the middle ages, it is quite common to see gold/silver ratios expressed as the ratio between 0.995 fine gold and 0.925 fine silver. This has the appeal of giving an exact ratio of 1:12 for the periods between June 1351 and March 1413, and March 1467 and November 1526, but for most purposes is evidently misleading, since it is not comparing like with like.

The third method, that which would have most interested a medieval trader, is the ratio between the value of gold and silver money that he would have received back from the mint in exchange for bullion; in other words minting costs would have entered into his calculations as well as the market values of the metals.

If we apply these three approaches to the indenture of June 1352 we get considerably different results:

Ratio between the values of pure silver and pure gold = 1:11.16
Ratio between the values of silver and gold coin   = 1:12.00
Ratio between the metals in net receipts   = 1:11.30

It is the first of these ratios that is used in this book, as its most important function here is to explain the preferential flow of one metal or the other into or out of the country.[341] The other ratios can usually be calculated if required.

INITIAL MARKS. The term used to describe any symbol at the commencement of the legend. This is preferred to the terms 'mint mark' or 'privy mark' since the mark may be neither of those. On the other hand, if, as with Mary's coinage, the mark appears other than in the initial position, it is referred to, *faut de mieux*, as a privy mark.

LIMITATIONS. This is a catalogue of a collection of gold coins and references to indentures and other sources concentrate on those aspects of them that deal with gold coinage. Many of these sources also cover silver coinage and there are others dealing with silver alone. Inferences should not be drawn for the coinage as a whole without reference to the appropriate works.[342]

MINT OPERATIONS.[343] Apart from the period between 1544 and 1572, the arrangements were as follows:

---

[340] 'Pure' is, of course, an ideal concept in this context. However, from 1344 onwards the mint indentures defined the standard of gold to be used (23 ct 3½ gr. (0.995 fine) until Henry VIII's debasements) thus recognising that it was not totally pure and defining with precision where it stood in relation to theoretically pure gold. Silver could easily be obtained at a greater fineness than 0.925 (see, for example, Mayhew and Walker 1977, 134).

[341] See n. 339.

[342] For example Challis 1992a and b.

[343] For a fuller description of these, see Challis 1992a, 230.

Production. This was undertaken by the master-worker (or master-moneyer) under the terms of an indenture (a form of contract) entered into by him with the crown. The master-worker employed the moneyers and other production staff. He bought the bullion and charged a rate on each pound of metal coined, in accordance with the indenture. So long as he adhered to the terms of the indenture, all profit he made he kept. Later in the period with which we are concerned the scope of the indentures was sometimes extended by the issue of a commission under authority of the Lord Treasurer.

Establishment. The mint buildings and equipment and the permanent staff establishment were the responsibility of the warden who was a full-time salaried crown officer. Among the staff were the comptroller/assayer, the chief clerk and the head porter, and their respective staffs. The costs of the establishment were met out of a charge on each pound of metal coined; any surplus (or deficit) belonged to the crown. This was the source of any legitimate profit the crown made out of coining operations (although the crown might make profit from bullion transactions, see pp. 89–90).

Die Engraving. The position of the engravers varied in the period with which we are concerned. Earlier they were treated as part of the master's responsibility and paid at a rate per dozen dies delivered. Later they were salaried and the master and warden had a joint responsibility for them.

During the period 1544 to 1572, initially prompted by the need to streamline mint operations to handle the huge throughput of the mid 1540s, and to ensure that all the profits of that came to the crown, all mint personnel, including the master-worker, were salaried and placed under the direction of an under-treasurer (who effectively replaced the warden).

MINT PRICE. This was the net amount received by a person bringing bullion to the mint after the master-worker's fee and the amount to be accounted for by the warden had been deducted. The crown could manipulate the mint price by raising or lowering the amount to be accounted for by the warden. This could be done either to make a profit for the crown (if the market would permit it) or to adjust the mint price to wider market rates, or both. The important considerations for a trader operating across frontiers would be whether a better mint price could be obtained for gold or silver, in what currency he needed to have the cash, where he needed the cash and in what form (gold or silver). Where different currencies are involved it facilitates comparison if the mint price is expressed as that which could be obtained for pure metal (see also Gold/silver ratio).

REMEDY. The margin of error in weight or alloy allowed in the production of the coins. The actual amount varied from time to time between $\frac{1}{16}$ and $\frac{1}{4}$ carat per pound weight. For many years in the middle ages it was $\frac{1}{8}$ carat per pound weight, that is, 28 grains in a Tower pound or just over 0.5%. If, when tested, the coin was found to be outside the limit of the remedy, the master worker had to melt and remake it at his own cost. It was a usual stipulation in an indenture that error could only arise by chance and not otherwise. It was the omission of this stipulation that opened the door for the manipulations of John Lonyson in the 1570s.[344]

WEIGHTS. Prior to 1526 the Mint used the Tower pound of 5,400 gr. From 1526 the Troy pound of 5,760 gr. was used. Both pounds divide into 12 ounces, each of 20 pennyweights. Thus a Tower pennyweight contains 22.5 gr., whereas a Troy pennyweight contains 24.0 gr. The highest common factor of both pounds is the grain (1.0 gr. = 0.0648 g).

[344] See p. 73 and n. 307.

HOARDS AND FINDS FROM BRITAIN AND
THE CONTINENT CONTAINING
ENGLISH GOLD COINS

THIS is a summary listing of hoards and single finds which, either definitely or possibly, included English gold coins (or their Continental imitations) issued between 1257 and 1603 and falling within the compass of this book.

The two most important single sources have been J. D. A. Thompson's *Inventory of British Coin Hoards, AD 600–1500* (Thompson 1956) and I. D. Brown and Michael Dolley's *Coin Hoards of Great Britain and Ireland, 1500–1967* (Brown and Dolley 1971). These have been extended by D. M. Metcalf's 'Some finds of medieval coins from Scotland and the north of England' in *BNJ* 30 (Metcalf 1960–1); I. D. Brown's 'First Addendum to the bibliography of coin hoards of Great Britain and Ireland' in *NCirc* 81 (Brown 1971); *Coin Hoards* 1972 – (*CH*); G. C. Boon's *Welsh Hoards* (Boon 1986); E. Besly's *English Civil War Coin Hoards* (Besly 1987); H. Manville's 'Additions and Corrections to Thompson's *Inventory* and Brown and Dolley's *Coin Hoards* – Part 1' in *BNJ* 63 (Manville 1993). The principal sources cited in these works have mostly been repeated here, although in some instances, where there are multiple sources, the lower quality ones have been omitted. The data from these valuable inventories has been augmented from various reports published in *NC*, *BNJ*, and elsewhere. Additionally information on hoards and finds discovered on the Continent has been added where this is relevant, although this aspect of the listing is certainly far from complete.

In cases where the full details of the content of hoards are not known, it has been assumed that those deposited up to 1649 may have included pre-1603 gold coins, since in cases where the content is known, a proportion of such coins is often present (see nos. 177, 179, 181 and 183). Hoards deposited later than 1649 have only been included when it is known for certain that they included pre-1603 gold.

The 197 entries are, in the first place, ordered and numbered according to their approximate date of deposit, where this can be inferred from the content of the hoard or find, or the date attributable to the issue of the latest coin (*tpq = terminus post quem*). In the latter case, of course, the coin may have been lost, or the hoard buried, appreciably later. The abbreviations *N* and *R* refer to gold and silver coins respectively. Following the chronological list, a listing in alphabetical order effectively provides an index to it.

Number	Deposit date or tpq	Find place	Find date	Content N	Content R	References
1.	1260?	Eaton Coppice, nr Leominster, Here.	1757	unknown	unknown N and R said to total 160	Manville 1993, 97, '160 pieces of gold and silver coin, some of King John'; *SM* 19 (Nov. 1757), 606.
2.	1344	Tyne, River, Northumb.	19th cent.	2 (double leopards)	–	Evans 1900.
3.	1350–1500	Bohemia (Czech Republic), various locations	to 1965	611, of which 3 English	–	Nohejlová-Pratová 1965.
4.	1351	Jawor, Legnica, Poland	1726	400, 12 English	–	Mikołajczyk 1987, find no. 42; Kiernowski 1976.
5.	1352	Northumb., unknown location	1862	1	–	Metcalf 1960–1, 115.
6.	1356	Belgium, unknown location	c. 1980	1	–	Schneider coll. **31**.
7.	1360	Shalford, Surrey	late 19th cent.	1	–	Schneider coll. **32**.
8.	1364	London (Beulah Hill)	1953	14	132	Thompson 1956, no. 241; Dolley 1953.
9.	"	Mirepoix, Ariège, France	1955	420, 126 described, none English, but thought that nobles were present	1497 described incl. 34 English	Saves and Villaronga 1974, no. 7.
10.	1369	Calder Abbey, Cumb.	1905	6	–	Thompson 1956, no. 67; *TCWAAS*[2] 14 (1905), 325.
11.	"	Ladram Bay, Devon	c. 1975	1	–	Shiel 1975.
12.	"	March, Cambs.	1994	2	–	Doolan 1995.
13.	"	Norwich, Ber Street, Norf.	1854	5	–	Thompson 1956, no. 292; *NorfolkArch* 4 (1854), 365–6.

Number	Deposit date or tpq	Find place	Find date	Content *N*	Content *R*	References
14.	"	Wrabness, Essex	1971	1	–	Sealy 1971.
15.	1373	Unna, Kr. Unna, Germany	1952	118, 1 English	–	Ilisch 1980, no. 115; Berghaus 1954.
16.	1377	Dolgellau, Mer.	unknown	1	2	Boon 1986, 124 n. 8; Thompson 1956, no. 121; *BNJ* 10 (1915), 352.
17.	"	East Raynham, Norf.	1910	200	–	Thompson 1956, no. 151; Brooke 1911.
18.	"	Furness Abbey, Lancs	1880; 1904	2	–	Metcalf 1960–1, 109; *TCWAAS* 1905, 303.
19.	"	Gdansk?, Poland	1772	1	–	Mikołajczyk 1987, find no. 43.
20.	"	Henstridge, nr Sherborne, Som.	1808	15–16	–	Manville 1993, 98; *GM* 78 (Jan. 1808), 40.
21.	"	London (Finchley Common)	1755	6+	–	Manville 1993, 100; *GM* 25 (May 1750), 253.
22.	"	Meols, Ches.	pre-1907	2	–	Metcalf 1960–1.
23.	"	Siddinghausen, Kr. Unna, Germany	1945	100+, 11 English	–	Ilisch 1980, no. 111 Berghaus 1954.
24.	"	Vejby, Frederiksborg Amt, Denmark	1976	110, 109 English	–, but 1 Æ	*DMS* no. 210; Crumlin-Pedersen 1976; *Danefæ* no. 78; *CH* III no. 376.
25.	1377?	Llandwrog, nr Caernarvon, Caer.	1827	2	–	Boon 1986, 124 n. 8.
26.	"	Sketty, nr Swansea, W. Glam.	1803	unknown	unknown	Manville 1993, 103, '*N* and *R* in great no.'; *GM* 73 (Nov. 1803), 1075.

Number	Deposit date or tpq	Find place	Find date	Content N	Content Æ	References
27.	1380	Balcombe, Sussex	1897	12	732	Thompson 1956, no. 22: Grueber and Lawrence 1898.
28.	"	Bredgar, Kent	1940	131	—	Thompson 1956, no. 57; Allen and Whitton 1947; *CH* VI, no. 381 re. additional details published in *Kent Life* July 1974, 59.
29.	"	London (Dean's Yard, Westminster)	1863	11	210	Thompson 1956, nos. 257 and 258; *NC²* 3 (1863), 215; *NC²* 4 (1864), 157.
30.	"	London (River Thames, Westminster)	1841	178	—	Thompson 1956, no. 259; *NC¹* 6 (1842), 133.
31.	"	Westbury, Wilts.	1877	32, 28 English	—	Thompson 1956, no. 375; *Arch.* 47 (1883), 137.
32.	1384	Coudekerke-Branche, Dunkirk, Nord, France	1911	145, 1 English	—	Thompson 1970; *RN* 1912, 284.
33.	"	Courtrai, Flanders, Belgium	1904	'about 200 English including some Anglo-Gallic'	—	Thompson 1970; *RN* 1904, 113; *GazNum* May 1905, 152; *RSN* 1906, 319.
34.	1385	Brinkbury Priory, Northumb.	1834	100s	—	Manville 1993, 94; Dolley 1964.
35.	1388	Pinchbeck (The), Lincs.	1987	99	—	Cook 1991; Christie sale 28.2.1989.
36.	1390	Fenwick Tower, Northumb.	1775	226+	—	Thompson 1956, no. 159; Dolley 1964; Manville 1993, 97; *GM* 45 (Sept 1775), 453.
37.	1395	Meopham, Kent	1973–6	14	—	Archibald and Connolly, 1977

Number	Deposit date or tpq	Find place	Find date	Content N	Content Æ	References
38.	1399	Mountain Ash, Glam.	pre-1910	3	—	Boon 1986, 121–2; Thompson 1956, no. 274 (erroneous find date).38.
39.	"	Poland?	pre-1972	14+	—	see Provenances, also Mickołajczyk 1987, find no. 45 and coins nos. 419, 424–34. The circumstantial evidence strongly suggests that Schneider coins **122** and **149** came from this source, too.
40.	1400	Lund, Malmøhus, Sweden	pre-1966	12, 6 English	—	Jacobsen and Morkholm 1966; Jensen 1973.
41.	"	Morsum, Sylt, Germany	to 1966	6	—	Jacobsen and Morkholm 1966; Jensen 1973.
42.	1400+	Dryburgh, Ber.	1820	unknown	—	Thompson 1956, no. 132; Lindsay (S), 267.
43.	1400–10	Rømø churchyard, Sønderjyllands amt, Denmark	1982	3, 1 English	—	*DMS* no. 245.
44.	1402	Llangynllo, Neuaddfach, Rad.	1804	80–90	—	Boon 1986, 123 n. 8; Thompson 1956, no. 238; *RCAHMW*, Radnorshire Inventory (1913), 99, no. 391.
45.	"	Sötenich, Eifel, Germany	1865	121, 2 English	—	Kluge 1981.
46.	1403	Glasgow (Cathedral)	1837	130, 67 English	—	Thompson 1956, no. 172; Lindsay (S), 269.
47.	1404	Dodford, Northants.	1955	1	—	Dolley 1955–7a.
48.	1410	Amiens, Somme, France	1950	1	—	Schneider coll. **191**.
49.	1411	Ashurst, nr Tunbridge Wells, Sussex.	c. 1955.	1	—	Dolley 1955–7b.

Number	Deposit date or tpq	Find place	Find date	Content *A*	Content *R*	References
50.	1412	Bratislava, Slovak Republic	1905	132, 7 English	–	Thompson 1970.
51.	1413	Bolton, Cockey Moor, Lancs.	1822	*A* and *R* together said to total 60	some.	*CH* III no. 334; *NCirc* 84 (1976), 13 and 374; *Times* 4.11.1822.
52.	"	Lublin province, Poland	pre-1914	2, both English	–	Mickołajczyk 1987, find no. 46; *NCirc* 22 (1914), 682 (nos. 24621–2).
53.	1419–24	Svendborg (II) (Møllergade), Fyns amt, Denmark	1885	51, 2 English	3779	*DMS* no. 253; Morkholm 1965.
54.	1420	Worth, nr Sandwich, Kent	1991	1	–	Coin Register 1991, no. 149
55.	1422	Barmby-on-the-Moor, Yorks.	1961	1	–	Dolley 1960–1.
56.	"	Exeter, Devon	c.1975	1	–	Shiel 1975.
57.	1423	Baarle-Nassau, North Brabant, Netherlands	1976	42, 1 English (Henry IV heavy noble)	–	*CH* IV, no. 451; R. L. Schulman 1977.
58.	1430	Biggleswade (Stratton House) Beds.	1770	300	–	Manville 1993, 94; *CH* IV no. 371; *CH* V no 289; Gaunt 1978; Heslip 1977; *LM* July 1770; *GM* June 1770, 276 bis, July 1770 372–3.
59.	"	Horsted Keynes, Sussex	1929	63	–	Thompson 1956, no. 194; Brooke 1929.
60.	1431	Bardsey Island, Caer.	c.1872–5	uncertain, perhaps only 1	–	Boon 1986, 122.
61.	1431	Barmouth, Mer.	1906	about 20	–	Boon 1986, 123.

Number	Deposit date or tpq	Find place	Find date	Content N	Content R	References
62.	"	Borth, Card.	1930	31	–	Boon 1986, 123; Thompson 1956, no. 48; Brooke 1931.
63.	"	Carham, Northumb.	pre-1901	1	4, certainly not all deposited together	Metcalf 1960–1, 107; PSAN 1901–2, 154.
64.	"	Tynwyn (nr), Mer.	1825	a few	220	Boon 1986, 123 n. 8.
65.	"	Wrekenton, Gateshead-on-Tyne, Durham	1954	2	–	Corbitt 1955–7.
66.	1434	Halsall, Lancs.	1923	20	–	Thompson 1956, no. 180; Brooke 1927.
67.	"	Huntington, Ches.	1986	1	41	Grosvenor Museum 1986.
68.	1450	Malvern (Abbey Hotel site), Worcs.	1849	4, 3 English, 1 pre-1603	25 plus 11 Æ	Dolley 1955–7c.
69.	1452	La Lucerne d'Outre Mer, Manche, France	1968	200+	–	Vinchon auctions 21.4.1969, 24.11.1969 and 9.3.1970; Thompson 1970.
70.	1455	Reigate (Wray Lane), Surrey	1972	3	982	Archibald 1978; CH I, no. 376; CH VI, no. 385.
71.	1460	Reigate (Brokes Road), Surrey	1992	125	6466	Preliminary information courtesy Dr Barrie Cook.
72.	1464–5	Fishpool, Blidworth, Notts.	1966	1237	–	NC[7] (1967), 133–46.
73.	1465	Diss, Norfolk	1871	2	323	Thompson 1956, no. 120; NorfolkArch 7 (1872) 341.
74.	1470	Aylesbury, Bucks.	1952	4	–	Thompson 1956, no. 17; Dolley 1952.

Number	Deposit date or tpq	Find place	Find date	Content Ạ	Content Ȓ	References
75.	1470	Congressbury, Som.	1828	23	115	Thompson 1956, no. 97; Manville 1993, 96; *GM* 98 (May 1828), 360.
76.	"	London (Tabard Inn, Southwark)	19th cent.	1	—	Sotheby sale catalogue 7.5.1901 (J. E. Moon). Schneider coll. **380.**
77.	"	Unknown	1899	35	—	Thompson 1956, no. 370; *NCirc.* 7 (1899), 3161–2.
78.	"	Wokingham, Berks.	1877	1+	—	Thompson 1956, no. 379; *NCirc.* 53 (1945), no. 34152.
79.	"	York, Yorks.	1938	2	—	Metcalf 1960–1, 103.
80.	1470?	St Andrews (Castle Wynd), Fife	1792	8	200+	Manville 1993, 102; *SM* 54 (March 1792), 151.
81.	1471	Kinsey Wood, Rad.	1852	2+	—	Thompson 1956, no. 219; *ACb²* 3 (1852), 314.
82.	"	Whitehills (New Deer), Aber.	c.1863	1	—	Metcalf 1960–1, 119; *PSAS* 1863, 298.
83.	1480	Llanarmon-dyffryn-Ceiriog, Mer.	1845	2+	unknown, said to be about 100 Ạ and Ȓ together	Boon 1986, 123 n. 3; Thompson 1956, no. 236; *ArchJ* 2 (1845), 270.
84.	"	Unknown	1900	5	301	Thompson 1956, no. 369; *BNJ* 1 (1904), 123.
85.	1488	Whitburn, W. Loth.	1488	unknown	unknown	*PSAS* 1921–2, 321. '248 Ạ, Ȓ and Bi. Scottish and English'.
86.	1498	Eglwys Brewis, Glam.	c. 1900	1	about 50	Boon 1986, 124.
87.	1500	Harrowgate, Yorks but possibly from Douglas, IOM (hd. 100)	1974	20+	—	Archibald 1977 (*CH* III, no. 313) augmented by *CH* V, no. 291.

Number	Deposit date or tpq	Find place	Find date	Content N	Content R	References
88.	"	Wick, Caith.	1881	30	2	Thompson 1956, no. 377; *PSAS* 16 (1882), 465.
89.	"	Wooburn, Beds.	1770	100+	–	Brown and Dolley, 1971, EP119; *TopBucks*, 138; *BNJ* 12 (1915), 115.
90.	1500–1600	Beffs, Cher, France	1870	17, 2 English	–	Brown and Dolley 1971, BR10; *ASFN* 3 (1868–70), 378.
91.	"	Bergues, Dunkirk, Nord, France	1911	192, some English	–	Brown and Dolley 1971, BR11; *RN*⁴, 15 (1911), 261.
92.	1500–1600	Domburg, Walcheren, Netherlands	1892	133, 1 English	–	Brown and Dolley 1971, AR2; *TMP* 1 (1893), 67.
93.	"	Masseré, Haure Vienne, France	1865	21, 8 English	uncertain	Brown and Dolley 1971, BR13; *ASFN* 1 (1866), 230.
94.	"	Montespuc-la-Conseillere, Haute Garonne, France	1898	27, some English	–	Brown and Dolley 1971, BR3; *RN*⁴ 18 (1899), 108.
95.	"	Preuves, Calais, France	1913	3	65, 2 English	Brown and Dolley 1971, BR2; *RN*⁴ 18 (1914), 118.
96.	"	River Meuse, Namur, Belgium	1900	1	100+	Brown and Dolley 1971, AR7; *GazNum* (1.10.1900), 36.
97.	"	Villers-Marmery, Reims, Marne, France	1912	18	102	Brown and Dolley 1971, BR12; *RN*⁴ 17 (1913), 109; *NCirc.* 21 (1913), 311.
98.	"	Vlissingen, Walcheren, Netherlands	1884	uncertain, 2 English	uncertain	Brown and Dolley 1971, AR6; *ProcNumSoc* 1884–5, 3.
99.	1500–44	London (London Bridge)	1832	40	–	Brown 1973, EL24; Hume 1955, 157.

Number	Deposit date or tpq	Find place	Find date	Content N	Content Æ	References
100.	1505	Douglas, I. of Man	1849	100+	–	Dolley and Cubbon 1970; Brown and Dolley 1971, EL21; Clay 1869, 41; *JMM* (1970), 140.
101.	1509	Henstridge, Som.	1936	4	–	Brown and Dolley 1971, EL3; Allen 1949–51.
102.	1510	Witchingham, Norfolk.	1805	2	15	Blunt and Dolley 1964.
103.	1515	North Hainaut, Belgium	1923	100+	100+	Brown and Dolley 1971, AR1; *RBN* 1923, 100.
104.	1520	St Albans (Park Street), Herts.	1886	221	–	Brown and Dolley 1971, EL12; *NC*³ 5 (1886), 173.
105.	1536	Calais, Pas de Calais, France	1852	6, all English	–	Brown and Dolley 1971, BR1; *NC*¹ 12 (1852), 59.
106.	"	Cefn Garw, Tregaer, Mon.	1962	9 or 10	–	Boon 1986, 125; Boon, *Mon. Antiquary* i (1964), 40–1.
107.	1538	Maidstone, Kent	1952	5	490	Dolley and Winstanley 1952–4.
108.	1542	Luxembourg-Eich, Luxembourg	1849	50, 1 English	–	Weiler 1975.
109.	1547	Kirtling, Saffron Waldron, Cambs.	1842	5	uncertain	Brown and Dolley 1971, EL7; *NC*¹ 5 (1842–3), 203; *ProcNumSoc* (1842–3), 98.
110.	"	London (The Cock and Tabard, Westminster)	1871	54	–	Brown and Dolley 1971, EL15; So 15.11.1880, lots 261, 275, 290; (not mentioned in *BNAC*).

Number	Deposit date or tpq	Find place	Find date	Content Æ	Content Æ	References
111.	"	Ormesby, Yorks.	1838	100+	—	Brown and Dolley 1971, EL18 but may be a later deposit date, see their EO16; Beard 1933, 276; JBAA 15 (1857), 103; Ord 1846, 143 & 557.
112.	"	Tregare, Mon.	1939	9	—	Brown and Dolley 1971, EL16; SWalesA (21.11.1962).
113.	1551	Hermeton sur Biert, Namur, Belgium	1893	6, 2 English	11	Brown and Dolley 1971, AR3; RBN 50 (1894), 276.
114.	1557	Amersfoort, Utrecht, Netherlands	1894	100+	100+	Brown and Dolley 1971, AR4; TMP 4 (1896), 103.
115.	"	Bourges, Berry, Cher, France	1930	13, 3 English	—	Brown and Dolley 1971, BR4; RN^4 35 (1932), 237.
116.	1558	London (The Angel and Crown, Whitechapel)	1752	100s	—	Manville 1993, 105, 'Queen Mary's gold coin amounting to upwards of £1,000'; SM 14 (June 1752), 315.
117.	1558–1603	London (Bear Tavern, Southwark)	1761	uncertain	uncertain	Burrows 1978.
118.	1559	Havre, Seine Inférieure, France	1932	72, some English	—	Brown and Dolley 1971, BR6; RN^4 35 (1932), 241.
119.	1560	Loughborough, Leics.	1981	1	—	Schneider coll. **752.**
120.	1561	Angers, Maine et Loire, France	1911	45+	—	Schneider 1968.
121.	"	Lough Ackrick, Cramorg, Rosc.	1967	unknown	unknown	Brown and Dolley 1971, IN14; NSIOP 5–9 (1969), 2.
122.	"	St Albans, Herts.	1872	29	—	Brown and Dolley 1971, EN1; NC^2 12 (1872), 186.

Number	Deposit date or tpq	Find place	Find date	Content N	Content R	References
123.	1561	Tracy-Bocage, Calvados, France	1936	87, 7 English	–	Brown and Dolley 1971, BR7; RN^5 1 (1937), 324.
124.	1562	Termonde, E. Flanders, Belgium	1927	uncertain, 4 English	uncertain, N and R together 255	Brown and Dolley 1971, AR5; RBN 79 (1927), 148.
125.	1564	London (River Thames, Blackfriars Bridge)	1840	unknown, but some	200	Brown and Dolley 1971, EN3; GM^2 14 (1840) ii, 415.
126.	"	Tommen (St Vith), Malmedy, Liege, Belgium	1900	71, 24 English	2	Brown and Dolley 1971, AR18; RN^4 15 (1911). 262.
127.	1565	Bisham Abbey, nr Maidenhead, Berks.	1878	318	–	Brown and Dolley EN4; NC^2 18 (1878), 304; $NCirc.$ 83 (1975), 161–2; CH II, (1976) no. 463.
128.	1566	Talmont, Vendee, France	1893	149, 9 English	6	Brown and Dolley 1971, BR9; RN^3 2 (1884), 271.
129.	1567	Glasgow (Taylor's Street)	1795	800+	–	Brown and Dolley 1971, SN17; Manville, 1993, 107; Lindsay (S) 264; SM 57 (Jan. 1795), 66–7.
130.	1568	Twisk, Medemblik, N. Holland, Netherlands	1975	12, one English	138	J. Schulman sale catalogue 263, 27.4.1976.
131.	1571	Hasselt, Limbourg, Belgium	1883	uncertain, some English	uncertain	Brown and Dolley 1971, AR8; $BMNA$ 2 (1882–3), 196.
132.	1573	Malines, Antwerp, Belgium	1838	75 including 2 English	–	CH IV, no. 418; Colaert 1976.
133.	1576	Joncret, Hainaut, Belgium	1850	132, 16 English	–	Brown and Dolley 1971, AR9; RBN^2 1 (1851), 91.
134.	1578	Neerpelt, Hasselt, Belgium	1883	3, 1 English	2	Brown and Dolley 1971, AR10; $BMNA$ 2 (1882–3), 167.

Number	Deposit date or tpq	Find place	Find date	Content N	Content Æ	References
135.	1580	Herentals, Antwerp,	1955	225, 20 English	22	Brown and Dolley 1971, AR11; Schneider 1955–7; *RBN* 101 (1955), 150; *RBN* 102 (1956), 174.
136.	"	Houghton-cum-Wyton, St Ives, Hunts.	1876	25	288	Brown and Dolley, 1971, EN10; *NC*[2] 17 (1877), 163.
137.	1585	Hulst, Antwerp, Belgium	1894	320, 3 English	–	Brown and Dolley 1971, AR12; *TMP* 4 (1896), 181; *RN*[3] 13 (1895), 103.
138.	1588	Elgin, Moray.	1759	unknown	–	Brown 1973, SO14; Lindsay (S), 260; *AnnR* 2 (1759), 109.
139.	1591	Kapelle, Zeeland, Netherlands	1881	unknown, 5 English	unknown, 1 English. *N* and Æ together 114	Brown and Dolley 1971, AR13; *RBN* 40 (1884), 211.
140.	1596	Huizinge, Groningen, Netherlands	1979	36, 1 English	171?	*CH* VII, no. 659; Schulman, Amsterdam, sale 21.11.1980.
141.	1600	Den Dungen, N. Brabant, Netherlands	1980	10, 1 English	–	*CH* VII, no. 661; van Osch 1981.
142.	1600?	Westbury (Old George Inn), Wilts.	1845	99	–	*CH* II, no. 477; *WAM* XXV, 49n. and XXXI, 336; *WiltsT* 2.3.1901.
143.	1603	London (River Thames)	1778	unknown	unknown	Brown and Dolley 1971, EN26; Sykes 1833, 1, 313.
144.	1603	Soest, Kr. Soest, Germany	1950	12, 3 English	251	Ilisch 1980, no. 252; *SoesterZ* 63 (1951), 70–3; Berghaus 1953.
145.	"	Wotton (Leith Hill), Surrey	1837	30	–	Brown and Dolley 1971, EN27; *VCH* Surrey 3, 154.

Number	Deposit date or tpq	Find place	Find date	Content *N*	Content *R*	References
146.	1603?	London (London Bridge)	1757	unknown	unknown	Manville 1993, 105, 'three pots of *N* and *R* money of Queen Elizabeth'; Burrows 1978; *GM* 27 (1757), 91.
147.	1606	Sheffield, Yorks.	1913	3	100	Brown and Dolley 1971, EO11; *NC*⁵ 7 (1927), 280.
148.	1607	Ney-Dieler, Rhineland, Germany	1939	64, 11 English	–	Brown and Dolley 1971, DS1; *RN*⁵ 8 (1945), 189. *BonnerJb* 147 (1942), 383.
149.	1619	Haynk, N. Brabant, Netherlands	1912	100+, 19 English	100+, 28 English	Brown and Dolley 1971, AS4; Schulman sale 20.5.1912, 87.
150.	1624	Fischenich, Koln, Westfalen, Germany	1908	124, 8 English	20	Brown and Dolley 1971, DS4; *NC*³ 13 (1893), 26.
151.	"	Warstein?, Kr. Arnsberg, Germany	1864?	3, 1 'rosenoble'	60	Ilisch 1980, no. 268; *NZ* 1864, Sp. 120 (sale advertisement).
152.	1625	Madeley Wood, Salop	1839	100+	–	Brown and Dolley 1971, EO8; *ShropshireJ* (Dec. 1839).
153.	"	Meschede, Kr. Meschede, Germany	1897	15, 1 English before 1603	–	Ilisch 1980, no. 270; *WestfZ* 55 (1897), 177–80.
154.	"	Ormesby, Yorks.	1838	100+	100+	Brown and Dolley 1971, EO16.
155.	"	Stamford (St Martins), Lincs.	1847	33	–	Brown and Dolley 1971, EO12; Simpson 1861, 369.
156.	"	Willesborough, nr Ashford, Kent	1970	17, 2 pre-1603	–	Archibald 1971.
157.	1625–49	Belfast (nr), Antrim/Down	1850	5?	–	Brown and Dolley 1971, IP29; *UJA* 1 (1853), 164.

Number	Deposit date or tpq	Find place	Find date	Content N	Content R	References
158.	"	Douglas, I. of Man	1880	4	55	Brown and Dolley 1971, EP97; *JBAA* 1 36 (1880), 373.
159.	"	Fethard, Tip.	1825	unknown	unknown	Brown and Dolley 1971, IP35; CI 135; *JRSAI* 4 (1856–7), 49.
160.	"	London (Tottenham)	1770	70+	—	Brown 1973; *AnnR* 13 (1770), 90.
161.	"	Sherborne Castle, Dorset	1972	unknown	unknown	Brown 1973; *NCirc.* 80 (1972), 278.
162.	"	Siibbertoft, Northants.	1866	unknown	—	Brown and Dolley 1971, EP111; *PSA2* 3 (1866), 346.
163.	1628	Werl, Kr. Soest, Germany	1898	574, 3 English before 1603, 38 'Continental' ryals	—	Ilisch 1980, no. 278; Berghaus 1958.
164.	1629	Monnikendam, N. Holland, Netherlands	1894	132, 2 English	—	Brown and Dolley 1971, AS6; *TMP* 4 (1896), 66 & 96.
165.	"	Unna, Kr. Unna, Germany	1899	uncertain, possibly included Continental ryals	uncertain	Ilisch 1980, no. 279; *Antiquitatenzeitung* 7 (1899), 18.
166.	1633	Botley (Tylers Hill) nr Chesham, Bucks.	1888	200	—	Besly 1987, no. A1; Brown and Dolley 1971, EP28; *NC*[3] 10 (1890), 48.
167.	"	Lissane (Clare Castle), Co. Clare	1958	1	14	Brown and Dolley 1971, IP3.
168.	1636	Muckleford, Bradford Peverell, Dorset	1935	115	—	Besly 1987, no. A3; Brown and Dolley 1971, EP35; *DNHASP* 57 (1935), 18; *NC*[5] 19 (1939), 184.

Number	Deposit date or tpq	Find place	Find date	Content N	Content AR	References
169.	1638	Farmborough, nr Bath, Avon	1953	3	517	Besly 1987, no. A2; Brown and Dolley 1971, EP34; NC[6] 13 (1953), 150; NC[6] 14 (1954), 218.
170.	1639	Childrey, Wantage, Berks.	1937	44	–	Besly 1987, no. B1; Brown and Dolley, EP31; BAJ 41 (1937), 82; NC[5] 19 (1939), 153.
171.	"	Newark, Notts.	1961	97 at least, possibly 161	–	Besly 1987, no. B2; Brown and Dolley 1971, EP21; Cun. (1969), 22; NTCWSW 74.
172.	1640	Cambridge (Pembroke College), Cambs.	1875	41, 2 before 1603	–	Besly 1987, no. C4; Brown and Dolley 1971, EP104.
173.	"	Lambourn (Woodland St Mary), Berks.	1949	60	–	Besly 1987, no. C7; Brown and Dolley 1971, EP29; NC[6] 9 (1949), 257.
174.	"	Whitchurch, Salop.	1945	4	39	Besly 1987, no. C10; Brown and Dolley 1971, EP18; NC[6] 5 (1945), 124.
175.	1641	Reading, Berks.	1934	17	–	Besly 1987, no. D23; Brown and Dolley 1971, EP4; NC[5] 19 (1929), 184.
176.	1643	Marlborough, Wilts.	1901	2	300	Besly 1987, no. D18.
177.	"	Newark (Crankley Point), Notts.	1957	17, 3 before 1603	466	Besly 1987, no. D19; Brown and Dolley 1971, EP20; Kent 1968.
178.	"	Wardour Castle, Tisbury, Wilts.	1643	100+	–	Besly 1987, no. D27; Brown and Dolley 1971, EP128; Ludlow, 1, 72, 85 & 93.
179.	"	Welsh Bicknor (Parkwood Cottage), Here.	1980	3, one before 1603	151	Besly 1987, no. E20; CH VII, no. 567.

Number	Deposit date or tpq	Find place	Find date	Content N	Content Æ	References
180.	1643–4	Oswestry, Salop.	1904	4	401	Besly 1987, no. E12; Brown and Dolley 1971, EP17; NC^4 5 (1905), 100.
181.	1644	Breckenbrough, N. Yorks.	1985	30, 1 before 1603	1552	Besly 1987, nos. 3 and E2.
182.	"	Catford, Kent	1937	110	–	Besly 1987, no. F6; Brown and Dolley, EP65; NC^5 19 (1939), 183.
183.	"	Sowerby, W. Yorks	1818	22, 2 before 1603	–	Besly 1987, no. E17; Crabtree 1836; 20 of the coins sold Spink Auction 50, 6.3.1986 (690–709).
184.	1645	London (Southend, Lewisham)	1837	420, perhaps 850	–	Besly 1987, no. H13; Brown and Dolley 1971, EP64; NC^1 1 (1839), 30; $GM2$ 10 (1838) ii, 307; GM April 1837, 413.
185.	"	Orston, Notts.	1952	2	1411	Besly 1987, no. D20; Brown and Dolley 1971, EP22; NC^6 12 (1952), 118.
186.	1648	Goldenhill, Oldcot, Wolstanton, Staffs.	1832	36	2 lbs.	Besly 1987, no. K47; Brown and Dolley 1971, EP131; Ward 1843, 122.
187.	1649	Bolam (Gallow Hill), Northumb.	1804	100+	–	Besly 1987, no. K7; Brown and Dolley 1971, EP123; Lewis 1845, 2, 275.
188.	"	Sandford, Chipping Norton, Oxon.	1768	100+	100+	Besly 1987, no. K55; Brown and Dolley 1971, EP72; GM 63 (1793), 83.
189.	"	Tullyhommon. Ferm.	1861	2	22	Brown and Dolley 1971, IP41; RIA Treasure Trove Register I, 9 and RIA Museum of Antiquities Register I, 101, both in NMI.

Number	Deposit date or tpq	Find place	Find date	Content N	Content R	References
190.	1649	Tunstall, Kent	1737	614+	–	Besly 1987, no. K68; Brown and Dolley 1971, EP126; Beard 1933, 252; Defoe 1753 1, 151.
191.	1695	Bridzor, Wardour, Wilts.	1786	£86 face value; included N of Elizabeth I	110	CH IV, no. 396 quoting undated cuttings in the library of the WANHS, book 24, 42 and book 26, 53 (bis).
192.	1725	London (Bank of England)	1978	4, 2 before 1603	1739	CH VII, no. 572.
193.	post-1355	Aalbeke, West Flanders, Belgium	1907	74, incl. 1 English	72+	CH V, no. 318; Vanderpijpen 1978.
194.	pre-1639	Horncastle, Lincs.	1844/5	15	–	Besly 1987, no. A3.
195.	uncertain	Llanelli (Red Lion Inn), Carm.	1820	16 ('nobles')	–	Boon 1986, 123 n. 8.
196.	unknown	Sprenge, Stomarn, Schleswig-Holstein, Germany	unknown	several	–	Hatz 1983, n. 61; HBN 14 (1960), 658.
197.	unknown, context of report suggests medieval	Caergwrle, Clwyd.	1757	unknown	unknown	Manville 1993, 95; SM 19 (May 1757), 258.

INDEX TO HOARDS AND FINDS

Find place	Number
Douglas, I. of Man	100, 158
Dryburgh, Ber.	42
East Raynham, Norf.	17
Eaton Coppice, nr Leominster, Here.	1
Eglwys Brewis, Glam.	86
Elgin, Moray	138
Exeter, Devon	56
Farmborough, nr Bath, Avon	169
Fenwick Tower, Northumb.	36
Fethard, Tip.	159
Fischenich, Koln, Westfalen, Germany	150
Fishpool, Blidworth, Notts.	72
Furness Abbey, Lancs.	18
Gdansk?, Poland	19
Glasgow (Cathedral)	46
Glasgow (Taylor's Street)	129
Goldenhill, Oldcot, Wolstanton, Staffs.	186
Halsall, Lancs.	66
Harrowgate, Yorks but possibly from Douglas, IOM (hd. 100)	87
Hasselt, Limbourg, Belgium	131
Havre, Seine Inferieure, France	118
Haynk, N. Brabant, Netherlands	149
Henstridge, nr Sherborne, Som.	20
Henstridge, Som.	101
Herentals, Antwerp, Belgium	135
Hermeton sur Biert, Namur, Belgium	113
Horncastle, Lincs	194
Horsted Keynes, Sussex	59
Houghton-cum-Wyton, St Ives, Hunts.	136
Huizinge, Groningen, Netherlands	140
Hulst, Antwerp, Belgium	137
Huntingdon, Ches.	67
Jawor, Legnica, Poland	4
Joncret, Hainaut, Belgium	133
Kapelle, Zeeland, Netherlands	139
Kinsey Wood, Rad.	81
Kirtling, Saffron Waldron, Cambs.	109
La Lucerne d'Outre Mer, Mance, France	69
Ladram Bay, Devon	11
Lambourn (Woodland St Mary), Berks.	173
Lissane (Clare Castle), Co. Clare	167
Llanarmon-dyffryn-Ceiriog. Mer.	83
Llandwrog, nr Caernarvon, Caer.	25
Llanelli (Red Lion Inn), Carm.	195
Llangynllo, Neuaddfach, Rad.	44
London (Bank of England)	192
London (Bear Tavern, Soutwark)	117
London (Beulah Hill)	8

Find place	Number
London (Dean's Yard, Westminster)	29
London (Finchley Common)	21
London (London Bridge)	99, 146
London (River Thames)	143
London (River Thames, Blackfriars Bridge)	125
London (River Thames, Westminster)	30
London (Southend, Lewisham)	184
London (Tabard Inn, Southwark)	76
London (The Angel and Crown, Whitechapel)	116
London (The Cock and Tabard, Westminster)	110
London (Tottenham)	160
Lough Ackrick, Cramorg, Rosc.	121
Loughborough, Leics.	119
Lublin province, Poland	52
Lund, Malmohus, Sweden	40
Luxembourg-Eich, Luxembourg	108
Madeley Wood, Salop	152
Maidstone, Kent	107
Malines, Antwerp, Belgium	132
Malvern (Abbey Hotel site), Worcs.	68
March, Cambs.	12
Marlborough, Wilts.	176
Massere, Haute Vienne, France	93
Meols, Ches.	22
Meopham, Kent	37
Meschede, Kr. Meschede, Germany	153
Mirepoix, Ariege, France	9
Monnikendam, N. Holland, Netherlands	164
Montespuc-la-Conseillere, Haute Garronne, France	94
Morsum, Sylt, Germany	41
Mountain Ash, Glam.	38
Muckleford, Bradford Peverell, Dorset	168
Neerpelt, Hasselt, Belgium	134
Newark (Crankley Point), Notts.	177
Newark, Notts.	171
Ney-Dieler, Rhineland, Germany	148
North Hainaut, Belgium	103
Northumb., unknown location	6
Norwich, Ber Street, Norf.	13
Ormesby, Yorks.	111, 154
Orston, Notts.	185
Oswestry, Salop	180
Pinchbeck (The), Lincs.	35
Poland?	39
Preuves, Calais, France	95
Reading, Berks.	174
Reigate (Brokes Road), Surrey	71
Reigate (Wray Lane), Surrey	70
River Meuse, Namur, Belgium	96
Romo churchyard, Sonderjyllands amt, Denmark	43

Find place	Number
Sandford, Chipping Norton, Oxon	188
Shalford, Surrey	7
Sheffield, Yorks.	147
Sherborne Castle, Dorset	161
Sibbertoft, Northants.	162
Siddinghausen, Kr. Unna, Germany	23
Sketty, nr Swansea, W. Glam.	26
Soest, Kr. Soest, Germany	144
Sotenich, Eifel, Germany	44
Sowerby, W. Yorks.	183
Sprenge, Stomarn, Schleswig-Holstein, Germany	196
St Albans (Park Street), Herts.	104
St Albans, Herts.	122
St Andrews (Castle Wynd), Fife	80
Stamford (St Martins), Lincs	155
Svendborg (II) (Mollergade), Fyns amt, Denmark	53
Talmont, Vendee, France	128
Termonde, E. Flanders, Belgium	124
Tommen (St Vith), Malmedy, Liege, Belgium	126
Tracy-Bocage, Calvados, France	123
Tregare, Mon.	112
Tullyhommon, Ferm.	189
Tunstall, Kent	190
Twisk, Medemblik, N. Holland, Netherlands	130
Tyne, River, Northumb.	2
Tynwyn (nr), Mer.	64
Unknown	77, 84
Unna, Kr. Unna, Germany	15, 165
Vejby, Frederiksborg Amt, Denmark	24
Villers-Marmery, Reims, Marne, France	97
Vlissingen, Walcheren, Netherlands	98
Wardour Castle, Tisbury, Wilts	178
Warstein?, Kr. Arnsberg, Germany	151
Welsh Bicknor (Parkwood Cottage), Here.	179
Werl, Kr. Soest, Germany	163
Westbury (Old George Inn), Wilts.	142
Westbury, Wilts.	31
Whitburn, W. Loth.	85
Whitchurch, Salop.	174
Whitehills (New Deer), Aber.	82
Wick, Caith.	88
Willesborough, nr Ashford, Kent	156
Witchingham, Norfolk.	102
Wokingham, Berks.	78
Wooburn, Beds.	89
Worth, nr Sandwich, Kent	54
Wotton (Leith Hill), Surrey	145
Wrabness, Essex	14
Wrekenton, Gateshead-on-Tyne, Durham	65
York, Yorks.	79

PROVENANCES

THIS section provides a key to the provenances cited in the catalogue section of this volume. These include hoards, collections, auction sales and dealers. The section also serves as an index to the catalogue, as for all provenances (except purchases from coin dealer's stock) the sylloge numbers in bold type are given for all coins coming from that source.

In the catalogue provenances are listed in chronological order starting with the earliest. Abbreviations used for auction houses are:

Ch. for Christie's (Christie, Manson & Woods Ltd, and their antecedents);
Gl. for Glendining & Co. Ltd;
So. for Sotheby's (Sotheby Parke Bernet & Co. Ltd, and their antecedents);
Sp. for Spink Auctions (Spink & Son Ltd).

The names of other auction houses are spelt out in full. Reference is also given to Manville and Robertson's invaluable work, *British Numismatic Auction Catalogues* (*BNAC*), cited by year and number, or as '*BNAC* App.' for collections dispersed privately and appearing in the appendix on pp. 375–9.

Addington, Samuel	Collection bought *en bloc* by H. Montagu, 1883 (*BNAC* App.). **649**, **701**.
Angers Hoard	Found 1911 'in a religious establishment not very far from Angers'. Consisted of 42 English coins from Edward III to Elizabeth I plus 3 imitations of English coins. Publication: Schneider 1968. Acquired by Spink in 1965 and dispersed by them. **231**, **372**, **464**, **557**, **558**, **726**, **732**, **887**, **888**.
Arnold, Dr F. O.	Collection dispersed by Spink from 1953 (some offered in *NCirc* 1953); (*BNAC* App.). **390**, **483**, **495**, **500**.
Astor, Viscount	Collection bought by Spink in the late 1960's (*BNAC* App.). **676**.
'Astronomer'	See McClean, Frank.
Baldwin	A. H. Baldwin & Sons Ltd, London, dealers.
Baptist College, Bristol	Coins acquired from the Rev. Andrew Gifford, DD, FSA and dispersed *c*.1962. **619**.
Barnes, James H.	Sold So. 26.6.1974 (*BNAC* 1974, 23). **180**.
Basmadjeff, L. A.	Sold Gl. 15.7.1953 (*BNAC* 1953, 16). **76**, **341**, **434**, **451**, **479**.
Beresford-Jones, R. Duncan	1. Coins sold privately *c*.1972: **99**, **115**, **163**, **218**, **265**, **503**, 2. Sold Sp. Auction 2.6.1983 (*BNAC* 1983, 28). **418**, **482**, **552**, **607**, **798**.
Bergne, John Brodribb	Sold So. 20.5.1873 (*BNAC* 1873, 14). **4**, **7**, **424**, **608**, **807**.
Bernstein, B. L.	Dispersed by Spink in the late 1960s. **128**, **344**, **518**, **801**.
Bieber, George W. E.	Sold So. 13.5.1889 (*BNAC* 1889, 14). **424**.

Birchmore, H. A.   Collection formed in the USA dispersed by Spink during the
                            1960s. **48, 59, 291, 810**.
Blake, E.   Sold So. 8.3.1895 (*BNAC* 1895, 7). **14**.
Bliss, T   Sold So. 22.3.1916 (*BNAC* 1916, 4). **74, 186, 803**.
Boord, Sir Thomas W.   Sold So. 27.1.1913 (*BNAC* 1913, 1).**571**.
Bourgey   Em. Bourgey, Paris, dealer and auctioneer. Miscellaneous or
                            anonymous sales.
                            1. 14.6.1971. **193**.
                            2. 28.10.1974. **148**
Brand, Virgil M.   Sold So. 26.5.1983 (*BNAC* 1983, 26), and So. 20.7.1983 (*BNAC*
                            1983, 38), and through dealers. **472**.
Brauner, Miss D.   Sold So. 11.7.1961 (*BNAC* 1961, 16). **858**.
Bredgar Hoard   Found in Kent in 1940.
                            Publication: Allen and Whitton 1947. Coins from the hoard sold
                            by J. F. H. Checkley through Gl. 10.2.1965 (*BNAC* 1965, 3), and
                            by R. H. Harvey through So. 28.9.1972 (*BNAC* 1972, 44). **111**.
Brice, William   Main collection purchased *en bloc* by H. Montagu in 1887.
                            Duplicates sold So. 15.6.1881 (*BNAC* 1881, 14). **4, 7, 192, 414,
                            418, 576, 608, 626, 627, 698, 807**.
Bridgewater House   Collection formed in the 17th and 18th cents. by the Earls of
                            Bridgewater. Sold So. 15.6.1972 (*BNAC* 1972, 30). **124, 175,**
British Museum   Sale of duplicates. So. 26.4.1811 (*BNAC* 1811, 3). **608**.
Bruun, Lars Emil   Sold So. 18.5.1925 (*BNAC* 1925, 9). **7, 120, 183, 212, 256, 264,
                            268, 310, 317, 318, 319, 328, 330, 332, 337, 407, 423, 460, 492,
                            567. 773**.
Burton, Major G. S. M.   Sold Gl. 18.11.1970 (*BNAC* 1970, 55). **456, 580, 588, 763, 844**
Bute, Marquis of   Sold Gl. 12.5.1959 (*BNAC* 1959, 10). **353, 484**.
Cabell, H. F.   Collection formed in America dispersed through Spink during
                            the 1960s. **168, 549, 613**.
Caine   Collection dispersed by Spink *c*. 1961. **133, 401, 454**.
Carlyon-Britton, Major   The coins in this collection do not appear to be amongst
   P. W. P.   those sold in the So. sale of 17.11.1913. Presumably they were
                            amongst those dispersed through Seaby during the 1930s. **14, 32,
                            112, 182, 190, 192, 212, 254, 263, 423, 434, 734**.
Carlyon-Britton, R.   Collection dispersed by Seaby from 1953 (*BNAC* App.). **393**.
Carter, Dr E. C.   Collection dispersed by Baldwin during the 1950s. **92, 137, 204,
                            243, 251, 275, 308, 345, 355, 385, 386, 391, 430, 431, 441, 455,
                            462, 465, 467, 473, 532, 551, 559, 561, 563, 566, 573, 611, 612,
                            623, 628, 649, 655, 668, 673, 675, 677, 689, 695, 701, 724, 742,
                            747, 748, 762, 783, 784, 800, 805, 807, 809, 842**.
Cartwright, E.   Collection dispersed by Spink in the 1970s. **40, 145, 189, 298,
                            665, 666, 670, 714**.
Cassal, Dr Raymon T.   Sold Gl. 3.12.1924 (*BNAC* 1924, 20). **443**.
Chadwick, C. R.   Sold So. 21.4.1920 (*BNAC* 1920, 8). **384**.
Christie's   London auction house. Micellaneous or anonymous sales:
                            1. 8.3.1960 (*BNAC* 1960, 6), **278**.
                            2. 21.3.1961 (*BNAC* 1961, 6), **279, 350, 364**.
                            3. 10.11.1967 (*BNAC* 1967, 22), **791**.

Clarke, Arthur D.	Sold (anonymously) Ch. 15.6.1891 (*BNAC* 1891, 23). **196**.
Clarke, Thornhill, T.	Sold Gl. 24.5.1937 (*BNAC* 1937, Bryan 13). **63, 481, 754**.
Clonterbrook Trust	Anglo-Saxon, English and Scottish coins purchased by Gerard Derek Lockett from the R. C. Lockett collection. Sold Gl./Baldwin 7.6.1974 (*BNAC* 1974, 18). **476**.
Cuff, James Dodsley	Sold So.8.6.1854 (*BNAC* 1854, 15). **2, 479, 669, 700**.
Dangar, H. C.	Sold Gl. 15.4.1953 (*BNAC* 1953, 7). **87, 222, 296, 351, 485, 562, 656**.
Davis, Dr J. B.	Sold So. 26.1.1883 (*BNAC* 1883, 1). **418**.
Dee, Mrs	Sold So. 10.12.1962 (*BNAC* 1962, 23). **826**.
Devonshire, Duke of	Sold Ch. 26.3.1844 (*BNAC* 1844, 5). **700**.
Dimsdale, Thomas	Sold So.6.7.1824 (*BNAC* 1824, 14). **576**.
Doubleday, Gordon V.	1. Sold Gl. 20.11.1961 (*BNAC* 1961, 32). **267, 272, 474, 486, 528, 823**.
	2. Sold Gl. 7.6.1972 (*BNAC* 1972, 26). **10, 11, 13, 19, 28, 33, 39, 57, 64, 92, 94, 95, 97, 101, 102, 103, 109, 111, 116, 117**.
Drabble, G. C.	Sold Gl. 4.7.1939 (*BNAC* 1939, 22). **314, 569**.
Dudman, John	Sold So. 15.12.1913 (*BNAC* 1913, 24). **379, 526**.
Dupree, David	Collection dispersed through Spink during the late 1980s. **170, 187, 188, 195, 303, 304, 420, 421, 422, 424, 446, 703**.
Durlacher, Alexander	Sold So. 20.3.1899 (*BNAC* 1899, 15). **196**.
Durrant, Lt.-Col. William	Sold So. 19.4.1847 (*BNAC* 1847, 7). **608**.
Dymock, Rev. T. F.	Sold So. 1.6.1858 (*BNAC* 1858, 18). **669**.
Evans, Sir John (d.1908)	Purchased *en bloc* by Spink and mostly resold to J. Pierrepont Morgan whose son disposed of the collection in 1915; the British Museum had first choice and many of the remainder were aquired by Lockett (*BNAC* App.). **1, 416, 418, 506, 574, 688, 756**.
Evans, Sir Arthur John	Sold So. 18.12.1911 (*BNAC* 1911, (d.1941) 23). **273**.
Fishpool Hoard	Found March 1966 in Nottinghamshire. Contained 1,237 gold coins. Preliminary publication Archibald 1967.
	1. 85 coins sold through Gl. 17.10.1968 (*BNAC* 1968, 30). **255, 260, 333, 336, 339**.
	2. 4 of the coins sold privately. **338**.
Fitch, Oswald	Collection purchased by Spink *c.* 1918 (*BNAC* App.).**1, 719**.
Forster, William	Sold So. 28.5.1868 (*BNAC* 1868, 16). **2**.
Foster, Richard Manley	Sold So. 3.11.1903 (*BNAC* 1903, 53). **212, 317**.
Galerie des Monnaies	Galerie des Monnaies S.A. Swiss dealer and auctioneer. Olten sale 4.2.1969. **452, 735**.
Gantz, Rev. W. L.	Part 2 sold Gl.23.6.1941 (*BNAC* 1941, 11). **638**.
Gibbs, James	Collection purchased by Spink before 1891 (*BNAC* App.). **493**.
Gifford, Rev. Andrew (1700–84)	Distinguished 18th-cent. antiquary and numismatist. Librarian of the British Museum. Gave or sold some coins to the Baptist College, Bristol. **619**.
Glendining	Glendining & Co., London auctioneers. Miscellaneous and/or anonymous sales:
	1. 28.4.1948 (*BNAC* 1948, 7). **152**.
	2. 14.7.1950 (*BNAC* 1950, 17). **617**.

3. 6.4.1954 (*BNAC* 1954, 6). **274, 387, 480, 819** (said on Mr Schneider's tickets to be 'ex Reynolds').
4. 28.6.1954 (*BNAC* 1954, 14). **174.**
5. 10.10.1955 (*BNAC* 1955, 16). **16.**
6. 10.2.1956 (*BNAC* 1956, 3). **470.**
7. 12.12.1956 (*BNAC* 1956, 21). **352.**
8. 30.10.1957 (*BNAC* 1957, 19). **360.**
9. 18.5.1960 (*BNAC* 1960, 13). **740.**
10. 21.9.1960 (*BNAC* 1960, 21). **843.**
11. 24.11.1960 (*BNAC* 1960, 26). **242.**
12. 10.2.1961 (*BNAC* 1961, 2). **78, 88.**
13. 17.3.1961 (*BNAC* 1961, 5). **287.**
14. 14.4.1961 (*BNAC* 1961, 8). **277, 284, 402, 578, 597.**
15. 8.2.1962 (*BNAC* 1962, 2). **440.**
16. 17.7.1962 (*BNAC* 1962, 13). **872.**
17. 19.5.1964 (*BNAC* 1964, 11). **302, 326, 397** (these coins not ex Lake).
18. 9.12.1964 (*BNAC* 1964, 27). **742, 816.** (possibly ex Hird).
19. 31.3.1965 (*BNAC* 1965, 10). **121, 229, 705.**(see also under Dr Kaufman, below).
20. 20.3.1968 (*BNAC* 1968, 7). **200.**
21. 25.9.1968 (*BNAC* 1968, 26). **108.**
22. 20.5.1969 (*BNAC* 1969, 31). **620.**
23. 12.3.1970 (*BNAC* 1970, 11). **161.**
24. 15.4.1971 (*BNAC* 1971, 12). **282, 294, 399, 553.**
25. 24.11.1976 (*BNAC* 1976, 47). **301, 820.**
26. 8.6.1983 (*BNAC* 1983, 30). **86.**

Goulburn, Maj.-Gen. E. H.	Sold Ch. 27.11.1962 (*BNAC* 1962, 20). **248, 441, 842.**
Graham, K. V.	Sold Gl. 12.6.1963 (*BNAC* 1963, 15). **170.**
Grantley, Lord	1. Private sale. **1.**
	2. Sale Gl. 29.11.1943 (*BNAC* 1943, 25). **202, 266, 384, 592, 794.**
Hall, Henry Platt	Catalogue prepared for his English, Scottish, Irish etc. for sale by Gl. 26–27.7.1950, but Spink bought the entire collection before the sale (*BNAC* 1950, 27). **38, 249, 854.**
Hall, W. M.	Sold Gl. 3.10.1963 (*BNAC* 1963, 25). **66, 617.**
Hastings, Lord	Sold anonymously So. 15.11.1880. The collection had been formed by Jacob Astley, 16th Baron Hastings (1797–1859), (*BNAC* 1880, 12). **379, 700.**
Haswell, J.	Sold So. 12.7.1926 (*BNAC* 1926, 12). **248.**
Hazeldine, Kendall	Sold So. 4.4.1914 (*BNAC* 1914, 8). **719.**
Herentals Hoard	Found in Antwerp, Belgium, in October 1955. Contained 225 gold and 22 silver coins. Published in *RBN* 1955 and 1956, and in *BNJ* 1955/57. **722, 733.**
Hird, Alderman Horace	1. Sold anonymously or privately. **493, 554, 637, 654, 671, 673, 675, 680, 703, 704, 707, 729, 756, 762, 768, 771, 780, 801, 806, 817, 821.**
	2. Sold Gl. 30.5.1961 (*BNAC* 1961, 12). **424, 445, 598, 661, 672, 682, 734, 744, 750, 754, 782, 788, 794, 810.**
Hirsch, Gerhard	Dealer and auctioneer in Munich, Germany. **691.**

Hoare, William	Sold So. 25.3.1850 (*BNAC* 1850, 3) or So. 19.5.1857 (*BNAC* 1857, 17). **653**.
Hodsoll, Edward	Collection purchased *en bloc* by Samuel Tyssen in the late 18th cent. (*BNAC* App.). **194**.
Huth, Reginald F.	Sold So. 4.4.1927 (*BNAC* 1927, 6). **493**.
Hylton, Lord	Sold Gl. 3.9.1975 (*BNAC* 1975, 32). **736**.
Jacson	Collection started by Roger Jacson in 1840 and subsequently added to by other family members. Sold Gl. 16.5.1962 (*BNAC* 1962, 7). **81**.
Jellard	Collection purchased by Spink in the 1950s. **341, 348**.
Jessop, Hugh R.	Private transaction. **11**.
Kaufman, Dr	Sold Gl. 31.3.1965 (anonymous sale, but this provenance identified by Mr Schneider's ticket), (*BNAC* 1965, 10). **705**.
Krondberg	(coll. sold by Schulman ?) **144**.
Krumbholz, Ernest	Sold So. 11.3.1897 (*BNAC* 1897, Charles 10). **611**.
La Lucerne Hoard	See Lucerne Hoard.
Lawrence, Dr L. A.	1. Sold Gl. 17.5.1950 (*BNAC* 1950, 11). **179, 294, 540, 596**.
	2. Edward III gold purchased *en bloc* by G. V. Doubleday. The following coins ultimately came into the Schneider collection: **13, 33, 39, 57, 64, 95, 101, 102, 109, 116, 117**.
Lawson, W.J.	Sold Gl.19.7.1954 (*BNAC* 1954, 16). **358, 593**.
Leslie-Ellis, Lt.-Col. Henry	Probably from the portion of the collection dispersed through Spink *c*.1919 (*BNAC* App.). **2, 355, 700**.
Lockett, Richard Cyril	1. Part III (Continental) sold Gl.29.2.1956 (*BNAC* 1956, 4). **835, 837**.
	2. Part IV (English 2) sold Gl.11.10.1956 (*BNAC* 1956, 15). **7, 9, 12, 15, 20, 21, 35, 58, 61, 74, 112, 139, 141, 166, 183, 186, 194, 215, 254, 256, 259, 268, 276, 306, 318, 319, 332, 337, 342, 346, 379, 394, 405, 407, 409, 412, 413, 416, 418, 424, 427, 449, 481, 496, 501, 502, 505, 506, 509, 514, 517, 525, 526, 537, 541, 549, 552, 570, 571, 574, 579, 589, 590, 599, 601, 608, 627, 639, 641, 652, 659, 660, 669, 671, 683, 690, 700, 707, 756, 787, 788, 793, 804, 816, 889**.
	3. Part VII (English 3) sold Gl. 4.11.1958 (*BNAC* 1958, 23). **42, 67, 89, 123, 138, 140, 171, 201, 217, 224, 317, 328, 330, 403, 414, 432, 442, 457, 460, 469, 498, 589, 622, 686, 741, 803, 824, 825**.
	4. Part X (English 4) sold Gl. 26.4.1960 (*BNAC* 1960, 10). **36, 55, 63, 113, 115, 182, 239, 321, 410, 453, 508, 522, 531, 538, 567, 585, 706, 776, 778, 789, 812, 822**.
	5. Part XIII (English 5) sold Gl. 17.10.1961 (*BNAC* 1961, 25). **18, 22, 32, 54, 60, 72, 157, 161, 253, 264, 271, 281, 297, 307, 365, 381, 400, 435, 463, 476, 499, 539, 684, 688, 721, 745**.
Lucerne Hoard	Found during restoration work on the ruins of the abbey of La Lucerne d'Outre Mer (Manche) in 1968. Sold by the Paris dealer and auctioneer, Jean Vinchon, mainly in three sales on 21.4.1969, 24.11.1969 and 9.3.1970 where described as the 'Trésor de l'abbé Philippe de Saint-Pierre'. The hoard has yet to be published. **207**.

Mangakis, D.   Collection of English coins dispersed by Spink in 1969 (*BNAC* App.). **215, 219, 227, 232.**

Marno, Capt. Cajetan L. M.   Collection dispersed by Spink in the 1920s. **14.**

McClean, Frank   Sold anonymously as 'Astronomer' So. 11.6.1906 (*BNAC* 1906, 26). **330**

Marsham (-Townshend),   Sold So. 19.11.1888 (*BNAC* 1888, 35). **196, 482, 611.**
  Hon. Robert W.

Martin, Rev. Joseph William   Sold So.23.5.1859 (*BNAC* 1859, 17). **2, 492.**

Menso, J. C. P. E.   Sold Jacques Schulman, Amsterdam, 9.3.1959. **779.**
  (of Ermelo, Netherlands)

Mitchell, Dominic   Sold Gl. 27.4.1949 (*BNAC* 1949, 8). **360.**

Montagu, Hyman   Sold So. 11.5.1896 (part 2), (*BNAC* 1896, 18). **2, 4, 7, 192, 196, 199** (possibly), **317, 414, 418, 476, 479, 526, 570, 576, 608, 626, 627, 648, 653, 698, 701, 807.**

Moon, J. E.   Sold So. 7.5.1901 (*BNAC* 1901, 20). **379, 700.**

Münzen und Medaillen   Münzen und Medaillen A.G., Basel. Swiss dealer and auctioneer. Sales of: 1. 17.6.1954. **70, 158.**
                                               2. 27.11.1964. **857.**

Murchison, Capt.   Sold So. 27.6.1864 (*BNAC* 1864, 20). **492, 648, 669, 701.**
  Roderick Maingey

Murdoch, John Gloag   Sold So. 31.3.1903 (part 1) (*BNAC* 1903, 18). **2. 196, 355, 441, 476, 570, 611, 648, 653, 701, 803.**

Mygind, H. H. S.   A number of coins of Richard II sold for incorporation in the Schneider collection, 1994. **124, 142, 147, 152, 156, 161, 162, 170, 172, 173, 175, 176, 182, 187, 188.**

Napier, Duncan S.   Sold Gl. 30.5.1956 (*BNAC* 1956, 9). **821.**

Noble, Mr and Mrs B. R.   Sold Gl./Sp. 11.12.1975 (*BNAC* 1975, 51). **770, 795.**

Northumberland, Duke of   Sold So. 12.11.1981 (part 3) (*BNAC* 1981, 54). The collection had been formed in the 18th cent. **331.**

Norweb, Mrs Emery   1. Sold Sp. 13.11.1985 (part 2). **535.**
  May Holden   2. Sold Sp. 19.11.1986 (part 3). **6, 641.**

Nunn, John Joseph   Sold So. 27.11.1896 (*BNAC* 1896, 36). **424.**

O'Byrne, James   Sold Ch. 14.5.1962 (part 1). (*BNAC* (d.1897) 1962, 5). **65, 154, 165, 662, 799,** 8**55.**

O'Hagan, Henry Osborne   Sold So. 16.12.1907 (*BNAC* 1907, 38). **424, 526, 576.**

Oman, C. C.   Sold Ch. 21.1.1969 (*BNAC* 1969, 3), or Ch. 12.10.1982 (*BNAC* 1982, 43). The collection was largely formed by his father, Professor Sir Charles William Chadwick Oman. **299, 658.**

Packe, Alfred Edmund   Sold So. 25.7.1921 (*BNAC* 1921, 21). **449, 482.**

Parsons, H. A.   Sold Gl. 11.5.1954 (*BNAC* 1954, 10). **181, 398.**

Pembroke, Lord Thomas   Sold So. 31.7.1848 (*BNAC* 1848, 24) **552.**
  Herebert, 8th Earl (d.1733)

Pinchbeck Hoard   Found between November 1985 and January 1987 in Lincolnshire. Contained 99 gold coins. Published Cook 1991. 76 of the coins sold Ch. 28.2.1989. **45, 52, 126, 131.**

PKP   Unknown source. Possibly a collection dispersed by Spink *c*.1967. **159, 202, 226, 490, 572.**

'Polish Hoard'	Coins dispersed through Switzerland *c*.1972–3 said to be from a hoard found in Poland. Twelve coins described in *SCBI* **37** (nos. 419, 424–34) will almost certainly come from this same provenance. **122, 149**.
Potter, W. J. W.	English coins dispersed to Baldwin, Seaby and Spink during the 1960s and, finally, *c*.1970–71 (*BNAC* App.). **28, 120, 167, 169, 380, 389, 521, 530, 536, 544, 556, 713**.
Powell, Sir F. S.	Sold So. 9.12.1929 (*BNAC* 1929, 30). **815**.
Price, F. G. Hilton	Sold So. 17.5.1909 (*BNAC* 1909, 18). **576, 760**.
Rashleigh, Evelyn William	Sold So. 21.6.1909 (*BNAC* 1909, 23). The collection was that of his father, Jonathan Rashleigh (1820–1905). **14, 194, 255, 460, 492, 552, 709**.
Rashleigh, Dr J. C. S.	Sold Gl. 10.6.1953 (part 3) (*BNAC* 1953, 13). **247, 503, 630, 814**.
Raynes, William Luard	Sold Gl. 15.2.1950 (*BNAC* 1950, 2). **4, 110, 162, 664, 702, 729, 754**.
Ready, William Talbot	Sold So. 15.11.1920 (*BNAC* 1920, 21). **68, 113, 259, 306, 423, 698**.
Reigate (Brokes Road) Hoard	Found 1992 close to Brokes Road, Reigate, Surrey. Contained 136 gold and 6,567 silver coins. 6,338 of the coins sold Gl. 8.12.1992. **258, 329**.
Reynolds	Noted by Mr Schneider, on his tickets, as the owner of the English gold coins sold in the Gl. anonymous sale of 6.4.1954, which see.
Rice, Brig. F. W.	Sale So. 9.4.1946 (*BNAC* 1946, 6), but the coin in this collection was apparently not in that sale. **41**.
'Ridgemount' collection	Sold Sp. 20.4.1989. **143**.
Rostron, Simpson	Sold So. 16.5.1892 (*BNAC* 1892, 18). **669**.
Roth, Bernard Mathias Simon	Sold So. 19.7.1917 (*BNAC* 1917, 11), or So. 14.10.1918 (*BNAC* 1918, 16). **342, 414, 479, 589, 627, 807**.
Ryan, Valentine John Eustace	Sold Gl. 28.6.1950 (*BNAC* 1950, 15). **1, 2, 30, 187, 190, 192, 212, 263, 310, 314, 327, 341, 392, 423, 434, 443, 445, 447, 451, 474, 492, 516, 548, 553, 569, 588, 593, 602, 626, 637, 645, 648, 651, 653, 678, 698, 699, 719, 731, 734, 737, 744, 750, 772, 773, 811, 815, 817**.
Saint-Pierre, Trésor de l'abbé Philippe de	See Lucerne Hoard.
St Oswald, Major the Lord	Sold Ch. 13.10.1964 (*BNAC* 1964, 22). **725**.
Sangorski, Alberto	Collection dispersed *c*.1925 (*BNAC* App.). **810**.
Seaby B. A.	B. A. Seaby Ltd. Dealers in London.
Schulman	Jacques Schulman B.V. Dealers and auctioneers in Amsterdam. Sales of:

1. 6.3.1958. **47, 779**.
2. 9.3.1959. **396, 433, 874**.
3. 20.5.1966. **144**.
4. unidentified date. **849**.

Serooskerke Hoard	Found on the island of Walcheren in 1966. Published Van Gelder 1965–6. The bulk of the hoard sold in Schulman sale 15.11.1966. **647**, **870**.
Sheffield	A collection of English gold coins sold by Spink Noble Numismatics Pty Ltd in Sydney, Australia, 17.11.1993. **110**, **419**.
Shepherd, Rev. Edward John	Sold So. 22.7.1885 (*BNAC* 1885, 27). **2**, **414**, **479**, **653**.
Sinkler, Wharton	Sold Gl. 24.2.1960 (*BNAC* 1960, 4). **201**, **497**.
Sotheby	London auction house. Miscellaneous or anonymous sale. 13.12.1978 (*BNAC* 1978, 55). **197**.
Spink	Spink & Son Ltd. London dealer and auctioneer. Miscellaneous or anonymous sales:
	1. 19.11.1990. **93**.
	2. 21.5.1991. **640**.
	3. 16.3.1992. **195**.
Spurgin, Cmdr J. B.	Sold Gl. 14.1.1944 (*BNAC* 1944, 1). **661**.
Spurway, J. W. and N. B.	Sold Gl. 9.4.1984 (*BNAC* 1984, 18). **533**, **534**, **546**, **605**. Also from this provenance but not in the above sale. **69**, **359**, **468**.
Strauss, Richard	Sold So. 26.5.1994. **578**, **700**.
Thelluson, Augustus	Sold So. 19.10.1931 (*BNAC* 1931, 13). **358**, **554**.
Thielau, Achim von	Auctioned by Schulman 28.3.1960. **47**, **343**, **839**. Dispersed by Schulman, not in the auction. **25**, **246**.
Thomas, Col.	Sold So. 28.3.1857 (*BNAC* 1857, 13). **576**.
Thompson, C. Dabney	Collection dispersed by Spink *c*.1965. **123**, **346**, **479**, **494**, **504**, **531**, **602**, **603**, **690**, **718**, **750**, **854**, **860**.
Thompson-Yates, Samuel Ashton	See Yates Thompson below.
Tyssen, Samuel	Sold So. 12.4.1802 (*BNAC* 1802, 2). **194**, **492**, **576**, **709**.
Vasallo, Dr H. F.	Sold Gl. 14.5.1957 (*BNAC* 1957, 8). **848**.
Vaughan Morgan, Sir Kenyon	Sold So. 17.6.1935 (*BNAC* 1935, 10). **571**, **707**, **759**, **817**.
Walters, Frederick Arthur	Sold So. 26.5.1913 (*BNAC* 1913, 10). **112**, **183**, **190**, **256**, **319**, **332**, **337**, **407**, **434**, **457**, **460**, **525**.
	(There are no coins in this collection recorded as being from the 1932 sale.)
Wertheimer, E.	Sold Gl. 24.1.1945 (*BNAC* 1945, 2). **30**.
Ward, Frank	Sold Ch. 8.3.1960 (*BNAC* 1960, 6). **283**.
Wellington, Duke of	Sold Gl. 18.6.1959 (*BNAC* 1959, 16). **46**, **51**.
Whitton, Cuthbert Alexander	Sold Gl. 5.10.1943 (*BNAC* 1943, 22). **9**, **21**, **322**.
Wigan, Edward Wright	Dispersed through Rollin and Feuerdent, the Paris dealers, in 1872 (*BNAC* App.). Collection formed by E. W. Wigan's uncle, John Alfred Wigan (1787–1869), **576**, **611**, **698**.
Williams, Francis	Sold Ch. 16.3.1965 (*BNAC* 1965, 9). **130**, **488**.
Winchester Cathedral	Coins donated anonymously for the benefit of Winchester Cathedral to be sold to help pay for restoration work in the 1960s. (*BNAC* -). **334**.
Winstanley, Edgar J.	Collection dispersed by Baldwin in the late 1950s. **104**, **174**, **181**.
Yates, Ernest E.	Collection puchased by Baldwin in 1938 (*BNAC* App). **602**.

Yates Thompson, Henry

Collection formed by Henry Yates Thompson (1838–1928) and/or his brother, Samuel Ashton Thompson-Yates (1843–1903) dispersed anonymously between 1900 and 1930. The fact that one of the coins in this collection, **698**, is ex Ready (sold 1920) is not conclusive evidence in favour of Henry Yates Thompson because Ready may have acquired the coin ex Thompson-Yates. **698, 701**.

Young, Mathew

Collection sold in ten parts by So. between 25.2.1839 (*BNAC* 1839, 2) and 2.12.1842 (*BNAC* 1842, 19). **192**.

ARRANGEMENT

DESIGN CONVENTIONS – NOBLES AND HALF-NOBLES. The noble was introduced under Edward III in 1344 and the same basic design continued to be used for 120 years until the reign of Edward IV. Thereafter the design was modified into the form used on the ryal ('rose-noble') and both forms of the design were copied on Continental imitations. There are a number of minor features which vary regularly at certain periods and which for simplicity of reference and economy of space can most conveniently be described in a summary way, for example: 'Ornaments, 11–11–11–11. Ropes, 3/3. Quatrefoils, 4/3. Lis, 3.'. These features, which are also indicated in Figure 2, are as follows:

Obverse

Ornaments. The sequence of lions and lis on the bulwarks of the ship is noted according to the position of the lis. Thus, 'lion, lis, lion, lis, lion, lis' is given as '1–1–1'.

Ropes. Numbers of ropes from the hull of the ship to the masthead on either side of the king are noted, for example, as 3/2.

Quatrefoils. All the quatrefoils on the sterncastle and on the forecastle are counted and noted, for example, as 2/3. Sometimes it is difficult to be certain of the presence of a quatrefoil on the face of the castle that is viewed obliquely and for this reason this criterion must be treated with caution.

Lis. The number refers to the number of lis in the first quarter of the shield. Until about 1365 the arms of France were a semée of lis (France Ancient), but they continued to appear in that form on English coins until the reign of Henry IV, so that there are sometimes visible on the shield several whole lis and fragments of others. The number given is that of complete lis, or substantially complete lis. The smaller fragments are not counted but, obviously, there is a subjective element in judging this, so again it is a criterion that should be treated with caution.

Bowsprit. This is usually present but is occasionally omitted. When it is omitted the fact is noted. Occasionally bracing spars are set along the bowsprit giving it the appearance of a comb.

Flag. Placed on the stern on some dies used at Calais but not present in every case.

Reverse

Lis in quarter. Usually by the lion's head in one of the four quarters but may be elsewhere .

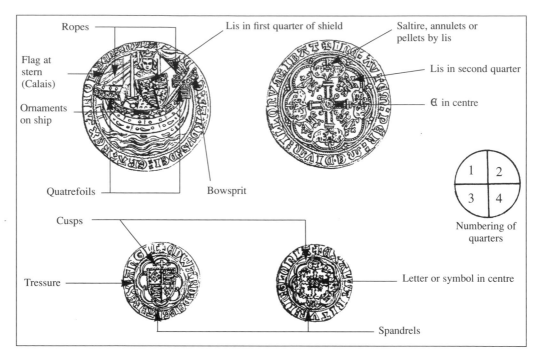

Figure 2. Terms used to define features on nobles and their fractions

Pellets (or annulets or saltires) by lis. Pellets, annulets or saltires by one or more of
the lis at the ends of the arms of the reverse cross.
E in centre. E, R or H (the initial of the king's name) usually appears in the centre
on London coins. Calais coins may have C in the centre but the other letters may
appear in its place.

Features on later medieval and sixteenth-century coins are referred to as they arise in
the catalogue and the descriptions are generally self-explanatory.

DIE-AXIS. This is expressed as the position of the reverse die relative to that of the
obverse when turned between the thumb and forefinger on the vertical axis, defined in
degrees. Thus, obverse ↑, reverse → gives 90°.

LEGENDS. In the catalogue, legends, including stops, are set out in full using an
extended version of the inscriptional type face described in *NC* 1982, 127–9. Generally
speaking, what is included in the legend is what can be read on the coin. An exception
to this is where there are two or more coins employing the same die, in which case the
opportunity is taken to secure the fullest reading possible. However, the shortcomings
of a particular piece in this collection may mean that there are stops or abbreviation

marks omitted that are recorded elsewhere. Conversely, there are a number of instances where coins in this collection have made it possible to amend earlier readings.

LETTERING. The specialised studies referred to in the catalogue at the beginning of each reign, in some cases, use the progressive replacement of letter punches as evidence for the chronological evolution of a series. Where reference is made to lettering (I_4, G_3 etc.) this refers to the study which has been mentioned. As an exception to this, for Edward III's fourth coinage reference is made to the letter forms illustrated in North 1991, 42–3.

QUARTERS. To assist in locating features, quarters of coins are numbered in accordance with heraldic convention, that is to say that, looking at the coin, the first quarter is the upper left hand side, the second quarter the upper right, the third quarter the lower left and the fourth quarter the lower right (see also Figure 2).

WEIGHTS. The coins listed in this Sylloge have been weighed in grams on a Sartorius electronic balance to the nearest milligram and rounded to two decimal places. Since the indentures to which the coins were made specified weights in grains, weights of coins are given in grains (gr.) and grams (g), the relationship being 1 grain = 0.0648 gram.

BIBLIOGRAPHY

ACb	*Archaeologia Cambrensis*
Allen 1937	D. F. Allen,'The coinage of Henry VI restored: notes on the London mint', *NC*[5] 17 (1937), 28–59
Allen 1949–51	D. F. Allen,'Henstridge, Somerset, 1936', *BNJ* 26 (1949–51), 91
Allen and Whitton	D. F. Allen and C. A. Whitton, 'The 1947 Bredgar find: with notes on the gold of Richard II', *NC*[6] 7 (1947), 160–70
ANum	*Acta Numismatica*
Angers Hoard	see Schneider 1968
AnnR	*Annual Register*
ANOH	*Aarboger før Nordisk Oldkyndighed og Historie*
Arch	*Archaeologia*
ArchJ	*Archaeological Journal*
Archibald 1967	M. M. Archibald, 'Fishpool, Blidworth (Notts) 1966 hoard', *NC*[7] 7 (1967), 133–46
Archibald 1971	M. M. Archibald, 'The Willesborough, Ashford, Kent, hoard', *BNJ* 40 (1971), 120
Archibald 1977	M. M. Archibald, 'A 15th century English gold hoard from an unknown site', *CH* III (1977), 124–7, no. 313
Archibald 1978	M. M. Archibald, 'The Reigate hoard', *BNJ* 48 (1978), 80
Archibald and Connolly 1977	M. M. Archibald and P. A. Connolly, 'The Meopham hoard of fourteenth-century gold coins', *Archaeologia Cantiana* 93 (1977), 47–53.
ASFN	*Annuaire de la Société Française de Numismatique et d'Archéologie*
BAJ	*Berkshire Archaeological Journal*
BAR	British Archaeological Reports
BB	See Borden and Brown 1983
BC 1	See Brown and Comber 1988
BC 2	See Brown and Comber 1989
Beard 1933	C. R. Beard, *Romance of Treasure Trove* (London 1933)
Berghaus 1953	P. Berghaus, 'Der Münzenfund aus der Marktstrasse zu Soest vom September 1950', *SoesterZ* 65 (1953), 31–40
Berghaus 1954	P. Berghaus, 'Westfälische Münzschatzfunde 1952–1953', *W* 32 (1954), 25–32 and 43
Berghaus 1958	P. Berghaus, 'Ein neuzeitlicher Münzschatzfund aus Werl', *W* 36 (1958), 227–42
Besly 1987	Edward Besly, *English Civil War Coin Hoards*, British Museum Occasional Paper 52 (London 1987)
Bispham 1985	J. Bispham, 'The base silver shillings of Edward VI', *BNJ* 55 (1985), 134–43
Blunt 1934–7	C. E. Blunt, 'The coinage of Edward V with some remarks on the later issues of Edward IV', *BNJ* 32 (1934–7), 213–26

Blunt 1941–4   C. E. Blunt, 'The heavy gold coinage of Henry IV', *BNJ* 24
                        (1941–4), 22–7

Blunt 1949–51   C. E. Blunt, 'An unpublished angel of Edward IV', *BNJ* 26
                        (1949–51), 221

Blunt 1967   C. E. Blunt, 'Unrecorded heavy nobles of Henry IV and some
                        remarks on that issue', *BNJ* 36 (1967), 106–13

Blunt and Brand 1970   C. E. Blunt and J. D. Brand, 'Mint output of Henry III', *BNJ* 39
                        (1970), 61–6

Blunt and Dolley 1964   C. E. Blunt and R. H. M. Dolley, 'The Witchingham, Norfolk,
                        XV-XVI c. hoard (1805)', *BNJ* 33 (1964), 107

Blunt and Whitton   C. E. Blunt and C. A. Whitton, 'The coinage of Edward IV
    1945–9 (BW)   and Henry VI restored', *BNJ* 25 (1945–9), 4–59, 130–82,
                        291–339

BM   British Museum
BMNA   *Bulletin Mensuel de Numismatique et d'Archéologie*
BNAC   H. E. Manville and T. J. Robertson, *British Numismatic Auction
                        Catalogues* (London, 1986)

BNJ   *British Numismatic Journal*
BNS   British Numismatic Society
BonnerJb   *Bonner Jahrbucher*
Boon 1986   George C. Boon, *Welsh Hoards* (Cardiff 1986)
Borden and Brown 1983 (BB) D. G. Borden and I. D. Brown, 'The milled coinage of
                        Elizabeth I', *BNJ* 53 (1983), 108–32

Brooke 1911   G. C. Brooke, 'A find of nobles of Edward III at East Raynham,
                        Norfolk', *NC*^{4} 11 (1911), 291–330

Brooke 1927   G. C. Brooke, 'Recently discovered English hoards: Halsall
                        treasure trove', *NC*^{5} 7 (1927), 279

Brooke 1929   G. C. Brooke, 'A find of nobles at Horsted Keynes, Sussex',
                        NC^5 9 (1929), 285

Brooke 1930   G. C. Brooke, 'Privy marks in the reign of Henry V', *NC*^{5} 10
                        (1930), 44–87

Brooke 1931   G. C. Brooke, 'A find of nobles at Borth (Cardiganshire)', *NC*^{5}
                        11 (1931), 53–61

Brooke 1950   G. C. Brooke. *English Coins*, 3rd edn (London, 1950)
Brown 1973   I. D. Brown, 'First addendum to the Bibliography of Coin
                        Hoards of Great Britain and Ireland 1500–1967', *NCirc* 81
                        (1973), 147–51

Brown 1984   I. D. Brown, 'A classification of the coinage of Elizabeth I',
                        NCirc 92 (1984), 116–8

Brown and Comber   I. D. Brown and C. H. Comber, 'Portrait punches used on the
    1988 (BC 1)   hammered coinage of Queen Elizabeth I', *BNJ* 58 (1988), 90–5
Brown and Comber   I. D. Brown and C. H. Comber,'Notes on the gold coinage of
    1989 (BC 2)   Elizabeth I', *BNJ* 59 (1989), 91–119
Brown and Dolley 1971   I. D. Brown and M. Dolley, *A Bibliography of Coin hoards of
                        Great Britain and Ireland 1500–1967* (London, 1971)

BullNum   *Bulletin de Numismatique*
Burrows 1978   O. Burrows, 'Two Elizabethan hoards discovered during
                        demolition work at London Bridge, 1757–61', *NCirc* 86
                        (1978), 10

BW	See Blunt and Whitton 1945–9
Carlyon-Britton 1925–6	R. Carlyon-Britton, 'The last coinage of Henry VII', *BNJ* 18 (1925–6), 1–62
Carpenter 1986	D. Carpenter, 'The gold treasure of King Henry III', *Thirteenth-Century England I. Proceedings of the Newcastle-upon-Tyne Conference 1985*, ed. P. R. Cross and S. D. Lloyd (Woodbridge, 1986), 61–8
Carpenter 1987	D. Carpenter, 'Gold and gold coins in England in the mid-thirteenth century', *NC* 147 (1987), 106–13
CCR	*Calendar of Close Rolls*
CENB	*Cercle d'Études Numismatiques Belges*
CH	*Coin Hoards*
Challis 1967	C. E. Challis, 'The debasement of the coinage, 1542–1551', *EcHR*² 20 (1967), 441–6
Challis 1968	C. E. Challis, 'Tower II 1545–1552', *BNJ* 37 (1968), 93–7
Challis 1975	C. E. Challis, 'Mint officials and moneyers of the Tudor period', *BNJ* 45 (1975), 51–76
Challis 1978	C. E. Challis, *The Tudor Coinage* (Manchester, 1978)
Challis 1989–90	C. E. Challis, Presidential addresses to the BNS dealing with the introduction of coinage machinery into the Royal Mint by Eloy Mestrell, *BNJ* 59 (1989), 256–62, and *BNJ* 60 (1990), 178–82
Challis 1990	C. E. Challis, 'The first gold sovereigns', *NCirc* 1990, 347–8
Challis 1992a	C. E. Challis, 'Lord Hastings to the great silver recoinage, 1464–1699', *A New History of the Royal Mint,* ed. C. E. Challis (Cambridge, 1992), ch. 3, 179–397
Challis 1992b	C. E. Challis, 'Mint output 1220–1985' and 'Mint contracts 1279–1817', *A New History of The Royal Mint,* ed. C. E. Challis (Cambridge, 1992), Appendices 1 and 2, 673–758
Challis and Harrison 1973	C. E. Challis and C. J. Harrison, 'A contemporary estimate of the production of silver and gold in England, 1542–1556', *EHR* 88 (1973), 821–35
Chronica Maiorum et Vicecomitum Londoniarum	ed. T. S. Stapleton (Camden Society, old series, 1846)
Clay 1869	C. C. Clay, *Currency of the Isle of Man etc.* (Douglas, 1869)
Coin Register	Coin Register [of single coin finds], *BNJ* 57– (1987–)
Colaert 1976	M. Colaert, 'Un Trésor de Monnaies d'or du XVIe siècle trouve a Malines', *RBN* 122 (1976), 153–65
Comber 1983	C. H. Comber, letter, *NCirc* 91 (1983), 341
Cook 1991	B. Cook, 'The Pinchbeck, Lincs., treasure trove', *NC* 151 (1991), 183–97
Corbitt 1955–7	J. H. Corbitt, 'Wrekenton (Gateshead) gold find', *BNJ* 28 (1955–7), 202–3
CPR	*Calendar of Patent Rolls*
Crabtree 1836	J. Crabtree, *Concise History of the Parish and Vicarage of Halifax* (1836)
Craig 1953	J. Craig, *The Mint, A History of the London Mint from A.D. 287 to 1948* (Cambridge, 1953)

134   BIBLIOGRAPHY

Crumlin-Pedersen 1976   O. Crumlin-Pedersen, 'Skattefund fra Havet', *NatMusArb* 1976,
                                183–4.
Crump and Johnson 1913   G. C. Crump and C. Johnson, 'Tables of bullion coined under
                                Edward I, II and III', *NC*[4] 13 (1913), 200–45
Cun   *Cunobelin*
Danefae   *Danefae* (Copenhagen 1980)
Dawson 1976   Veronica Dawson, letter in *NCirc* 84 (1976), 374
Defoe 1753   D. Defoe, *A Tour through the Whole Island of Great Britain*, 5th
                                edn (London, 1753)
DMS   *Danmarks middelalderlige skattefund c. 1050–c. 1550* (Copen-
                                hagen, 1992)
DNHASP   *Dorset Natural History and Archaeological Society Proceedings*
Dolley 1952   R. H. M. Dolley, 'Aylesbury Treasure Trove', *NC*[6] 12 (1952),
                                125
Dolley 1955–7a   R. H. M. Dolley, 'Dodford (Northants.) Treasure Trove', *BNJ* 28
                                (1955–7), 201
Dolley 1955–7b   R. H. M. Dolley, 'The heavy Calais quarter-noble of Henry IV',
                                BNJ 28 (1955–7), 416
Dolley 1955–7c   R. H. M. Dolley, 'A group of medieval and modern coins from a
                                site in Malvern', *BNJ* 28 (1955–7), 662–5
Dolley 1960–1   R. H. M. Dolley, 'A late noble of Henry V recently found in
                                Yorkshire', *BNJ* 30 (1960–1), 365
Dolley 1964   R. H. M. Dolley, 'Two neglected Northumbrian hoards of late
                                14th-century gold coins', *BNJ* 33 (1964), 90–3
Dolley and Cubban 1970   Michael Dolley and A. M. Cubban, 'The 1846 find of English
                                gold coins from Seneschal Lane, Douglas', *JMM* VII 86 (1970),
                                140–3
Dolley and Winstanley   R. H. Dolley and E. J. Winstanley, 'Maidstone treasure trove',
    1952–4   *BNJ* 27 (1952–4), 58
Doolan 1995   S. Doolan, 'A find of two Edward III nobles from
                                Cambridgeshire', *NCirc* 103 (1995), 141
Duplessy 1989   J. Duplessy, *Les Monnaies Françaises Royales de Hugues Capet
                                à Louis XVI (987–1793)*, 2. (*François I–Louis XVI*) (Paris and
                                Maastricht, 1989)
EcHR   *Economic History Review*
EHR   *English History Review*
Evans 1900   J. Evans, 'The first gold coins of England', *NC*[3] 20 (1900),
                                218–51
Gaunt 1978   D. J. Gaunt, letter referring to Heslip 1977, *NCirc* 86 (1978), 11.
GazNum   *Gazette Numismatique*
GM   *Gentleman's Magazine*
Grierson 1951   P. Grierson, 'Oboli de musc', *EHR* 66 (1951), 75–81 (reprinted
                                in his *Later Medieval Numismatics (11th-16th Centuries)*
                                (London, 1979), art. VII)
Grierson 1963   P. Grierson, 'Carat-grains and grains in 16 century assaying',
                                NCirc 71 (1963), 139.
Grierson 1964   P. Grierson, 'The origin of the English sovereign and the sym-
                                bolism of the closed crown', *BNJ* 33 (1964), 118–34

Grosvenor Museum 1986	Grosvenor Museum (Chester) press release 'The Huntington hoard', reproduced in *NCirc* 94 (1986), 263
Grueber and Lawrence 1898	H. A. Grueber and L. A. Lawrence, 'The 1898 Balcombe Find', *NC*[3] 18 (1898), 8–72
Hatz 1983	G. Hatz, 'Finds of English medieval coins in Schleswig-Holstein', *Studies in Numismatic Method*, ed. Brooke, Stewart, Pollard and Volk (Cambridge, 1983), 205–24
HBN	*Hamburger Beiträge zur Numismatik*
Heslip 1977	R. J. Heslip, 'A gold hoard from Bedfordshire', *NCirc* 85 (1977), 358
HSLCAS	*Historical Society of Lancashire and Cheshire Antiquarian Society*
Hume 1955	I. N. Hume, *Treasure in the Thames* (Mueller, 1955)
Ilisch 1980	Peter Ilisch, *Münzfunde und Geldumlauf in Westfalen in Mittelalter und Neuzeit* (Munster, 1980)
Ives 1941	H. E. Ives, *Foreign Imitations of the English Noble*, American Numismatic Society's Numismatic Notes and Monographs 93 (New York, 1941)
Jacobsen and Morkholm 1966	A. Jacobsen and O. Morkholm, 'Danske guldmontfund fra middelalderen', *ANOH* 1966, 78
JBAA	*Journal of the British Archaeological Association*
Jensen 1973	J. S. Jensen, *MS* 6 (1973), 161–71
JMM	*Journal of the Manx Museum*
JMP	*Jaarboek voor Munt- en Penningkunde*
JRSAI	*Journal of the Royal Society of Antiquaries of Ireland*
Kent 1963	J. P. C. Kent, 'Five Tudor notes', *BNJ* 32 (1963), 161–4
Kent 1968	J. P. C. Kent, 'Hoard reports XVI-XX centuries: Newark, Notts, (Crankley Point) treasure trove', *BNJ* 37 (1968), 138–45
Kent 1981	J. P. C. Kent, 'A new type of George noble of Henry VIII', *Collectanea Historica, essays in memory of Stuart Rigold* (Maidstone, 1981), 231–4
Kenyon 1884	R. L. Kenyon, *The Gold Coins of England* (London, 1884)
Kiersnowski 1976	R. Kiersnowski, 'Floreny slaskie z XIV w. i ich obieg w Europie', *WN* 20 (1976), 145–76
Kluge 1981	B. Kluge, 'Der spätmittelalterliche Goldmünzenfund von Sötenich/Eifel (1865) vergraben nach 1402. Eine Rekonstruction', *Lagom, Festschrift fur Peter Berghaus*, ed. T. Fischer and P. Ilisch (Munster, 1981), 221–48
Lawrence 1912	L. A. Lawrence, 'The long cross coinage of Henry III and Edward I', *BNJ* 9 (1912), 145–80
Lawrence 1918	L. A. Lawrence, 'The coinage of Henry VII', *NC*[4] 18 (1918), 205–61
Lawrence 1926–33	L. A. Lawrence, 'The coinage of Edward III from 1351', *NC*[5] 6 (1926), 417–69; *NC*[5] 9 (1929), 106–68; *NC*[5] 12 (1932), 96–174; *NC*[5] 13 (1933), 15–79
Lawrence 1937	L. A. Lawrence, *The Coinage of Edward III from 1351* (London, 1937) [a reprint of Lawrence 1926–33, with a supplement and corrigenda by D. Allen]

Lewis 1845   S. Lewis, *Topographical Dictionary of England* (London, 1845)
Liddell 1989a   Douglas Liddell, 'Obituary, Herbert Schneider', *NCirc* 97 (1989), 189–90
Liddell 1989b   D. G. Liddell, 'Obituary, Herbert Schneider', *BNJ* 59 (1989), 245–6
Lindsay (I)   J. Lindsay, *A View of the Coinage of Ireland* (Cork, 1839)
Lindsay (S)   J. Lindsay, *A View of the Coinage of Scotland* (Cork, 1845)
Lloyd 1977   T. H. Lloyd, *English Wool Trade in the Middle Ages* (Cambridge, 1977)
LM   *London Magazine*
LP   *Letters and Papers, Foreign and Domestic, of the Reign of Henry VIII*, ed. J. S. Brewer, J. Gairdner and J. H. Brodie (1862–1932)
Ludlow   *Memoires of Edmund Ludlow* (Vivay, Switzerland, 1698)
Mackie 1962   J. D. Mackie, *The Earlier Tudors* (Oxford, 1952; reprinted with corrections 1962)
Manville 1993   H. E. Manville, 'Additions and corrections to Thompson's *Inventory* and Brown and Dolley's *Coin Hoards*', *BNJ* 63 (1993), 91–113
Mate 1978   M. Mate, 'The role of gold coinage in the English economy, 1338–1400', *NC*[7] 18 (1978), 126–41
Mayhew 1992   N. J. Mayhew, 'From regional to central minting, 1158–1464', *A New History of the Royal Mint*, ed. C. E. Challis (Cambridge, 1992), ch. 2, 83–178
Mayhew and Walker 1977   N. J. Mayhew and D. R. Walker, 'Crockards and pollards: imitation and the problem of fineness in a silver coinage', *Edwardian Monetary Affairs (1279–1344)*, ed. N. J. Mayhew, BAR British ser. 36 (Oxford, 1977), 125–46
Metcalf 1960–1   D. M. Metcalf, 'Some finds of medieval coins from Scotland and the north of England', *BNJ* 30 (1960–1), 88–123
Metcalf 1976   D. M. Metcalf, *Ashmolean Museum, Oxford*, III. *Coins of Henry VII* (SCBI 23; London, 1976)
Mikołajczyk 1987   Andrzej Mikołajczyk, *Polish Museums* (SCBI 37; London, 1987).
Miles 1974   A. Miles and K. Miles, [additional background details relating to the Bredgar hoard], *Kent Life*, July 1974, 59
Mitchell 1972   [P. D. Mitchell], *The Gordon V. Doubleday Collection of coins of Edward III (1327 to 1377)* (Glendining & Co., London, auction, 7 June 1972)
Montagu 1895   H. Montagu, 'The coinage of Edward V', *NC*[3] 15 (1895), 117–34
Morkholm 1965   O. Morkholm, 'Gold aus dem Meer', *Dona Numismatica*, ed. P. Berghaus and G. Hatz (Hamburg, 1965), 255–9
Morrieson 1916   H. W. Morrieson, 'The silver coins of Edward VI', *BNJ* 12 (1916), 137–80
MS   *Medieval Skandinavia*
Munro 1972   J. H. Munro, *Wool, Cloth, and Gold* (Brussels and Toronto, 1972)
Munro 1981   J. H. Munro, 'Mint policies, ratios and outputs in the Low Countries and England, 1335–1420: Some reflections on new data', *NC* 141 (1981), 71–116

Naster 1955	P. Naster, 'Trouvaille de monnaies des XV et XVI siècles a Herentals (1955)', *RBN* 102 (1955), 150–8
Naster 1956	P. Naster, 'Encore la trouvaille de monnaies des XV et XVI siècles a Herentals (1955)', *RBN* 103 (1956), 174–85
NatMusArb	*Nationalmuseets Arbejdsmark*
NC	*Numismatic Chronicle*
NCirc	*Numismatic Circular*
NMI	National Museum of Ireland
Nohejlová-Pratová 1965	E. Nohejlová-Pratová, 'Dukaten (Florentiner) und Goldgulden in den mittelalterlichen Munzfunden Bohmens', *Dona Numismatica*, ed. P. Berghaus and G. Hatz (Hamburg 1965), 233–41
NorfolkArch	*Norfolk Archaeology*
North 1991	J. J. North, *English Hammered Coinage*, 2, Edward I to Charles II 1272–1662, 3rd edn (London, 1991)
North 1994	J. J. North, *English Hammered Coinage*, 1, Early Anglo-Saxon to Henry III, 3rd edn (London, 1994)
Norweb 1	*The Norweb Collection of English Coins—Part 1* (Spink Coin Auctions No. 45, London, 13 June 1985)
NSIOP	*Numismatic Society of Ireland Occasional Papers*
NTCWSW	*Newark on Trent, the Civil War Siege Works* (Royal Commission on Historic Monuments 1964, 72–3, reprinted in *Cun* 1969, 22–5)
NZ	*Numismatische Zeitung*
Ord 1846	J. W. Ord, *History and Antiquities of Cleveland* (London, 1846)
PA	*Public Advertiser*
Parker 1977	G. Parker, *The Dutch Revolt* (London, 1977)
Potter 1955–7	W. J. W. Potter, 'Henry VIII-the sequence of marks in the second coinage', *BNJ* 28 (1955–7), 560–7
Potter 1958–9	W. J. W. Potter, 'The silver coinages of Richard II, Henry IV and Henry V', *BNJ* 29 (1958–9), 334–52
Potter 1962	W. J. W. Potter, 'The coinage of Edward VI in his own name', *BNJ* 31 (1962), 125–37
Potter 1963	W. J. W. Potter, 'The gold coinages of Edward III', NC^7 3 (1963), 107–28
Potter 1964	W. J. W. Potter, 'The gold coinages of Edward III, cont'd', NC^7 4 (1964), 305–18
Potter and Winstanley 1960–3 (PW)	W. J. W. Potter and E. J. Winstanley, 'The coinage of Henry VII', *BNJ* 30 (1960–1), 262–301; BNJ 31 (1962), 109–24; *BNJ* 32 (1963), 140–60
PRO	Public Record Office, London
ProcNumSoc	*Proceedings of the Numismatic Society* (part of *NC*)
PSA	*Proceedings of the Society of Antiquaries*
PSAN	*Proceedings of the Society of Antiquaries of Newcastle-upon-Tyne*
PSAS	*Proceedings of the Scottish Society of Antiquaries*
PW	See Potter and Winstanley 1960–3
Ramsey 1953–4	P. Ramsey, 'Overseas trade in the reign of Henry VII: the evidence of the custom accounts', $EcHR^2$ 6 (1953–4), 173–82

RBN	*Revue Belge de Numismatique*
RCAHMW	Royal Commission on Ancient and Historical Monuments in Wales
Reddaway 1967	T. T. Reddaway, 'The king's mint and exchange in London 1343–1543', *EHR* 82 (1967), 1–23
RIA	Royal Irish Academy
RN	*Revue Numismatique*
Rot.Parl.	*Rotuli Parliamentorum; ut et petitiones et placita in parliamento [1278–1503]*, 6 vols. (n.p., n.d.)
Rymer 1816–30	T. Rymer, *Foedera* etc. (Record Edition, London, 1816–30)
Saves and Villaronga 1974	G. Saves and L. Villaronga, 'Les Monnaies de la Peninsule Iberique trouvees en France dans la region midi-Pyrenees (II)', *ANum* 4 (1974), 235–57
SCBI	*Sylloge of Coins of the British Isles*
SCBI 23	See Metcalf 1976
SCBI 37	See Mikołajczyk 1987
Schneider 1952–4	H. Schneider, 'A note on Mr. Whitton's paper "The coinages of Henry VIII and Edward VI in Henry's name, to which are added certain addenda and corrigenda', *BNJ* 27 (1952–4), 195–203
Schneider 1955–7a	H. Schneider, 'An angel of Edward V in the Herentals (Belgium) treasure trove', *BNJ* 28 (1955–7), 312
Schneider 1955–7b	H. Schneider, 'A new half sovereign mule of Henry VIII / Edward VI', *BNJ* 28 (1955–7), 658
Schneider 1965	H. Schneider, 'Chronological problems of the Pinecone-Mascle coinage of Henry VI', *BNJ* 34 (1965), 118–20
Schneider 1968 or Angers Hoard	H. Schneider, 'The significance of the archaeological evidence in a review of a French hoard of English gold coins', *BNJ* 37 (1968), 73–84
Schneider 1974	H. Schneider, 'A note on "The Rose Group" angels of Henry VII', *NC*[7] 14 (1974), 193–7
Schneider 1983	H. Schneider, 'Lot 216', *NCirc* 91 (1983), 221–2
Schulman 1966	J. Schulman, Sale catalogue 244, Amsterdam, 15 November 1966
R. L. Schulman	R. L. Schulman, 'Muntvondst Baarle Nassau', *De Beeldenar* 1:3 (1977), 6–7
SCMB	*Seaby's Coin and Medal Bulletin*
Seaby 1993	B. A. Seaby Ltd, *Standard Catalogue of British Coins*, vol. 1, 28th edn, ed. S. Mitchell (London, 1993)
Sealy 1971	D. L. F. Sealy, 'A half-noble find at Wrabness', *BNJ* 40 (1971), 173–4
Shiel 1975	N. Shiel, 'Finds of gold coins', *NCirc* 83 (1975), 475
ShropshireJ	*Shropshire Journal*
Simpson 1861	J. Simpson, *Obituary and Records for the Counties of Lincoln, Rutland and Northampton* (Stamford, 1861)
SM	*The Scots Magazine*
Snelling 1763	T. Snelling, *A View of the Gold Coin and Coinage of England, from Henry the Third to the Present Time* (London, 1763)
SNR	*Schweizerische Numismatische Rundschau (Revue Suisse de Numismatique)*

SoesterZ	*Soester Zeitschrift*
Spooner 1972	F. C. Spooner, *The International Economy and Monetary Movements in France, 1493–1725* (Cambridge, Massachusetts, 1972)
Spufford 1963	P. Spufford, 'Continental coin in late medieval England', *BNJ* 32 (1963), 127–39
Spufford 1988	P. Spufford, *Money and its Use in Medieval Europe* (Cambridge, 1988)
Statutes	*Statutes of the Realm* (Record Edition, 1810–28)
Stewart 1974	I. Stewart, 'Problems of the early coinage of Henry VII', *NC*[7] 14 (1974), 125–47
Stokes 1929	E. Stokes, 'Tables of bullion coined from 1377 to 1550', *NC*[5] 9 (1929), 27–69
SWalesA	*South Wales Argus*
Sykes 1833	J. Sykes, *Local records etc., in Northumberland, Durham, Newcastle-upon-Tyne and Berwick-upon-Tweed* (Newcastle, 1833; reprinted 1866)
Symonds 1911	H. Symonds, 'The coinage of Queen Mary Tudor, 1553–1558; illustrated from the Public Records', *BNJ* 8 (1911), 179–202
Symonds 1913	H. Symonds, 'The documentary evidence for the English royal coinages of Henry VII and Henry VIII', *BNJ* 10 (1913), 127–72
Symonds 1915	H. Symonds, 'The English coinages of Edward VI', *BNJ* 11 (1915), 123–68
Symonds 1916	H. Symonds, 'The mint of Queen Elizabeth and those who worked there', *NC*[4] 16 (1916), 61–105
TCWAAS	*Transactions of the Cumberland and Westmoreland Antiquarian and Archaeological Society*
Thompson 1941	J. D. A. Thompson, 'Elizabethan ryals and their Dutch imitations', *NC*[6] 1 (1941), 139–68
Thompson 1945–8	J. D. A. Thompson, 'Continental imitations of the rose noble of Edward IV', *BNJ* 25 (1945–8), 183–208
Thompson 1956	J. D. A. Thompson, *Inventory of British Coin Hoards AD 600–1500* , Royal Numismatic Society, s.p.1 (London, 1956)
Thompson 1970	J. D. A. Thompson, 'A heavy noble of Henry IV from Czechoslovakia', *BNJ* 39 (1970), 91–7
TMP	*Tijdschrift van het Nederlandsch Genootschap voor Munt- en Penningkunde*
TopBucks	*Topography and Statistical Account of Buckingham* (London, n.d.)
Tudor Royal Proclamations	*Tudor Royal Proclamations*, ed. P. L. Hughes and J. F. Larkin (New Haven and London, 1964–9)
UJA	*Ulster Journal of Archaeology*
Vanderpijpen 1978	W. Vanderpijpen, '(Aalbeke hoard)', *CENB* 15:4, (1978), 71–3
Van Gelder 1965–6	E. van Gelder, 'Muntvondst Serooskerke 1966', *JMP* 1965–6, 127–205
Van Gelder 1980	E. van Gelder, 'Die Klop van 1573/4', *JMP* 1980, 101–6
Van Gelder and Hoc 1960	H. E. van Gelder and M. Hoc, *Les Monnaies des Pays-Bas Bourguignons et Espagnols, 1434–1713* (Amsterdam, 1960)

Van Osch 1981   H. van Osch, 'Muntvondst Den Dungen, 1980', *De Beeldenaar*, Jan/Feb. 1981, 26

VCH   *Victoria County History*
W   *Westfalen*
Walters 1904   F. A. Walters, 'The coinage of Richard II', NC^4 4 (1904), 326–52
Walters 1905   F. A. Walters, 'The coinage of Henry IV', NC^4 5 (1905), 247–307
WAM   *Wiltshire Archaeological Magazine*
WANHS   Wiltshire Archaeological and Natural History Society
Ward 1843   J. Ward, *The Borough of Stoke-upon-Trent* (London, 1843)
Webb Ware 1985   T. G. Webb Ware, 'Dies and designs: the English gold coinage 1465–1485', *BNJ* 55 (1985), 95–133

Weiler 1975   Raymond Weiler, *La Circulation monétaire et les Trouvailles numismatiques du Moyen Âge et de Temps modernes au Pays de Luxembourg* (Luxembourg, 1975)

WestfZ   *Westfälische Zeitschrift*
Whicher 1938   S. Whicher, 'Types of throne treatment on the 'fine' sovereigns of Elizabeth during the period 1584 to 1597', *NCirc* 46 (1938), 131–2

Whitton 1938–41   C. A. Whitton, 'The heavy coinage of Henry VI', *BNJ* 23 (1938–41), 59–90, 206–67, 399–439 and 'Addenda and corrigenda' in *BNJ* 24 (1941–4), 118–19

Whitton 1941–4a   C. A. Whitton, 'A note on the post-treaty nobles of Edward III', *BNJ* 24 (1941–4), 110–2

Whitton 1941–4b   C. A. Whitton, 'Die links between Edward IV, Edward V and Richard III', *BNJ* 24 (1941–4), 175–8

Whitton 1944   C. A. Whitton, 'Additional notes on Edward III and Henry V', NC^6 4 (1944), 116–20

Whitton 1949   C. A. Whitton, 'Elizabeth's hammered gold', *NCirc* 55 (1949), 58

Whitton 1949–51   C. A. Whitton, 'The coinages of Henry VIII and Edward VI in Henry's name', *BNJ* 26 (1949–51), 56–89, 171–212, 290–332

Williams 1976   J. C. Williams, letter in *NCirc* 84 (1976), 13
WiltsT   *Wiltshire Times*
Winstanley 1941–4   E. J. Winstanley, 'The angels and groats of Richard III', *BNJ* 24 (1941–4), 179–89

WN   *Wiadomości Numizmatyczne*
Woodhead 1979   P. Woodhead, 'Calais and its mint: part II', *Coinage in the Low Countries (880–1500)*, ed. N.J Mayhew, BAR International Ser. 54 (Oxford, 1979), 185–202

Woodhead 1989a   P. Woodhead, 'The early coinage of Edward III (1327–43)' in J.J.North, *Edwardian English Silver Coins 1279–1351*, SCBI 39 (London, 1989), 54–78

Woodhead 1989b   Peter Woodhead, 'Publications of Herbert Schneider', *BNJ* 59 (1989), 246

PLATES

HENRY III

(28 October 1216–16 November 1272)

No official indenture is known, although the coins were proclaimed in 1257 at a value of 20 sterlings. According to a contemporary chronicle the coins were made of 'pure' gold, struck at the weight of two silver sterlings.[345] All known specimens have the London mint signature and the name of the moneyer William of Gloucester. Classified according to Evans 1900 and Lawrence 1912.

London mint only

1 Gold penny of twenty pence

Obv.: h./ƐИRIɑ / RƐӾ ·I·I·I' The Ɛ of hƐИRIɑ appears to have been struck over an h.

Rev.: WILL//ƐM:O//NLV//NDƐ: Small dashes on the cross bar of the Ns.

Weight		
g	*gr.*	*Die-axis*
2.96	45.7	180°

Evans 3; Lawrence type I; North 1000; Seaby 1376. Fineness determined by XRF analysis, Au 99.3%, Ag 0.6%, Cu 0.1%.[346] Ex Ryan (2); ex Fitch; ex Sir John Evans, who bought it from Lord Grantley, who had acquired it in Rome.

EDWARD III

(25 January 1327–21 June 1377)

THIRD COINAGE, FIRST PERIOD (January to July 1344).
This is Potter's first (gold) coinage.

Fine gold coinage issued at a nominal weight of 108 gr. (7.00 g) to the double-leopard of 6s 0d. Denominations struck were double-leopard, leopard, and half, the helm. The standard classification is that of Evans 1900.

No coins of this issue are represented in this collection (see p. 11 for an illustration of the three denominations).

THIRD COINAGE, SECOND PERIOD (1344–6).
This is Potter's second (gold) coinage.

Fine gold coinage issued at a nominal weight of 136.7 gr. (8.86 g) to the noble of 6s 8d. Denominations struck were noble and quarter-noble.
Classified according to Potter 1963.

Characteristics: Large lettering with Gothic П. L in centre of reverse cross. ᚼVTƐM omitted. The quarter-noble has a tressure of six arches on the obverse and a single line tressure of eight arches on the reverse.

London mint only

2 Quarter-noble
2.19	33.8	350°

Obv.: ✚ƐDWᚼR,'RƐӾ,'ᚼNGL,'Ƨ,'FRᚼNɑ,'D,'hYB
Rev.: ✚:ƐӾᚼLTᚼBITVR:IN:GLORIᚼ:
Potter 3;[347] North 1109; Seaby 1480. Ex Ryan (3); ex Leslie-Ellis; ex Murdoch (290); ex Montagu (428); ex Shepherd (135); ex Forster (19); ex Martin (83); ex Cuff (828).

[345] See Introduction, p. 4.
[346] See Introduction, p. 4 and Appendix 1, pp. 78–9.
[347] Potter 1963 lists four specimens of which two are the same coins (Grueber 262 = Brooke pl. XXIX, 3). The coin in the Schneider collection is no. 3 on his list.

[*continued overleaf*]

PLATE 1

× 1.6 : 1

1

2

3

4

5

6

7

8

9

Plate 1 (*cont.*)

THIRD COINAGE, THIRD PERIOD (1346–51).
This is Potter's third (gold) coinage.

Gold coinage issued at a fineness of 23 ct 3½ gr. (0.995 fine) at a nominal weight of 128.6 gr. (8.33 g) to the noble of 6s 8d. Denominations struck were noble, half-noble and quarter-noble. Classified according to Potter 1963.

Characteristics: Large lettering with Gothic Ⲛ and chevron-barred Ⴀ. Introduces a closed Ⴂ in the centre of the reverse, but on the obverse retains the spelling ⴂDWႱR (later nobles and half-nobles have ⴂDWႱRD). The quarter-noble has a tressure of six arches on the obverse and a double line tressure of eight arches on the reverse.

London mint only

3 Noble
    7.30   112.6   100°
    (clipped)

Obv.: ⴂD/WႱR:D:GRႱ:RⴂX:ႱNGL:Ⴟ:FRႱNႵ:DNS:hYB
    Potter lettering B.
Rev.: +:IhႵ:TRႱNSIⴂNS:PⴂR:MⴂDIVM:ILLORVM:IRႱT: Lettering as on obverse. R for B in IBႱT.
Potter I(a), 2 (but this specimen not recorded by him); North 1110; Seaby 1481. Bt Baldwin 1979.

4 Noble
    8.28   127.8   280°

Obv.: ႵD/WႱR':D:GRႱ:RⴂX:ႱNGL:Ⴟ:FRႱNႵ:DNS:hYB
    Potter lettering B. Ⴀ for Ⴂ in ⴂD/WႱR.
Rev.: +:IhႵ:TRႱNSIⴂNS:PⴂR:MⴂDIVM:ILLORVM:IBႱT: Larger lettering (Potter C). Large Ⴂ in centre.
Potter I(b), 5 (this coin); North 1110; Seaby 1481. Ex Raynes (6); ex Montagu (409); ex Brice; ex Bergne (372).

5 Half-noble
    4.13   63.7   270°

Obv.: ⴂD/WႱR:D:GRႱ:RⴂX:ႱNGL:Ⴟ:FRႱNႵ:DNS:hYB
Rev.: +:DOMINⴂ:Nⴂ:IN:FVRORⴂ TVO:ႱRGVႱS:Mⴂ:
As the nobles of Potter I(b), lettering B/C;[348] North 1111; Seaby 1482. Bt Spink 1964.

6 Half-noble
    4.13   63.7   180°

Obv.: ⴂD/WႱR:D:GRႱ:RⴂX:ႱNGL:Ⴟ:FRႱNႵ:DNS:hYB
Rev.: +:DOMINⴂ:Nⴂ:IN:FVRORⴂ TVO:ႱRGVႱS:Mⴂ:
As the nobles of Potter I(b), lettering B/C; North 1111; Seaby 1482. Ex Norweb 3 (850).

7 Quarter-noble
    2.06   31.7   180°

Obv.: +:ⴂDWႱR:R:ႱNGL:Ⴟ:FRႱNႵ:D:hYB:
Rev.: +:ⴂXႱLTႱBITVR:IN:GLORIႱ: Large Ⴂ in centre.
North 1112; Seaby 1483. Ex Lockett (1226); ex Bruun (291); ex Montagu (429); ex Brice; ex Bergne (373).

8 Quarter-noble
    2.08   32.1   80°

Obv.: +:ⴂDWႱR:R:ႱNGL:Ⴟ:FRႱNႵ:D:hYB:
Rev.: +:ⴂXႱLTႱBITVR:IN:GLORIႱ: Large Ⴂ in centre.
North 1112; Seaby 1483. Bt Baldwin 1961.

---

[348] Neither this coin nor **6** were known to Potter who recorded four half-nobles, all in the British Museum.

Plate 1 (*cont.*)

FOURTH COINAGE (1351–77)

This is Potter's fourth (gold) coinage.

Gold coinage issued at a fineness of 23 ct 3½ gr. (0.995 fine) and at a nominal weight of 120 gr. (7.78 g) to the noble. Denominations struck were noble, half-noble and quarter-noble. Mints at which gold coins were struck are London and Calais (from 1363).

Classified according to Lawrence 1937 (including the supplement and corrigenda prepared by Derek Allen) and with reference to the letter forms conveniently illustrated in North 1991. Some references to the Doubleday sale catalogue (Mitchell 1972) are included and the Post Treaty coins are set out according to the amended classification used therein.

Pre-Treaty Period (1351–61)

SERIES A (1351)

No true gold coins are known of this series. Reverses are found muled with obverses of Series B (**9** and **10**) and Series C (**14**). These are characterised by the omission of the word ᴀVTᴇM from the legend, as in the previous coinage (**3** and **4**), double saltire punctuation, a small saltire each side of the lower terminal lis of the cross and, sometimes, by having a closed inverted ᴇ in the centre.

SERIES B/A (1351)

Characteristics: *obv.* see below (Series B), *rev.* see above (Series A).

London mint

9 Noble			*Obv.:*	ᴇ/DWᴀRD꞉DEI∘GRᴀ∘REX∘ᴀNGL꞉ꝛ∘FRᴀNC∘D∘hYB.
	7.37	113.7	190°	Ornaments, 11–11–11–11. Ropes, 3/3. Quatrefoils, 4/3. Lis, 3.
			Rev.:	✠Ihᴄ꞉TRᴀNSIᴇNS꞉PᴇR꞉MᴇDIVM꞉ILLORVM꞉IBᴀT꞉ Lis, ✠. Saltires each side of all four terminal lis. Closed inverted ᴇ in centre.
				Lawrence D/5; North 1139; Seaby 1485. Ex Lockett (1231), ex Whitton (16).

FOURTH COINAGE (*cont.*)

Pre-Treaty Period (*cont.*)

SERIES B/A (*cont.*)

London mint (cont.)

10 Half-noble

	Weight		
	g	*gr.*	*Die-axis*
	3.83	59.1	45°

Obv.: ЄD/WΛRD⫶GRΛ∘REX∘ΛПGL'⁊ FRΛ∘D⫶hУB
Ornaments, 11–11–1. Ropes, 3/3.
Quatrefoils, 3/2. Lis, 3.
Rev.: ✠⫶DOMIПЄПЄ⫶IП⫶FVRORЄ⫶TVO⫶ΛRGVΛS⫶MЄ
Lis, ✠. Є in centre not inverted.
Lawrence 6, where ΛRGVS is a misprint for the actual reading of ΛRGVΛS, as can be seen from the BM coin he cites; North 1140; Seaby 1491. Ex Doubleday (15).

SERIES B (1351)

Characteristics: I.m. cross 1. Roman M and N, reversely barred or unbarred. Open Gothic C and Є (North 1). Wedge tailed R (North 11). Annulet stops. With this series and henceforth the quarter-noble has a tressure of eight arches on the obverse.

London mint

11	Noble		
	7.65	118.0	300°

Obv.: ЄD/WΛD' DЄI GRΛ REX ΛПGL' ⁊ FRΛПC' D hУBЄ
Ornaments, 1–11–11–11. Ropes, 3/3. Quatrefoils, 5/3. Lis, 3. No stops.
Rev.: ✠IhC⫶TRΛПCIЄПS⫶PЄR⫶MЄDIVM⫶ILLOREM⫶ IBΛT⫶ΛM   Lis ✠.
Lawrence C/6; North 1138; Seaby 1484. Ex Doubleday (19); ex Schneider (exchange 1951); ex Jessop.

12	Noble		
	7.64	117.8	80°

Obv.: Є/DWΛRD⫶DЄI∘GRΛ∘REX∘ΛПGL⫶⁊∘FRΛПC∘D∘hIB'
Ornaments, 11–11–11–1. Ropes, 3/3. Quatrefoils, 4/3. Lis,4.
Rev.: ✠IhЄS'⫶ΛVTEM⫶TRΛПCIЄПS⫶PЄR⫶MЄDIVM⫶ILLORV⫶IBΛ Lis ✠.
Lawrence E/-; North 1138; Seaby 1484. Ex Lockett (1230).

13	Quarter-noble		
	1.88	29.1	290°

Obv.: ✠ЄDWΛR⫶R∘ΛПGL'⁊ FRΛПC⫶D∘hУBЄR
Pellet below shield. Omits D.G. Same die as 20.
Rev.: ✠ЄXΛLTΛBITVR⫶IП⫶GLORIΛ⫶Λ The Λ at the end of the legend stands for 'amen'.
Lawrence 3/3; North 1141; Seaby 1495. Ex Doubleday (24); ex Lawrence.

SERIES C/A (1351–2)

Characteristics: obv. see below (Series C); rev. see above (Series A).

London mint

14	Half-noble		
	3.84	59.2	170°

Obv.: Є/DWΛR⫶DЄI⫶G⫶REX∘ΛПGL⫶⁊∘FRΛПC⫶D
Ornaments, 1–1–1. Ropes, 3/3. Quatrefoils, 3/3. Lis, 4.
Rev.: ✠DOMIПЄ ПЄ⫶IП⫶FVRORЄ⫶TVO⫶ΛRGVΛS⫶MЄ
Lis in eighth spandrel and another in the second quarter over the lion's tail.
Lawrence 1 (p. 25); North 1145; Seaby 1492. Ex Marno; ex P. W. P. Carlyon-Britton; ex E. W. Rashleigh (663); ex Blake (2).

[*continued overleaf*]

PLATE 2

Plate 2 (*cont.*)

Characteristics: obv. see above (Series B); rev. see below (Series C)

London mint

15 Noble
    7.73   119.2   170°
    Obv.: Є/DWARD∘DЄI∘GR͂A∘REX×ANGL⦂∘FRANC⦂D∘ҺɎB
              Ornaments, 11–11–11–11. Ropes, 3/3. Quatrefoils, 4/3. Lis, 3.
    Rev.: ✠IҺ͡Ꮯ∘AVTЄM∘TRANꝄIЄN∘P∘MЄDIVM∘ILLORVM∘IBA∘
              Lis, ✠. Closed Є in centre.
              Similar to Lawrence D, but without abbreviation mark over R of GRA and reverse
              reading not noted by him; North 1138/1144; Seaby 1484/1486. Ex Lockett (1232).

Characteristics: I.m. Cross 1. Gothic Ϻ. Closed ᴄ and Є (North 2). Roman Ꞑ reversely barred. Wedge-tailed R (North 11). Annulet stops.

London mint

16 Noble
    7.71   119.0   200°
    Obv.: Є/DWARD⦂DЄI∘GRA∘REX∘ANGL⦂∘FR∘ANꝄ⦂D∘ҺɎB'
              Ornaments, 1–1–1–1. Ropes, 3/3. Quatrefoils, 4/4. Lis, 4.
    Rev.: ✠IҺЄSV⦂AVTЄM∘TRANꝄIЄNS∘PЄR∘MЄDIṼ∘ILLORṼ∘IBAT
              Lis, ✠. Open Є in centre.
               Lawrence G/12, with abbreviation marks over V of MЄDIV and ILLORV (see his
              pl. XVI, 11); North 1144; Seaby 1486. Ex Glendining sale 10.10.1955 (1).

17 Noble
    7.73   119.3   60°
    Obv.: Є/DWARD⦂DЄI∘GRA∘REX∘ANGL⦂∘FRANꝄ∘D∘ҺɎB
              Ornaments, 1–1–1–1. Ropes, 4/4. Quatrefoils, 5/5. Lis, 4.
    Rev.: ✠IҺЄS⦂AVTЄM∘TRANꝄIЄNS∘PЄR∘MЄDIṼ∘ILLORṼ∘IBAT
              Lis, ✠. Open Є in centre.
               Lawrence I/16; North 1144; Seaby 1486. No provenance.

18 Noble
    7.67   118.3   210°
    Obv.: Є/DWARD⦂DЄI∘GRA∘REX∘ANGL⦂∘FRANꝄ∘D∘ҺɎB
              Ornaments, 1–11–11–1. Ropes, 3/3. Quatrefoils, 4/4. Lis, 4.
    Rev.: ✠IҺ͡Ꮯ∘AVTЄM∘TRANꝄIЄNS∘P∘MЄDIVϺ∘ILLORVM∘IBAT
              Lis, ✠. Closed Є in centre.
               Lawrence L/26 var. but different dies from Pinchbeck (1); North 1144; Seaby 1486. Ex
              Lockett (4251).

Characteristics: obv. see above (Series C); rev. see below (Series D).

London mint

19 Noble
    7.72   119.1   260°
    Obv.: Є/DWARD∘DЄI∘GR∘A∘REX∘ANGL⦂∘FRANꝄ⦂D∘ҺɎB'
              Ornaments, 11(?)–11–11–11. Ropes, 3/3. Quatrefoils, 4/4. Lis, 3.
    Rev.: ✠IҺ͡Ꮯ∘AVTЄM∘TRAIIꝄIЄNS∘P∘MЄDIVM∘ILLORꝄM∘IBAT
              Lis, ✠. Small closed Є in centre. Note spelling ILLORꝄM.
             Lawrence N/-; North 1151; Seaby 1487. Ex Doubleday (45).

FOURTH COINAGE (*cont.*)

Pre-Treaty Period (*cont.*)

London mint (*cont.*)

SERIES D (1352–3)

Characteristics: I.m. cross 1 or 1a. New plain lettering with small serifs. Gothic Ⅿ. Closed Ⅽ and Ⅽ (North 2). Roman N often unbarred. R with curled tail (North 12). Annulet stops.

On the gold coins this series is only known from reverse dies muled with obverses of Series C (**19**).

SERIES B/E (1354–5)

Characteristics: obv. see above (Series B); rev. see below (Series E).

London mint

20	Quarter-noble		
	Weight		
	g	*gr.*	*Die-axis*
	1.90	29.3	220°

Obv.: ✠ƐDWⱯR⦂R⦂Ɐ∩GL ͘꒱ ∘FRⱯ∩Ⅽ⦂D∘hYBƐR
Pellet under shield. Omits D·G. Same die as **13**.
Rev.: ✠ƐXⱯLTⱯBITVR∘Ⅲ∘GLORⅠⱯ   Pellet in centre. North R14.
Lawrence 10/10 var. with annulet before GLORⅠⱯ; North 1162; Seaby 1495/1497. Ex Lockett (1241).

SERIES C/E (1354–5)

Characteristics: obv. see above (Series C); rev. see below (Series E).

London mint

21	Noble		
	7.67	118.3	160°

Obv.: Ɛ/DWⱯRD⦂DƐⅠ GRⱯ∘RƐX∘Ɐ∩GL⦂꒱∘FRⱯ∩Ⅽ∘D̄∘hYB
Ornaments, 1–11–11–11. Ropes, 3/3 with mast end of stern ropes visible to right of crown. Quatrefoils, 4/4. Lis, 3. North R14.
Rev.: ✠ⅠhⅭ∘ⱯVTƐⅯ∘TRⱯⅡⅭⅠƐⅡS∘P∘ⅯƐDⅠVⅯ∘ⅠLLORVⅯ∘ⅠBⱯT
Lis, ✠. R with curled tail (North 12). Small closed Ⅽ in centre.
Lawrence N/-, similar to 35; North 1144/1160; Seaby 1486/1488. Ex Lockett (1239); ex Whitton (19).

22	Half-noble		
	3.73	57.5	0°

Obv.: Ɛ/DWⱯR⦂DƐⅠ∘G⦂RƐX∘Ɐ∩GL⦂꒱∘FRⱯ∩Ⅽ D
Ornaments, 1–1–1. Ropes, 3/3. Quatrefoils 3/3. Lis, 4.
Rev.: ✠DOⅯⅠ∩ƐNƐ⦂Ⅰ∩⦂RVRORƐ⦂TVO⦂ⱯRGVⱯS⦂ⅯƐ
Lis, ✠. R for F in FVRORƐ. Small closed Ⅽ in centre. Pellet trefoils in spandrels.
Lawrence p. 25, pl. III (XVIII), 25 but this coin from different dies; North 1145/1161; Seaby 1492/1493. Ex Lockett (4267).

[*continued overleaf*]

PLATE 3

20

21

22

23

24

25

26

27

28

Plate 3 (*cont.*)

Characteristics: I.m. cross 2. Lettering similar to Series D but Ɑ and Ɛ are often broken at the bottom (North 4, 5). V sometimes has a nick in the right limb. R may have a curled tail (North 12), a horizontal wedge tail (North 13), or, more usually, a forked tail (North 14). Stops may be annulets or saltires.

London mint

23 Noble

7.67   118.3   180°

Obv.: ƐDWARD⁝DƐI·GRA·RƐX AIIGL 7 FRAIIƆ·D hI
Ornaments, 1(?)–11–11–1. Ropes, 3/3 with the mast end of the stern ropes visible to right of crown. Quatrefoils, 3/4. Lis, 3. North R14.

Rev.: +IhƆ·AVTƐM·TRAIIƐIƆIIS·P·MƐDIVM LLIORVM·IBAT
Lis, +. Note Ɛ in place of Ɑ in IhƆ, Ɛ and Ɑ transposed in TRAVƆIƐVS and I placed after LL in ILLORVM. Small closed Ɛ in centre.
Lawrence V/47–48 var.; North 1160; Seaby 1488. Bt Spink 1953.

24 Noble

Obv.: ƐDWARD°DƐI·GRA·RƐX°AIIGL⁝7·FRAIIƆ·DhY/B
Ornaments, –1–11–11–1. Ropes, 3/3 with mast end of stern ropes visible to right of crown. Quatrefoils, 3/3. Lis, 3. North R14.

Rev.: +IhƆ·AVTƐM·TRAIIƆIƐIIS·P·MƐDIVM·ILLORVM·IBAT
Lis, +. Small closed Ɛ in centre.
Similar to Lawrence AA (see Doubleday 63) / Lawrence 53; North 1160; Seaby 1488. Bt Spink 1955.

25 Noble

7.65   118.1   270°

Obv.: ƐDWARD°DƐI·GRA·RƐX°AIIGL⁝7·FRAIIƆ·DhY/B
Ornaments, 1–11–11–(?). Ropes, 3/2. Quatrefoils, 4/3. Lis, 3. North R14.

Rev.: +IhƐ·AVTƐM·TRAIIƆIƐIIS·P·MƐDIVM·ILLORVM·IBAT   Lis, +. Ɛ for Ɑ in IhƆ. Ɑ and Ɛs broken except for Ɛ in AVTƐM. Small closed Ɛ in centre.
Lawrence –/62; North 1160; Seaby 1488. Bought Schulman 1960, ex von Thielau (not in auction).

26 Noble

7.48   115.4   100°

Obv.: ƐDWARD⁝DƐI·GRA·RƐX·AIIGL⁝7·FRAIIƆ·D hY/B
Ornaments, –11–11–. Ropes, 3/3. Quatrefoils, 3/4. Lis, 3. Saltire over sail. No bowsprit. North R14.

Rev.: +IhƆ·AVTƐM·TRAIIƆIƐIIS·P·MƐDIVM·ILLORVM·IBAT
Lis, +. Small closed Ɛ in centre. RA of TRAIIƆIƐIIS over ƆM(?).
Lawrence AC/63 (similar); North 1160; Seaby 1488. Bought Spink 1960.

27 Noble

7.64   117.9   190°

Obv.: ƐDWARD×DƐI·GRA·RƐX·AIIGL⁝7·FRAIIƆ·D hY/B
Ornaments, –11–11–. Ropes, 3/0. Quatrefoils, 3/4. Lis, 3. No bowsprit. All Ɛs and Ɑs broken. North R14.

Rev.: +IhƆ·AVTƆM·TRAIIƆIƐIIS·P·MƐDIVM×ILLORVM·IBAT   Lis, +. All Ɛs and Ɑs broken. North R14. Small closed Ɛ in centre.
Lawrence AH/66; North 1160; Seaby 1488. No provenance.

28 Half-noble

3.85   59.4   0°

Obv.: ƐDWAR×DƐI·G RƐX AIIGL⁝7 FRAIIƆ·D
Ornaments, probably 1–1–1. Ropes, 3/1. Quatrefoils, 3/3. Lis, 3. No bowsprit. All Ɛs and Ɑs broken. North R14.

Rev.: +DOMINƐIIƆ⁝IN⁝RVRORƐ⁝TVO⁝ARGVAS⁝MƐ   Lis, +. Ɛs and Ɑs not broken. North R14. Last A of ARGVAS struck over S giving the impression of being barred.
Lawrence p. 79; North 1161; Seaby 1493. Ex Doubleday (76); ex Potter.

FOURTH COINAGE (*cont.*)

Pre-Treaty Period (*cont.*)

SERIES E/F (1356)

Characteristics: obv. see above (Series E); rev. see below (Series F).

London mint

29 Noble

	Weight	
g	*gr.*	*Die-axis*
7.69	118.6	270°

Obv.: Ɛ/DWⱯRD×DƐI×GRⱯ×RƐX×ⱯIIGL⁚Ⅎ×FRⱯIIⱰ D hɎ+B
Ornaments, 1–11–11–1. Ropes, 3/0. Quatrefoils, 3/4. Lis, 3. Ɛs and Ɑs broken at bottom (North 5). No bowsprit. North R14. No saltire after FRⱯNⱰ and with a cross between Ɏ and B of hɎB.

Rev.: ⚓IhⱰ ⱯVTƐM°TRⱯIIⱰIƐIIS°P°MƐDIVM°ILLORVM°IBⱯT　Lis, ✠.
Ɛs and Ɑs not broken. Large closed Ɛ in centre. North R14. No annulet after IhⱰ and very weak after MƐDIVM.
Lawrence -/75; North 1160/1173; Seaby 1488/1489.
No provenance.

30 Noble
| 7.64 | 117.9 | 300° |

Obv.: Ɛ/DWⱯRD×DƐI×GRⱯ×RƐX×ⱯIIGL×Ⅎ×FRⱯIIⱰ×DhɎ×B
Ornaments, –11–11–. Ropes, 3/3. Quatrefoils, 3/3. Lis, 3. Ɛs and Ɑs not broken. Initial Ɛ is Ɑ with cross-bar added afterwards. F of FRⱯNⱰ struck over an inverted F.

Rev.: ⚓IhⱰ°ⱯVTƐM°TRⱯIIⱰIƐIIS°P°MƐDIVM°ILLORVM·IBⱯT　Lis, ✠.
Ɛs and Ɑs not broken. North R14. Large closed Ɛ in centre.
Lawrence AL/72; North 1160/1173; Seaby 1488/ 1489. Bt Baldwin 1957; ex Wertheimer (80); ex Ryan (7).

SERIES F/E (1356)

Characteristics: obv. see below (Series F); rev. see above (Series E).

London mint

31 Noble
| 7.63 | 117.7 | 260° |

Obv.: ×Ɛ/DWⱯRD×DƐI×GRⱯ×RƐX×ⱯIIGL⁚Ⅎ×FRⱯIIⱰ Dh×/ɎB
Ornaments, –11–11–. Ropes, 3/1. Quatrefoils, 3/4. Lis, 3. Ɑs and Ɛs broken (North 6). North R14.

Rev.: ✠IhⱰ×ⱯVTƐM×TRⱯIIⱰIƐIIS×P°MƐDIVM°ILLORVM·IBⱯT　No lis.
Ɛs and second Ɑ broken (North 5). North R14. Small closed Ɛ in centre.
Lawrence AP/66** (supp.) without lis in *rev.* quarter; North 1173/1160; Seaby 1489/1488. Bt Baldwin 1982, said to have been found in Belgium.

SERIES F (1356)

Characteristics: I.m. crown. Ɑ and Ɛ often broken at top (North 6). Saltire/annulet stops.

London mint

32 Noble
| 7.62 | 117.6 | 0° |

Obv.: ×Ɛ/DWⱯRD×DƐI×GRA×RƐX×AIIGL⁚Ⅎ×FRAIIⱰ×Dh×/×ɎB
Ornaments, (?)–11–11–.Ropes, 3/1. Quatrefoils, 3/4. Lis, 3. Ɛs and Ɑs broken at top.

Rev.: ⚓IhⱰ°ⱯVTⱰM°TRⱯIIⱰIƐIIS°P°MƐDIVM°ILLORVM IBⱯT
Lis, ✠. Ɑs and Ɛs not broken. Ɑ for Ɛ in ⱯVTƐM. Large closed Ɛ in centre.
Lawrence AP/78; North 1173; Seaby 1489. Ex Lockett (4256); ex P. W. P. Carlyon-Britton. Stated on the Lockett ticket to have been found at Shalford, Surrey.

PLATE 4

29 30 31 32

33 34 35 36 37

38 39

Plate 4 (*cont.*)

SERIES B/Gd (1356–61)

Characteristics: obv. see above (Series B); rev. see below (Series Gd).

London mint

33 Quarter-noble
   1.86   28.7   350°

Obv.: +ЄDWΛR ⠅D ⠅G ⠅RЄX∘ΛIIGL ⠅⁊∘FRΛIIC
Pellet below shield.

Rev.: +ЄXΛLTΛBITVR×III∘GΛhLORI   Broken Ꝯ (North 8). Annulet by lion's head in second quarter.

Lawrence B no. 4/Gd no. 1* (p. 271); North 1141/1190; Seaby 1495/1498. Ex Doubleday (80); ex Lawrence.

SERIES E/Gc (1356–61)

Characteristics: obv. see above (Series E); rev. see below (Series Gc).

London mint

34 Noble
   7.71   118.9   260°

Obv.: ×Ꝯ/DWΛRD×DЄI×GRΛ×RЄX×ΛIIGL ⠅⁊×FRΛIIꝯ×DhⱯ×/B
Ornaments, –1–1–. Ropes, 3/1. Quatrefoils, 4/4. Lis, 3. ꝯ and Ꝯs broken at bottom (North 5).

Rev.: +Ihꝯ×ΛVTЄM×TRΛIIꝯIЄIIS×P×MЄDIVM×ILLORVM×IBΛT   Lis, ✠.
ꝯs and Ꝯs broken at bottom (North 7). Small closed Ꝯ in centre.

Lawrence AJ (see pl. III which confirms the saltire before Ꝯ/DWΛRD)/15 var. (p. 141); also see Doubleday 96; North 1160/1180; Seaby 1488/1490. Bought Schulman 1958.

SERIES Ga/E (1356/61)

Characteristics: obv. see below (Series Ga); rev. see above (Series E).

London mint

35 Quarter-noble
   1.91   29.4   10°

Obv.: +ЄDWΛR ⠅R∘ΛNGL∘⁊∘FRΛNꝯ∘D ⠅hⱯ
Ꝯ unbroken. Four lis in first quarter of shield.

Rev.: +ЄXΛLTΛBITVR∘IIIGhLORIΛ∘   Pellet in centre. North E3. No stop between III and GHLORIΛ.

Lawrence 1/– (a new rev. die); North 1189/1162. Seaby 1498/1497. Ex Lockett (1243).

SERIES F/Gb or c (1356–61)

Characteristics: obv. see above (Series F); rev. see below (Series Gb).

London mint

36 Noble
   7.64   118.3   290°

Obv.: ×Ꝯ/DWΛRD×DЄI×GRΛ×RЄX×ΛIIGL×⁊×FRΛIIꝯ×Dh×/×ⱯB
Ornaments.–11–11–. Ropes, 3/1. Quatrefoils, 3/4. Lis, 3. ꝯ and Ꝯs broken (North 6).

Rev.: +Ihꝯ·ΛVTЄM·TRΛIIꝯIЄII·S·MЄDIVM·ILLORVM·IBΛT·   Lis, ✠. ꝯs and Ꝯs broken (North 7). Small closed Ꝯ in centre. P omitted between TRΛNꝯIЄNS and MЄDIVM.

Lawrence AP/86*; North 1173/1180; Seaby 1489/1490. Ex Lockett (3973).

Plate 4 (*cont.*)

SERIES F/Gg (1356–61)

Characteristics: obv. see above (Series F); rev. see below (Series Gg).

London mint

37 Noble
    7.73   119.3   10°

Obv.: ꓰ/DWᚪRD·Dꓰl·GRᚪ·RꓰX·ᚪIIGL⸱⁊·FRᚪᚪIIꓚ·DhƳ/B
Ornaments, –11–11–. Ropes, 3/3. Quatrefoils, 3/4. Lis, 3. ꓚ and ꓰs broken (North 6). R with curled tail (North 12). Double ᚪ in FRᚪNꓚ. Same die as next coin, **38**.

Rev.: ✠IhꓰꓺᚪVTꓰM·FRᚪIIꓚlꓰIIS⁚P·MꓰDIVM⁚ILLORVM⁚IBᚪ   Lis, ✠. ꓰ with cross-bar (North 9). Large pellets either side of the lis ending the top of the reverse cross. Large closed ꓰ in centre. ꓰ for ꓚ in Ihꓚ. F for T in TRᚪIIꓚlꓰIIS.

Lawrence AQ (saltire before ꓰ/DWᚪRD uncertain: see also Doubleday 89)/–; North 1173/1183; Seaby 1489/1490. Bt Spink 1955.

38 Noble
    7.73   119.2   280°

Obv.: Same die as last coin, **37**.

Rev.: ✠IhꓰꓺᚪVTꓰM·TRᚪIIꓚlꓰIIS⁚P·MꓰDIVM·ILLORVM·IBᚪT   Lis, ✠. ꓰ with cross-bar (North 9). Pellets, left high, either side of the top lis ending the top of the reverse cross. Large closed ꓰ in centre. ꓰ for ꓚ in Ihꓚ.

Lawrence AQ (saltire before ꓰ/DWᚪRD uncertain)/similar to 91 but reads IBᚪT, not ƳBᚪT; North 1173/1183; Seaby 1489/1490. Bt Spink; ex H. P. Hall (25 or 26).

SERIES Ga/F (1356–61)

Characteristics: obv. see below (Series Ga); rev. see above (Series F).

London mint

39 Noble
    7.67   118.3   45°

Obv.: ꞏꓰ/DWᚪRD Dꓰl·GRᚪ·RꓰX ᚪIIGLꞏ⁊ꞏFRᚪIIꓚ·DhƳ/B
Ornaments, –11–11–. Ropes, 3/1. Quatrefoils, 3/4. Lis, 5. ꓚ and ꓰs unbroken.

Rev.: ✍IhꓚꞏᚪVTꓰM·TRᚪIIꓚIꓰIISꞏPꞏMꓰDIVMꞏILLORVMꞏIBᚪT   Lis, ✠. ꓚs and ꓰs unbroken. Large closed ꓰ in centre with pellet on cross-bar.

Lawrence ᚪR/80; North 1179/1173; Seaby 1490/1489. Ex Doubleday (89); ex Lawrence.

FOURTH COINAGE (*cont.*)

Pre-Treaty Period (*cont.*)

SERIES G (1356–61)

General characteristics: I.m. cross 3. ᛖ with broad arched top. ᛆ and Ɇ often with a piece cut from the top (North 7).

SUB-SERIES Ga: obv. annulet before ƐDWᛅRD, small annulet stops (nobles); rev. large annulet stops, large Ɇ in centre.

London mint

40 Noble

	Weight		
g	*gr.*	*Die-axis*	
7.67	118.3	110°	

Obv.: °ᛆ/DWᛅRD°DƐI°GRᛅ°ᛅIIGL°ℱ°FRᛅIIᛅ°D°hY°B°Ɇ
Ornaments, –11–11–. Ropes, 3/1. Quatrefoils, 3/4. Lis, 5. ᛆ for Ɇ in ƐDWᛅRD. ᛆ and Ɇs not cut. No RƐX.
Rev.: ✠Ihᛆ°ᛅVTƐᛉ°TRᛅIIᛅIƐIIS°P°ᛉƐDIVᛉ°ILLORVᛉ°IBᛅT   Lis, ✠.
ᛆs and Ɇs not cut.
Lawrence AU/2; North 1179; Seaby 1490. Bt Spink 1972; ex Cartwright.

41 Half-noble (Ga or Gb, these sub-classes are not differentiated for this denomination).

Obv.: Ɇ/DWᛅR ⸪DƐI°G°RƐX°ᛅIIGL°ℱ°FRᛅIIᛅ°D/[hYB(?)]
| 3.82 | 59.0 | 180° | |

Ornaments, –1–1–. Ropes, 3/3. Quatrefoils, 3/3. Lis, 4. Ɇs not cut. No bowsprit. Same die as **42.**
Rev.: ✠DOᛉINƐNƐ°IN°RVRORƐ°TVO°ᛅRGVᛅS°ᛉƐ°   Lis, ✠. R for F in FVRORƐ. Small Ɇ in centre.
Lawrence 3/3; North 1184; Seaby 1494. Ex Brigadier F. W. Rice (though acquired in 1962 and apparently not in the 1946 sale).

42 Half-noble

Obv.: Same die as last coin, **41**. Unfortunately, on this coin, the letters following D are no clearer than on **41**.
| 3.78 | 58.3 | 200° | |

Rev.: ✠DOᛉINƐNƐ°IN°RVRORƐ°TVO°ᛅRGVᛅS°ᛉƐ°   Lis, ✠. R for F in FVRORƐ. Small closed Ɇ in centre.
Lawrence 1/4; North 1184; Seaby 1494. Ex Lockett (3014).

SUB-SERIES Ga/Gb or Gc (these sub-classes are not differentiated for the noble): obv. no annulet before ƐDWᛅRD. Small annulet stops.

London mint

43 Noble
| 7.52 | 116.0 | 30° | |

Obv.: ᛆ/DWᛅRD°DƐI°GRᛅ°RᛆX°ᛅIIGL°ℱ°FRᛅIIᛅ°D˙hY/B
Ornaments, –1–1–. Ropes, 2/1. Quatrefoils, 3/3. Lis, 5. ᛆ for Ɇ in Ɇ/DWᛅRD and RƐX. ᛆs and Ɇs not cut.
Rev.: ✠Ihᛆ ᛅVTƐᛉ TRᛅIIᛅIƐIIS P ᛉƐDIVᛉ ILLORVᛉ IBᛅT   Lis, ✠.
ᛆs and Ɇs cut on top (North 7). No stops; same die as Doubleday 90. Small Ɇ in centre.
Lawrence AS/11; North 1179/1180; Seaby 1490. Bt Spink 1955.

SUB-SERIES Ga/Gd: obv. see above; rev. see below.

London mint

44 Quarter-noble
| 1.19 | 29.4 | 180° | |

Obv.: ✠ƐDWᛅR ⸴R ⸴ᛅNGL' ℱ°FRᛅNᛆ⸴D⸴hY
Ɇ unbroken. Four lis in first quarter of shield.
Rev.: ✠ƐXᛅLTᛅBITVR×III×GᛅhᛃORI   Annulet to r. of upper lis. Small Ɇ or pellet (?) in centre.
Lawrence 1/1 (pp. 146–7); North 1189/1190; Seaby 1498. Bt Seaby 1959.

[*continued overleaf*]

PLATE 5

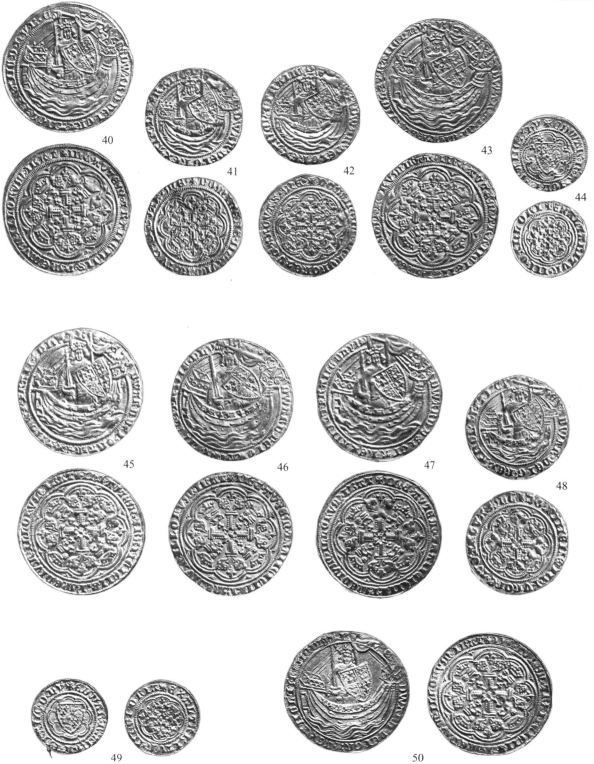

40

41

42

43

44

45

46

47

48

49

50

Plate 5 (*cont.*)

SUB-SERIES Gb and Gc/Gd: obv. see above; rev. see below.

London mint

45 Noble
7.63   117.8   30°

Obv.: ·Ɛ/DWⱯRD·DƐI·GRⱯ×RƐX×ⱯIIGL·⁊·FRⱯIIɊ·DhɎ/B
Ornaments, –1–1–. Ropes, 3/1. Quatrefoils, 3/3. Lis, 5. Ɋ and Ɛs cut at top (North 7).

Rev.: ✦IhɊ˙×ⱯVTƐM×TRⱯIIɊIƐIIS⦂P·MƐDIVM×ILLORVM×IBⱯT   Lis, ✚.
Initial cross flawed. Ɋs and Ɛs broken at bottom (North 8). Annulet to r. of lis ending the top of the central cross. Small Ɛ in centre.
Lawrence BA/24–30; North 1180/1181; Seaby 1490. Ex Christie sale 28.2.1989 (14); ex Pinchbeck hoard.

SUB-SERIES Gd: obv. large annulet or saltire stops with an annulet or pellet before ƐDWⱯRD; rev. saltire stops and an annulet or pellet alongside the lis ending the top arm of the central cross.

London mint

46 Noble
7.36   113.6   310°

Obv.: °Ɛ∘/DWⱯRD·DƐI·GRⱯ·RƐX×ⱯIIGL·⁊·FRⱯIIɊ·DhɎ/B
Ornaments, 1–1–1–1. Ropes, 3/1. Quatrefoils, 4/4. Lis, 4. Ɋ and Ɛs not cut. A weak annulet (misplaced ?) after Ɛ of ƐDWⱯRD.

Rev.: ✦IhɊ×ⱯVTƐM×TRⱯIIɊIƐIIS⦂P·MƐDIVM×ILLORVM×IBⱯT   Lis. ✚.
Ɋs and Ɛs broken below (North 8). Annulet to the right of the lis ending the top of the reverse cross. Small Ɛ in centre.
Similar to Lawrence BF/31 but rev. variety and different from Doubleday 105; North 1181; Seaby 1490. Ex Wellington (2).

SUB-SERIES Ge. No gold coins are known which can be attributed to this sub-series.

SUB-SERIES Gb and Gc/Gf: obv. see above; rev. see below.

London mint

47 Noble
7.64   117.9   10°

Obv.: Ɛ/DWⱯRD·DƐI·GRⱯ·RƐX×ⱯIIGL·⁊·FRⱯIIɊ DhɎB   Ornaments, –1–1–.
Ropes, 2/3. Quatrefoils, 3/3. Lis, 5. Ɋ and Ɛs not cut.

Rev.: ✦IhƐ×ⱯVTƐM×TRⱯIIɊIƐIIS⦂P·MƐDIVM×ILLORVM×IBⱯT   Lis, ✚. Ɋ and Ɛs long. One annulet each side (to the right double cut) of lis ending the top arm of the reverse cross. Small Ɛ in centre.
Lawrence AY/32–38 etc.; North 1180; Seaby 1490. Ex von Thielau (1513); ex Schulman sale 6.3.1958 (3298).

SUB-SERIES Gf: obv. saltire stops, sometimes a saltire before ƐDWⱯRD on the noble; rev. pellet on each side of the lis at the end of the top arm of the central cross.

London mint

48 Half-noble
3.80   58.6   100°

Obv.: Ɛ/DWⱯR⦂DƐI·G⦂RƐX×ⱯИGL⦂⁊×FRⱯИɊ·D'/×   Ornaments, 1(?)–1–1–1.
Ropes, 4/4. Quatrefoils, 3/4. Lis, 4. Saltire above crown. Nails on ship's side are annulets.

Rev.: ✚DOMIИƐIIƐ×IИ×FVRORƐ×TVO×ⱯRGVⱯS⦂MƐ   Lis, ✚. Large pellets on each side of the lis ending the top of the reverse cross. Fleur trefoils in spandrels. Ɋ and Ɛ long as on the nobles. Last Ɛ of DOMIИƐИƐ struck over a saltire(?).
Dies not listed by Lawrence; North 1186; Seaby 1494. Bt Spink 1965; ex Birchmore.

Plate 5 (*cont.*)

49 Quarter-noble
    1.92   29.6   75°

Obv.: +ƐDWⱯR⦂R˟ⱯIIGL⦂7˟FRⱯIIꝀ˟D⦂hY'
Rev.: +ƐXⱯLTⱯBITVR˟III˟GLORIⱯ   Pellet either side of upper lis. Small Ɛ in centre.
Lawrence 4/3; as Doubleday 155; North 1191; Seaby 1498. Bt Spink 1963.

SUB-SERIES Gg/Gd: obv. see below; rev. see above.

London mint

50 Noble
    7.76   119.7   130°

Obv.: ˟Ɛ⦂/DWⱯRD˟DƐI˟GRⱯ˟RƐX˟ⱯIIGL⦂7˟FRⱯIIꝀ˟DhY/B
        Ornaments, 1–1–1–1. Ropes, 3/1. Quatrefoils, 4/3. Lis, 4. North E10.
Rev.: +IhꝀ⦂ⱯVTƐM˟TRⱯIIꝀIƐIIS⦂P˟MƐDIVM˟ILLORVM˟IBⱯT   Lis, +.
        Ꝁs and Ɛs broken below (North 8). Annulet to the right of the lis ending the top of the central cross.
Lawrence BQ/24–30; North 1183/1181; Seaby 1490. Bt Spink 1948.

FOURTH COINAGE (*cont.*)

Pre-Treaty Period (*cont.*)

SERIES G (*cont.*)

SUB-SERIES Gg: obv. as Gf; rev. similar to Gf but large Є in centre.

London mint

51 Noble

	Weight		
	g	gr.	Die-axis
	7.74	119.4	70°

Obv.: Є/DWΛRD×DЄI×GRΛ×REX×ΛIIGL⁞Ƒ×FRΛIIꟼ×DhY/B
Ornaments, 1–1–1–1. Ropes, 3/2. Quatrefoils, 4/4. Lis, 4. X broken.
Rev.: +IhЄ⁚ΛVTЄM×TRΛIIꟼIЄNS⁚P⁚MЄDIVM×ILLORVM×YBΛT
Lis, ✚. Pellet on each side of the lis ending the top of the centre cross. North E9.
Lawrence BR/51; Doubleday 128–9/124; North 1183; Seaby 1490. Ex Wellington (4).

SUB-SERIES Gh/Gg: obv. see below; rev. see above.

London mint

52 Noble

	7.86	121.2	210°

Obv.: Є/DWΛRD×DЄI×GRΛ×REX×ΛIIGL⁞Ƒ×FRΛIIꟼ×DhY/B
Ornaments, 1–1–1–1. Ropes, 3/1. Quatrefoils, 4/4. Lis, 4. Open Єs (North 10) except in DЄI.
Rev.: +IhЄ×ΛVTЄM×TRΛIIꟼIЄIIS⁚P⁚MЄDIVM×ILLORVM×IBΛT
Lis, ✚. North E9. Pellets at each side of the lis ending the top arm of the reverse cross. Large Є in centre.
Lawrence – (as Doubleday 126)/57, pl.VII, 6; North -/1183; Seaby 1490. Ex Christie sale 28.2.1989 (30); ex Pinchbeck hoard.

53 Half-noble

	3.82	58.9	270°

Obv.: Є/DWΛR⁚DEI×G⁚REX×ΛIIGL⁞Ƒ×FRΛIIꟼ D
Ornaments, 1–1–1–1. Ropes, 3/1. Quatrefoils, 3/3. Lis, 4. Open Єs (North 10).
Rev.: +DOMIИЄИЄ×IИ·FVRORЄ×TVO×ΛRGVΛS⁚MЄ
No lis in quarter. Pellet at each side of the lis ending the top arm of the reverse cross. North E9. Pellet trefoils in spandrels. Closed ꟼ in centre. Lawrence 13/13; Doubleday 141; North 1188/1187; Seaby 1494. Bt Spink 1981.

SUB-SERIES Gh: obv. open Єs (North 10); rev. pellet at each side of the lis ending the top arm of the reverse cross.

London mint

54 Half-noble

	3.83	59.1	230°

Obv.: Є/DWΛR⁚DЄI·G×REX×ΛIIGL⁞Ƒ⁚FRΛIIꟼ⁚D'
Ornaments, 1–1–1–(?). Ropes, 3/1. Quatrefoils, 3/3. Lis, 4.
Rev.: +DOMIИЄИЄ×IИ·FVRORЄ×TVO×ΛRGVΛS⁚MЄ
No lis in quarter. Pellet on each side of the lis ending the top of the centre cross.
Lawrence 16/16, pl.VIII, 4; North 1188; Seaby 1494. Ex Lockett (4268).

[continued overleaf]

PLATE 6

51   52   53   54

55   56   57   58

59   60   61   62   63

Plate 6 (*cont.*)

Treaty Period (1361–9)

TRANSITIONAL TREATY SERIES (1361–3)

Characteristics: I.m. cross potent. Saltire stops. Sometimes Gothic Пs. Sometimes with letters F, h, I, П and P of abnormal size.

London mint

55 Noble	7.68	118.6	60°

Obv.: Є/DWЛRD⫶DЄI⫶GRЛ⫶RЄX⫶ЛNGL⫶DПS⫶hIB⫶Ƶ⫶Л
Ornaments, 1–1–1–1. Ropes, 3/3. Quatrefoils, 4/3. Lis, 5. Ship's planks divided. Same die as next coin, **56**.
Rev.: +IhЄ⫶ЛVTЄ⫶TRЛNSIЄVS⫶P⫶MЄDIVM⫶ILLORR⫶IBЛT
Lis, ✚. Central panel with annulets. No large letters. Reads TRЛNSIЄVS.
Lawrence Cc/5; North 1222; Seaby 1499. Ex Lockett (3976).

56 Noble	7.72	119.1	180°

Obv.: Same die as last coin, **55**.
Rev.: +IhЄ⫶ЛVTЄM⫶TRЛNSIЄNS⫶PЄR⫶MЄD⫶ILLORR⫶IBЛT Lis, ✚.
h, I and P large. Central panel with annulets.
Lawrence Cc/8; North 1222; Seaby 1499. Bt Glendining sale 18.2.1954 (5).

57 Noble	7.67	118.3	80°

Obv.: Є/DWЛRD⫶DЄI⫶GRЛ⫶RЄX⫶ЛNGL⫶DПS⫶hIB⫶Ƶ⫶ЛꝊ⫶
Ornaments, 1–11–11–1. Ropes, 3/3. Quatrefoils, 4/3. Lis, 5(?). h, I and Пs large. Ship's planks divided.
Rev.: +IhꝎⴼⴼⴼЛVTЄM⫶TRЛПꝎIЄNS⫶P⫶MЄDIVM⫶ILLORR⫶IBЛT
Lis, ✚. h, I and P large. Small lions. Central panel with pellets.
Lawrence Cg/15; North 1222; Seaby 1499. Ex Doubleday (167); ex Lawrence.

58 Half-noble	3.73	57.5	210°

Obv.: Є/DWЛRDVS⫶DЄI⫶G⫶RЄX/ЛNGL⫶D Ornaments, 1–1–1–. Ropes, 3/2. Quatrefoils, 3/3. Lis, 3. Annulet over crown. No large letters.
Rev.: +DOMIПЄ⫶IN⫶FVRORЄ⫶TVO⫶ЛRGVЛS M Lis, ✚. First П Gothic, second N Roman. No large letters. Trefoils in spandrels formed of three pellets, as later series G (g or h). Central panel with annulets.
Lawrence a/3; North 1223; Seaby 1500. Ex Lockett (1250).

59 Half-noble	3.87	59.6	0°

Obv.: Є/DWЛRDI⫶DЄI⫶G⫶RЄX/⫶ЛNGL⫶D' Ornaments, 1–1–1–.
Ropes, 3/2. Quatrefoils, 4/3. Lis, 3. annulet over crown. No large letters. Ship's planks divided. No bowsprit.
Rev.: +DOMIПЄ⫶IN⫶FVRORЄ⫶TVO⫶ЛRGVTS⫶MЄ Lis, ✚. Large F and I. Fleurs in spanrels. Central panel with annulets.
Lawrence b/9; North 1223; Seaby 1500. Bt Spink 1965; ex Birchmore.

60 Half-noble	3.83	59.1	90°

Obv.: Є/DWЛRD⫶DЄI⫶GRЛ⫶RЄ/X⫶ЛNG Ornaments, 1–1–1–1. Ropes, 2/3. Quatrefoils, 3/3. Lis, 3. No large letters. Ship's planks divided. No bowsprit.
Rev.: +DOMIПЄ⫶IN⫶FVRORЄ⫶TVO⫶ЛRGVTS⫶MЄ Lis, ✚. Large F and I. Central panel with annulets.
Lawrence d/8, this coin; North 1223; Seaby 1500. Ex Lockett (4269).

61 Half-noble	3.82	58.9	60°

Obv.: Є/DWЛRDV⫶DЄI⫶G⫶RЄX/ЛNGL⫶D' Ornaments, 1–1–1–. Ropes, 3/2. Quatrefoils, 4/4. Lis, 3. No large letters. Ship's planks divided. No bowsprit. Same die as next coin, **62**.
Rev.: +DOMIПЄ×IN⫶FVRORЄ⫶TVO⫶ЛRGVЛS⫶M' Lis, ✚. Large F and I. Central panel with annulets.
Lawrence e/11; North 1223; Seaby 1500. Ex Lockett (1240).

62 Half-noble	3.79	58.4	60°

Obv.: Same die as last coin, **61**.
Rev.: +DOMIПЄ×IN⫶FVRORЄ⫶TVO×ЛRGVTS×MЄ Lis, ✚. Large F and I. Central panel with annulets.
Lawrence e/16; North 1223; Seaby 1500. Bt Spink 1953.

Plate 6 (*cont.*)

63 Half-noble
  3.85   59.3   45°

Obv.: Ɇ/DWⱯRD ⁝DƐI⸳G RƐX ˣ Ʌ∏/GL ⁝ D ⁝ ҺB'   Ornaments, 1–1–1–1.
      Ropes, 3/3. Quatrefoils, 4/3. Lis, 3. Large H and I. Ship's planks divided.
Rev.: ✠DOⱭⱭIIƐ ˣ I∏⁝FVRORƐ ˣ TVO⁝ⱯRGVTS⁝ⱭƐ   No lis in quarter. Large F
      and I. Central panel with annulets.
Lawrence g/- but rev. similar to his 13, only with double saltire before FVRORɆ;
similar to Doubleday 181; North 1223; Seaby 1500. Ex Lockett (3978); ex
Clarke-Thornhill (10).

FOURTH COINAGE (*cont.*)

Treaty Period (*cont.*)

TRANSITIONAL TREATY SERIES (*cont.*)

London mint (cont.)

	Weight		
	g	*gr.*	*Die-axis*

64 Half-noble
3.85 59.4 180°

Obv.: Є/DWΛRD⦂DЄI·G⦂RЄX×ΛП/GL⦂D⦂hIB
Ornaments, 1–1–1–1. Ropes, 3/3. Quatrefoils, 5/3. Lis, 3. Large h and I.
Ship's planks divided.
Rev.: ✠DOMIПЄ×IП·FVRORЄ·TVO×ΛRGVΛS×MЄ No lis in quarter. Large F
and I. Central panel with pellets.
Lawrence l/19; North 1223; Seaby 1500. Ex Doubleday (186); ex Lawrence.

65 Half-noble
3.81 58.8 190°

Obv.: Є/DWΛRD⦂DЄI·G⦂RЄX×ΛПGL/×D⦂hIB⦂ Ornaments, 1–1–1–1.
Ropes, 3/3. Quatrefoils, 5/3. Lis, 3. Large h and I. Ship's planks divided.
Rev.: ✠DOMIПЄ⦂IП⦂FVRORЄ⦂TVO⦂ΛRGVTS⦂MЄ Lis, ✠. Large F and I.
Central panel with annulets.
Lawrence m/-; As Doubleday 187; North 1223; Seaby 1500. Ex O'Byrne I (1).

66 Half-noble
3.78 58.3 0°

Obv.: Є/DWΛRD⦂DЄI·G⦂RЄX×ΛПGL⦂D⦂hIB Ornaments, 1–1–1–1.
Ropes, 3/3. Quatrefoils, 3/3. Lis, 3. Large h and I. The sterncastle does not cut
the legend. Ship's planks divided.
Rev.: ✠DOMIПЄ×IП·FV[RORЄ×TVO×ΛR]GVTS×MЄ Lis, ✠. Large F and I.
Central panel with annulets.
Lawrence p/17; rev. as Doubleday 185; North 1223; Seaby 1500. Ex W.M.Hall (15).

67 Quarter-noble
1.92 29.6 210°

Obv.: ✠ЄDWR⦂R⦂ΛПGLIЄ⦂Ƶ⦂DПVS⦂hУ Fleur trefoils in spandrels and pellets
at the cusps of the tressure. Same die as next coin, **68**.
Rev.: ✠ЄXΛLTΛBITVR⦂IП⦂GLORIΛ×× Pellet trefoils in spandrels of tressure.
Large Є in centre.
Lawrence a/1; North 1224 (i); Seaby 1501. Ex Lockett (3020).

68 Quarter-noble
1.88 28.9 60°

Obv.: same die as last coin, **67**.
Rev.: ✠ЄXΛLTΛBITVR⦂IП⦂GLORIΛ Lis above lion in fourth quarter (this
feature was not commented on in Lawrence 1937 or in Potter 1964 but is
clearly visible on the coin illustrated by the former – Pl. XVI(XII), no. 5).
Pellet trefoils in the spandrels of the tressure. Large letter I. In centre is a small
cross potent with annulets in its angles and centre.
Lawrence a/4; North 1224 (ii); Seaby 1501. Bt Baldwin 1980, ex Ready (probably 330,
part).

69 Quarter-noble
1.93 29.7 300°

Obv.: ✠ЄDWΛR⦂DЄI⦂GRΛC⦂RЄX⦂ΛПGL⦂D' Pellet trefoils in spandrels
and annulets on cusps of tressure.
Rev.: ✠ЄXΛLTΛBITVR⦂IП⦂GLORIΛ⦂ Pellets in spandrels of tressure. In centre
a small cross potent with annulets in angles and a pellet in the centre.
Lawrence c/5, however on this coin the letters I and П do not have the appearance of
being larger than the other letters; North 1224; Seaby 1501. Bt Spink 1962; ex
Spurway.

70 Quarter-noble
1.89 29.2 160°

Obv.: ✠ЄDWΛR⦂DЄI⦂GRΛC⦂RЄX⦂ΛПGL⦂D' Trefoils in spandrels and on
cusps of tressure. May be large I (top off flan).
Rev.: ✠ЄXΛLTΛBITVR⦂IП⦂GLRIΛ⦂ Pellets in spandrels of tressure. Large
letter I. In centre, a small cross potent with annulets in the angles and in its
centre. Same die as next coin, **71**.
Lawrence b/6; North 1224; Seaby 1501. Bt Munzen und Medaillen sale 17.6.1954
(87).

[*continued overleaf*]

PLATE 7

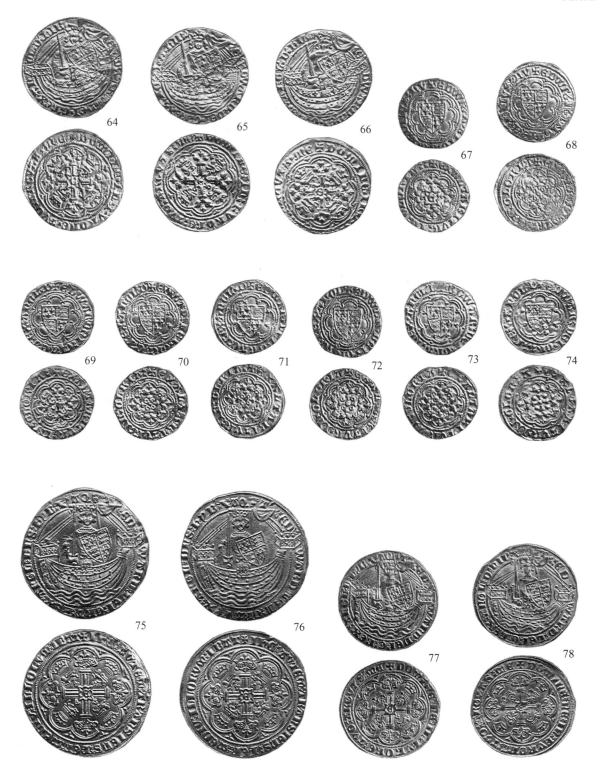

64

65

66

67

68

69

70

71

72

73

74

75

76

77

78

Plate 7 (*cont.*)

71 Quarter-noble
     1.95   30.1   320°

Obv.: ✠ЄDWѦR×DЄI⋮GRѦɑ⋮RЄX×ѦNGL⋮D Pellets in spandrels and pellet trefoils on cusps of tressure. Probably large letter I (top off flan).
Rev.: same die as last coin, **70**.
Lawrence d/6; North 1224; Seaby 1501. No provenance.

72 Quarter-noble
     1.89   29.1   60°

Obv.: ✠ЄDWѦR⋮DЄI×GRѦɑ⋮RЄX×ѦNGL' Pellets in spandrels and annulets on cusps of tressure. Large letter I.
Rev.: ✠ЄXѦLTѦBITVR×IN×GLORIѦ Pellets in spandrels of tressure. In centre a small cross potent with annulets in the angles and a pellet in its centre.
Lawrence g/12, this coin cited; North 1224; Seaby 1501. Bt Spink 1975; ex Lockett (4272).

73 Quarter-noble
     1.87   28.8   350°

Obv.: ✠ЄDWѦR⋮DЄI×GRѦ⋮RЄX×ѦNGL'D' Pellets in spandrels and pellet trefoils on cusps of tressure. Large letter I.
Rev.: ✠ЄXѦLTѦBITVR⋮IN×GLORIѦ Pellet trefoils in spandrels of tressure. Large Is (but not in GLORIѦ). In centre a small cross potent with annulets containing pellets in the quarters and a voided quatrefoil with a pellet punched over it in its centre.
Lawrence p/2; North 1224; Seaby 1501. Bt Spink 1955.

74 Quarter-noble
     1.91   29.4   160°

Obv.: ✠ЄDWѦR⋮DЄI×GRѦ⋮RЄX×ѦNGL⋮D No ornament in the spandrels of the tressure but trefoils on the cusps. Large letter I.
Rev.: ✠ЄXѦLTѦBITVR×IN×GLORIѦ Pellets in spandrels of tressure. Large Is and N. In centre, a small cross potent with large pellets in the quarters and centre.
Lawrence q/18; North 1224; Seaby 1501. Ex Lockett (1256); ex Bliss (200).

Plate 7 (*cont.*)

Characteristics: I.m. cross potent. New lettering with Treaty X (North 17) or curule-shaped X (North 16, on gold only). Saltire stops.

London mint

Group a – saltire before ᕕDWᛉRD (nobles and half-nobles) or nothing before ᕕDWᛉR(D) (quarter-nobles).

75 Noble
   7.70   118.7   190°

      Obv.: ×ᕕD/WᛉRD⁑DᕕI⁑GRᛉ⁑RᕕX⁑ᛉNGL⁑DNS⁑hYB⁑Σ×ᛉQ/T
      Ornaments, –11–11. Ropes, 3/2. Quatrefoils, 4/4. Lis, 4. The saltire before
      ᕕDWᛉRD is *below* the fold of the sail.
      Rev.: +Ihᕊ⁑ᛉVTᕕM⁑TRᛉNSIᕕNS⁑PᕕR⁑MᕕDIV⁑ILLORVM⁑IBᛉT
      Lawrence 1; North 1231; Seaby 1502. Bt Spink 1960.

76 Noble
   7.72   119.1   340°

      Obv.: ×ᕕD/WᛉRD'⁑DᕕI⁑GRᛉ⁑RᕕX⁑ᛉNGL⁑DNS⁑hYB⁑Σ×ᛉQ/T'
      Ornaments, –11–11. Ropes, 3/2. Quatrefoils, 4/4. Lis, 4. The saltire before
      ᕕDWᛉRD is *above* the fold of the sail.
      Rev.: +Ih'ᕊ⁑ᛉVTᕕM⁑TRᛉNSIᕕNS⁑PᕕR⁑MᕕDIVᕊ⁑ILLORVM⁑IBᛉT
      Lawrence 7; North 1231; Seaby 1502. Ex Basmadjieff (2).

77 Half-noble
   3.71   57.2   330°

      Obv.: ×ᕕD/WᛉRD⁑DᕕI⁑G⁑RᕕX⁑ᛉNGL⁑D⁑hYB„Σ×ᛉQ/T'
      Ornaments, –11–11. Ropes, 3/2. Quatrefoils, 4/2. Lis, 4.
      Rev.: +DOMINᕕ⁑NᕕᛉIN⁑FVRORᕕ⁑TVO⁑ᛉRGVᛉS⁑Mᕕ
      Lawrence 1; North 1238; Seaby 1506. Bt Spink 1960.

78 Half-noble
   3.87   59.7   330°

      Obv.: ×ᕕD/WᛉRD⁑DᕕI⁑G⁑RᕕX⁑ᛉNGL⁑D⁑hIB„Σ×ᛉO/T
      Ornaments, –11–11. Ropes, 3/2. Quatrefoils, 4/4. Lis, 4. hIB instead of hYB.
      O for Q in ᛉO/T.
      Rev.: +DOMINᕕ⁑NᕕᛉIN⁑FVRORᕕ⁑TVO⁑ᛉRGVᛉS⁑Mᕕ
      Lawrence 1 var. with spelling hIB; North 1238; Seaby 1506. Bt Glendining sale
      10.2.1961 (12).

79 Half-noble

	Weight	
g	*gr.*	*Die-axis*
3.78	58.4	330°

Obv.: ·ƎD/WⱯRD⁑DƎI⁑G⁑RƎX⁑ⱯNGL⁑D⁑hƳB Ƨ ⱯO/T
Ornaments, 11–11–. Ropes, 3/2. Quatrefoils, 4/4. Lis, 4. No punctuation after hƳB and before ⱯQ/T. O for Q in ⱯQ/T.
Rev.: ✠DOMINƎ⁑NƎ⁑IN⁑FVRORƎ⁑TVO⁑ⱯRGVⱯS⁑mƎ
Similar to Lawrence 1 but with variations in punctuation, spelling and the arrangement of the ship's ornaments; obverse as Doubleday 235; North 1238; Seaby 1506. Bt Spink 1940.

80 Half-noble

3.75	57.8	160°

Obv.: ·ƎD/WⱯRD⁑DƎI⁑G RƎX⁑ⱯNGL D⁑hƳB.Ƨ·ⱯQ/T
Ornaments, –11–11. Ropes, 3/2. Quatrefoils, 4/4. Lis, 4. Curved I for Ƴ in hƳB. No punctuation between G and RƎX, ⱯNGL and D.
Rev.: ✠DOMINƎ⁑NƎ⁑IN⁑FVRORƎ⁑TVO⁑ⱯRGVⱯS⁑mƎ
Lawrence 3 var.; North 1238; Seaby 1506. Bt Spink 1960.

81 Quarter-noble

1.90	29.2	180°

Obv.: ✠ƎDWⱯRD⁑DƎI⁑GRⱯ⁑RƎX⁑ⱯNGL' Treaty X (North 17).
Rev.: ✠ƎXⱯLTⱯBITVR⁑IN⁑GLORIⱯ Treaty X (North 17). Lis in centre.
Lawrence 1/1; North 1243; Seaby 1510. Ex Jacson (5).

82 Quarter-noble

1.87	28.8	60°

Obv.: ✠ƎDWⱯRD⁑DƎI⁑GRⱯ⁑RƎX⁑ⱯNGL Treaty X (North 17).
Rev.: ✠ƎXⱯLTⱯBITVR⁑IN⁑GLORIⱯ Treaty X (North 17). Lis in centre.
Lawrence 1/1; North 1243; Seaby 1510. Bt Spink 1959.

83 Quarter-noble

1.72	26.5	340°

Obv.: ✠ƎDWⱯRD⁑DƎI⁑GRⱯ⁑RƎX⁑ⱯNGL' Treaty X (North 17). Same die as next coin, **84**.
Rev.: ✠ƎX⁑ⱯLTⱯBTVR⁑IN⁑GLORIⱯ Curule X (North 16). Lis in centre.
Lawrence 4/4 var. with : after X and BTVR; North 1243; Seaby 1510. Bt Baldwin 1976.

84 Quarter-noble

1.92	29.5	170°

Obv.: same die as last coin, **83**.
Rev.: ✠ƎXⱯLTⱯBITVR⁑IN⁑GLORIⱯ Curule X (North 16). Lis in centre.
Lawrence 4/4; North 1243; Seaby 1510. Bt Seaby 1953.

Group b/a – annulet before ƎDWⱯRD

85 Noble

7.69	118.6	30°

Obv.: ·ƎD/WⱯRD⁑DƎI⁑GRⱯ⁑RƎX⁑ⱯNGL'⁑DNS⁑hƳB.Ƨ·ⱯQ/T
Ornaments, –11–11. Ropes, 3/1. Quatrefoils, 4/4. Lis, 4. Stops before and after Ƨ weak ('omitted' in Lawrence).
Rev.: ✠IhƎ ⱯVTƎM TRⱯNSIƎNS PƎR MƎDIVM ILLORV IBⱯT
No stops. Ǝ in centre supine.
Lawrence 3; North 1232; Seaby 1503. Bt Baldwin 1966.

[*continued overleaf*]

PLATE 8

79

80

81

82

83

84

85

86

87

88

89

90

91

Plate 8 (*cont.*)

Group b – annulet before ЄDWᴧRD, ᴧ barred in IBᴧT, ᴧRGVᴧS and GLORIᴧ.

86 Noble
    7.71   118.9   0°
Obv.: °ЄD/WᴧRD×DЄI×GRᴧ×RЄX×ᴧNGL×DNS×hYB.Ƶ×ᴧQ/T
        Ornaments, –11–11. Ropes, 3/2. Quatrefoils, 4/4. Lis, 4.
Rev.: +IhꞪ×ᴧVTЄM×TRᴧNSIЄNS×PЄR×MЄDIV×ILLORVM×IBᴧT
Lawrence 2/1; North 1232; Seaby 1503. Bt Glendining sale 8.6.1983 (5).

87 Noble
    7.73   119.3   190°
Obv.: °ЄD/WᴧRD×DЄI×GRᴧ×RЄX×ᴧNGL×DNS×hYB.Ƶ×ᴧQ/T
        Ornaments, –11–11. Ropes, 3/2. Quatrefoils, 4/2. Lis, 4.
Rev.: +IhꞪ×ᴧVTЄM×TRᴧNSIЄNS×PЄR×MЄDIV×ILLORVM×IBᴧT
Lawrence 3; North 1232; Seaby 1503. Ex Dangar (82).

88 Half-noble
    3.86   59.5   130°
Obv.: °ЄD/WᴧRD×DЄI×G×RЄX×ᴧNGL×D×hYB.Ƶ×ᴧQ/T'
        Ornaments, –11–11. Ropes, 3/2. Quatrefoils, 3/2. Lis, 4.
Rev.: +DOMINЄ×NЄ×IN×FVRORЄ×TVO×ᴧRGVᴧS×MЄ
Lawrence 1; North 1239; Seaby 1507. Bt Glendining sale 10.2.1961 (11).

89 Half-noble
    3.80   58.6   160°
Obv.: °ЄD/WᴧRD×DЄI×G×RЄX×ᴧNGL×D×hYB.Ƶ×ᴧQ/T'
        Ornaments, –11–11. Ropes, 3/2. Quatrefoils, 3/2. Lis, 4.
Rev.: +DOMINЄ×NЄ×IN×FVRORЄ×TVO×ᴧRGVᴧS×MЄ
Lawrence 1 (but different dies from **88**); North 1239; Seaby 1507. Ex Lockett (3018).

90 Quarter-noble
    1.84   28.3   310°
Obv.: +°ЄDWᴧRD×DЄI×GRᴧ×RЄX×ᴧNGL   Curule Ӿ (North 16).
Rev.: +ЄӾᴧLTᴧBITVR×IN×GLORIᴧ   Curule Ӿ (North 16). Lis in centre.
Lawrence 1; North 1244; Seaby 1511. Bt Spink 1960.

91 Quarter-noble
    1.87   28.8   330°
Obv.: +°ЄDWᴧRD×DЄI×GRᴧ×RЄX×ᴧNGL   Curule Ӿ (North 16).
Rev.: +ЄӾᴧLTᴧBITVR×IN×GLORIᴧ   Curule Ӿ (North 16). Lis in centre.
Lawrence 2, var. with ᴧ in GRᴧ barred; North 1244; Seaby 1511. No provenance.

FOURTH COINAGE (*cont.*)

Treaty Period (*cont.*)

REGULAR TREATY SERIES (*cont.*)

Calais mint

Characteristics: obv. (a) flag at the stern of the ship on some coins.
                  (b) trefoils either side of Ƨ on all except Group d (with quatrefoils before ꬃD, which does not occur for
                    London).
         rev.   letter Ɑ in centre.

Group a – saltire before ꬃDWⱯRD.

92 Noble			
	Weight		*Die-axis*
	g	*gr.*	
	7.09	109.4	0°

Obv.: ×ꬃD/WⱯRDːDꬃIːGRⱯ×RꬃXːⱯ∩GLːDΠSːhƴB·Ƨ·Ɐꝺ/T
Ornaments, –11–11. Ropes, 3/2. Quatrefoils, 4/4. Lis, 4. Saltire before
ꬃDWⱯRD alongside fold of sail. No flag at stern. Same die as
next coin, **93**.
Rev.: ✠Ih·Ɑː ⱯVTꬃMːTRⱯ∩SIꬃ∩SːPꬃR×MꬃDIVːILLORVMːIBⱯT
Lawrence 1; North 1234; Seaby 1505. Ex Doubleday (264); ex Carter.

93 Noble			
	7.68	118.5	350°

Obv.: same die as last coin, **92**.
Rev.: ✠Ih·Ɑː ⱯVTꬃMːTRⱯ∩SIꬃ∩SːPꬃR×MꬃDIVːILLORVMːIBⱯT
Lawrence 1; North 1234; Seaby 1505. Bt Spink auction 81, 19.11.1990 (6).

94 Noble			
	7.75	119.6	40°

Obv.: ×ꬃD/WⱯRDːDꬃIːGRⱯ×RꬃXːⱯ∩GLːDΠSːhƴB·Ƨ·Ɐꝺ/T·
Ornaments, –11–11. Ropes, 3/2. Quatrefoils, 3/2. Lis, 4. Flag at stern. Saltire
before ꬃDWⱯRD *above* fold of sail.
Rev.: ✠Ih·Ɑː ⱯVTꬃMːTRⱯ∩SIꬃ∩SːPꬃR×MꬃDIVːILLORVMːIBⱯT
Lawrence 2; North 1234; Seaby 1504. Ex Doubleday (265).

95 Half-noble			
	3.16	48.7	10°
	(clipped)		

Obv.: ×ꬃD/[WⱯRD·DꬃI·G·RꬃX×Ɐ∩GL]ːDːhƴB·Ƨ·Ɐꝺ/T
Ornaments, –11–11. Ropes, 3/2. Quatrefoils, 3/2(?). Lis, 4. Flag at stern.
Rev.: ✠DOMIꬃ[∩ꬃ× ∩·FVORꬃ]ːTVOːⱯRGVⱯSːMꬃ
Lawrence 2; North 1240; Seaby 1508. Ex Doubleday (270); ex Lawrence.

Group b – no mark before ꬃDWⱯRD.

96 Noble			
	7.74	119.4	80°

Obv.: ꬃD/WⱯRDːDꬃIːGRⱯ×RꬃXːⱯ∩GLːDΠSːhƴB·Ƨ·Ɐꝺ/T
Ornaments, –11–11. Ropes, 3/2. Quatrefoils, 4/4. Lis, 4. No flag at stern.
Rev.: ✠IhɑːⱯVTꬃMːTRⱯ∩SIꬃ∩SːPꬃR×MꬃDIVːILLORVM×IBⱯT
Lawrence 3; North 1235; Seaby 1505. Bt Spink 1971.

97 Noble			
	7.71	119.0	270°

Obv.: ꬃD/WⱯRD×DꬃIːGRⱯ×RꬃXːⱯ∩GLːDΠSːhƴB·Ƨ·Ɐꝺ/T
Ornaments, –11–11. Ropes, 3/2. Quatrefoils, 4/4. Lis, 4. Flag at stern.
Rev.: ✠IhɑːⱯVTꬃMːTRⱯ∩SIꬃ∩SːPꬃR×MꬃDIVːILLORVM×IBⱯT
Lawrence 4; North 1235; Seaby 1505. Ex Doubleday (267).

98 Half-noble			
	3.86	59.5	270°

Obv.: ꬃD/WⱯRDːDꬃIːG·RꬃXːⱯ∩GLːDːhƴB·Ƨ·Ɐꝺ/T·
Ornaments, –11–11. Ropes, 3/2. Quatrefoils, 3/2. Lis, 4. Flag at stern.
Rev.: ✠DOMIꬃː∩ꬃ×I∩·FVRORꬃːTVOːⱯRGVⱯSːMꬃ
Lawrence 4; North 1241; Seaby 1508. Bt Spink 1971.

[*continued overleaf*]

PLATE 9

92　　　　　　93　　　　　　94

96　　　　　　97

95　　　　　　98

99　　　　　　100　　　　　　101

Plate 9 (*cont.*)

99 Quarter-noble
    1.86   28.7   0°

Obv.: ✚ⰄDWⰀRD⫶DⰄI⫶GRⰀ⫶RⰄX⫶ⰀⲚGL'   Curule X
    (North 16). Cross in circle over shield. Dotted L in ⰀⲚGL.
Rev.: ✚ⰄXⰀLTⰀBITVR⫶IⲚ⫶GLORIⰀ   Curule X (North 16). Annulet in centre.
Lawrence 2; North 1245; Seaby 1513. Bt Spink 1972, ex Beresford-Jones.

100 Quarter-noble
    1.83   28.1   180°

Obv.: ✚˙ⰄDWⰀRD⫶DⰄI⫶GRⰀ⫶RⰄX⫶ⰀⲚGL'   Large pellet before ⰄDWⰀRD.
    Curule X (North 16). Cross in circle over shield. Dotted L in ⰀⲚGL.
Rev.: ✚ⰄXⰀLTⰀBITVR⫶IⲚ⫶GLORIⰀ   Curule X (North 16). Annulet in centre.
Lawrence 3; North 1245; Seaby 1513. Bt Baldwin 1973.

101 Quarter-noble
    1.79   27.6   140°

Obv.: ✚ⰄDWⰀRD⫶DⰄI⫶GRⰀ⫶RⰄX⫶ⰀⲚGL   Plain cross over shield.
Rev.: ✚ⰄXⰀLTⰀBITVR⫶IⲚ˟GLORIⰀ   Voided quatrefoil in centre.
Lawrence 4; North 1246; Seaby 1514. Ex Doubleday (278); ex Lawrence.

FOURTH COINAGE (*cont.*)

Treaty Period (*cont.*)

REGULAR TREATY SERIES (*cont.*)

Calais mint (cont.)

Group d – voided quatrefoil before ЄDWΛRD on the noble and half-noble and in the centre of the reverse on the quarter-noble.

102 Noble

	Weight		
	g	*gr.*	*Die-axis*
	7.19	110.9	10°

Obv.: ✣ЄD/WΛRD꞉DЄI꞉GRΛ꞉RЄX꞉ΛNGL꞉DNS꞉hУB·Σ˙ΛQ/T
Ornaments, –11–11. Ropes, 3/2. Quatrefoils, 3/2(?). Lis, 4. Flag at stern.
Saltires either side of Σ.
Rev.: ✚IhC꞉ΛVTЄM꞉TRΛNSIЄNS꞉PЄR꞉MЄDIV꞉ILLORVM꞉IBΛT
Lawrence 5; North 1236; Seaby 1504. Ex Doubleday (269); ex Lawrence.

103 Half-noble
3.49   53.8   270°

Obv.: ✣ЄD/WΛR[ ]DЄI꞉G꞉RЄX꞉ΛNGL꞉D꞉hУB·Σ˙ΛQ/T
Ornaments, –11–11. Ropes, 3/2. Quatrefoils, 3/2. Lis, 4. Flag at stern.
Saltires either side of Σ.
Rev.: ✚DOMINЄ꞉NЄ꞉IN꞉FVRORЄ꞉TVO꞉ΛRGVΛS꞉MЄ
Same die as 110. Lawrence 5; North 1242; Seaby 1508. Ex Doubleday (273).

104 Quarter-noble
1.90   29.3   220°

Obv.: ✚˙ЄDWΛRD꞉DЄI꞉GRΛ꞉RЄX꞉ΛNGL'   Annulet before ЄDWΛRD.
Curule X (North 16). Crescent over shield. Same die as next coin, **105**.
Rev.: ✚ЄXΛLTΛBITVR꞉IN꞉GLORIΛ   Curule X (North 16). Voided quatrefoil
in centre. Same die as next coin, **105**.
Similar to Lawrence 5, who illustrated the variety on pl. XX(IV), 12 (same dies as this
coin) but did not describe it; North 1246; Seaby 1515. Bt Baldwin 1972, ex
Winstanley.

105 Quarter-noble
1.86   28.6   200°

Obv.: same die as last coin, **104**.
Rev.: same die as last coin, **104**.
Although a die duplicate of the last coin both are included as each shows features not
visible on the other. Similar to Lawrence 5 (see above); North 1246; Seaby 1515. Bt
Spink 1991.

Calais/London mule

106 Half-noble
3.85   59.4   160°

Obv.: ЄD/WΛRD꞉DЄI꞉G꞉RЄX꞉ΛNGL꞉D꞉hУB·Σ˙ΛQ/T'
Ornaments, –11–11. Ropes, 3/2. Quatrefoils, 3/2. Lis, 4. No mark before
ЄDWΛRD. No flag at stern. Trefoils either side of Σ.
Rev.: ✚DOMINЄ꞉NЄ꞉IN꞉FVRORЄ꞉TVO꞉ΛRGVΛS꞉MЄ
Є in centre. Weak trefoil in second spandrel of first quarter. Second Λ of
ΛRGVΛS barred as usual for this group. S of ΛRGVΛS with pellet at waist.
Obverse of Group b, Lawrence 3 (Calais), pl. XX(IV), 5 (same die) used with a
normal Calais reverse with Cl in the centre. Reverse of Group b, Lawrence 1–3
(London). Same obverse die as Doubleday 271. North 1241/1239; Seaby 1509/1507.
Bt Seaby April 1970 (*SCMB* April 1970, no. G413).

[*continued overleaf*]

PLATE 10

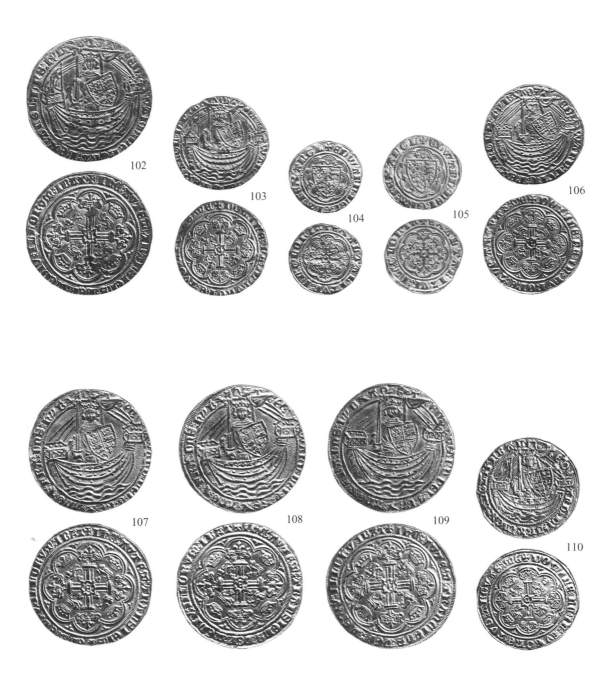

102

103

104

105

106

107

108

109

110

Plate 10 (*cont.*)

Post Treaty Period (1369–77)

As noted by Mitchell in the Doubleday sale catalogue,[349] the second of Lawrence's three groups consists of mules between the first and third groups. Furthermore, Lawrence omits to number the headings for the London nobles in his lists (pp. 221–2). Accordingly, for this section, the same ordering has been adopted as that used by Mitchell, and London coins are grouped on the same basis as that used for the Calais pieces; that is to say:

Group I: obverse lettering of Treaty style but with French title, FRΛ. Reverse as Treaty issues (sometimes considered mules). Of 9 obverse dies listed by Potter, 6 have a crescent on the forecastle.

Group III: tall Post-Treaty lettering. French title FRΛNC. Fore- and stern-castles crenellated (nobles only).

GROUP I

London mint

107 Noble
7.71 119.0 260°

Obv.: ◦ED/WΛRD⁝DEI⁝G⁝RE×X×ΛNG⁝Σ×FRΛ⁝DNS⁝hYB⁝Σ×ĀQ/T
Ornaments, –11–11. Ropes, 3/2. Quatrefoils, 4/4. Lis, 3(?). Annulet before EDWΛRD. Saltire between E and X of REX. Crescent on forecastle. Ā of ĀQ/T barred. With bowsprit. Same die as next coin, **108**.
Rev.: +Ih'C⁝ΛVTEM⁝TRΛNSIENS⁝PER⁝MEDIV⁝ILLORVM⁝IBĀT
Ā of IBĀT barred. E in centre.
Similar to Lawrence group I, 1–3 but another variety. Lawrence illustrates a coin from the same dies as this one on his pl. XIX(III), 1 which is not listed in detail and is erroneously described in the key to the plate as a Treaty/Post Treaty mule, instead of the other way about. This was corrected by Whitton in his *Additional Notes*.[350] The same obverse die is also illustrated by Lawrence on his pl. XX(IV), 1 used with a reverse with an inverted C in the centre and thus attributed to Calais. Potter 1964 cites the coin here described as well as another from the same dies in the Doubleday collection (lot 281 in the sale) and designates the obverse die as his no. 2. North 1277; Seaby 1517. Bt Spink 1953.

108 Noble
7.57 116.8 300°

Obv.: same die as last coin, **107**, but now in a rusty condition.
Rev.: +IhC⁝ΛVTEM⁝TRΛNSIENS⁝PER⁝MEDIV⁝ILLORVM⁝IBĀT
Ā of IBĀT barred. E in centre.
For the obverse see the notes on the previous coin, **107**. The reverse, too, is very similar to that used on the last coin, even to the extent of using some of the same letter punches (for example, M with a flawed centre upright) but is definitely from a different die.
Potter obverse 2; North 1277; Seaby 1517. Bt Glendining sale 25.9.1968 (8).

Calais mint

109 Noble
7.76 119.7 90°

Obv.: ◦ED/WΛRD⁝DEI⁝G⁝REX⁝ΛNG××Σ××FRΛ⁝DNS⁝hYB⁝Σ×ΛQ/T
Ornaments, –11–11. Ropes, 3/2. Quatrefoils, 4/4. Lis, 4. No flag at stern. Crescent on forecastle.
Rev.: +IhC⁝ΛVTEM⁝TRΛNSIENS⁝PER⁝MEDIV̇⁝ILLORV⁝IBĀT Ā of IBĀT barred. C struck over a pellet in the centre (rather than an E). Pellet at the base of the top lis.
Lawrence 2 (Calais); Potter obv. die 9 (London); same obv. die as Doubleday 282 – see also the note under that lot no.; North 1279; Seaby 1522. Ex Doubleday (296); ex Lawrence.

[349] Mitchell 1972.
[350] Whitton 1941–4a.

Plate 10 (*cont.*)

Calais mint

110 Half-noble
    3.89   60.0   300°

Obv.: Є'DW/ΛRD⁝DĪ·GRΛ⁝RЄX×ΛΠGL⁝Ƨ·FRΛΠC
Ornaments, 1–1–1. Ropes, 3/1. Quatrefoils, 3/2 (?). Lis, 4/3. Fore- and stern-castles plain. Annulet at base of shield. Flag at stern.

Rev.: +DOMIΠЄ⁝ΠЄ⁝⁝IΠ⁝FVRORЄ⁝TVO⁝ΛRGVΛS⁝MЄ   Ɑ in centre. Λs unbarred. Same die as **103**. Lawrence group III/Treaty d; North 1283/1242; Seaby 1525. Ex Spink Noble sale, Sydney, 17.11.1993 (2627); ex Raynes (19).

FOURTH COINAGE (*cont.*)

Post-Treaty Period (*cont.*)

MULE GROUP III/GROUP I (i.e. Lawrence's Group II)

Calais mint

111 Noble			
	Weight		
	g	*gr.*	*Die-axis*
	7.71	119.0	270°

Obv.: ✠/ƐDW/ΛRD ⁚ DI × GRΛ × RƐX × ΛNGL ⁚ Ⱶ × FRΛNƆ ⁚ DNS × ⱵIB ⁚ Ⱶ ⁚ ΛQVIT ⁚
Ornaments, 1–1–1–1. Ropes, 3/1. Quatrefoils, 5/4.
Lis, 4. Post-treaty lettering. Flag at stern. Quatrefoil above sail.

Rev.: ✠IⱵƆ ⁚ ΛVTƐM ⁚ TRΛNSIƐNS ⁚ PƐR ⁚ MƐDIV ⁚ ILLORVM ⁚ IBΛT
Late Treaty style. Ⱥ in IBΛT barred. Probably Ɔ in centre.
Obverse similar to Lawrence Group II, 2 (pl. XX(IV), 2) but this coin has no pellets visible below the shield. The reverse is similar to the same coin, but from other dies. Potter reported three obverse dies of this type. North 1280/1232–3; Seaby 1520. Ex Doubleday (300); ex Bredgar hoard.

GROUP III

London mint

112 Noble		
7.65	118.1	0°

Obv.: °ƐDW/[ΛRD × D ⁚ GRΛ × RƐX]× ΛNGL ⁚ Ⱶ × FRΛNƆ ⁚ DNS × ⱵIB ⁚ Ⱶ × ΛQ
Bracketted section of the legend is somewhat 'scrambled' due to double striking. Ornaments, 1–1–1–1. Ropes, 3/1. Quatrefoils, 4/4. Lis, 4. Annulet over sail. With bowsprit.

Rev.: ✠IⱵƆ ⁚ ΛVTƐM ⁚ TRΛNSIƐNS ⁚ PƐR ⁚ MƐDIVM ⁚ ILLORVM ⁚ IBΛT ⁚
Annulet at the point of the tressure under IⱵƆ. Small cross in front the central Ɛ. Pellet at base of top lis. Ⱥ in IBΛT is chevron barred.
Lawrence 5 and pl. XIX(III), 4, this coin; North 1278; Seaby 1519. Ex Lockett (1265); ex P. W. P. Carlyon-Britton; ex Walters, 1913 (130).

113 Noble		
7.77	118.8	260°

Obv.: °/ƐDW/ΛRD ⁚ DI × GRΛ × RƐX × ΛNGL ⁚ Ⱶ × FRΛNƆ ⁚ DNS × ⱵIB ⁚ Ⅎ × ΛQVIT
Ornaments, 1–1–1–1. Ropes, 3/1. Quatrefoils, 5/4. Lis, 4. With bowsprit.

Rev.: ✠IⱵƆ ⁚ ΛVTƐM ⁚ TRΛNSIƐNS ⁚ PƐR ⁚ MƐDIVM ⁚ ILLORVM ⁚ IBΛT   Ⱥ in IBΛT is chevron barred. Small cross in front of central Ɛ. Small pellets at base and sides of top lis.
Lawrence 8 and pl. XIX (III), 5; Doubleday 291; North 1278; Seaby 1519. Ex Lockett (3980); ex Ready (311).

114 Noble		
7.71	119.0	180°

Obv.: ƐDW/ΛRD × DI ⁚ GR̄Λ × RƐX × ΛNGL × Ⅎ × FRΛNƆ ⁚ DNS × ⱵIB ⁚ Ⱶ × ΛQV/T
Ornaments, 1–1–1–1. Ropes, 3/1. Quatrefoils, ?/4. Lis, 4. No annulet before ƐDWΛRD. With bowsprit.

Rev.: ✠IⱵƆ ⁚ ΛVTƐM ⁚ TRΛNSIƐNS ⁚ PƐR ⁚ MƐDIVM ⁚ ILLORV ⁚ IBΛT   Ⱥ of IBΛT is chevron barred. Pellet in front of the central Ɛ.
Lawrence does not record the reading ΛQV/T but another example is Pinchbeck 65. The reverse is Lawrence 15. Potter (p. 317) has one die with the reading ΛQVT. North 1278; Seaby 1518. No provenance.

[*continued overleaf*]

PLATE 11

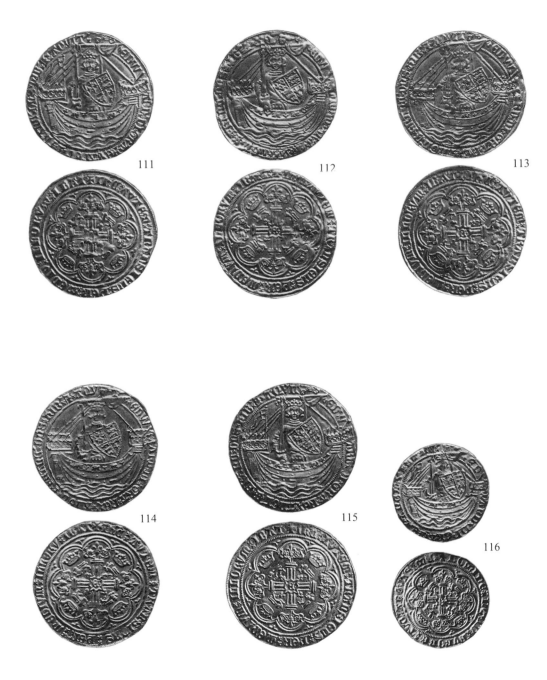

111

112

113

114

115

116

Plate 11 (*cont.*)

Calais mint

115 Noble
   7.74 119.4   250°

Obv.: ✥/ƐDW/ΛRD·DĪ·GRΛ×RƐX×ΛΠGL⦂Ħ·FRΛΠꝈ⦂DΠ̄S·ҺIB⦂Ħ×ΛꝒVIT
Ornaments, 1–1–1–1. Ropes, 3/1. Quatrefoils, 5/4. Lis, 4. Flag at stern.
Quatrefoil above sail. Two tiny pellets below shield,

Rev.: ✠IҺꝈ⦂ΛVTƐM⦂TRΛΠSIƐΠS⦂PƐR⦂MƐDIVM⦂ILLORVM⦂IBΛT
Λ of IBΛT barred. Pellet in front of central Ɛ. Small pellets either side and at
the base of upper and lower lis.
Obverse similar to Lawrence Gp. III, 2 but no saltire after IBΛT and Λ of IBΛT
unbarred. Potter reports six obverse dies of this type. North 1281; Seaby 1521. Bt
Spink 1972; ex Beresford-Jones; ex Lockett (3988). Said to have been found in
Canterbury.

116 Half-noble
   3.87   59.7   20°

Obv.: ✠/ƐD/WΛRD⦂DI·GRΛ·RƐX·ΛΠGL·Ꙅ·FRΛꝈ⦂
Ornaments, 1–1–1. Ropes,3/1. Quatrefoils, 3/3. Lis, 4. Flag at stern. Quatrefoil
over sail. No crenellations on the fore- and stern-castles and no pellets at rope
ends.

Rev.: ✠DOMIΠƐ⦂ΠƐ⦂IΠ⦂FVRORƐ⦂TVO⦂ΛRGVΛS⦂MƐ×
The letter in the centre is possibly from a broken Ɛ punch
Lawrence 3; Potter obverse die 3; North 1283; Seaby 1524. Ex Doubleday (312); ex
Lawrence.

RICHARD II (22 June 1377–29 September 1399)

Gold coins issued at a fineness of 23 ct 3½ gr. (0.995 fine) and a nominal weight of 120 gr. (7.78 g) to the noble. Denominations issued were noble, half-noble and quarter-noble. Gold coins were struck at the mints of London and Calais.

Classified according to Webb Ware (not yet published but see p. xxx for a summary based on his paper read to the British Numismatic Society and the notes then circulated).

Edward III/Richard II mules

Calais mint

117 Noble

	Weight		
	g	*gr.*	*Die-axis*
	6.95	107.2	160°
	(clipped)		

Obv.: ΕDW/ΛRD·DI·GRΛ·RΕX·ΛNGL[-]FRΛNΘ·DNS×hIB·Ꝛ×ΛQVIT
Ornaments, 1–1–1–1. Ropes, 3/1. Quatrefoils, 5/4. Flag at stern. Quatrefoil above sail (off flan on this specimen).

Rev.: +IhΘ×ΛVTΕM×TRΛNSIΕNS×PΕR·MΕDIVM×ILLORV×IBΛT
R in centre. Letter forms of new Richard II type (Type I).
Lawrence Group 3,8/Webb Ware 1b; North 1280/1306; Seaby 1520/1659. Ex Doubleday (315); ex Lawrence.

118 Half-noble
3.85   59.4   130°

Obv.: ΕDW/ΛRD⋮DI·GRΛ·RΕX ΛNGL·Σ·FRΛNΘ
Ornaments, 1–1–1. Ropes, 3/1. Quatrefoils, perhaps 3/3. Lis, 3(?). Flag at stern. Voided quatrefoil over sail.

Rev.: +DOMINΕ×NΕ⋮IN×FVRORΕ⋮TVO⋮ΛRGVΛS⋮MΕ   R in centre. Letter forms of Edward III type.
Lawrence this die pl. XX(IV), 6 (post-treaty)/Webb Ware 1a; North 1283/1313; Seaby 1524/1668. Bt Spink 1981.

Richard II/Edward III mules

London mint

119 Half-noble
3.78   58.3   100°

Obv.: RIΘ/ΛRD×DI·GRΛ·RΕX·ΛNGL⋮[   ]   (end of legend jumbled through double striking). Ornaments, none. Ropes, 3/1. Quatrefoils, 2/2(?). RIΘ struck over ΕDW. Uncertain symbol over sail.

Rev.: +DOMINΕ×NΕ⋮IN[   ]×ΛRGVΛS⋮MΕ   Ε and pellet in centre of reverse.
The obverse die is Webb Ware 1a. The reverse die is similar to the Post Treaty die described in Lawrence 1937 on p. 223. For the obverse die see also Whitton 1944 which suggests that in its unaltered form this is an unfinished Post Treaty die of Edward III. North 1309/1282; Seaby 1664/1523. Bt Baldwin 1959.

True coins of Richard II

FIRST ISSUE (Edward III style)

TYPE 1a

Characteristics: Edward III lettering; nobles and half-nobles with lis over sail and with French title. Ropes are 3/1. Quarter-nobles with R in centre of reverse.

London mint only

120 Noble
7.76   119.7   45°

Obv.: RIΘ·/ΛRD⋮DI·GRΛ·RΕX·ΛNGL⋮Ꝛ·FRΛNΘ⋮DNS×hIB⋮Ꝛ·ΛQ'
Ornaments, 1–1–1–1. Quatrefoils, 5/4. Same die as next two coins, **121, 122**.

Rev.: +IhΘ⋮ΛVTΕM⋮TRΛNSIΕNS⋮PΕR⋮MΕDIVM⋮ILLORVM⋮IBΛT⋮
Last Λ̄ chevron-barred.
Webb Ware 1a; North 1301; Seaby 1654. Ex Potter; ex Bruun (351).

121 Noble
7.73   118.5   110°

Obv.: same die as last and next coins, **120, 122**.

Rev.: +IhΘ×ΛVTΕM×TRΛNSIΕNS×PΕR×MΕDIVM×ILLOR V̄×IBΛT
Last Λ̄ chevron-barred.
Webb Ware 1a; North 1301; Seaby 1654. Ex Glendining sale 31.3.1965 (115).

[continued overleaf]

PLATE 12

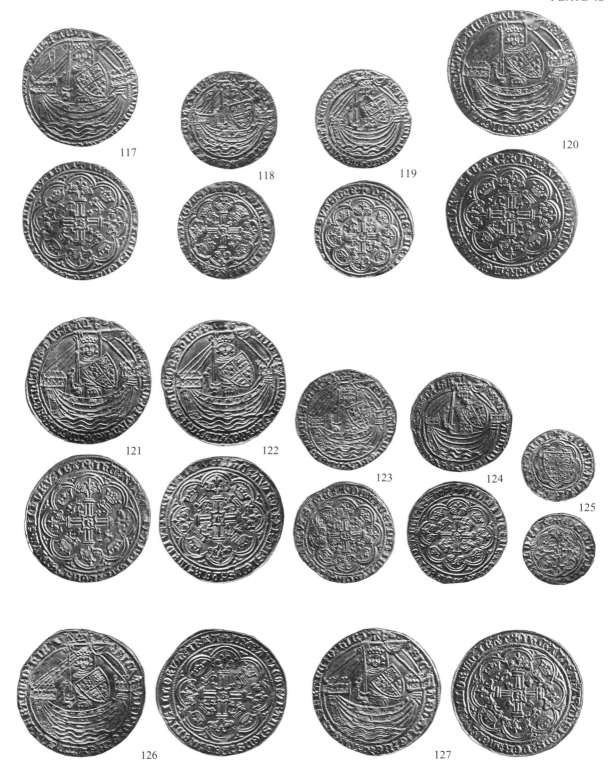

117

118

119

120

121

122

123

124

125

126

127

Plate 12 (*cont.*)

122 Noble
7.68 118.5 0°

Obv.: same die as last two coins, **120**, **121**.
Rev.: +IhC:AVTEM:TRANSIENS:PER:MEDIV:ILLORV:IBĀT
Last Ā chevron-barred.
Webb Ware 1a; North 1301; Seaby 1654. Bt Baldwin 1973, ex 'Polish Hoard'.

123 Half-noble
3.78 58.3 160°

Obv.: RIC/ARD:DI×G×REX×ANGL:7×F×DNS×hIB:7×AQ'
Ornaments, –1–1–1–. Quatrefoils, 2/4. RIC struck over EDW. Uncertain whether lis over sail.
Rev.: +DOMINE:NE:IN:FVRORE:TVO:ARGVAS:ME:
Webb Ware 1a; North 1309; Seaby 1664. Bt Spink 1965; ex Thompson; ex Lockett (3051).

124 Half-noble
3.86 59.6 45°

Obv.: RIC/ARD:DI×GRA×REX×ANGL:7×FR:D×h:A× No lis or lions on side of ship. Quatrefoils, 3/4. Annulet over sail. RIC over EDW. In spite of apparent differences may be same die as **119**.
Rev.: +DOMINE:NE:IN:FVRORE:TVO:ARGVAS:ME R in centre struck over E.
Webb Ware 1a; North 1309; Seaby 1664. Ex Mygind; ex Bridgewater House (7).

125 Quarter-noble
1.80 27.8 30°

Obv.: +RICARD:DEI:GRA:REX:ANGL
Rev.: +EXALTABITVR:IN:GLORIA×
Webb Ware 1a; North 1317; Seaby 1672. No provenance.

TYPE 1b

Characteristics: new lettering, annulet (London) or quatrefoil (Calais) over sail on nobles and half-nobles.

London mint

126 Noble
7.77 120.0 50°

Obv.: RIC/ARD:D:G:REX:ANGL:Σ×FRANC:D:hIB:Σ×AQ'
Ornaments, 1–1–1–1. Quatrefoils, 5/4.
Rev.: ✠IhC:AVTEM:TRANSIENS:PER:MEDIV:ILLORVM:IBĀT
Last Ā chevron-barred.
The distinctive reverse i.m. is known from one die from which three coins are in the BM and two were in the Lockett sale (lots 1327 and 4281). See also the quarter-noble, **139**. Webb Ware 1b; North 1302; Seaby 1655. Bt Christie sale 28.2.1989 (74); ex Pinchbeck Hoard.

127 Noble
7.64 117.9 130°

Obv.: RIC/ARD:DI:G:REX:ANGL:Σ:FRANC:D:hIB×Σ×A
Ornaments, 1–1–1–1. Quatrefoils, 5/4. Same die as next coin, **128**.
Rev.: +IhC:AVTEM:TRANSIENS:PER:MEDIV:ILLORVM:IBAT
Webb Ware 1b; North 1302; Seaby 1655. No provenance.

FIRST ISSUE (Edward III style) (*cont.*)

TYPE 1b (*cont.*)

London mint (cont.)

128 Noble			
	Weight		
	g	*gr.*	*Die-axis*
	7.71	119.9	260°

Obv.: same die as last coin, **127**.
Rev.: +IhᏟᎥᎯVTᎬMᎥTRᎯNSIᎬNSᎥPᎬRᎥMᎬDIVMᎥILLORVᎥIBᎯT

Webb Ware 1b; North 1302; Seaby 1655. Bt Spink 1968; ex Bernstein.

129 Noble		
7.64	117.9	200°

Obv.: RIᏟ/RDᎥᎥDᎥGᎥRᎬXᎥᎯNGLᎥᎥᏚᎥFRᎯNᏟᎥDᎥhIBᎥᎥᏚᎥᎯᏟ
Ornaments, 1–1–1–1. Quatrefoils, 5/4. Same die as next coin, **130**.
Rev.: +IhᏟᎥᎯVTᎬMᎥTRᎯNSIᎬNSᎥPᎬRᎥMᎬDIV̄ᎥILLORV̄ᎥIBᎯT
Last Ᏼ̄ chevron-barred.
Webb Ware 1b; North 1302; Seaby 1655. No provenance.

130 Noble		
7.71	119.0	280°

Obv.: same die as last coin, **129**. Annulet over sail not visible.
Rev.: +IhᏟᎥᎯVTᎬMᎥTRᎯNSIᎬNSᎥPᎬRᎥMᎬDIVᎥILLORVᎥIBᎯT
Last Ᏼ̄ chevron-barred.
Webb Ware 1b; North 1302; Seaby 1655. Ex Williams (148).

131 Noble		
7.75	119.6	70°

Obv.: RIᏟ/ᎯRDᎥDᎥGᎥRᎬXᎥᎯNGLᎥᎥᏚᎥFRᎯNᏟᎥDᎥhIBᎥᎥᏚᎥᎯᏟ'
Ornaments, 1–1–1–1. Quatrefoils, 5/4. Same die as next coin. **132**.
Rev.: +IhᏟᎥᎯWTᎬMᎥTRᎯNSIᎬNSᎥPᎬRᎥMᎬDIVᎥILLORVMᎥIBᎯ
Webb Ware 1b; North 1302; Seaby 1655. Bt Christie sale 28.2.1989 (76); ex Pinchbeck Hoard.

132 Noble		
7.76	119.7	350°

Obv.: same die as last coin, **131**.
Rev.: +IhᏟᎥᎯVTᎬMᎥTRᎯNSIᎬNSᎥPᎬRᎥMᎬDIVᎥILLORVᎥIBᎯT
Last Ᏼ̄ chevron-barred.
Webb Ware 1b; North 1302; Seaby 1655. Bt Spink 1955.

133 Noble		
7.71	119.9	190°

Obv.: RIᏟ/ᎯRDᎥDIᎥGᎥRᎬXᎥᎯNGLᎥᎥᏚᎥFRᎯNᏟᎥDᎥhIBᎥᎥᏚᎥᎯᏟ'
Ornaments, 1–1–1–1. Quatrefoils, 5/4. No mark clearly visible over sail.
Rev.: +IhᏟᎥᎯVTᎬMᎥTRᎯNSIᎬNSᎥPᎬRᎥMᎬDIVᎥILLORVMᎥIBᎯT
Legend starts at 11 o'clock.
Webb Ware 1b; North 1302; Seaby 1655. Bt Spink 1961; ex Caines.

134 Noble		
7.75	119.1	350°

Obv.: RIᏟ/ᎯRDᎥDᎥGᎥRᎬXᎥᎯNGLᎥᎥᏚᎥFRᎯNᏟᎥDᎥhIBᎥᎥᏚᎥᎯᏟ'
Ornaments, 1–1–1–1. Quatrefoils, 5/4.
Rev.: +IhᏟᎥᎯVTᎬMᎥTRᎯNSIᎬNSᎥPᎬRᎥMᎬDIVᎥILLORVMᎥIBᎯT
Webb Ware 1b; North 1302; Seaby 1655. Bt Spink.

135 Half-noble		
3.78	58.4	20°

Obv.: RIᏟ/ᎯRDᎥDIᎥGᎥRᎬXᎥᎯNGLᎥᎥᏚᎥFRᎯNᏟᎥDᎥh
Ornaments, 1–1–1. Quatrefoils, 3/4. No annulet visible above sail.
Rev.: +DOMINᎬᎥNᎬᎥIN FVRORᎬᎥTVOᎥᎯRGVᎯSᎥMᎬ
Same die as next coin, **136**.
Webb Ware 1b; North 1310 var. because no annulet above sail; Seaby 1665 var. for the same reason. No provenance.

136 Half-noble		
3.77	58.2	310°

Obv.: RIᏟ/ᎯRDᎥDᎥGᎥRᎬXᎥᎯNGLᎥᎥᏚᎥFᎥDᎥhIBᎥᎥᏚᎥᎯ
Ornaments, –1–1–. Quatrefoils, 4/3. Saltire (or crosslet) above sail.
Rev.: same die as last coin, **135**.
Webb Ware 1b; North 1310 var. because saltire instead of annulet over sail; Seaby 1665 var. for same reason. No provenance.

137 Half-noble		
3.85	59.3	140°

Obv.: RIᏟ/ᎯRDᎥDᎥGᎥRᎬXᎥᎯNGLᎥᎥᏚᎥFᎥDᎥhIBᎥᎥᏚᎥᎯᏟ
Ornaments, –1–1–. Quatrefoils, 3/3(?). Saltire over sail.
Rev.: +DOMINᎬᎥNᎬᎥINᎥFVRORᎬᎥTVOᎥᎯRGVᎯSᎥMᎬˣ   R over Ꭼ in centre.
Webb Ware 1b; North 1310 var. because saltire instead of annulet over sail; Seaby 1665 var. for the same reason. Bt Baldwin; ex Carter.

PLATE 13

128

129

130

131

132

133

134

135

136

137

FIRST ISSUE (Edward III type) (*cont.*)

TYPE 1b (*cont.*)

London mint (cont.)

138 Quarter-noble			
	Weight		*Die-axis*
	g	*gr.*	
	1.91	29.4	330°

Obv.: ✠RIⴵARD⦂DⴲI⦂GRⴷ⦂RⴲX⦂ⴷNGL
Rev.: ✠ⴲXⴷLTⴷBITVR⦂IN⦂GLORIⴷ

Webb Ware 1b; North 1318 (4); Seaby 1673. Ex Lockett (3053).

139 Quarter-noble		
1.95	30.1	130°

Obv.: ✠RIⴵARD⦂DI⦂GRⴷ⦂RⴲX⦂ⴷNG⦂ Same die as next coin, **140**, and **157**.
Rev.: ✠ⴲXⴷLTⴷBITVR⦂IN⦂GLORIⴷ For a similar initial cross see also the noble, **126**.
Webb Ware 1b; North 1318 (4) var. with pellets around the initial cross; Seaby 1673 var. for the same reason. Ex Lockett (1338).

140 Quarter-noble		
1.72	26.5	40°

Obv.: same die as last coin, **139**, and **157**.
Rev.: ✠ⴲXⴷLTⴷBITVR⦂IN⦂GLORIⴷ
Webb Ware 1b; North 1318 (4); Seaby 1673. Ex Lockett (3054).

141 Quarter-noble		
1.93	29.8	230°

Obv.: ✠RIⴵARD⦂D⦂GRⴷ⦂RⴲX⦂ⴷNGL⦂Σ⦂F'
Slipped trefoil (or lis?) over shield.
Rev.: ✠ⴲXⴷLTⴷBITVR⦂IN⦂GLORIⴷ'
Webb Ware 1b; North 1318 (2); Seaby 1677. Ex Lockett (1337).

Calais mint (flag at stern)

142 Noble		
7.51	116.0	160°

Obv.: RIⴵ/ARD⦂D⦂G⦂RⴲX⦂ⴷNGL⦂Σ⦂FRⴷNⴵ⦂D⦂hIB⦂Σ⦂ⴷⵕ
Ornaments, 1–1–1–1. Quatrefoils, 5/4.
Rev.: ✠Ihⴵ⦂ⴷVTⴲM⦂TRⴷNSIⴲNS⦂PⴲR⦂MⴲDIV⦂ILLORV̄⦂IBⴷT
Webb Ware 1b; North 1306; Seaby -. Ex Mygind.

143 Half-noble		
3.87	59.8	80°

Obv.: RIⴵ/ARD⦂D⦂G⦂RⴲX⦂ⴷNGL⦂Σ⦂F⦂D⦂hIB⦂Σ⦂ⴷⵕ'
Ornaments, 1–1–1. Quatrefoils, 4/3. Voided quatrefoil over sail.
Rev.: ✠DOMINⴲ⦂Nⴲ⦂IN FVRORⴲ⦂TVO⦂ARGVⴷS⦂Mⴲ
Webb Ware 1b; North 1314; Seaby 1669. Ex 'Ridgemount' (139)

SECOND ISSUE (French title omitted)

TYPE 2a

Characteristics: crude style; noble and half-noble with saltire over sail (London) or no marks (Calais).

London mint

144 Noble		
7.75	119.6	190°

Obv.: RIⴵ/ARD⦂DⴲI⦂GRⴷ⦂RⴲX⦂ⴷNGL⦂DNS⦂hIB⦂Σ⦂ⴷⵕ
Ornaments, 1–1–1–1. Ropes, 3/2. Quatrefoils, 5/4. No mark clearly visible above sail.
Rev.: ✠Ihⴵ⦂ⴷVTⴲM⦂TRⴷNSIⴲNS⦂PⴲR⦂MⴲDIV⦂ILLORV⦂IBⴷT
Struck on a small flan so that the tops of the letters and some punctuation cannot always be seen. Webb Ware 2a; North 1302; Seaby 1655. Bt Schulman 1966; ex Krondberg.

145 Noble		
7.78	120.1	70°

Obv.: RIⴵ/ARD⦂DⴲI⦂GRⴷ⦂RⴲX⦂ⴷNGL⦂DNS⦂hIB⦂Σ⦂ⴷ/ⵕ
Ornaments, 1–1–1–1. Ropes, 3/2. Quatrefoils, 4/4. No mark clearly visible above sail.
Rev.: ✠Ihⴵ⦂ⴷVTⴲM⦂TRⴷNSIⴲNS⦂PⴲR⦂MⴲDIV⦂ILLORM⦂IBⴷT
Webb Ware 2a; North 1307 (1); Seaby 1661. Bt Spink 1972; ex Cartwright.

PLATE 14

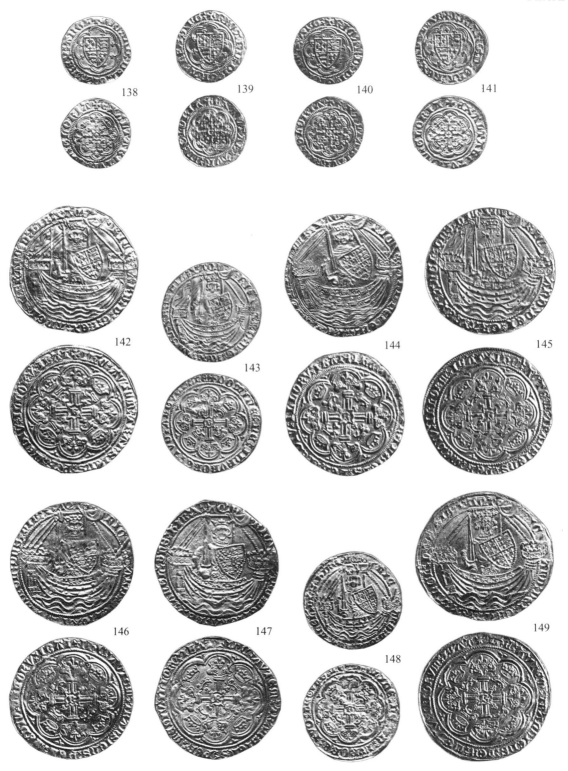

138   139   140   141

142   143   144   145

146   147   148   149

Plate 14 (*cont.*)

146 Noble
7.57   116.9   330°

Obv.: RIꞒ/ꞀRD⸭DꬴI⸭GRꞀ⸭RꬴX⸭ꞀNGL⸭DNS⸭ħIB⸭Ƨ⸭ꞀQT
Ornaments, 1–1–1–1. Ropes, 3/1. Quatrefoils, 4/4. Saltire clearly visible above sail.
Rev.: ✠IħꞒ⸭ꞀVTꬴM⸭TRꞀNSIꬴNS⸭PꬴR⸭MꬴDIV⸭ILLORV⸭IBꞀT
Webb Ware 2a; North 1304 (2, probably); Seaby 1658. Bt Seaby 1952.

147 Noble
7.59   117.2   270°

Obv.: RIꞒ/ꞀRD⸭DꬴI⸭GRꞀ⸭RꬴX⸭ꞀNGL⸭DNS⸭ħIB⸭Ƨ⸭ꞀQT
Ornaments, –1–1–1. Ropes, 3/1. Quatrefoils, 4/4.
Rev.: ✠IħꞒ⸭ꞀVTꬴM⸭TRꞀNSIꬴNS⸭PꬴR⸭MꬴDIV⸭ILLORV⸭IBꞀT
Webb Ware 2a showing transitional features towards 2b; North 1304 (2); Seaby 1658. Ex Mygind.

148 Half-noble
3.84   59.2   70°

Obv.: RIꞒ/ꞀRD⸭D⸭GRꞀ⸭RꬴX⸭ꞀNGL⸭DNS⸭ħIB⸭Ƨ⸭ꞀQ
Ornaments, –1–1–. Ropes, 3/1. Quatrefoils, 2/4. No mark clearly visible above sail.
Rev.: ✠DOMINꬴ⸭Nꬴ⸭IN⸭FVRORꬴ⸭TVO⸭ꞀRGVꞀS⸭Mꬴ
Webb Ware 2a; North 1312 var. without crescent on rudder; Seaby 1667 var. for the same reason. Bt Spink 1975; ex Bourgey sale 28.10.1974 (482).

TYPE 2b

Characteristics: robust style; nobles with trefoil over sail (both London and Calais). Ropes, 3/1.

London mint

149 Noble
7.78   119.9   50°

Obv.: RIꞒ/ꞀRD⸭DꬴI⸭GRꞀ⸭RꬴX⸭ꞀNGL⸭DN[   ]IB⸭Ƨ⸭ꞀQT
Ornaments, 1–1–1–1. Quatrefoils, 4/4. Slipped trefoil over sail.
Rev.: ✠IħꞒ⸭ꞀVTꬴM⸭TRꞀNSIꬴNS⸭PꬴR⸭MꬴDIV⸭ILLORVM⸭IBꞀT
Webb Ware 2b; North 1304 (2); Seaby 1658. Bt Spink 1973; ex 'Polish Hoard'.

SECOND ISSUE (French title omitted) (*cont.*)

TYPE 2b (*cont.*)

London mint (*cont.*)

150 Noble

	Weight		
	g	*gr.*	*Die-axis*
	7.69	118.7	210°

Obv.: RIꝃ/ꞍRD ⁖DEI⁖GRꞧ ⁖REX⁖ꞧNGL ⁖DNS ⁖ꞍIB⁖Ƨ×ꞧQT
Ornaments, 1–1–1–1. Quatrefoils, 4/4. Slipped trefoil over sail.
Rev.: ✠IꞍꝃ⁖ꞧVTEM⁖TRꞧNSIENS⁖PER⁖MEDIV ⁖ILLORV ⁖IBꞧT
Webb Ware 2b; North 1304 (2); Seaby 1658. Bt Spink 1960.

151 Noble
        7.72   119.1   200°

Obv.: RIꝃ/ꞧRD⁖DEI⁖GRꞧ⁖REX⁖ꞧNGL ⁖DNS ⁖ꞍIB ⁖Ƨ×ꞧQT
Ornaments, 1–1–1–1. Quatrefoils, 4/4. Slipped trefoil over sail.
Rev.: ✠IꞍꝃ⁖ꞧVTEM⁖TRꞧNSIENS⁖PER⁖MEDIV ⁖ILLORV ⁖IBꞧT
Webb Ware 2b; North 1304 (2); Seaby 1658. No provenance.

Calais mint (flag at stern)

152 Noble
        7.71   119.0   310°

Obv.: RIꝃ/ꞧRD ×DEI⁖GRꞧ ×REX⁖ꞧNGL ⁖DNS ⁖ꞍIB ⁖Ƨ×ꞧQT
Ornaments, 1–1?? Quatrefoils, 4/3. Trefoil of pellets over sail.
Rev.: ✠IꞍꝃ ⁖ꞧVTEM⁖TRꞧNSIENS⁖PER⁖MEDIV M⁖ILLORV M⁖IBꞧT
Webb Ware 2b; North 1308; Seaby 1660 var. Ex Mygind; ex Glendining sale
29.4.1948 (89).

TYPE 2c

Characteristics: porcine style of face; nobles with no marks (both London and Calais). Ropes, 3/1.

London mint

153 Noble
        7.76   119.7   190°

Obv.: RIꝃ/ꞧRD ⁖DEI⁖GRꞧ ⁖REX×ꞧNGL×DNS×ꞍYB⁖꒞×ꞧQVIT
Ornaments, 1–1–1–1. Quatrefoils, 4/4.
Rev.: ✠IꞍꝃ ⁖ꞧVTEM⁖TRꞧNSIENS⁖PER⁖MEDIV ⁖ILLORV ⁖IBꞧT
Webb Ware 2c; North 1303 (1); Seaby 1656. No provenance.

154 Noble
        7.69   118.7   250°

Obv.: RIꝃ/ꞧRD ⁖DEI⁖GRꞧ ⁖REX×ꞧNGL×DNS⁖ꞍYB⁖꒞×ꞧQVIT
Ornaments, 1–1–1–1. Quatrefoils, 4/4. Same die as next coin, **155**, prior to the
addition of the flag.
Rev.: ✠IꞍꝃ ×ꞧVTEM⁖TRꞧNSIENS⁖PER⁖MEDIV M⁖ILLORV M⁖IBꞧT
Webb Ware 2c; North 1303 (1); Seaby 1656. Ex O'Byrne (6).

Calais mint (flag at stern)

155 Noble
        7.71   119.0   320°

Obv.: same die as last coin, **154**, but with flag added.
Rev.: ✠IꞍɛ⁖ꞧVTEM⁖TRꞧNSIENS⁖PER⁖MEDIV M⁖ILLORV M⁖IBꞧT
        ɛ for ꝃ in IꞍꝃ.
Webb Ware 2c; North 1307 (1); Seaby 1661. Bt Baldwin 1973.

156 Noble
        7.72   119.2   0°

Obv.: RIꝃ/ꞧRD ⁖DEI⁖GRꞧ ⁖REX×ꞧNGL⁖DNS⁖ꞍYB⁖꒞×ꞧQVIT
Ornaments, 1–1–1–1. Quatrefoils, 4/3. With non-porcine, realistic, portrait.
Rev.: ✠IꞍꝃ⁖ꞧVTEM⁖TRꞧNSIENS.PER⁖MEDIV ⁖ILLORV M⁖IBꞧT
Webb Ware 2c; North 1307; Seaby 1661. Ex Mygind.

[*continued overleaf*]

PLATE 15

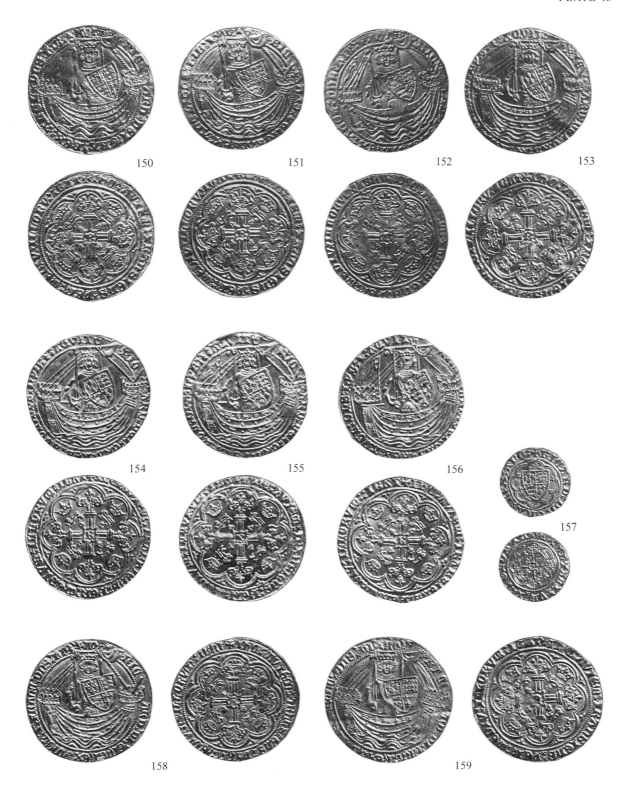

150   151   152   153

154   155   156   157

158   159

Plate 15 (*cont.*)

THIRD ISSUE (French title resumed)

MULE, TYPES 1b/3a

Characteristics: obv. as 1b, see above; rev. as 3a, see below.

London mint

157 Quarter-noble
    1.71   26.4   80°

Obv.: ✠RIᴄ∧RD⦂DI⦂GR∧⦂RⒺX⦂∧NG⦂. Same die as **139** and **140** but now in rusty state.
Rev.: ✠ⒺX∧LT∧BITVR⦂IN⦂GLORI∧ Fishtail letters (Type II). Pellet in centre.
Webb Ware 1b/3a; North 1318 (4)/1319; Seaby 1673. Ex Lockett (4284)

TYPE 3a

Characteristics: nobles and half-nobles of London and Calais with no marks; ropes, 3/1; quarter-nobles, presumably of London, with pellet in centre of reverse.

London mint

158 Noble
    7.73   119.2   210°

Obv.: RIᴄ/∧RD⦂DI⦂GR∧⦂RⒺX⦂∧NGL⦂Σ⦂FR∧Nᴄ⦂DNS⦂hIB⦂Σ×∧Q/T
Ornaments, −1−1−. Quatrefoils, 4/4.
Rev.: ✠Ihᴄ⦂∧VTⒺM⦂TR∧NSIⒺNS⦂PⒺR⦂MⒺDIVM⦂ILLORVM⦂IB∧T
Webb Ware 3a; North 1303 (1); Seaby 1656. Ex Münzen und Medaillen sale, Basel, 17.6.1954.

159 Noble
    7.73   119.3   270°

Obv.: RIᴄ/∧RD⦂DI⦂GR∧⦂RⒺX⦂∧NGL×Σ×FR∧Nᴄ⦂DNS⦂hI⦂Σ ∧Q
Ornaments, −1−1−. Quatrefoils, 4/4(?).
Rev.: ✠Ihᴄ⦂∧VTⒺM⦂TR∧NSIⒺNS⦂PⒺR⦂MⒺDIV⦂ILLORVM⦂IB∧T
Webb Ware 3a; North 1303 (1); Seaby 1656. Bt Spink 1967; ex PKP.

THIRD ISSUE (French title resumed) (*cont.*)

TYPE 3a (*cont.*)

London mint (cont.)

160 Noble

Weight		
g	*gr.*	*Die-axis*
7.65	118.1	80°

Obv.: RIᏟ/ᏗRD·D×G·RᏋX⁝ᏗNGL·Σ×FRN·DNS×hIB·Σ×ᏗᎲ/T
Ornaments, −1−1−. Quatrefoils, 4/4. Same die as **162**.
Rev.: +IhᏟ⁝ᏗVTᏋM⁝TRᏗNSIᏋNS⁝PᏋR⁝MᏋDIV⁝ILLORV⁝IBᏗT
Webb Ware 3a; North 1303 (1); Seaby 1656. Bt Spink 1959.

161 Noble
7.21	111.3	50°

Obv.: RIᏟ/ᏗRD⁝DI⁝GRᏗ⁝RᏋX⁝ᏗNGL⁝Σ×FRᏗNᏟ⁝DNS×hIB·Σ×ᏗᎲ/T
Ornaments, −1−1−1. Quatrefoils, 4/4. This die was later used at Calais with a
flag added at the stern, **168**.
Rev.: +IhᏟ⁝ᏗVTᏋM⁝TRᏗNSIᏋNS⁝PᏋR⁝MᏋDIV⁝ILLORVM⁝IBᏗT
Webb Ware 3a; North 1303 (1); Seaby 1656. Ex Mygind; ex Glendining sale 12.3.1970
(5); ex Lockett (4280).

162 Noble
7.72	119.1	260°

Obv.: RIᏟ/ᏗRD⁝D⁝G⁝RᏋX⁝ᏗNGL⁝Z×FRN⁝DNS×hIB·Z×ᏗᎲ/T
Ornaments, −1−1−. Quatrefoils, 4/4. Same die as **160**.
Rev.: +IhᏟ⁝ᏗVTᏋM⁝TRᏗNSIᏋNS⁝PᏋR⁝PᏋR⁝MᏋDIV⁝ILLORV×IBᏗ
The word **PᏋR** is duplicated.
Webb Ware 3a; North 1303 (1); Seaby 1656. Ex Mygind; ex Raynes (21).

163 Half-noble
3.78	58.3	260°

Obv.: RIᏟ/ᏗRD⁝DI⁝G⁝RᏋX⁝ᏗNGL⁝Σ×FRᏗN⁝D⁝hI⁝Ꮧ/T
Ornaments, 1−1−1−1. Quatrefoils, 3/3.
Rev.: +DOMINᏋ⁝NᏋ⁝IN⁝FVRORᏋ⁝TVO⁝ᏗRGVᏗS⁝MᏋ
Webb Ware 3a; North 1311 var. without lion on rudder; Seaby 1666 var. for same
reason. Bt Spink 1959.

164 Half-noble
3.82	58.9	210°

Obv.: RIᏟ/ᏗRD⁝DI·G·RᏋX×ᏗNGL·Σ×F·DNS hIB Ꮧ
Ornaments, 1−1−1−1 (probably). Quatrefoils, 3/3(?).
Rev.: +DOMINᏋ⁝NᏋ⁝IN⁝FVRORᏋ⁝TVO⁝ᏗRGVᏗS⁝MᏋ
Webb Ware 3a; North 1311 var. without lion on rudder; Seaby 1666 var. for same
reason. Bt Baldwin 1965.

165 Half-noble
3.91	60.3	30°

Obv.: RIᏟ/ᏗRD×DI×GRᏗ×RᏋX×ᏗNGL⁝Σ×FRᏗNᏟ⁝D⁝h⁝Σ×ᏗᎲ/T
Ornaments, −1−1−. Quatrefoils, 4/4.
Rev.: +DOMINᏋ⁝NᏋ⁝IN⁝FVRORᏋ⁝TVO⁝ᏗRGVᏗS⁝MᏋ
Webb Ware 3a; North 1312 var. without crescent on rudder; Seaby 1667 var. for same
reason. Ex O'Byrne (7).

166 Quarter-noble
1.98	30.5	160°

Obv.: +RIᏟᏗRD⁝DᏋI⁝GRᏗ⁝RᏋX⁝ᏗNGL' **RIᏟ** overstruck, possibly, on a
blundered version of the same letters. This coin has previously been described
as having an obverse die of Edward III altered to Richard. The small irregular
style of the lettering (type III) makes this impossible as do the traces of the
under-lettering (for example, the letter under the **R** seems to have started with a
straight vertical upright).
Rev.: +ᏋXᏗLTᏗBITVR⁝IN⁝GLORIᏗ Pellet in centre.
Webb Ware 3a; North 1319 (4); Seaby 1674. Ex Lockett (1339).

[*continued overleaf*]

PLATE 16

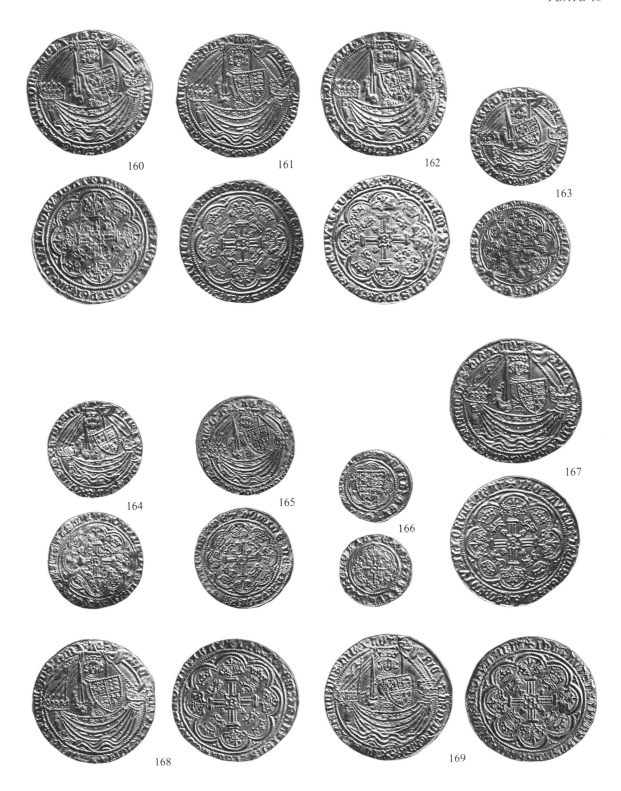

160

161

162

163

164

165

166

167

168

169

Plate 16 (*cont.*)

Calais mint (flag at stern)

167 Noble
    7.74   119.4   50°

Obv.:   RIC/ARD⁚DI⁚GRA⁚REX⁚ANGL⁚Σ⁚FRANC⁚DNS⁚hIB⁚Σ⁚AQT
          Ornaments, –1–1–. Quatrefoils, 4/4.
Rev.:   +IhC⁚AVTEM⁚TRANSIENS⁚PER⁚MEDIV⁚ILLORVM⁚IBAT
Webb Ware 3a; North 1307; Seaby 1661. Bt Spink 1972; ex Beresford-Jones; ex
Potter.

168 Noble
    7.70   118.9   130°

Obv.:   RIC/ARD⁚DI⁚GRA⁚REX⁚ANGL⁚Σ⁚FRANC⁚DNS⁚hIB'⁚Σ⁚AQ/T
          Ornaments, –1–1–1. Quatrefoils, 4/4. Same die as **161**, above, London, but with
          flag added at stern.
Rev.:   +IhC⁚AVTEM⁚TRANSIENS⁚PER⁚MEDIV⁚ILLORVM⁚IBAT
Webb Ware 3a; North 1307; Seaby 1661. Bt Spink 1972; ex Cabell.

169 Noble
    7.64   117.9   220°

Obv.:   RIC/ARD⁚DI⁚GRA⁚REX⁚ANGL⁚Σ⁚FRANC⁚DNS⁚hIB⁚Σ⁚AQT
          Ornaments, –1–1–1. Quatrefoils, 4/4. Triangle of three annulets above sail.
Rev.:   +IhC⁚AVTEM⁚TRANSIENS⁚PER⁚MEDIVM⁚ILLORVM⁚IBAT
Webb Ware 3a; North 1307 var. with this mark above the sail; Seaby 1661 var. for the
same reason. Bt Spink 4.3.1974; ex Potter.

THIRD ISSUE (French title resumed) (*cont.*)

TYPE 3a (*cont.*)

Calais mint (*cont.*)

170 Half-noble

	Weight		
g	*gr.*	*Die-axis*	
3.71	57.3	310°	

Obv.: RIC/ΛRD×DI G[   ]FRΛNCͰD·h·Σ·ΛΩ/T
Ornaments, –1–1–. Quatrefoils, 3/3(?).

Rev.: +DOMINɆːNɆːINͰFVRORɆːTVOːΛRGVΛS MɆ

Webb Ware 3a; North –; Seaby –. Ex Mygind; ex Dupree; ex Graham (5).

TYPE 3b

Characteristics: lis on rudder (London), lion on rudder (Calais). Ropes, 3/1.

London mint

171 Noble
    7.68   118.5   250°

Obv.: RICΛ/RD:DI·GRΛ:RɆX:ΛNGL:Σ·FRΛNC:DNS·hIB·Σ·ΛΩ/T
Ornaments, 1–1–1–1. Quatrefoils, 4/4. Trefoil stops.

Rev.: +IhC×ΛVTɆM×TRΛNSIɆNS×PɆR×MɆDIV×ILLORVM:IBΛT

Webb Ware 3b; North 1303 (2); Seaby 1657. Ex Lockett (3047).

172 Noble
    7.66   118.2   0°

Obv.: RIC/ΛRD·DI×GRΛ:RɆX×ΛNGL:Σ·FRΛNC×DNS·hIB Σ×ΛΩ
Ornaments, 1–1–1–1. Quatrefoils, 4/4. This die was reused in type 3c with a slipped trefoil added by the shield, see **175**.

Rev.: +IhC   ΛVTɆM×TRΛNSIɆNS×PɆR×MɆDIV×ILLORVM:IBΛT

Webb Ware 3b; North 1303 (3); Seaby 1657. Ex Mygind.

173 Half-noble
    3.87   59.7   190°

Obv.: RICΛ/RD×D·G×RɆX×ΛNGL×Z×FRΛNC×D·hY·D×ΛΩ
Ornaments, –1–1–. Quatrefoils, 2/2(?). Lion on rudder (usually a Calais feature in this type).

Rev.: +DOMINɆːNɆːINːFVRORɆːTVO×ΛRGVΛS·M

Webb Ware 3b; North 1311; Seaby 1666. Ex Mygind.

Calais mint (flag at stern)

174 Noble
    7.27   112.2   340°
    (clipped)

Obv.: RICΛ/RD:DI:GRΛ:RɆX:ΛNGL:Σ:FRΛNC:DNS:hIB Σ ΛΩ
Ornaments, 1–1–1–1. Quatrefoils, 4/4. Trefoil stops. Same die as **180** before the addition of pellets above and below the shield.

Rev.: +IhC ΛVTɆM×TRΛNSIɆNS×PɆR×MɆDIVM×ILLORVM×IBΛT

Webb Ware 3b; North 1307 (2); Seaby 1662. Bt Baldwin 1973; ex Winstanley; ex Glendining sale 28.6.1954 (possibly lot 91 although description varies and not illustrated).

[*continued overleaf*]

PLATE 17

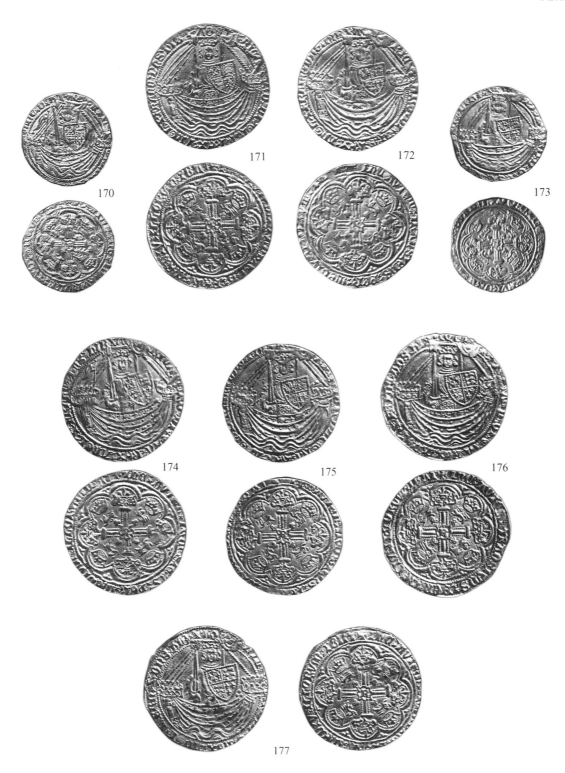

170

171

172

173

174

175

176

177

Plate 17 (*cont.*)

TYPE 3c

Characteristics: nobles with trefoil by shield (London) or two pellets by shield (Calais); half-noble (Calais) with saltire to left of rudder; quarter-noble (?London) with trefoils in obverse spandrels. Ropes, 3/1 except where stated otherwise.

London mint

175 Noble
    7.02   108.3   170°
    (clipped)

Obv.: RIⒸ/ᛉRD×DI×GRᛉꞏREX×ᛉꞤGL ᛏ×FRᛉꞤⒸ×DꞤS×ʰIB Σ×ᛉꞞ
Ornaments, 1–1–1–1. Quatrefoils, 4/4(?). Lis on rudder. Same die as **172** but with a slipped trefoil added by the shield.
Rev.: ✠IʰⒸ×ᛉVTEMꞏTRᛉꞤSIEꞤSꞏPER[   ]DIV×ILLORVMꞏIBᛉT
Webb Ware 3c; North 1303 (4); Seaby 1656. Ex Mygind; ex Bridgewater House (6).

176 Noble
    7.58   116.9   310°

Obv.: RIⒸ/ᛉRD ᛏDI×GRᛉ×REX×ᛉꞤGL ᛏΣ×FRᛉꞤⒸ×DꞤS×ʰIB ᛉꞞ/T
Ornaments, –1–1–1. Quatrefoils replaced by annulets, 4/6. Slipped trefoil by shield. The die later used in type 4a with an escallop added on the rudder, see **182**.
Rev.: ✠IʰⒸ ᛏᛉVTEMꞏTRᛉꞤSIEꞤSꞏPERꞏMEDIV ᛏILLORVMꞏIBᛉT
Webb Ware 3c; North 1303 (4); Seaby 1656. Bt Baldwin 1953.

177 Noble
    7.68   118.4   140°

Obv.: RIⒸ/ᛉRD×D×G×REX×ᛉꞤGL ×Σ×FRꞤ×Σ×DꞤS×ʰIB×Σ×ᛉꞞ
Ornaments, –1–1–. Quatrefoils, 4/4. Trefoil by shield.
Rev.: ✠IʰⒸ ᛏᛉVTEM×TRᛉꞤSIEꞤSꞏPER×MEDIV ᛏILLORVMꞏIBᛉT
Webb Ware 3c; North 1303 (4); Seaby 1656. No provenance.

THIRD ISSUE (French title resumed) (*cont.*)

TYPE 3b (*cont.*)

London mint (cont.)

178 Quarter-noble

	Weight	
g	*gr.*	*Die-axis*
1.89	29.1	320°

Obv.: +RICARD[ ] DI⁙GRA×REX×ANGL⁚Ƨ·F
Double struck. Trefoils in spandrels. Fishtail letters of Type 2.
Rev.: +EXALTABITVR⁚IN⁚GLORIA
Pellet in centre. Mainly small irregular letters of Type 3.
Webb Ware 3c; North 1319 var. with trefoils in spandrels; Seaby 1673. No provenance.

179 Quarter-noble
1.89   29.2   240°

Obv.: +RICARD⁚DI⁚G⁚REX⁚ANGL·Ƨ FRANC
Trefoil of annulets over shield. Nothing in spandrils; trefoils on cusps.
Rev.: +EXALTABITVR×IN⁚GLORIA   Nothing in spandrils.
Webb Ware 3c; North 1319 (1); Seaby 1676. Ex Mygind; ex Lawrence (13).

Calais mint (flag at stern)

180 Noble
7.73   119.3   60°

Obv.: RICA/RD⁚DI⁚GRA⁚REX×ANGL⁚Ƨ⁚FRANC⁚DNS⁚hIB Ƨ AQ
Ornaments, 1–1–1–1. Quatrefoils, 4/4. Trefoil stops. Same die as **174** but with pellets added above and below shield.
Rev.: +IhC ⁚ AVTEM·TRANSIENS⁚PER⁚MEDIVM⁚ILLORVM⁚IBAT
Webb Ware 3c; North 1307 (2), var. with pellets above and below shield; Seaby 1662 var. for the same reason. Ex Barnes (93).

181 Half-noble
3.79   58.5   100°

Obv.: RICA/RD·D·G·ANGL·Ƨ×FRANC⁚D⁚h AQ/T
Ornaments unclear. Ropes, 2/1. Quatrefoils uncertain. Saltire to left of rudder.
Rev.: +DOMINE⁙NE⁚IN⁚FVRORE⁚TVO⁚ARGVAS⁚ME
Webb Ware 3c; North 1316 (4); Seaby 1671. Bt Baldwin 1973; ex Winstanley; ex Parsons (9).

FOURTH ISSUE (Henry IV style)

TYPE 4a

Characteristics: nobles and half-nobles with scallop on rudder. Ropes, 3/1.

London mint only

182 Noble
7.09   109.4   150°

Obv.: RIC/ARD⁚DI⁚GRA×REX×ANGL⁚Ƨ⁚FRANC·DNS×hIB AQ/T
Ornaments, −1–1–1. Quatrefoils, 4/4. Slipped trefoil between shield and forecastle. From an old die of type 3c with a scallop added on the rudder, see **176**.
Rev.: +IhC×AVTEM×TRANSIENS⁚PER⁚MEDIV ⁚ILLORVM⁚IBAT
Webb Ware 4a; North 1304; Seaby 1658. Ex Mygind; ex Lockett (3987); ex P. W. P. Carlyon-Britton.

183 Noble
7.77   118.2   310°

Obv.: RIC/ARD·DEI·G×REX×ANGL⁚Ƨ·F⁚DNS⁚hIB⁚Ƨ×AQ/T'
Ornaments, 1–1–1–1. Quatrefoils, 4(?)/4. Scallop on rudder and slipped trefoil by shield. Same die as next coin, **184**.
Rev.: +IhC ⁚ AVTEM⁚TRANSIENS⁚PER⁚MEDIV ⁚ILLORVM⁚IBAT
Webb Ware 4a; North 1304 (1); Seaby 1658. Ex Lockett (1331); ex Bruun (352); ex Walters, 1913 (196).

184 Noble
7.59   117.2   10°

Obv.: same die as last coin, **183**.
Rev.: +IhC ⁚ AVTEM⁚TRANSIENS⁚PER⁚MEDIV ⁚ILLORVM⁚IBAT⁚
Saltires after IBAT.
Webb Ware 4a; North 1304 (1); Seaby 1658. Bt Baldwin 1979.

PLATE 18

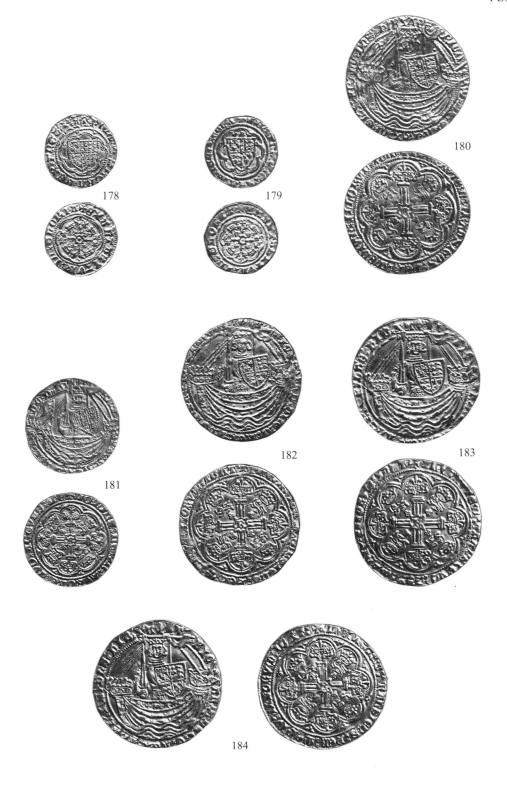

178

179

180

181

182

183

184

RICHARD II (*cont.*)

FOURTH ISSUE (Henry IV style) (*cont.*)

TYPE 4a (*cont.*)

London mint (cont.)

185 Quarter-noble

	Weight	
g	*gr.*	*Die-axis*
1.84	28.4	170°

Obv.: ✠RIᏟᎪRD⫶DЄI⫶GRᎪ⫶RЄX⫶ᎪNGL⫶   Scallop over shield.
Rev.: ✠ЄXᎪLTᎪBITVR⫶IN⫶GLORIᎪ   Pellet in centre.

Webb Ware 4a; North 1319 (2); Seaby 1675. No provenance.

TYPE 4b

Characteristics: nobles with crescent on rudder. Ropes, 3/1.

London mint only

186 Noble

6.82	105.2	20°

Obv.: RIᏟ/ᎪRD⫶DI⫶GRᎪ⫶RЄX⫶ᎪNGL⫶Ƨ FRᎪNᏟ⫶D⫶hIB⫶Ƨ ᎪᏚ/T
Ornaments, 1–1–1–1. Quatrefoils, 4/4. 2 extra pellets in each lis quarter of shield.

(clipped)

Rev.: ✠IhᏟ⫶ᎪVTЄM⫶TRᎪNSIЄNS⫶PЄR⫶MЄDIV⫶ILLORVM⫶IBᎪT
Webb Ware 4b; North 1304 (3); Seaby 1658. Ex Lockett (1333); ex Bliss (205).

187 Noble

7.69	118.6	200°

Obv.: RIᏟ/ᎪRD⫶DЄI⫶GRᎪ⫶RЄX⫶ᎪNGL⫶Ƨ⫶FRᎪNᏟ⫶D⫶hIB⫶Ƨ⫶ᎪᏚ/T
Ornaments, –1–1–1. Quatrefoils, 4/4(?). 4 extra pellets in each lis quarter of shield.

Rev.: ✠IhᏟ⫶ᎪVTЄM⫶TRᎪNSIЄNS⫶PЄR⫶MЄDIV⫶ILLORVM⫶IBᎪT
Webb Ware 4b; North 1304 (3); Seaby 1658. Ex Mygind; ex Dupree; ex Ryan (18).

188 Half-noble

3.85	59.4	310°

Obv.: RIᏟ/ᎪRD⫶DI⫶G⫶RЄX⫶ᎪNGL⫶Ƨ⫶FRᎪᏟ⫶D⫶h′ᎪᏚ
Ornaments, 1–1–1–1. Quatrefoils, 2/?. Crescent on rudder.

Rev.: ✠DOMINЄ⫶NЄ⫶IN⫶FVRORЄ⫶TVO⫶ᎪRGVᎪS⫶MЄ
Webb Ware 4b; North 1312; Seaby 1667. Ex Mygind; ex Dupree.

HENRY IV (30 September 1399–20 March 1413)

FIRST OR HEAVY COINAGE (1399–1409)
Gold coinage issued at a fineness of 23 ct 3½ gr. (0.995 fine) and at a nominal weight of 120 gr. to the noble. Denominations struck were noble, half-noble and quarter-noble. Mints striking gold were London and Calais.

Classified according to Blunt 1941–4 and Blunt 1967.

TYPE Ia

Characteristics: On the nobles and half-nobles, crescent (London) or crown (Calais) on rudder. On the quarter-nobles, crescent over shield (London) or crown as reverse initial mark (Calais). Four lis in the first quarter of the shield.

London mint

189 Noble

7.65	118.1	260°

Obv.: hЄN/RIᏟ⫶DЄI⫶GRᎪ⫶RЄX⫶ᎪNGL⫶Ƨ⫶FRᎪNᏟ⫶D⫶hIB⫶Ƨ ᎪᏚT
Ornaments, 1–1–1–1. Ropes, 3/1. Quatrefoils, 4/4. Crescent on rudder. Nails on ship's side point to left.

Rev.: ✠IhᏟ⫶ᎪVTЄM⫶TRᎪNSIЄNS⫶PЄR⫶MЄDIV⫶ILLORVM⫶IBᎪT
Blunt Ia, 1; North 1336; Seaby 1705. Bt Spink 1972; ex Cartwright.

[continued overleaf]

PLATE 19

185

186

187

188

189

190

191

192

193

194

Plate 19 (*cont.*)

190 Noble
    7.68   118.5   10°

Obv.: hEN/RIɑ⋮DI⋮GRⱯ⋮REX⋮ⱯNGL⋮Ƹ⋅FRⱯNɑ⋮DNS⋮hI'Ƹ⋅ⱯQ/(T?)
Ornaments, 1–1–1–1. Ropes, 3/1. Quatrefoils, 4/4. Crescent on rudder. Four extra pellets in first and one extra pellet in fourth quarter of shield. Nails on ship's side point to right.
Rev.: ✚Ihɑ⋅ⱯVTEM⋮TRⱯNSIENS⋮PER⋮MEDIV⋮ILLORVM⋮IBⱯT
Blunt Ia, 5 (this coin); North 1336; Seaby 1705. Ex Ryan (23); ex P. W. P. Carlyon-Britton; ex Walters, 1913 (223).

191 Half-noble
    3.87   59.7   130°

Obv.: hEN/RIɑ⋮DI⋮G⋮REX⋮ⱯNGL⋮Ƹ⋅FRN⋮D⋮hI' ⱯQ/T
Ornaments, –1–1–1. Ropes, 3/1. Quatrefoils, 3(?)/3. Crescent on rudder.
Rev.: ✚DOMINE⋮NE⋮IN⋮FVRORE⋮TVO⋮ⱯRGVⱯS⋮ME
Blunt (1967) 2 (this coin). Possibly the only known heavy half-noble of London of Type Ia. The specimen in the BM ex Ryan and the other specimen in this collection, **195**, are clearly of Type Ib (with three lis in the French arms). Exhibited by A. H. Baldwin at the BNS meeting of 23 April 1952 and illustrated in *BNJ* 27 (1952–4), pl. VIII. North 1340; Seaby 1709. Bt Baldwin 1952. Found in Amiens, May 1950.

192 Quarter-noble
    1.89   29.1   260°

Obv.: ✚hENRIɑVS⋮DI⋮GRⱯ⋅ⱯNGL⋮Ƹ⋅FRⱯN
Crescent over shield. Pellet in centre of initial cross. Three extra pellets in first and two extra pellets in fourth quarter of shield.
Rev.: ✚EXⱯLTⱯBITVR⋮IN⋮GLORIⱯ   Pellet in centre. Nothing after GLORIⱯ.
Blunt 1 (this coin); North 1343; Seaby 1712. Ex Ryan (26); ex P. W. P. Carlyon-Britton; ex Montagu (477); ex Brice; ex Young.

Calais mint

193 Noble
    7.68   118.5   340°

Obv.: hEN/RIɑ⋮DEI⋮GRⱯ⋮REX⋮ⱯNGL⋮Ƹ⋅FRⱯNɑ⋮D⋮hIB'Ƹ ⱯQ/T
Ornaments, 1–1–1–1. Ropes, 3/1. Quatrefoils, 4/4. Flag on stern. Crown placed horizontally on rudder.
Rev.: ✚IhɑⱯVTEM⋮TRⱯNSIENS⋮PER⋮MEDIV⋮ILLORVM⋮IBⱯT
Blunt IIa; North 1338 var. with crown horizontal; Seaby 1707. Bt Bourgey sale 24.6.1971 (318).

TYPE Ib

Characteristics: crescent on rudder; French arms in first quarter of shield with lis positioned ✚ ✚ ✚ .

London mint

194 Noble
    7.71   118.8   130°

Obv.: hEN/RIɑ⋮DI⋮GRⱯ⋮REX⋮ⱯNGL⋮Ƹ⋮FRⱯNɑ⋮DNS⋮hIB'Ƹ ⱯQ
Ornaments, 1–1–1–1. Ropes, 3/1. Quatrefoils, 4/4. Crescent on rudder.
Rev.: ✚Ihɑ⋮ⱯVTEM⋮TRⱯNSIENS⋮PER⋮MEDIV⋮ILLORVM⋮IBⱯT
I.m. is pierced cross. h in centre possibly punched over another letter (Mr Schneider wondered if this could be an R).
Blunt Ib, 2 (this coin); North 1337; Seaby 1706. Ex Lockett (1367); ex E. W. Rashleigh (691); ex Tyssen (1198); ex Hodsol.

FIRST OR HEAVY COINAGE (*cont.*)

TYPE Ib (*cont.*)

London mint (cont.)

195 Half-noble

Weight

g	*gr.*	*Die-axis*
3.08	47.7	270°
(clipped)		

Obv.: hEN[   ]ˣFRⱭ NꝘ D h ˣ Ⱥ
Ornaments, 1–1–1. Ropes, 2/1. Quatrefoils, (?). Crescent on rudder.
Rev.: [   ] ЄNЄ[   ]ˣFⱯRORЄˣTVO[   ]
Blunt Ib but this coin unknown to him. It is similar to the Ryan specimen (now BM) illustrated in Blunt 1941–4, no. 5 on the plate though from different dies. North 1341; Seaby 1710. Bt Spink sale 90, 16.3.1992 (4); ex Dupree.

TYPE Ic

Characteristics: crescent on rudder, French arms in first quarter of shield with three lis positioned ⚜⚜⚜.

London mint

196 Noble

7.75	119.6	260°

Obv.: hEN/RIꝘˣDIˣGRⱯˣREXˣⱭNGLˣƩˣFRⱭNꝘˣDˣhIB'Ʃ ⱭꝘ/T'
Ornaments, 1–1–1–1. Ropes, 3/1. Quatrefoils, 4/4. Crescent on rudder.
Rev.: ✠IhꝘˣⱭVTЄMˣTRⱭNSIЄNSˣPЄRˣMЄDIVMˣILLORVˣIBⱭT
Blunt Ic, 6 (this coin). Mr Blunt noted that the lis in the French arms had been over-struck and suggested that this might be an attempt at 'France ancient'. The present writer is of the opinion that three lis were at first struck using the very small lis punches used on the side of the ship. The engraver then overstruck them using the larger lis punches found on other dies having three lis. North 1337; Seaby 1707. Bt Spink 1965; ex Murdoch (310); ex Durlacher (53); ex Montagu (475); ex Clarke (37); ex Marsham (312).

TYPE IIa

Characteristics: lis on rudder. Annulet stops. Three lis in first quarter of shield ⚜⚜⚜.

London mint

197 Noble

7.74	119.5	170°

Obv.: hEN/RIꝘˣDЄIˣGRⱭˣREXˣⱭNGL°ˣFRⱭNꝘˣDˣhIBˣⱭꝘ'/°
Ornaments, –(I)–I–. Ropes, 3/1. Quatrefoils, 4/4. Broken annulet stops. Slipped trefoil on side of ship. Lis on rudder (not visible on this coin but confirmed by die duplicates – see Blunt 1967, p. 168). See **198** below for the same die used for the light coinage, with an annulet added on the side of the ship.
Rev.: ✠IhꝘˣⱭVTЄMˣTRⱭNSIЄNSˣPЄRˣMЄDIVMˣILLORṼˣIBⱭT
Slipped trefoil by lion's tail in fourth quarter.
Blunt II, 1 (same obverse die); North 1337; Seaby 1706. Bt Baldwin; ex Glendining sale 13.12.1978 (95).

[*continued overleaf*]

PLATE 20

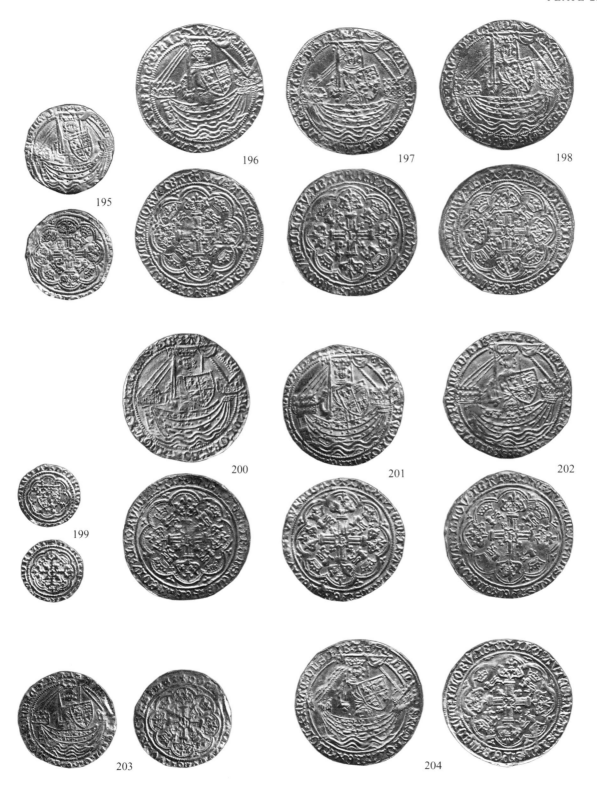

195

196

197

198

199

200

201

202

203

204

Plate 20 (*cont.*)

SECOND OR LIGHT COINAGE (1412–13)

Gold coinage issued at a fineness of 23 ct $3\frac{1}{2}$ gr. (0.995 fine) and at a weight of 108 gr. to the noble. Denominations struck were noble, half-noble and quarter-noble. London was the only mint at which gold was struck. Classified according to the extended Blunt classification, see p. 22.

TYPE IIb

Characteristics: as IIa with annulet and slipped trefoil added to the side of the ship and a slipped trefoil added in one quarter of the reverse.

London mint

198 Noble
6.91   106.6   190°

Obv.: hEN/RIႶ∶DEI∶GRႣ∶REX∶ႬNGL∘Ⴟ∘FRႬNႶ∶D∶hIB∶ႬႶ'/°
Ornaments, –1–1–. Ropes, 3/1. Quatrefoils, 4/4. Broken annulet stops. Lis on rudder. Annulet and slipped trefoil on side of ship. See **197** above for the same die used for the heavy coinage without the annulet on the side of the ship.

Rev.: ✠IhႶ∶ႬVTEM∶TRႬNSIENS∶PER∶MEDIVM∶ILLORႮ∶IBႬT∶
Slipped trefoil by lion's head in fourth quarter.
Blunt II (same obverse die); North 1355; Seaby 1715. Bt Spink 1963.

199 Quarter-noble
1.51   23.3   350°
(clipped)

Obv.: ✠hENRIႶ∙DEI∙GRႬ∙REX∙ႬNGL   Trefoil stops. Nothing beside or above shield. Four lis in first quarter of shield.

Rev.: ✠EXႬLTႬBITVR∙IN∙GLORIႬh   Lis in centre. h after Ⴌ in GLORIႬ. It is uncertain whether the stops are trefoils or quatrefoils.
It is by no means certain that this is the correct place to put this coin. The four lis in the arms suggest an early die, but one without a crescent over the shield appears to be otherwise unrecorded. The lis in the centre of the reverse is normal for the light coinage. Unfortunately, being clipped, weight is not a reliable guide. A die-link, if it could be found, might help to solve the problem. In the meantime, the coin is placed here as it can be seen as a bridge between the heavy and light coinages.
Blunt –; North –; Seaby –. Provenance unsure but possibly ex Montagu (481)
(Mr Schneider noted on his ticket that the coin might be ex Montagu).

TYPE IIIb

Characteristics: Pellet or saltire on rudder. New form of ampersand. Slipped trefoil in one quarter of the reverse.

London mint

200 Noble
6.93   106.9   130°

Obv.: hEN/RIႶ∶DI∶GRႬ∶REX∶ႬNGL∘Ⴟ∘FRႬNႶ∙DNS∶hIB∙Ⴟ ႬႶ
Ornaments, (?)–1–1–1. Ropes, 3/1. Quatrefoils, 3(?)/4. Saltire on rudder. Annulet and slipped trefoil on side of ship. Lis in first quarter of shield are ✚.

Rev.: ✠IhႶ×ႬVTEM×TRႬNSIENS∶PER∶MEDIႮ×ILLORVM∶IBႬT
Slipped trefoil by lion's head in third quarter. Pellet before h in centre.
Although the disposition of the lis in the French arms points to an early, heavy, die, the lettering, for example the ampersand, is of the later type introduced on dies of Blunt III. North 1355; Seaby 1715. Ex Glendining sale 20.3.1968 (2).

Plate 20 (*cont.*)

TYPE IV

Characteristics: Nothing on rudder. Slipped trefoil or annulet and slipped trefoil on side of ship. Still with crennelated fore- and stern-castles as on previous types.

London mint

201 Noble
    6.82   105.2   110°
    (clipped)

Obv.: hEN/RIႱ:DI:GRᴀ:REX ᴀ∩GL∙Σ∙FRᴀႱ∙D∩S∙hIB∶Σ/ᴀႱ
    Ornaments, 1–1–1–1. Ropes, 3/1. Quatrefoils, 3/3. Nothing on rudder
    (Mr Schneider considered that there was a pellet on the rudder. In the writer's
    opinion this is very doubtful, the possible pellet being the lower bracket of the
    rudder hinge. A clearer specimen from the same die could resolve the ques-
    tion). Slipped trefoil on the side of the ship.
Rev.: ✠IhႱ∗ᴀVTEM∶TRᴀ∩SIE∩S:PER:MEDIV∙ILLORVM∶IBᴀT
    Slipped trefoil by lion's tail in the second quarter.
North 1355; Seaby 1715. Ex Sinkler (668); ex Lockett (3069).

202 Noble
    6.94   107.1   240°

Obv.: hEN/RIႱ:DI∙GRᴀ∙REX∙ᴀ∩GL∶Σ∙FRᴀ∩Ⴑ:D∶hIB∶Σ∙ᴀ/Ⴑ
    Ornaments, 1–1–1–. Ropes, 3/1. Quatrefoils, 3/3. Nothing on rudder. Annulet
    and slipped trefoil on side of ship.
Rev.: ✠IhႱ:ᴀVTEM∶TRᴀ∩SIE∩S:PER:MEDIVM∶ILLOVⁱ:IBᴀT∗
    Slipped trefoil by lion's head in second quarter. Pellet to left of h in centre.
North 1355; Seaby 1715. Bt Spink 1963; ex PKP; ex Grantley (19).

203 Half-noble
    3.34   51.5   200°

Obv.: hEN/RIႱ:DI∙G∙REX∙ᴀ∩GL∶Σ∙FRᴀႱ D∶h'ᴀႱ
    Ornaments, 1–1–1–1. Ropes, 2/1. Quatrefoils, 2/(?). Probably nothing on
    rudder. Annulet (filled) and slipped trefoil on side of ship.
Rev.: ✠DOM[   ]∙IN∙FVRORE∙TVO∶ᴀRGVᴀS∶MEⁱ
    Slipped trefoil by tail of lion in fourth quarter. Pellet to left of h in centre.
North 1356; Seaby 1716. Bt Spink February 1974

TYPE V

Characteristics: Ship's fore- and stern-castles not crenellated. Nothing on rudder. Annulet and slipped trefoil, or slipped trefoil and annulet, or trefoil alone on side of ship. Slipped trefoil in one quarter of the reverse. Usually pellet to left of the h in the centre of the reverse.

London mint

204 Noble
    7.01   108.2   110°

Obv.: hEN/RIႱ:Dᵀ∙GRᴀ∙REX∙ᴀ∩GL∶Σ∙FRᴀႱ:D∩ˉS∶hIB∶Σ∗/ᴀႱ
    Ornaments, –11–1. Ropes, 3/1. Quatrefoils, 3/3. Annulet and slipped trefoil on
    side of ship. Same die as next coin, **205**.
Rev.: ✠IhႱ:ᴀVTEM∶TRᴀ∩SIEΓIS∶PER∶MEDIVM∶ILLORVˉ:IBᴀT
    Slipped trefoil by head of lion in third quarter. Pellet to left of h in centre.
North 1355; Seaby 1715. Bt Baldwin 1956; ex Carter.

SECOND OR LIGHT COINAGE (*cont.*)

TYPE V (*cont.*)

London mint (*cont.*)

	Weight		
	g	*gr.*	*Die-axis*

205 Noble
6.98 107.6 10°

Obv.: Same die as last coin, **204**.
Rev.: +IhՇ꞉ΛVTЄM꞉TRΛNSIЄNS꞉PЄR꞉MЄDIVM꞉ILLORVM꞉IBΛT
Slipped trefoil by head of lion in second quarter.
Pellet to left of **h** in centre.
North 1355; Seaby 1715. Bt Spink 1960.

206 Noble
6.98 107.7 180°

Obv.: hЄ/ՈRIՇ꞉DꞀ꞉GRΛ×RЄX×ΛNGL×Ӿ×FRΛՇ꞉DՈ‾S꞉hIB꞉Ʒ/ΛՉ
Ornaments, –11–1. Ropes, 3/1. Quatrefoils, 3/4. Slipped trefoil and annulet on
side of ship. Same die as next coin, **207**.
Rev.: +IhՇ꞉ΛVTЄM꞉TRΛNSIЄNS꞉PЄR꞉MЄDIVM꞉ILLOR̄V꞉IBΛT⁕
Slipped trefoil at the end of the legend and another by the lion's head in the
fourth quarter. Pellet to left of **h** in centre.
North 1355; Seaby 1715. Bt Spink.

207 Noble
6.91 106.6 180°

Obv.: Same die as last coin, **206**, but somewhat double-struck
Rev.: +IhՇ꞉ΛVTЄM꞉TRΛNSIЄNS꞉PЄR꞉MЄDIVM꞉ILLORVM꞉IBΛT
Slipped trefoil by lion's head in first quarter. Pellet to left of **h** in centre.
North 1355; Seaby 1715. Ex Vinchon sale 9.3.1970 (74); ex Lucerne hoard (Trésor de
l'abbé Philippe de Saint-Pierre).

208 Noble
6.99 107.8 40°

Obv.: hЄՈ/RIՇ꞉DI×GRΛ×RЄX×ΛNGL×Ӿ×FRΛ‾Ç꞉DՈS꞉hIB꞉Ӿ Λ/Q
Ornaments, 1–11–1. Ropes, 3/1. Quatrefoils, 3/3. Trefoil alone on side of ship.
Same die as next coin, **209**.
Rev.: +IhՇ꞉ΛVTЄM꞉TRΛNSIЄNS꞉PЄR꞉MЄDIVM꞉ILLORV×IBΛT
Slipped trefoil by lion's head in second quarter. Pellet to left of **h** in centre.
North 1355; Seaby 1715. Bt Spink 1970.

209 Noble
6.91 106.6 160°

Obv.: Same die as last coin, **208**.
Rev.: +IhՇ꞉ΛVTЄM꞉TRΛNSIЄNS꞉PЄR꞉MЄDIVM꞉ILLORV×IBΛT
Slipped trefoil by lion's head in first quarter. Pellet to left of **h** in centre.
North 1355; Seaby 1715. Bt Baldwin May 1970.

210 Noble
6.88 106.2 350°

Obv.: hЄՈ/RIՇ꞉DI×GRΛ×RЄX×ΛNGL×Ӿ×FRΛՇ꞉D꞉hIB꞉Ӿ Λ/Q
Ornaments, –11–. Ropes, 3/1. Quatrefoils, 3/3. Annulet and slipped trefoil on
side of ship.
Rev.: +IhՇ꞉ΛVTЄM꞉TRΛNSIЄNS꞉PЄR꞉MЄDIVM꞉ILLORV꞉IBΛT
Slipped trefoil by lion's head in first quarter. Pellet to left of **h** in centre.
North 1355; Seaby 1715. Bt Baldwin 1960.

211 Noble
6.85 105.7 20°

Obv.: hЄՈR/IՇ꞉DꞀ×GRΛ×RЄX×ΛNGL×Ӿ×FRΛՇ꞉DՈS꞉hyB꞉Ӿ Λ/Q'
Ornaments, –11–11. Ropes, 3/1. Quatrefoils, 3/3. Annulet and slipped trefoil on
side of ship.
Rev.: +IhՇ꞉ΛVTЄM꞉TRΛNSIЄNS꞉PЄR꞉MЄDIVM꞉ILLORV꞉IBΛT
Slipped trefoil by lion's head in second quarter. Pellet to left of **h** in centre.
North 1355; Seaby 1715. Bt Spink 1963.

212 Quarter-noble
1.72 26.5 280°

Obv.: +hЄՈRIՇ꞉꞉DI꞉GRΛ꞉RЄX꞉ΛNGL' Lis above shield. Slipped trefoil above
annulet on both sides of shield.
Rev.: +·ЄXΛLTΛBITVR꞉IN꞉GLORIΛ꞉ Lis in centre.
North 1357; Seaby 1717. Ex Ryan (29); ex P. W. P. Carlyon-Britton; ex Bruun (373);
ex Foster (26).

[*continued overleaf*]

PLATE 21

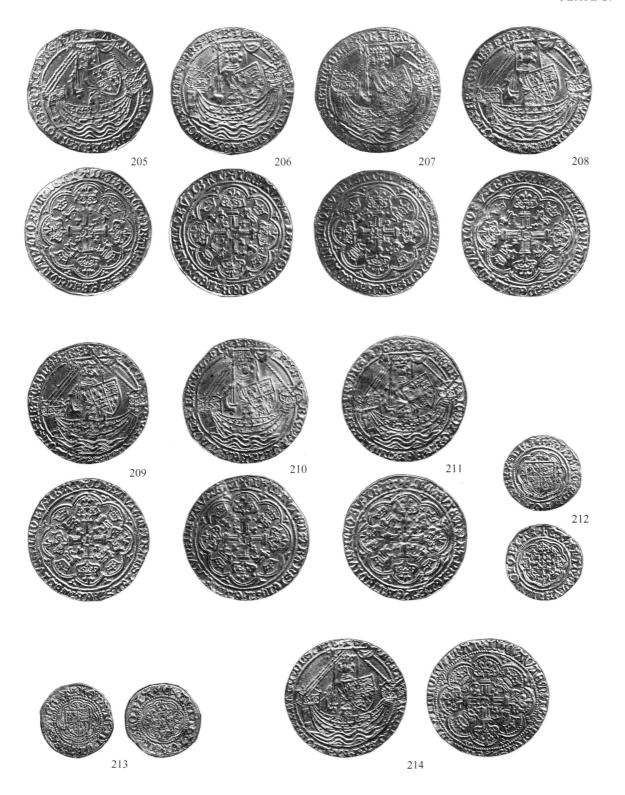

205

206

207

208

209

210

211

212

213

214

Plate 21 (*cont.*)

HENRY V (21 March 1413–1 September 1422)

Gold coinage issued at a fineness of 23 ct 3½ gr. (0.995 fine) and at a weight of 108 gr. (6.998 g) to the noble of 6s 8d. Denominations struck were noble, half-noble and quarter-noble. During most of the reign the only mint for gold was London, but Calais reopened in July 1422 (see p. 24). Arranged according to the classification of Brooke 1950, classes A–G, with that of Brooke 1930, classes I–IX, in parenthesis.

CLASS A (I)

Characteristics: Short, broad, lettering. On nobles and half-nobles quatrefoil over sail; nothing on rudder; quatrefoil above lion's head in second quarter of reverse. On quarter-noble quatrefoil and annulet each side of shield.

This rare class is represented in this collection by a single quarter-noble, **213**. There were three nobles in the Fishpool Hoard of which one is illustrated in *NC* 1967, pl. IX, 32.

London mint only

213 Quarter-noble
1.72   26.6   220°

Obv.: ✙ hЄNRIQ⦂DI⦂GRΛ⦂RЄX×ΛNG Ᵹ×F
Large trefoils at ponts of tressure. Lis above and quatrefoil and annulet each side of shield. Letters Brooke 1.

Rev.: ✙ ЄXΛLTΛBITVR⦂IN⦂GLORIΛ   Stars at angles of centre panel. Letters of Brooke 1.

This coin appears to be a die-duplicate of the BM specimen which is illustated in Brooke 1930, pl. V. The differences in punctuation are accounted for by the outer part of the legends of the BM coin being removed by clipping Brooke A (I); North 1381/1; Seaby 1754. Bt Spink 1993.

CLASS B (II and III)

Characteristics: Taller lettering (Brooke no. 2, though on Brooke II and IIIa letters I, m and S are of a distinctive form (Brooke no. 1a) which gives way to Brooke no. 2 throughout on IIIb. Quatrefoil over sail, but no other marks (II) or annulet on rudder (IIIa and b). Quatrefoil above lion's head in second quarter of reverse.

HENRY IV/CLASS B MULE

London mint only

214 Noble
6.80   104.9   110°
(clipped)

Obv.: hЄNR/IQ⦂DI⦂GRΛ×RЄX×ΛNGL×Ᵹ×FRΛNQ×DNS⦂hIB×Ᵹ/Λ
Ornaments, 1–11–1. Ropes, 3/1. Quatrefoils, 3/3.
Die of Henry IV's light coinage with ship's fore- and stern-castles not crenellated (Type V). Slipped trefoil on side of ship.

Rev.: ✙ IhQ ⦂ΛVTЄm⦂TRΛNSIЄNS×PЄR×mЄDIV×ILLORV×IBΛT
Lettering of Brooke 1a for I, m and S, otherwise lettering of Brooke 2.
Brooke -/B (II); North 1355/1370; Seaby 1715/1740. Bt Baldwin 1965.

CLASS B (II and III) (*cont.*)

CLASS B/HENRY IV MULES

London mint only

215 Noble

	Weight	
g	*gr.*	*Die-axis*
6.80	104.9	260°

Obv.: hЄΝRIႺ⦂DI⦂GRⱯ⦂RЄX×ⱯΝGL×Ⱦ×FRⱯΝ'ႺˣDΝS⦂hYB
Ornaments, –11–11. Ropes, 3/2. Quatrefoils, 3/3. Slipped trefoil (and not a quatrefoil) above sail. Annulet on rudder. Letters of Brooke 2.

Rev.: ✠IhˋႺˣⱯVTЄMˣTRⱯΝSIЄΝSˣPЄRˣMЄDIVMˣILLORVˣIBⱯTˣ
Die of Henry IV's light coinage (Type V). Plain initial cross. Slipped trefoil above lion's head in second quarter and at end of legend. Pellet to left of h in centre.

Brooke B/– (IIIb/–); North 1370/1355; Seaby 1740/1715. Ex Mangakis; ex Lockett (1379).

216 Half-noble

3.44	53.1	60°

Obv.: hЄΝRIႺ⦂DI⦂GRⱯ⦂RЄX×ⱯΝGL×Ⱦ×FRⱯ×D/hYB
Ornaments, –11–. Ropes, 3/2. Quatrefoils, 3/3. No marks visible above sail or on rudder. Lettering is basically Brooke 2; h is similar to Brooke h2 but not quite identical with any of his drawings; Ν is a variety not recorded by Brooke but seems to be a mixture of his Ν1 and Ν2; I is unmistakably Ia with top and bottom finished in palmate form.

Rev.: ✠DOMIΝЄ×ΝЄ×IΝ×FVRORЄ⦂TVO×ⱯRGVⱯS MЄ   Die of Henry IV light coinage (Type V). Slipped trefoil above lion's head in second quarter. No saltire stops after ⱯRGVⱯS and MЄ. Late h and pellet in centre.

Brooke B/– (II/–); North 1376/1356; Seaby 1748/1716. Bt Seaby 1958.

TRUE COINS OF CLASS B

London mint only

217 Noble

6.93	106.9	0°

Obv.: hЄΝRIႺˋˣDI⦂GRⱯˋˣRЄX×ⱯΝGL×Ⱦ×FRⱯΝႺ⦂DΝS⦂hYB
Ornaments, –11–11. Ropes, 3/2. Quatrefoils, 3/3. No annulet on rudder. Lettering of Brooke 1a for I, M and S, otherwise lettering of Brooke 2.

Rev.: ✢ IhˋႺˣⱯVTЄMˣTRⱯΝSIЄΝSˣPЄRˣMЄDIVMˣILLORVˣIBⱯT
Letters I, M (except for M in ⱯVTЄM) and S are of Brooke 1a, otherwise lettering is of Brooke 2.

Brooke B (II); North 1370; Seaby 1740. Ex Lockett (3078).

218 Noble

7.00	108.0	170°

Obv.: hЄΝRIႺ⦂DI⦂GRⱯ⦂RЄX×ⱯΝGL⦂Ⱦ×FRⱯΝႺ⦂ˋDΝS⦂hYB'
Ornaments, –11–11. Ropes, 3/2. Quatrefoils, 3/4. No annulet on rudder. Letters I, M and S are of Brooke 1a, otherwise lettering is of Brooke 2.

Rev.: ✠IhˋႺˣⱯVTЄMˣTRⱯΝSIЄΝSˣPЄRˣMЄDIVˣILLORVˣIBⱯT
Plain initial cross. Letters I, M and S are of Brooke 1a, otherwise lettering is of Brooke 2.

Brooke B (II); North 1370; Seaby 1740. Bt Spink, ex Beresford Jones.

219 Noble

6.84	105.5	160°

Obv.: hЄΝRIႺ⦂D'IˣGRⱯˋˣRЄX×ⱯΝGL⦂Ⱦ×FRⱯΝႺ⦂DΝS⦂hYB'
Ornaments unclear (one lis visible). Ropes, 3/2. Quatrefoils, 3/4. No annulet on rudder. Letters I, M and S are of Brooke 1a, otherwise lettering is of Brooke 2.

Rev.: ✢ IhˋႺˣⱯVTЄMˣTRⱯΝSIЄΝSˣPЄRˣMЄDIVˣILLORVˣIBⱯT
Letters of Brooke 2.

Brooke B (II/IIIb); North 1370; Seaby 1740. Ex Mangakis 1969.

220 Noble

6.93	106.9	200°

Obv.: hЄΝRIႺ⦂DI×GRⱯ×RЄX×ⱯΝGL×Ⱦ×FRⱯΝႺ⦂DΝS×hYB'
Ornaments, –11–11. Ropes, 3/2. Quatrefoils, 3/4. Annulet on rudder. Letters of Brooke 2.

Rev.: ✢ IhႺ⦂ⱯVTЄMˣTRⱯΝSIЄΝSˣPЄRˣMЄDIVˋˣILLORVˣIBⱯT
Letters M and S of Brooke 1a, letter I and other letters of Brooke 2.

Brooke B (IIIa); North 1370; Seaby 1740. Bt Spink 1952.

[*continued overleaf*]

PLATE 22

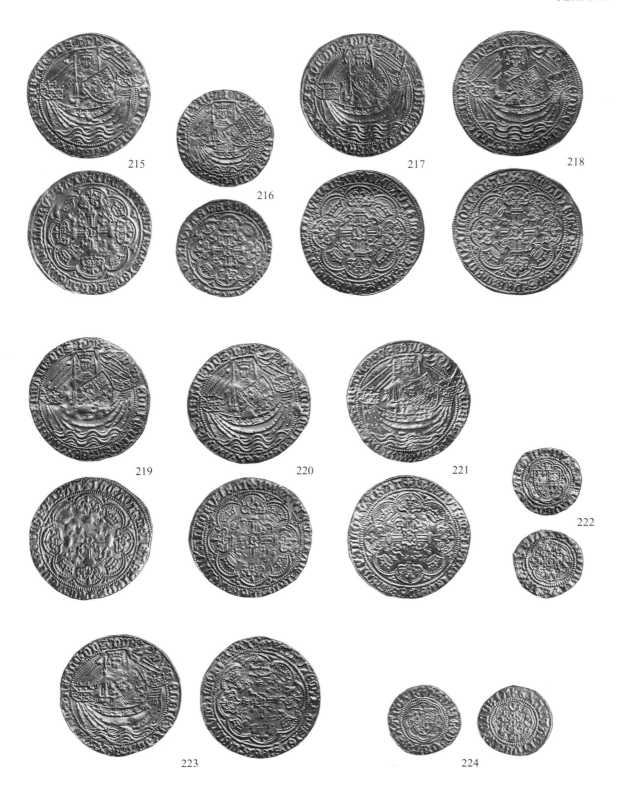

215

216

217

218

219

220

221

222

223

224

Plate 22 (*cont.*)

221 Noble
    6.83   105.4   190°

Obv.: hΛ€NRΙCΛDΙΛGRΛΛR€XΛΛNGLΛΣΛFRΛNCΛDN'SΛhYB
Ornaments, –11–11. Ropes, 3/2. Quatrefoils, 3/4. Annulet on rudder. Letters of Brooke 2.

Rev.: ✠lh'CΛΛVT€MΛTRΛNSI€NSΛP€RΛM€DIVΛILLORVΛIBΛT
Letters of Brooke 2.

Brooke B (IIIb); North 1370; Seaby 1740. Bt Spink 1958.

222 Quarter-noble
    1.64   25.3   100°

Obv.: ✠h€NRICΛDIΛGRΛΛR€XΛΛNGLΛ꙳ F
Large trefoils at points of tressure. Lis over shield. Quatrefoils and annulets beside shield. Letters, Brooke I_2, h_2 and N_2.

Rev.: ✠€XΛLTΛBITVRΛINΛGLORIΛ   Trefoils at angles of central panel. Letters, Brooke I_2 and N_2.

Brooke B (III); North 1381/2; Seaby 1754/–. Ex Dangar (95, part).

CLASS C (IVa–b and Va–t)
Characteristics: Cinquefoil (mullet) in obverse field, by the king's wrist on the nobles, over the shield on the half-nobles and alongside the shield on the quarter-nobles. Annulet on rudder (IV) or broken annulet on the ship's side (V). Quatrefoil over sail. Letters of Brooke 2 (IVa) or with large C, €, and I (IVb) or with the progressive introduction of other letter forms (Va–t, see individual coin descriptions). Quatrefoil above lion's head in second quarter of reverse (nobles) or broken annulet in the same position on the half-nobles.

CLASS C/HENRY IV MULE

London mint only

223 Noble
    6.93   106.9   180°

Obv.: hΛ€NRICΛDIΛGRΛΛR€XΛΛNGLΛΣΛFRΛNCΛDN'SΛhYB'
Ornaments, –11–11. Ropes, 3/2. Quatrefoils, 3/4. Annulet on rudder. Large letters C, € and I.

Rev.: ✠lh'CΛΛVT€MΛTRΛNSI€NSΛP€RΛM€DIVMΛILLORVΛIBΛT
Die of Henry IV light coinage. Plain initial cross. Slipped trefoil (described by Mr Schneider on his ticket as a lis) in first quarter by lion's head. Pellet to left of h in centre.

Brooke C (IVb)/–; North 1371/1355; Seaby 1741/1715. Bt Spink 1964.

CLASS C/B MULE

London mint only

224 Quarter-noble
    1.69   26.1   0°

Obv.: ✠h€NRICΛDIΛGRΛΛR€XΛΛN'GΛ꙳ΛFΛ
Annulets at points of tressure. Lis above and quatrefoils on each side of shield. Mullet below shield to right. Letters Brooke 2.

Rev.: ✠€XΛLTΛBITVRΛINΛGLORIΛ   Trefoils at angles of the central panel. Letters Brooke 2.

Brooke C/B (IV_2/III); North 1382/1381/2; Seaby 1755/–. Ex Lockett (3082).

CLASS C (IVa–b and Va–t) (*cont.*)

TRUE COINS OF CLASS C

London mint only

225 Noble

	Weight	
g	*gr.*	*Die-axis*
6.95	107.2	60°

Obv.: h/ENRIC×DI×GRA×REX×ANGL×ɜ×FRANC×DNS×hYB
Ornaments, –11–11. Ropes, 3/2. Quatrefoils, 3/3. Annulet on rudder.
Letters Brooke 2. Mr Schneider considered this to be an old die of
Brooke IIIb with a cinquefoil added at the wrist.
Rev.: ✚IhC×AVTEM×TRANSIENS×PER×MEDIV×ILLORV×IBAT
Plain (but perhaps filled-in) initial cross. Letters Brooke 2.
Brooke C (IVa); North 1371; Seaby 1741. No provenance.

226 Noble
6.97　107.6　30°

Obv.: h/ENRIC×DI×GRA×REX×ANGL×ɜ×FRANC×DN'S×hYB'
Ornaments, –11–11. Ropes, 3/2. Quatrefoils, 3/3. Annulet on rudder. Broken
annulet on side of ship. Large C, E and I, otherwise letters of Brooke 2.
Rev.: ✚IhC×AVTEM×TRANSIENS×PER×MEDIV×ILLORV×IBAT
Large C, E and I, letter Brooke P_3, otherwise letters of Brooke 2.
Brooke C (IVb); North 1371; Seaby 1742. Bt Spink 1967; ex PKP.

227 Noble
6.90　106.6　280°

Obv.: h/ENRIC×DI×GRA×REX×ANGL×ↄ×FRANC×DN'S×hYB'
Ornaments, –11–11. Ropes, 3/2. Quatrefoils, 3/3. Nothing on rudder. Broken
annulet on side of ship. Large C, E and I, otherwise letters of Brooke 2.
Rev.: ✚IhC×AVTEM×TRANSIENS×PER×MEDIV×ILLORV×IBAT
Large C, E and I, letter Brooke P_3, otherwise letters of Brooke 2.
Brooke C (IVb); North 1371; Seaby 1742. Bt Spink; ex Mangakis.

228 Noble
6.88　106.2　250°

Obv.: h/ENRIC×DI×GRA×REX×ANGL×ɜ×FRANC×DNS×hYB
Ornaments, –11–11. Ropes, 3/2. Quatrefoils, 3/3. Nothing on rudder. Broken
annulet on side of ship. Letters Brooke N_6, h_4 (mended), I_4 and C reversed for
D.
Rev.: ✚IhC×AVTEM×TRANSIENS×PER×MEDIV×ILLORV×IBAT
Letters Brooke I_4, h_5, N_6 and P_8.
Brooke C (Vp/Vr); North 1371; Seaby 1742. Bt Spink 1960.

229 Noble
6.85　105.7　310°

Obv.: h/ENRIC×DI×GRA×REX×ANGL×ɜ×FRANC×DN'S×hYB'
Ornaments, –11–11. Ropes, 3/2. Quatrefoils, 3/3. Nothing on rudder. Broken
annulet on side of ship. Letters Brooke h_4, I_3 and N_6.
Rev.: ✚Ih'C×AVTEM×TRANSIENS×PER×MEDIV×ILLORV×IBAT
Letters Brooke h_4, I_4, N_6 and P_8.
Brooke C (Vb/Vs); North 1371; Seaby 1742. Bt Glendining sale 31.3.1965 (115).

230 Noble
6.89　106.4　160°

Obv.: h/ENRIC×DI×GRA×REX×ANGL×ɜ×FRANC×DN'S×hYB'
Ornaments, –11–11. Ropes, 3/2. Quatrefoils, 3/3. Nothing on rudder. Annulet
on side of ship doubtful. Letters Brooke C_4, h_4, I_3, N_4 and Y_2.
Rev.: ✚IhC×AVTEM×TRANSIENS×PER×MEDIV×ILLORV×IBAT
Letters Brooke h_3, I_3, N_4 and P_7.
Brooke C (Vh/Vi); North 1371; Seaby 1742. Bt Spink 1957.

231 Noble
6.73　103.8　120°

Obv.: h/ENRIC×DI×GRA×REX×ANGL×ɜ×FRANC×DNS×hIB
Ornaments, –11–11. Ropes, 3/2. Quatrefoils, 3/3. Nothing on rudder. Broken
annulet on side of ship. Reads hIB. Letters Brooke C_3, large E, I_3 and N_3.
Rev.: ✚IhC×AVTEM×TRANSIENS×PER×MEDIV×ILLORV×IBAT
Letters Brooke C_3, large E, I_3, N_3 and larger T. Flaw in M punch.
Brooke C (Vb/Va); North 1371; Seaby 1742. Bt Spink 1967; ex Angers Hoard.

[*continued overleaf*]

PLATE 23

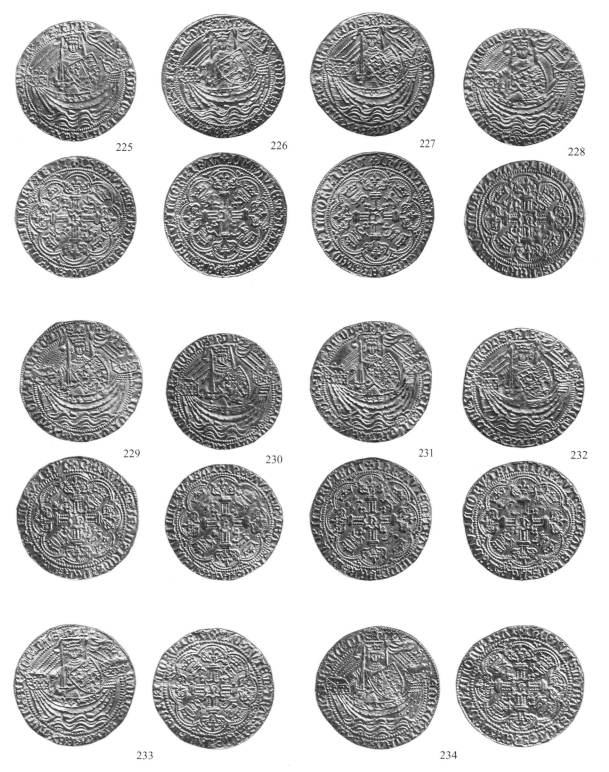

225   226   227   228

229   230   231   232

233   234

Plate 23 (*cont.*)

232 Noble
    6.95   107.3   180°

Obv.: hⒺNRIⒶ⦂DI⦂GRᴧ×RⒺX×ᴧNGL⦂Ƨ×FRᴧNⒶ⦂DNS⦂hIB
Ornaments, –11–11. Ropes, 3/2. Quatrefoils, 3/3. Nothing on rudder. Broken annulet on side of ship. Letters Brooke $\mathrm{Ⓐ}_3$, large Ⓔ, I_3 and N_3.

Rev.: ✙Ih'Ⓐ×ᴧVTⒺM⦂TRᴧNSIⒺNS⦂PⒺR⦂MⒺDIV⦂ILLORV⦂IBᴧT
Letters Brooke N_4 and P_5. Flaw in h in centre of reverse mended but that in IhⒶ not mended.
Brooke C (Vb/Vg); North 1371; Seaby 1742. Bt Spink 1969; ex Mangakis.

233 Noble
    6.90   106.5   20°

Obv.: hⒺNRIⒶ×DI⦂GRᴧ⦂RⒺX×ᴧNGL⦂Ƨ×FRᴧNⒶ⦂DN'S×hYB
Ornaments, –11–11. Ropes, 3/2. Quatrefoils, 3/3. Nothing on rudder. Broken annulet on side of ship. Letters Brooke h_5, I_3, N_6 and Y_3.

Rev.: ✙Ih'Ⓐ×ᴧVTⒺM⦂TRᴧNSIⒺNS⦂PⒺR⦂MⒺDIV⦂ILLORV⦂IBᴧT
Letters Brooke h_5, I_4, N_6 and Y_3.
Brooke C (Vs [similar]/Vt); North 1371; Seaby 1742. No provenance.

234 Noble
    6.88   106.2   170°

Obv.: hⒺNRIⒶ⦂DI⦂GRᴧ⦂RⒺX×ᴧNGL⦂Ƨ FRᴧNⒶ⦂DN'S×hYB'
Ornaments, –11–11. Ropes, 3/2. Quatrefoils, 3/3. Nothing on rudder. Broken annulet on side of ship: Letters Brooke h_5, I_4, N_7 and Y_3.

Rev.: ✙Ih'Ⓐ×ᴧVTⒺM⦂TRᴧNSIⒺNS⦂PⒺR⦂MⒺDIV⦂ILLORV⦂IBᴧT
Letters Brooke h_5, I_4 and P_8.
Brooke C (Vt/Vt); North 1371; Seaby 1742. Bt Spink 1958.

CLASS C (IVa–b and Va–t) (*cont.*)

TRUE COINS OF CLASS C (*cont.*)

London mint only (cont.)

235 Noble

	Weight	
g	gr.	Die-axis
6.80	105.0	60°

Obv.: h/ENRIC⦂DI⦂GRA⦂REX×ANGL⦂ᵴ×FRANC⦂DNS×hYB
Ornaments, –11–11. Ropes, 3/2 Quatrefoils, 3/3. Nothing on rudder.
Broken annulet on side of ship. Letters Brooke h_4, I_3, N_5 and Y_2.
Rev.: ✠IhC×AVTEM·TRANSIENS⦂PER⦂MEDIV⦂ILLORV⦂IBAT
Letters Brooke h_3 (centre), h_4 (IhC), I_3 but N_6. C reversed for D. Flaw in M.
Brooke C (Vm var./VI); North 1371; Seaby 1742. Bt Spink 1960.

236 Noble

6.80 105.0 110°

Obv.: h/ENRIC⦂DI⦂GRA⦂REX×ANGL⦂ᵴ×FRANC⦂DN'S×hYB'
Ornaments, –11–11. Ropes, 3/2. Quatrefoils, 3/3. Nothing on rudder. Broken
annulet on side of ship. Letters Brooke C_3, large E, I_3 and N_3.
Rev.: ✠IhC×AVTEM⦂TRANSIENS⦂PER⦂MEDIV⦂ILLORV⦂IBAT
Letters Brooke N_4 and P_4. Flaw in h mended in central compartment but not in
IhC.
Brooke C (Va/Vf); North 1371; Seaby 1742. Bt Spink 1961.

237 Half-noble

3.37 52.0 40°

Obv.: h/ENRIC×DI⦂GRA⦂REX×ANGL⦂ᵴ×FR⦂D⦂hYB
Ornaments, –11(?). Ropes, 3/1. Quatrefoils, 3/3. Broken annulet on side of ship.
Letters Brooke C_4, h_3 in hYB, h_4 in hENRIC, I_3 and N_4.
Rev.: ✠DOMINE×NE⦂IN⦂FVRORE⦂TVO⦂ARGVAS⦂ME   Letters Brooke I_3
and N_4.
Brooke C (Ve–h/Vd); North 1377, later variety; Seaby 1749. Bt Seaby 1956.

238 Half-noble

3.33 51.4 340°

Obv.: h/ENRIC×DI×GRA×REX×ANGL⦂ᵴ×FR⦂D⦂hYB'
Ornaments, –11–11. Ropes, 3/1. Quatrefoils, 3/3. Broken annulet on side of
ship. Letters Brooke C_4, h_4, I_3 and N_5.
Rev.: ✠DOMINE⦂NE⦂IN⦂FVRORE⦂TVO⦂ARGVAS⦂ME   Letters Brooke I_3
and N_4.
Brooke C (Vm/Vd); North 1377, later variety; Seaby 1749. No provenance.

239 Half-noble

3.44 53.1 260°

Obv.: h/ENRIC×DI×GRA×REX×ANGL⦂ᵴ×FR⦂hYB
Ornaments, –11(?). Ropes, 3/1. Quatrefoils, 3/3. Quatrefoil (?) before
hENRIC. Broken annulet on side of ship. Letters Brooke h_5, I_4, N_6 and Y_3.
Rev.: ✠DOMINE×NE⦂IN⦂FVRORE⦂TVO⦂ARGVAS⦂ME   Letters Brooke I_3
and N_6.
Brooke C (Vs/Vs); North 1377, later variety; Seaby 1749. Ex Lockett (4001).

240 Quarter-noble

1.73 26.7 280°

Obv.: ✠hENRIC⦂REX×ANGL⦂ᵴ×FRANC   Plain initial cross.
Annulets at points of tressure. Lis above shield. Broken annulet to left and
mullet to right of shield. Letters Brooke 2 but with large C, E and I.
Rev.: ✠EXALTABITVR⦂IN⦂GLORIA   Trefoils at angles of the central panel.
Letters Brooke 2 but with large E and I_3.
Brooke C (Va/IV); North 1382; Seaby 1756. No provenance.

241 Quarter-noble

1.27 19.6 210°
(clipped)

Obv.: hENRIC⦂REX×ANGL×ᵴ×FRANC×   Apparently no initial cross.
Annulets at points of tressure. Lis above shield. Broken annulet to left and
cinquefoil to right of shield. Letters Brooke C_3, large E, I_3 and N_3.
Rev.: ✠EXALTABITVR⦂IN⦂GLORIA   Trefoils at angles of the central panel.
Letters Brooke large E, I_3 and N_2.
Brooke C (Va/IV); North 1382; Seaby 1756 var. Bt Spink 1953.

[*continued overleaf*]

PLATE 24

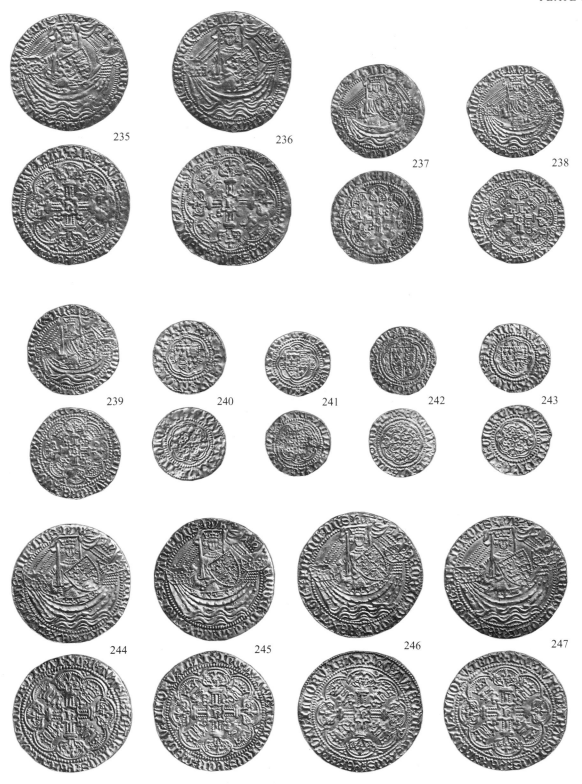

235   236   237   238

239   240   241   242   243

244   245   246   247

Plate 24 (*cont.*)

242 Quarter-noble
    1.46   22.5   180°

Obv.: ✠hЄNRIᗡ×DI⦂GRᗩ⦂RЄX×ᗩNG×Ƨ×   Plain initial cross.
Annulets at points of tressure. Lis above shield. Annulet to left and cinquefoil to right of shield. Mullet below shield to left. Letters Brooke h_4, I_3 and N_4.

Rev.: ✠ЄXᗩLTᗩBITVR⦂IN⦂GLORIᗩ   Trefoils at angles of central panel. Letters Brooke I_3 and N_3.

Brooke C (Vd–i/Va); North 1382; Seaby 1756 var. Ex Glendining sale 24.11.1960 (259).

243 Quarter-noble
    1.77   27.1   200°

Obv.: ✠hЄNRIᗡ⦂RЄX×ᗩNGL⦂Ƨ×FRᗩNᗡ   Plain initial cross.
Annulets at points of tressure. Lis above shield. Broken annulet to left and mullet to right of shield. Letters Brooke h_5, I_4 and N_6.

Rev.: ✠ЄXᗡVLTᗩBITVR⦂IN⦂GLORIᗩ   Note mispelling of ЄXᗩLTᗩBITVR. Trefoils at angles of central panel. Lettering Brooke I_4 and N_6.

Brooke C (Vs/Vr–s); North 1382; Seaby 1756 var. Bt Baldwin 1952; ex Carter.

CLASS D (VI)

Characteristics: Trefoil added by shield. cinquefoil (mullet) and annulet either side of wrist. Quatrefoil above sail. Broken annulet on side of ship. Letter P on the reverse always of Brooke 9. Quatrefoil by head of lion in second quarter of reverse.

CLASS D/C MULE

London mint only

244 Noble
    6.89   106.3   280°

Obv.: h/ЄNRIᗡ×DI⦂GRᗩ×RЄX×ᗩNGL⦂Ƨ×FRᗩNᗡ⦂DN'S×hУB'
Ornaments, –11–11. Ropes, 3/2. Quatrefoils, 3/3. Broken annulet on side of ship. Letters Brooke $ᗡ_4$, ordinary D, h_5, I_4 and N_7.

Rev.: ✠Ih'ᗡ×ᗩVTЄM⦂TRᗩNSIЄNS⦂PЄR⦂MЄDIV⦂ILLORV⦂IBᗩT   Letters Brooke $ᗡ_4$, h_5 (unbroken in centre), N_7 and P_8.

Brooke D/C (VI/Vt); North 1371/1372; Seaby 1743/1742. Bt Spink 1958.

TRUE COIN OF CLASS D

London mint only

245 Noble
    6.95   107.2   230°

Obv.: h/ЄNRIᗡ⦂DI⦂GRᗩ⦂RЄX×ᗩNGL⦂Ƨ×FRᗩNᗡ⦂DN'S×hУB'
Ornaments, –11–11. Ropes, 3/2. Quatrefoils, 3/3. Broken annulet on side of ship. Letters Brooke $ᗡ_4$, ordinary D, h_5, I_4 and N_7.

Rev.: ✠Ih'ᗡ×ᗩVTЄM⦂TRᗩNSIЄNS⦂PЄR⦂MЄDIV⦂ILLORV⦂IBᗩT
Letters Brooke $ᗡ_4$, h_5, N_7 and P_9.

Brooke D (VI); North 1372; Seaby 1743. Bt Spink 1957.

Plate 24 (*cont.*)

CLASS E (VIIa–d)
Characteristics: Pellet added at sword point. Trefoil by shield. Quatrefoil and annulet by wrist. Quatrefoil above sail. Annulet on side of ship, sometimes broken, sometimes not. On the reverse pellet by tail of lion in the first quarter and quatrefoil by head of lion in the second quarter.

CLASS E/D MULES

London mint only

246 Noble
     6.99   107.8   220°

Obv.: hЄNRIꝀ⁚DI⁚GRⱭ⁚RЄX×ⱭNGL⁚ϟ×FRⱭNꝀ⁚DN'S×hYB'
Ornaments, –11–11. Ropes, 3/2. Quatrefoils, 3/3. Broken annulet on side of ship. Letters Brooke h_5, l_4, n_8 and y_4.
Rev.: ✠Ih'Ꝁ×ⱭVTЄM⁚TRⱭNSIЄNS⁚PЄR×MЄDIV⁚ILLORV⁚IBⱭT
Letters Brooke h_5, l_4 and P_9.
Brooke E/D (VII/VI); North 1373/1372; Seaby 1744/1743. Ex von Thielau 1960 (not in sale).

247 Noble
     6.90   106.5   50°

Obv.: hЄNRIꝀ⁚DI⁚GRⱭ⁚RЄX×ⱭNGL⁚ϟ×FRⱭNꝀ⁚DN'S×hYB'
Ornaments, –11–11. Ropes, 3/2. Quatrefoils, 3/3. Unbroken annulet on side of ship. Letters Brooke h_5, l_4, n_8 and y_4.
Rev.: ✠Ih'Ꝁ×ⱭVTЄM⁚TRⱭNSIЄNS⁚PЄR×MЄDIV⁚ILLORV⁚IBⱭT
Letters Brooke h_5, l_4 and P_9.
Brooke E/D (VIIb/VI); North 1373/1372; Seaby 1744/1743. Ex J. C. S. Rashleigh (6).

CLASS E (VIIa–d) (*cont.*)

CLASS E/D MULES (*cont.*)

London mint only (cont.)

	Weight		
	g	*gr.*	*Die-axis*

248 Noble

6.93   106.9   300°

Obv.: h/ENRIC⁚DI⁚GRA⁚REX⁚ANGL⁚ᵴ×FRANC⁚DN'S×hYB'
Ornaments, –11–11. Ropes, 2/1. Quatrefoils, 3/3. Broken annulet on side of ship. Letters Brooke A_5, h_5, N_7 and Y_4.

Rev.: ✠Ih'C×AVTEM⁚TRANSIENS⁚PER⁚MEDIV⁚ILLORV⁚IBAT
Letters Brooke h_5, I_4, N_7 and P_9. Mr Schneider noted 'this reverse with N_7 is rather disturbing'.
Brooke E/D (VIIc/VI); North 1373/1372; Seaby 1744/1743. Ex Goulburn (236); ex Haswell (76).

TRUE COINS OF CLASS E

London mint only

249 Noble

6.98   107.7   130°

Obv.: h/ENRIC⁚DI⁚GRA×REX⁚ANGL⁚ᵴ×FRANC⁚DN'S×hYB'
Ornaments, –11–11. Ropes, 3/2. Quatrefoils, 3/3. Unbroken annulet on side of ship. Letters Brooke h_5, I_4, N_8 and Y_4.

Rev.: ✠Ih'C×AVTEM⁚TRANSIENS⁚PER⁚MEDIV⁚ILLORV⁚IBAT
Letters Brooke h_5, I_4, N_9 and P_8.
Brooke E (VIIb/VII); North 1373; Seaby 1744. Ex Hall (42).

250 Noble

6.94   107.1   140°

Obv.: h/ENRIC⁚DI⁚GRA⁚REX×ANGL⁚ᵴ×FRANC⁚DN'S×hYB'
Ornaments, 1–11–1. Ropes, 2/1. Quatrefoils, 3/3. Ship has no mast. Y in hYB is altered from I. Unbroken annulet on side of ship. Letters Brooke h_5, I_4 and N_8.

Rev.: ✠Ih'C×AVTEM⁚TRANSIENS⁚PER⁚MEDIV⁚ILLORV⁚IBAT
Letters Brooke h_5, N_8 and P_9.
Brooke E (VIIc var./VII); North 1373; Seaby 1744. Bt Spink 1958.

251 Noble

6.96   107.4   50°

Obv.: h/ENRIC×DI⁚GRA×REX×ANGL⁚ᵴ×FRANC⁚DN'S×hYB
Ornaments, 1–1–. Ropes, 2/1. Quatrefoils, 3/3. Unbroken annulet on side of ship. Letters Brooke h_5, I_4 and N_8.

Rev.: ✠Ih'C×AVTEM⁚TRANSIENS⁚PER⁚MEDIV×ILLORV×IBAT
Late type of fleurs in spandrels. letters Brooke h_5, I_4 and N_8.
Brooke E (VIIc/VII); North 1373; Seaby 1744. Bt Baldwin 1952; ex Carter.

252 Noble

6.91   106.7   50°

Obv.: h/ENRIC⁚DI⁚GRA⁚REX⁚ANGL⁚ᵴ×FRANC⁚DN'S×hYB'
Ornaments, –11–11. Ropes, 2/1. Quatrefoils, 3/3. Broken annulet on side of ship. Letters Brooke N_8 and Y_4.

Rev.: ✠Ih'C×AVTEM⁚TRANSIENS⁚PER⁚MEDIV⁚ILLORV⁚IBAT
Letters Brooke N_8 and P_9.
Brooke E (VIIc/VII); North 1373; Seaby 1744. Bt Spink 1961.

[*continued overleaf*]

PLATE 25

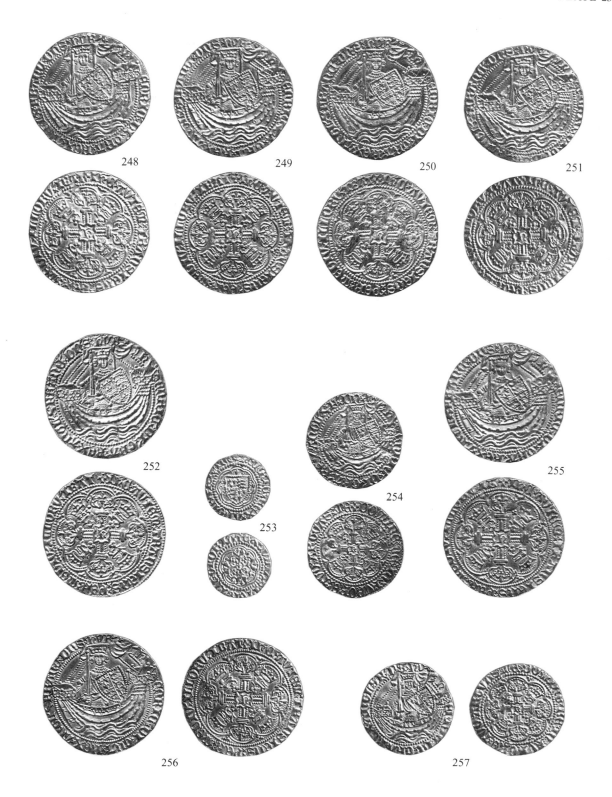

248   249   250   251

252   253   254   255

256   257

Plate 25 (*cont.*)

CLASS F (VIIIa and b)
Characteristics: No longer pellet at sword point. Trefoil by shield. Quatrefoil above sail. Cinquefoil (VIIIa) or cinquefoil and annulet (VIIIb) by wrist. Annulet (VIIIa) or trefoil (VIIIb) on side of ship. On reverse trefoil by tail of lion in first quarter and quatrefoil by head of lion in second quarter. Quarter-noble with trefoil to left and cinquefoil to right of shield.

CLASS C/F MULE

London mint only

253 Quarter-noble
   1.55   23.9   220°

Obv.: ✠hENRIΓ⦂REX×ΛNGL⦂ჴ FRΛNΓ
Annulets at points of tressure. Lis above shield. Broken annulet to left and cinquefoil to right of shield. Letters Brooke h_5, I_4 and N_8.
Rev.: ✠EXΓVLTΛBITVR⦂IN⦂GLORIΛ   Trefoils at angles of the central panel. Letters Brooke h_5, I_4 and N_8.
Brooke C/F (Vs/VIII); North 1382/1383; Seaby 1756/1757. Ex Lockett (4293).

CLASS F/D MULE

London mint only

254 Half-noble
   3.41   52.7   200°

Obv.: h/ENRIΓ⦂DI⦂GRΛ⦂REX×ΛNGL⦂ჴ×F⦂DN⦂hY
Ornaments, –11–11. Ropes, 2/1. Quatrefoils, 3/3. Mullet above and trefoil to right of shield. No quatrefoil visible above sail. No annulet on side of ship. Letters Brooke N_7 and Y_4.
Rev.: ✠DOMINE⦂NE⦂IN⦂FVRORE⦂TVO⦂ΛRGVΛS⦂ME
Unbroken annulet above lion's head in second quarter. Letters Brooke I_4 and N_7.
Brooke F/D (VIII$_1$/VIa); North 1379/–; Seaby 1751/–. Ex Lockett (1400); ex P. W. P. Carlyon-Britton.

CLASS E/F MULES

London mint only

255 Noble
   6.88   106.2   320°

Obv.: h/ENRIΓ⦂DI⦂GRΛ⦂REX×ΛNGL⦂ჴ×FRΛNΓ⦂DNS⦂hYB
Ornaments, –11–1. Ropes, 2/1. Quatrefoils, 3/3. Pellet at sword point. No mark above sail (may be off-flan). Trefoil by shield. Unbroken annulet on side of ship. Letters Brooke N_7 (apparently) and Y_4.
Rev.: ✠IhΓ×ΛVTEM⦂TRΛNSIENS⦂PER×MEDIV×ILLORV×IB
Apparently Λ struck over B of IB. Letters Brooke N_8 and P_9.
Brooke E/F (VIIc/VIII); North 1373/1374; Seaby 1744/1746. Ex Glendining sale 17.10.1969 (32); ex Fishpool Hoard.

256 Noble
   6.91   106.7   220°

Obv.: h/ENRIΓ⦂DI⦂GRΛ⦂REX×ΛNGL'ჴ FRΛNΓ⦂DNS⦂hYB'
Ornaments, –11–1. Ropes, 2/1. Quatrefoils, 3/3. Pellet at sword point. Quatrefoil (probably) above sail. Cinquefoil and annulet either side of wrist. Trefoil by shield. Trefoil on side of ship. Letters Brooke h_5, I_4 and N_6.
Rev.: ✠Ih'Γ×ΛVTEM⦂TRΛNSIENS⦂PER⦂MEDIV×ILLORV⦂IBΛT
Letters Brooke h_5, I_4, N_6 and P_9.
Brooke E/F (VIId/VIIIa); North 1373/1374; Seaby 1745/1746. Ex Lockett (1398); ex Bruun (384); ex Walters, 1913 (272).

Plate 25 (*cont.*)

London mint only

257 Half-noble   *Obv.*: hⱰⱰRIⱰ×DI⟨GRꓵ⟨RⱰX×ꓵⱰGL⟨Ʂ×F⟨DS⟨hꓬ'
    3.51   54.1   310°   Ornaments, –11–1. Ropes, 2/1. Quatrefoils, 3/3. No trefoil to right of shield. Nothing on side of ship. S of DS struck over ꓵ. Letters Brooke h_5, I_4, $ꓵ_7$ and $ꓬ_4$.

                   Rev.: DOMIⱰⱰ×ⱰⱰ×IⱰ⟨FVRORⱰ×TVO⟨ꓵRGVꓵS×MⱰ× No initial cross. Pellet above lion's tail in first quarter and annulet above lion's head in second quarter. Letters Brooke normal D, I_4 and $ꓵ_7$.

        Brooke F/E (VIII2/VIIe); North 1379/1378; Seaby 1752. Ex E. W. Rashleigh (702).

CLASS F (VIIIa and b) (*cont.*)

TRUE COINS OF CLASS F (?)

London mint only

258 Quarter-noble

	Weight	
g	gr.	Die-axis
1.69	26.1	20°

Obv.: ✠hЄNRIᏟ⫶RЄX×ᴧNGL⫶Ꙅ×FRᴧᏟ'
Annulets at points of tressure. Lis above shield. Trefoil to left and cinquefoil to right of shield. Letters Brooke h_5 and N_7.

Rev.: ✠ЄXᴧLTᴧBITVR⫶IN⫶GLORIᴧ   Trefoils at angles of central panel. Letter Brooke N_8.

Brooke F (VIII/VIIIa); North 1383; Seaby 1757. Ex Glendining sale 8.12.1992 (39); ex Reigate, Brokes Road, hoard.

259 Quarter-noble

1.67	25.7	0°

Obv.: ✠hЄNRIᏟ⫶RЄX×ᴧNGL⫶Ꙅ×FRᴧN
Annulets at points of tressure. Lis above shield. Trefoil to left and cinquefoil to right of shield. Letters Brooke h, I_4 and N_8.

Rev.: ✠ЄXᴧLTᴧBITVR×IN×GLORIᴧ   Trefoils at angles of central panels. Letters Brooke h, I_4 and N_8.

Brooke F (VIII/VIIIa); North 1383; Seaby 1757. Ex Lockett (1404); ex Ready (407).

CLASS G (IX)

Characteristics: No marks in fields. No symbol over sail. Mullet after the first word on each side. Punctuation is annulets in place of the saltires used on earlier classes.

CLASS F/G MULES

London mint only

260 Noble

6.94	107.1	140°

Obv.: h/ЄNRIᏟ⫶DI⫶GRᴧ⫶RЄX×ᴧNGL⫶Ꙅ×FRᴧNᏟ⫶DN'S×hYB'
Ornaments, –11–1. Ropes, 2/1. Quatrefoils, 3/3. Quatrefoil above sail. Cinquefoil and annulet either side of wrist. Trefoil by shield. Trefoil on side of ship. Letter Brooke N_8.

Rev.: ✠Ih'Ꮯ★ᴧVTЄM⫶TRᴧNSIЄNS°PЄR°MЄDIV⫶ILLORV⫶IBᴧT
Earlier form of letter h in centre. Letters Brooke I_4, N_8 and P_9.

Brooke F/G (VIIIb/IX); North 1374/1375; Seaby 1746/1747. Ex Glendining sale 17.10.1968 (33); ex Fishpool hoard.

261 Noble

6.94	107.1	230°

Obv.: h/ЄNRIᏟ⫶DI⫶GRᴧ⫶RЄX×ᴧNGL⫶Ꙅ×FRᴧNᏟ⫶DN'S⫶hYB'
Ornaments, –11–1. Ropes, 2/1. Quatrefoils, 3/3. Quatrefoil above sail. Cinquefoil and annulet either side of wrist. Trefoil by shield. Trefoil on side of ship. Letter Brooke N_8.

Rev.: ✠Ih'Ꮯ★ᴧVTЄM°TRᴧNSIЄNS°PЄR°MЄDIV⫶ILLORV⫶IBᴧT
Later form of letter h in centre. Letters Brooke I_4, N_8 and P_9.

Brooke F/G (VIIIb/IX); North 1374/1375; Seaby 1746/1747. Bt Spink 1962.

CLASS G/F MULE

London mint only

262 Noble

6.97	107.5	280°

Obv.: h/ЄNRIᏟ★DI⫶GRᴧ⫶RЄX°ᴧNGL'[   ]ᴧNᏟ⫶DN'S°hYB'
Ornaments, –11–1. Ropes, 2/1. Quatrefoils, 3/3. Annulet stops. Letters Brooke h_6, I_4, N_4 (?) and Y_5.

Rev.: ✠Ih'Ꮯ×ᴧVTЄM⫶TRᴧNIЄNS⫶PЄR⫶MЄDIV⫶ILLORV⫶IBᴧT
Trefoil by lion's tail in first quarter and quatrefoil by lion's head in second quarter. Ꙅ omitted from TRᴧNSIЄNS. Letters Brooke h_5, I_4, N_8 and P_9.

Brooke G/F (IX/VIII); North 1375/1374; Seaby 1747/1746. Bt Spink 1993.

[*continued overleaf*]

PLATE 26

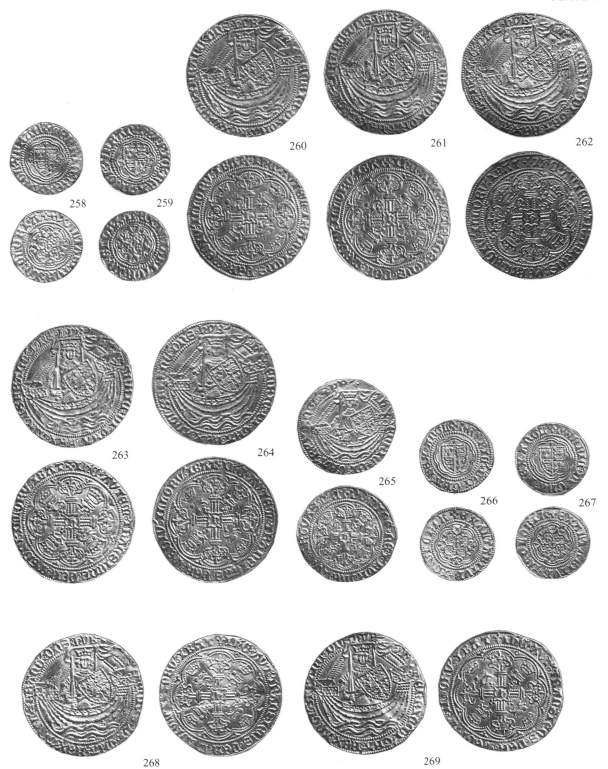

258

259

260

261

262

263

264

265

266

267

268

269

Plate 26 (*cont.*)

London mint only

263 Noble
    6.92   106.8   70°

Obv.: hᗺПRIᏟ★DIᒐGRᗅᒐᐧRᗺX°ᗅПGLᐧᔓᐧFRᗅПᏟᒐᐧDПᐧSᐧhᎩB'
Ornaments, –11–1. Ropes, 2/1. Quatrefoils, 3/3. Letters Brooke h_6, I_4, N_3 and Y_5.

Rev.: ✚Ih'Ꮯ★ᗅVTᗺᙢᐧTRᗅПSIᗺПSᐧPᗺRᐧᙢᗺDIVᒐᐧILLORVᒐᐧIBᗅT
Small fleurs in spandrels. Letters Brooke I_4, N_8 and P_9.
Brooke G (IX/IX); North 1375; Seaby 1747. Ex Ryan (33); ex P. W. P. Carlyon-Britton.

264 Noble
    6.88   106.2   290°

Obv.: hᗺПRIᏟ★DIᒐGRᗅᒐᐧRᗺX°ᗅПGLᒐᔓᐧFRᗅПᏟᒐᐧDПᐧSᐧhᎩB'
Ornaments, –11–1. Ropes, 2/1. Quatrefoils, 3/3. The mullet after hᗺПRIᏟ is struck over an annulet. Letters Brooke h_6, I_4, N_3 and Y_5.

Rev.: ✚Ih'Ꮯ★ᗅVTᗺᙢᐧTRᗅПSIᗺПSᐧPᗺRᐧᙢᗺDIVᒐᐧILLORVᒐᐧIBᗅT
Large fleurs in spandrels. Letters Brooke I_4, N_8 and P_9.
Brooke G (IX/IX); North 1375; Seaby 1747. Ex Lockett (4291); ex Bruun (388).

265 Half-noble
    3.42   52.8   10°

Obv.: hᗺПRIᏟ★DIᒐGRᗅᒐᐧRᗺX°ᗅПGLᒐᔓᐧFR'
Ornaments, –11–1. Ropes, 2/1. Quatrefoils, 3/3. Quatrefoil above sail. Letter Brooke I_4.

Rev.: ✚DOᙢIПᗺ★ПᗺᐧIᒐᐧFVRORᗺᐧTVOᐧᗅRGVᗅSᐧᙢᗺ
Letter Brooke I_4.
Brooke G (IX/IX, his dies IX_2/IX_a); North 1380; Seaby 1753. Ex Beresford-Jones 1972.

266 Quarter-noble
    1.72   26.6   0°

Obv.: ✚hᗺПRIᏟ★DᗺIᐧGRᗅᒐᐧRᗺX°ᗅПGL'
Lis above shield. Nothing on points of tressure. Letters Brooke h_6, I_4 and N_7.

Rev.: ✚ᗺXᗅLTᗅBITVR★IПᐧGLORIᗅ   Trefoils at angles of the central panel. Letter Brooke I_4.
Brooke G (IX/IXa); North 1384; Seaby 1758. Ex Grantley (25).

267 Quarter-noble
    1.68   26.0   230°

Obv.: hᗺПRIᏟ★DIᒐGRᗅᒐᐧRᗺX°ᗅПGL'
Lis above shield. Nothing on points of tressure. Letters Brooke h_6, I_4, N_7.

Rev.: ✚ᗺXᗅLTᗅBITVR★IПᐧGLORIᗅ   Trefoils at angles of the central panel. Letter Brooke I_5.
Brooke G (IX/IXb); North 1384; Seaby 1758. Ex Doubleday (44).

Plate 26 (*cont.*)

HENRY VI, FIRST REIGN (1 September 1422–deposed 4 March 1461)

Gold coinage issued at a fineness of 23 ct 3½ gr. (0.995 fine) and at a nominal weight of 108 gr. (6.999 g) to the noble. Denominations struck were noble, half-noble and quarter-noble. Gold coins were struck at the London, Calais and York mints. The classification used is that set out in Whitton 1938–41 and 1941–4.

ANNULET ISSUE (1422–30)[351]

Characteristics: Annulet by wrist. Lis after hЄПRIɑ and at the commencement of the reverse legend. Mullet after Ihɑ. Calais coins have flag at stern (nobles and half-nobles, quarter-nobles with three lis about the shield are attributed to that mint). York nobles and half-nobles have a lis on the stern of the ship.

MULE OF HENRY V, CLASS F AND HENRY VI, ANNULET ISSUE

London mint

268 Noble			
6.91	106.7	260°	

Obv.: h/ЄПRIɑ ⋮ DI ⋮ GRɅ ⋮ RЄX × ɅПGL ⋮ ⋩ × FRɅПɑ ⋮ DПS ⋮ hƳB'
Ornaments, –11–1. Ropes, 2/1. Quatrefoils, 3/3. Cinquefoil and annulet either side of wrist. Trefoil on side of ship. Quatrefoil above sail. Letter Brooke Пₐ.

Rev.: ✠ Ih'ɑ ★ ɅVT ⋮ TRɅПSIЄПS ∘ PЄR ∘ MЄDIVM ∘ ILLORV ⋮ IBɅT
Annulet in first spandrel of second quarter, trefoils of Whitton 1 in other spandrels. Letters Whitton П₁ and P₁.
Brooke F (VIIIb)/Whitton 1a; North 1374/1414; Seaby 1800. Ex Lockett (1426); ex Bruun (402).

MULES OF HENRY V, CLASS G AND HENRY VI, ANNULET ISSUE

London mint

269 Noble			
6.94	107.1	200°	

Obv.: h/ЄПRIɑ★DI ⋮ GRɅ ⋮ RЄX ∘ ɅПGL ⋮ ⋩ × FRɅПɑ ⋮ DПS hƳB'
Ornaments, –11–1. Ropes, 2/1. Quatrefoils, 3/3. No marks in field or legend. Letters Brooke h₅, I₄ and Пₐ. Same die as next coin, **270**.

Rev.: ✠ Ih'ɑ ★ ɅVT ⋮ TRɅПSIЄПS ∘ PЄR ∘ MЄDIVM ∘ ILLORV ⋮ IBɅT
Annulet in first spandrel of second quarter, trefoils of Whitton 1 in other spandrels. Letters Whitton П₁ and P₁.
Brooke G (IX)/Whitton 1a; North 1375/1414; Seaby 1800. Bt Spink 1955.

---

[351] For a discussion of the chronology of Henry VI's early issues see Appendix 2, pp. 80–4, above).

ANNULET ISSUE (1422–30) (*cont.*)

MULES OF HENRY V, CLASS G, AND HENRY VI, ANNULET ISSUE (*cont.*)

London mint (cont.)

270 Noble

	Weight	
g	*gr.*	*Die-axis*
6.79	104.8	330°

Obv.: same die as last coin, **269**.
Rev.: ✠ Ih'Ɑ ★ ΛVTːTRΛNSIƐNS·PƐR·MƐDIVM·ILLORVːIBΛT
Annulet in first spandrel of second quarter, *all other spandrels empty*.
Letters Whitton Π₁ and P₁. I of IBΛT over Π.
Brooke G (IX)/Whitton 1a var. This is the coin cited in Whitton's Addenda and
Corrigenda in *BNJ* 24, p.118. North 1375/1414; Seaby 1800. Bt Baldwin.

271 Noble
6.94	107.0	170°

Obv.: h/ƐNRIɑ★DIːGRΛːRƐX·ΛNGLːᔓ·FRΛNɑːDN'S·hIB'
Ornaments, −11−1. Ropes, 2/1. Quatrefoils, 3/3. I of hIB over Ƴ. No marks in
field or legend. Letters Brooke h₆, I₄ and Π₈.
Rev.: ✠ Ih'Ɑ ★ ΛVTːTRΛNSIƐNS·PƐR·MƐDIVM·ILLORVːIBΛT
Annulet in first spandrel of second quarter and trefoils of Whitton 1 in other
spandrels. Letters Whitton Π₁ and P₁.
Brooke G (IX)/Whitton 1a; North 1375/1414; Seaby 1800. Bt Spink 1983; ex Lockett
(4296).

272 Half-noble
3.42	52.8	90°

Obv.: h/ƐNRIɑ✦DIːGRΛːRƐX·ΛNGLːᔓ·FR'
Ornaments, −11−1. Ropes, 2/1. Quatrefoils, 3/3. Quatrefoil above the sail
off-flan. No marks in field. Letters Brooke h₆, I₄ and Π₈. Same die as next coin,
273.
Rev.: ✠ DOMINƐ★NƐ·IN·FVRORƐ·TVO·ΛRGVΛS·MƐ
Annulet in first spandrel of second quarter, trefoils in other spandrels. Letter
Whitton F₁.
Brooke G (IX)/Whitton 1; North 1380/1417; Seaby 1806. Ex Doubleday 1961 (45).

273 Half-noble
3.50	53.9	260°

Obv.: Same die as last coin, **272**; the quatrefoil above the sail is clearly visible.
Rev.: ✠ DOMINƐ★NƐ·IN·FVRORƐ·TVO·ΛRGVΛS·MƐ
Annulet in first spandrel of second quarter, trefoils in other spandrels. Letter
Whitton F₁.
Brooke G (IX)/Whitton 1; North 1380/1417; Seaby 1806. Ex Sir Arthur Evans (1438).

TRUE COINS OF THE ANNULET ISSUE

London mint

274 Noble
6.93	106.9	200°

Obv.: h/ƐNRIɑ'✦DI·GRΛːRƐX·ΛNGLːᔓ·FRΛNɑːDNS·hƳB'
Ornaments, −11−1. Annulet by wrist. Letters Whitton F₁ and Π₂.
Rev.: ✠ Ih'Ɑ ★ ΛVTːTRΛNSIƐNS·PƐR·MƐDIVM·ILLORVːIBΛT
Annulet in first spandrel of second quarter and trefoils of Whitton 1 in other
spandrels. Letters Whitton Π₁ and P₁.
Whitton 3a; North 1414; Seaby 1799. Ex Glendining sale 6.5.1954 (8) (Mr Schneider's
ticket refers to this as the Reynolds collection).

275 Noble
6.90	106.5	200°

Obv.: h/ƐNRIɑ'✦DI·GRΛːRƐX·ΛNGLːᔓ·FRΛNɑːDN'S·hƳB'
Ornaments, 1−1−1. Annulet by wrist. Letters Whitton F₁ and Π₂.
Rev.: ✠ Ih'Ɑ ★ ΛVTːTRΛNSIƐNS·PƐR·MƐDIVM·ILLORVːIBΛT
Annulet in first spandrel of second quarter and trefoils of Whitton 1 in other
spandrels. Trefoil in second quarter by lion's paw. Letters Whitton Π₁ and P₁.
Whitton 4b; North 1414; Seaby 1799. Bt Baldwin; ex Carter.

[*continued overleaf*]

PLATE 27

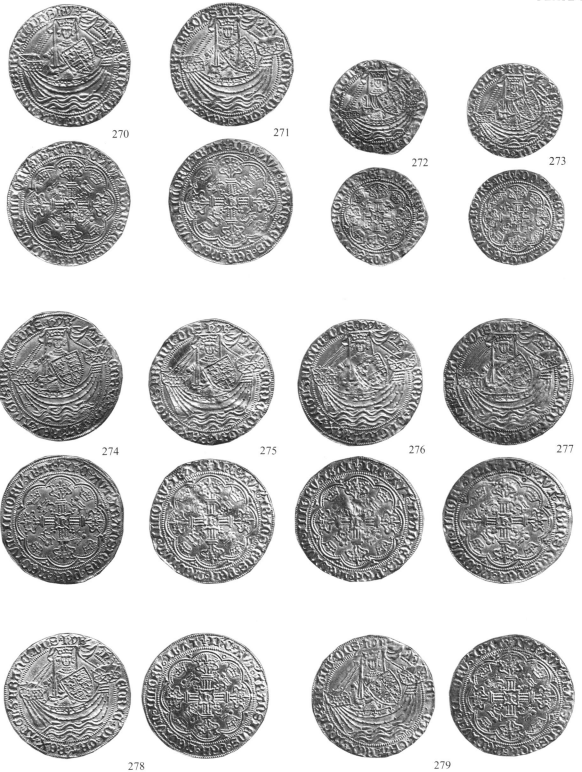

270

271

272

273

274

275

276

277

278

279

Plate 27 (*cont.*)

276 Noble
 6.95 107.3 40°

Obv.: hɛNRIɑ'✚DI꞉GRꟲ꞉RɛX·ꟲNGL꞉Ʂ·FRꟲNɑ꞉DN'S·hYB'
   Ornaments, 1–1–1. Annulet by wrist. Letters Whitton F$_1$ and N$_2$.

Rev.: ✚Ih'ɑ★ꟲVT꞉TRꟲNIɛNS·PɛR·MɛDIVM·ILLORV꞉IBꟲT
   First S omitted from TRꟲNSIɛNS. Annulet in first spandrel of second quarter
   and trefoils of Whitton 1 in other spandrels. Trefoil in second quarter by lion's
   paw. Letters Whitton N$_1$ and P$_1$.

Whitton 4b var. (with spelling TRꟲNIɛNS); North 1414; Seaby 1799. Ex Lockett
(1430).

277 Noble
 6.86 105.8 210°

Obv.: hɛNRIɑ'✚DI꞉GRꟲ꞉RɛX·ꟲNGL꞉Ʂ·FRꟲNɑ꞉DN'S·hYB'
   Ornaments, 1–1–1. Annulet by wrist. Letters Whitton F$_1$ and N$_2$.

Rev.: ✚Ih'ɑ★ꟲVT꞉TRꟲNSIɛNS·PɛR·MɛDIVM·ILLORV꞉IBꟲT
   Annulet in first spandrel of second quarter and trefoils of Whitton 2 in other
   spandrels. Pellet in second quarter by lion's paw. Letters Whitton N$_1$ and P$_1$.

Whitton 4d; North 1414; Seaby 1799. Ex Glendining sale 14.4.1961 (10).

278 Noble
 6.95 107.2 250°

Obv.: hɛNRIɑ'✚DI꞉GRꟲ꞉RɛX·ꟲNGL꞉Ʂ·FRꟲNɑ꞉DN'S·hYB'
   Ornaments, 1–1–1. Annulet by wrist. Letters Whitton F$_1$ and N$_2$.

Rev.: ✚Ih'ɑ★ꟲVT꞉TRꟲNSIɛNS·PɛR·MɛDIVM·ILLORV꞉IBꟲT
   Annulet in first spandrel of second quarter and trefoils of Whitton 2 in other
   spandrels. Trefoil in second quarter by lion's paw. Letters Whitton N$_1$ and P$_1$.

Whitton 4e var. (with N$_1$ on reverse); North 1414; Seaby 1799. Ex Christie sale
8.3.1960 (99).

279 Noble
 6.96 107.4 340°

Obv.: hɛNRIɑ'✚DI꞉GRꟲ꞉RɛX·ꟲNGL꞉Ʂ·FRꟲNɑ꞉DN'S·hYB'
   Ornaments, 1–1–1. Annulet by wrist. Letters F$_1$ and N$_2$.

Rev.: ✚Ih'ɑ★ꟲVT꞉TRꟲNSIɛNS·PɛR·MɛDIVM·ILLORV꞉IBꟲT
   Annulet in first spandrel of second quarter and trefoils of Whitton 2 in other
   spandrels. No marks in field. Letters Whitton N$_1$ and P$_1$.

Whitton 4f; North 1414; Seaby 1799. Ex Christie sale 21.3.1961 (96).

ANNULET ISSUE (1422–30) (*cont.*)

London mint (cont.)

280 Noble

	Weight		
	g	*gr.*	*Die-axis*
	6.89	106.4	120°

Obv.: h/ƐNRIɑ'✚DI⸫GR⅄⫶RƐX·⅄NGL⫶ϩ·FR⅄Nɑ⫶DN'S·hYB'
Ornaments, 1–1–1. Annulet by wrist. Letters Whitton F_1 and N_3.

Rev.: ✚Ih'ɑ★⅄VT⫶TR⅄NSIƐNS∘PƐR∘MƐDIVM∘ILLORV⫶IB⅄T
Annulet in first spandrel of second quarter and trefoils of Whitton 2 in other spandrels. No marks in field. Letters Whitton N_3 and P_1.

Whitton 6a; North 1414; Seaby 1799. Bt Baldwin 1961.

281 Noble

6.91 106.7 40°

Obv.: h/ƐNRIɑ'✚DI⸫GR⅄⫶RƐX·⅄NGL⫶ϩ·FR⅄Nɑ⫶DNS·hYB
Ornaments, 1–1–1. Annulet by wrist. Letters Whitton F_1 and N_3.

Rev.: ✚Ih'ɑ★⅄VT⫶TR⅄NSIƐNS∘PƐR∘MƐDVM∘ILLORV⫶IB⅄T
Letter I omitted from MƐDIVM. Annulet in first spandrel of second quarter and trefoils of Whitton 2 in other spandrels. No marks in field. Letters Whitton N_3 and P_1.

Whitton 6c; North 1414; Seaby 1799. Ex Lockett (4279).

282 Noble

6.96 107.4 30°

Obv.: h/ƐNRIɑ'✚DI⸫GR⅄⫶RƐX·⅄NGL⫶ϩ·FR⅄Nɑ⫶DNS·hYB'
Ornaments, 1–1–1. Annulet by wrist. Letters Whitton F_1 and N_3.

Rev.: ✚Ihɑ★⅄VT⫶TR⅄NSIƐNS∘PƐR∘MƐDIVM∘ILLORV⫶IB⅄T
Annulet punctuation mark after TR⅄NSIƐNS punched-in over mullet. Annulet in first spandrel of second quarter and trefoils of Whitton 2 in other spandrels. No marks in field. Letters Whitton N_4 and P_1.

Whitton 6c; North 1414; Seaby 1799. Ex Glendining sale 15.4.1971 (50).

283 Noble

6.93 107.0 170°

Obv.: h/ƐNRIɑ'✚DI⸫GR⅄⫶RƐX·⅄NGL⫶ϩ·FR⅄Nɑ⫶DN'S·hYB'
Ornaments, 1–1–1. Annulet by wrist. Letters Whitton F_1 and N_4.

Rev.: ✚Ih'ɑ★⅄VT⫶TR⅄NSIƐNS∘PƐR∘MƐDIVM∘ILLORV⫶IB⅄T
Annulet in first spandrel of second quarter and trefoils of Whitton 2 in other spandrels. Letters Whitton N_3 and P_1.

Whitton 7a/6a; North 1414; Seaby 1799. No provenance.

284 Noble

6.88 106.1 300°

Obv.: h/ƐNRIɑ'✚DI⸫GR⅄⫶RƐX·⅄NGL⫶ϩ·FR⅄Nɑ⫶DN'S·hYB'
Ornaments, 1–1–1. Annulet by wrist. Letters Whitton F_1 and N_4.

Rev.: ✚Ihɑ★⅄VT⫶TR⅄NSIƐNS∘PƐR∘MƐDIVM∘ILLORV⫶IB⅄T
Annulet in first spandrel of second quarter and trefoils of Whitton 2 in other spandrels. Letters Whitton N_4 and P_2.

Whitton 7c; North 1414; Seaby 1799. Ex Glendining sale 14.4.1961 (11).

285 Noble

6.97 107.6 110°

Obv.: h/ƐNRIɑ'✚DI⸫GR⅄⫶RƐX·⅄NGL⫶ϩ·FR⅄Nɑ⫶DN'S·hYB'
Ornaments, 1–1–1. Annulet by wrist. Letters Whitton F_1 and N_4.

Rev.: ✚Ihɑ★⅄VT⫶TR⅄NSIƐNS∘PƐR∘MƐDIVM∘ILLORV⫶IB⅄T
Annulet in first spandrel of second quarter and trefoils of Whitton 3 in other spandrels. Letters Whitton N_4 and P_2.

Whitton 7d; North 1414; Seaby 1799. Bt Schulman 1952.

[*continued overleaf*]

PLATE 28

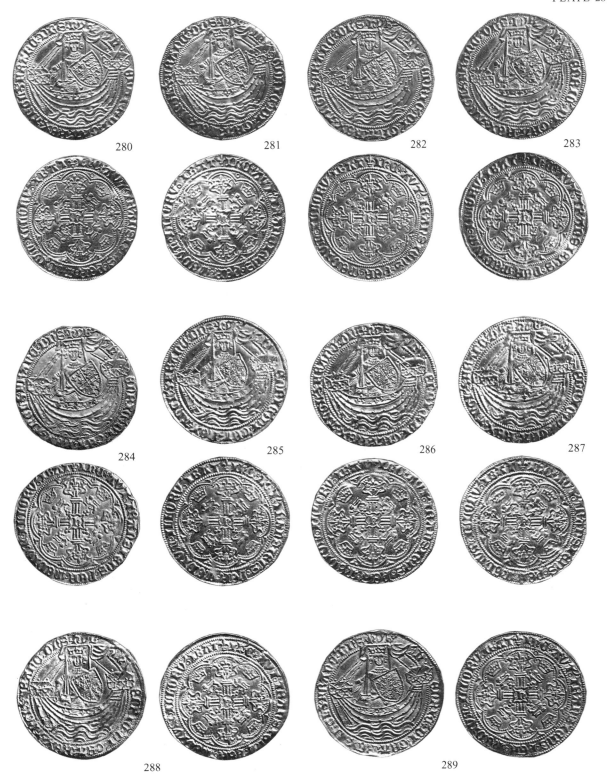

280   281   282   283

284   285   286   287

288   289

Plate 28 (*cont.*)

286 Noble

6.98   107.7   330°

Obv.: hⱭNRIɑ'✚DIːGRⱯːRⱭX·ⱯNGLːꝺ·FRⱯNɑːDNꞋSꞏhƔBꞋ
Ornaments, 1–1–1. Annulet by wrist. Letters Whitton F_1, N_4 and broken R.

Rev.: ✚IhꞋɑ★ⱯVTːTRⱯNSIⱭNSꞏPⱭRꞏMⱭDIVMꞏILLORVːIBⱯT
Annulet in first spandrel of second quarter and trefoils of Whitton 3 in other spandrels. Letters N_4, P_2 and broken R.

Whitton 8a; North 1414; Seaby 1799. Ex Ward (128).

287 Noble

6.91   106.6   170°

Obv.: hⱭNRIɑ'✚DIːGRⱯːRⱭX·ⱯNGLːꝺ·FRⱯNɑːDNꞋSꞏhƔBꞋ
Ornaments, 1–1–1. Annulet by wrist. Letters Whitton F_1, N_4 and broken R and E.

Rev.: ✚IhꞋɑ★ⱯVTːTRⱯNSIⱭNSꞏPⱭRꞏMⱭDIVMꞏILLORVːIBⱯT
Annulet in first spandrel of second quarter and trefoils of Whitton 3 in other spandrels. Letters Whitton N_4, P_2 and broken R and E.

Whitton 9; North 1414; Seaby 1799. Ex Glendining sale 17.3.1961 (95).

288 Noble

6.98   107.7   200°

Obv.: hⱭNRIɑːDIːGRⱯːRⱭX·ⱯNGL·ꝺ·FRⱯNɑːDNꞋSꞏhƔB
Ornaments, 1–1–1. Ordinary trefoil stop instead of lis after hⱭNRIɑ. Annulet by wrist. Letters Whitton F_1, N_4 and broken E.

Rev.: ✚IhꞋɑ★ⱯVTꞏTRⱯNSIⱭNSꞏPⱭRꞏMⱭDIVMꞏILLORVːIBⱯT
Annulet in first spandrel of second quarter and trefoils of Whitton 3 in other spandrels. Letters Whitton N_4, P_x and broken E.

Whitton 11/10; North 1414; Seaby 1799. Bt Spink 1962.

289 Noble

6.95   107.3   300°

Obv.: hⱭNRIɑ'✚DIːGRⱯːRⱭX·ⱯNGL·ꝺ·FRⱯNɑːDNꞋSꞏhƔBꞋ
Ornaments, 1–1–1. Annulet by wrist. Letters Whitton F_1 and N_4.

Rev.: ✚IhꞋɑ★ⱯVTꞏTRⱯNSIⱭNSꞏPⱭRꞏMⱭDIVMꞏILLORVːIBⱯT
Annulet in first spandrel of second quarter and trefoils of Whitton 3 in other spandrels. Letters Whitton N_4 and P_2.

Whitton 13; North 1414; Seaby 1799. Bt Spink 1961.

ANNULET ISSUE (1422–30) (*cont.*)

London mint (cont.)

290 Noble

Weight		
g	*gr.*	*Die-axis*
6.86	105.9	220°

Obv.: h/ENRIC'✠DI⫶GRA⫶REX·ANGL⫶⪦·FRANC⫶DNS·hYB
Ornaments, 1–1–1. Annulet by wrist. Letters Whitton F_2 and N_4.
Rev.: ✠Ih'C★AVT⫶TRANSIENS∘PER∘MEDIVM∘ILLORV⫶IBAT
Annulet in first spandrel of second quarter and trefoils of Whitton 3 in other spandrels. Letters Whitton N_4 and P_2.
Whitton 14; North 1414; Seaby 1799. Bt Spink 1961.

291 Half-noble
3.42   52.8   170°

Obv.: h/ENRIC✠DI⫶GRA⫶REX·ANGL⫶⪦·FRAN'
Ornaments, –11–1. Annulet by wrist. Letters Whitton F_1 and N_1.
Rev.: ✠DOMINE★NE∘IN∘FVRORE∘TVO∘ARGVAS∘ME
Annulet in first spandrel of second quarter. Letter Whitton F_1.
Whitton 1; North 1417; Seaby 1805. Bt Spink 1965; ex Birchmore.

292 Half-noble
3.48   53.7   170°

Obv.: h/ENRIC'✠DI⫶GRA'REX·ANGL⫶⪦·FRANC⫶
Ornaments, 1–1–1. Annulet by wrist. Letter Whitton F_1.
Rev.: ✠DOMINE★NE∘IN∘FVRORE∘TVO∘ARGVAS∘ME
Annulet in first spandrel of second quarter. Letter Whitton F_1.
Whitton 2/3b; North 1417; Seaby 1805. No provenance.

293 Half-noble
3.48   53.7   10°

Obv.: h/ENRIC'✠DI⫶GRA⫶REX·ANGL⫶⪦·FRANC⫶
Ornaments, 1–1–1. Annulet by wrist. Letter Whitton F_1.
Rev.: ✠DOMINE★NE∘IN∘FVRORE∘TVO∘ARGVAS∘ME
Annulet in first spandrel of second quarter. Letter Whitton F_1.
Whitton 3d; North 1417; Seaby 1805. Bt Spink 1965.

294 Half-noble
3.45   53.3   170°

Obv.: h/ENRIC'✠DI⫶GRA⫶REX·ANGL⫶⪦·FRANC⫶
Ornaments, 1–1–1. No annulet by wrist. Apparently trefoil stop at the end of the obverse legend. Letter Whitton F_2.
Rev.: ✠DOMINE★NE∘IN∘FVRORE∘TVO∘ARGVAS∘ME
Annulet in first spandrel of second quarter. Letter Whitton F_2.
Whitton 5 var. with trefoil after FRANC'; North 1417; Seaby 1805. Ex Glendining sale 15.4.1971 (52); ex Lawrence (40).

295 Quarter-noble
1.72   26.6   190°

Obv.: ✠hENRIC'✠DI⫶GRA⫶REX·ANGL' I.m. large lis.
Lis above shield.
Rev.: ✠EXALTABITVR★IN∘GLORIA I.m. large lis. Mullet after EXALTABITVR.
Whitton 1; North 1420; Seaby 1810. No provenance.

296 Quarter-noble
1.75   26.9   80°

Obv.: ✠hENRIC'✠DI⫶GRA⫶REX·ANGLI I.m. large lis.
Small lis above, and trefoil below, shield.
Rev.: ✠EXALTABITVR★IN∘GLORIA I.m. large lis. Mullet after EXALTABITVR.
Whitton 3; North 1420; Seaby 1811. Ex Dangar (95).

297 Quarter-noble
1.72   26.6   10°

Obv.: ✠hENRIC'✠DI⫶GRA⫶REX·ANGL' I.m. large lis.
Small lis above, and pellet below, shield.
Rev.: ✠EXALTABITVR★IN∘GLORIA I.m. large lis. Mullet after EXALTABITVR.
Whitton 4; North 1420; Seaby 1812. Ex Lockett (4301).

[*continued overleaf*]

PLATE 29

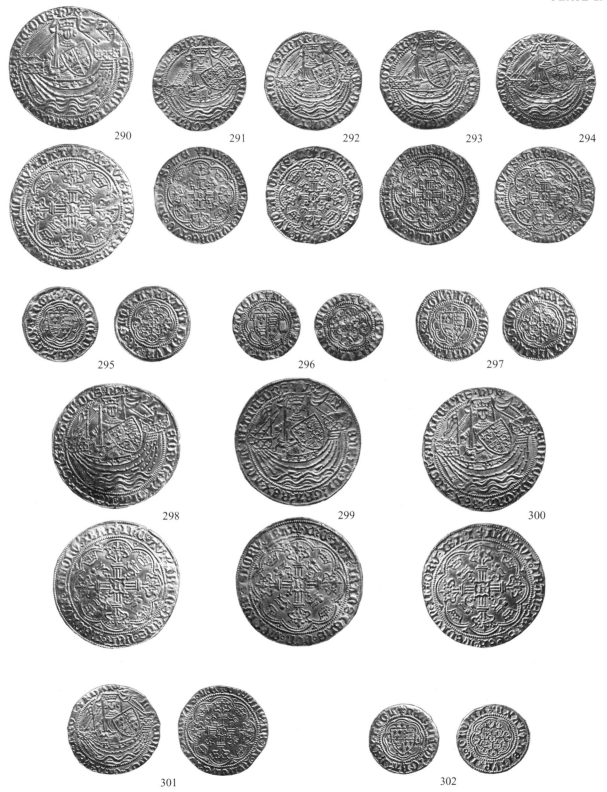

290

291

292

293

294

295

296

297

298

299

300

301

302

Plate 29 (*cont.*)

Calais mint (all with flag at stern)

298 Noble
6.95   107.3   240°

Obv.: h/ƐNRIⵏ'✚DIːGRⵏːRƐXⵏⵏNGLːᛋ·FRⵏNⵏːDN'SᐧhYB'
Ornaments, 1–1–1. Annulet by wrist. Letters Whitton F₁ and N₂.

Rev.: ✚Ih'ⵏ★ⵏVTːTRⵏNSIƐNS∘PƐR∘MƐDIVM∘ILLORVːIBⵏT
ⵏ in centre of reverse. Annulet in first spandrel of second quarter and trefoils of Whitton 1 in the other spandrels. Letters Whitton N₁ and P₁.
Whitton 4a; North 1415; Seaby 1802. Bt Spink 1972; ex Cartwright.

299 Noble
6.91   106.7   30°

Obv.: h/ƐNRIⵏ'✚DIːGRⵏːRƐXⵏⵏNGLːᛋ·FRⵏNⵏːDNSᐧhYB'
Ornaments, 1–1–1. Annulet by wrist. Letters Whitton F₁ and N₄.

Rev.: ✚Ih'ⵏ★ⵏVTⵏTRⵏNSIƐNS∘PƐR∘MƐDIVM∘ILLORVːIBⵏT
h in centre of reverse. Annulet in first spandrel of second quarter and trefoils of Whitton 2 in other spandrels. Letters Whitton N₃ and P₁.
Whitton 7a; North 1415; Seaby 1803. Bt Spink 1973; ex Oman (140).

300 Noble
6.94   107.1   160°

Obv.: h/ƐNRIⵏ'✚DIːGRⵏːRƐXⵏⵏNGLːᛋ·FRⵏNⵏːDN‾SᐧhYB'
Ornaments, 1–1–1. Annulet by wrist. Letters Whitton F₁ and N₄.

Rev.: ✚Ih'ⵏ★ⵏVTⵏTRⵏNSIƐNS∘PƐR∘MƐDIVM∘ILLORVːIBⵏT
h in centre of reverse. Annulet in first spandrel of second quarter and trefoils of Whitton 2 in the other spandrels. Letters Whitton N₄ and P₁.
Whitton 7b; North 1415; Seaby 1803. Bt Spink 1971.

301 Half-noble
3.38   52.1   170°

Obv.: h/ƐNRIⵏ✚DIᐧGRⵏᐧRƐXᐧⵏNGLᐧᛋᐧFRⵏNⵏᐧ
Ornaments, 1–1–1. Annulet by wrist. Letter Whitton F₁.

Rev.: ✚DOMINƐ★NƐ∘INᐟFVRORƐᐧTVO∘ⵏRGVⵏSᐧMƐ
h in centre of reverse. Annulet in first spandrel of second quarter. Letter Whitton F₁.
Whitton 2; North 1418; Seaby 1808. Ex Glendining sale 24.11.1976 (53).

302 Quarter-noble
1.70   26.3   320°

Obv.: ✚hƐNRIⵏ'✚DIːGRⵏːRƐXᐧⵏNGL' I.m. large lis.
Three lis about shield. Later lettering with Whitton N₄.

Rev.: ✚ƐXⵏLTⵏBITVR★IN∘GLORIⵏ I.m. large lis. Mullet after ƐXⵏLTⵏBITVR.
Whitton 6; North 1421; Seaby 1814. Ex Glendining sale 19.5.1964 (284).

ANNULET ISSUE (1422–30) (*cont.*)

York mint (lis at stern)

303 Half-noble

	Weight		
	g	*gr.*	*Die-axis*
	3.43	53.0	130°

Obv.: hЄNRIC✚DI·GRA꞉RЄX·ANGL·S·FRANC꞉
Ornaments, 1–1–1. Lis over sterncastle.
Annulet by wrist. Letter Whitton F₁.

Rev.: ✚DOMINЄ★NЄ·IN◦FVRORЄ·TVO·ARGVAS◦MЄ
h in centre of reverse. Annulet in first spandrel of second quarter. Letter
Whitton F₁.
Whitton 1; North 1419; Seaby 1809. Bt Spink 1989; ex Dupree.

304 Quarter-noble
1.72   26.6   150°

Obv.: ✚hЄNRIC·✚DI꞉GRA꞉RЄX꞉ANGL'   `I.m.large lis.
Two lis over shield.

Rev.: ✚ЄXALTABITVR★IN◦GLORIA'   Mullet after ЄXALTABITVR
and annulet after IN.
Whitton 1; North 1422; Seaby 1816. Bt Spink 1989; ex Dupree.

ROSETTE-MASCLE ISSUE (1430–1)
Characteristics: Lis by wrist and in second quarter of reverse. Punctuation rosettes only on earlier dies but on later dies with one or,
rarely, two rosettes replaced by a mascle.

London mint

305 Noble
6.92   106.8   330°

Obv.: hЄNRIC◦DI◦GRA◦RЄX◦ANGL◦S◦FRANC◦DN'S◦hYB◦
Ornaments, 1–1–1. Lis by wrist. No mascle.

Rev.: ✚IhC◦AVT◦TRANSIЄNS◦PЄR◇MЄDIVM◦ILLORV◦IBAT
Mascle after PЄR punched over a rosette. Lis by head of lion in second quarter.
Same die as next coin, **306**.
Whitton 16c; North 1439; Seaby 1817. No provenance.

306 Noble
6.95   107.2   40°

Obv.: hЄNRIC◦DI◦GRA◦RЄX◦ANGL◦S◦FRANC◦DN'S◦hYB◦
Ornaments, 1–1–1. Lis by wrist. No mascle.

Rev.: same die as last coin, **305**.
Whitton 16c; North 1439; Seaby 1817. Ex Lockett (1431); ex Ready (423).

307 Noble
6.96   107.4   330°

Obv.: hЄNRIC◦DI◦GRA◇RЄX◦ANGL◦S◦FRANC◦DNS◦hYB'
Ornaments, 1–1–1. Lis by wrist. Mascle after GRA.

Rev.: ✚IhC◦AVT◦TRANCIЄNS◦PЄR◇MЄDIVM◦ILLORV◦IBAT
Mascle after PЄR. Lis by head of lion in second quarter.
Whitton 17a; North 1439; Seaby 1817. Ex Lockett (4299).

308 Noble
6.94   107.1   160°

Obv.: hЄNRIC◦DI◦GRA◦RЄX◇ANGL◦S◦FRANC◦DN'S◦hYB◦
Ornaments, 1–1–1. Lis by wrist. Mascle after RЄX punched over a rosette.

Rev.: ✚IhC◦AVT◦TRNCIЄNS◦PЄR◇MЄDIVM◦ILLORV◦IBAT
A omitted from TRANCIЄNS. Lis by head of lion in second quarter. Mascle
after PЄR.
Whitton 19 var. with omission of A from TRANCIЄNS; North 1439; Seaby 1817.
Bt Baldwin 1952; ex Carter.

309 Half-noble
3.46   53.4   180°

Obv.: hЄNRIC◦DI◦GRA◦RЄX◦ANGL◦S◦FRNC◦
Ornaments, 1–1–1. A omitted from FRANC. Lis by wrist. No mascle.

Rev.: ✚DOMINЄ◦NЄ◦IN◦FVRORЄ◦TVO◦ARGVAS◇MЄ
Lis by head of lion in second quarter. Mascle after ARGVAS.
Whitton – (this is an early variety unknown to Whitton that, more or less, corresponds
to the nobles without a mascle in the obverse legend of Whitton 16); North 1441;
Seaby 1819. Bt Schulman 1958.

[*continued overleaf*]

PLATE 30

303

304

305

306

307

308

309

310

311

312

313

314

Plate 30 (*cont.*)

310 Half-noble
    3.44   53.1   30°

Obv.: hΛ/ENRIᗡᵒDIᵒGRΛᗡ◊ REXᵒΛNGLᵒⱾᵒFRΛNᗡᵒ
Ornaments, 1–1–1. Ropes, 2/0. Lis by wrist. Mascle after GRΛ punched-in over a rosette stop.

Rev.: ✠DOMINEᵒNE◊ INᵒFVROREᵒTVOᵒΛRGVΛS◊ ME
Lis by head of lion in second quarter. Mascles after NE and ΛRGVΛS, the latter over a rosette.

Whitton 16a; North 1441; Seaby 1819. Ex Ryan (52); ex Bruun (421).

311 Half-noble
    3.15   48.6   250°

Obv.: hΛ/ENRIᗡᵒDIᵒGRΛᗡ◊ REXᵒΛNGLᵒⱾᵒFRΛNᗡᵒ
Ornaments, 1–1–1. Ropes, 2/1. Lis by wrist. Mascle (not over rosette) after GRΛ.

Rev.: ✠DOMINEᵒNE◊ INᵒFVROREᵒTVOᵒΛRGVΛS◊ ME
Lis by head of lion in second Mascles after NE and ΛRGVΛS.

Whitton 16a var., with mascle not over rosette and ropes 2/1; North 1441; Seaby 1819. Bt Baldwin 1960.

312 Quarter-noble
    1.73   26.7   200°

Obv.: ✠hENRIᗡᵒDIᵒGRΛᗡ◊ REXᵒΛNGL   Lis over shield. Mascle after GRΛ.

Rev.: ✠EXΛLTΛBITVRᵒINᵒGLORIΛ   Lis in centre. No mascle.

Whitton 6a; North 1443; Seaby 1821. Bt Spink 1989; ex Dupree.

313 Quarter-noble
    1.70   26.3   290°

Obv.: ✠hENRIᗡᵒDIᵒGRΛᵒREXᵒΛNGL'   Lis above and rosettes beside shield. No mascle.

Rev.: ✠EXΛLTΛBITVRᵒINᵒGLORIΛ   No mascle.

Whitton *Calais* no. 7. Schneider noted on the ticket for this coin that the example illustated by Whitton had the same reverse die as his London 6a, so that the attribution to Calais was unlikely. North 1444 (Calais); Seaby 1823 (Calais). Bt Spink 1959.

314 Quarter-noble
    1.71   26.4   180°

Obv.: ✠hENRIᗡᵒDIᵒGRΛᵒREX◊ ΛNGL   No lis above shield. Mascle after REX.

Rev.: ✠EXΛLTΛBITVRᵒIN◊ GLORIΛ   Mascle after IN.

Whitton 8a; North 1443; Seaby 1822. Ex Ryan (54); ex Drabble (106).

ROSETTE-MASCLE ISSUE (1430–1) (*cont.*)

Calais mint (flag at stern)

315 Noble

Weight		
g	*gr.*	*Die-axis*
6.84	105.5	160°

Obv.: h/ENRIᏟ⚬DI⚬GRᏗ⚬REX⚬ᏗNGL⚬S⚬FRᏗNᏟ⚬DN'S⚬hYB⚬
Ornaments, 1–1–1. Flag at stern. Lis by wrist.
No mascle. Same die as next coin, **316**.
Rev.: ✠IhᏟ⚬ᏗVT⚬TRᏗNSIENS⚬PER◊ MEDIVM⚬ILLORV⚬IBᏗT
h in centre. Lis over lion's head in second quarter. Mascle punched-in over rosette after PER.
Whitton 16a; North 1440; Seaby 1818. Bt Spink 1972; ex Cartwright.

316 Noble
| 6.82 | 105.3 | 230° |

Obv.: same die as last coin, **315**.
Rev.: ✠IhᏟ⚬ᏗVT⚬TRᏗNSIENS⚬PER◊ MEDIVM⚬ILLORV⚬IBᏗT
h in centre. Lis by lion's head in second quarter. Mascle punched-in over rosette after PER.
Whitton 16b; North 1440; Seaby 1818. Bt Spink 1982.

317 Half-noble
| 3.48 | 53.7 | 210° |

Obv.: h/ENRIᏟ⚬DI⚬GRᏗ⚬REX⚬ᏗNGL⚬S⚬FRᏗNᏟ⚬
Ornaments, 1–1–1. Flag at stern. Lis by wrist. No mascle.
Rev.: ✠DOMINE⚬NE⚬IN⚬FVRORE⚬TVO⚬ᏗRGVᏗS⚬ME   h in centre of reverse. Lis by lion's head in second quarter. No mascle.
Whitton 3 (this coin); North 1442; Seaby 1820. Bt Spink 1993; ex Lockett (3095); ex Bruun (422); ex Foster (36); ex Montagu (517).

For a quarter-noble of this issue attributed by Whitton to the Calais mint, see **313** above (London).

PINECONE-MASCLE ISSUE (1431–2)
Characteristics: No longer a lis by the wrist but that in the second quarter of the reverse remains. Pinecone punctuation with one or two pinecones in each legend replaced by a mascle.

MULES OF ROSETTE-MASCLE AND PINECONE-MASCLE ISSUES

London mint only

318 Noble
| 6.99 | 107.9 | 120° |

Obv.: h/ENRIᏟ⚬DI⚬GRᏗ⚬REX◊ ᏗNGL⚬S⚬FRᏗNᏟ⚬DNS⚬hIB
Ornaments, 1–1–1. Lis by wrist. Mascle after REX. I in hIB.
Rev.: ✠IhᏟ⚬ᏗVT⚬TRᏗNSIENS⚬PER◊ MEDIVM⚬ILLORV⚬IBᏗT
Lis by head of lion in second quarter. Mascle after PER. Cones of Whitton 3.
Whitton 20a (this coin cited); North 1439/1457; Seaby 1817/1824. Ex Lockett (1432); ex Bruun (411).

319 Half-noble
| 3.42 | 52.8 | 90° |

Obv.: h/ENRIᏟ⚬DI⚬GRᏗ◊ REX⚬ᏗNGL⚬S⚬FRᏗNᏟ⚬
Ornaments, 1–1–1. Lis by wrist. Mascle over rosette after GRᏗ.
Rev.: ✠DOMINE⚬NE⚬IN⚬FVRORE⚬TVO◊ ᏗRGVᏗS⚬ME   No lis in field. Mascle after TVO. Cones of Whitton 1.
Whitton 6b (this coin cited); North 1458; Seaby 1825. Ex Lockett (1441); ex Bruun (423); ex Walters (308).

320 Quarter-noble
| 1.72 | 26.6 | 20° |

Obv.: ✠hENRIᏟ⚬DI⚬GRᏗ⚬REX◊ ᏗNGL   No lis above shield.
Mascle after REX.
Rev.: ✠EXᏗLTᏗBITVR⚬IN◊ GLORIᏗ   Mascle after IN. Cone of Whitton 8.
Whitton 8b; North 1443/1459; Seaby 1822/1826. Bt Spink 1957.

[*continued overleaf*]

PLATE 31

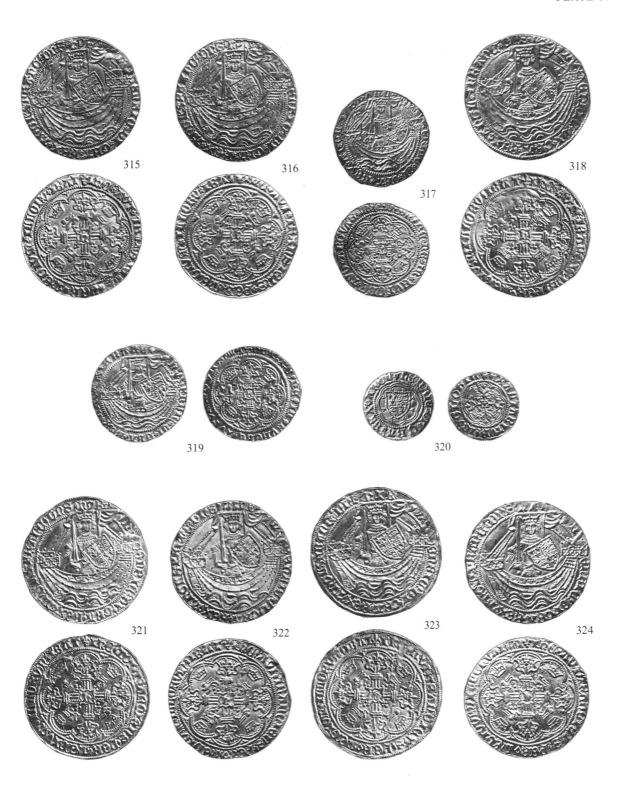

315

316

317

318

319

320

321

322

323

324

Plate 31 (*cont.*)

TRUE COINS OF THE PINECONE-MASCLE ISSUE

London mint only

321 Noble
6.93   107.0   40°

Obv.:   hƐNRIꞆ'𝔭DI'𝔭GRᴧ'𝔭RƐX◊ᴧNGL×Ꮥ×FRᴧNꞆ𝔭DNS'𝔭hꓭB'
Ornaments, 1–1–1. Mascle after RƐX. Cones of Whitton 1a.
Rev.:   ✠IhꞆ'𝔭ᴧVT𝔭TRᴧNꞆIƐNS𝔭PƐR𝔭MƐDIVM𝔭ILLORVM◊IBᴧT
Lis by head of lion in second quarter. Mascle over pinecone after ILLORVM.
Cones of Whitton 2.

Whitton 22/23b; North 1457; Seaby 1824. Ex Lockett (4008).

322 Noble
6.94   107.1   10°

Obv.:   hƐNRIꞆ'𝔭DI'𝔭GRᴧ'𝔭RƐX◊ᴧNGL×Ꮥ×FRᴧNꞆ𝔭DNS𝔭hꓭB'
Ornaments, 1–1–1. Mascle after RƐX. Cones of Whitton 3.
Rev.:   ✠IhꞆ𝔭ᴧVT𝔭TRᴧNꞆIƐNS𝔭PƐR◊MƐDIVM𝔭ILLORVM𝔭IBᴧT
Lis by head of lion in second quarter. Mascle after PƐR. Cones of Whitton 3
and 8.

Whitton 25d; North 1457; Seaby 1824. Ex Whitton (54).

323 Noble
6.96   107.4   260°

Obv.:   hƐNRIꞆ'𝔭DI'𝔭GRᴧ'𝔭RƐX◊ᴧNGL×Ꮥ×FRᴧNꞆ'𝔭DNS'hꓯB
Ornaments, 1–1–1. Mascle after RƐX. Cones of Whitton 8. Same die as next
two coins, **324, 325.**
Rev.:   ✠IhꞆ𝔭ᴧVT𝔭TRᴧNꞆIƐNS𝔭PƐR◊MƐDIVM𝔭ILLORVM𝔭IBᴧT
Lis by head of lion in second quarter. Mascle after PƐR. Cones of Whitton 4.

Whitton 29a/25d var. with cones of Whitton 4 (not recorded by him on any gold
coins); North 1457; Seaby 1824. Bt Baldwin 1964.

324 Noble
6.94   107.1   40°

Obv.:   same die as last and next coins, **323, 325.**
Rev.:   ✠IhꞆ𝔭ᴧVT𝔭TRᴧNꞆIƐNS𝔭PƐR◊MƐDIVVM𝔭ILLORVM IBᴧT
Reads MƐDIVVM. Lis by head of lion in second quarter. Mascle after PƐR.
Cones of Whitton 8.

Whitton 29b var. with aberrant spelling of MƐDIVM and, on this coin, it is difficult to
see whether or not there is a cone under the I of IBᴧT; North 1457; Seaby 1824.
Bt Spink 1966.

PINECONE-MASCLE ISSUE (1431–2) (*cont.*)

TRUE COINS OF THE PINECONE-MASCLE ISSUE (*cont.*)

London mint (cont.)

325 Noble

	Weight	
g	*gr.*	*Die-axis*
6.83	105.4	100°

Obv.: same die as last two coins, **323**, **324**.
Rev.: ✠ IhꞀ ℗ ꓥVT' ℗ TRꓥꞀ꓉IꤲNS℗ PꤲR◊ MꤲDIVM℗ ILLORVM IBꓥT
Lis by head of lion in second quarter. Mascle after PꤲR. Cones of Whitton 8.
Possibly cone under I of IBꓥT.
Whitton 29b; North 1457; Seaby 1824. Bt Schulman 1965.

326 Noble

6.91	106.7	190°

Obv.: h/ꤲNRIꞀ'℗ DI'℗ GRꓥ℗ RꤲX◊ ꓥNGL'I꙳ FRꓥN꓉℗ DNS℗ hIB
Ornaments, 1–1–1. Ampersand not struck from a regular punch but assembled
from a small letter I with a wedge and a pinecone. Mascle after RꤲX. Some
cones apparently of a design not in Whitton but possibly an early version of 3.
There is a cone of Whitton 2 after FRꓥN꓉.
Rev.: ✠ IhꞀ '℗ ꓥVT℗ TRꓥN꓉IꤲNS℗ PꤲR℗ MꤲDIVM◊ ILLORV℗ IBꓥT
No lis in reverse field. Cones of Whitton 3. Mascle after MꤲDIVM.
Schneider 1967 (this coin described); Whitton – (this coin is quite different from any
of this issue published by him); North 1457; Seaby 1824. Ex Glendining sale
19.5.1964 (283).

327 Quarter-noble

1.48	22.8	100°
(clipped)		

Obv.: ✠ hꤲNRIꞀ'℗ DI℗ GRꓥ℗ RꤲX◊ ꓥNGL   Lis above shield. Mascle after
RꤲX. Cones of Whitton 1.
Rev.: ✠ ꤲXꓥLTꓥBITVR◊ IN℗ GLORIꓥ   Mascle after ꤲXꓥLTꓥBITVR.
Cone of Whitton 1.
Whitton 9 (this coin cited); North 1459; Seaby 1826. Ex Ryan (55).

LEAF-MASCLE ISSUE (1433–6)
Characteristics: Leaf in waves on the noble and under shield on half-noble; leaf above the lion's tail in the first quarter of the reverse
on the half-noble. On the quarter-noble lis above shield and leaf under R of GLORIꓥ. Punctuation is by saltires with mascles after
RꤲX on the obverse (noble and half-noble) and, on the reverse, after PꤲR (noble), FVRORꤲ (half-noble) and ꤲXꓥLTꓥBITVR
(quarter-noble).

London mint only

328 Noble

6.96	107.4	300°

Obv.: h/ꤲNRIꞀ⁖DI×GRꓥ×RꤲX◊ ꓥNGL×꙳×FRꓥN꓉⁖DNS hYB
Ornaments, 1–1–1. Leaf in waves. Mascle after RꤲX.
Rev.: ✠ IhꞀ⁖ꓥVT⁝TRꓥN꓉IꤲNS⁝PꤲR◊ MꤲDIVM⁝ILLORV IBꓥT
Mascle after PꤲR.
Whitton 30a (this coin cited, however Whitton describes it as having a pinecone after
ꓥVT, which is certainly not the case); North 1472; Seaby 1827. Ex Lockett (3093);
ex Bruun (416).

329 Half-noble

3.46	53.4	150°

Obv.: h/ꤲNRIꞀ⁝DI×GRꓥ⁝RꤲX×◊ ꓥNGL⁝꙳×FRꓥNꞀ⁝
Ornaments, 1–1–1. Leaf below shield and another in waves below ship.
Rev.: ✠ DOMINꤲ⁝Nꤲ⁝IN⁝FVRORꤲ◊ TVO⁝ꓥRGVꓥS Mꤲ
Leaf above lion's tail in first quarter of reverse.
Whitton –. This denomination of this issue was first known from the single specimen
in the Fishpool Hoard (Archibald 1967) which is now in the BM. This is the second
recorded specimen. North –; Seaby 1828. Ex Glendining sale 8.12.1992 (88); ex
Reigate (Brokes Road) Hoard.

330 Quarter-noble

1.73	26.7	180°

Obv.: ✠ hꤲNRIꞀ⁝DI×GRꓥ⁝RꤲX◊ ꓥNG'   Lis above shield. Mascle after RꤲX.
Rev.: ✠ ꤲXꓥLTꓥBITVR◊ IN⁝GLORI   Leaf below R of GLORI. Mascle after
ꤲXꓥLTꓥBITVR.
Whitton 10; North 1473; Seaby 1829. Ex Lockett (3097); ex Bruun (427); ex
'Astronomer' (21).

[*continued overleaf*]

PLATE 32

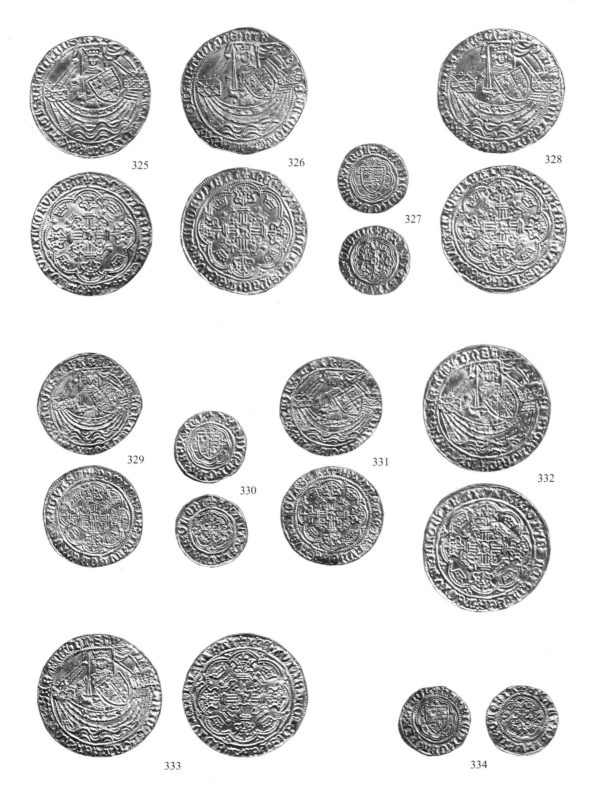

325 326 327 328

329 330 331 332

333 334

LEAF-TREFOIL ISSUE (1436–8)
Characteristics: Leaf punctuation with trefoils after one or two words on the obverse and reverse.

MULE OF LEAF-TREFOIL AND ANNULET ISSUES

London mint only

331 Half-noble
3.48   53.7   50°

Obv.: hⲦ𝖦NRIꝄ '◈DI◈GRꙅ◈RⲦX·ꙅNGL⦂𝖘×FRꙅNꝄ⦂
Ornaments, 1–1–1. Trefoils after RⲦX and FRꙅNꝄ.
Rev.: ✠DOMINⲦ★NⲦ·IN·FVRORⲦ·TVO·ꙅRGVꙅS·MⲦ
Annulet in first spandrel of second quarter. Letter Whitton F₂.
Whitton –/4 or 5, no leaf-trefoil half-noble die was known to him; North –/1417;
Seaby 1830A/1805. Ex Northumberland (2).

TRUE COINS OF THE LEAF-TREFOIL ISSUE

London mint only

332 Noble
6.96   107.4   180°

Obv.: hⲦNRIꝄ '◈DI◈GRꙅ◈RⲦX·ꙅNGL⦂𝖘·FRꙅNꝄ '◈DNS·hYB'
Ornaments, 1–1–1. Y of hYB over I. Trefoil after RⲦX. Same die as next
coin, **333**.
Rev.: ✠IhꝄ '◈ꙅVT '◈TRꙅNꝄIⲦNS◈PⲦR·MⲦDIVM·ILLOR '◈IBꙅT◦
Trefoils after PⲦR and MⲦDIVM, annulet after IBꙅT.
Whitton 31, this coin cited; North 1482/1; Seaby 1830. Ex Lockett (1434); ex Bruun
(414); ex Walters (303).

333 Noble
6.93   106.9   20°

Obv.: same die as last coin, **332**.
Rev.: ✠IhꝄ◈ꙅVT '◈TRꙅNꝄIⲦNS◈PⲦR·MⲦDIVM ILLORV◈IBꙅT
Trefoil after PⲦR only.
Whitton 31 var. with differences in reverse legend; North 1482/1; Seaby 1830. Ex
Glendining sale 17.10.1968 (66); ex Fishpool Hoard.

334 Quarter-noble
1.74   26.8   310°

Obv.: ✠hⲦNRIꝄ '◈DI '◈GRꙅ '◈RⲦX·ꙅNGL'
Lis above shield. Trefoil after RⲦX.
Rev.: ✠ⲦXꙅLTꙅBITVR◈◈IN·GLORIꙅ Two leaves (as stops) one above the
other after ⲦXꙅLTꙅBITVR. Trefoil after IN.
Whitton – (no quarter-noble of this issue was recorded by him); North 1483; Seaby
1831. Bt Spink; ex Winchester Cathedral.

TREFOIL ISSUE (1439–41)
Characteristics: Trefoil to left of shield. Punctuation saltires on obverse and saltires and trefoils on the reverse. Only the noble is known for this issue.

London mint only

335	Noble			
	Weight			
	g	*gr.*	*Die-axis*	
	6.94	107.1	300°	

Obv.: h/ƐПRIƆ∺DI∺GRⱯ∺RƐX∺ⱯПGL∗S∗FRⱯПƆ'DS hIB∺
Ornaments, –1–1–1. Trefoil to left of shield. No П in DПS.

Rev.: ✠Ih'Ɖ∺ⱯVTO∺TRⱯПSIƐПS PƐR∙MƐDIV ILLO' IBⱯT
Trefoils after ⱯVTO and PƐR.

Whitton 32 var. from different dies; North 1495; Seaby 1832. Bt Baldwin 1959.

TREFOIL-PELLET ISSUE (1441–5)
No gold coins are known from this issue.

LEAF-PELLET ISSUE (1445–54)
Characteristics: Only nobles are known. There are two varieties of which only the second was recorded by Whitton. The first variety was first recorded from the Fishpool hoard (Archibald 1967).
   (i) leaf to left of shield; saltire and pellet punctuation (**336**).
   (ii) annulet, lis and leaf to left of shield; annulet, pellet and trefoil punctuation (**337**).
Both varieties have a pellet before the **h** in the centre of the reverse. The noble is the only gold denomination known.

London mint only

336	Noble		
	6.92	106.8	160°

Obv.: h/∗ƐПRIƆ'DI GRⱯ RƐX ⱯПGL S FRⱯПƆ DПS hY∗./B
Leaf to left of shield.

Rev.: IhƆ∗ⱯVT∗TRⱯПSIƐПS PƐR MƐDIVM ILLORV'IBⱯT∗
No initial mark (or, possibly, T of IBⱯT struck over lis). Pellet before **h** in centre.

Whitton –; North 1502; Seaby 1833. Ex Glendining sale 17.10.1968 (67); ex Fishpool hoard.

337	Noble		
	6.98	107.7	200°

Obv.: ∙h∙/ƐПRIƆ∺DI∺GRⱯ∘RƐX∙ⱯПGL∗S∗FRⱯПƆ∘DПS hY
Annulet, lis and leaf to left of shield.

Rev.: ✠Ih'Ɖ∗ⱯVT∗TRⱯПSIƐПS∗PƐR MƐDIVM∗ILLORV IBⱯT
h in centre supine with pellet above. Letter Ɱ of type found on late coins of the Leaf-pellet issue.

Whitton 33c, this coin cited; North 1502; Seaby 1833. Ex Lockett (1435); ex Bruun (417); ex Walters (304).

UNMARKED, CROSS-PELLET AND LIS-PELLET ISSUES (1454–60)
No gold coins were known that could be attributed to these issues until the appearance, in the Fishpool hoard (Archibald 1967), of six nobles with saltires to the left of the shield and mascles in the obverse and reverse legends. These can possibly be equated with the Cross-pellet issue, the groats of which normally have saltires by the neck and some of which have mascles in the obverse legend. The six Fishpool nobles are all in the BM.

[continued overleaf]

PLATE 33

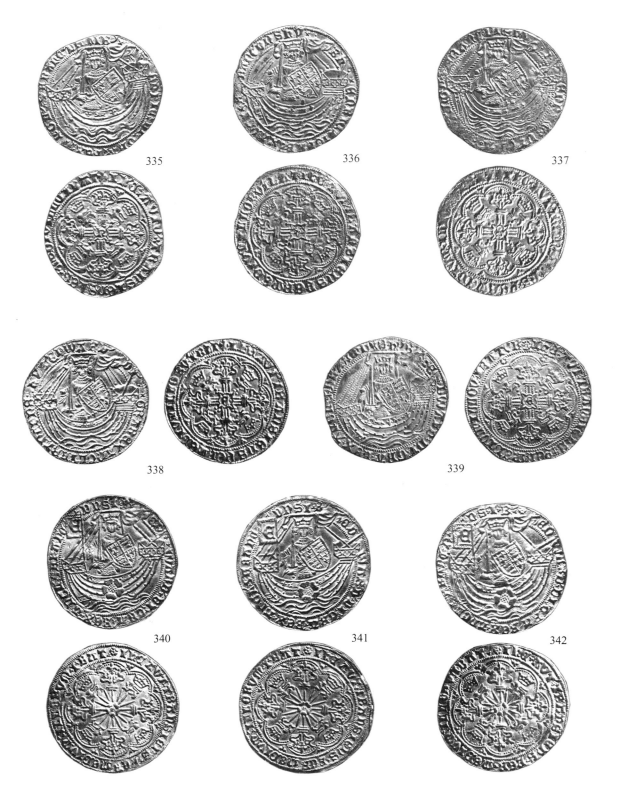

335

336

337

338

339

340

341

342

Plate 33 (*cont.*)

EDWARD IV, FIRST REIGN (4 March 1461–deposed 3 October 1470)

FIRST OR HEAVY COINAGE (1461–March 1465)

Gold coinage issued at a fineness of 23 ct 3½ gr. (0.995 fine) and at a nominal weight of 108 gr. (6.998 g) to the noble of 6s 8d (8s 4d after 13 August 1464). Denominations known are noble and quarter-noble. Classified in accordance with Blunt and Whitton 1945–8 (BW).

Characteristics: Initial marks lis or rose.

London mint only

338 Noble
    6.98   107.7   100°

Obv.: ЄDWΛRD'/DI/·GRΛ RЄX ΛПGL S FRΛПCI DПS·ҺУB'
Ornaments, 1–1–1. Ropes, 4/2. Legend starts at 11 o'clock. Lis below shield.
Rev.: ✚IҺCI 'ΛVT'TRΛПSIЄПS PЄR MЄDIVM ILLORV⁙IBΛT
Є and pellet in centre.
Blunt and Whitton type I (same dies as *BNJ* 25, pl.2, 18 [BM coin]); North 1527; Seaby 1946. Bt Spink; ex Fishpool hoard (not in the 1968 auction).

339 Noble
    6.98   107.7   290°

Obv.: ☉Є/⁺DWΛRD⁚DI⁚GRΛ⁚RЄX×ΛПGL×S×FRΛПCI×DПS×ҺУB'
Ornaments, 1–1–1. Ropes, 4/1. Legend begins at 2 o'clock. Quatrefoil of 4 pellets below king's wrist.
Rev.: ☉IҺCI‡ΛVT⁚TRΛПSIЄПS‡PЄR MЄDIVM×ILLOV'‡IBΛTVR
I of IҺCI struck over G? Roses in first and last spandrels instead of trefoils.
Blunt and Whitton –, but relates to their type III. This variety was first known from the Fishpool hoard which contained two specimens of which this is one; the other is in the BM. North 1528; Seaby 1948. Ex Glendining sale 17.10.1968 (77); ex Fishpool hoard.

SECOND OR LIGHT COINAGE (March 1465–October 1470)

Gold coin issued at a fineness of 23 ct 3½ gr. (0.995 fine) and at a nominal weight of 120 gr. (7.776 g) to the ryal of 10s 0d and 80 gr. (5.184 g) to the angel of 6s 8d. Denominations struck were ryal, half-ryal, quarter-ryal and angel. Gold coinage was struck at the mints of London, Bristol, Coventry, Norwich and York. Classified according to Blunt and Whitton 1945–8 (BW) and Webb Ware 1985.

Characteristics:

    Ryal and Half-ryal. King standing facing in a ship, as on the noble, but with a rose on the ship's side and a banner containing the letter Є on the stern. Reverse is similar to that of the noble except that there is a large radiant sun containing a rose at the centre.

    Quarter-ryal. Obverse similar to the quarter-noble but only rarely with 8 arches to the tressure (Blunt and Whitton types V and VI – not represented in this collection) and usually with a tressure of 4 arches. Lis below shield.

    Angel. St Michael standing facing and spearing a dragon. Reverse ship with a large cross on its mast on which is a shield bearing the royal arms. To the left of the mast is a sun, to the right, a rose.

Initial marks: rose (V)   1464–5
                           sun (VI)   1465–6
                           crown (VII)   1466–7
                           crown and sun combined (VIII)   1467–8
                           crown and rose combined (IX)   1468–9
                           long cross fitchée (X–XI)   1469–70
                           (Roman numerals refer to Blunt and Whitton types)

Plate 33 (*cont.*)

London mint

340 Ryal
     7.72   119.2   40°
            I.m. none/rose.
            Obv.: ЄD/··WᴧRD᛬DI ᛬GRᴧ᛬RЄ·X·ᴧNGL᛬S·FRᴧႶ/·DႶS᛬I·B᛬
                     Letter BW R_3. Same die as **343**.
            Rev.: ☉IhႶ ᴧVT·TRᴧႶSIЄႶS·PЄR MЄDIVM᛬ILLORVM·I·BᴧT·
                     Large fleurs in spandrels. Letter BW R3. Same die as next coin, **341**.
            Blunt and Whitton type V, variant 2; Webb Ware dies 1/V, 2; North 1549; Seaby 1950.
            Bt Spink 1957.

341 Ryal
     7.70   118.9   70°
            I.m. none/rose.
            Obv.: ЄD/WᴧRD᛬DI ᛬GRᴧ᛬RЄ·X·ᴧNGL᛬S·FRᴧႶ/·DႶS᛬I·B
                     Letter BW R_3.
            Rev.:   same die as last coin, **340**.
            Blunt and Whitton type V, variant 2; Webb Ware dies 2/V, 2; North 1549; Seaby 1950.
            Bt Spink 1954; ex Jellard; ex Basmadjeff (15); ex Ryan (67).

342 Ryal
     7.67   118.4   340°
            I.m. rose both sides.
            Obv.: ☉/ЄD/WᴧRD᛬DI ᛬GRᴧ᛬RЄX·ᴧNGL·S·FRᴧႶ·D·/·ႶS᛬I·B᛬
                     Letter BW R_2.
            Rev.: ☉IhႶ ·ᴧVT᛬TRᴧႶSIЄႶS·PЄR·MЄDIVM᛬ILLORVM BᴧT᛬
                     I of IBᴧT under M of ILLORVM. Large fleurs in spandrels. Letter BW R_2.
            Blunt and Whitton type V, variant 1; Webb Ware dies 6/V, 5; North 1549; Seaby 1950.
            Ex Lockett (1523); ex Roth (211 in the first sale or 196 in the second, neither
            illustrated).

SECOND OR LIGHT COINAGE (March 1465–October 1470) (*cont.*)

London mint (cont.)

	Weight		
	g	*gr.*	*Die-axis*

343 Ryal

7.55   116.5   200°

I.m. none/sun.

Obv.: same die as **340**.

Rev.: ✱IhᄃːЛVTˑTRЛNSI∈NSːP∈RˑM∈DIVMːILLORVMːNIˑBЛTˑ
Ν before I of IᴧBAT. Large fleurs in spandrels. Letter BW R$_3$. Same die as **356**.

Blunt and Whitton type V/VI, variant 2(a), var. with reverse legend that is recorded for 1(a); Webb Ware dies 1/VI, 19; North 1549; Seaby 1950.
Ex von Thielau (1536).

344 Ryal

7.64   117.9   70°

I.m. rose/sun.

Obv.: ☉/∈D/WЛRDːDIːGRЛˑR∈XˑЛNGL`SˑFRЛNᄃˑDˑ/ˑNSːIˑBː
I.m. above sail. Letter BW R$_1$? Same die as next coin, **345**.

Rev.: ✱IhᄃːЛVTːTRЛNSI∈NSˑP∈RˑM∈DIVM ILLORVˑIˑBЛT
Large fleurs in spandrels. Letter BW R$_2$.

Blunt and Whitton type V/VI; Webb Ware dies 6/V, 2; North 1549; Seaby 1950. Bt Spink 1968; ex Bernstein.

345 Ryal

7.71   119.0   170°

I.m. rose/sun.

Obv.: same die as last coin, **344**.

Rev.: ✱IhᄃˑЛVTˑTRЛNSI∈NSˑP∈Rː M∈DIVMˑILLORVMˑIˑBЛTˑ
Large fleurs in spandrels but fleur missing from first spandrel in second quarter. Letter BW R$_2$.

Blunt and Whitton type V/VI; Webb Ware dies 6/VI, 12(?); North 1549; Seaby 1950.
Bt Baldwin 1952; ex Carter.

346 Ryal

7.71   119.0   100°

I.m. none/sun.

Obv.: ∈D/WЛRDːDIːGRЛːR∈XˑЛNGLˑSˑFRЛNᄃː/⊕DNSˑIˑBˑ⊕ˑ
Lis before DNS and after B'. Letter BW R$_3$.

Rev.: ✱IhᄃːЛVTːTRЛNSI∈NSːP∈Rː M∈DIVMːILLORVMˑIˑBЛT
Large fleurs in spandrels. Letter BW R$_4$.

Blunt and Whitton type V/VI, variant 2(b)1; Webb Ware dies 7/VI, 6; North 1549; Seaby 1950. Bt Spink 1965; ex Thompson; ex Lockett (1526).

347 Ryal

7.64   117.9   50°

I.m. none/rose.

Obv.: ∈D/ˑWЛRDːDIːGRЛːR∈XˑЛNGLˑSˑFRЛNᄃ`/ˑDNSˑIB`··
Letter BW R$_3$. Same die as next coin, **348**.

Rev.: ☉IhᄃˑЛVTˑTRЛNSIː∈NSˑP∈RˑM∈DIVMːILLORVMˑIˑBЛT
Large fleurs in spandrels. Letter BW R$_3$.

Blunt and Whitton type VI/V; Webb Ware dies 8/V, 3; North 1549; Seaby 1950. Bt Spink 1959.

[*continued overleaf*]

PLATE 34

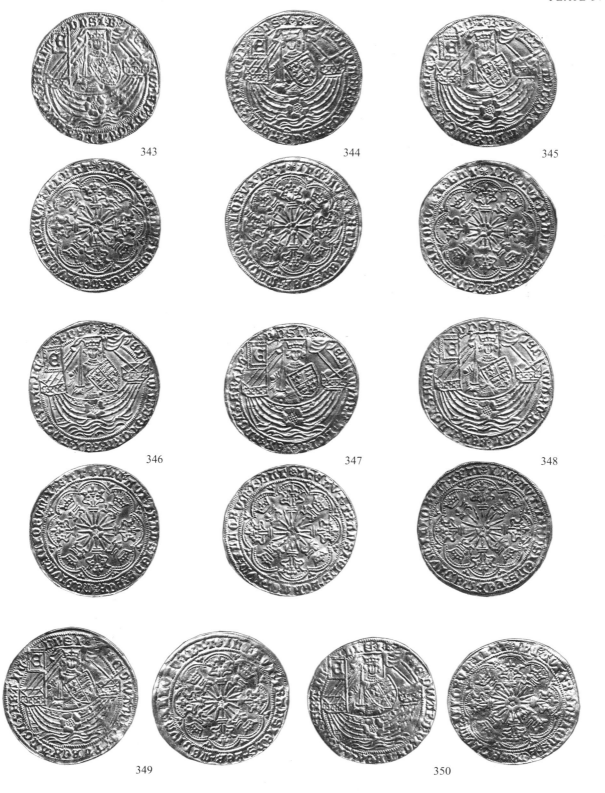

343

344

345

346

347

348

349

350

Plate 34 (*cont.*)

348 Ryal
    7.72   119.2   230°

I.m. none/rose.
Obv.: same die as last coin, **347**.
Rev.: ⊙IhႠ·ႬVT·TRႬNSIᕮNS∶PᕮR MᕮDIVM∶ILLORVM·I·BႬT
      Large fleurs in spandrels. Letter BW R$_2$.
Blunt and Whitton type VI/V, variant 2; Webb Ware dies 8/V, 6; North 1549; Seaby 1950. Bt Spink 1954; ex Jellard.

349 Ryal
    7.72   119.2   300°

I.m. sun/rose.
Obv.: ✳ᕮ/DWႬRD∶DI∶GRႬ·RᕮX·ႬNGL∶S·FRႬNႠ∶/·DNS∶I·B∶
      I.m. below sail. Letter BW R$_3$. Same die as next two coins, **350**, **351**.
Rev.: ⊙IhႠ∶ႬVT∶TRႬNSIᕮNS·PᕮR·MᕮDIVM∶ILLORV∶IBႬT
      Large fleurs in spandrels. Letter BW R$_3$.
Blunt and Whitton type VI/V, variant 1; Webb Ware dies 10/V, 7; North 1549; Seaby 1950. Bt Seaby 1951.

350 Ryal
    7.53   116.2   30°

I.m. sun both sides.
Obv.: same die as last and next coins, **349**, **351**.
Rev.: ✳IhႠ∶ႬVT'TRႬNSIᕮNS·PᕮR MᕮDIVM∶ILLORVM∶IBႬT
      Large fleurs in spandrels. Letter BW R$_3$.
Blunt and Whitton type VI, variant 1a; Webb Ware dies 10/VI, 15; North 1549; Seaby 1950. Ex Christie sale 21.3.1961 (98).

SECOND OR LIGHT COINAGE (March 1465–October 1470) (*cont.*)

London mint (cont.)

	Weight		
	g	*gr.*	*Die-axis*

351 Ryal
    7.38   113.9   100°

I.m. sun both sides.
Obv.: same die as last two coins, **349, 350**.
Rev.: ✳IhꞒ:ᴧVT:TRᴧNSIЄNS:PЄR:MЄDIVM ILLORV:I·Bᴧ
    Large fleurs in spandrels. Letter BW R$_3$.
Blunt and Whitton type VI, variant 1a; Webb Ware dies 10/VI, 16; North 1549; Seaby 1950. Ex Dangar (96).

352 Ryal
    7.58   117.0   10°

I.m. sun both sides.
Obv.: ✳/ЄD/WᴧRD:DI·GRᴧ:RЄX·ᴧNGL:S·FRᴧNꞒ:✚/·DNS:I·B:
    I.m. above sail. Lis after FRᴧNꞒ. Letter BW R$_1$.
Rev.: ✳IhꞒ:ᴧVT:TRᴧNSIЄNS·PЄR·MЄDIVM:ILLORVM:IBᴧT'
    Large fleurs in spandrels. Letter BW R$_1$.
Blunt and Whitton type VI, variant 1b var. with lis after FRᴧNꞒ; Webb Ware dies 12/VI, 20; North 1549; Seaby 1950. Ex Glendining sale 12.12.1956 (64).

353 Ryal
    7.69   118.6   100°

I.m. sun both sides.
Obv.: ✳/ЄD/WᴧRD:DI·GRᴧ·RЄX·ᴧNGL·S·FRᴧNꞒ/DNS:I·B:
    I.m. above sail. Letter BW R$_1$.
Rev.: ✳IhꞒ:ᴧVT:TRᴧNSIЄNS:PЄR·MЄDIVM:I·LLORVM·IBᴧT
    Trefoil between I and L of ILLORVM. Large fleurs in spandrels. Letter BW
    R$_1$.
Blunt and Whitton type VI, variant 1b; Webb Ware dies 13/VI, 23; North 1549; Seaby 1950. Ex Bute (41).

354 Ryal
    7.58   117.0   80°

I.m. sun both sides.
Obv.: ✳/ЄD/WᴧRD:DI·GRᴧ:RЄX·ᴧNGL:S·FRᴧNꞒ:/·DNS·I·B:
    I.m. above sail. Letter BW R$_3$.
Rev.: ✳·IhꞒ:ᴧVT·TRᴧNSIЄNŜ:PЄR·MЄDIVM:ILLORVM:IBᴧT·
    Large fleurs in spandrels. Letter BW R$_3$.
Blunt and Whitton type VI, variant 1b citing *NC* 1909, pl. XII, 5. This coin is from different dies, however. Webb Ware dies –/–; North 1549; Webb Ware dies –/–; North 1549; Seaby 1950. Bt Spink 1962.

355 Ryal
    7.70   119.8   100°

I.m. none/sun.
Obv.: ЄD/WᴧRD:DI·GRᴧ·RЄX·ᴧNGL:S·FRᴧNꞒ:/✚DNS I B'
    Lis before DNS. Letter BW R$_3$.
Rev.: ✳IhꞒ:ᴧVT:TRᴧNSIЄNS·PЄR:MЄDIVM:ILLORVM:I·BᴧT:
    Large fleurs in spandrels, the first one in the first quarter missing. Letter BW
    R$_3$.
Blunt and Whitton type VI, variant 2(b)3; Webb Ware dies 14/VI, 31; North 1549; Seaby 1950. Bt Baldwin 1951; ex Carter; ex Leslie-Ellis; ex Murdoch I (344).

356 Ryal
    7.69   118.6   190°

I.m. none/sun.
Obv.: ЄD/WᴧRD:DI:GRᴧ·RЄX·ᴧNGL·S·FRᴧNꞒ:/·DNS:I⸱Bⁱ⸱
    Letter BW R$_3$.
Rev.: same die as **343**.
Blunt and Whitton type VI, variant 2(a) var. with reverse reading that is recorded for 1(a); Webb Ware dies 15/VI, 19; North 1549; Seaby 1950. Bt Spink 1954 (*NCirc* 7201).

[*continued overleaf*]

PLATE 35

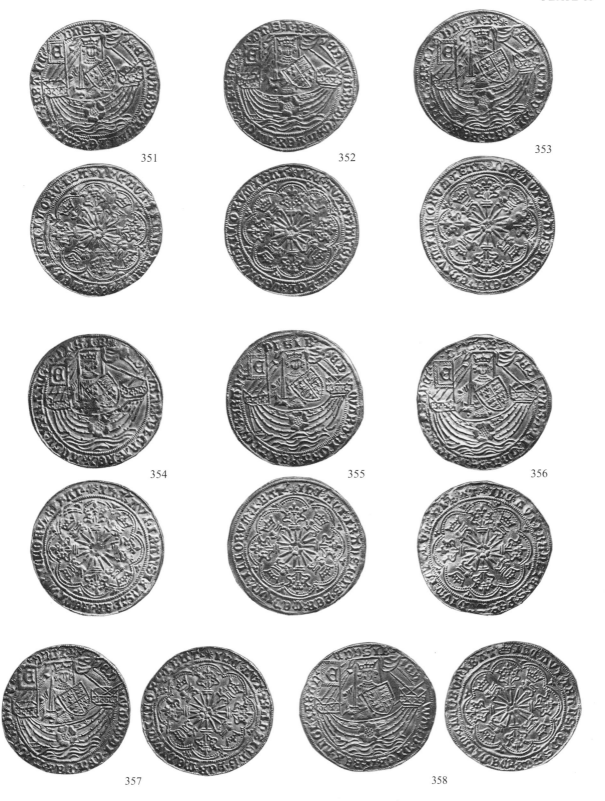

351

352

353

354

355

356

357

358

Plate 35 (*cont.*)

357 Ryal
    7.73   119.3   110°

I.m. none/sun.
Obv.: ED/WARD:DI ·GRA:REX ·ANGL:S ·FRANC·/·DNS:I·B:
    Letter BW R_1.
Rev.: ✸ IhC:AVT:TRANSIENS ·PER·MEDIVM·ILLORV·IBAT:
    Large fleurs in spandrels. Letter BW R_2.
Blunt and Whitton type VI, variant 2(a) var. of punctuation; Webb Ware dies 17/VI, 37; North 1549; Seaby 1950. Bt Spink 1953.

358 Ryal
    7.72   119.1   30°

I.m. none/crown.
Obv.: ED/WARD:DI ·GRA:REX ·ANGL:S ·FRAN·/C DNS:I B'
    Letter BW R_4.
Rev.: ⚓ IhC:AVT:TRANSIENS ·PER·MEDIVM·ILLORVM·IBAT
    Letter M broken. Large fleurs in spandrels. Letter BW R_4.
Blunt and Whitton type VII; Webb Ware dies 19/VII, 6; North 1549; Seaby 1950. Ex Lawson (27); ex Thelluson (17).

SECOND OR LIGHT COINAGE (March 1465–October 1470) (*cont.*)

London mint (cont.)

	Weight g	*gr.*	*Die-axis*	
359 Ryal	7.70	118.8	170°	I.m. none/crown. *Obv.*: EDWARD'DI GRA·REX·ANGL:S·FRANC:·:·/·DNS·I·B' Quatrefoil of four pellets after FRANC. Letter BW R_4. *Rev.*: crown IhC:AVT:TRANSIENS·PER MDIVM·ILLORVM·IBAT Punctuation after AVT is two abbreviation marks, one inverted. E omitted from MEDIVM. Large fleurs in spandrels. Letter BW R_4. Blunt and Whitton type VII, obverse variant 2, reverse variant 5; Webb Ware dies 21/VII, 7; North 1549; Seaby 1950. Bt Spink 1962; ex Spurway.
360 Ryal	7.74	119.4	30°	I.m. none/crown. *Obv.*: ED/··WARD:DI·GRA:REX·ANGL:S·FRAN·/·C DNS:I·B: Ornaments are 1– –11. Letter BW R_4. *Rev.*: crown IhC:AVT:TRANSIES·PER·MEDIVM ILLORVM:I:BAT N omitted from TRANSIENS. Large fleurs in spandrels. Letter BW R_4. Blunt and Whitton type VII, variant 1; Webb Ware dies 28/VII, 22; North 1549; Seaby 1950. Ex Glendining sale 30.10.1957 (8) and in the catalogue said to be ex Dominic Mitchell (7 or 8?).
361 Ryal	7.72	119.1	320°	I.m. none/crown. *Obv.*: ED/WARD·DI GRA·REX·ANGL:S·FRANC/·DNS·I·B: Letter BW R_4. *Rev.*: crown IhC:AVT:TRANSIENS·PER ·MEDIVM·ILLORVM·IBAT Punctuation after AVT is two abbreviation marks, one inverted (but not the same die as **359**). Large fleurs in spandrels. Letter BW R_4. Blunt and Whitton type VII, variant 5; Webb Ware dies 29/VII, 39; North 1549; Seaby 1950. No provenance.
362 Ryal	7.68	118.5	280°	I.m. none/crown. *Obv.*: ED/··WARD:DI·GRA:REX·ANGL:S·FRANC/·DNS:I·B: Letter BW R_4. Same die as **364**. *Rev.*: crown IhC'AVT:TRANSIENS·PER MEDIVM:ILLORVM:IBAT Large fleurs in spandrels but those in the second spandrel of the first quarter and the first spandrel of the second quarter are omitted. Letter BW R_2. Blunt and Whitton type VII var. with the two fleurs omitted; Webb Ware dies 30/VII, 40; North 1549; Seaby 1950. Bt Spink 1974.
363 Ryal	7.61	117.5	70°	I.m. none/crown. *Obv.*: ED/WARD:DI·GRA'REX·ANGL:S·FRANC:/·DNS'IB' Letter BW R_4. *Rev.*: crown IhC:AVT·TRANSIENS·PER·MEDIVM·ILLORVM IBAT Large fleurs in spandrels. Letter BW R_4. Blunt and Whitton type VII; Webb Ware dies 33/VII, 41; North 1549; Seaby 1950. Bt Spink 1960.

[*continued overleaf*]

PLATE 36

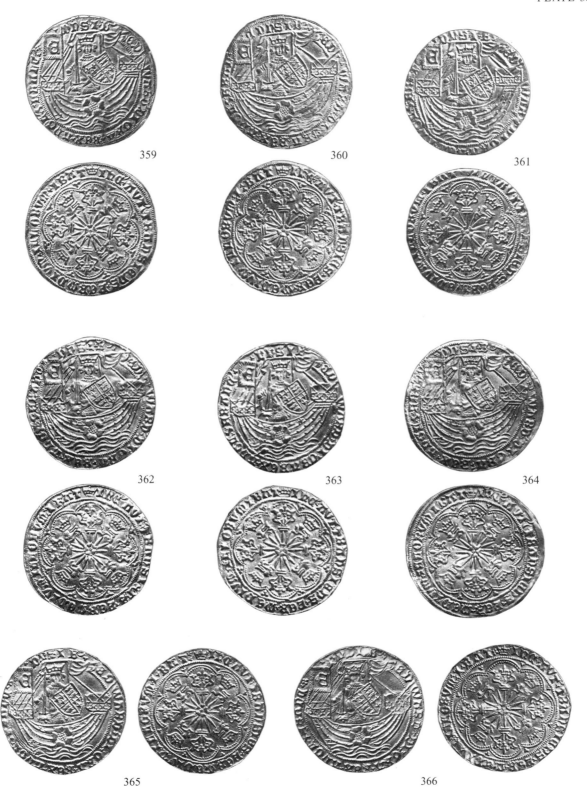

359   360   361

362   363   364

365   366

364 Ryal
7.67 118.3 190°

I.m. none/crown.
Obv.: same die as **362**.
Rev.: [crown] IhC⁝ΛVT⁝TRΛNSIЄNS·PЄR·MЄDIVM·ILLORVM IBΛT
Punctuation after ΛVT is two abbreviation marks, one inverted. Small trefoils in spandrels.
Blunt and Whitton type VII/VIII(A); Webb Ware dies 30/VIII, 2; North 1549; Seaby 1951. Ex Christie sale 21.3.1961 (49).

365 Ryal
7.65 118.0 30°

I.m. none/crown.
Obv.: ЄD/WΛRD⁝DI⁝GRΛ·RЄX·ΛNGL·S FRΛNC·∷/·DNS I B⁝
Pellet by shield. Quatrefoil after FRΛNC·. Letter BW R_4. Same die as next coin, **366**.
Rev.: [crown] IhC·ΛVT·TRΛNSIЄS·PЄR MЄDIVM·ILLORVM·I·BΛT⁝
Second N omitted from TRΛNSIЄNS. Small trefoils in spandrels. Letter BW R_4. Blunt and Whitton type VIII(A), variant 1; Webb Ware dies 36/VIII, 9; North 1549; Seaby 1951. Ex Lockett (4303).

366 Ryal
7.75 119.6 140°

I.m. none/crown.
Obv.: same die as last coin, **365**.
Rev.: [crown] IhC⁝ΛVT⁝TRΛNSIЄNS·PЄR·MЄDIVM ILLORVM⁝I·BΛT·∴
Second N of TRΛNSIЄNS over S. I of ILLORVM over ? giving the appearance of U. Quatrefoil after IBΛT. Small trefoils in spandrels. Letter BW R_4.
Blunt and Whitton type VIII(A), obverse as variant 1; Webb Ware dies 36/VIII, 31; North 1549; Seaby 1951. Bt Spink 1962.

SECOND OR LIGHT COINAGE (March 1465–October 1470) (*cont.*)

London mint (cont.)

	Weight		
	g	*gr.*	*Die-axis*

367 Ryal

7.72 119.1 130°

I.m. none/crown.
Obv.: ED/·WΛRD:DI ·GRΛ:REX·ΛNGL:S FRΛNC/·DNS:I·B:
Pellet by shield. Letter BW R$_4$.
Rev.: ⚓IhC:ΛVT:TRΛNSIENS·PER:MEDIVM·ILLORV:I·BΛT
Small trefoils in spandrels. Letter BW R$_4$.
Blunt and Whitton type VIII(A), similar to variant 1 but no quatrefoil between
FRΛNC and DNS; Webb Ware dies 38a/VIII, 34(?); North 1549; Seaby 1951. Bt
Spink 1957. Seaby 1951. Bt Spink 1957.

368 Ryal

7.71 119.0 200°

I.m. none/crown.
Obv.: ED/WΛRD·DI ·GRΛ·REX·ΛNGL:S·FRΛNC/·DNS·I B'
Hinges on ship's rudder omitted. No pellet by shield. Letter BW R$_4$.
Rev.: ⚓IhC:ΛVT TRΛNSIENS·PER·MEDIVM·ILLORVM·IBΛT·
Small trefoils in spandrels. Letter BW R$_4$.
Blunt and Whitton type VIII(A), variant 4. Webb Ware dies 41/VIII, 32; North 1549;
Seaby 1951. Bt Schulman 1965.

369 Ryal

7.63 117.7 200°

I.m. none/crown.
Obv.: ED/·WΛRD:DI ·GRΛ:REX·ΛNGL:S·FRΛNC·/·DNS'IB:××
R of GRΛ struck over a G. Two saltires at end of legend. No pellet by shield.
Letter BW R$_4$.
Rev.: ⚓IhC:ΛVT:TRΛNSIENS:PER·MEDIVM ILLORM·IBΛT
TRΛNSIENS has been corrected from TRΛSNINS by punching the correct
letters over the wrong ones. V omitted from ILLORVM. Small trefoils in
spandrels. Letter BW R$_4$.
Blunt and Whitton type VIII(A), variant 5; Webb Ware dies 44/VIII, 20; Same dies as
Lockett 1528; North 1549; Seaby 1951. No provenance.

370 Ryal

7.73 119.3 160°

I.m. none/crown.
Obv.: ED/WΛRD:DI GRΛ:REX·ΛNGL·S·FRΛNC·/·DNS I·B'[·?]
No pellet by shield. Letter BW R$_4$.
Rev.: ⚓IhC·ΛVT·TRΛNSIES·PER·MEDIVM·ILLORVM I·BΛT:
Second N omitted from TRΛNSIENS. Small trefoils in spandrels. Letters BW
R$_4$ and M broken.
Blunt and Whitton type VIII(A), variant 3; possibly, but not certainly, Webb Ware dies
49a/VIII, 33; North 1549; Seaby 1951. No provenance.

371 Ryal

7.66 118.2 260°

I.m. none/crown.
Obv.: ED/·WΛRD:DI ·GRΛ:REX·ΛNGL:S FRΛNC·/·DNS:I·B:
No pellet by shield. Letter BW R$_4$.
Rev.: ⚓IhC:ΛVT:TRΛNSIENS ‡PER·MEDIVM·ILLORVM·IBΛT
Two saltires before PER. Small trefoils in spandrels. Letter BW R$_4$.
Blunt and Whitton type VIII(A), variant 6; Webb Ware dies 51/VIII, 30; North 1549;
Seaby 1951. Bt Schulman 1958.

[*continued overleaf*]

PLATE 37

367

368

369

370

371

372

373

374

Plate 37 (*cont.*)

372 Ryal
    7.54   116.3   20°

I.m. none/sun.

Obv.: Ɛ Ð /WⱯR Ð: Ð I ‡GR Ʌ:RƐX × ⱯNGL:S × FR Ʌ/NꝈ ' ƉNS I B:
Ornaments, lion, lion (no lis). All Ds are reversed Ɛs. 'Comb' on bowsprit. Saltire stops. Letter R s abnormal.

Rev.: ✱ IhꝈ : ⱯVT: TRⱯNSIƐNS : PƐR ⱭƐDIVⱭ · ILLORVⱭ: I · BⱯT
Small trefoils in spandrels. Letter R s abnormal.

Blunt and Whitton –, but described and attributed to their type VIII(B) in Schneider 1968. This coin is no. 9 in the list of coins given in that paper and is illustrated on plate I thereto. In spite of the abnormal letters, others, for example P, are from the normal fount which confirms the coin as part of the regular series. Webb Ware dies 63/VIIIb, 1; North 1549; Seaby 1951 var. this i.m. Bt Spink 1967; ex Angers hoard.

373 Ryal
    7.55   116.5   50°

I.m. sun/sun.

Obv.: ✱ Ɛ/DWⱯRD:DI:GRⱯ:RƐX × ⱯNGL:S × FRⱯ/NꝈ ƉNS'IB'
Ornaments, lion lion (no lis). I.m. below sail. 'Comb' on bowsprit. Ship's planks divided, and four on hull. Letter BW R$_5$.

Rev.: ✱ IhꝈ : ⱯVT: TRⱯNSIƐNS · PƐR · ⱭƐDIV:ILLORV: I · BⱯT
Small trefoils in spandrels. Probably letter BW R$_5$ though this is not very clear.

Blunt and Whitton type X/VIII(B); Webb Ware dies 64/VIIIb, 2; North 1549; Seaby 1951 *var.* this i.m. Bt Baldwin 1961.

374 Ryal
    7.70   118.8   260°

I.m. none/long cross fitchée.

Obv.: Ɛ/DWⱯRD DI GRⱯ RƐX · ⱯNGL:S · FRⱯNꝈ/DNS · I · B'
Letter BW R$_5$.

Rev.: ⴱ IhꝈ : ⱯVT: TRⱯNSIƐNS · PƐR · ⱭƐDIVⱭ · ILLORVⱭ · I · BⱯT'
Small trefoils in spandrels. Letter BW R$_5$.

Blunt and Whitton type X; Webb Ware dies 52/X, 5; North 1549; Seaby 1951. Bt Spink 1971 (*NCirc* 10395).

SECOND OR LIGHT COINAGE (*cont.*)

London mint (cont.)

375 Ryal

	Weight		
	g	*gr.*	*Die-axis*
	7.67	118.3	290°

I.m. none/long cross fitchée.
Obv.: ЄD/:·WᴧRD'DI ·GRᴧ REX ᴧNGL·S ·FRᴧNᏟ·/·DNS'IB'
 Letter BW R$_5$.
Rev.: ✠IhᏟ∶ᴧVT∶TRᴧNSIЄNS ·PЄR ·MЄDIVM·ILLORV'I ·BᴧT'
 Small trefoils in spandrels. Letter BW R$_5$.
Blunt and Whitton type X; Webb Ware dies 54/X, 19; North 1549; Seaby 1951. Bt Baldwin 1952.

376 Ryal

7.47	115.3	60°

I.m. none/long cross fitchée.
Obv.: Є·/DWᴧRD∶DI GRᴧ∶REX ᴧNGL∶S ·FRᴧNᏟ·/·DNS·I·B'
 Letter BW R$_5$. Same die as next two coins, **377, 378**.
Rev.: ✠IhᏟ∶ᴧVT∶TRᴧNSIЄNS ·PЄR ·MЄDIVM·ILLORV∶IBᴧT
 Small trefoils in spandrels except that the one in the second spandrel in the second quarter is omitted. Letter BW R$_5$.
Blunt and Whitton type X, variant 3; Webb Ware dies 56/X, 12; North 1549; Seaby 1951. No provenance.

377 Ryal

7.76	119.7	190°

I.m. none/long cross fitchée.
Obv.: same die as last and next coins, **376, 378**.
Rev.: ✠IhᏟ∶ᴧVT∶TRᴧNSIЄNS ·PЄR MЄDIVM∶ILLORV∶I·BᴧT
 Small trefoils in spandrels, that in the second spandrel of the first quarter omitted. Letter BW R$_5$.
Blunt and Whitton type X, variant 3; Webb Ware dies 56/X, 20; North 1549; Seaby 1951. Bt Spink 1979.

378 Ryal

7.76	119.7	30°

I.m. none/long cross fitchée.
Obv.: same die as last two coins, **376, 377**.
Rev.: ✠IhᏟ∶ᴧVT∶TRᴧNSIЄNS ·PЄR MЄDIVM·I·LLORV·I·BᴧT
 Small trefoils in spandrels. Letter BW R$_5$.
Blunt and Whitton type X; Webb Ware dies 56/X, 15; North 1549; Seaby 1951. Bt Spink 1956 (*NCirc* 9377).

379 Ryal

7.74	119.4	10°

I.m. none/long cross fitchée.
Obv.: ЄD/·WᴧRD∶DI GRᴧ·REX·ᴧNGL·S FRᴧNᏟ·/·DNS'I B∶
 Ornaments, lion lion (no lis). Letter BW R$_5$.
Rev.: ✠IhᏟ·ᴧVT∶TRᴧNSIЄNS ·PЄR MЄDIVM∶ILLORV I·BᴧT
 Small trefoils in spandrels. Letter BW R$_5$.
Blunt and Whitton type X, variant 2; Webb Ware dies 59/X, 16; North 1549; Seaby 1951. Ex Lockett (1529); ex Dudman (36); ex Moon (76); ex Hastings (261). Said in the Moon catalogue to have been found during the demolition of the Tabard Inn, Southwark.

380 Ryal

7.39	114.1	90°

I.m. none/long cross fitchée.
Obv.: ЄD/·WᴧRD∶DЄI ·GRᴧ∶REX·ᴧNGL∶⁄·FRᴧNᏟ·/·DNS∶I·B∶
 Reads DЄI. No rudder hinges. Two ropes at stern. Small lettering.
Rev.: ✠IhᏟ·ᴧVT∶TRᴧNSIЄNS ·PЄR MЄDIVVM·ILLORV IBᴧT
 Reads MЄDIVVM. Small trefoils in spandrels. Letter BW R$_5$.
Blunt and Whitton type X, variant 1; Webb Ware dies 60/X, 21; North 1549; Seaby 1951. Ex Potter 1961.

[*continued overleaf*]

PLATE 38

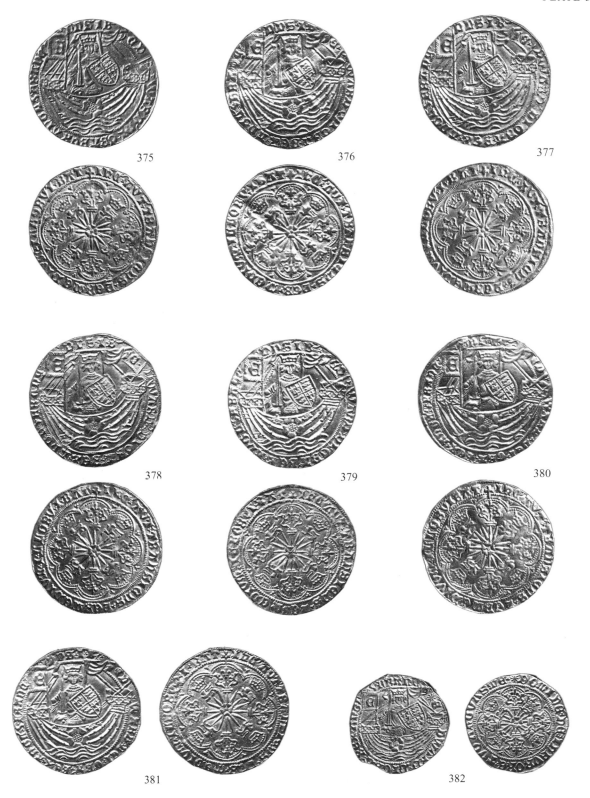

375

376

377

378

379

380

381

382

Plate 38 (*cont.*)

381 Ryal
    7.70   118.9   110°

I.m. none/pierced long cross fitchée.

Obv.: ЄD/·WᴀRD·DЄI·GRᴀ·RЄX·ᴀNGL·S·FRᴀnᴄ·/·DnS·I·B·

Reads DЄI. No rudder hinges. Two ropes at stern. Small lettering.

Rev: ✠Ihᴄ·ᴀVT·TRᴀnSIЄnS·PЄR·mЄDIVm·ILLORVm·I·BᴀT

The long cross fitchee is not only pierced but is indented at the ends of the arms. Small trefoils in spandrels. Letter BW R_5.

Blunt and Whitton type X, variant 1; Webb Ware dies 62/X, 21; North 1549; Seaby 1951. Ex Lockett (4304).

382 Half-ryal
    3.84   59.3   320°

I.m. sun both sides.

Obv.: ✹Є/DWᴀRD·DI·GRᴀ·RЄX·ᴀNGL'/·S·FRᴀnᴄ

I.m. below sail. Saltire stops. Letter BW R_1.

Rev.: ✹DOMInЄ·nЄ·In FVRORЄ·TVO ᴀRGVᴀS mЄ·   Trefoil stops. Letter BW R_1.

Blunt and Whitton type VI(A); Webb Ware dies 2/3; North 1554; Seaby 1959. Bt Seaby 1966.

SECOND OR LIGHT COINAGE (*cont.*)

London mint (cont.)

	Weight		
	g	*gr.*	*Die-axis*

383 Half-ryal
3.83   59.1   70°

I.m. none/crown.
Obv.: ЄD/WARD·DI GRA·RЄX ANGL·S·/FRANC   Letter BW R$_4$.
Rev.: ⚜DOMINЄ·NЄ ·IN FVRORЄ·TVO ARGVAS·MЄ·
     Letter BW R$_4$.
Blunt and Whitton type VII; Webb Ware dies 3/–; North 1554; Seaby 1959. Bt Baldwin 1961.

384 Half-ryal
3.87   59.8   80°

I.m. none/crown.
Obv.: ЄD/WARD·DЄI [.]GRA[.]RЄX ANGL·/S FANC   It is unclear from this coin whether the stops in brackets are trefoils or quatrefoils although what can be seen seems more to favour the former. Reads DЄI. R omitted from FRANC.
Rev.: ⚜DOMINЄ·NЄ ·IN FVRORЄ[?]TVO ARGVAS MЄ·   There appears to be a letter between FVRORЄ and TVO which cannot be determined from this specimen. No trefoils in spandrels. Letter BW R$_4$.
Blunt and Whitton type VII, variant 4; Webb Ware dies 12/13; North 1554; Seaby 1959. Ex Grantley (29); ex Chadwick (141).

385 Half-ryal
3.78   58.4   170°

I.m. none/crown.
Obv.: Є/DWARD·DI ·GRA·RЄX·ANGL·S·/FRANC·   Letter BW R$_4$.
Rev.: ⚜DOMINЄ·NЄ ·IN FVRORЄ·TVO ARGVAS MЄ   Letter BW R$_4$.
Blunt and Whitton type VII; Webb Ware dies 13/–; North 1554; Seaby 1959. Bt Baldwin 1952; ex Carter.

386 Half-ryal
3.84   59.3   90°

I.m. none/crown.
Obv.: ЄD/WARD·DI ·GRA·RЄX·ANGL·S·/✠ FRANC   Quatrefoil before FRANC. Letter BW R$_4$.
Rev.: ⚜DOMINЄ·NЄ ·IN ·FVRORЄ·TVO ARGVAS MЄ   Letter BW R$_4$.
Blunt and Whitton type VII, variant 1; Webb Ware dies 15a/12a; North 1554; Seaby 1959. Bt Baldwin 1952; ex Carter.

387 Half-ryal
3.86   59.5   310°

I.m. none/crown.
Obv.: ЄD/WARD·DI ·GRA RЄX·ANGL·S·/FRANC·   It is uncertain whether the symbol before FRANC is a trefoil or a quatrefoil. Letter BW R$_4$.
Rev.: ⚜DOMINЄ·NЄ ·IN·FVRORЄ·TVO:ARGVAS MЄ   Letter BW R$_4$.
Blunt and Whitton type VII; Webb Ware dies –/–; North 1554; Seaby 1959. Ex Glendining sale 6.4.1954 (11) (Mr Schneider's ticket refers to this as the Reynolds collection).

388 Half-ryal
3.40   52.4   260°

I.m. none/crown.
Obv.: ЄD/WARD[   ]GRA·RЄX·ANGL·/FRANC   Lis in waves. Letter BW R$_4$.
Rev.: ⚜DOMINЄ·NЄ ·IN FVRORЄ TVO·ARGVAS MЄ   Letter BW R$_4$.
Blunt and Whitton type VIII(A), variant 1. Webb Ware lis group, dies 1/1; North 1554; Seaby, see parenthetical reference after no. 1962. Bt Spink 1989.

389 Half-ryal
3.73   57.6   10°

I.m. none/crown.
Obv.: ЄD/WARD·DI ·GRA·RЄX·ANGL·/·S FRANC   Lis in waves. Letter BW R ?.
Rev.: ⚜DOMINЄ·NЄ ·IN·FVRORЄ·TVO·ARGVAS MЄ   Letter BW R$_4$.
Blunt and Whitton type VIII(A), variant 1; Webb Ware, obverse, lis group die 2, reverse, non lis group die 5; North 1554; Seaby, see reference under last coin. This important coin establishes a die link between the series with lis in waves and those without. Ex Potter.

[*continued overleaf*]

PLATE 39

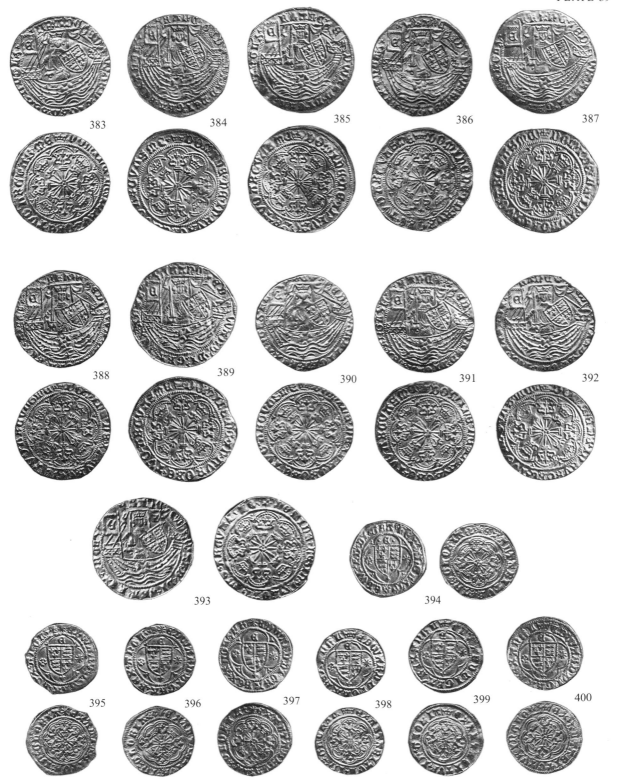

383   384   385   386   387

388   389   390   391   392

393   394

395   396   397   398   399   400

Plate 39 (*cont.*)

390 Half-ryal
3.79 58.5 0°

I.m. rose towards end of legend/crown.
Obv.: ЄD/WΛRD·DI GRΛːRЄX·ΛNGL·S·FR/[Λ]Nꝶ⊕✚
Lis in waves. Quatrefoil, after rose, at end of legend. The Λ in FRΛNꝶ, apparently omitted on this coin, is known to be present from a coin from the same die in the BM which is illustrated in *NC* 1909, pl. XIV, 6. Both coins also show that Blunt and Whitton were wrong to record two trefoils between the rose and the quatrefoil. The Schneider coin lacks the pellet above shield feature recorded by Blunt and Whitton from the coin illustrated in *NC*. That pellet was, no doubt accidentally, artificially raised on the coin with a sharp instrument!
Rev.: ⚓DOMINЄ·NЄ IN·FVRORЄ TVO ΛRGVΛS MЄ Letters BW R$_4$. Blunt and Whitton type IX, variant 1; Webb Ware lis group dies 3/1; North 1554; Seaby 1959. Bt Spink 1957; ex Arnold.

391 Half-ryal
3.83 59.1 40°

I.m. sun towards end of legend/crown.
Obv.: ЄD/WΛRD·DI·GRΛ·RЄX·ΛNGL·Sꞏ·F/·RΛNꝶ✳ ː ✚
Quatrefoil at end of legend. Pellet below shield. Letter BW R$_4$.
Rev.: ⚓DOMINЄ·NЄ ·IN·FVRORЄ·TVO·ΛRGVΛS MЄ Letter BW R$_4$.
Blunt and Whitton type VIII(C); Webb Ware dies 16/–; North 1554; Seaby 1959. Bt Baldwin 1952; ex Carter.

392 Half-ryal
3.85 59.4 180°

I.m. rose towards end of legend/crown.
Obv.: ЄD/WΛRD·DI GRΛ·RЄX·ΛNGL S F/·RΛNꝶ⊕ Small lis in waves. Small lettering.
Rev.: ⚓DOMINЄ NЄ ·IN FVRORЄ TVO ΛRGVΛS·MЄ✚
Quatrefoil at end of legend. Letter BW R$_4$.
Blunt and Whitton type IX, variant 2; Webb Ware lis group dies 4/4; North 1554; Seaby 1959. Ex Ryan (77).

393 Half-ryal
3.85 59.4 180°

I.m. none/pierced long cross fitchée.
Obv.: ЄD/WΛRDːDI ·GRΛ·RЄX·ΛNGL·Sꞏ/FRΛNꝶ· Small lettering.
Rev.: ✟DOMINЄ·NЄ ·IN·FVRORЄ·TVO·ΛRGVΛS·MЄꞏ Pellets (not trefoils) in spandrels. Small lettering.
Blunt and Whitton type X; Webb Ware dies 18/21; North 1554; Seaby 1959. Bt Seaby 1962; ex R. Carlyon-Britton.

394 Quarter-ryal
1.90 29.3 60°

I.m. rose/sun.
Obv.: ⊕ЄDWΛRD·DI ·GRΛːRЄX ΛNGLːSꞏFꞏ Legend starts at bottom of coin. Є above, rose to left and sun to right of shield. Trefoils in spandrels.
Rev.: ✳ЄXΛLTΛBITVR⊕IN⊕GLORIΛ⊕ Stops are large roses.
Blunt and Whitton type V/VI; Webb Ware dies 3/3; North 1560; Seaby 1965. Ex Lockett (1543).

395 Quarter-ryal
1.85 28.5 60°

I.m. sun both sides.
Obv.: ✳ЄDWΛRDːDI ·GRΛ ːRЄX·ΛNGL⊕ Rose at end of legend. Є above, rose to left and sun to right of shield. Trefoils in spandrels. Same die as next coin, **396**.
Rev.: ✳ЄXΛLTΛBITVR‡INːGLORIΛ Double saltire stops.
Blunt and Whitton type VI, variant 2; Webb Ware dies 4/4; North 1560; Seaby 1965. No provenance.

Plate 39 (*cont.*)

396 Quarter-ryal
    1.90   29.3   220°

I.m. sun both sides.
Obv.:   same die as last coin, **395**.
Rev.:   ✳ ЄXΛLTΛBITVR׃IN׃GLORIΛ☼׃ Rose at end of legend. Double trefoil stops.
Blunt and Whitton type VI but a major variety with the rose at the end of the reverse legend which also has double trefoil punctuation; Webb Ware dies 4/–; North 1560; Seaby 1965. Ex Schulman sale 9.3.1959 (1780).

397 Quarter-ryal
    1.90   29.3   330°

I.m. sun both sides.
Obv.:   ✳ ЄDWΛRD DI ·GRΛ·RЄX·ΛNGL·S·FR Є above, rose to left and sun to right of shield. Trefoils in spandrels.
Rev.:   ✳ ЄXΛLTΛBITVR׃IN ·∴·GLORIΛ
Blunt and Whitton type VI, variant 1, var. with 4 trefoils after IN on reverse; Webb Ware dies 6/7; North 1560; Seaby 1965. Ex Glendining sale 19.5.1964 (287).

398 Quarter-ryal
    1.94   29.9   260°

I.m. crown both sides.
Obv.:   ⚜ ЄDWΛRD·DI·GRΛ·RЄX ΛNGL Є above, rose to left and sun to right of shield. Nothing in spandrels. Same die as next two coins, **399, 400**.
Rev.:   ⚜ ЄXΛLTΛBITVR·IN☼GLORIΛ Blunt and Whitton type VII, variant 8 but without quatrefoil before reverse i.m.; Webb Ware dies 8/18; North 1560; Seahy 1965. Ex Parsons (19, part).

399 Quarter-ryal
    1.93   29.8   200°

I.m. crown both sides.
Obv.:   same die as last and next coins, **398, 400**.
Rev.:   ⚜ ЄXΛLTΛBTTVR·IN·GLORIΛ T for I in ЄXΛLTΛBITVR.
Blunt and Whitton type VII, variant 9; Webb Ware dies 8/19; North 1560; Seaby 1965. Ex Glendining sale 15.4.1971 (58).

400 Quarter-ryal
    1.92   29.6   50°

I.m. crown both sides.
Obv.:   same die as last two coins, **398, 399**.
Rev.:   ⚜ ЄX·ΛLTΛBITVTVR IN GLOR Trefoil stop between X and Λ. TV twice in ЄXΛLTΛBITVR. Lis missing from second cross end.
Blunt and Whitton type VII, variant 8–9/2; Webb Ware dies 8/20; North 1560; Seaby 1965. Ex Lockett (4308).

SECOND OR LIGHT COINAGE (*cont.*)

London mint (cont.)

401 Quarter-ryal

	Weight		
	g	*gr.*	*Die-axis*
	1.91	29.4	10°

I.m. crown both sides.
Obv.: ⚜ ЄDWΛRD'DI +GRΛ'RЄX ΛNGL'˙S×
ℰ above, rose to left and sun to right of shield. Saltire stops.
Nothing in spandrels.
Rev.: ⚜ ЄXΛLTΛBITVR✠IN✠GLORIΛ✠ Stops are lis.
Blunt and Whitton type VII, variant 6; Webb Ware dies 10/22; North 1560; Seaby 1965. Bt Spink 1961; ex Caine.

402 Quarter-ryal

1.89	29.1	220°

I.m. crown both sides.
Obv.: ⚜ ЄDWΛRD·DI·GRΛ'RЄX·ΛNGL' ℰ above, rose to left and sun to
right of shield. Trefoils in spandrels.
Rev.: ⚜ ЄX·ΛLTΛBITVTVR IN GLOR Trefoil stop between X and Λ. TV
twice in ЄXΛLTΛBITVR. Lis missing from first and second cross ends.
Blunt and Whitton type VII, variant 2; Webb Ware dies 11/20a; North 1560; Seaby 1965. Ex Glendining sale 14.4.1961 (18).

403 Quarter-ryal

1.89	29.2	20°

I.m. crown both sides.
Obv.: ⚜ ЄDWΛRD·DI·GRΛ'RЄX·ΛNGL' ℰ above, rose to left and sun to
right of shield. Trefoils in spandrels.
Rev.: ⚜ ЄXΛLTΛBITVR⊙IN·GLORIΛ
Blunt and Whitton type VII, variant 3 (same dies as the coin illustrated on their pl. IX, 11); Webb Ware dies 11/10; North 1560; Seaby 1965. Ex Lockett (3132).

404 Quarter-ryal

1.91	29.5	70°

I.m. crown both sides.
Obv.: ⚜ ЄDWΛRD·DI·GRΛ'RЄX·ΛNGL'˙S˙ ℰ between two pellets above,
rose to left and sun to right shield. Pellets in spandrels.
Rev.: ⚜ ЄXΛLTΛBITVR·IN GLORIΛ⊙ (the probable reading; there is
considerable double striking) Rose at end of legend.
Blunt and Whitton type VII, variant 1 var. with trefoil stop and rose on reverse; Webb Ware dies 13/27; North 1560; Seaby 1965. No provenance.

405 Quarter-ryal

1.90	29.3	340°

I.m. crown both sides.
Obv.: ⚜ ЄDWΛRD✠DI✠GRΛ'✠RЄX✠ΛNGL'✠ Stops are lis. ℰ before, sun
to left and rose to right of shield. Nothing in spandrels.
Rev.: ⚜ ЄXΛLTΛBITVR'IN⊙GLORIΛ⊙▴ Stops are roses and a trefoil.
Blunt and Whitton type VII, variant 10, who illustrate this coin (pl. X, 8). However it is clear from the coin that, contrary to what they say in their table on pp. 178–9, there is nothing in the spandrels (they give trefoils) and the obverse stops are lis only (they give trefoil and lis). Also the object before the reverse i.m. appears to be a trefoil rather than a quatrefoil, as they state. Webb Ware dies 14/29; North 1560; Seaby 1965. Ex Lockett (1544).

406 Quarter-ryal

1.88	29.0	90°

I.m. crown both sides.
Obv.: ⚜ ЄDWΛRD'✠DI✠GRΛ'✠RЄX✠ΛNGL' Stops are lis. ℰ above, sun to
left and rose right of shield. Nothing in spandrels.
Rev.: ⚜ ЄXΛLTΛBITVR✠IN✠GLORIΛ✠ Stops are lis.
Blunt and Whitton type VII, variant 13; Webb Ware dies 15/28; North 1560; Seaby 1965. Bt Spink 1973.

[*continued overleaf*]

PLATE 40

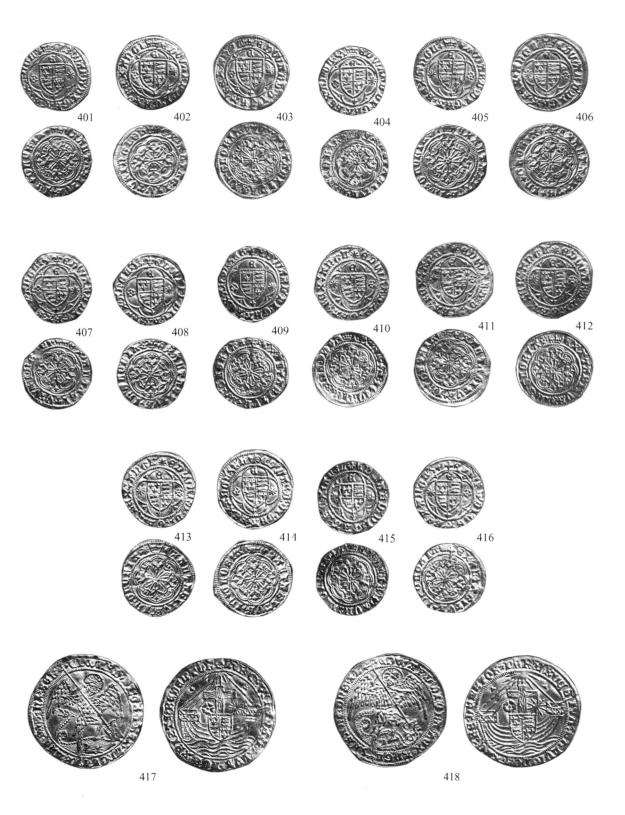

401   402   403   404   405   406

407   408   409   410   411   412

413   414   415   416

417   418

Plate 40 (*cont.*)

407 Quarter-ryal
1.97 30.4 160°

I.m. lis/crown.
Obv.: ✚ EDWARD'DI ·GRA:REX·ANGL:S· E above, rose to left and sun to right of shield. Trefoils in spandrels.
Rev.: ⚓ EX·ALTABITVTVR IN GLOR Trefoil stop between X and A. TV twice in EXALTABITVR. Lis missing from second cross end.
Blunt and Whitton type VII, variant 16 and pl. XI, 14 (this coin); Webb Ware dies 21/36; North 1560; Seaby 1965. Ex Lockett (1548); ex Bruun (498, part); ex Walters, 1913 (383).

408 Quarter-ryal
1.77 27.3 130°

I.m. lis both sides.
Obv.: ✚ EDWARD'DI ×GRA REX×ANGL:S: Single saltire stops. E above, rose to left and sun to right of shield. Nothing in spandrels.
Rev.: ✚ EXALTABITVR·IN·GLORIA⊙ Rose at end of legend. Lis missing from second cross end.
Blunt and Whitton type VII, variant 15–17/–, no reverse legend having i.m. lis and ending with a rose is recorded by them; Webb Ware dies –/–; North 1560; Seaby 1965. No provenance.

409 Quarter-ryal
1.93 29.8 80°

I.m. lis both sides.
Obv.: ✚ EDWARD:DI ·GRA:REX ANGL S FR E above, rose to left and sun to right of shield. Trefoils in spandrels.
Rev.: ✚ ·EXALTABITVR·IN·GLORIA✿ Cinquefoil (?) at end of legend.
Blunt and Whitton type VII, variant 17; Webb Ware dies 20/34; North 1560; Seaby 1965. Ex Lockett (1549).

410 Quarter-ryal
1.90 29.3 10°

I.m. sun/crown.
Obv.: ✱ EDWARD:DI :GRA':REX:ANGL' E above, sun to left and rose to right of shield. Trefoils in spandrels. Pellet in first quarter of shield. Same die as next three coins, **411, 412, 413**.
Rev.: ⚓ EXALTABITVR✚IN⊙GLORIA
Blunt and Whitton type VIII, variant 6; Webb Ware dies 7/9; North 1560; Seaby 1965. Ex Lockett (4023).

411 Quarter-ryal
1.86 28.7 290°

I.m. sun/crown.
Obv.: same die as last and next two coins, **410, 412, 413**.
Rev.: ⚓ EXALTABITVR✚IN✚GLORIA✚ Stops are lis.
Blunt and Whitton type VIII, variant 2; Webb Ware dies 7/14; North 1560; Seaby 1965. Bt Spink 1951.

412 Quarter-ryal
1.92 29.7 350°

I.m. sun/crown.
Obv.: same die as last two and next coins, **410, 411, 413**.
Rev.: ⚓ EXATABITVR⊙IN⊙GLORIA⊙ Stops are large roses. L omitted from EXALTABITVR.
Blunt and Whitton type VIII, variant 5 and pl. X, 11 (this coin); Webb Ware dies 7/15; North 1560; Seaby 1965. Ex Lockett (1545).

413 Quarter-ryal
1.90 29.3 350°

I.m. sun/crown.
Obv.: same die as last three coins, **410, 411, 412**.
Rev.: ⚓ EXALTABITVR:IN:GLORIA·✱
Blunt and Whitton type VIII, variant 8; Webb Ware dies 7/16; North 1560; Seaby 1965. Ex Lockett (1546).

414 Quarter-ryal
1.90 29.3 280°

I.m. sun over crown/sun over crown.
Obv.: ✱ EDWARD:DI :GRA:REX ANGL:S·FR E above, rose to left and sun to right of shield. Nothing in spandrels.
Rev.: ✱ EXALTABITVR✚IN✚GLORIA Stops are lis.
Blunt and Whitton type VIII, variant 1; Webb Ware dies 17/31; North 1560; Seaby 1965. Ex Lockett (3131); ex Roth (217); ex Montagu (590); ex Brice; ex Shepherd (178).

Plate 40 (*cont.*)

415 Quarter-ryal
    1.00   15.5   90°

I.m. sun/crown.
Obv.: ✳ ЄDWⱯRD:DI :GRⱯ:RЄX ⱯNGL Є above, sun to left and rose to right of shield. Trefoils in spandrels.
Rev.: ⚓ ЄXⱯLTⱯBITVR:IN GLORIⱯ·
Blunt and Whitton type VIII, variant 3. The very light weight of this coin, especially as it does not appear to be clipped, taken together with its poor colour, make it likely that this is a forgery, probably contemporary. The dies are of good workmanship and from his ticket it appears that Mr Schneider regarded the coin as being genuine (however, there is no indication that he was aware of the low weight). Blunt and Whitton state that all coins of type VIII, variants 2–8, are from the same obverse die. This coin is from a different die which, in the circumstances, supports the case for its falseness. Webb Ware dies –/–. Bt Spink 1962.

416 Quarter-ryal
    1.85   28.6   230°

I.m. long cross fitchée both sides.
Obv.: ✠ЄDWRD'DI GRⱯ'RЄX ⱯNGL'S· Ɐ omitted from ЄDWⱯRD. Є above, sun to right and rose to left of shield. Trefoils in spandrels.
Rev.: ✠ЄXⱯLTⱯBITVR·IN·GLORIⱯ☉ Trefoil and rose stops
Blunt and Whitton type IX, variant 2 and pl. XI, 15 (this coin); Webb Ware dies 19/33; North 1560; Seaby 1965. Ex Lockett (1547); ex Sir John Evans.

417 Angel
    5.15   79.4   160°

I.m. none/rose.
Obv.: ЄDWⱯRD:DI :GRⱯ:RЄX·ⱯNGL:S·FRⱯNC·DNS:hI·BЄR'
Dragon with two heads (the second attached to its tail). Letter BW R_3.
Rev.: ☉PЄR CRVCЄ/TVⱯ:SⱯLVⱯ·NOS·XPISTЄ·RЄDЄPTOR
Large rose to left and large sun to right of cross. Two small trefoils in field outside the ropes of the mast.
Blunt and Whitton type V, early (perhaps the earliest) variety which, with the two-headed dragon, was not known to them when their paper was written. This coin was first published in Blunt 1950. Webb Ware dies 2/1; Neither North nor Seaby list this variety. No provenance.

418 Angel
    5.07   78.2   260°

I.m. none/rose.
Obv.: ЄDWⱯRD:DI :GRⱯ:RЄX ⱯNGL:·S FRⱯNC:DNS:I·B'
Letter BW R_3.
Rev.: ☉PЄR :CRVCЄ'/TVⱯ:SⱯLVⱯ·NOS·XPC:RЄ·DЄMPTOR
Large rose to left and larger sun to right of cross. Two small trefoils in field outside ropes of mast. Letter BW R_3.
Blunt and Whitton type V, variant 2; Webb Ware dies 3/2; North 1561; Seaby 1967. Ex Beresford-Jones (11); ex Lockett (1550); ex Sir John Evans; ex Montagu (592); ex Brice; ex Davis (309).

SECOND OR LIGHT COINAGE (cont.)

Bristol mint

419 Ryal

	Weight		
	g	*gr.*	*Die-axis*
	7.51	115.9	350°

I.m. none/crown.
Obv.: ЄD/·ꞂWΛRD·DI·GRΛ꞉RЄX·ΛNGL·S·FRΛNɊ·/·DNS·I·B··
        B in waves below ship. Letter BW R$_4$.
Rev.: ⚓IhɊ꞉ΛVT꞉TRΛNSIЄNS꞉PЄR·MЄDIVM꞉ILLORVM IBΛT
        Letter BW R$_4$.
Blunt and Whitton type VIII; North 1550; Seaby 1954. Ex Spink Noble sale, Sydney, 17.11.1993 (2648).

420 Half-ryal

3.89	60.0	80°

I.m. none/sun and crown.
Obv.: ЄD/WΛRD꞉DI·GRΛ·RЄX·ΛNGL✚·S✚/✚FRΛNɊ·
        B in waves. Three lis in legend. Letter BW R$_4$.
Rev.: ⚓DOMINЄ·NЄ·IN·FVRORЄ·TVO·ΛRGVS·mЄ✱
        Second Λ omitted from ΛRGVΛS. Letter BW R$_4$(?).
Blunt and Whitton type VII/VIII(D); North 1555; Seaby 1960. Bt Spink 1989; ex Dupree.

Coventry mint

421 Ryal

7.66	118.2	90°

I.m. none/sun.
Obv.: ЄD/WΛRD꞉DI꞉GRΛ·RЄX ΛNGL·S·FRNɊ ✚ /DNS꞉I·B꞉
        Ɋ in waves. Λ omitted from FRΛNɊ. Letters BW R$_2$ and R$_3$ (in FRNɊ).
Rev.: ✱IhɊ·ΛVT·TRΛNSIЄNS·PЄR·mЄDIVM·ILLORV·IBΛT·
        Large fleurs in spandrels. Letter BW R$_2$.
Blunt and Whitton type VI, variant 1; North 1551; Seaby 1955. Bt Spink 1989; ex Dupree.

Norwich mint

422 Ryal

7.52	116.1	180°

I.m. none/sun.
Obv.: ЄD/WΛRD꞉DI꞉GRΛ꞉RЄX·ΛNGL[ ]FRNɊ ✚ /·DNS·I·B·
        N in waves. Λ omitted from FRΛNɊ. Quatrefoil after FRNɊ. Letter BW R$_3$.
Rev.: ✱IhɊ꞉ΛVT꞉TRΛNSIЄNS·PЄR·mЄDIVM·ILLORVM·I·BΛT
        Large fleurs in spandrels. Letter BW R$_3$.
Blunt and Whitton type VI, variant as there noted (pl. X, 6); North 1552; Seaby 1956. Bt Spink 1989; ex Dupree.

423 Half-ryal

3.81	58.8	230°

I.m. none/rose.
Obv.: ЄD/WΛRD·DI·GRΛ·RЄX ΛNGL S·/·FRΛNɊ·
        Ornaments, lion lion (no lis). N in waves. Letter BW R$_2$.
Rev.: ⊕DOMINЄ·NЄ·IN·FVRORЄ TVO꞉ΛRGVΛS mЄ꞉   Letter BW R$_2$.
Blunt and Whitton type V (from the only pair of dies known); North 1557; Seaby 1962. Ex Ryan (29); ex Bruun (491); ex Ready (463); ex P. W. P. Carlyon-Britton.

York mint

424 Half-ryal

3.85	59.4	50°

I.m. none/sun.
Obv.: ЄD/WΛRD꞉DI꞉GRΛ꞉RЄX·ΛNGL꞉S·FR/ΛNɊ DNS
        Ɇ in waves. Small lettering.
Rev.: ✱DOMINЄ·NЄ·IN FVRORЄ꞉TVO꞉ΛRGVS꞉mЄ☉꞉
        Rose after mЄ. Second Λ omitted from ΛRGVΛS. Letter BW R$_2$.
Blunt and Whitton type VI, variant 1 (pl. XI, 9 this coin). However, the trefoil they record as being after FR in the obverse legend cannot be seen with any confidence on this specimen. North 1558; Seaby 1963. Bt Spink 1989; ex Dupree; ex Hird (1); ex Lockett (1538); ex O'Hagan (46); ex Nunn (272); ex Bieber (32); ex Bergne (460).

[*continued overleaf*]

PLATE 41

419

420

421

422

423

424

425

426

427

428

Plate 41 (*cont.*)

425 Half-ryal
    3.33   51.4   100°

I.m. none/sun.
Obv.: Ɛ[D?]/WⱯRD·DI·GRⱯ:RƐX ⱯNGL·S·/FRⱯNɊ Ɛ in waves. Letter BW R₂. An apparent pellet below the shield has, in fact, been raised as a result of a blow from a sharp object.
Rev.: ✱DOMINƐ·NƐ IN FVRORƐ·TVO ⱯRGVⱯS MƐ Letter BW R₂.
Blunt and Whitton type VI; Webb Ware dies 4/8; North 1558; Seaby 1963. Bt Spink 1989.

HENRY VI, SECOND REIGN (3 October 1470–11 April 1471)

Gold coins issued at a fineness of 23 ct 3½ gr. (0.995 fine) and at a nominal weight of 80 gr. (5.184 g) to the angel of 6s 8d. Denominations were angels and half-angels. Gold was struck at the mints of London, Bristol, Coventry, Norwich and York. Classified according to Allen 1937, Blunt and Whitton 1945–8 and, where appropriate, Webb Ware 1985.

Characteristics: Both angels and half-angels are similar to the angels of Edward IV's first reign, except that in place of the sun and rose beside the ship's mast there is now a letter **h** and a lis. Punctuation is normally by trefoils; any departures from this are noted in the descriptions of individual coins. Normally a cross in the nimbus round the saint's head.

Initial marks: Cross pattée
                     Pierced (restoration) cross
                     Lis

London mint

426 Angel
    5.04   77.8   200°

I.m. none/cross pattée.
Obv.: ·hƐNRIɊ·DI·GRⱯ:RƐX·ⱯNGL·S·FRⱯNɊ/· Same die as next three coins, **427, 428** and **429**.
Rev.: ✠PƐR ɊRVSƐ:TVⱯ·SⱯLVⱯNO:XPɊ·RƐDƐMTOR
      No bowsprit.
Allen dies A/a; Blunt and Whitton type 1/1; North 1613; Seaby 2078. Bt Baldwin 1964.

427 Angel
    5.11   78.8   80°

I.m. none/cross pattée.
Obv.: same die as last and next two coins, **426, 428, 429**.
Rev.: ✠PƐR ɊRVSƐ TVⱯ·SⱯLVⱯ·NOS XPɊ:RƐDƐ·TOR
      No bowsprit.
Allen dies A/b; Blunt and Whitton type 1/2; North 1613; Seaby 2078. Ex Lockett (1605).

428 Angel
    5.13   79.2   190°

I.m. none/pierced ('restoration') cross.
Obv.: same die as last two and next coin, **426, 427** and **429**.
Rev.: ✠PƐR·/ɊRVSƐ·TVⱯ·SⱯLVⱯ NOS XPɊ·RƐD·Ɛ·T·
Allen dies A/e; Blunt and Whitton type 1/4; North 1613; Seaby 2078. No provenance, bt 1956.

London mint (cont.)

429 Angel

Weight

g	gr.	Die-axis
5.14	79.3	270°

I.m. none/pierced ('restoration') cross.
Obv.: same die as last three coins, **426, 427, 428**.
Rev.: ✤PꞒR/··ꞒRVSꞒ·TVꜼ·SꜼLVꜼ·ⁿOS·XPꞒ·ⁱRꞒDʼꞒ·T
    Two trefoils before ꞒRVSꞒ, otherwise pellet stops. Same die as **431**.
Allen dies A/f; Blunt and Whitton type 1/5; North 1613; Seaby 2078. No provenance.

430 Angel

5.11	78.9	100°

I.m. none/cross pattée.
Obv.: ·hꞒⁿRIꞒʼDI·GRꜼⁱRꞒX·ꜼⁿGLʼⁱS·FRꜼⁿꞒ/·
    Same die as next three coins, **431, 432, 433**.
Rev.: ✤PꞒR·ꞒRVSꞒⁱ·TVꜼ·ʼSꜼLVꜼ·ⁿOS·XPꞒⁱRꞒDꞒ·TOR
    Pellet after ꞒRVSꞒ. Trefoils before and after XPꞒ. No bowsprit.
Allen dies B/d; Blunt and Whitton type 1/3; North 1613; Seaby 2078. Bt Baldwin; ex Carter.

431 Angel

5.12	79.0	150°

I.m. none/pierced ('restoration') cross.
Obv.: same die as last coin and next two, **430, 432, 433**.
Rev.: Same die as **429**. Mark radiant sun stamped into field to right of ship's hull.
Allen dies B/f; Blunt and Whitton type 1/5; North 1613; Seaby 2078. Bt Baldwin 1952; ex Carter.

432 Angel

5.12	79.0	130°

I.m. none/pierced ('restoration') cross.
Obv.: same die as last two and next coins, **430, 431, 433**.
Rev.: ✤PꞒR/··ꞒRVSꞒ·TVꜼ·SꜼLVꜼ·ⁿOS·XPꞒ·RꞒDꞒ·Tʼ
Allen dies B/g; Blunt and Whitton type 1/7; North 1613; Seaby 2078. Ex Lockett (3154).

433 Angel

5.10	78.7	120°

I.m. none/pierced ('restoration') cross.
Obv.: same die as last three coins, **430, 431, 432**.
Rev.: ✤/PꞒR·ꞒRVSꞒ·TVꜼ·SꜼLVꜼ·ⁿOS·XPꞒ·RꞒDꞒ·TOR
Allen dies B/l; Blunt and Whitton type 1/8; North 1613; Seaby 2078. Ex Schulman sale 9.3.1959 (1779).

434 Angel

5.09	78.6	340°

I.m. none/cross pattée.
Obv.: ·hꞒⁿRIꞒVS·DI·GRꜼⁱRꞒX·ꜼⁿGLʼⁱS·FRꜼⁿꞒIꞒ/·
    Same die as next two coins, **435, 436**.
Rev.: ✤PꞒR·ꞒRVSꞒ·TVꜼⁱSꜼLVꜼ·ⁿOS·XPꞒⁱRꞒDꞒ·TOR
    No bowsprit.
Allen dies C/c; Blunt and Whitton type 2/2; North 1613; Seaby 2078. Ex Basmadjieff (14); ex Ryan (60); ex P. W. P. Carlyon-Britton; ex Walters, 1913 (427).

435 Angel

4.94	76.2	250°

I.m. none/pierced ('restoration') cross.
Obv.: same die as last and next coins, **434, 436**.
Rev.: ✤/PꞒR·ꞒRVSꞒⁱTVꜼⁱSꜼLVꜼ·ⁿOS·XPꞒ·RꞒDꞒ·TOR   I.m. to left of mast.
Allen dies C/i; Blunt and Whitton type 2/8; North 1613; Seaby 2078. Ex Lockett (4317).

436 Angel

5.12	78.9	340°

I.m. none either side.
Obv.: same die as last two coins, **434, 435**.
Rev.: PꞒR·ꞒR/VꞒSꞒⁱTVꜼⁱSꜼLVꜼ·ⁿOS·XPꞒ·RꞒDꞒ·TOR
Allen dies C/o; Blunt and Whitton type 2/11; North 1613; Seaby 2078. Bt Spink 1952.

[*continued overleaf*]

PLATE 42

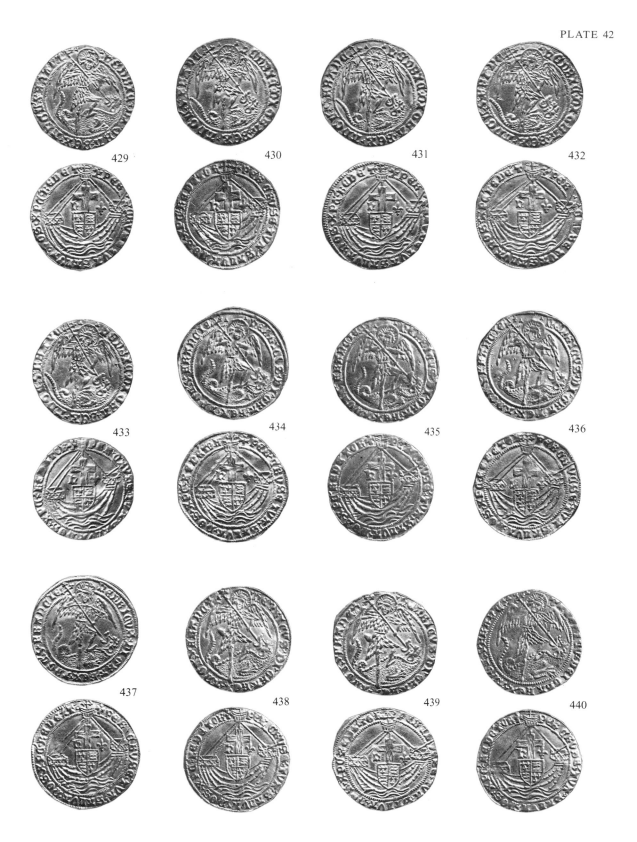

429 430 431 432

433 434 435 436

437 438 439 440

Plate 42 (*cont.*)

437 Angel
    5.15   79.5   190°

I.m. none/pierced ('restoration') cross.
Obv.: hENRICVS·DI GR A :REX·ANGL:S·FRANCIE
Rev.: ✚PER/CRVSE:TV A :SALVA·NOS·XPC :REDE :T: Pellet stops.
Allen dies D/n; Blunt and Whitton type 2/10; North 1613; Seaby 2078. Bt Baldwin 1958.

438 Angel
    5.14   79.3   0°

I.m. pierced ('restoration') cross both sides.
Obv.: ✚/hENRICVS·DI·GR A :REX·ANGL:S·FRANC   I.m. to left of spear
    shaft. Same die as next coin, **439**.
Rev.: ✚/PER CRVSE:TV A :SALVA·NOS·XPC·REDE'TOR   I.m. to left of
    mast.
Allen dies F/j; Blunt and Whitton type 3/8; North 1613; Seaby 2078. Bt Schulman 31.1.1956.

439 Angel
    5.10   78.7   110°

I.m. pierced ('restoration') cross/none.
Obv.: Same die as last coin, **438**.
Rev.: PER CR/VCSE:TV A :SALVA·NOS·XPC·REDE:TOR
Allen dies F/p; Blunt and Whitton type 3/11; North 1613; Seaby 2078. No provenance.

440 Angel
    5.03   77.6   130°

I.m. pierced ('restoration') cross both sides.
Obv.: ✚hENRICV·DEI GR A 'REX·ANGL·S·FRANC:·/·
Rev.: ✚/PER CRVSE:TV A :SALVA·NOS·XPC·REDE'TOR   I.m. to left of
    mast.
Allen dies I/k; Blunt and Whitton type 6/8; North 1613; Seaby 2078. Ex Glendining sale 8.2.1962 (25).

London mint (cont.)

441 Angel
          Weight

g	gr.	*Die-axis*
5.15	79.4	210°

I.m. pierced ('restoration') cross (filled in on this coin)/none.
Obv.: ✠hЄNRIꝆV'ꝒЄI·GRꝆ'RЄX ꝆNGL·S·FRꝆꝆ:
Rev.: PЄR ꝆRVꝆЄ'TVꝆ'SꝆLVꝆ·NOS·XPꝆ:RЄꝒЄ'TO'
Allen dies K/r; Blunt and Whitton type 6/13; North 1613; Seaby 2078. Ex Goulburn (242); ex Carter; ex Murdoch (337).

442 Angel

5.14	79.3	0°

I.m. pierced ('restoration') cross/none.
Obv.: ·✠hЄNRIꝆV:ꝒI GRꝆ·RЄX·ꝆNGL·S·FRꝆꝆ··/·
Rev.: PЄR·ꝆR/VꝆЄ:TVꝆ SꝆLVꝆ·NOS·XPꝆ'RЄꝒЄ'TOR
Allen dies –/–; Webb Ware dies L/r; Blunt and Whitton type 7/14; North 1613; Seaby 2078. Ex Lockett (3153).

443 Half-angel

2.57	39.7	250°

I.m. none/lis at end of legend.
Obv.: hЄRIꝆ:ꝒЄI GRꝆ·RЄX ꝆNGL·S·[FR?]
Rev.: O ꝆRV·/·X ꝆVЄ·SPЄS V·:NIꝆꝆ·✠: h and lis by shield instead of by mast.
Allen dies A/a; Blunt and Whitton type 1/1; North 1615; Seaby 2080. Ex Ryan (64); ex Cassal (190).

444 Half-angel

2.53	39.0	310°

I.m. none/cross pattée.
Obv.: ·hЄNRIꝆ:ꝒI GRꝆ RЄX ꝆNGL·S FR/Ꝇ'
Rev.: ✠O :/ꝆRVX ꝆVЄ·SPЄS·V·NIꝆꝆ
Allen dies B/– (similar to his die b); Blunt and Whitton type 2/2 var. of punctuation; North 1615; Seaby 2080. Bt Baldwin 1948.

445 Half-angel

2.48	38.3	280°

I.m. none/pierced ('restoration') cross.
Obv.: ·hЄNRIꝆVS[   ]I GRꝆ:RЄX·ꝆNGL[   ]/··
Rev.: ✠+O +/·ꝆRVX ꝆVЄ+SPЄꝆЄ V NIꝆꝆ   Saltire stops.
Allen dies C/c; Blunt and Whitton type 3/3; North 1615; Seaby 2080. Ex Hird (3); ex Ryan (65).

Bristol mint

446 Angel

5.20	80.2	160°

I.m. none either side.
Obv.: ·hЄNRIꝆV:ꝒI·GRꝆ:RЄX·ꝆNGL:S·FRꝆN[   ]NS/·
Rev.: PЄR ꝆR/VꝆЄ:TVꝆ·SꝆLVꝆ·NOS·XPꝆ[   ]ЄꝒЄ:TOR B in waves.
Allen dies B/c; Blunt and Whitton type 2/3; North 1614; Seaby 2079. Bt Spink 1989; ex Dupree.

Lis group (see p. 38)

447 Angel

4.98	76.9	300°

I.m. none/lis.
Obv.: hЄNRIꝆVS×ꝒЄI×GRꝆ:RЄX ꝆNGL×S×FRꝆꝆ
    Saltire stops. Same die as next coin, **448**.
Rev.: ✠/PЄR ꝆRVꝆ:TVꝆ'SꝆLVꝆ NOS·XPꝆ'RЄꝒЄM·TOR
    Same die as **449**. I.m. to left of mast.
Allen dies G/m; Blunt and Whitton type 4/9; North 1613; Seaby 2078. Bt Spink 1952; ex Ryan (58).

448 Angel

4.98	76.9	250°

I.m. none either side.
Obv.: same die as last coin, **447**.
Rev.: PЄR ꝆR/VꝆЄ:TVꝆ'SꝆLVꝆ·NOS XPꝆ'RЄꝒЄMTOR·
Allen dies G/n; Blunt and Whitton type 5/9; North 1613; Seaby 2078. No provenance.

[*continued overleaf*]

PLATE 43

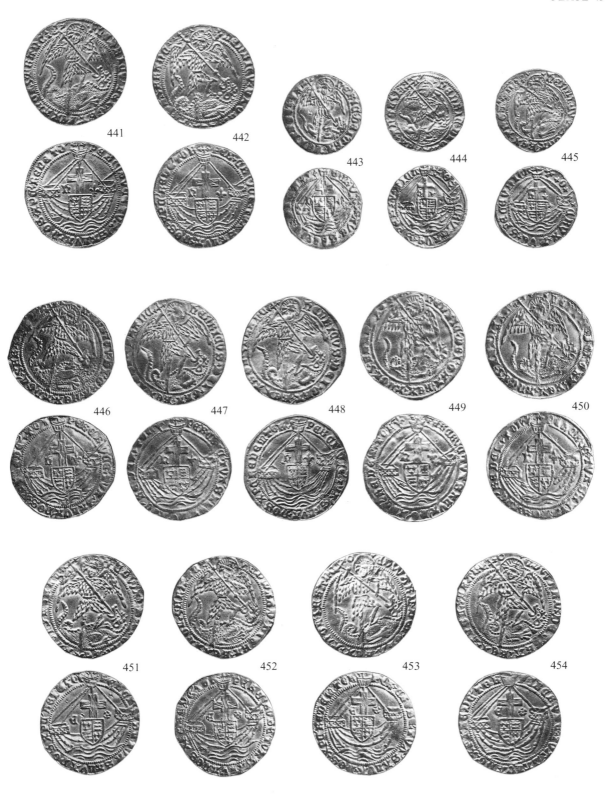

441 442 443 444 445

446 447 448 449 450

451 452 453 454

Plate 43 (*cont.*)

449 Angel
    5.05   77.9   210°

I.m. none/lis.
Obv.: ·hᴇNRIα:Dᴇl·GRᴧ:Rᴇx·ᴧNGL·'S·FRᴧNαIᴇ·/·
Trefoil rather than cross in nimbus. Same die as next coin, **450**.
Rev.: same die as **447**.
Allen dies H/m; Blunt and Whitton type 5/9; North 1613; Seaby 2078. Ex Lockett (1606); ex Packe (57).

450 Angel
    5.10   78.7   290°

I.m. none/lis.
Obv.: same die as last coin, **449**.
Rev.: ✠/PᴇR αRV/α·TVᴧ'SᴧLVᴧ·NOS·XPα'RᴇDᴇM·TOR   I.m. to left of mast.
Allen dies H/–, the reverse is similar to his die m but this variety has a trefoil after NOS; Blunt and Whitton type 5/9 var. with reading NOS instead of NO; North 1613; Seaby 2078. Bt Baldwin 1960.

EDWARD IV, SECOND REIGN (11 April 1471–9 April 1483)

Gold coinage issued at a fineness of 23 ct 3½ gr. (0.995 fine) and at a nominal weight of 80 gr. (5.184 g) to the angel of 6s 8d. Denominations struck were angels and half-angels. Gold was struck at the London and Bristol mints, although the latter is not represented here. Classified according to Webb Ware 1985 and Blunt and Whitton 1945–8.

Characteristics: The h and lis beside the ship's mast of Henry VI is now replaced by an ᴇ and a rose. The earliest varieties of the half-angel have the religious legend on the obverse and the royal name on the reverse (**470**, **471**), but this was quickly corrected, and there are mules between the earlier and later dies with the king's name on both sides (**472**, **473**). Stops are initially trefoils but soon change to saltires and there are also a few dies with pellet stops or no stops at all. Because of these variations, the type of punctuation is mentioned in the description of each coin.

Initial marks:		
Short cross fitchée (XII)	⎫	April 1471
Small annulet (XIV)	⎬	to
Pellet in annulet (XV)	⎭	late 1472
Cross with pellet in each quarter (XVI)	⎫	
Pierced cross (XVII)	⎪	Late 1472
Cross with pellet in one quarter (XVIII)	⎬	to
Pierced cross with central pellet (XIX)	⎭	late 1475
Cinquefoil (XXI)		Late 1475 to Feb. 1483
Sun and rose (XXII)		Feb. 1483 to April 1483

(these are the marks known on the gold coins, Roman numerals refer to Blunt and Whitton classes, dates are ex Webb Ware 1985)

London mint

451 Angel
    5.11   78.8   320°

I.m. pierced short cross fitchée to right of head/none.
Obv.: ✠ᴇDWᴧRD'DI·GRᴧ·Rᴇx·ᴧNGL·'S·FRᴧNα·
Trefoil stops. Cross in nimbus.
Rev.: PᴇR αR/Vsᴇ'TVᴧ'SᴧLVᴧ NOS XPα'RᴇDᴇ'TOR   No stops.
Webb Ware dies 1/3; Blunt and Whitton type XII, variant 2; North 1626; Seaby 2091. Ex Basmadjieff (19); ex Ryan (82).

452 Angel
    5.12   79.0   260°

I.m. short cross fitchée to right of head/none.
Obv.: ✠ᴇDWᴧRD·DI GRᴧ:Rᴇx·ᴧNGL·'S·FRᴧNα·
Trefoil stops. Cross in nimbus.
Rev.: PᴇR α/RVsᴇ'TVᴧ'SᴧLVᴧ NOS XPα RᴇDᴇ'TOR   No stops.
Webb Ware dies 3/2; Blunt and Whitton type XII, variant 2/variant 1; North 1626; Seaby 2091. Ex Galeries de Monnaies sale, Olten, 4.2.1969 (33).

Plate 43 (*cont.*)

453 Angel
    5.08   78.4   160°

I.m. annulet to left of head/none.
Obv.: O/·ƐDWⱯRD:DƐI·GRⱯ·RƐX·ⱯⴖGL'S FRⱯⴖႪ
    Trefoil stops. Cross in nimbus.
Rev.: PƐR·ႪRVSƐːTVⱯ'SⱯLVⱯ·ⴖOS·XPႪ'RƐ·DƐMTOR   Trefoil stops. No
    bowsprit. Same die as **455**.
Webb Ware dies 5/12; Blunt and Whitton type XIV, variant 2 but var. with trefoil after
RƐ; North 1626; Seaby 2091. Ex Lockett (4031).

454 Angel
    5.08   78.4   230°

I.m. annulet to left of head/none.
Obv.: O/·ƐDWⱯRD:DƐI·GRⱯ:RƐX·ⱯⴖGL·S·FRⱯⴖႪ
    Trefoil stops. Cross in nimbus.
Rev.: PƐR ႪR/VSƐːTVⱯ'SⱯLVⱯ ⴖOːXPႪ'RƐDƐ'TOR   Trefoil stops.
Webb Ware dies 6/8; Blunt and Whitton type XIV, variant 1–3 but they do not record
this combination of punctuation and spelling; North 1626; Seaby 2091. Bt Spink 1961;
ex Caine.

London mint (cont.)

455 Angel

	Weight		
	g	*gr.*	*Die-axis*
	5.11	78.8	340°

I.m. annulet to right of head/none.
Obv.: O ЄDWᴀRD:DЄI GRᴀ REX ᴀNGL:S FRᴀNᴄ'
  Trefoil stops. Cross in nimbus. Same die as next coin, **456**.
Rev.: PЄR·ᴄRVSЄ:TVᴀ'Sᴀ̵LVᴀ·NOS·XPᴄ RЄ·DЄMTOR   Trefoil stops. No
  bowsprit. Same die as **453**.
Webb Ware dies 8/12; Blunt and Whitton type XIV, variant 4; North 1626; Seaby
2091. Bt Baldwin 1952; ex Carter.

456 Angel

| 5.17 | 79.8 | 190° |

I.m. annulet to right of head/none.
Obv.: same die as last coin, **455**.
Rev.: PЄR ᴄR/SЄM·TVᴀ·Sᴀ̵LVᴀ·NOS·XPᴄ'RЄDЄ'TOR·   Trefoil stops.
Webb Ware dies 8/14; Blunt and Whitton type XIV, variant 4/–. The reverse is similar
to variant 13 because of the reading ᴄR/SЄM, but it has a trefoil after RЄDЄ'TOR
instead of between the Є and the T of that word. North 1626; Seaby 2091. Ex Burton
(23).

457 Angel

| 5.11 | 78.9 | 80° |

I.m. annulet to right of head/none.
Obv.: O ЄDWᴀRD:DЄI·GRᴀ REX ᴀNGL:S·FRᴀNᴄ✠
  Trefoil stops. Trefoil in nimbus. Lis after FRᴀNᴄ. Same die as next coin, **458**.
Rev.: PЄR·ᴄRV/SЄ'TVᴀ:Sᴀ̵LVᴀ·NOS·XPᴄ:RЄDЄTOR   Trefoil stops.
Webb Ware dies 10/16; Blunt and Whitton type XIV, variant 13/–. Reverse variety with
the bowsprit dividing ᴄRVSЄ after V. This is not, however, the same die as that used
on the next coin, **458**. North 1626; Seaby 2091. Ex Lockett (3161); ex Walters, 1913
(probably 443).

458 Angel

| 5.16 | 79.7 | 290° |

I.m. annulet to right of head/none.
Obv.: same die as last coin, **457**.
Rev.: PЄR ᴄRV/SЄ:TVᴀ'Sᴀ̵LVᴀ NOS XPᴄ'RЄDЄ'TOR   Trefoil stop after
  ᴄRVSЄ.
Webb Ware dies 10/17; Blunt and Whitton type XIV, variant 13/–. Reverse variety with
the bowsprit dividing ᴄRVSЄ after the V. North 1626; Seaby 2091. Bt Spink 1962.

459 Angel

| 5.13 | 79.2 | 220° |

I.m. annulet to right of head/none.
Obv.: O ЄDWᴀRD:DЄI·GRᴀ REX ᴀNGL:S·FRᴀNᴄ·/·   Trefoil stops. Trefoil
  in nimbus.
Rev.: PЄR·ᴄR/VSЄ'TVᴀ:Sᴀ̵LVᴀ·NOS·XPᴄ'RЄDЄ'TO'   Trefoil stops.
Webb Ware dies 12/21; Blunt and Whitton type XIV, variant 13/11; North 1626; Seaby
2091. Bt Baldwin 1975.

460 Angel

| 5.13 | 79.1 | 280° |

I.m. annulet to right of head/annulet enclosing pellet.
Obv.: O ЄDWᴀRD:DЄI·GRᴀ:REX ᴀNGL·S FRᴀNᴄ·×   Trefoil stops. Saltire at
  end of legend. Cross(?) in nimbus.
Rev.: OPЄR[ ]/ᴄRVᴄЄM×TVᴀ:Sᴀ̵LVᴀ×NOS×XPЄ:RЄDЄMPT'
  Saltire stops. Rose in field struck over sun.
Webb Ware dies 16/28; Blunt and Whitton type XV, variant 2; North 1626; Seaby
2091. Ex Lockett (3162); ex Bruun (503); ex Walters, 1913 (442); ex E. W. Rashleigh
(735).

461 Angel

| 5.08 | 78.4 | 160° |

I.m. annulet enclosing pellet/none.
Obv.: OЄDWᴀRD:DЄI×GRᴀ:REX×ᴀNGL:S FRᴀNᴄ×   Saltire stops. Nothing
  in nimbus.
Rev.: PЄR ᴄR/VSЄM TVᴀ·Sᴀ̵LVᴀ×NOS XPᴄ'RЄDЄ'TOR
  Saltire stops.
Webb Ware dies 17/25; Blunt and Whitton type XV, variant 1 but var. with punctuation
in reverse legend; North 1626; Seaby 2091. Bt Spink 1990.

[continued overleaf]

PLATE 44

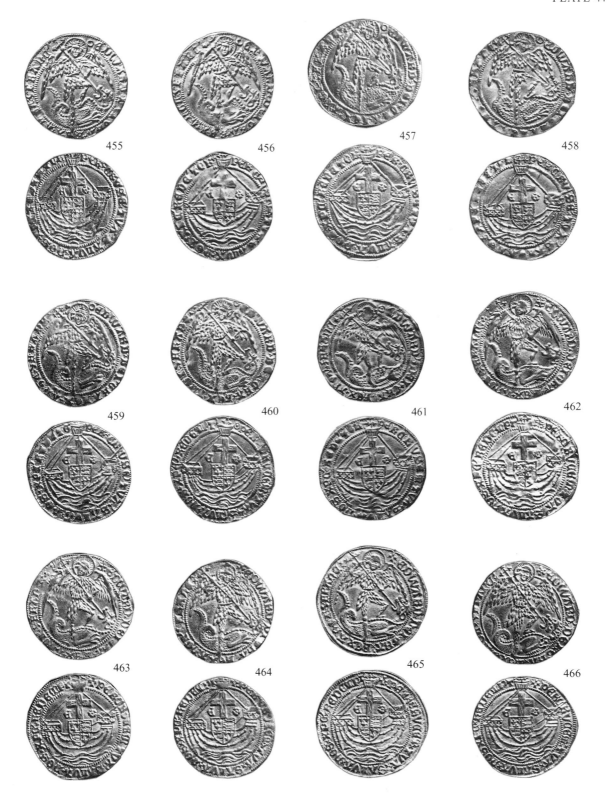

455 456 457 458

459 460 461 462

463 464 465 466

Plate 44 (*cont.*)

462 Angel
 5.15   79.5   350°   I.m. cross with pellet in each quarter both sides.
 Obv.: ✠ЄDW∀RD·DЄI GR∀⸪RЄX×∀ΠGL⸪Ꙅ×FR∀ΠᏆ⸭▴⸭
   Saltire stops, trefoil between double saltire stops at end of legend. Nothing in
   nimbus. Same die as next coin, **463**.
 Rev.: ✠PЄR Ꙅ/RVᏆЄM TV∀'S∀LV∀ ΠOS XPЄ'RЄDЄMPT'   No stops.
 Webb Ware dies 19/30; Blunt and Whitton type XVI, variant 2; North 1626; Seaby
 2091. Bt Baldwin 1952; ex Carter.

463 Angel
 5.11   78.8   60°   I.m. cross with pellet in each quarter/pierced cross with pellet in first quarter.
 Obv.: same die as last coin, **462**.
 Rev.: ✠PЄRᏟ/RVᏆЄM TV∀'S∀LV∀×ΠOS×XPЄ⸪RЄDЄMPT'   Saltire stops.
 Webb Ware dies 19/36; Blunt and Whitton type XVI/XVIII(a); North 1626; Seaby
 2091. Ex Lockett (4320).

464 Angel
 4.98   76.8   10°   I.m. cross with pellet in fourth quarter/pierced cross with pellet in fourth quarter.
 Obv.: ✠ЄDW∀RD'DI GR∀'RЄX ∀ΠGL'Ꙅ FR∀ΠᏆ⸭
   Double saltire stop after FR∀ΠᏆ. Nothing in nimbus.
 Rev.: ✠PЄR ᏆRVᏆЄM·TV∀×S∀LV∀·ΠOS×XPᏆ·RЄDЄMPT'   Saltire stops.
 Webb Ware dies 30/57; Blunt and Whitton type XVIIIb, variant 3; North 1626; Seaby
 2091. Bt Spink 1967; ex Angers hoard.

465 Angel
 5.12   79.0   60°   I.m. pierced cross with pellet in fourth quarter both sides.
 Obv.: ✠ЄDW∀RD×DЄI·GR∀⸪RЄX ∀ΠGL⸪Ꙅ×FR∀ΠᏆ⸭×
   Saltire stops with a triangle of three saltires after FR∀ΠᏆ. Nothing in nimbus.
 Rev.: ✠PЄR×/ᏆRVᏆЄM·TV∀⸪S∀LV∀×ΠOS×XPᏆ⸪RЄDЄMPT'   Saltire stops.
 Webb Ware dies 32/54; Blunt and Whitton type XVIIIb, variant 4 but a var. with the
 third saltire after FR∀ΠᏆ; North 1626; Seaby 2091. Bt Baldwin 1952; ex Carter.

466 Angel
 5.12   79.0   180°   I.m. cinquefoil/pierced cross.
 Obv.: ✠ЄDW∀RD⸪DЄI⸪GR∀×RЄX×∀ΠGL'Ꙅ FR∀ΠᏆ⸪
   Saltire stops. Nothing in nimbus.
 Rev.: ✠PЄRᏆ/RVᏆЄM⸭TV∀⸪S∀LV∀·ΠOS×XPᏆ×RЄDЄMPT'   Saltire stops.
 Webb Ware A/ rev. die 68; Blunt and Whitton type XXI/XIX, variant 1; North 1626;
 Seaby 2091. No provenance.

London mint (cont.)

467 Angel

	Weight	
g	*gr.*	*Die-axis*
5.12	79.0	160°

I.m. cinquefoil both sides.
Obv.: ✠ ЄDWЛRD⦂DЄI·GRЛ⦂RЄX×ЛNGL⦂S FRЛNꝯ/⦂
Saltire stops. Nothing in nimbus.
Rev.: ✠PЄR ꝯRVꝯЄM⦂TVЛ⦂SЛLVЛ·NOS XPꝯ'RЄDЄMT' Saltire stops.
Webb Ware A; Blunt and Whitton type XXI, variant 1 but var. with P omitted from RЄDЄMPT; North 1626; Seaby 2091. Bt Baldwin 1952; ex Carter.

468 Angel

| 5.16 | 79.7 | 130° |

I.m. cinquefoil both sides.
Obv.: ✠ ЄDWЛRD⦂DЄI GRЛ×/RЄX ЛNGL×S FRЛNꝯ
Saltire stops. Nothing in nimbus. Saint's foot divides legend.
Rev.: ✠PЄR/ꝯRVꝯЄM TVЛ'SЛLVЛ NOS XPꝯ'RЄDЄMT No stops.
Webb Ware B; Blunt and Whitton type XXI, variant 2; North 1626; Seaby 2091. Bt Spink 1962; ex Spurway.

469 Angel

| 5.12 | 79.0 | 140° |

I.m. sun and rose dimidiated both sides (sun and rose 1).
Obv.: ✸ЄDWЛRD⦂DЄI⦂GRЛ⦂RЄX×ЛNGL⦂S FRЛN/⦂
Saltire stops. Nothing in nimbus. Saint's foot divides legend.
Rev.: ✸PЄR/ꝯRVꝯЄM TVЛ SЛLVЛ NOS XPꝯ' RЄDЄMP'⦂
Double saltire stop at end of legend only. Same die as **482** (Edward V).
Webb Ware B; Blunt and Whitton type XXII, variant 7; North 1626; Seaby 2091. Ex Lockett (3137).

470 Half-angel

| 2.57 | 39.6 | 120° |

I.m. pierced short cross fitchée/none.
Obv.: ✠O ꝯRVX·ЛVЄ·SPЄS·V·NIꝯЛ· Trefoil stops. Cross in nimbus. Same die as next coin, **471**.
Rev.: ЄDW/ЛRD'DI GRЛ'RЄX·ЛNGL⦂S·FRЛ Pellet stops.
Webb Ware dies 1/1; Blunt and Whitton type XII, variant 2; North 1628; Seaby 2094. Ex Glendining sale 10.2.1956 (1).

471 Half-angel

| 2.58 | 39.8 | 60° |

I.m. pierced short cross fitchée/none.
Obv.: same die as last coin, **470**.
Rev.: ЄD/WЛRD'DI GRЛ⦂RЄX·ЛNGL'S FR Trefoil stops. Same die as next coin, **472**.
Webb Ware dies 1/3; Blunt and Whitton type XII, variant 1/types XIV-XII, variant 2. This is, in fact, the true coin of which the reverse die was only known to Blunt and Whitton as a mule with type XIV. Had they known of it, they would presumably have designated it 'type XII, variant 3'. North 1628; Seaby 2094. Bt Schulman 1956.

472 Half-angel

| 2.58 | 38.8 | ↲50° |

I.m. annulet/none.
Obv.: O ЄDWЛRD'DI GRЛ RЄX×ЛNGL'⦂ Saltire stops. Cross in nimbus. Same die as next coin, **473**.
Rev.: same die as last coin, **471**.
Webb Ware dies 2/3; Blunt and Whitton type XIV/XII, variant 2; North 1629; Seaby 2095. Bt Spink 1958; ex Virgil Brand.

473 Half-angel

| 2.54 | 39.2 | 190° |

I.m. annulet/none.
Obv.: same die as last coin, **472**.
Rev.: ЄDW/ЛRD'DI GRЛ⦂RЄX·ЛNGL⦂S·FR Pellet stops.
Webb Ware dies 2/2; Blunt and Whitton type XIV/XII, variant 3; North 1629; Seaby 2095. Bt Baldwin 1952; ex Carter.

[*continued overleaf*]

PLATE 45

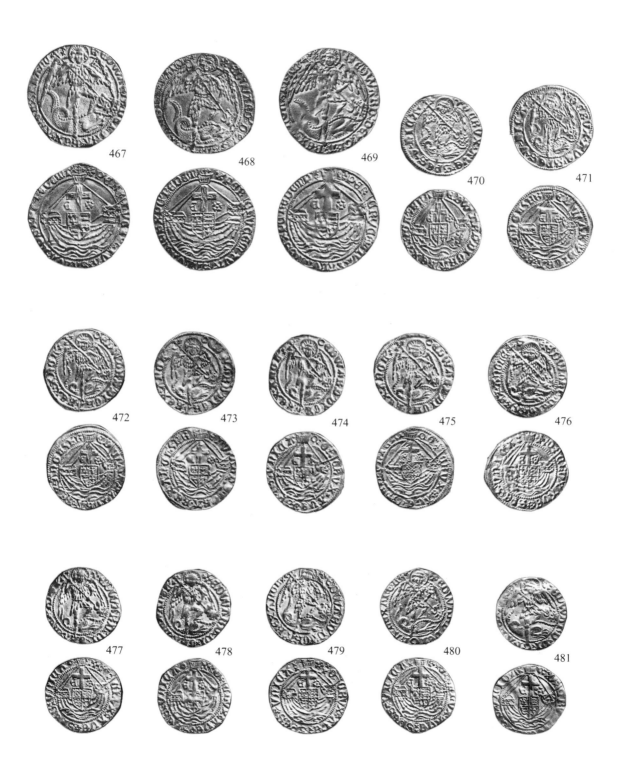

467   468   469   470   471

472   473   474   475   476

477   478   479   480   481

Plate 45 (*cont.*)

474 Half-angel
    2.54   39.2   10°

I.m. annulet both sides.
Obv.: O ƐDWⱯRD'DI GRⱯ RƐX⁚ ⱯꟼGL'⁚   Saltire stops. Cross in nimbus.
    Same die as next coin, **475**.
Rev.: O ⁚O⁚ˣ/ꟼRVX×ⱯVƐ⊕SPƐS⁚VꟼIꟼⱯ   Saltire stops. Rose after ⱯVƐ.
Webb Ware dies 2/4; Blunt and Whitton type XIV, variant 1/–. The reverse was not recorded by them with the three saltires after O and the rose after ⱯVƐ. North 1630; Seaby 2093. Ex Doubleday 1 (64); ex Ryan (88).

475 Half-angel
    2.54   39.2   30°

I.m. annulet both sides.
Obv.: same die as last coin, **474**.
Rev.: O O⁚/ꟼRVX⊕ⱯVƐ·SPƐS·VꟼIꟼⱯ·   Trefoil stops. Rose after ꟼRVX.
Webb Ware dies 2/5; Blunt and Whitton type XIV, variant 1/–. The reverse differs from variant 1 by having two trefoils after the O instead of two saltires. North 1630; Seaby 2093. Bt Baldwin 1952.

476 Half-angel
    2.49   38.4   270°

I.m. cross on annulet both sides.
Obv.: ⊕ ƐDWⱯRD×DƐI GRⱯ'RƐX×ⱯꟼGLƐ/ˣ   Saltire stops. Nothing in
    nimbus.
Rev.: ⊕ ‡O‡/ꟼRVX ⱯVƐ⊕SPƐS×VꟼIꟼⱯ‡   Saltire stops. Rose after ⱯVƐ.
Webb Ware dies 3/6; Blunt and Whitton type XVI (their pl. XIV, 13; same dies and possibly the same coin); North 1630; Seaby 2093. Ex Clonterbrook (108); ex Lockett (4323); ex Murdoch (360); ex Montagu (599).

477 Half-angel
    2.54   39.2   300°

I.m. pierced cross with pellet in fourth quarter/pierced cross with pellet in third quarter.
Obv.: ✚ƐDWⱯRD⁚DI×GRⱯ⁚RƐX×ⱯꟼGL'   Saltire stops. Nothing in nimbus.
    Same die as next coin, **478**.
Rev.: ✚⁚O⁚/ꟼRVX⁚ⱯVƐ⊕SPƐS⁚VꟼIꟼⱯ✱
    Double saltire stops with rose after ⱯVƐ and pierced sun (spur rowel ?) after
    VꟼIꟼⱯ.
Webb Ware dies 4/10; Blunt and Whitton type XVIIIb, variant 2 but var. with additional saltire stops in the obverse legend; North 1630; Seaby 2093. No provenance.

478 Half-angel
    2.53   39.1   170°

I.m. pierced cross with pellet in fourth quarter/pierced cross with pellet in third quarter.
Obv.: same die as last coin, **477**.
Rev.: ✚⁚O⁚/ꟼRVX⁚ⱯVƐ⊕SPƐS⁚VꟼIꟼⱯ✱
    Double saltire stops with rose after ⱯVƐ and pierced sun (spur rowel ?) after
    UꟼIꟼⱯ. A different die from the last coin.
Webb Ware dies 4/9; Blunt and Whitton type XVIIIb, variant 2 but var. with additional saltire stops in the reverse legend; North 1630; Seaby 2093. Bt Baldwin 1975.

Plate 45 (*cont.*)

479 Half-angel
    2.58   39.8   10°

I.m. cinquefoil both sides.
Obv.: ✤ EDWARD·DI GRA·REX ANGL×   Saltire stop after ANGL. Nothing in nimbus.
Rev.: ✤ ⁞O/CRVX⊗AVE⁞SPES⊕VNICA⁞   Double saltire stops. Roses after CRVX and SPES. Five-line ship.
Webb Ware dies 6/22; Blunt and Whitton type XXI, variant 2; North 1630; Seaby 2093. Bt Spink 1965; ex Thompson; ex Basmadjieff (21); ex Roth (219); ex Montagu (600); ex Shepherd (177); ex Cuff (926).

480 Half-angel
    2.51   38.7   190°

I.m. cinquefoil both sides.
Obv.: ✤ EDWARD DEI GRA REX ANGL   No stops. Nothing in nimbus.
Rev.: ✤ ×O×/CRVX⊗AVE⁞SPES⊕VNICA⁞   Saltire stops. Roses after CRVX and SPES. Five-line ship.
Webb Ware dies 7/20; Blunt and Whitton type XXI, variant 6/5; North 1630; Seaby 2093. Ex Glendining sale 6.4.1954 (16).

481 Half-angel
    2.47   38.1   290°

I.m. sun and rose dimidiated both sides.
Obv.: ✣ EDWARD×DI×GRA REX ANG   Saltire stops. Nothing in nimbus.
Rev.: ✣ ⁞O⁞/CRV[ ]AVE[ ]SPES×VNICA⁞   Double saltire stops. Four line ship.
Webb Ware dies 8/24. Blunt and Whitton type XXII who knew of two specimens from the same dies, of which this is one; the other is in the BM. The reading they give differs from that given above in minor respects relating to punctuation, presumably due to the weakness of this specimen. Webb Ware's more recent but, as yet, unpublished work suggests that it may be more appropriate to attribute this coin to Edward V – see pp. 41–2 above. North 1630; Seaby 2145 (Edward IV or V). Ex Lockett (1646); ex Clarke-Thornhill (38).

EDWARD V (9 April 1483–26 June 1483)

Gold coinage issued at a fineness of 23 ct 3½ gr. (0.995 fine) and at a nominal weight of 80 gr. (5.184 g) to the angel of 6s 8d. Denominations struck were angels and half angels. Classified according to Webb Ware (paper read to the British Numismatic Society on 23.6.1987, as yet unpublished; see pp. 41–2 for a summary of his conclusions).

London mint only

	Weight		
	g	*gr.*	*Die-axis*
	5.14	79.3	90°

482 Angel

I.m. sun and rose 1 both sides.
Obv.: ❋ЄDWΛRD⠇DI⠇GRΛ⠇RЄX×ΛNGL⠇S FRΛNΛₓˣ
Same die as next coin, **483** (Richard III), before alteration of the initial mark.
Rev.: ❋PЄR/ΛRVΛЄM TVΛ SΛLVΛ NOS XPΛ'RЄDЄMP'⠇
Same die as **469**.
Webb Ware (Richard III paper referred to above)/Webb Ware 1985 B; Blunt and Whitton type XXII, no. 8 (this coin); other specimens from different dies are known from the Drabble 1 and Duveen sales. North 1626 (Edward IV); Seaby 2144 (Edward IV or V). Ex Beresford-Jones (16); ex Packe (61); ex Marsham (354).

For a possible half-angel of this reign see **481** above.

RICHARD III (26 June 1483–22 August 1485)

Gold coinage issued at a fineness of 23 ct 3½ gr. (0.995 fine) and at a nominal weight of 80 gr. to the angel of 6s 8d. Denominations struck were angels and half-angels. Classified according Winstanley 1941–4 and Webb Ware (paper read to the British Numismatic Society on 23.6.1987, as yet unpublished; see pp. 41–2 for a summary of his conclusions).

TYPE 1
Characteristics: coins reading RIΛRD DI GRΛ with initial mark sun and rose 1. These are known from one die only. There is no specimen in the Schneider collection.

TYPE 2a
Characteristics: coins reading ЄDWΛRD DI GRΛ, or with the die of Type 1 reading RIΛRD DI GRΛ, but in all cases with the initial mark sun and rose 1 overstruck on the obverse with boar's head 1.[352]

London mint only

483 Angel
5.14   79.3   130°

I.m. boar's head 1 over sun and rose 1/sun and rose 1.
Obv.: ❧ЄDWΛRD⠇DI⠇GRΛ⠇RЄX×ΛNGL×S FRΛNΛₓˣ
Same die as **482** after alteration of the initial mark.
Rev.: ❋PЄR/ΛRVΛЄM TVΛ SΛLVΛ NOS XPΛ RЄDЄMPT'   No stops.
The former attribution of this coin to Edward V has been revised as a result of the recent work by Webb Ware (see pp. 41–2). The obverse is probably from the same die as no. 4 on the plate with Blunt 1934–7. The reverse is as Blunt and Whitton 1945–9 pl. XXII, 9. The coin is an obverse and reverse die-duplicate of Lockett lot 1645 and Parsons lot 23. North 1670 (Edward V); Seaby 2149 (Edward V). Bt Spink 1954; ex Arnold.

484 Angel
5.03   77.6   200°

I.m. boar's head 1 over sun and rose 1/sun and rose 1.
Obv.: ❧RIΛRD⠇DI⠇GRΛ 'RЄX×ΛNGL×S×FRΛNΛ
Letter Winstanley I₁. Same die as next three coins, **485**, **486**, **487**.
Rev.: ❋PЄR/ΛRVΛЄM×TVΛ×SΛLVΛ×NOS XPΛ×RЄDЄMPT
Large cross. R beside cross over Є. Letter Winstanley V₁.
Webb Ware dies 1'/1; Winstanley pl.I, 5, same dies; North 1676; Seaby 2157. Bt Spink 1962; ex Bute (10).

[352] Initial marks sun and rose 1, 2 and 3, and boar's head 1 and 2 are illustrated in Winstanley 1941–44 and North 1991.

[continued overleaf]

PLATE 46

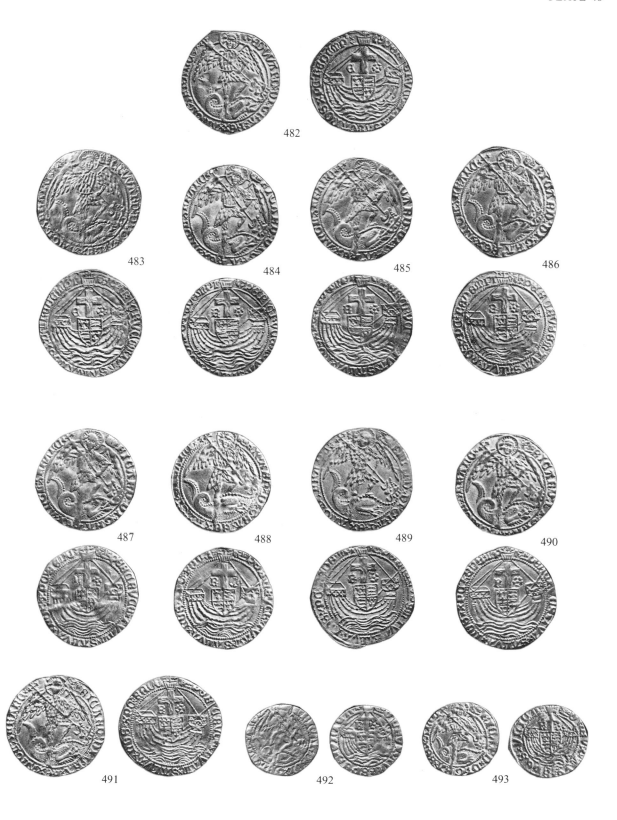

482

483   484   485   486

487   488   489   490

491   492   493

Plate 46 (*cont.*)

485 Angel
    5.09   78.6   210°

I.m. boar's head 1 over sun and rose 1/sun and rose 1.
Obv.:   same die as last and next two coins, **484, 486, 487**.
Rev.:   ✠ PΣR/ᴄRVᴄΣM×TVΛ×SΛLVΛ×ПOS XPᴄ×RΣDΣMPT
      Large cross. R beside cross over Σ. Letter Winstanley V$_1$.
Webb Ware dies 1'/3; Winstanley pl. I, 4, same obv. die/ pl. I, 1, same rev. die); North
1676; Seaby 2156. Ex Dangar (101).

486 Angel
    5.12   79.0   50°

I.m. boar's head 1 over sun and rose 1/boar's head 2.
Obv.:   same die as last two coins and next coin, **484, 485, 487**.
Rev.:   ✠ PΣR/ᴄRVSΣM TVΛ SΛLVΛ×ПOS XPᴄ'RΣDΣMPT
      Large cross. R beside cross over rose(?). Letter Winstanley V$_1$.
Webb Ware dies 1'/6; Winstanley pl. I, 4, same obv. die/ pl. I, 7, same rev. die); North
1676; Seaby 2157. Ex Doubleday.

487 Angel
    5.01   77.3   280°

I.m. boar's head 1 over sun and rose 1/boar's head 2.
Obv.:   same die as last three coins, **484, 485, 486**.
Rev.:   ✠ PΣR/ᴄRVᴄΣ×TVΛM×SΛLVΛ×ПOS×XPᴄ×RΣDΣ×
      Large cross. R beside cross over Σ. Letter Winstanley V$_1$.
Webb Ware dies 1'/13; Winstanley pl.I, 4 same obv., rev.-; North 1676; Seaby 2157. Bt
Schulman 1953.

TYPE 2b
Characteristics: coins reading RIᴄΛRD DI GRΛ and with an unaltered boar's head 1 or boar's head 2 initial mark.

London mint only

488 Angel
    5.02   77.5   190°

I.m. boar's head 1/boar's head 2.
Obv.:   🐗 RIᴄΛRD×DI×GRΛ×RΣX ΛПGL×S FRΛПᴄ×
      Letter Winstanley I$_1$.
Rev.:   ✠ PΣR/ᴄRVᴄΣ×TVΛM×SΛLVΛ×ПOS×XPᴄ×RΣDΣ×
      Large cross. Letter Winstanley V$_1$.
Webb Ware dies 2/12; Winstanley pl. I, 6, same dies; North 1676; Seaby 2156. Ex
Williams.

489 Angel
    5.17   79.8   130°

I.m. boar's head 2 both sides.
Obv.:   ✠ RIᴄΛRD×DI×GRΛ×RΣX ΛПGL×S FRΛПᴄ×/×
      RIᴄ struck over ΣDW. Letter Winstanley I$_1$.
Rev.:   ✠ PΣR/ᴄRVSΣM TVΛ SΛLVΛ×ПOS XPᴄ×RΣDΣMPT
      Large cross. R by cross over rose. Letter Winstanley V$_1$.
Webb Ware dies 4/8; Winstanley pl. I, 7, same dies; North 1676; Seaby 2156. Bt Seaby
1960.

490 Angel
    5.15   79.4   170°

I.m. boar's head 2 both sides.
Obv.:   ✠ RIᴄΛRD×DIׄGRΛ×RΣX ΛПGL×S FRΛПᴄ×
      Letter Winstanley I$_1$. Same die as next coin, **491**.
Rev.:   ✠ PΣR ᴄRVᴄΣ×TVΛ×SΛLVΛ×ПOS×XPᴄ RΣDΣMP
      Large cross. R by cross over rose. Letter Winstanley V$_1$.
Webb Ware dies 6/6; dies not illustrated by Winstanley; North 1676; Seaby 2156. Bt
Spink 1967; ex PKP.

Plate 46 (*cont.*)

491 Angel
    5.14   79.3   240°

I.m. boar's head 2 both sides.
Obv.: same die as last coin, **490**.
Rev.: ✠ PER/ɑRVɑE×TVʌM×SʌLVʌ×nOS×XPɑ⸱REDE'
    Large cross. Letter Winstanley V₁.
Webb Ware dies 6/14; Winstanley pl. I, 8, same dies; North 1676; Seaby 2156. No provenance.

492 Half-angel
    2.44   37.6   50°

I.m. boar's head 2 both sides.
Obv.: ✠ RIɑʌRD×DI⸱GRʌ×REX×ʌNGL
Rev.: ✠ O/ɑRVX×ʌVE×SPES×VNIɑʌ×
Webb Ware dies 1/1; North 1678; Seaby 2158. Ex Ryan (102); ex Bruun (524); ex E. W. Rashleigh (749); ex Murchison (108); ex Martin (125); ex Tyssen (probably 1428).

493 Half-angel
    2.57   39.6   60°

I.m. boar's head 2 both sides.
Obv.: ✠ RIɑʌRD⸱DI⸱GRʌ×REX×ʌNGL
Rev.: ✠ O/ɑRVX⸱ʌVE×SPES×VNIɑʌ×
Webb Ware dies 2/3; North 1678; Seaby 2158. Ex Hird (private sale); ex Huth (28); ex Gibbs.

London mint (cont.)

TYPE 3

Characteristics: reintroduction of the sun and rose initial mark using a new punch, sun and rose 2.

TYPE 2b/3 MULES

London mint

	Weight		
	g	gr.	Die-axis

494 Angel

5.03 77.6 80°

I.m. boar's head 2/sun and rose 2.
Obv.: ❦ RICARD⦂DI⸱GRA×REX ANGL⦂S FRANC
Letter Winstanley I$_1$.
Rev.: ✱ PER/CRVCE×TVA⸱SALVA NOS XPC×REDEMP
Small cross. Letter Winstanley V$_2$.
Webb Ware dies 3/25; Winstanley illustrates a similar coin but from different dies on pl. I, 12; North 1677; Seaby 2156. Bt Spink 1965; ex Thompson.

495 Angel

5.17 79.8 210°

I.m. boar's head 2/sun and rose 2.
Obv.: ❦ RICARD⦂DI⦂GRA×REX ANGL⦂S ×FRANC×
A in RICARD over T(?). Letter Winstanley I$_1$.
Rev.: ✱ PER/CRVCE⦂TVA⦂SALVA NOS XPC⦂REDEDMT
Large cross, Letter Winstanley V$_1$. Ware dies 6/21; Winstanley pl. I, 9, same dies; North 1677; Seaby 2156. Bt Spink 1957; ex Arnold.

TYPE 3/2b MULE

London mint

496 Angel

5.02 77.5 100°

I.m. sun and rose 2/boar's head 2.
Obv.: ✱ RICAD⸱DI×GRA×REX ANGL⸱S FRANC⦂
Second R omitted from RICARD. Letter Winstanley I$_2$.
Rev.: ❦ PER/CRVCE×T[   ]SALVA×NOS×XPC⦂REDE×
Large cross. Letter Winstanley V$_1$.
Webb Ware dies 10/12; Winstanley pl. I, 10. this coin; North 1677; Seaby 2156. Ex Lockett (1652).

TRUE COINS OF TYPE 3

London mint

497 Angel

5.07 78.2 30°

I.m. sun and rose 2 both sides.
Obv.: ✱ RICARD⸱DI×GRA×REX ANGL⸱S FRANC×/×
Letter Winstanley I$_1$.
Rev.: ✱ PER/CRVCE×TVA×SALVA NOS XPC×REDEMPT
Small cross. Letter Winstanley V$_2$.
Webb Ware dies 8/18; Winstanley pl. I, 11, same dies; North 1677; Seaby 2156. Ex Wharton Sinkler (673).

498 Angel

5.11 78.9 320°

I.m. sun and rose 2 both sides.
Obv.: ✱ RICAD⦂DI×GRA×REX ANGL⸱S FRANC⦂
Second R omitted from RICARD. Letter Winstanley I$_2$.
Rev.: ✱ PER/CRVCE⦂TVA⦂SALVA NOS XPC⸱REDEMPT
Small cross. Letter Winstanley V$_2$.
Webb Ware dies 13/27; Winstanley pl. I, 13, this coin; North 1677; Seaby 2156. Ex Lockett (3178).

[*continued overleaf*]

PLATE 47

494

495

496

497

498

499

500

501

502

503

504

Plate 47 (*cont.*)

HENRY VII (22 August 1485–21 April 1509)

Gold coin issued at a fineness of 23 ct 3½ gr. (0.995 fine) and at a nominal weight of 240 gr. (15.552 g) to the sovereign of 20s 0d, 120 gr. (7.776 g) to the ryal of 10s 0d and 80 gr. (5.184 g) to the angel of 6s 8d. Denominations struck were sovereign, ryal, angel and half-angel. Rare multiple sovereigns exist and were probably used for diplomatic gifts.

Classified according to Potter and Winstanley 1960–3 (PW) and Metcalf 1967 (*SCBI* 23). With regard to the former, care must be taken in interpreting their die reference numbers because they numbered their reverse dies starting at one for every obverse die with which it was found. Thus any number quoted for a reverse die only makes sense if it is related to an obverse die number. It should be noted that the sovereigns and the ryal use a different series of initial marks from those used on the angels and half-angels and, in consequence, the former are listed separately at the end of the catalogue of coins of this reign.

Angels and half-angels

TYPE I
Characteristics: Early form of St Michael with feathers. Saltire stops. PW lettering A.

A. WITH COMPOSITE INITIAL MARKS

Sun and rose 3 ⎫
Lis on rose   ⎬   Aug. 1485–Summer 1487
Lis on sun and rose ⎭

London mint only

499	Angel			I.m. sun and rose 3 both sides.
	5.08	78.4	250°	*Obv.*: ✱hENRIꓵ·DI·GRꓕ∶REX ꓕNGL·S FRꓕNꓵ∶/∶ Saltire stops double after FRꓕNꓵ and between spear shaft and nimbus.

Rev.: ✱PꟾR/ꓵRVSꟾM∶TVꓕM∶SꓕLVꓕ·NOS·XPꓵ RꟾD
h by cross possibly struck over R.
PW type I, 10 (dies 3/5), this coin; *SCBI* 23, 1, different dies; North 1694; Seaby 2179. Ex Lockett (4328).

500	Angel			I.m. sun and rose 3/lis on rose.
	5.04	77.7	0°	*Obv.*: ✱hENRIꓵ·DI∶GRꓕ·REX ꓕNGL∶S FRꓕNꓵ∶/∶

Saltire stops, double after FRꓕNꓵ and between spear shaft and nimbus.
Rev.: ✿PꟾR/ꓵRVꓵꟾM TVꓕ'SꓕLVꓕ NOS XPꓵ'RꟾDꟾM   No stops.
PW type I, coin no. 6 (sun and rose die 1/lis on rose die 1), this coin; *SCBI* 23, 3, same dies; North 1694; Seaby 2179. Bt Spink 1953; ex Arnold.

501	Angel			I.m. lis on sun and rose/sun and rose 3.
	5.17	79.8	350°	*Obv.*: ✱hENRIꓵ·DI∶GRꓕ∶REX ꓕNGL×S FRꓕNꓵ∶/∶

hENRIꓵ over RIꓵꓕRD. Saltire stops, double after FRꓕNꓵ and between spear shaft and nimbus. Same die as next coin, **502**.
Rev.: ✿PꟾR/ꓵRVSꟾM∶TVꓕM∶SꓕLVꓕ·NOS×XPꓵ RꟾDꟾ×
Saltire stops, double after ꓵRVSꟾM and TVꓕM. h by cross over R.
PW type I, 11 (dies, lis on sun and rose 1/sun and rose 4), this coin. *SCBI* 23, –; North 1694; Seaby 2180. Ex Lockett (1670).

502	Angel			I.m. lis on sun and rose/lis on rose.
	5.12	79.0	290°	*Obv.*: same die as last coin, **501**.

Rev.: ✿PꟾR/ꓵRVꓵꟾM TVꓕ'SꓕLVꓕ NOS XPꓵ'RꟾDꟾM   No stops.
PW type I, 12 (dies, lis on sun and rose 1/lis on rose 3), this coin; *SCBI* 23, –; North 1694; Seaby 2180. Ex Lockett (1669).

Plate 47 (*cont.*)

503 Angel

    5.04   77.8   280°

I.m. lis on sun and rose/sun and rose 3.

Obv.: ✤ hᗺПRIᗤ⦂DI⨯GRᗅ⨯RᗺX ᗅПGL'S FRᗅПᗤ⨯/⦂
hᗺПRIᗤ over RIᗤᗅRD. Saltire stops, double after FRᗅПᗤ and between spear shaft and nimbus.

Rev.: ✤ PᗺR ᗤ/RVSᗺ⦂TVᗅ⦂SᗅLVᗅ[   ]ᗤ⨯RᗺDᗺMPT
h possibly over R.

PW type I, 14 (dies, lis on sun and rose 2/sun and rose 3, 6), this coin; *SCBI* 23, –; North 1694; Seaby 2180. Bt Spink 1977; ex Beresford-Jones; ex J. C. S. Rashleigh (18).

504 Angel

    5.16   79.6   340°

I.m. lis on rose both sides.

Obv.: ✤ hᗺПRIᗤ⦂DI⦂GRᗅ⦂RᗺX⨯ᗅПGL⨯S⨯FRᗅПᗤ⦂
Saltire stops double after DI and FRᗅПᗤ. Same die as next coin, **505**.

Rev.: ✤ PᗺR/ᗤRVᗤᗺM TVᗅ'SᗅLVᗅ ПOS XPᗤ RᗺDᗺM   No stops.

PW type I, 16 (lis on rose dies 2/1); *SCBI* 23, –/3; North 1694; Seaby 2179. Bt Spink 1965; ex Thompson.

Angels and half-angels (*cont.*)

TYPE I (*cont.*)

A. WITH COMPOSITE INITIAL MARKS (*cont.*)

London mint (*cont.*)

505 Angel   I.m. lis on rose both sides.

	Weight		
g	*gr.*	*Die-axis*	
5.14	79.3	190°	

Obv.: same die as last coin, **504**.

Rev.: ✤PER/ɑRVɑEM TVʌM SʌLVʌ ΠOS XPɑ·REDET   No stops.

PW type I, 20 (lis on rose dies 2/5), this coin; *SCBI* 23, –; North 1694; Seaby 2179. Ex Lockett (1672).

506 Half-angel   I.m. sun and rose 3/lis on sun and rose.

2.45	37.8	350°	

Obv.: ✽ hENRIɑ×DI×GRʌ·REX·ʌΠGL

Rev.: ✿ ×O×/ɑRVX×ʌVE×SPES×VΠIɑʌ

PW type I, 5 (dies 2/2), this coin; *SCBI* 23, –; North 1699; Seaby 2188. Ex Lockett (1673); ex Sir John Evans.

B. WITH SINGLE INITIAL MARK

     Rose   Summer 1487–*c*. Feb. 1488

There are no true coins of this variety in the Schneider collection (but see mule, **507**, below). In his note on the rose group angels (Schneider 1974), Schneider records five specimens, two in the BM, one each in the Ashmolean and Manx museums and one in a private collection in Luxembourg. He also argues in favour of assigning this variety to Type II, instead of Type I, on the grounds that it has closer affinities to the earlier coins of Type II (trefoil stops, three ropes from stern to mast, legends).

TYPE II

Characteristics: Early form of angel. Trefoil stops. Lettering of PW type A.

Initial marks:	None either side	*c*. Feb. 1488–Spring or Summer 1489
	Heraldic cinquefoil	Spring or Summer 1489–Spring 1493

London mint only

507 Angel   I.m. rose/none.

5.10	78.7	20°	

Obv.: ⊕hENRIɑ·DI×GRʌ×REX ʌΠGL·S·FRʌΠɑ·DΠS I/B'·'

Rev.: PER ɑ/RVɑE·TVʌ×SʌLVʌ·ΠOS·XPɑ·REDE·TOR

     Three (instead of two) ropes from stern to mast.

PW type I/II mule, obv. die as their pl. IX, 4; *SCBI* 23, 4 (same dies); North 1694/1695; Seaby 2179/2181. Bt Spink 1973.

508 Angel   I.m. none either side.

5.12	79.0	330°	

Obv.: ×hENRIɑ DI×GRʌ·REX·ʌΠGL·S FRʌΠɑ·DΠS'/×

     Saltires at commencement and end of legend.

Rev.: PER ɑR/VɑE·TVʌM·SʌLVʌ ΠOS·XPɑ REDTOR

     The reading of the last word is uncertain.

PW type II, dies 1/1, this coin; *SCBI* 23, –; North 1695; Seaby 2181. Ex Lockett (4040).

509 Angel   I.m. none either side.

5.07	78.2	350°	

Obv.: ×hENRIɑ·DI GRʌ·REX·ʌΠGL×S·FRʌΠɑ DΠS/I

     Saltire before **h**. Same die as next coin, **510**.

Rev.: PER·ɑR/VSE·TVʌ×SʌLVʌ·ΠOS·XPɑ·REDE·TOR

PW type II, dies 4/1, this coin; *SCBI* 23, 5/6; North 1695; Seaby 2181. Ex Lockett (1674).

[*continued overleaf*]

PLATE 48

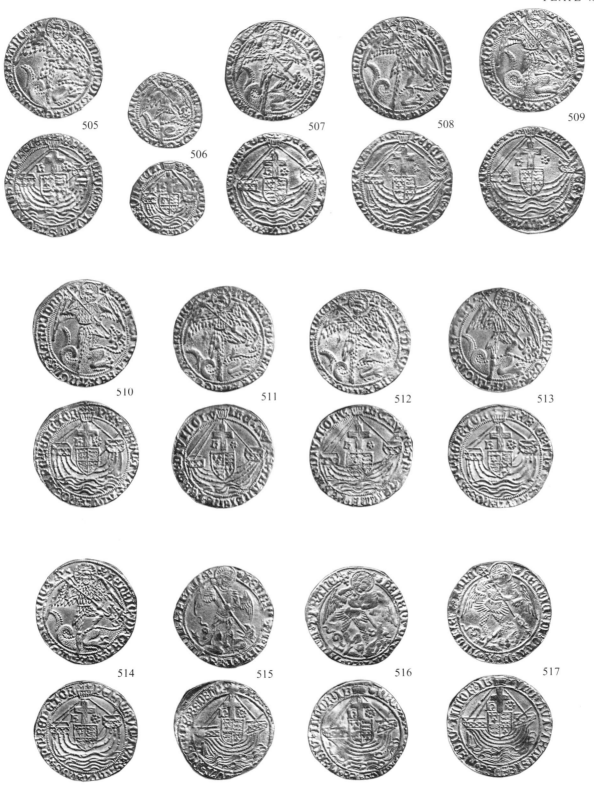

505

506

507

508

509

510

511

512

513

514

515

516

517

Plate 48 (*cont.*)

510 Angel
    5.14   79.3   60°

I.m. none either side.
Obv.: Same die as last coin, **509**.
Rev.: PER/ᏟRVᏟ:TVᏗ·SᏗLVᏗ·NOS·XPᏟ:RᏗDᏗ'TOR
    h by cross possibly over another letter.
PW type II, dies 4/–; *SCBI* 23, –; North 1695; Seaby 2181. Bt Baldwin 1964.

511 Angel
    5.03   77.6   270°

I.m. none either side.
Obv.: ×hᏗNRIᏟ·DI·GRᏗ·RᏗX·ᏗNGL·S·FRᏗNᏟ·DNS/×
    Saltires at commencement and end of legend, otherwise trefoil stops. Same die as next coin, **512**.
Rev.: IhᏟ:ᏗV/TᏗ:TRᏗNSIᏗNS·PᏗR MᏗDIV ILORV
PW type II, dies 5/2, this coin; *SCBI* 23, 6/5; North 1695; Seaby 2182. Bt Baldwin.

512 Angel
    5.07   78.2   110°

I.m. none either side.
Obv.: same die as last coin, **511**.
Rev.: IhᏟ:ᏗV/TᏗ:TRᏗNSIᏗNS·PᏗR MᏗDIV ILORV·
PW type II, dies 5/–; *SCBI* 23, as 5 but different dies; North 1695; Seaby 2182. Bt Munzen und Medaillen, Basel, 1965.

513 Angel
    5.09   78.6   80°

I.m. cinquefoil/none.
Obv.: ✠ hᏗNRIᏟ·DI·GRᏗ:RᏗX·ᏗNGL·S FRᏗNᏟ·S·
Rev.: PᏗR/ᏟRVᏟ·TVᏗ·SᏗLVᏗ·NOS·XPᏟ:RᏗDᏗ'TOR
PW type II, dies 1/2, this coin; *SCBI* 23, 8/–; North 1695; Seaby 2181. No provenance.

514 Angel
    5.11   78.9   60°

I.m. cinquefoil/none.
Obv.: ✠ hᏗNRIᏟ:DI:GRᏗ·RᏗX·ᏗNGL·S FRᏗNᏟ·S /·
Rev.: PᏗR/ᏟRVᏟ:TVᏗ:SᏗLVᏗ·NOS·XPᏟ:RᏗDᏗ'TOR
PW type II, dies 2/2, this coin; *SCBI* 23, 9 and 10/-; North 1695; Seaby 2181. Ex Lockett (1675).

Plate 48 (*cont.*)

TYPE III

Characteristics: Transitional (with i.m. scallop) then later form of angel. Rosette (earlier) or saltire (later) stops. Lettering of PW forms B–E.

Initial marks:	Scallop	Spring 1493–Autumn 1495
	Pansy	Autumn 1495–Michaelmas 1498 or later
	Lis issuant	Michaelmas 1498 or later –
	from rose	Michaelmas 1499
	Anchor	Michaelmas 1499–Michaelmas 1502

London mint only

515 Angel
  5.12 79.0 260°
  I.m. scallop both sides.
  Obv.: ✿ hENRIΩ⊙DI⊙GRΛ⊙REX⊙ΛNGL⊙Z⊙FRΛN
  Rosette stops. Cross with hammer ends. Letters PW B.
  Rev.: ✿ PER⊙Ω[   ]LVΛ⊙NOS⊙XPE'⊙REDEMP
  Rosette stops. Letters PW B.
  PW type III, class I, apparently from dies not known to them; *SCBI* 23, 12 var.; North 1696; Seaby 2183. Bt Baldwin 1975.

516 Angel
  4.97 76.7 80°
  I.m. scallop both sides.
  Obv.: ✿ hENRIΩ⊙DI⊙GRΛ⊙REX⊙ΛNGL'⊙S'⊙FRΛNΩ'/⊙
  Rosette stops, including one each side of nimbus. Cross crosslet spear shaft. Angel design 3. Letters PW $Ω_1$.
  Rev.: ✿ IhΩ⊙ΛVT⊙TRΛNSIES⊙PE'⊙MEDIV'⊙ILLOR'⊙IB
  Rosette stops. No second N in TRΛNSIENS. Letters PW $Ω_1$.
  PW type III, class II (reverse die IIb), this coin; *SCBI* 23, 13 (different dies)/–; North 1696; Seaby 2184. Ex Ryan (113).

517 Angel
  5.10 78.7 230°
  I.m. scallop both sides.
  Obv.: ✿ hENRIΩ'⊙DI'⊙GRΛ'⊙REX⊙ΛNGLIE⊙Z⊙FΛNΩ
  Rosette stops. R omitted from FRΛNΩ. Angel design 3. Letters PW $Ω_1$ (of half groats).
  Rev.: ✿ IhΩ⊙ΛVT'⊙TRΛNSIES'⊙PE'⊙MEDIV'⊙ILLOR'⊙IB
  Rosette stops. no second N in TRΛNSIENS. Letters PW $Ω_1$.
  PW type III, class III, obv. (a)/rev. die IIb, this coin; *SCBI* 23, –; North 1696; Seaby 2184. Ex Lockett (1677).

Angels and half-angels (*cont.*)

TYPE III (*cont.*)

London mint (*cont.*)

518	Angel			

	Weight		Die-axis
	g	*gr.*	
	5.15	79.5	230°

I.m. pansy, intermediate type, both sides.
Obv.: ✠ hɛNRIɑ⸰DI⸰GRꓘ⸰RɛX⸰ꓘNGL⸰Z⸰FR'
Rosette stops. Cross crosslet spear shaft. Letters PW ɛ$_1$ (of half-groats).
Rev.: ✠ PɛR⸰ɑRVɑɛ'⸰TVꓘ⸰SꓘLVꓘ⸰NOS⸰XPɛ⸱Rɛ'
Rosette stops. Letters PW ɛ$_2$.
PW type IIIB/C; *SCBI* 23, –; North 1696; Seaby 2183. Bt Spink 1968; ex Bernstein.

519	Angel		
	4.98	76.9	350°

I.m. pansy, intermediate type, both sides.
Obv.: ✠ hɛNRIɑ⸱DI⸱GRꓘ×RɛX×ꓘNGL⸱Z FRꓘNɑ'
Saltire stops. Hammer cross spear shaft. Letter PW ɛ$_2$.
Rev.: ✠ PɛR⸱ɑRVɑɛ⸱TVꓘ⸱SꓘLVꓘ⸱NOS⸱XPɛ⸱RɛDɛM'
Saltire stops, double after PɛR, SꓘLVꓘ and NOS. Letter PW ɛ$_2$.
Countermarked with a lion rampant in an oval of pellets (Holland, Van Gelder type H2).[353]
PW type IIIC; *SCBI* 23, –; North 1696; Seaby 2183. No provenance.

520	Angel		
	5.22	80.3	250°

I.m. pansy, intermediate type, both sides.
Obv.: ✠ hɛNRIɑ⸱DIꓘ⸱GRꓘ⸱RɛX×ꓘNGLI⸱Z⸱FR⸱
Saltire stops, double after RɛX and Z. Hammer cross spear shaft. Letter PW ɛ$_2$.
Rev.: ✠ PɛR⸱ɑRVɑɛ⸱TVꓘ⸱SꓘLVꓘ⸱NOS×XPɑ⸱Rɛ
Saltire stops, double after PɛR. Letter PW ɛ$_2$.
PW type IIIC; *SCBI* 23, –; North 1696; Seaby 2183. Bt 1963.

521	Angel		
	5.12	79.0	280°

I.m. pansy, intermediate type, both sides.
Obv.: ✠ hɛNRIɑ⸱DI⸱GRꓘ⸱RɛX×ꓘNGL⸱Z⸱FRꓘNɑ'
Saltire stops. Hammer cross spear shaft. Letter PW ɛ$_2$.
Rev.: ✠ PɛR×ɑRVɑɛ⸱TVꓘ⸱SꓘLVꓘ⸱NOS×XPɑ⸱RɛD⸱
Saltire stops. Letters PW ɛ$_2$, fishtail letters with broken ɛ.
PW type IIIC; *SCBI* 23, –; North 1696; Seaby 2183. Ex Potter.

522	Angel		
	5.04	77.7	80°

I.m. pansy, intermediate type, both sides.
Obv.: ✠ hɛNRIɑ×DI⸱GRꓘ×RɛX×ꓘNGL⸱Z⸱FRꓘN⸱
Saltire stops. Hammer cross spear shaft. Letter PW ɛ$_2$.
Rev.: ✠ PɛR⸰ɑRVɑ'⸰TVꓘ⸰SꓘLVꓘ⸰NOS×XPɛ⸰RɛDɛ⸰
Rosette stops. Letter PW ɛ$_2$.
PW type IIIC; *SCBI* 23, 21/–; North 1696; Seaby 2183. Ex Lockett (4041).

---

[353] Van Gelder 1980.

[*continued overleaf*]

PLATE 49

518 519 520 521

522 523 524 525 526

527 528 529 530 531

Plate 49 (*cont.*)

523 Half-angel
  2.60 40.1 100°

I.m. pansy, early type, both sides.
Obv.: ✠ hENRIQ×DI×GRA⁝REX×AGL⁝Z×F'
  Saltire stops. Hammer cross spear shaft.
Rev.: ∘✠⁝O⁝/QRVX⁝AVE⁝SPES⁝VNIQA⁝∘
  (this reading is not very clear because of double striking). Double rosette stops.
PW type III; *SCBI* 23, –; North 1700; Seaby 2189. Bt Spink 1953.

524 Angel
  5.17 78.9 350°

I.m. lis issuant from rose/pansy, late type.
Obv.: ✿hENRIQ⁝DI⁝GRA⁝REX×ANGL⁝Z×FRR∘
  Saltire stops. Hammer cross spear shaft. Reads FRR'. Letter PW E₂. Same die as next coin, **525**.
Rev.: ✠ PER⁝QRVQ×TVA⁝SALVA⁝NOS×XPE⁝RED⁝
  Double saltire stops, single after QRVQ', TVA' and SALVA'.
PW type III; *SCBI* 23, 25/–; North 1696; Seaby 2183. Bt Spink 1970.

525 Angel
  5.00 77.1 160°

I.m. lis issuant from rose both sides.
Obv.: same die as last coin, **524**.
Rev.: ✿PER×QRVQE×TVA⁝SALVA⁝NOS×XPE⁝RE'
  Saltire stops, double after SALVA, NOS and XPE. Letter PW E₂.
PW type III; *SCBI* 23, 25/–; North 1696; Seaby 2183. Ex Lockett (1682); ex Walters, 1913 (482).

526 Angel
  5.06 78.0 340°

I.m. anchor inverted/pansy, late type.
Obv.: ⳨hENRIQ⁝DI⁝GRA⁝REX×ANGL⁝Z×FRA'
  Saltire stops. Cross pommée spear shaft. Letter PW E₂.
Rev.: ✠ PER⁝QRVQ×TVA⁝SALVA⁝NOS×XPE⁝RED⁝
  Saltire stops, double after PER, NOS and XPE. Letter PW E₂.
PW type III and pl. IX, 13, this coin; *SCBI* 23, –; North 1682; Seaby 2183. Ex Lockett (1683); ex Dudman (45); ex O'Hagan (60); ex Montagu (662).

527 Angel
  5.09 78.6 240°

I.m. anchor inverted both sides.
Obv.: ⳨hENRIQ⁝DI⁝GRA⁝REX×AGL⁝Z×FRA⁝
  Saltire stops. No N in ANGL. Cross pommée spear shaft. Letter PW E₂.
Rev.: ⳨PER⁝QRVQ×TVA⁝SALVA⁝NOS×XPE⁝REDE'
  Saltire stops, double after PER, SALVA and NOS. Letter PW E₂.
PW type III; *SCBI* 23, –; North 1696; Seaby 2183. Bt Spink 1984.

528 Angel
  5.15 79.4 120°

I.m. anchor upright both sides.
Obv.: ⳨hENRIQ⁝DI⁝GRA⁝REX×AGLI⁝Z×FR⁝/×
  Saltire stops, probably double after FR' (one arm of the saltire is weak making it look like a trefoil in one or two positions). Hammer head spear shaft. Letter PW E₂.
Rev.: ⳨PER×QRVQE⁝TVA⁝SALVA⁝NOS⁝XPE⁝RE'
  Saltire stops, double after SALVA and NOS. Letter PW E₂.
PW type III; *SCBI* 23, –/26 and 27; North 1696; Seaby 2183. Ex Doubleday 1961.

529 Half-angel
  2.52 38.9 110°

I.m. anchor inverted/pansy, late variety.
Obv: ⳨hENRIQ⁝DI⁝GRA×REX×AGL Z Saltire stops.
Rev: ✠⁝O⁝ QRVX⁝AVE⁝SPES⁝VNIQA Double saltire stops.
PW type III; *SCBI* 23, 72; North 1700; Seaby 2189. Bt Seaby 1966.

Plate 49 (*cont.*)

TYPE IV

Characteristics: Late angel, saltire stops, lettering PW Є and F.

Initial mark: Greyhound's head   Michaelmas 1502–Spring 1504

London mint only

530 Angel
     5.12   79.0   80°

I.m. greyhound's head 1 both sides.

Obv.: ◄ hЄNRIᗓ ⦂DI ⦂GRᛉ ⦂RЄX⦂ᛉGL ⦂Z·F'

Saltire stops, double after RЄX. Cross crosslet spear shaft. Letter PW Є.

Rev.: ◄ PЄR⦂ᗓRVᗓЄ⦂TVᛉ⦂SᛉLVᛉ⦂NOS⦂XP'

Saltire stops, double after PЄR and NOS. Abbreviation mark struck over saltire after XP. Letter PW Є.

PW type IV (GH1, obv. die 2/ rev. of die 1 which is used with obv. GH2 die 1); reverse die as Lockett lot 1686; *SCBI* 23, 34/39; North 1697; Seaby 2185. Ex Potter 1961.

531 Angel
     5.18   79.9   330°

I.m. greyhound's head 1/greyhound's head 2.

Obv.: ◄ hЄNRI⦂DI⦂GRᛉ⦂RЄX×ᛉGL⦂Z·FR'⦂

Saltire stops, double after ГR'. Cross crosslet spear shaft. Letters PW Є₂.

Rev.: ◄ PЄR×ᗓRVᗓЄ⦂TVᛉ⦂SᛉLVᛉ·NOS×XPЄ×RЄD'

Saltire stops. Letters PW F (but R is different).

PW type IV (GH1, obv. die 4/ rev. pl. IX, 15); *SCBI* 23, 37/– and 38/38; North 1697; Seaby 2185. Bt Spink 1965; ex Thompson; ex Lockett (4043).

Angels and half-angels (*cont.*)

TYPE IV (*cont.*)

London mint (*cont.*)

532 Angel   I.m. greyhound's head 2 both sides.

| | *Weight* | | *Obv.*: ◀ hENRIꞘ∴DI∴GR𝔸∴REX×𝔸GL∴Z×FR𝔸'   Saltire stops. |

Obv.: ◀ hENRIꞘ∴DI∴GR𝔸∴REX×𝔸GL∴Z×FR𝔸' Saltire stops.
Cross crosslet spear shaft. Letters PW **F**

g	*gr.*	*Die-axis*
5.14	79.3	170°

Rev.: ◀PER×ꓚRVꓚE∴TV𝔸∴S𝔸LV𝔸∴NOS×XPE∴RE Saltire stops.
Letters PW **F**.
PW type IV (obv. die 2/rev. 1, this coin cited); *SCBI* 23, 40/– and 41/-; North 1697;
Seaby 2185. Bt Baldwin 1951; ex Carter.

TYPE V
Characteristics: late angel, saltire stops, letters PW G.

Initial marks:	Cross crosslet	Spring 1504–20 November 1504?
	Pheon	20 November 1504?–April 1509

London mint only

533 Angel   I.m. cross crosslet both sides.

5.11	78.9	290°

Obv.: ✚hENRIꓚ∴DI∴GR𝔸∴REX∴𝔸NGLI∴Z×FR𝔸' Saltire stops,
double after REX. Hammer head spear shaft. Nothing by nimbus. Small **h** in
hENRIꓚ. Letters PW **G₂**.

Rev.: ✚PER∴ꓚRVꓚ∴TV𝔸∴S𝔸LV𝔸∴NOS×XPE∴RED'
Saltire stops, double after PER and NOS. Letters PW **G₂**.
PW type V (class I(a), dies 1/1); *SCBI* 23, –; North 1698; Seaby 2186. Bt Spink 1962;
ex Spurway.

534 Angel   I.m. cross crosslet both sides.

5.16	79.6	250°

Obv.: ✚hENRIꓚ∴DI∴GR𝔸∴REX×𝔸NGLIE∴Z×FR𝔸' Saltire stops,
double after REX. Hammer head spear shaft. Nothing by nimbus. Normal **h** in
hENRIꓚ. Letters PW **G₄**.

Rev.: ✚PER×ꓚRVꓚ∴TV𝔸∴S𝔸LV𝔸×NOS×XPE×RED' Saltire stops,
double after PER and NOS. Letters PW **G₄**.
PW type V (class I(b), obv. die 6 and corresponding rev.); *SCBI* 23, –; North 1698;
Seaby 2186. Bt Spink 1962; ex Spurway.

535 Angel   I.m. cross crosslet both sides.

5.11	78.8	110°

Obv.: ✚hENRIꓚ'∴DI'∴GR𝔸'∴REX∴𝔸GLIE'∴Z×FR𝔸'/×   Double saltire stops.
Cross crosslet spear shaft. One saltire by nimbus. Letters PW **G₃b**.

Rev.: ✚PER×ꓚRVꓚE∴TV𝔸∴S𝔸LV𝔸×NOS×XPE∴RED∴ Saltire stops.
Letters PW **G₃b**. PW type V (class II(b)2, dies 10/2); *SCBI* 23, –; North 1698;
Seaby 2186. Ex Norweb 2 (302).

536 Angel   I.m. cross crosslet both sides.

5.15	79.5	340°

Obv.: ✚hENRIꓚ'∴DI'∴GR𝔸'∴REX∴𝔸GLIE'∴Z×FR𝔸∴/×   Double saltire stops.
Cross crosslet spear shaft. One saltire by nimbus. Letters PW **G₃b**.

Rev.: ✚PER×ꓚRVꓚE'∴TV𝔸'∴S𝔸LV𝔸×NOS×XPE'∴RED'
Double saltire stops. Letters PW **G₃b**.
PW type V (class II(b)2, dies 12/4, this coin); *SCBI* 23, 49/–. North 1698; Seaby 2186.
Ex Potter 1961.

[*continued overleaf*]

PLATE 50

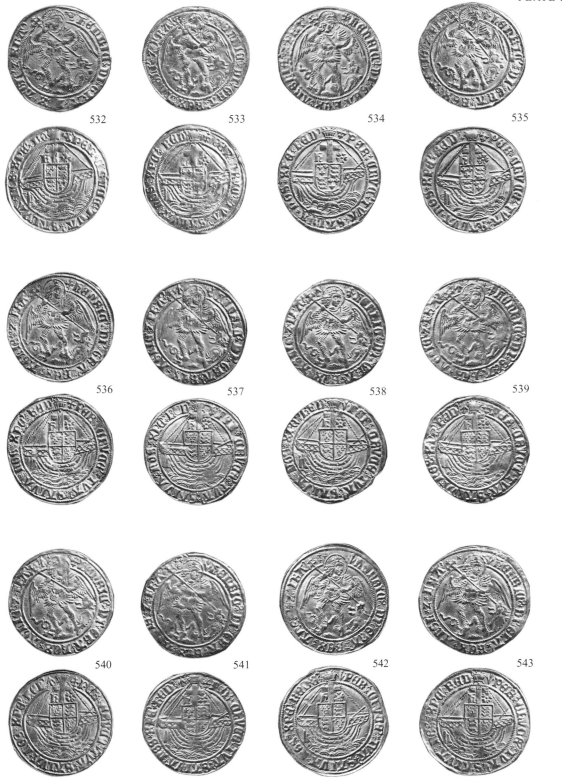

532   533   534   535

536   537   538   539

540   541   542   543

Plate 50 (*cont.*)

537 Angel
    5.15   79.4   280°
          I.m. cross crosslet and pheon upwards/cross-crosslet alone.
          Obv.: +✠ hЄNRIꝘ ?×DI?×GRA?×RЄX×AGLIЄ?×Z×FR A?×/✦
              Saltire stops. Large crook-shaped abbreviation marks. Saltire (faint) by nimbus.
              Cross crosslet spear shaft. Same die as next coin, **538**.
          Rev.: ✠· PЄR×ꝘRVꝘЄ'×TVA'×SALVA×NOS×XPЄ'×RЄD×
              Double saltire stops, single after RЄD'.
          PW type V (class III(a), dies 1/2, this coin); *SCBI* 23, –; North 1698; Seaby 2187. Ex
          Lockett (1691).

538 Angel
    5.12   79.0   270°
          I.m. cross crosslet and pheon upwards/pheon down.
          Obv.: same die as last coin, **537**.
          Rev.: ↓ PЄR×ꝘRVꝘЄ'×TVA'×SALVA×NOS×XPЄ'×RЄD×
              Double saltire stops, single after RЄD'.
           PW type V (class III(a), dies 1/3, this coin); *SCBI* 23, –; North 1698; Seaby 2187. Ex
          Lockett (4044).

539 Angel
    5.14   79.4   120°
          I.m. cross crosslet and pheon upwards both sides.
          Obv.: +✠ hЄNRIꝘ ?×DI?×GRA?×RЄX×AGLIЄ?×Z×FR A?×/×✦×
              Saltire stops. Large crook-shaped abbreviation marks. Cross crosslet spear
              shaft.
          Rev.: ✠PЄR×ꝘRVꝘЄ×TVA×SALVA×NOS×XPЄ×RЄD'×✦
          PW type V (class III(b), dies 2/1, this coin cited); *SCBI* 23, 52; North 1698; Seaby
          2187. Bt Spink 1962; ex Lockett (4330).

540 Angel
    5.14   79.3   350°
          I.m. cross crosslet and pheon upwards both sides.
          Obv.: ×✠ hЄNRIꝘ ?×DI?×GRA?×RЄX×AGLIЄ?×Z×FR A?/×✦×
              Saltire stops. Large crook-shaped abbreviation marks. Cross crosslet spear
              shaft.
          Rev.: ✠PЄR×ꝘRVꝘЄ×TVA×SALVA×NOS×XPЄ×RЄD×✦
          PW type V (class III(b), dies 3/1, this coin); *SCBI* 23, 53; North 1698; Seaby 2187. Ex
          Lawrence (probably lot 107 which is not illustrated, lot 106, which is of the same type
          and i.m. is from different dies).

541 Angel
    5.14   79.3   130°
          I.m. pheon down/cross crosslet and pheon upwards.
          Obv.: ↓ hЄNRIꝘ ?×DI?×GRA?×RЄX×AGLIЄ?×Z×FR A?/× ×
              Double saltire stops, except after hЄNRIꝘ'. Large crook-shaped abbreviation
              marks. Cross crosslet spear shaft.
          Rev.: ✠PЄR×ꝘRVꝘЄ×TVA×SALVA×NOS×XPЄ×RЄD'× ✦ ×
          PW type V (class III(c), dies 5/5, this coin); *SCBI* 23, –; North 1698; Seaby 2187. Ex
          Lockett (1692).

542 Angel
    5.18   80.0   250°
          I.m. pheon down both sides.
          Obv.: ↓ hЄNRIꝘ ?×DI?×GRA?×RЄX×ANGL?×Z×FR A?/×××
              Double saltire stops. Large crook-shaped abbreviation marks. Cross crosslet
              spear shaft.
          Rev.: ↓ PЄR×ꝘRVꝘЄ'×TVA×SALVA×NOS×XPЄ×RЄDЄ×
              Saltire stops, double after PЄR, ꝘRVꝘЄ' and NOS.
          PW type V (pheon mark both sides, ANGL, 3 saltires); *SCBI* 23, –; North 1698; Seaby
          2187. No provenance.

543 Angel
    5.15   79.5   60°
          I.m. pheon down both sides.
          Obv.: ↓hЄNRIꝘ ?×DI?×GRA?×RЄX×ANGL?×Z×FR A?/×
              Saltire stops. Large crook-shaped abbreviation marks. Cross crosslet spear
              shaft.
          Rev.: ↓ PЄR×ꝘRVꝘЄ'×TVA'×SALVA×NOS×XPЄ'×RЄD'
              Double saltire stops.
          PW type V (pheon mark both sides, ANGL, 1 saltire); *SCBI* 23, –; North 1698; Seaby
          2187. Bt Baldwin 1963.

Angels and half-angels (*cont.*)

TYPE V (*cont.*)

London mint (cont.)

	Weight			
	g	*gr.*	*Die-axis*	

544 Angel

5.15   79.4   170°

I.m. pheon down both sides.
Obv.: ↓hENRIϹ℔·DI℔·GRᴧ℔·REX·ᴧGL℔·Z·FRᴧ℔·/℔   Saltire stops. Large crook-shaped abbreviation marks. Cross crosslet spear shaft.
Rev.: ↓PER·ϹRVϹE℔TVᴧ℔SᴧLVᴧ·nOS·XPE℔RED℔
PW type V (pheon mark both sides, ᴧGL, 2 saltires); *SCBI* 23, –; North 1698; Seaby 2187. Ex Potter 1961.

545 Half-angel

2.55   39.4   30°

I.m. rose/cross crosslet and rosette.
Obv.: ⊕hENRIϹ℔·DI℔·GRᴧ·REX·ᴧN   Rosette stops. Hammer head spear shaft.
Rev.: ✠·O·ϹRVX·ᴧVE·SPES℔VNNIϹᴧ℔∘℔   Saltire stops.
PW type V, pl. IX, 21, this coin; *SCBI* 23, 74/–; North 1702; Seaby 2191. Bt Seaby 1952.

546 Half-angel

2.54   39.2   80°

I.m. pheon down both sides.
Obv.: ↓hENRIϹ℔·DI℔GRᴧ℔REX·ᴧGL℔Z/×   Saltire stops. Large crook-shaped abbreviation mark after hENRIϹ. Hammer head spear shaft.
Rev.: ↓O℔ϹRVX℔ᴧVE℔SPES℔VNIϹᴧ℔   Double saltire stops.
PW type V; *SCBI* 23, 76; North 1702; Seaby 2192. Bt Spink 1962; ex Spurway.

547 Half-angel

2.48   38.3   190°

I.m. pheon down both sides.
Obv.: ↓hENRIϹ℔·DI℔·GRᴧ℔·REX℔ᴧGL℔·Z   Double saltire stops, except after ᴧGL and Z. Large crook-shaped abbreviation marks. Hammer head spear shaft.
Rev.: ↓O℔ϹRVX℔ᴧVE℔SPES℔VNIϹᴧ℔   Double saltire stops.
PW type V; *SCBI* 23, 75/–; North 1702; Seaby 2192. No provenance.

Sovereigns and ryal

The initial marks used on these denominations differ from those used on other coins of the reign. Following *SCBI* 23 the chronology for these is considered to be as follows:

Initial marks:
Cinquefoil	(P W II)	28 October 1489–*c.* November 1492
Cross fitchée	(P W I)	*c.* November 1492–*c.* Spring 1493
Dragon	(P W III)	*c.* Spring 1493–*c.* Autumn 1495
Small lis/ Dragon	(P W IV)	Michaelmas 1502–Spring 1504
Small lis/ Cross crosslet	(P W IV)	Spring 1504–20 November 1505?
Small lis/ Pheon	(P W IV)	20 November 1505?–April 1509

London mint only

548 Sovereign

15.22   234.9   40°

I.m. cross fitchée on reverse.
Obv.: hENRIϹVS℔DI·GRᴧϹIᴧ·REX·ᴧNGLIE·ET·FRᴧNϹ·DNS I·BᴧR' Saltire stops. Chevron-barred ᴧs.
Rev.: ✠IhϹ ᴧVTEM℔TRᴧNSϹIENS·PER·MEDIVM℔ILLORVM℔IBᴧT NE Trefoil stops, double after ᴧVTEM, MEDIVM and ILLORVM. Chevron-barred ᴧs.
PW type I, pl. X, 1 same dies; *SCBI* 23, –; North 1689; Seaby 2172. Ex Ryan (104).

[*continued overleaf*]

PLATE 51

544

545

546

547

548

549

550

551

Plate 51 (*cont.*)

549 Sovereign
    15.29   236.0   10°

I.m. dragon both sides.
Obv.: hENRICVS:DEI:GRACIA:REX:ANGLIE:ET:FRANCIE: DNS:IBAR   Mullet stops.
Rev.: IhESVS*AVTEM*TRANSIENS:PER:MEDIVM: ILLORVM:IBAT::   Mullet stops.
PW type III, pl. X, 3 same dies; *SCBI* 23, 78; North 1691; Seaby 2174. Bt Spink; ex Cabell; ex Lockett (1676).

550 Sovereign
    15.43   238.1   10°

I.m. small lis/dragon.
Obv.: +hENRICVS·DEI·GRA×REX×ANGL·ET·FRAN·DNS×hIB'N' Saltire stops. As unbarred.
Rev.: :IhESVS:AVTEM:TRANSIENS:PER:MEDIVM: ILLORVM:IBAT:o:
Double saltire stops. As unbarred. Roman Ms, other letters of Gothic form.
PW type IV (obv. die 2), pl. X, 5; *SCBI* 23, 79 and 80; North 1692/1; Seaby 2175. Bt Baldwin 1951.

551 Sovereign
    15.49   239.1   240°

I.m. small lis/cross crosslet.
Obv.: +hENRICVS:DEI:GRACIA:REX/ANGLIE:ET·FRANC'·DNS:hIB: Saltire stops. As unbarred.
Rev.: +:IhESVS:AVTEM:TRANSIENS:PER:MEDIVM:ILLORVM:IBAT: Saltire stops. As unbarred. Roman Ms, other letters of Gothic form.
PW type IV, pl. X, 6 this die; *SCBI* 23, 82; North 1692/2; Seaby 2176. Bt Baldwin 1951, ex Carter.

Sovereigns and ryal (*cont.*)

London mint (*cont.*)

552 Ryal

Weight		Die-axis
g	*gr.*	
7.52	116.0	350°

I.m. cross fitchée on reverse.
Obv.: hɛႮ/RI/Ⴍ·DI·GRᗉ·Rɛx·ᗉႮGL·S·FRᗉႮႭ·DႮS·I/Bᗉᗉ
Trefoil stops. ᗉs chevron-barred. Dragon in banner at stern of ship.
Rev.: ✠IhႭ∴ᗉVTɛᙏ·TRᗉႮSIɛႮS·Pɛᖇ ᙏɛDIV·ILLORV·IBᗉT
Trefoil stops. Second two ᗉs chevron-barred.
PW pl. X, 7 same dies; *SCBI* 23, 84; North 1693; Seaby 2178. Ex Beresford-Jones
(25); ex Lockett (1668); ex E. W. Rashleigh (758); ex Pembroke (106).

HENRY VIII (22 April 1509–28 January 1547)

FIRST PERIOD (6 August 1509–22 August 1526)

Gold coinage issued at a fineness of 23½ ct 3 gr. (0.995 fine) and at a nominal weight of 240 gr. (15.552 g) to the sovereign of 20s 0d, 120 gr. (7.776 g) to the ryal of 10s 0d and 80 gr. (5.184 g) to the angel of 6s 8d. Denominations struck were sovereign, ryal, angel and half-angel. Classified according to Whitton 1949–51.

Sovereigns

Characteristics: Similar to the last type of Henry VII but with i.m. crowned portcullis both sides. The date of the introduction of this i.m. on this denomination is not known.

London mint only

553 Sovereign
        15.44   238.3   170°

I.m. crowned portcullis both sides.
Obv.: ⊞ hɛႮRIႭVS∷DɛI∷GRᗉႭIᗉ∷Rɛx/·ᗉႮGLIɛ∷ɛT∷FRᗉႮႭ∷DႮS·∷hIB'
Double saltire stops, except after Rɛx and hIB'. Broken ɛ. Same die as next
coin, **554,**
Rev.: ⊞ IhɛSVS∷ᗉVTɛᙏ∷TRᗉႮႭIɛႮS∷Pɛᖇ∷ᙏɛDIVᙏ∷ILLORVᙏ∷IBᗉT'
Double saltire stops, except after IBᗉT'. ɛ unbroken. TRᗉႮႭIɛႮS with Ⴀ.
Whitton no. 1, dies 01a/R1; North 1759/1; Seaby 2264. Ex Glendining sale 15.4.1971
(66); ex Ryan (133).

554 Sovereign
        15.38   237.3   320°

I.m. crowned portcullis both sides.
Obv.: same die as last coin, **553.**
Rev.: ⊞ IhɛSVS∷ᗉVTɛᙏ∷TRᗉႮSIɛႮS∷Pɛᖇ∷ᙏɛDIVᙏ∷ILLORVᙏ∷IBᗉT'
Double saltire stops, except after IBᗉT'. Broken ɛ. TRᗉႮSIɛႮS with S.
Whitton no. 3, dies 01a/R3a; North 1759/1; Seaby 2264. Ex Hird (private sale); ex
Thelluson (31).

[*continued overleaf*]

PLATE 52

552

553

554

555   556   557   558

Plate 52 (*cont.*)

Angels and half-angels

Characteristics: Numeral after the king's name VIIJ, sometimes with dots above the digits, sometimes with pellets between the digits or VIII plain (i.m. portcullis). Normally with large crook-shaped abbreviation marks after hЄПRIᏟ and VIII (often after hЄПRIᏟ only on the half-angels). Gothic lettering.

Initial marks:	Pheon	probably for a short period in 1509
	Castle	1509–*c.*1513[354]
	Portcullis	*c.*1513–26

London mint only

555 Angel			I.m. pheon, down both sides.
4.90	75.6	300°	*Obv.:* ↓ hЄПRIᏟ ⁹ˣVIIJ⁹ˣDI ˣGRᴧ⋮RЄXˣᴧGL⋮ZˣFRᴧ'/⋮
			Saltire stops, double after spear. VIIJ plain.
			Rev.: ↓ PЄRˣᏟRVᏟЄˣTVᴧ⋮SᴧLVᴧˣПOSˣXPЄ'⋮RЄD⋮
			Saltire stops, double after PЄR, SᴧLVᴧ and XPЄ'. Initial mark rather indistinct.
			Whitton (i); North 1760; Seaby 2265. Bt Spink 1960.

556 Angel			I.m. pheon, down both sides.
5.10	78.7	190°	*Obv.:* ↓ hЄПRIᏟ ⁹⋮VˑIˑIˑJ⁹ˣDI ⋮GRᴧ⋮RЄXˣᴧGL⋮ZˣF'ˣ/⋮
			Saltire stops, double after hЄПRIᏟ', RЄX and the spear.
			Rev.: ↓ PЄRˣᏟRVᏟЄˣTVᴧ⋮SᴧLVᴧˣПOSˣXPЄ⋮RЄD Saltire stops.
			Whitton (i); North 1760; Seaby 2265. Bt Spink 1961; ex Potter.

557 Angel			I.m. castle with pellet before on both sides.
5.06	78.1	140°	*Obv.:* ·⚜hЄПRIᏟ ⁹⋮VIIJ⁹ˣDI ⋮GRᴧ⋮RЄX⋮ᴧGL'⋮Z⋮FRᴧ'/⋮
			Saltire stops, double after hЄПRIᏟ', RЄX, ᴧGL' and Z. VIIJ dotted.
			Rev.: ·⚜PЄRˣᏟRVᏟЄ⋮TVᴧ⋮SᴧLVᴧˣПOSˣXPЄ⋮RЄDЄ'
			Saltire stops, double after PЄR, SᴧLVᴧ and ПOS.
			Whitton (ii), variant 3; North 1760; Seaby 2265. Bt Spink 1967; ex Angers hoard.

558 Angel			I.m. castle with pellet before/castle plain.
4.98	76.9	80°	*Obv.:* ·⚜hЄПRIᏟ ⁹ˣVIIJ⁹ˣDI ⋮GRᴧ⋮RЄX⋮ᴧGL Z⋮FR/⋮
			Saltire stops, double after spear. VIIJ dotted.
			Rev.: ⚜PЄRˣᏟRVᏟЄˣTVᴧ⋮SᴧLVᴧˣПOSˣXPЄ⋮RЄDЄ⋮ Saltire stops.
			Whitton (ii), variant 3/1; North 1760; Seaby 2265. Bt Spink 1967; ex Angers hoard.

[354] The evidence for the date of replacement of the i.m. castle with i.m. portcullis is rather tenuous. It is based on a groat die where the T for Tournai is overstruck by the portcullis mark, presumably a die originally destined for Tournai converted for use in London. See Whitton 1949–51, 189.

FIRST PERIOD (*cont.*)

Angels and half-angels (*cont.*)

London mint only (*cont.*)

559 Angel

	Weight		
	g	*gr.*	*Die-axis*
	5.08	78.4	20°

I.m. castle with H flanked by saltires, both sides.
Obv.: ×✠×hꞬNRIƆ ᵖ×V·I·I·Jᵖ×DI ⁝GRꞀ⁝RꞬX×ꞀGL⁝Z×FR'/⁝
  Saltire stops, double after spear.
Rev.: ×✠×PꞬR×ƆRVƆꞬ⁝TVꞀ⁝SꞀLVꞀ×NOS⁝XPꞬ'⁝RꞬDꞬ'
  Saltire stops, double after NOS and XPꞬ'.
Whitton (ii), variant 4; North 1760; Seaby 2265. Bt Baldwin; ex Carter.

560 Angel

| | 5.12 | 79.0 | 250° |

I.m. castle with H flanked by saltires/castle plain.
Obv.: ×✠×hꞬNRIƆ ᵖ×V iIJᵖ×DI ⁝GRꞀ⁝RꞬX⁝ꞀGL⁝Z×FR'/⁝
  Saltire stops, double after spear.
Rev.: ✠PꞬR⁝ƆRVƆꞬ'⁝TVꞀ'⁝SꞀLVꞀ⁝NOS⁝XPꞬ'⁝RꞬDꞬT' Double saltire
  stops.
Whitton (ii), variant 4/1; North 1760; Seaby 2265. Bt Spink.

561 Angel

| | 5.13 | 79.1 | 80° |

I.m. crowned portcullis with chains, both sides.
Obv.: ⊞hꞬNRIƆ ᵖ×VIIIᵖ×DI ⁝GRꞀ⁝RꞬX×ꞀGL⁝Z×F'/⁝× Saltire stops,
  treble after spear.
Rev.: ⊞PꞬR×ƆRVƆꞬ⁝TVꞀ⁝SꞀLVꞀ×NOS×XPꞬꞬ×RꞬDꞬ' Saltire stops
Whitton (iii), variant 1; North 1760; Seaby 2265. Bt Baldwin; ex Carter.

562 Angel

| | 5.14 | 79.3 | 210° |

I.m. crowned portcullis with chains and saltire before/crowned portcullis with chains.
Obv.: ×⊞hꞬNRIƆ ᵖ×VIIIᵖ×DI ⁝GRꞀ⁝RꞬX×ꞀGL⁝Z×FR'/× Saltire stops.
Rev.: ⊞PꞬR×ƆRVƆꞬ⁝TVꞀ⁝SꞀLVꞀ×NOS×XPꞬ⁝RꞬDꞬ⁝ Saltire stops.
Whitton (iii), variant 2; North 1760; Seaby 2265. Ex Dangar (105 or 106).

563 Angel

| | 5.13 | 79.1 | 40° |

I.m. crowned portcullis without chains/crowned portcullis with chains.
Obv.: ⊞hꞬNRIƆ ᵖ×VIIIᵖ×DI ⁝GRꞀ⁝RꞬX×ꞀGL⁝Z×FRꞀ'/⁝ Saltire stops.
Rev.: ⊞PꞬR×ƆRVƆꞬ⁝TVꞀ⁝SꞀLVꞀ×NOS×XPꞬ⁝RꞬD' Saltire stops.
Whitton (iii), variant 3/1; North 1760; Seaby 2265. Bt Baldwin 1952; ex Carter.

564 Half-angel

| | 2.54 | 39.2 | 20° |

I.m. castle, plain both sides.
Obv.: ⊞hꞬNRIƆ ᵖ×DI ⁝GRꞀ⁝RꞬX×ꞀGL⁝Z/× Saltire stops. King's numeral
  omitted. Large crook-shaped abbreviation mark after hꞬNRIƆ only.
Rev.: ⊞O ⁝ƆRVX⁝ꞀVꞬ⁝SPꞬS⁝VNIƆꞀ⁝ Double saltire stops.
Whitton (i), variant 1; North 1761; Seaby 2266. No provenance.

565 Half-angel

| | 2.55 | 39.3 | 200° |

I.m. castle, plain both sides.
Obv.: ⊞hꞬNRIƆ ᵖ×VIIJᵖ×DI ⁝GRꞀ⁝RꞬX×Ꞁ'L⁝ Saltire stops.
Rev.: ⊞×O ⁝ƆRVX⁝ꞀVꞬ⁝SPꞬS×VNIƆꞀ Saltire stops, double after O, ƆRVX
  and ꞀVꞬ.
Whitton (i), variant 2; North 1761; Seaby 2266. No provenance.

566 Half-angel

| | 2.53 | 39.1 | 190° |

I.m. castle, plain both sides.
Obv.: ⊞hꞬNRIƆ ᵖ×VIIJᵖ×DI ⁝GRꞀ⁝RꞬX×ꞀGL'/Z Saltire stops. VIIJ pelleted.
Rev.: ⊞O ⁝ƆRVX⁝ꞀVꞬ⁝SPꞬS⁝VNIƆꞀ× Double saltire stops, single after
  VNIƆꞀ.
Whitton (i), variant 2; North 1761; Seaby 2266. Bt Baldwin 1952; ex Carter.

[*continued overleaf*]

PLATE 53

559   560   561   562   563

564   565   566   567   568

569   570   571

Plate 53 (*cont.*)

567 Half-angel
    2.55   39.3   240°

I.m. crowned portcullis with chains, both sides.
Obv.: ⊞ hⒺNRIⒶ [ ]DI ⁝GRⒶ⁝RⒺX×ⒶGL⁝Z/×   Saltire stops. No numeral after king's name. Abbreviation mark after hⒺNRIⒶ not visible and that after DI is not large and crook-shaped.
Rev.: ⊞ O ⁝ⒶRVX⁝ⒶVⒺ⁝SPⒺS⁝VNIⒶ⁝   Double saltire stops.
Whitton (ii), variant 1; North 1761; Seaby 2266. Ex Lockett (4055); the Lockett catalogue states the the coin is ex Bruun but it is not included in the Bruun sale catalogue.

568 Half-angel
    2.51   38.7   190°

I.m. crowned portcullis with chains/crowned portcullis without chains.
Obv.: ⊞ hⒺNRIⒶ ᵠ×VIĩᵠ×DI [ ]GRⒶ⁝RⒺX⁝ⒶGL'/   Saltire stops. VIII dotted.
Rev.: ⊞ O ⁝ⒶRVX⁝ⒶVⒺ⁝SPⒺS⁝VNIⒶ⁝   Double saltire stops.
Whitton (ii), variant 2/2, var. without chains to portcullis; North 1761; Seaby 2266. Bt Spink 1962.

SECOND PERIOD (22 August 1526–28 May 1544)

Gold coins were issued at three standards of fineness during this period.

A. Fine, 23 ct 3½ gr. (0.995 fine), gold coinage was issued at 240 gr. (15.552 g) to the sovereign of 22s 0d (22s 6d after 5 November 1526), 80 gr. (5.184 g) to the angel of 7s 4d (7s 6d after 5 November 1526) and 71.1 gr. (4.607 g) to the george noble of 6s 8d (after November 1526). Denominations struck were sovereign, angel, half-angel, george noble and half-george noble.
B. 23 ct (0.958 fine) gold coins were issued at 53 gr. (3.434 g) to the crown of the rose of 5s 0d (August to November 1526 only).
C. Crown, 22 ct (0.917 fine), gold coinage was issued at 57.3 gr. (3.713 g) to the crown of the double rose of 5s 0d (from November 1526). Denominations struck were the crown of the double rose and its half.

The classification used is that set out in Whitton 1949–51.

A. FINE GOLD COINAGE

Sovereigns

Characteristics: Similar to sovereigns of the first period but with different initial marks.

Initial marks: Sunburst   1537–8
                          Lis   1538–41
                          Arrow[355]   1541–2

London mint only

569 Sovereign
    15.24   235.2   330°

I.m. lis over sunburst both sides.
Obv.: ×✚ hⒺNRIⒶVS⁝DⒺI⁝GRⒶⒸIⒶ⁝RⒺX/×ⒶNGLIⒺ⁝ⒺT⁝FRⒶNⒸIⒺ⁝ DNS'⁝hIB'   Double saltire stops. Saltire before initial mark. This is the same die that was used for the next coin, **570**, before renovation.
Rev.: ✚ IhⒺSVS⁝ⒶVTEM⁝TRⒶNSIⒺNS⁝PⒺR⁝MⒺDIVM⁝ILLORVM⁝IBⒶT Double saltire stops. Double tressure.
Whitton 2, dies O1c/R3c; North 1782; Seaby 2267. Ex Ryan (135).

[355] Although generally called an arrow, this mark has more the appearance of a cross-bow bolt.

Plate 53 (*cont.*)

570 Sovereign
    15.44   238.2   310°

Obv.: ⸱✠ hᏀNRIᏀVS⸱DᏀI⸱GRᎯᏀIᎯ⸱RᏀX/⸱ᎯNGLIᏀ⸱ᏀT⸱FRᎯNᏀ⸱ DNS'⸱hIB' Double saltire stops, single after FRᎯNᏀ'. Saltire before initial mark. This is the same die that was used for the last coin, **569**, after renovation (see Whitton).

Rev.: ⸴IhᏀSVS⸱ᎯVTEM⸱TRᎯNSIᏀNS⸱PᏀR⸱MᏀDIVM⸱ILLORVM⸱IBᎯT Double saltire stops. Double tressure.

I.m. lis over sunburst/arrow.

Whitton 5, dies O1d/R7; North 1782; Seaby 2267. Ex Lockett (1750); ex Murdoch (406); ex Montagu (234).

571 Sovereign
    15.36   237.1   140°

I.m. lis (new) both sides.

Obv.: ⸱✠ hᏀNRIᏀVS⸱DᏀI⸱GRᎯᏀIᎯ⸱RᏀX/ᎯNGLIᏀ⸱ᏀT⸱FRᎯNᏀ⸱ DNS⸱hIB⸱ Saltire before i.m. This is the same die as the next coin, **572**, after the error FRᎯNᏀ was corrected to FRᎯNᏀ.

Rev.: ✠ IhᏀSVS⸱ᎯVTEM⸱TRᎯNSIᏀNS⸱PᏀR⸱MᏀDIVM⸱ILLORVM⸱IBᎯT Double saltire stops. Saltires in spandrels of normal size. Double tressure.

Whitton 3, dies O2 var./R4a, the mispelling FRᎯNᏀ on the examples of this obverse die recorded by Whitton has, on this specimen, been corrected to FRᎯNᏀ; North 1782; Seaby 2267. Ex Lockett (1749); ex Vaughan-Morgan (2); ex Boord (178).

SECOND PERIOD (*cont.*)

A. FINE GOLD COINAGE (*cont.*)

Sovereigns (*cont.*)

London mint (*cont.*)

572 Sovereign

	Weight		
	g	*gr.*	*Die-axis*
	15.40	237.6	340°

I.m. lis (new)/arrow.
Obv.: ⁘✠h€NRICVS⁙D€I⁙GRΛCIΛ⁙R€X/ΛNGLI€⁙€T⁙FRΛN€⁙
DNS⁙hIB⁙ Double saltire stops, single after €T, FRΛN€', DNS' and hIB'.
This is the same die as the last coin, **571**, but before the error FRΛN€ was
corrected to FRΛNC.
Rev.: ⅃Ih€SVS⁙ΛVT€M⁙TRΛNSI€NS⁙P€R⁙M€DIVM⁙ILLORVM⁙IBΛT
Double saltire stops. Double tressure.
Whitton 6, dies O2/R7; North 1782; Seaby 2267. Bt Spink 1967; ex PKP.

573 Sovereign
15.40 237.6 210°

I.m. lis over sunburst/arrow (B).
Obv.: ✠h€NRICVS⁙D€I⁙GRΛCIΛ⁙R€X/·ΛNGLI€⁙€T⁙FRΛNC⁙
DNS'⁙hIB⁙ Double saltire stops, single after FRΛNC' and hIB'. No saltire
visible before i.m.
Rev.: ⅃⁙Ih€SVS⁙ΛVT€M⁙TRΛNSI€NS⁙P€R⁙M€DIVM⁙ILLORVM⁙IBΛT·
Double saltire stops, single after IBΛT. Single tressure. No lions, lis or saltires
in spandrels.
Whitton 5, die O1d but var. with the cross and orb on the crown recut. The saltire
before the i.m. seems to have been filled-in in the recutting process. However, judging
from his pl. I, this is not the recutting that gives the variety that Whitton cites as
O1e/R8. North 1782; Seaby 2267. Bt Baldwin 1952; ex Carter.

Angels and half-angels

Characteristics: Similar to angels and half-angels of the first period but with different initial marks.

Initial marks:	Lis	*c.* 1529–32, 1538–41
	Sunburst	1537–8

London mint only

574 Angel
5.15 79.5 300°

I.m. lis both sides.
Obv.: ✠hCNRIC⁹·VIII⁹·D⁙G⁙R⁙ΛGL⁙Z⁙FRΛNCC
Saltire stops. No cross-bars visible in €s.
Rev.: ✠P€R⁙CRVC€'⁙TVΛ⁙SΛLVΛ⁙NOS⁙XPC'⁙R€D€' Double saltire
stops, single after TVΛ' and R€D€'. Very faint cross-bars in €s.
Whitton (ii); North 1783; Seaby 2268. Ex Lockett (1762); ex Sir John Evans.

575 Half-angel
2.54 39.2 300°

I.m. lis both sides.
Obv.: ✠h€NRIC⁹·VIII⁹·D⁙G⁙R⁙ΛGL⁙Z⁙FR' Saltire stops.
Rev.: ✠O⁙CRVX⁙ΛV€⁙SP€S⁙VNICΛ⁙ Double saltire stops.
Whitton, sole type and his pl. XII, 8, same dies; North 1784; Seaby 2269. Bt Seaby
1955.

[*continued overleaf*]

PLATE 54

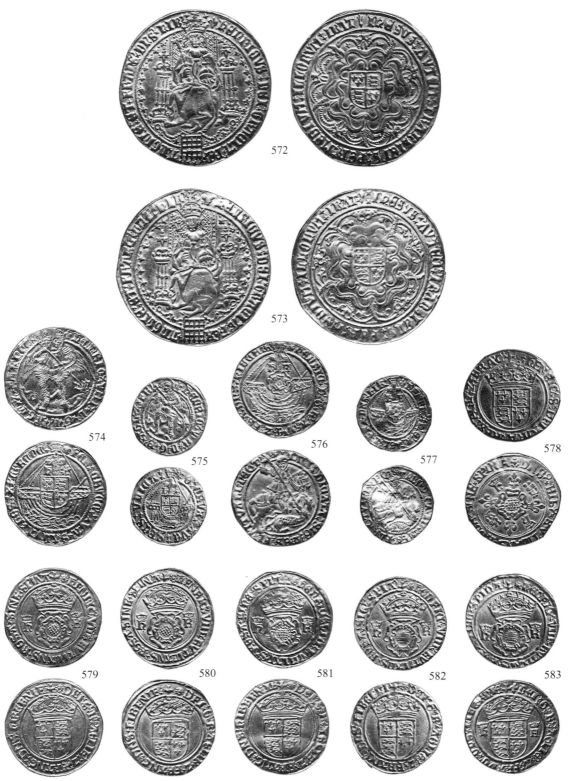

572

573

574

575

576

577

578

579

580

581

582

583

Plate 54 (*cont.*)

George Noble and its half

Characteristics: Obverse, ship with rose on mast and cross above with H-K at sides; reverse, Saint George on horseback spearing dragon.

Initial mark: Rose   November 1526–*c*.1529
                       Lis   *c*.1529–32
                       (these dates are those proposed by Whitton 1949–51, for a discussion of the possibility that i.m. rose ended in November 1527 see Kent 1981)

London mint only

576 George noble   I.m. rose both sides.
     4.62   71.3   330°   *Obv.*: ✿ hЄNRIꝲ ⁚D⁚G⁚ ᚛GLIЄ⁚Z×FR᚛⁚DNS⁚hIBЄRIЄ'
                                           Saltire stops, double after DNS'.
                                  Rev.: ✿ ×T᚛LI⁚DIꝲ᚛T᚛⁚SIG⁰×mЄS⁚FLVCTV᚛RI⁚NЄꝲT'
                                           Double saltire stops, single before T᚛LI and after SIG⁰.
                                  Whitton, p. 187, sole type although several dies with minor legend variations are
                                  known; North 1785; Seaby 2270. Ex Price (91); ex O'Hagan (76); ex Montagu (717);
                                  ex Brice; ex Wigan; ex Thomas (215); ex Dimsdale (497); ex Tyssen (1541).

577 Half-george noble   I.m. lis/rose.
     2.27   35.0   30°   *Obv.*: ✚ hЄNRIꝲ ?⁚D⁚G⁚R'⁚AGL⁚Z×FRA⁚DNS⁚hIB⁚
                                           Saltire stops, double after hЄNRIꝲ? and R'.
                                  Rev.: ✿ T᚛LI×DIꝲA×SIG⁚mЄS⁚FLV/ꝲTV᚛RI⁚NЄꝲT'   Single saltire stops.
                                  The only specimen of this denomination known to Whitton (p. 186) was that in the
                                  BM with i.m. rose both sides. The discovery of this example extends the period during
                                  which the denomination was issued into that of i.m. lis. The i.m. rose looks more like a
                                  cinquefoil, but as the latter mark does not fit into the known sequence of marks of the
                                  period it is taken to be a degenerate rose punch; cf. the BM specimen illustrated by
                                  Whitton. North 1786 var. this i.m.; Seaby 2271 var. this i.m. Bt Spink 1994; ex a
                                  recent metal-detector find.

B. 23ct GOLD COINAGE

Crown of the rose

Characteristics: obverse, shield crowned; reverse, rose on cross with arms ending in lis, **h**s and lions in angles. There are two varieties of reverse legend, one starting with the king's name as described by Whitton, the other, of which the Schneider specimen appears to be the only recorded example, with the legend starting DNS⁹×HIb⁹×.

Initial mark: Rose   August–November 1526

London mint only

578 Crown of the rose   I.m. rose both sides.
     3.35   51.7   320°   *Obv.*: ✿ hЄNRIꝲ⁚8×DEI⁚GRA×REX⁚AGL'⁚Z×FRA'C'   Double saltire stops, single
                                           after hЄNRIꝲ, none after FRA'C'. Wire-line circle within beaded inner circle.
                                  Rev.: ✿ DNS⁹×HIb⁹×RVTILANS×ROSA×SINE×SPINA   Single saltire stops, none
                                           after SPINA. Wire-line circle within beaded inner circle.
                                  Whitton pp.171–2 and 180; North 1787/1; Seaby 2272 but the var. with this reverse
                                  legend not described. Ex Strauss (65); ex Glendining 14.4.1961 (22).

Plate 54 (*cont.*)

C. CROWN GOLD COINAGE

Crown of the double rose and half-crown

Characteristics: Obverse, rose; reverse, shield. Initials in field on obverse or both sides, crowned on the crown, uncrowned on the half-crown. Large crook-shaped abbreviation marks after hENRIႧ and VIII. Mixed Roman and Gothic lettering.

Initial marks:	Rose	initials H–K	November 1526–1529
	Lis	initials H–K	1529–32
	Arrow	initials H–K	1532–3
		initials H–A	1533–6
		initials H–I	1536–7
		initials H–R	1537–42
	Pheon	initials H–R	1542

London mint only

579 Crown of the double rose
    3.68   56.8   340°

I.m. rose both sides.
Obv.: ✿hENRIႧ⁹×VIiⅰ⁹×RVTILⲀNS×ROSⲀ×SINE×SPINⲀ
Saltire stops. VIII pelleted. Crowned h–K by rose. Mixed Roman and Gothic letters.
Rev.: ✿DEI⦂G·×R·×ⲀGLIE·×Z⦂FRⲀNႧ·DNS⦂hIBERNIE× Double saltire stops, single after DNS' and hIBERNIE. Mixed Roman and Gothic letters.
Whitton (i); North 1788; Seaby 2273. Ex Lockett (1769).

580 Crown of the double rose
    3.64   56.1   10°

I.m. rose both sides.
Obv.: ✿hENRIႧ⁹×VIII⁹×RVTILⲀNS×ROSⲀ×SINE×SPINⲀ
Saltire stops. Crowned h–K by rose. Mixed Roman and Gothic letters.
Rev.: ✿DFI⦂G·R⦂ⲀGLIF·Z⦂FRⲀNႧ·DNS⦂hIBFNIF⦂ Saltire stops, double after DFI, DNS and hIBFNIF. R omitted from hIBERNIE. Letter E punch with a broken arm giving the appearance of F. Mixed Roman and Gothic letters.
Whitton (i); North 1788; Seaby 2273. Ex Burton (29).

581 Crown of the double rose
    3.70   57.1   240°

I.m. rose both sides.
Obv.: ✿hENRIႧ⁹×VIII⁹×RVTILⲀNS×ROSⲀ×SINE×SPIⲀ'
Saltire stops. Crowned h–K by rose. Gothic letters.
Rev.: ✿DEI⦂G·R'×ⲀGLIE'Z⦂FRⲀNႧ'×DNS⦂hIBERNIE Saltire stops, double after R', Z, FRⲀNႧ' and DNS'. Mixed Roman and Gothic letters.
Whitton (i); North 1788; Seaby 2273. Ex Lockett (3220).

582 Crown of the double rose
    3.69   56.9   50°

I.m. rose both sides.
Obv.: ×✿hENRIႧ⁹×VIII⁹×RVTILⲀNS×ROSⲀ×SIE·×SPIⲀ'
Saltire before initial mark. Saltire stops, double after ROSⲀ and SIE'. Crowned h–K by rose. Gothic letters.
Rev.: ✿DEI⦂G·R⦂ⲀGLIE·Z⦂FRⲀNႧ⦂DNS⦂hIBERNI' Saltire stops, double after DEI. Gothic letters.
Whitton (i); North 1788; Seaby 2273. No provenance.

583 Crown of the double rose
    3.71   57.2   0°

I.m. rose/lis.
Obv.: ✿hENRIႧ⁹×VIII⁹×RVTILⲀNS×ROSⲀ×SINE×SPINⲀ×
Saltire stops. Crowned h–K by rose. Gothic letters.
Rev.: ✠DEI⦂G·×R·×ⲀGLIE·×Z⦂FRⲀNႧ·×DNS⦂hIBERNIE Double saltire stops. Crowned h–K by shield. Gothic letters.
Whitton (ii); North 1788; Seaby 2274. No provenance.

SECOND PERIOD (*cont.*)

C. CROWN GOLD COINAGE (*cont.*)

Crown of the double rose and half-crown (*cont.*)

London mint (cont.)

584	Crown of the double rose		
	Weight		
	g	*gr.*	*Die-axis*
	3.70	57.1	230°

I.m. lis both sides.
Obv.: ·✠ hƐNRIƆ⁹ᣵVⅰⅰⅰ⁹ᣵRVTILⱭNSᣵROSⱭᣵSINEᣵSPIⱭ'
Saltire before i.m. Double saltire stops, single after hƐNRIƆ' and VIII'. VIII pelleted. Crowned h–K by rose. Gothic letters.
Rev.: ✠ DƐIᣵG'ᣵRᣵⱭGLIƐᣵZᣵFRⱭNƆᣵDNS'ᣵhIBƐRNIƐ   Double saltire stops, single after FRⱭNƆ'. Crowned h–K by shield. Gothic letters.
Whitton (iii); North 1788; Seaby 2274. No provenance.

585	Crown of the double rose		
	3.75	57.8	170°

I.m. lis/lis over rose.
Obv.: ✠ hƐNRIƆ⁹ˣVⅰⅰⅰ⁹ᣵRVTILⱭNSᣵROSⱭᣵSIƐ'ˣSPIⱭ'
Double saltire stops, single after hƐNRIƆ' and VIII'. VIII dotted. Crowned h–K by rose. Roman Ns, other letters Gothic.
Rev.: ✠ DƐIᣵG'ˣRˣⱭGLIƐᣵZᣵFRⱭᣵDNS'ˣhIBƐRNIƐ   Double saltire stops, single after ⱭGLIƐ' and FRⱭ'. Crowned h–K by shield. Gothic letters.
Whitton (iii), var.; North 1788; Seaby 2274. Ex Lockett (4057).

586	Crown of the double rose		
	3.48	53.7	10°

I.m. lis both sides.
Obv.: ✠ hƐNRIƆ⁹ˣVIII⁹ᣵRVTILⱭNSˣROSⱭˣSIƐᣵSPIⱭ'
Saltire stops. Crowned h–K by rose. Roman Ns, other letters Gothic.
Rev.: ✠ DƐIᣵG'ᣵRˣⱭGLIƐᣵZᣵFRⱭNƆƐᣵDNSˣhIBƐRI'   Double saltire stops, single after G', and ⱭGLIƐ'. Crowned h–K by shield. Roman Ns, other letters Gothic.
Whitton (iii), var.; North 1788; Seaby 2274. No provenance.

587	Crown of the double rose		
	3.67	56.6	170°

I.m. arrow both sides.
Obv.: ↓hƐNRIƆ⁹ˣVIII⁹ᣵRVTILⱭNSˣROSⱭˣSIƐᣵSPIⱭ'
Double saltire stops, single after hƐNRIƆ' and SIƐ'. Crowned h–K by rose. Gothic letters.
Rev.: ↓DƐIᣵG'ᣵRᣵⱭGLIƐˣZᣵFRⱭNƆˣDNSᣵhIBƐRNI'   Double saltire stops, single after G', R' and DNS'. Crowned h–K by shield. Gothic letters.
Whitton (iv), 1; North 1788; Seaby 2274. No provenance.

588	Crown of the double rose		
	3.68	56.8	10°

I.m. arrow both sides.
Obv.: ↓hƐNRIƆ⁹ˣVIII⁹ᣵRVTILⱭNSˣROSⱭˣSIƐᣵSPIⱭ'
Saltire stops. Crowned h–K by rose. Gothic letters.
Rev.: ↓DƐIᣵG'ᣵRˣⱭGLIƐᣵZᣵFRⱭNƆ'DNSᣵhIBƐRNIƐᣵ   Double saltire stops, single after G' and DNS'. Crowned h–Ɑ by shield. Gothic letters.
Whitton (iv), 2; North 1788/1789; Seaby 2275. Ex Burton (32); ex Ryan (158).

589	Crown of the double rose		
	3.69	57.0	340°

I.m. arrow both sides.
Obv.: ↓hƐNRIƆ⁹ˣVIII⁹ᣵRVTILⱭNSˣROSⱭˣSIƐᣵSPINⱭ
Saltire stops, double after RVTILⱭNS. Tops of abbreviation marks after hƐNRIƆ and VIII broken. Crowned h–Ɑ by rose. Gothic letters.
Rev.: ↓DƐIᣵG'ᣵRˣⱭGLIƐᣵZᣵFRⱭNƆ'DNSᣵhIBƐRNIƐᣵ   Double saltire stops, single after G' and DNS'. Crowned h–Ɑ by shield. Gothic letters.
Whitton (iv), 4; North 1789; Seaby 2277. Ex Lockett (1773); ex Drabble (131); ex Roth (220, part).

[*continued overleaf*]

PLATE 55

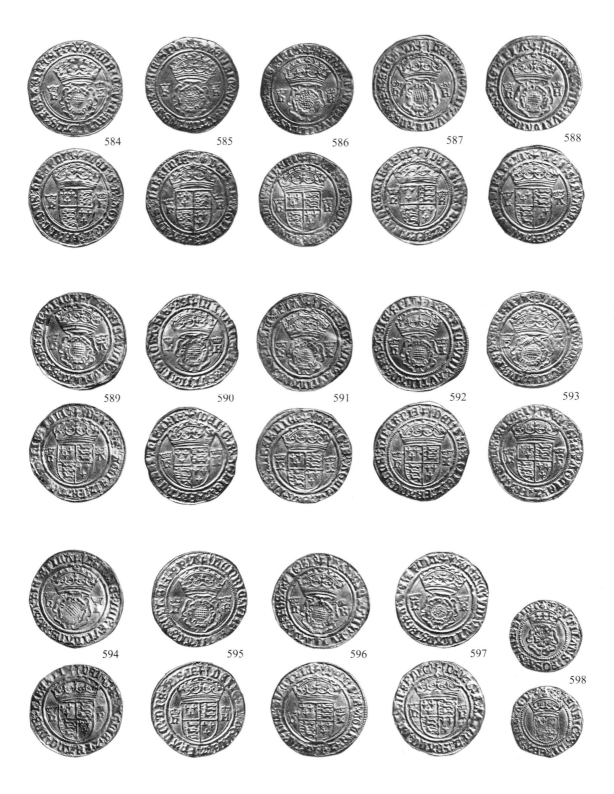

584 585 586 587 588

589 590 591 592 593

594 595 596 597

598

Plate 55 (*cont.*)

590 Crown of the double rose
    3.73   57.6   10°

I.m. arrow both sides.
Obv.: ↓hЄNRIC⁹×VIII⁹×RVTILⅯNS×ROSⅯ×SIЄ×SPI'
Saltire stops. Tops of abbreviation marks after hЄNRIC and VIII broken. Crowned h–K by rose. Gothic letters.
Rev.: ↓DЄI×G×R×ⅯGLIЄ×Z×FRⅯNC×DNS'×hIBЄRIЄ   Saltire stops, double after DЄI and DNS'. Crowned h–I by shield. Gothic letters.
Whitton (iv), 5; North 1788/1790; Seaby 2280. Ex Lockett (1775).

591 Crown of the double rose
    3.64   56.1   230°

I.m. arrow both sides.
Obv.: ↓hЄNRIC⁹×VIII⁹×RVTILⅯNS×ROSⅯ×SIЄ×SPIⅯ'
Saltire stops, double after RVTILⅯNS. Crowned h–I by rose. Gothic letters.
Rev.: ↓DЄI×G'×R'×ⅯGLIЄ×Z×FRⅯ×DNS'×hIBЄRNIЄ×   Double saltire stops, single after G', ⅯGLIЄ', FRⅯ' and hIBЄRNIЄ'. Crowned h–I by shield. Gothic letters.
Whitton (iv), 6; North 1790; Seaby 2279. Bt Baldwin 1968.

592 Crown of the double rose
    3.70   57.1   240°

I.m. arrow both sides.
Obv.: ↓hЄNRIC⁹×VIII⁹×RVTILⅯNS×ROSⅯ×SIЄ×SPIⅯ
Saltire stops. Tops of abbreviation marks after hЄNRIC and VIII broken. Crowned h–I by rose. Gothic letters.
Rev.: ↓DЄI×G'×R×ⅯGLIЄ'×Z×FRⅯNC×DNS'×hIBЄRNIЄ'   Double saltire stops, single after FRⅯNC'. Crowned h–I by shield. Gothic letters.
Whitton (iv), 6; North 1790; Seaby 2279. Ex Grantley (51).

593 Crown of the double rose
    3.59   55.4   320°

I.m. arrow both sides.
Obv.: ↓hЄNRIC⁹×VIII⁹×RVTILⅯNS×ROSⅯ×SIЄ×SPIⅯ×
Saltire stops, double after RVTILⅯNS. The stop after SPIⅯ is above the cross on the orb of the crown. Crowned h–Ⅾ by rose. Gothic letters.
Rev.: ↓DЄI×G'×R'×ⅯGLIЄ×Z×FRⅯNC×DNS×hIBЄRI'   Saltire stops, double after DЄI',G' and R'. Crowned h–R by shield. Gothic letters.
Whitton (iv), 7; North 1789/91; Seaby 2278. Ex Lawson (36); ex Ryan (159).

594 Crown of the double rose
    3.68   56.8   330°

I.m. arrow both sides.
Obv.: ↓hЄNRIC⁹×VIII⁹×RVTILⅯNS×ROSⅯ×SIЄ×SPINⅯ
Saltire stops, double after RVTILⅯNS. Crowned h–I by rose. Gothic letters.
Rev.: ↓DЄI×G×R×ⅯGLIЄ×Z×FRⅯNC×DNS×hIBЄRIЄ   Saltire stops. Crowned h–R by shield. Gothic letters.
Whitton (iv), –; Schneider 1952–4, p.201; North 1790/1791; Seaby 2276. Bt Spink 1951.

595 Crown of the double rose
    3.68   56.8   130°

I.m. arrow both sides.
Obv.: ↓hЄNRIC⁹×VIII⁹×RVTILⅯNS×ROSⅯ SIЄ×SPIⅯ'
Saltire stops. Crowned h–R by rose. Gothic letters.
Rev.: ↓DЄI×G'×R'×ⅯGLIЄ×Z×FRⅯNC×DNS×hIBЄR'   Double saltire stops, single after DNS'. Crowned h–K by shield. Gothic letters.
Whitton (iv), –; Schneider 1952–4, pp.201–2; North 1791/1788; Seaby 2276. Bt Spink 1950.

596 Crown of the double rose
    3.71   57.3   0°

I.m. arrow both sides.
Obv.: ↓hЄNRIC⁹×VIII⁹×RVTILⅯNS×ROSⅯ×SIЄ×SP'
Saltire stops, double after RVTILⅯNS. Crowned h–R by rose. Gothic letters.
Rev.: ↓DЄI×G'×R×ⅯGLIЄ×Z×FRⅯNC×DNS×hIBЄRNIЄ   Saltire stops, double after DЄI', G' and FRⅯNC'. Crowned h–I by shield. Gothic letters.
Whitton (iv), 8; North 1791/1790; Seaby 2281. Ex Lawrence (118).

Plate 55 (*cont.*)

597 Crown of the double rose
      3.74   57.7   340°

I.m. arrow both sides.

Obv.: ☩hƐNRIꝯ⁹×VIII⁹×RVTILⱯNS፥ROSⱯ፥SIƐ፥SPINⱯ
Saltire stops, double after RVTILⱯNS and ROSⱯ. Broken tops to abbreviation marks after hƐNRIꝯ and VIII. Crowned h–R by rose. Gothic letters.

Rev.: ☩DƐI፥G'፥R፥ⱯGLIƐ'፥Z፥FRⱯNꝯ፥DNS፥hIBƐRNIƐ' Double saltire stops, single after R', FRⱯNꝯ' and DNS'. Crowned h–R by shield. Gothic letters.

Whitton (iv), 9; North 1791; Seaby 2282. Ex Glendining sale 14.4.1961 (23).

598 Half-crown
      1.81   27.9   270°

I.m. rose both sides.

Obv.: ✿RVTILⱯNS፥ROSⱯ፥SINE፥SPINⱯ Double saltire stops. No initials by rose. Mixed Roman and Gothic letters.

Rev.: ✿hENRIꝯ⁹×8×DI'፥GRⱯ፥REX፥ⱯGL፥Z× Saltire stops, double after DI and REX. No initials by shield. Mixed Roman and Gothic lettering.

Whitton (i), 1; North 1793; Seaby 2284. Ex Hird (9).

SECOND COINAGE (*cont.*)

C. CROWN GOLD COINAGE (*cont.*)

Crown of the double rose and half-crown (*cont.*)

London mint (*cont.*)

	Weight		
	g	*gr.*	*Die-axis*

599 Half-crown
1.82 28.2 250°

I.m. rose both sides.
Obv.: ✿ RVTILⱭNS⁝ROSⱭ⁝SINE⁝SPINⱭ⁝ Double saltire stops. h–K by rose; small mark above the letter K. Mixed Roman and Gothic letters.
Rev.: ✿ hENRIⱭ⁹×8·DI⁝GRⱭ⁝REX⁝ⱭGL'⁝Z⁝F' Saltire stops, double after REX, ⱭGL' and Z. No initials by shield. Mixed Roman and Gothic letters.
Whitton (i), 2; North 1794; Seaby 2285. Ex Lockett (1781).

600 Half-crown
1.84 28.4 210°

I.m. rose both sides.
Obv.: ✿ RVTILⱭNS⁝ROSⱭ⁝SINE⁝SPINⱭ× Double saltire stops, single after SPINⱭ. h–K by rose. Gothic letters.
Rev.: ✿ hENRIⱭ⁹×8⁝DI'×G'×R'×ⱭGL'×Z⁝FRⱭ' Double saltire stops. No initials by shield. Gothic letters.
Whitton (i), 2; North 1794; Seaby 2284. No provenance.

601 Half-crown
1.83 28.2 50°

I.m. rose/lis over rose.
Obv.: ✿ RVTILⱭNS⁝ROSⱭ⁝SINE⁝SPINⱭ× Double saltire stops, single after SPINⱭ. h–K by rose. Flaw over h. Gothic letters.
Rev.: ✚ hENRIⱭ⁹×8·DI⁝G⁝R⁝ⱭGL⁝Z·FRⱭ' Saltire stops. h–K by shield. Gothic letters.
Whitton (ii); North 1794; Seaby 2286. Ex Lockett (1784).

602 Half-crown
1.81 27.9 20°

I.m. lis/lis over rose.
Obv.: ✚ RVTILⱭNS⁝ROSⱭ×SINE⁝SPINⱭ× Double saltire stops, single after ROSⱭ(?) and SPINⱭ. h–K by rose. Gothic letters.
Rev.: ✚ hENRIⱭ⁹×8·DI⁝G⁝R⁝ⱭGL⁝Z·FRⱭ' Saltire stops. h–K by shield. Gothic letters.
Whitton (iii), but not noted with overstruck i.m. on reverse; North 1794; Seaby 2286. Bt Spink; ex Yates; ex Ryan (179); ex Thompson.

603 Half-crown
1.86 28.7 10°

I.m. lis both sides.
Obv.: ✚ RVTILⱭNS⁝ROSⱭ⁝SINE⁝SPINⱭ× Double saltire stops, single after SPINⱭ. h–K by rose. Gothic letters.
Rev.: ✚ hENRIⱭ⁝8⁝DI'×G⁝R⁝ⱭGL⁝Z·FRⱭNⱭE⁝ Saltire stops, double after 8, DI', G and FRⱭNⱭE. Small abbreviation mark after hENRIⱭ⁝ h–K by shield. Roman N in FRⱭNⱭE, all other letters Gothic.
Whitton (iii), variant with Roman N on reverse; North 1794; Seaby 2286. Bt Spink 1965; ex Thompson.

604 Half-crown
1.81 28.1 300°

I.m. arrow/arrow over lis.
Obv.: ↓RVTILⱭNS⁝ROSⱭ×SINE⁝SPINⱭ⁝ Double saltire stops, single after ROSⱭ. h–K by rose. Gothic letters.
Rev.: ↓hENRIⱭ⁹×8·DI⁝G'×R⁝ⱭGL⁝Z·FRⱭNⱭ' Saltire stops, double after G'. h–K by shield. Gothic letters.
Whitton (iv), 1(pl. X, 4, same dies); North 1794; Seaby 2286. Bt Spink 1975.

605 Half-crown
1.81 27.9 310°

I.m. arrow both sides.
Obv.: ↓RVTILⱭNS⁝ROSⱭ×SINE⁝SPINⱭ Double saltire stops. h–I by rose. Gothic letters.
Rev.: ↓hENRIⱭ⁹×8·D⁝G⁝R×ⱭGL⁝Z·FRⱭNⱭ' Saltire stops. h–I by shield. Gothic letters.
Whitton (iv), 2; North 1795; Seaby 2287. Bt Spink 1962; ex Spurway.

[*continued overleaf*]

PLATE 56

599   600   601   602   603

604   605   606

607   608   609

610

Plate 56 (*cont.*)

606 Half-crown
    1.84   28.4   60°
                                      I.m. arrow both sides.
                                      Obv.: ʃRVTILⱯNS⁚ROSⱧ⁚SINꞬ⁚SPINⱯ   Double saltire stops. h–I by rose. Gothic letters.
                                      Rev.: ʃhꞬNRIɑ⁚8⁚DI⁚G⁚R⁚ⱯGL'⁚Z⁚FRⱯ⁚   Saltire stops, double after hꞬNRIɑ, 8 and ⱯGL'. h–I by shield. Gothic letters.

                                      Whitton (iv), 2; North 1795; Seaby 2287. Bt Baldwin.

THIRD PERIOD (13 May 1544–28 January 1547)

A period of progressive debasement in which various standards of fineness and weight were used, see details under each type heading. The gold denominations struck were sovereign, half-sovereign, angel, half-angel, quarter-angel, crown of the double rose and half-crown. The mints at which gold was struck were Tower 1, Tower 2, Southwark and Bristol. The classification used continues to be that of Whitton 1949–51.

Sovereigns

Tower I and II mints

Characteristics: Bearded king upon throne with double rose below. Shield with supporters on reverse, **HR** below. Large module.

TYPE I. Large Module. Nominal fineness 23 ct (0.958 fine) and weight 200 gr. (12.960 g). Value 20s 0d. Straight sided throne.

Initial mark: Large lis.

607 Sovereign
    12.79   197.4   170°
                                      I.m. large lis both sides.
                                      Obv.: ⁕✠hꞬNRIɑᵖ⁚8⁚DI⁚GRⱯ⁚ⱯNGLIꞬ⁕/⁕FRⱯNɑIꞬ⁚ꞬT⁚hIB'Ꞵ⁚RꞬX⁚
                                      Saltire stops, double after FRⱯNɑIꞬ and hIB'Ꞵ. Large hook-shaped abbreviation mark after hꞬNRIɑ. Ⱨ of GRⱧ struck over V. Gothic letters.
                                    Rev.: ✠IhꞬSVS⁚ⱯVTꞬM⁚TRⱯNɑIꞬNS⁚PꞬR⁚MꞬDIVM⁚ILLORV'⁚IBⱯT
                                      Double saltire stops. Roman **M**s, other letters Gothic.
                                    Whitton, Tower, type I, pl. III, Aa, same dies; North 1823; Seaby 2289. Tooled in the neighbourhood of the cross on the king's crown; apparently not plugged so perhaps at one time mounted. Ex Beresford-Jones (34).

TYPE IIa. Small module. Nominal fineness 23 ct (0.958 fine) and weight 200 gr. (12.960 g). Value 20s 0d. Curved sided throne.

Initial mark: Small lis

608 Sovereign
    12.72   196.3   130°
                                        I.m. small lis both sides.
                                      Obv.: ✠hꞬNRIɑᵖ⁕8⁕DI'⁕GRⱧ⁕ⱯNGL'⁕/⁕FRⱯNɑIꞬ⁕Z⁕hIBꞬRN'⁕RꞬX⁕
                                      Slipped trefoil stops, double after FRⱯNɑIꞬ. Large crook-shaped abbreviation mark after hꞬNRIɑ. Gothic letters.
                                    Rev.: ✠IhS'⁕ⱯVTꞬM⁕TRNSIꞬNS⁚PꞬR⁚MꞬDIVM⁚ILLORVM⁚IBⱯT⁚
                                      Double slipped trefoil stops, single after IhS' and ⱯVTꞬM'. Ⱨ omitted from TRⱯNɑIꞬNS. Roman **M**s, other letters Gothic.
                                    Whitton, Tower, type II(a), pl. III, Bb; North 1824; Seaby 2290. Ex Lockett (1752); ex Montagu (707); ex Brice; ex Bergne (522); ex Durrant (402); ex British Museum dups. (203).

Plate 56 (*cont.*)

TYPE IIb. Small module. Nominal fineness 22 or 20 ct (0.917 or 0.833 fine) and weight 192 gr. (12.441 g). Distinguishable from type IIa by reason of lighter weight.

Initial marks: Small lis
                Annulet with pellet

609 Sovereign
    12.26   189.2   340°

I.m. small lis both sides.

Obv.: ✠ hɛNRIᘓ ⸱8ℨDI⸱GRᴧ⸱ᴧGL⸱/⸱FRᴧNᘓIɛℨZℨhIBɛR 'ℨRɛXℨ
Double sleeve stops, single after hɛNRIᘓ', DI', GRᴧ', ᴧGL' and /. Curved sided throne. Roman R, other letters Gothic.

Rev.: ✠ IhSℨᴧVTɛMℨTRᴧNSIɛNS ℨPɛR MɛDIVMℨILLORV⸱IBᴧTℨ
Double sleeve stops, single after ILLORV. Roman R, other letters Gothic.

Whitton, Tower, type II(b), 2, pl. III, Ce; North 1824; Seaby 2290. Bt Spink 1969.

610 Sovereign
    12.37   190.9   270°

I.m. annulet with pellet/small lis.

Obv.: ☉ hɛNRIᘓ'ℨ8ℨDI'×GRᴧ'×ᴧGL'/ℨFRᴧNᘓIɛℨZℨhIBɛR 'ℨRɛXℨ
Double slipped trefoil stops, single after DI' and GRᴧ'. Curved sided throne. Roman E and R, other letters Gothic.

Rev.: ✠ IhSℨᴧVTɛMℨTRᴧNᘓIɛNS ℨPɛR MɛDIVℨILLORV'×IBᴧT×
Double slipped trefoil stops, single after ILLORV' and IBᴧT. Roman E, M and R, other letters Gothic.

Whitton, Tower, type II(b), 3, pl. III, Dd, same dies; North 1824; Seaby 2290. No provenance.

THIRD PERIOD (*cont.*)

Sovereigns (*cont.*)

Southwark mint (opened June 1545)

Characteristics: as for Tower coins, but with distinctive initial marks, and sometimes with E below shield on reverse.

Initial marks: S
                   E

TYPE IIb. Small module. Nominal fineness 20 ct (0.833 fine) and weight 192 gr. (12.441 g). Value 20s 0d.

611 Sovereign		
Weight		
g	*gr.*	*Die-axis*
12.09	186.6	20°

I.m. S both sides.

Obv.: S hENRIꝈ∶8∶DI∶GRA∶ΛGL'/∶FRΛNꝈIE'∶Z∶hIBERN∶REX
Trefoil stops, some slipped, double after 8, ΛGL'/, FRΛNꝈIE' and Z. Roman E and R, other letters Gothic.

Rev.: S IhS'∗ΛVTEM∗TRΛNSIENS∗PER MEDIVM∗ILLOR'∗IBΛT∗
Slipped trefoil stops, double after ΛVTEM, TRΛNSIENS and MEDIVM. Roman E, M and R, other letters Gothic. The i.m. appears to be struck over something else.

Whitton, Southwark, as Tower type II(b), 1, pl. III, Ef, same dies; North 1825; Seaby 2291. Bt Spink 1972; ex Carter; ex Murdoch (410); ex Krumbholz (6); ex Marsham (377); ex Wigan.

Half-sovereigns

The half-sovereigns are classified on the same lines as the sovereigns, except that no half-sovereign is known of Tower type I (large module).

Tower I and II mints

TYPE IIa Nominal fineness 23 ct (0.958 fine) and weight 100 gr. (6.480 g). Value 10s 0d.

Initial mark: lis

There is no specimen of this issue in the Schneider collection. The only specimen recorded by Whitton is in the Fitzwilliam Museum.

TYPE IIb Nominal fineness 22 or 20 ct (0.917 or 0.833 fine) and weight 96 gr. (6.221 g). Value 10s 0d.

Initial mark: Annulet-with-pellet

612 Half-sovereign		
6.09	94.0	50°

I.m. annulet-with-pellet both sides.

Obv.: ☉ HENRIꝈ∗8∗D'∗GRA ∗AGL'/∶FRANCIE∗Z∶HIBERNI∶REX∗
Small double saltire stops, single after HIBERNI'. All letters small Roman, H with ornamental cross-bar. King's portrait contained within inner circle.

Rev.: ☉ IHS∶AVTEM∗TRANSIENS ∗PER∗MEDIVM∗ILLORVM∗IBA
Small double saltire stops. All letters small Roman, H with ornamental cross-bar.

Whitton, Tower, type II(b), 1; North 1827; Seaby 2294. Bt Baldwin; ex Carter.

613 Half-sovereign		
6.16	95.0	60°

I.m. annulet-with-pellet both sides.

Obv.: ☉ HENRIꝈ⁹∗8∗DI∶GRA∶AGL'/∶FRANꝈIE∶Z∶HIBE∶REX∗
Trefoil stops, double after AGL'/ and FRANꝈIE. All letters small Roman. Ꝺ is reversed D, perhaps over another letter. H with ornamental cross-bar. Top of crown breaks inner circle.

Rev.: ☉ IHS'∶AVTEM∗TRANꝈIENS ∗PER∗MEDIVM∗ILLORV∶IBAT
Small double saltire stops. All letters small Roman. Ꝺ is reversed D. H with ornamental cross-bar.

Whitton, Tower, type II(b), 2/1; North 1827; Seaby 2294. Bt Spink 1972; ex Cabell.

[*continued overleaf*]

PLATE 57

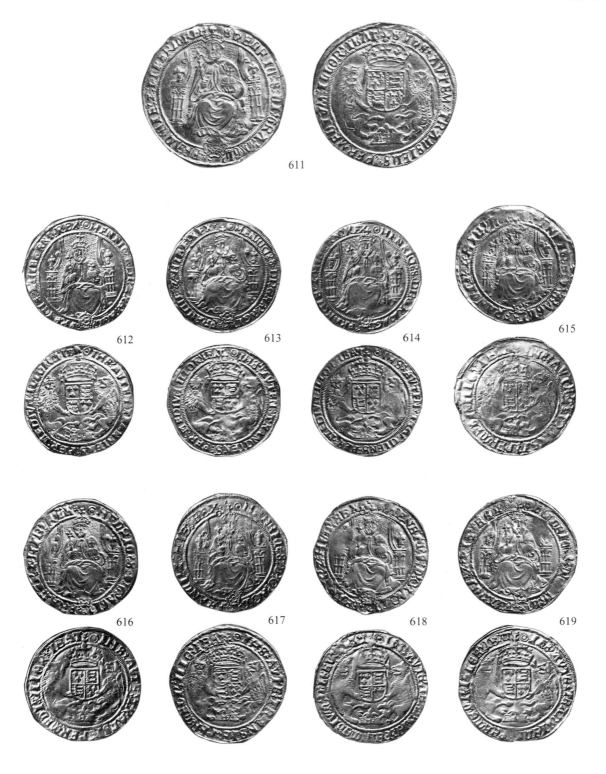

611

612   613   614   615

616   617   618   619

Plate 57 (*cont.*)

614 Half-sovereign
    6.20   95.9   110°

I.m. annulet with pellet both sides.
Obv.: ☉ HENRIႠꝰ·8·DI·GRA·AGL'/·FRANႠIE·Z·HIBERN·REX
Trefoil stops. Large crook-shaped abbreviation mark after HENRIႠ. All letters small Roman. H with ornamental cross-bar. Top of crown breaks inner circle.
Rev.: ☉ IHS:AVTEM·TRANႠIENS ·PER·MEDIVM·ILLOR·IBAT
Trefoil stops. All letters small Roman. H with ornamental cross bar.
Whitton, Tower, type II(b), 2; North 1827; Seaby 2294. Bt Spink 1951.

615 Half-sovereign
    6.14   94.7   350°

I.m. annulet with pellet both sides.
Obv.: ☉ HENRIႠ:8:D':G:AGL':FRANႠI:I:Z·HIB·RX·
Trefoil stops, double after 8, D' and AGL'. Additional letter I between FRANႠI' and Z. No E in REX. Mixed Roman and Gothic letters.
Rev.: ☉ IHS:AVTE:TRANSI:PERMEDI:ILLO:⁑IBAT
Trefoil stops. Roman letters except for Gothic M.
Whitton, Tower, type II(b), 3; North 1827; Seaby 2294. No provenance.

616 Half-sovereign
    6.15   94.9   320°

I.m. annulet with pellet both sides.
Obv.: ☉ HENRIႠꝰ·8·D:G:AGL':FRANႠI:Z·HIB:REX
Trefoil stops, double after AGL'. Large crook-shaped abbreviation mark after HENRIႠ. Mixed Roman and Gothic letters.
Rev.: ☉ IHS:AVTE:TRANSI :PERMEDI':ILLOR':IBAT·
Trefoil stops, double after MEDI' and ILLOR'. Mixed Roman and Gothic letters.
Whitton, Tower, type II(b), 3; North 1827; Seaby 2294. No provenance.

617 Half-sovereign
    6.17   95.2   190°

I.m. annulet with pellet both sides.
Obv.: ☉ HENRIႠꝰ·8:D:G:AGL'/:FRANႠI:Z:HIB:REX:
Saltire stops, double after 8, AGL', Z, HIB and REX. Large crook-shaped abbreviation mark after HENRIႠ. Roman letters. Annulet on inner circle by X.
Rev.: ☉ IHS:AVTE:TRANSIE:PERMEDI:ILLO:IBAT
Saltire stops, double after MEDI'. Roman letters except Gothic M in MEDI. Annulet on inner circle under B.
Whitton, Tower, type II(b), 4; North 1827; Seaby 2295. Ex W. M. Hall (114).

618 Half-sovereign
    6.08   93.8   160°

I.m. annulet with pellet both sides.
Obv.: ☉ HENRIႠꝰ·8:D:G:AGL':FRANႠI:Z:HIB:REX:
Saltire stops, double after 8, AGL', Z, HIB' and REX. Large crook-shaped abbreviation mark after HENRIႠ. Roman letters. Annulet on inner circle after REX.
Rev.: ☉ IHS:ΛVTE:TRΛNSIE:PER:MEDIVM:ILLORV:IBAT·
Trefoil stops, double after MEDIVM. Gothic lettering. Annulet on inner circle under I of IBAT.
Whitton, Tower, type II(b), 4; North 1827; Seaby 2295. Bt Spink 1958.

619 Half-sovereign
    6.09   94.0   50°

I.m. annulet with pellet both sides.
Obv.: ☉ hENRIႠ:8·D:G:ΛGL':FRΛNႠI:Z·hIB:REX·
Trefoil stops, double after ΛGL' and REX. Gothic letters. Annulet on inner circle after REX.
Rev.: ☉ IhS·ΛVTE:TRΛNSIENS:PERMEDI:ILLOR:IBΛT·
Trefoil stops, the stop after IBΛT on cross of crown. Gothic letters. No annulet on inner circle.
Whitton, Tower, type II(b), 6; North 1827; Seaby 2295 var. Bt Spink 1962; ex Baptist College, Bristol; ex Gifford.

THIRD PERIOD (*cont.*)

Half-sovereigns (*cont.*)

Tower I and II mints (*cont.*)

TYPE IIb (*cont.*)

620 Half-sovereign			
	Weight		
g	*gr.*	*Die-axis*	
6.04	93.2	120°	

I.m. annulet with pellet both sides.
Obv.: Ⓞ hꞓNRIꞀ⸴8⸴D⸴G⸴ⱭGL⸴⸴FRⱭNꞀI⸴Z⸴hIB⸴RꞓXⰞ
Sleeve stops, double after ⱭGL', hIB and RꞓX. Gothic letters.
Rev.: Ⓞ IhS⸴ⱭVTꞓ⸴TRⱭNSIꞓNS⸴PꞓRMꞓDI⸴ILLOR⸴IBⱭT
Sleeve stops. Gothic letters.
Whitton, Tower, type II(b), 7; North 1827; Seaby 2294. Ex Glendining sale 20.5.1969 (5).

Southwark mint

TYPE IIb. Nominal fineness 20ct (0.833 fine) and weight 96gr. (6.221g). Value 10s 0d.

Initial marks:　　　　　S
　　　　　　　　　　　E

621 Half-sovereign			
5.98	92.3	30°	

I.m. S both sides.
Obv.: S HENRIꞀ⁚8⁚D⁚G⁚AGL'⁚FRⱭNꞀI⁚[ ]⁚[ ]IB⁚REX⁚
Saltire stops, double after 8 and possibly elsewhere, but not visible.
Mixed large Roman and Gothic letters.
Rev.: S⁚IhS⁚ⱭVTꞓ⁚TRⱭNSI⁚PꞓRMꞓDIVM⁚ILLOR⁚IBⱭT⁚
Trefoil stops. Gothic letters. ꞓ below shield.
Whitton, Southwark, type II(b), i.m. S(b), 1/3; North 1828; Seaby 2296. Bt Spink 1975.

Angel, half- and quarter-angel

Issued at a nominal fineness of 23 ct (0.958 fine) and weight of 80 gr. (5.184 g) for the angel of 8s 0d.

Initial mark:　　　　　Lis　　　　　May 1542–March 1545 (when the coinage of 23 ct gold ceased)

Tower mint

622 Angel			
5.18	79.9	110°	

I.m. lis both sides.
Obv.: ✠ hꞓNRIꞀᵖ⸴8⸴D⸴G⸴ⱭGL⸴FRⱭ⸴Z⸴hIB⸴RꞓXⰞ/°
Slipped trefoil stops. Large crook-shaped abbreviation mark after hꞓNRIꞀ.
Annulet by head. Gothic letters.
Rev.: ✠ PꞓR⸴ꞀRVꞀꞓ⸴TVⱭ⸴SⱭLVⱭ⸴NOS⸴XPꞓ⸴RꞓDꞓ⸴
Slipped trefoil stops. Annulet on ship. Gothic letters.
Whitton, standard type; North 1830; Seaby 2299. Ex Lockett (3215).

623 Angel			
5.15	79.5	70°	

I.m. lis both sides.
Obv.: ✠ hꞓNRIꞀᵖ⸴8⸴D⸴G⸴ⱭGL⸴FRⱭ⸴Z⸴hIB⸴RꞓX⸴
Slipped trefoil stops. Large crook-shaped abbreviation mark after hꞓNRIꞀ. No annulet by head. Gothic letters.
Rev.: ✠ PꞓR⸴ꞀRVꞀꞓ⸴TVⱭ⸴SⱭLVⱭ⸴NOS⸴XPꞓ⸴RꞓDꞓ⸴
Slipped trefoil stops. No annulet on ship. Gothic letters.
Whitton, variant – (but published in Schneider 1952–4 and there designated as variant 3); North 1830; Seaby 2300. Bt Baldwin; ex Carter.

[*continued overleaf*]

PLATE 58

620 621 622 623

624 625 626 627 628 629

630 631 632 633 634

Plate 58 (*cont.*)

624 Angel
    5.18   79.9   10°

I.m. lis both sides.
Obv.: ✚hᏮNRIᏇ⁹×8×D'×G×ᏗGL'×FRᏗ'×Z×hI'×RᏮX/°
Slipped trefoil stops. Large crook-shaped abbreviation mark after hᏮNRIᏇ.
Annulet by head. Gothic letters.
Rev.: ✚PᏮR×ᏇRVᏇᏮ×TVᏗ'×SᏗLVᏗ'×ⴖOS×XPᏮ'×RᏮDᏮ'×
Slipped trefoil stops. Annulet on ship. Gothic letters.
Whitton, standard type; North 1830; Seaby 2300. No provenance.

625 Half-angel
    2.48   37.8   290°

I.m. lis both sides.
Obv.: ✚hᏮ'RIᏇ⁹×8×D'×G'×ᏗL'×FR'×Z×hB'×RᏮX
Slipped trefoil stops (possibly from a damaged saltire punch). Large crook-
shaped abbreviation mark after hᏮ'RIᏇ. Gothic letters.
Rev.: ✚O×ᏇRVX×ᏗVᏮ×SPᏮS×VⴖIᏗ×   Double saltire stops. Gothic letters.
Whitton, variant 1; North 1831; Seaby 2302. Bt Spink 1958.

626 Half-angel
    2.52   38.9   340°

I.m. lis both sides.
Obv.: ✚hᏮNRIᏇ'×8×D'×G'×ᏗGL'×FR'×Z×hIB'×RᏮX
Slipped trefoil stops. Gothic letters.
Rev.: ✚O°ᏇRVX°ᏗVᏮ°SPᏮS°VⴖIᏗ°   Annulet stops. Annulet on ship. Gothic
letters.
Whitton, variant 3 but var. with trefoil stops on obverse; North 1831; Seaby 2301. Ex
Ryan (200); ex Montagu (727); ex Brice.

627 Half-angel
    2.58   39.8   200°

I.m. lis both sides.
Obv.: ✚hᏮNRIᏇ⁹×8×D×G×ᏗGL×FR×Z×hIB×RᏮX
Saltire stops. Large crook-shaped abbreviation mark after hᏮNRIᏇ. Gothic
letters.
Rev.: ✚O°ᏇRVX°ᏗVᏮ°SPᏮS°VⴖIᏗ°   Annulet stops. Three annulets on ship.
Gothic letters.
Whitton, variant 1; North 1831; Seaby 2303. Ex Lockett (1745); ex Roth (219); ex
Montagu (728); ex Brice.

628 Quarter-angel
    1.32   20.3   270°

I.m. lis both sides.
Obv.: ✚hᏮNRIᏇVS VIII DᏮI GRᏗ ᏗGL/I   No stops. Roman N in
hᏮNRIᏇVS, other letters Gothic. Angel of early style.
Rev.: ✚FRᏗNᏇIᏮ×ᏮT×hIBᏮRNIᏮ×RᏮX   Slipped trefoil stops. Roman Ns, other
letters Gothic.
Whitton, variant 1; North 1832; Seaby 2304. Bt Baldwin; ex Carter.

629 Quarter-angel
    1.21   18.7   200°

I.m. lis both sides.
Obv.: ✚hᏮNRIᏇVS×VIII×DI×GRᏗ×ᏗGLIᏮ×   Slipped trefoil stops. Roman Ns,
other letters Gothic. Angel of early style.
Rev.: ✚FRᏗNᏇ×ᏮT×hIBᏮRNIᏮ×RᏮX×   Slipped trefoil stops. Roman Ns, other
letters Gothic.
Whitton, variant 1; North 1832; Seaby 2304. No provenance.

630 Quarter-angel
    1.29   19.9   260°

I.m. lis both sides.
Obv.: ✚hᏮNRIᏇVS×VIII×DᏮI×GRᏗ×ᏗGLII/Ꮾ   Slipped trefoil stops. Gothic let-
ters. Angel of late style.
Rev.: ✚FRᏗNᏇIᏮ××ᏮT××hIBᏮRNIᏮ×RᏮX   Slipped trefoil stops. Gothic
letters.
Whitton, variant 2; North 1833; Seaby 2304A. Ex J. C. S. Rashleigh (27).

Plate 58 (*cont.*)

Crown of the double rose and half-crown

Issued at a nominal fineness of 22 or 20 ct (0.917 or 0.833 fine) and a weight of 48 gr. (3.110 g) to the crown of the double rose of 5s 0d.

Initial mark: Annulet with pellet

Tower I and II mints

631 Crown of the double rose
     3.07   47.4   350°

I.m. annulet with pellet both sides.
Obv.: ☉ hЄNRIɑ'⸰8⸸ROSɅ⸸SINЄ⸴SPINЄ⸴
Double sleeve stops, single after hЄNRIɑ' and SPINЄ. Є of SPINЄ punched over an Є on its side. RVTILɅNS omitted. Crowned h–R by rose. Gothic letters.
Rev.: ☉ DЄI'⸴GRɅ'⸴ɅGL'⸴FRɅ'⸴Z⸴hIB'⸴RЄX
Sleeve stops, double after GRɅ'. Crowned h–R by shield. Gothic letters.
Whitton, Tower, variant 1; North 1834; Seaby 2306. No provenance.

632 Crown of the double rose
     3.00   46.3   10°

I.m. annulet with pellet both sides.
Obv.: ☉ ⸰hЄNRIɑ'⸱8⸱ROSɅ⸸SINЄ⸸SPINЄ⸸
Double slipped trefoil stops, single after hЄNRIɑ' and 8'. Pellet before hЄNRIɑ'. RVTILɅNS omitted. Crowned h–R by rose. Gothic letters.
Rev.: ☉ DЄI⸸GRɅ'⸱ɅGL'⸸FRɅ'⸱ЄT⸸hIB'RЄX⸱
Slipped trefoil stops, double after DЄI, ɅGL' and ЄT. Reads ЄT (in place of Z). Crowned H–R by shield. Gothic letters.
Whitton, Tower, variant 1; North 1834; Seaby 2306. No provenance.

633 Crown of the double rose
     3.13   48.3   160°

I.m. annulet with pellet both sides.
Obv.: ☉ hЄNRIɑ'⸱8⸱ROSɅ⸸SINЄ⸸SPIN   Slipped trefoil stops, double after ROSɅ and SINЄ. RVTILɅNS omitted. Crowned h–R by rose. Annulet on inner circle under S of SPIN. Gothic letters.
Rev.: ☉ ⸱DЄI'⸱GRɅ'⸱ɅGL'⸸FRɅ'⸱Z⸱hIB'⸸RЄX⸸   Slipped trefoil stops, double after ɅGL', hIB' and RЄX. Crowned h R by shield. Annulet on inner circle under Є of RЄX. Gothic letters.
Whitton, Tower, variant 2; North 1834; Seaby 2307. Bt Baldwin 1968.

634 Crown of the double rose
     3.13   48.3   130°

I.m. annulet with pellet both sides.
Obv.: ☉ hЄNRIɑ'⸱8⸱RVTILɅ'⸱ROSɅ⸱SINЄ⸱SPI⸱   Slipped trefoil stops. Crowned Roman H–R by rose, otherwise Gothic letters.
Rev.: ☉ DI'⸱GRɅ'⸱ɅGLI'⸱FRɅNɑ'⸱Z⸱hIB'⸱RЄX⸱   Slipped trefoil stops. Crowned Roman H–R by shield, otherwise Gothic letters.
Whitton, Tower, variant 3; North 1834; Seaby 2305. No provenance.

THIRD PERIOD (*cont.*)

Crown of the double rose and half-crown (*cont.*)

Tower I and II mints (*cont.*)

635 Crown of the double rose

	Weight	
g	*gr.*	*Die-axis*
3.09	47.7	150°

I.m. annulet with pellet both sides.
Obv.: ☉ hENRIɑ⁹×8×RVTILA̶'×ROSA̶×SINE×SPI'×   Slipped trefoil stops. Large crook-shaped abbreviation mark after hENRIɑ. Crowned h–R by rose. Gothic letters.
Rev.: ☉ DI'×GRA̶'×A̶GLI'×FRA̶Nɑ'×Z×hIB'×REX×   Slipped trefoil stops. Crowned Roman H–R by shield, otherwise Gothic letters.
Whitton, Tower, variant – (but this variety with the Roman H in the reverse field is published in Schneider 1952–4 where it is designated variant 4); North 1834; Seaby 2305 var. No provenance.

636 Half-crown

1.53	23.6	290°

I.m. annulet with pellet both sides.
Obv.: ☉ RVTILA̶NS×ROSA̶×SINE×SPIN   Slipped trefoil stops. h–R by rose. Gothic letters.
Rev.: ☉ hENRIɑ⁹×8×D×G×A̶G'×FR'×Z×hIB'×REX×   Slipped trefoil stops. Large crook-shaped abbreviation mark after hENRIɑ. h–R by shield. Annulet on inner circle below R of REX. Gothic letters.
Whitton, Tower, variant 1 (but legend variety unknown to him and published in Schneider 1952–4); North 1837; Seaby 2312. No provenance.

637 Half-crown

1.57	24.2	270°

I.m. annulet with pellet both sides.
Obv.: ☉ RVTILA̶NS⁝ROSA̶⁝SINE⁝SPINA̶   Double slipped trefoil stops. h–R by rose. Gothic letters.
Rev.: ☉ hENRIɑ⁹×8×D'×G'×A̶GL'×FR'×Z×hB'×REX   Slipped trefoil stops. Large crook-shaped abbreviation mark after hENRIɑ. h–R by shield. Gothic letters.
Whitton, Tower, variant 2 (but legend variety unknown to him and published in Schneider 1952–4); North 1837; Seaby 2311. Ex Hird private sale); ex Ryan (182).

638 Half-crown

1.55	24.0	330°

I.m. annulet with pellet both sides.
Obv.: ☉ RVTILA̶NS⁝ROSA̶⁝SINE'[   ]   Double saltire stops. h–R by rose. Gothic letters.
Rev.: ☉ h[   ]⁹×8×D⁝G⁝A̶GL⁝FR⁝Z×hIB⁝REX   Saltire stops. Large crook-shaped abbreviation mark after hENRIɑ. h–R by shield. Gothic letters.
Whitton, Tower, variant 2; North 1837; Seaby 2311. Ex Gantz (1165).

639 Half-crown

1.50	23.2	170°

I.m. annulet with pellet both sides.
Obv.: ☉ RVTILANS⁝ROSA⁝SINE⁝SPIN×   Double slipped trefoil stops, single after SPIN. h–R by rose, otherwise Roman letters.
Rev.: ☉ HENRIɑ'×8 D'×G×AGL'×FR'×Z×HI×REX   Slipped trefoil stops. h–R by shield. Mixed, mainly Roman letters. H with ornamental cross-bar.
Whitton, Tower, variant 4; North 1837; Seaby 2311. Ex Lockett (1786).

[*continued overleaf*]

PLATE 59

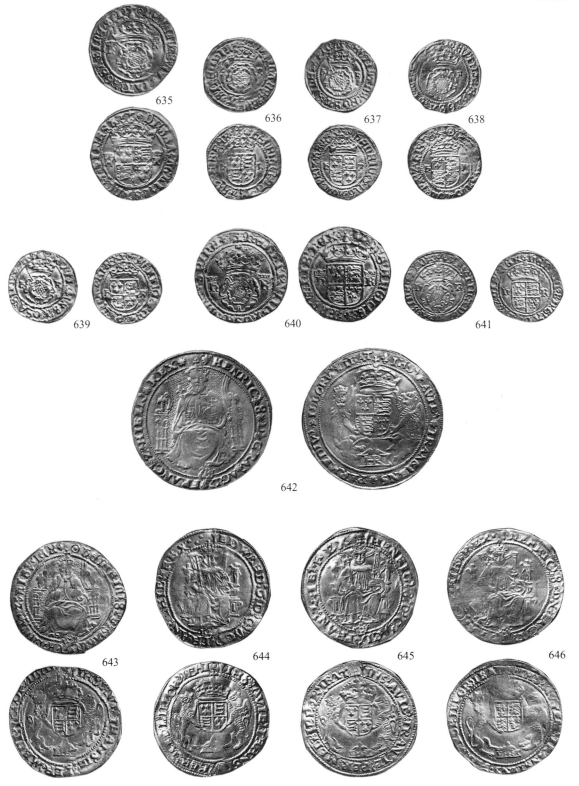

635

636

637

638

639

640

641

642

643

644

645

646

Plate 59 (*cont.*)

Bristol mint

Issued at a nominal fineness of 20 ct (0.833 fine) and weight of 48 gr. (3.110 g) to the crown of the double rose of 5s 0d.

Characteristics: Usually double saltire stops on the obverse and pellet stops on the reverse. Distinctive Bristol (Gothic) lettering.

Initial mark: WS monogram

640 Crown of the double rose   I.m. none/WS monogram.
     3.16   48.7   80°   *Obv.*: ×hENRIɊ. VIIIₒROSA·SINEₒSPINA+×
                                   A variety of stops. Bristol lettering. Crowned h–R by rose.
                             Rev.: .VS̸ .D˸.G˸.ANGLIE×˸FRA˸.Z.hIB˸.REX: Pellet stops varied by saltires
                                   and a cross after ANGLIE. Crowned h–R by shield.
                              Whitton, Bristol, variant 2; North 1836; Seaby 2309. Ex Spink auction 21.5.1991 (12).

641 Half-crown   I.m. WS monogram/none.
     1.63   25.1   120°   *Obv.*: .VS̸ .RVTILANS˸ROSA˸SINE×SPINA   Single saltire stop after SINE.
                                 h–R by rose.
                             Rev.: hENRIɊ⁹8.D˸.G˸.ANG.FR˸.Z.hIB˸.REX   h–R by shield.
                              Whitton, Bristol, sole type; North 1839; Seaby 2315. Ex Norweb (905); ex Lockett
                              (1790).

EDWARD VI (28 January 1547–19 July 1553)

FIRST PERIOD (5 April 1547–24 January 1549)

Gold coinage of 20 ct (0.833 fine) issued at a nominal weight of 192 gr. (12.441 g) to the sovereign of 20s 0d and 48 gr. (3.110 g) to the crown of 5s 0d. Denominations struck were sovereign, half-sovereign, crown and half-crown. These coins continue to be classified according to Whitton 1949–51.

Characteristics: Roman letters. Most coins in the name of Henry VIII, a few in the name of Edward VI (**644, 648, 653, 665** in this collection). All half-sovereigns, however, have the face of Edward VI. Crowns usually have Roman **H–R** by shield and rose (except that the coins in the name of **EDWARD** have **E–R**); half-crowns more often have Gothic letters in these positions.

Tower I mint

Initial marks: Lis florencée. Sovereign only.
                              Arrow, lozenge stops, some in Edward's name
                              Àrrow, pierced cross stops
                              Lis, pellet stops

642 Sovereign   I.m. lis florencée both sides.
     12.34   190.5   30°   *Obv.*: ✠HENRIC˸8ₒD˸GRA˸AGL˸FRANC˸Z ₒHIBER˸REXₒ
                                   Rosette stops.
                             Rev.: ✠IHSₒAVTEₒTRANCIENSₒPERMEDIVₒILLORVₒIBAT
                                 Rosette stops. C of TRANCIENS over S.
                              Whitton p. 87, pl. VI, 1/3, same dies; North 1863; Seaby 2389. Bt Seaby 1952.

Plate 59 (*cont.*)

643 Half-sovereign
    6.24   96.3   310°

I.m. annulet with pellet/arrow (mule Henry VIII/Edward VI).

Obv.:   ⊙ hENRIꓚ'⸝8'⸝D'⸝G'⸝ᴧGL'⸝FRᴧΠꓚI ZᔕhIB'⸝REX⸝
        Legend unclear, in part due to double striking. Sleeve stops, double after Z and
        hIB'. Gothic letters.

Rev.:   ⫯IHSᵖ◇AVT⁝TRANSIE⁝PER⁝MEDI⁝ILLOR⁝IBAT⁝
        Legend unclear, in part due to double striking. Lozenge stops. Roman letters.

This is the coin referred to in Schneider 1955–7b. Whitton, Tower, Henry VIII, II(b),
variant 7/ Tower, Edward VI, variant 2 with E not broken; North 1827/1865; Seaby
2294/2391. Bt Spink 1958.

644 Half-sovereign
    6.07   93.7   310°

I.m. arrow both sides.

Obv.:   ⫯EDWARD⁝6⁝D⁝G⁝AG◇⁝FRAN'⁝Z⁝HIB'⁝REX◇◇◇ With Edward's name.
        Lozenge stops, double after FRAN', HIB' and REX.

Rev.:   ⫯IHS⁝AVTE⁝TRANSIE⁝PER⁝MEDI⁝ILLOR⁝IBAT◇
        Lozenge stops, double after PER.

Whitton, Tower, p. 88, variant 1; North 1892; Seaby 2429. Bt Spink 1951.

645 Half-sovereign
    6.12   94.4   50°

I.m. arrow both sides.

Obv.:   ⫯HENRIꓚ⁝8⁝D⁝G⁝AGL◇⁝FRAN⁝Z HIB'⁝REX(◇◇◇?)
        Lozenge stops, double after HIB' and, perhaps, REX.

Rev.:   ⫯IHS⁝AVTE⁝TRANSIE⁝PER⁝MEDI⁝ILLOR⁝IBAT
        Lozenge stops, double after PER.

Whitton, Tower, p. 88, variant 2; North 1865; Seaby 2391. Ex Ryan (206).

646 Half-sovereign
    6.21   95.9   100°

I.m. arrow/lis.

Obv.:   ⫯HENRIꓚ⁝8◇D⁝G⁝AGL⁝FRANC◇Z⁝HIB⁝REX◇
        Lozenge stops.

Rev.:   ✚IHS:AVTEM:TRANSIENS:PERMEDI:ILLOR:IBAT
        Pellet stops.

Whitton, Tower mule, p. 88; North 1865; Seaby 2391. Bt Baldwin 1961.

FIRST PERIOD (*cont.*)

Tower I mint (cont.)

	Weight		
	g	*gr.*	*Die-axis*

647 Half-sovereign
5.97   92.1   190°

I.m. lis both sides.
Obv.: ✠ HENRIC⦂8⦂D᾽G⦂.AGI᾽⦂FRANCIE⦂Z⦂HIB᾽⦂REX⦂
Double pellet stops, single after HENRIC᾽ and G᾽, none after D᾽.
Rev.: ✠ IHS⦂AVTE⦂TRANSIE⦂PERMEDI⦂ILLOR᾽IBA
Pellet stops.
Whitton, Tower, p. 88; North 1865; Seaby 2391. Ex Schulman sale 15.11.1966 (702);
ex Serooskerke hoard.

648 Crown
3.12   48.1   310°

I.m. arrow both sides.
Obv.: ⌇RVTILANS⦂ROSA⦂SINE⦂SPINE⦂◊⦂◊◊   Double lozenge stops. King's
name and numeral omitted and in the resulting spare space five additional
lozenges are inserted at the end of the legend. Crowned Roman E–R by rose.
Rev.: ⌇EDWARD᾽⦂6⦂D◊G᾽⦂AG᾽⦂FR᾽⦂Z⦂HIB᾽⦂REX◊
Reads EDWARD. Double lozenge stops, single after D᾽, HIB᾽ and REX.
Crowned Roman E–R by shield.
Whitton, Tower, p. 180, variant 1; North 1894; Seaby 2431. Ex Ryan (226); ex
Murdoch (458); ex Montagu (787); ex Addington; ex Murchison (158).

649 Crown
3.28   50.6   260°

I.m. arrow both sides.
Obv.: ⌇HENRIC⦂8⦂RVTILA⦂ROSA⦂SINE⦂SPI
Double lozenge stops, single after HENRIC᾽. Crowned Roman H–R by rose.
Rev.: ⌇DEI⦂GRA◊AGL◊FRA◊Z HIB◊REX⦂◊
Lozenge stops, triple after REX.
Crowned Roman H–R by shield.
Whitton, Tower, p. 180, normal type; North 1867; Seaby 2395. Bt Baldwin; ex Carter.

650 Crown
3.03   46.7   310°

I.m. arrow both sides.
Obv.: ⌇HENRIC⦂8◊RVTILA◊ROS᾽⦂SIN◊SPI◊
Lozenge stops, double after ROS᾽. Crowned Roman H–R by rose.
Rev.: ⌇HENRIC⦂D⦂G⦂RVTILANS.ROSA.SINE.SP   Pellet stops. Crowned
Roman H–R by shield.
Whitton, Tower, p. 180, normal type/variant 2 (this combination not recorded by him);
North 1867; Seaby 2396. Bt Seaby 1962.

651 Half-crown
1.44   22.2   130°

I.m. annulet with pellet both sides.
Obv.: ⊙ RVTILANS◊ROSA᾽⦂SINE⦂SPI⦂   Double lozenge stops, single after
RVTILANS. Gothic h–R by rose.
Rev.: ⊙ HENRIC⦂8⦂C⦂G⦂AGI⦂FR◊Z◊HIB᾽   Double lozenge stops, single after Z.
C for D[ei]. Gothic h–R by shield.
Whitton, Tower, p. 181, Henry VIII variant 4 (attributed by him to Edward VI on the
grounds of the lozenge stops); North 1837 (Henry VIII); Seaby –. Ex Ryan (183).

652 Half-crown
1.49   23.0   0°

I.m. annulet with pellet/arrow.
Obv.: ⊙ RVTILANS⦂RSA◊SINE⦂SPI◊◊   Double lozenge stops, single after
RSA. Gothic h–R by rose.
Rev.: ⌇HENRIC⦂8⦂D◊G◊AG◊FR◊Z HI◊REX   Lozenge stops, double after 8,
none after Z. Gothic h–R by shield.
Whitton, Tower, p. 181, mule; North 1837/1869; Seaby 2311/2399. Ex Lockett (1848).

[*continued overleaf*]

PLATE 60

647

648

649

650

651

652

653

654

655

656

657

658

659

Plate 60 (*cont.*)

653 Half-crown
    1.58   24.4   320°

I.m. arrow both sides.
Obv.: ⚑RVTILANS⚬⚬ROSA⚬⚬SINE⚬SPIN[ ]   Double lozenge stops, single after SINE. Roman E–R by rose.
Rev.: ⚑EDWARD⚬⚬6⚬D⚬G⚬AG⚬FR⚬Z HI⚬REX   Reads EDWARD. Lozenge stops. Roman E–R by shield. On his ticket and in his paper in *BNJ* 1952–4, p. 202, Mr Schneider refers to this coin as having an annulet on the inner circle of the reverse at 4 o'clock. In the opinion of the writer this is without doubt the punctuation lozenge between EDWARD' and D' punched in a little lower than normal.
Whitton, Tower, p. 181, variant 1; Schneider 1952–4, p. 202; North 1895; Seaby 2432. Ex Ryan (227); ex Murdoch (459); ex Montagu (788); ex Shepherd (238); ex Hoare (219).

654 Half-crown
    1.49   23.0   100°

I.m. arrow both sides.
Obv.: ⚑RVTILANS⚬ROSA⚬SINE SP'   Lozenge stops. Gothic h–R by rose.
Rev.: ⚑HENRIC⚬⚬8⚬D⚬G⚬AG⚬FR Z⚬HB⚬RE   Lozenge stops. Gothic h–R by shield.
Whitton, Tower, p. 181, standard type; North 1869; Seaby 2399. Ex Hird (private sale).

655 Half-crown
    1.47   22.7   160°

I.m. arrow/arrow inverted.
Obv.: ⚑RVTILANS⚬ROSA⚬SINE⚬SPI   Lozenge stops. Gothic h–R by rose.
Rev.: ⚑HENRIC×8×D×G×AG×FR×Ɛ×HI×REX   Saltire stops. Ampersand ET ligated. Gothic h–R by shield.
Whitton, Tower, p. 182, variant 2; Schneider 1952–4, p. 202; North 1869; Seaby 2399. Bt Baldwin 1952; ex Carter.

Tower II mint

Initial marks: K, lozenge stops
    Grapple, lozenge, then pellet stops
    Martlet, pellet stops

656 Half-sovereign
    6.17   95.2   280°

I.m. none either side but with K below shield.
Obv.: HENRIC⚬⚬8⚬⚬DEI⚬GRA'AGL⚬FRA⚬Z⚬HIB⚬REX   Lozenge stops, double after 8, none after GRA'.
Rev.: IHS⚬AVTEM⚬TRANSIENS⚬PERMEDI⚬ILLOR⚬IBAT⚬   Lozenge stops. K below shield.
Whitton, Tower, p. 88; North 1865; Seaby 2392. Ex Dangar (111).

657 Half-sovereign
    6.22   96.0   190°

I.m. none/K and another K below shield.
Obv.: HENRIC⚬8⚬⚬D⚬G⚬AGL⚬⚬FRA⚬Z⚬HIB⚬⚬REX⚬⚬   Lozenge stops, double after 8, AGL' and triple after REX.
Rev.: K⚬IHS⚬AVTEM⚬TRANSIENS⚬PER⚬MEDIV⚬ILLO⚬IBAT⚬   Lozenge stops. K below shield.
Whitton, Tower, p. 88; North 1865; Seaby 2392. No provenance.

658 Half-sovereign
    6.10   94.2   130°

I.m. none either side but with grapple below shield.
Obv.: HENRIC⚬8⚬D⚬G⚬AGL⚬⚬FRANC⚬Z HIB⚬REX⚬   Lozenge stops, double after AGL'.
Rev.: ⚬IHS⚬AVTE⚬TRANSIE⚬PER⚬MEDIV⚬ILLOR⚬IBA⚬   Very small lozenge stops or pellets. Grapple below shield.
Whitton, Tower, p. 88, but lozenge stops not recorded by him for the grapple mark; North 1865; Seaby 2393. Ex Oman (173).

659 Half-sovereign
    6.25   96.4   340°

I.m. grapple both sides and under shield.
Obv.: ⚷HENRIC·8·DEI·GRA·AGL:FRA:Z·HIB·REX·   Pellet stops.
Rev.: ⚷IHS·AVTE:TRANSIEN·PER:MEDIV:ILLO:IBAT·   Pellet stops. Grapple below shield.
Whitton, Tower, p. 88; North 1865; Seaby 2393. Ex Lockett (1843).

FIRST PERIOD (*cont.*)

Tower II mint (*cont.*)

660 Half-sovereign

	Weight	
g	*gr.*	*Die-axis*
6.22	96.0	250°

I.m. martlet both sides.
Obv.: ❦HENRI.·C·: 8·.·D: G: AGL': FRA: ZHIB: REX
Pellet stops, double after **HENRI, C**, and **AGL'**. Triple after 8.
Rev.: ❦IHS: AVTE: TRANSIENS: PER·MEDIV: ILLO: IBAT
Pellet stops. No mark below shield.
Whitton, Tower, p. 88; North 1865; Seaby 2391. Ex Lockett (1844).

661 Crown
3.03	46.8	170°

I.m. none/K.
Obv.: HENRIC◊8◊RVTILANS◊ROSA◊SINE◊SPI◊   Lozenge stops. Crowned Roman **H–R** by rose.
Rev.: K◊DEI◊GRA◊AGL◊FRANC◊Z◊HIB◊REX   Lozenge stops. Crowned Roman **H–R** by shield.
Whitton, Tower, p. 180; North 1867; Seaby 2395. Ex Hird (17); ex Spurgin (7).

662 Crown
3.10	47.9	190°

I.m. martlet both sides.
Obv.: ❦HENRIC: 8·.·RVTILANS: ROSA: SIN: SP   Pellet stops, triple after 8. Crowned Roman **H–R** by rose.
Rev.: ❦DEI: GRA: AGL: FRA: Z·HIBE: REX   Pellet stops. Crowned Roman **H–R** by shield.
Whitton, Tower, p. 181; North 1867; Seaby 2395. Ex O'Byrne (24).

663 Half-crown
1.57	24.3	140°

I.m. martlet both sides.
Obv.: ❦RVTILANS·ROSA·SIN·SP   Pellet stops. Roman **H–R** by rose.
Rev.: ❦HENRIC: 8: D: G: AG: FR: Z·HI REX   Pellet stops. Roman **H–R** by shield.
Whitton, Tower, p. 182; North 1869; Seaby 2399. Bt Baldwin 1953.

664 Half-crown
1.56	24.0	190°

I.m. martlet both sides.
Obv.: ❦RV.TILANS·ROSA·SINE·SPI.   Pellet stops; pellet between **V** and **T** of **RVTILANS**. Roman **H–R** by rose.
Rev.: ❦HENRIC: 8 D: G: AG: FR: Z·HI: REX   Pellet stops. Roman **H–R** by shield.
Whitton, Tower, p. 182; North 1869; Seaby 2399. Ex Raynes (89).

Southwark mint

Initial marks: E
                 S

665 Half-sovereign
6.02	92.9	120°

I.m. Roman E over arrow/Roman E.
Obv.: E◊EDWARD⅜6◊D◊G◊AG◊FRAN◊Z◊HIB◊REX◊◊◊   Reads **EDWARD**. Lozenge stops, double after **EDWARD**, triple after **REX**.
Rev.: E◊IHS◊AVTEM◊TRANSIES◊PERMEDI◊ILLOR◊IBAT◊   Lozenge stops. E below shield.
Whitton, Southwark, p. 88, variant 1; North 1893; Seaby 2430. Bt Spink 1972; ex Cartwright.

666 Half-sovereign
6.05	93.4	0°

I.m. Roman E both sides.
Obv.: E◊HENRIC◊8⅜D⅜G⅜AGL⅜FRANC◊Z◊HIB⅜REX⅜   Double lozenge stops, single after E, **HENRIC'**, **FRANC** and **Z**.
Rev.: E◊IHS◊AVTEM◊TRANSIES◊PERMEDI◊ILLOR◊IBAT◊   Lozenge stops. E below shield.
Whitton, Southwark, pp. 88–9, standard type; North 1866; Seaby 2394. Bt Spink 1972; ex Cartwright.

[*continued overleaf*]

PLATE 61

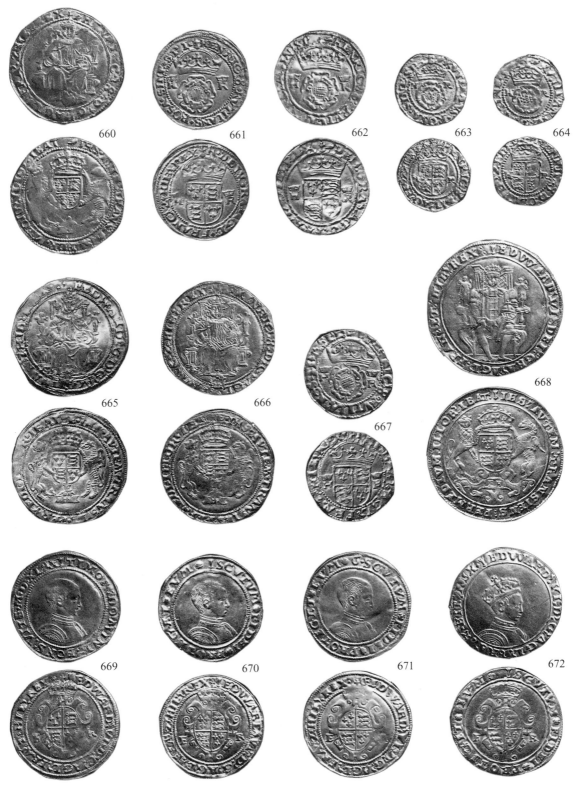

660   661   662   663   664

665   666   667   668

669   670   671   672

Plate 61 (*cont.*)

667 Crown
    2.84   43.8   60°   I.m. Roman E/none.
                                            Obv.: E HENRIC⸲8⬦RVTILA'ROS⸲SIN⸲SPI⸲ Lozenge stops. Crowned Roman
                                            H–R by rose.
                                          Rev.: DEI⬦GRA'⸲AGL'⬦FRA'⬦Z⬦HIB'⬦REX⬦ Lozenge stops. Crowned Roman
                                            H–R by shield.
                                          Whitton, Southwark, p. 181, variant 1 (also discussed by him on p. 176); North 1868;
                                          Seaby 2398. Bt Baldwin 1970.

SECOND PERIOD (24 January 1549–18 December 1550)

Gold coinage of 22 ct (0.917 fine) issued at a nominal weight of $169\frac{7}{17}$ gr. (10.977 g) to the sovereign of 20s 0d and 43 gr. (2.786 g) to the crown of 5s 0d. Denominations struck were sovereign, half-sovereign, crown and half-crown. Gold was struck at the mints of Tower I, Tower II, Durham House and Southwark. The classification used is that put forward in Potter 1962.

Characteristics: Roman letters. Sovereigns continue to be of the seated, facing king type; other denominations have the king's bust to right, on earlier varieties the bust is bare headed, on later varieties the bust is crowned.

Tower I mint

Initial marks: Arrow
                     6 (placed here provisionally, see p. 64)
                     Swan

668 Sovereign
    10.90   168.2   30°   I.m. arrow both sides.
                                          Obv.: ⸸EDWARD'VI:DEI:GRA:AGL:FRAN:ET:HIB':REX:
                                          Small square stops, single after GRA', AGL' and FRAN'.
                                          Rev.: IHS:AVTEM:TRANSIENS:PERMEDIVM:ILLOR:IBAT.
                                          Small square stops, single after IHS', ILLOR' and IBAT.
                                          Potter, p. 135; North 1906; Seaby 2433. Bt Baldwin 1951; ex Carter.

669 Half-sovereign, 1549
    5.42   83.7   230°   I.m. arrow both sides.
                                          Obv.: ⸸TIMOR:DOMINI:FONS:VITE.M.D.XL.IX
                                          Uncrowned bust. Small square stops, double after TIMOR, DOMINI and
                                          FONS.
                                          Rev.: ⸸EDWARD:VI.D:G:AGL:FRA:Z.HIB:REX. Small square stops.
                                          Potter, p. 135, type 1(a); North 1907; Seaby 2434. Ex Lockett (1859); ex Rostron
                                          (130); ex Murchison (165); ex Dymock (255); ex Cuff (1021).

670 Half-sovereign
    5.36   82.7   340°   I.m. arrow both sides.
                                          Obv.: ⸸SCVTVM✠FIDEI✠PROTEGET✠EVM✠ Uncrowned bust. Rosette stops.
                                          Rev.: ⸸EDWARD:VI.D:G:AGL:FRA:Z.HIB:REX Small square stops, double
                                          after VI.
                                          Potter, p. 135, type 1(b); North 1908; Seaby 2435. Bt Spink 1972; ex Cartwright.

671 Half-sovereign
    5.31   81.9   70°   I.m. 6 both sides.
                                          Obv.: 6.SCVTVM✠FIDEI✠PROTEGET✠EVM✠ Uncrowned bust. Rosette stops,
                                          except for small square stop between the i m and SCVTVM.
                                          Rev.: 6.EDWARD:VI.D:G:AGL:FRA:Z.HIB:REX. Small square stops.
                                            Potter, p. 135, type 1(b); North 1908; Seaby 2435. Ex Hird (private sale); ex Lockett
                                          (1861).

672 Half-sovereign
    4.76   73.5   0°   I.m. arrow both sides.
                                          Obv.: ⸸EDWARD:VI:D:G:AGL:FRA:Z.HIB:REX. Crowned bust. Small square
                                          stops, double after VI. Plain breast armour.
                                          Rev.: ⸸SCVTVM✠FIDEI✠PROTEGET✠EVM✠ Rosette stops.
                                          Potter, p. 135, type 2(a); North 1911; Seaby 2438. Ex Hird (22).

SECOND PERIOD (*cont.*)

Tower I mint (cont.)

673 Half-sovereign

Weight		
g	gr.	Die-axis
5.39	83.2	80°

I.m. swan/arrow.
Obv.: ✿.EDWARD:VI:D:G:AGL:FRA:Z:HIB:REX. Crowned bust. Small square stops, double after **VI** and **Z**. Decorated breast armour.
Rev.: ↓✿SCVTVM✿FIDEI✿PROTEGET✿EVM✿ Rosette stops. EGET✿E struck over wrongly placed **SCVTVM**. Potter, p. 135, type 2(b); North 1911; Seaby 2438. Ex Hird (private sale); ex Carter.

674 Half-sovereign

4.83	74.6	50°

I.m. swan both sides.
Obv.: ✿EDWARD:VI:D:G:AGL:FRA:Z:HIB:REX Crowned bust. Small square stops, double after **VI**. Decorated breast armour.
Rev.: ✿SCVTVM✿FIDEI✿PROTEGET✿EVM✿ Rosette stops.
Potter, p. 135, type 2(b); North 1911; Seaby 2438. No provenance.

675 Half-sovereign

5.40	83.3	180°

I.m. swan both sides.
Obv.: ✿EDWARD:VI:D:G:AGL':FRA:Z:HIB:REX Crowned bust. Small square stops, double after **VI** and **Z**. Decorated breast armour.
Rev.: ✿:SCVTVM:FIDEI:PROTEGET:EVM: Double small square stops.
Potter, p. 135, type 2(b); North 1911; Seaby 2438. Ex Hird (private sale); ex Carter.

676 Crown

2.70	41.6	80°

I.m. arrow/none.
Obv.: ↓SCVTVM:FIDEI:PROTEGET:EVM: Uncrowned bust. Double small square stops.
Rev.: EDWARD:VI:D:G:AGL:FR.Z.HIB:REX Double small square stops, single after **FR** and **Z**. Potter, p. 135, type 1(b); North 1913; Seaby 2441. Bt Spink 1967; ex Viscount Astor.

677 Crown

2.68	41.3	130°

I.m. arrow both sides.
Obv.: ↓EDWARD:VI:D:G:AG:FRA:Z:HIB:REX. Crowned bust. Double small square stops, single after **EDWARD**' and **REX**. Plain breast armour.
Rev.: ↓.SCVTVMFIDEI:PROTEGET:EVM Double small square stops, single after i.m.
Potter, p. 135, type 2(a); North 1914; Seaby 2442. Bt Baldwin; ex Carter.

678 Half-crown

1.31	20.2	60°

I.m. arrow/none.
Obv.: ↓SCVTVM.FIDEI.PROTEGET.EVM Uncrowned bust. Small square stops.
Rev.: EDWAR:VI.D:G:AGL:FR:Z.H:R' Small square stops. Interior of crown frosted.
Potter, p. 135, type 1(b); North 1915; Seaby 2443. Ex Ryan (244).

679 Half-crown

1.37	21.1	20°

I.m. arrow/none.
Obv.: ↓EDWARD.VI.D.G.AG.FR.Z HI.REX Crowned bust. Small square stops.
Rev.: SCVTVM:FIDEI:PROTE:EVM Double square stops.
Potter, p. 135, type 2(a); North 1916; Seaby 2444. Bt Spink 1950.

680 Half-crown

1.39	21.5	350°

I.m. arrow both sides.
Obv.: ↓EDWARD.VI.D.G.AG.FR.Z HI.REX Crowned bust. Small square stops.
Rev.: ↓.SCVTVM.FIDEI.PROTEGET.EVM. Small square stops.
Potter, p. 135, type 2(a); North 1916; Seaby 2444. Ex Hird (private sale).

[*continued overleaf*]

PLATE 62

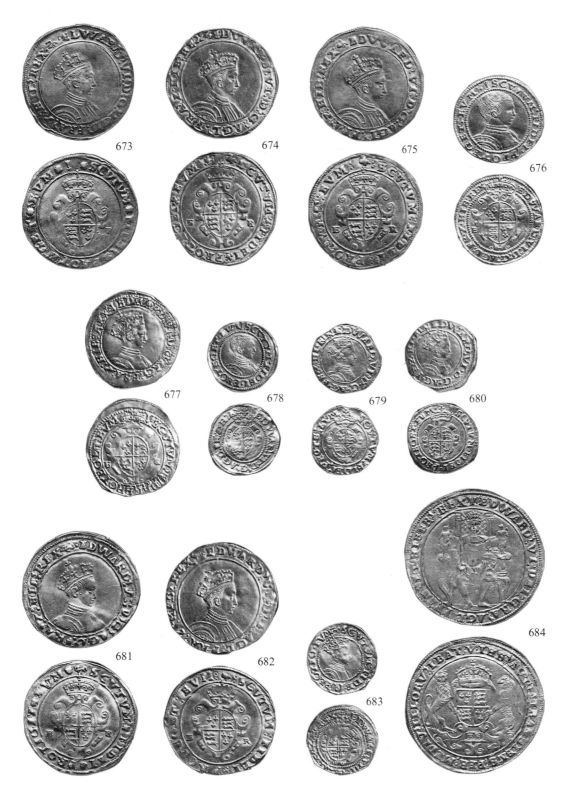

673

674

675

676

677

678

679

680

681

682

683

684

Plate 62 (*cont.*)

Tower II mint

Initial marks: Grapple
                                     Martlet

681 Half-sovereign
      5.38   83.0   330°

I.m. grapple both sides.
Obv.: ℭᵒ.EDWARD:VI:D:G:AGL:FRA:Z:HIB:REX Crowned bust. Small square stops, double after VI and Z. Plain breast armour.
Rev.: ℭᵒSCVTVM✠FIDEI✠PROTEGET✠EVM✠ Rosette stops.
Potter, p. 135, type 2(a); North 1911; Seaby 2438. No provenance.

682 Half-sovereign
      4.92   75.9   0°

I.m. martlet both sides.
Obv: ⚑.EDWARD:VI:D:G:AGL:FRA:Z:HIB:REX Crowned bust. Small square stops, double after VI and Z. Decorated breast armour.
Rev.: ⚑SCVTVM:FIDEI:PROTEGET:EVM: Double small square stops.
Potter, p. 135, type 2(b); North 1911; Seaby 2438. Ex Hird (23).

683 Half-crown
      1.37   21.2   350°

I.m. grapple/none.
Obv.: ℭᵒSCVTVM:FIDEI:PROTEG.EVM Crowned bust. Double small square stops, single after PROTEG. Plain breast armour. Inner circle of small pellets instead of a wire-line.
Rev.: EDWARD.VI D.G.AG.FR Z H.REX Small square stops.
Potter, p. 135, type 2(a) var. with legends transposed between obverse and reverse and with the obverse inner circle of small pellets; North 1916; Seaby 2445. Ex Lockett (1872).

Southwark mint

Initial marks: Y
                           Lis

684 Sovereign
     10.91   168.4   30°

I.m. Y both sides.
Obv.: Y.EDWARD:VI:DEI:GRA:AGL:FRAN:ET:HIBER'.REX.
Small square stops, double after VI, DEI, ET and HIBER'.
Rev.: Y.IHS:AVTE:TRANSIENS:PER:MEDIV:ILLORV:IBAT:
Small square stops, double after TRANSIENS, PER and IBAT.
Potter, p. 133; North 1900; Seaby 2433. Ex Lockett (4340).

SECOND PERIOD (*cont.*)

Southwark mint (cont.)

685 Sovereign

	Weight		
	g	*gr.*	*Die-axis*
	11.12	171.6	130°

I.m. Y both sides.
Obv.: Ⴤ EDWARD:VI:D:G:AGL':FRAN':ET:HIB':REX⊙:
Double, small, square stops, single after **EDWARD'**, **D'** and **G'**.
Rose after **REX**.
Rev.: Ⴤ IHS:AVTEM.TRANSIENS:PERMEDI:ILLOR':IBAT.
Small square stops, double after **TRANSIENS** and **ILLOR'**
Potter, p. 135; North 1906; Seaby 2433. No provenance.

686 Half-sovereign

| | 5.52 | 85.2 | 50° |

I.m. Y both sides.
Obv.: Ⴤ SCVTVM⊛FIDEI⊛PROTEGET⊛EVM⊛ Uncrowned bust. Rosette stops.
Rev.: Ⴤ:EDWARD':VI:D:G:AGL:FRA:Z.HIB':REX. Small square stops, double
after i.m., **EDWARD'**, **VI** and **HIB'**.
Potter, p. 135, type 1(b); North 1908; Seaby 2435. Ex Lockett (3247).

687 Half-sovereign

| | 5.49 | 84.7 | 200° |

I.m. Y both sides.
Obv.: Ⴤ.EDWARD:VI:D:G:AGL:FRA:Z:HIB:REX. Crowned bust. Small square
stops, double after **VI** and **Z**. Plain breast armour.
Rev.: Ⴤ.⊛SCVTVM⊛FIDEI⊛PROTEGET⊛EVM⊛ Rosette stops except for a
small square stop after **Ⴤ**.
Potter, p. 135, type 2(a); North 1911; Seaby 2438. Bt Spink 1965.

688 Crown

| | 2.47 | 38.1 | 200° |

I.m. Y both sides.
Obv.: Ⴤ.EDWARD:VI:D:G:AGL:FRA:Z.HIB.REX Crowned bust. Double small
square stops, single after **Y**, **Z** and **HIB**. Large **V** and **W**. Plain breast armour.
Rev.: Ⴤ.SCVTVM:FIDEI:PROTEG:EVM: Double small square stops, single
after i.m.
Potter, p. 135, type 2(a); North 1914; Seaby 2442. Ex Lockett (4362); ex Sir John
Evans.

Durham House mint

Initial mark: Bow

There are no coins of this mint in the Schneider collection.

THIRD PERIOD (15 December 1550–6 July 1553)

Gold coinage was issued at two standards of fineness:

A. Fine gold of 23 ct 3½ gr. (0.995 fine)[356] at a nominal weight of 240 gr. (15.552 g) to the sovereign of 30s 0d and 80 gr. (5.184 g) to the angel of 10s 0d. Denominations struck were the sovereign, angel and half-angel.
B. Crown gold of 22 ct (0.917 fine) at a nominal weight of 174.6 gr. (11.314 g) to the sovereign of 20s 0d and 43.6 gr. (2.825 g) to the crown of 5s 0d. Denominations struck were the sovereign, half-sovereign, crown and half-crown.

Gold coins were struck at Tower I, Tower II and Southwark mints. See p. 61 above for observations on the attribution of the coins with i.m. ostrich head to the Southwark mint. Otherwise classified according to North 1991.

Characteristics: Fine gold coinage of conventional design. Crown gold coinage with a half length figure of the king facing right, holding in his right hand an orb and in his left a sword, which rests on his shoulder. All coins normally have Gothic letters.

---

[356] Actually given in the indenture as 23 ct 10½ gr. See n. 275.

[*continued overleaf*]

PLATE 63

685

686

687

688

689

690

691

692

693

Plate 63 (*cont.*)

A. Fine gold coinage

Tower I and Tower II mints

Initial marks: Y
                    Tun

689 Angel
     5.15   79.5   150°

I.m. tun over ostrich head both sides.
Obv.: ⊖ЄDWЖRD⁹×VI×D×G×ЖGL×FRЖ×Z×HIB×RЄX× Double saltire stops, single after ЄDWЖRD', Z and RЄX.
Rev.: ⊖PЄR:CRVCЄ:TVЖ:SЖL'ПOS:XPЄ:RЄD': Small square stops, double after ПOS and RЄD'.
If, as appears likely, the i.m. ostrich head coins were struck at Southwark mint (see p. 61), then this coin will have been made from dies altered so that they could be used at the Tower after Southwark closed in August 1551.
North 1931; Seaby 2448. Bt Baldwin 1960; ex Carter.

B. Crown gold coinage

Tower I and Tower II mints

Initial marks: Y
                    Tun

690 Sovereign of 20s
    11.27   174.0   160°

I.m. Y both sides.
Obv.: Y:ЄDWЖRD:VI:D:G:ЖGL':FRЖП':Z:hIB':RЄX: Double pellet stops, single after ЄDWЖRD, D and G. Wire-line inner circle.
Rev.: Y·IhS:ЖVTЄM:TRЖПCI:PЄRMЄDI':ILLOR:IBЖT. Double pellet stops, single after i.m., IhS', TRЖПCI', ILLOR' and IBЖT.
North 1927; Seaby 2450. Bt Spink 1965; ex Thompson; ex Lockett (1875).

691 Sovereign of 20s
    11.20   172.8   350°

I.m. tun both sides, possibly over Y on reverse.
Obv.: ⊖:ЄDWЖRD:VI:D:G:ЖGL':FRЖ:Z:hIBЄR':RЄX: Double pellet stops, single after ЄDWЖRD', G' and FRЖ'. Wire-line inner circle.
Rev.: ⊖::IhS:ЖVTЄ:TRЖПCI:PЄR:MЄDIV:ILLOR:IBЖT· Pellet stops, double after i.m. and PЄR. North 1927; Seaby 2450. Bt Hirsch (Munich) 1962.

692 Sovereign of 20s
    11.24   173.5   290°

I.m. tun both sides.
Obv.: ⊖:ЄDWЖRD:VI:D':G:ЖGL':FRЖ:Z:hIBЄR':RЄX: Double pellet stops, single after ЄDWЖRD', G' and FRЖ'. Wire-line inner circle.
Rev.: ⊖·IhS:ЖVTЄM·TRЖПSIЄПS:PЄRMЄDI:ILLORV:IBЖT· Pellet stops. Double inner circle the inner of which is a wire-line.
North 1927; Seaby 2450. Bt Spink 1970.

693 Half-sovereign
    5.61   86.5   280°

I.m. Y both sides.
Obv.: Y:ЄDWЖRD:VI:D:G:ЖGL':FRЖ:Z:hIB:RЄX: Pellet stops, double after i.m., VI, ЖGL', Z and RЄX. Large letters.
Rev.: Y:IhS:ЖVTЄ:TRЖПCI:PЄRMЄD:ILLO':IBЖT Pellet stops, double after i.m. and ILLO'. Large letters. Crown band plain and interior not frosted.
North 1928; Seaby 2451. Bt Spink 1958.

THIRD PERIOD (*cont.*)

B. Crown gold coinage (*cont.*)

Tower I and Tower II mints (*cont.*)

694 Half-sovereign

	Weight		
	g	*gr.*	*Die-axis*
	5.57	85.9	10°

I.m. tun both sides.
Obv.: ☒ƐDWⴹRD:VI:D:G:ⴹGL:FRⴹ:Z:hIB':RƐX:
Pellet stops, double after VI, hIB' and RƐX. Large letters.
Rev.: ☒IhS:ⴹVTƐM:TRⴹNSIƐ:PƐRMƐ:ILLOR:IBⴹT Pellet stops, double after ⴹVTƐM. Large letters. Crown band plain and interior not frosted.
North 1928; Seaby 2451. Bt Spink 1965.

695 Half-sovereign
5.69 87.8 290°

I.m. tun both sides.
Obv.: ☒ƐDWⴹRD:VI:D:G:ⴹGL:FRⴹNCI:Z:hIBƐ':RƐX: Pellet stops, double after VI, hIBƐ' and RƐX. Small letters.
Rev.: ☒IhS:ⴹVTƐM·TRⴹNSIƐNS·PƐRMƐDI:ILLOR:IBⴹT· Pellet stops. Small letters. Plain band to crown and interior not frosted.
North 1928; Seaby 2451. Bt Baldwin 1957; ex Carter.

696 Half-sovereign
5.49 84.8 310°

I.m. tun both sides.
Obv.: ☒ƐDWⴹRD:VI:D:G:ⴹGL':FRⴹ:Z:hIB':RƐX: Double pellet stops, single after ƐDWⴹRD', D', G' and hIB'. Small letters.
Rev.: ☒IhS:ⴹVTƐM:TRⴹNSIƐ:PƐRMƐDI:ILLO:IBⴹT Pellet stops, double after ⴹVTƐM. Small letters. Crown band jewelled and interior frosted.
North 1928; Seaby 2451. Bt Spink 1960.

697 Half-sovereign
5.57 85.9 260°

I.m. tun both sides.
Obv.: ☒ƐDWⴹRD:VI:D:G:ⴹGL':FRⴹNCI:Z.hIB':RƐX: Pellet stops, double after VI, ⴹGL', hIB' and RƐX. Small letters.
Rev.: ☒.IhS:ⴹVTƐM:TRⴹNCI:PƐRMƐDI:ILLOR:IBⴹT. Pellet stops, double after ⴹVTƐM. Small letters. Crown band jewelled and interior frosted.
North 1928; Seaby 2451. No provenance.

698 Crown
2.90 44.8 350°

I.m. tun both sides.
Obv.: ☒:Ɛ.DWⴹRD:VI:D."G:ⴹGL':FRⴹ:Z:hIB:RƐX Small square stops, double after i.m., VI, ⴹGL' and Z.
Rev.: ☒.SCVTVM:FIDƐI:PROTƐGƐT:ƐVM:· Double small square stops, single after i.m., treble after ƐVM. Small letters.
North 1929; Seaby 2452. Ex Ryan (254); ex Yates-Thompson; ex Ready (possibly 577); ex Montagu (811); ex Brice; ex Wigan.

699 Half-crown
1.32 20.3 340°

I.m. tun both sides.
Obv.: ☒ƐDWⴹRD:VI.D:G'ⴹ:FRⴹ.Z hIB:RƐ/X. Small square stops.
Rev.: ☒SCVTVM.FIDƐI.PROTƐG.ƐVM. Small square stops.
North 1930; Seaby 2453. Ex Ryan (255).

[*continued overleaf*]

PLATE 64

694

695

696

697

698

699

701

702

703

Plate 64 (*cont.*)

700

Southwark mint

Initial mark: Ostrich head

700 Double-sovereign of 60s
    30.90   476.8   350°

I.m. ostrich head both sides
Obv.: 𝟐ЄDWⱯRD⁹×VI⁹×D⁝G⁝ⱯNGLIЄ/FRⱯNᏟIЄ⁝Z⁝hIBЄRNIЄ⁝RЄX⁝
Double saltire stops, single after ЄDWⱯRD' and VI'. Same die as next coin, **701**.
Rev.: 𝟐IhЄSV⁹×ⱯVTЄM⁝TRⱯNSIЄNS⁝PЄR⁝MEDIVM⁝ILLORVM⁝IBAT⁝
Double saltire stops, single after IhЄSV⁹. Roman Ms, otherwise Gothic letters. Same die as next coin, **701**.
North –; Seaby 2447. Ex Strauss (70); ex Lockett (1874); ex Leslie-Ellis; ex Moon (112); ex Lord Hastings (297); ex Cuff (1027); ex Duke of Devonshire (233).

701 Sovereign of 30s
    15.31   236.3   170°

I.m. ostrich head both sides.
Obv.: Same die as last coin, **700**.
Rev.: Same die as last coin, **700**.
North 1926; Seaby 2446. Bt Baldwin 1951; ex Carter; ex Yates-Thompson; ex Murdoch (480); ex Montagu (805); ex Addington; ex Murchison (171).

702 Angel
    5.01   77.3   230°

I.m. ostrich head both sides.
Obv.: 𝟐ЄDWⱯRD⁹VI⁝D⁝G⁝ⱯGL⁝FR⁝Z⁝hIB⁝RЄX
Double saltire stops, single after Z.
Rev.: 𝟐PЄR⁝ᏟRVᏟЄ⁝TVⱯ⁝SⱯLVⱯ⁝NOS⁝XPЄ⁝RED⁝
Double saltire stops, single after ᏟRVᏟЄ', TVⱯ' and XPЄ'.
North 1931; Seaby 2448. Ex Raynes (100).

703 Angel
    5.11   78.9   80°

I.m. ostrich head both sides.
Obv.: 𝟐ЄDWⱯRD⁝VI⁝D⁝G⁝ⱯGL⁝FRⱯ⁝Z⁝hIB⁝RЄX.
Small square stops, double after VI.
Rev.: 𝟐PЄR⁝ᏟRVᏟЄ⁝TVⱯ⁝SⱯLVⱯ.NOS XPЄ'RED
Small square stops.
North 1931; Seaby 2448. Bt Spink 1991; ex Dupree; ex Hird (private sale).

MARY ALONE (19 July 1553–25 July 1554),

WITH PHILIP (25 July 1554–17 November 1558)

Fine gold coinage of 23 ct 3½ gr. (0.995 fine)[357] struck on the basis of 240 gr. (15.552 g) to the sovereign of 30s 0d. Denominations struck were sovereign, ryal of 15s 0d, angel of 10s 0d and half-angel. The coins are classified in accordance with pp. 68–9, above.

Sovereigns and ryal

Characteristics: Sovereign. Conventional design with Gothic letters. Dated 1553, 1554 or undated (probably later). Privy mark after MARIA on obverse and DNO' on reverse. At first annulet stops, later pellet stops.

Ryal. Conventional design with Gothic letters. Dated 1553. Privy mark (pomegranate only) after MARIA on obverse only. Annulet stops.

| Privy marks: | Pomegranate | 1553–4 |
| | Halved rose and castle | 1554–? |

London mint only

704 Sovereign, 1553

	Weight		*Die-axis*
	g	gr.	
	15.19	234.4	350°

P.m. pomegranate both sides.
Obv.: ⦂MARIA⦂❧⦂D'⦂G'⦂ANG⦂FRA/Z⦂hIB'⦂REGINA⦂M⦂D⦂LIII
Double annulet stops, single after ANG'. Same die as **706** before the privy mark was altered.
Rev.: A⦂DNO❧FACTV⦂EST⦂ISTV⦂Z⦂EST⦂MIRA⦂IN⦂OQVL'⦂NRIS⦂
Double annulet stops, single after FACTV', ISTV', MIRA' and NRIS'.
North 1956; Seaby 2488. Ex Hird (private sale).

705 Sovereign, 1554

| 15.20 | 234.4 | 20° |

P.m. pomegranate both sides.
Obv.: MARIA'❧D⦂G⦂ANG⦂FRAN⦂/Z⦂hIB⦂REGINA⦂M⦂D⦂LIIII
Broken annulet stops after Z, REGINA, M and D.
Rev.: A⦂DNO❧⦂FACTV⦂EST⦂ISTV⦂Z⦂EST⦂MIRA⦂IN⦂OQVL⦂NRIS⦂⦂°
Small unbroken annulet stops, double after ❧, EST, Z, EST and IN, and four in a diamond configuration after NRIS'.
North 1956; Seaby 2488. Ex Glendining sale 31.3.1965 (2); ex Kaufmann.

706 Sovereign, 1553

| 15.47 | 238.7 | 350° |

P.m. halved rose and castle over pomegranate/pomegranate.
Obv.: ⦂MARIA⦂⬛⦂D'⦂G'⦂ANG⦂FRA/Z⦂hIB'⦂REGINA⦂M⦂D⦂LIII
Double annulet stops, single after ANG'. Same die as **704**, but with altered p.m. and as **707** in this state.
Rev.: A⦂DNO❧FACTV⦂EST⦂ISTV⦂Z⦂EST⦂MIRA⦂IN⦂OQVL'⦂NRIS'⦂
Double annulet stops, single after FACTV', ISTV' and MIRA'.
North 1956; Seaby 2488. Ex Lockett (4084).

707 Sovereign, 1553

| 15.38 | 237.3 | 80° |

P.m. halved rose and castle over pomegranate/halved rose and castle.
Obv.: ⦂MARIA⦂⬛⦂D⦂G'⦂ANG⦂FRA/Z⦂hIB'⦂REGINA⦂M⦂D⦂LIII
Double annulet stops, single after ANG'. Same die as **704** with the p.m. altered and thus in the same state as **706**.
Rev.: A⦂DNO⦂⬛FACTV⦂EST⦂ISTV⦂Z⦂EST⦂MIRA⦂INOQVL'⦂NRIS'⦂
Double pellet stops, single after FACTV', ISTV' and MIRA'. Same die as next coin, **708**.
North 1956; Seaby 2488. Ex Hird (private sale); ex Lockett (1923); ex Vaughan Morgan (23).

[357] See n. 275.

[*continued overleaf*]

PLATE 65

704

705

706

707

708

709

Plate 65 (*cont.*)

708 Sovereign, no date
    14.86   229.4   10°

P.m. halved rose and castle both sides.
Obv.: ：ΜΛRIΛ：✠：D：：G：ΛΝG：FRΛ/Z hIBERΝIE：REGINΛ：
    Double pellet stops, single after G' and ΛΝG'.
Rev.: Λ：DΝO：✠FΛQTV：EST：ISTV：Z：EST：ΜIRΛ：INOQVL'：ΝRIS：
    Double pellet stops, single after Λ', DΝO', FΛQTV', ISTV' and ΜIRΛ'.
    Same die as last coin, **707**.
North 1956; Seaby 2488. No provenance.

709 Ryal, 1553
    7.74   119.9   80°

P.m. pomegranate/none.
Obv.: ΜΛRIΛ∘✚∘D∘G'ΛΝG：FRΛ：Σ∘hIB：REGINΛ∘/Μ∘D∘L/III∘
    Annulet stops.
Rev.: Λ∘DΝO∘FΛQTV∘EST∘ISTVD∘Σ∘EST∘ΜIRΛBI∘IN∘OQVL∘ΝRIS∘
    Annulet stops, double after Λ, EST, ISTVD and Σ.
North 1957; Seaby 2489. Ex E. W. Rashleigh (827); ex Tyssen (1663).

Angels and half-angels

These are arranged in the four classes proposed on pp. 68–9. The characteristics are:

1. P.m. pomegranate; large Gothic letters; annulet stops.
2. P.m. pomegranate; small or mixed large and small Gothic letters; pellet stops.
3. P.m. halved rose and castle; large Roman letters; pellet stops.

The above are all in Mary's name alone. The privy marks on the angels are after MΛRIΛ on the obverse and ISTVD on the reverse. the privy marks on the half-angels are after MΛRIΛ on the obverse and EST on the reverse. The fourth class covers the coins in the name of both Philip and Mary:

4. P.m. lis; smaller Roman letters; pellet stops. The privy marks on this class revert to the initial position on both sides.

CLASS 1

London mint only

710 Angel			P.m. pomegranate both sides.
	Weight		*Obv.:* MΛRIΛ⦂✚⦂D⦂G⦂ΛNG⦂FRΛ⦂Σ⦂hIB⦂REGI⦂
	g	*gr.*	*Die-axis*	Annulet stops, double after MΛRIΛ, p.m. and Σ. Same die as next coin, **711**.
	5.07	78.3	230°	*Rev.:* Λ⦂DNO⦂FΛΩTV⦂EST⦂ISTVD✚Z⦂EST⦂'MIRΛBI⦂ช
				Annulet stops, double after EST and EST. Patterns on ship's fore- and stern-castles.
				North 1958; Seaby 2490. Bt Baldwin 1959.

711 Angel			P.m. pomegranate both sides.
	5.11	78.8	120°	*Obv.:* same die as last coin, **710**.
				Rev.: Λ⦂DNO⦂FΛΩTV⦂EST⦂ISTVD'✚Z⦂EST⦂MIRΛBI⦂ช
				Annulet stops, double after EST and EST. Patterns on ship's fore- and stern-castles.
				North 1958; Seaby 2490. Bt Baldwin 1961.

712 Angel			P.m. pomegranate both sides.
	5.14	79.3	260°	*Obv.:* ⦁MΛRIΛ⦁✚⦁D⦂G⦂ΛNG⦂FRΛ⦂Σ⦂hIB⦂R‾EGI⦁
				Annulet stops, double after Z.
				Rev.: Λ⦁DNO⦂FΛΩTV⦂EST⦂ISTVD✚Z⦂EST⦂MIRΛBI⦂ช
				Annulet stops, double after Z.
				North 1958; Seaby 2490. No provenance.

713 Angel			P.m. pomegranate both sides.
	5.03	77.6	150°	*Obv.:* MΛRIΛ⦂✚⦂D⦂G⦂ΛNG⦂FRΛ⦂Σ⦂hIB⦂REGIN⦂
				Annulet stops, double after MΛRIΛ and Σ.
				Rev.: Λ⦁DNO⦂FΛΩTV⦂EST'ISTVD✚Z⦂EST⦂MIRΛBI⦂ช
				Annulet stops, double after Z.
				North 1958; Seaby 2490. Bt Spink 1967; ex Potter.

714 Angel			P.m. pomegranate both sides.
	5.13	79.1	60°	*Obv.:* ⦁MΛRIΛ⦂✚⦁D⦂G⦂ΛNG⦂FRΛ⦂Z⦂hIB⦂REGI⦂
				Annulet stops, double after Z.
				Rev.: Λ⦁DNO⦂FΛΩTV⦂EST⦁ISTVD⦁✚⦁Σ⦂EST⦁MIRΛBI⦂ช
				Annulet stops.
				North 1958; Seaby 2490. Bt Spink 1972; ex Cartwright.

715 Angel			P.m. pomegranate both sides.
	5.10	78.7	240°	*Obv.:* ⦁MΛRIΛ⦁✚⦁D⦂G⦂ΛNG⦂FRΛ⦂Z⦂hIB⦂REGIN⦂ Annulet stops.
				Rev.: ⦁Λ⦁DNO⦂FΛΩTV⦂EST⦂ISTVD✚Z⦂EST⦂MIRΛBI⦂ช
				Annulet stops, double after Z.
				North 1958; Seaby 2490. Bt Baldwin 1970.

[*continued overleaf*]

PLATE 66

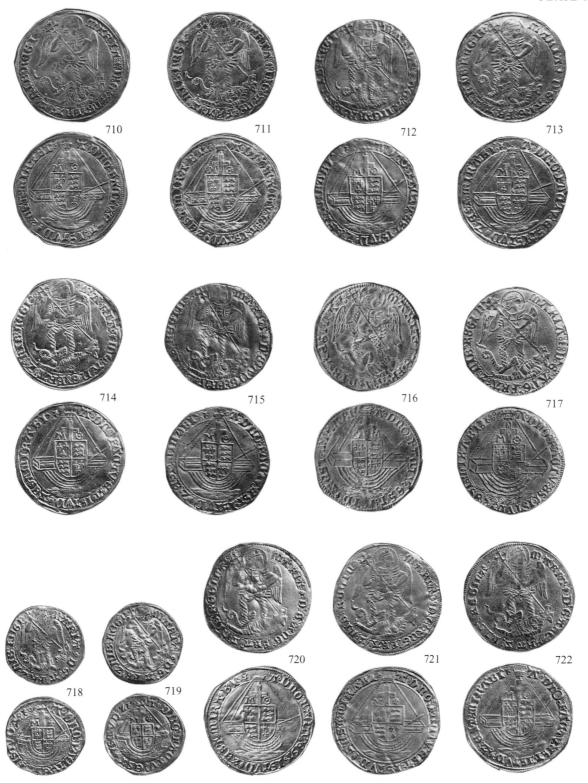

710   711   712   713

714   715   716   717

720   721   722

718   719

Plate 66 (*cont.*)

716 Angel
4.91   75.7   180°

P.m. pomegranate both sides.
Obv.: ∘MⱯRIⱯ∘♣∘D∘G∘FRⱯ∘Σ∘hIB∘REGINⱯ∘ƌ∘
Annulet stops, double after Σ. ⱯNG omitted.
Rev.: Ⱥ∘DNO∘FⱯⱯTV∘EST∘ISTD♣∘Σ∘EST∘MIRⱯBI ƌ
Annulet stops, after ISTD and Σ. No V in ISTVD. Rose to left and M to right of the cross on the ship's mast, the reverse of the normal.
North 1958; Seaby 2490. Bt Spink 1976.
N.B. The slightly light weight and the abnormal variations on both obverse and reverse of this coin mean that it must be regarded with grave suspicion. As the general style is not really abnormal, it has been decided to leave it in this position.

717 Angel
5.00   77.2   90°

P.m. pomegranate both sides.
Obv.: MⱯRIⱯ♣∘D∘G∘ⱯNG∘FRⱯ∘Z∘hIB∘REGIN'
Annulet stops, double after MⱯRIⱯ, p.m. and Z. Letter Є is reversed B.
Rev.: Ⱥ∘DNO∘FⱯⱯTV∘EST∘ISTVD♣∘Z∘EST∘MIRⱯBI∘ƌ∘
Annulet stops, double after ISTVD and ƌ. Letter Єs are reversed Bs.
North 1958; Seaby 2490. Bt Baldwin 1966.

718 Half-angel
2.62   40.4   160°

P.m. pomegranate both sides.
Obv.: MⱯRIⱯ♣D∘G∘Ⱥ∘FR∘Z∘hIB∘REGI'
Annulet stops. Same die as next coin, **719**.
Rev.: Ⱥ∘DNO∘FⱯⱯTV∘EST∘♣∘ISTVD∘Σ∘ƌ∘   Annulet stops, double after ISTVD and Σ.
North 1959; Seaby 2491. Bt Spink 1965; ex Thompson.

719 Half-angel
2.49   38.5   20°

P.m. pomegranate both sides.
Obv.: same die as last coin, **718**.
Rev.: Ⱥ∘DNO∘FⱯⱯTV∘EST♣ISTVD∘Z ƌ   Annulet stops, double after ISTVD.
North 1959; Seaby 2491. Ex Ryan (263); ex Fitch; ex Hazeldine (105).

CLASS 2/CLASS 1 MULES

London mint only

720 Angel
5.10   78.7   100°

P.m. pomegranate both sides.
Obv.: .MⱯRIⱯ.♣.D∘G∘ⱯNG∘FRⱯ∘Σ∘hIB∘REGINⱯ.
Pellet stops, double after Σ. Small Gothic letters.
Rev.: Ⱥ∘DNO∘FⱯⱯTV∘EST∘ISTVD♣Z∘EST∘MIRⱯBI∘ƌ
Annulet stops. Patterns on ship's fore- and stern-castles.
North 1958; Seaby 2490. Bt Spink 1969.

721 Angel
5.37   82.8   350°

P.m. pomegranate both sides.
Obv.: .MⱯRIⱯ.♣∘D∘G∘ⱯNG∘FRⱯ∘Σ∘hIB∘REGIN∘
Pellet stops, double after p.m. and Σ. Small Gothic letters.
Rev.: Ⱥ∘DNO∘FⱯⱯTV∘EST∘ISTVD∘♣∘Σ∘EST∘MIRⱯBI∘ƌ
Annulet stops, double after EST, Σ and EST.
Note the unusually heavy weight of this coin.
North 1958; Seaby 2490. Ex Lockett (4379).

722 Angel
4.97   76.7   220°

P.m. pomegranate both sides.
Obv.: MⱯRIⱯ.♣.D∘G∘ⱯNG∘FRⱯ∘Σ∘hIB∘REGINⱯ.
Pellet stops, double after Σ. Mostly small Gothic letters but M, Ⱥ, D, G and R large. Same die as next coin, **723**.
Rev.: ∘Ⱥ∘DNO∘FⱯⱯTV∘EST∘ISTVD∘♣∘Z∘EST∘MIRⱯBI∘ƌ
Stops are a mixture of annulets with pellets inside, annulets, and pellets in the form of small triangular wedges. Double stops after DNO and Z. There is a mixture of small and large Gothic letters, Ⱥ and O being large.
North 1958; Seaby 2490. Ex Herentals hoard (no. 245 in Naster 1956).

Angels and half-angels (*cont.*)

CLASS 2

London mint only

	Weight		
723 Angel			
	g	*gr.*	*Die-axis*
	4.98	76.9	250°

P.m. pomegranate both sides.
Obv.: same die as last coin, **722**.
Rev.: .ᚦ.DᑎO:FᚪᑕTV:ᴇST.ISTVD.ᶘ.Z.ᴇST.ᛗIRᚪBI:ᵹ
Pellet stops. Mostly small Gothic letters except D, C, V and M large. Same die as **725**.
North 1958; Seaby 2490. Bt Seaby 1957.

724 Angel			
	5.14	79.3	120°

P.m. pomegranate both sides.
Obv.: .ᛗᚪRIᚪ.ᶘ.D:G:ᚪᑎG:FRᚪ:Ƨ:hIB:RᴇGIᑎ:
Pellet stops, double after Ƨ. Mostly small Gothic letters except M, D, G and E large.
Rev.: ᚦ.DᑎO:FᚪᑕTV:ᴇST.ISTVD.ᶘ:Z.ᴇST.ᛗIRᚪBI:ᵹ:
Pellet stops, double after p.m. and ᵹ. Mostly small Gothic letters except D, C, V and M large.
North 1958; Seaby 2490. Bt Baldwin 1957; ex Carter.

CLASS 3/CLASS 2 MULE

London mint only

725 Angel			
	5.06	78.1	350°

P.m. halved rose and castle/ pomegranate.
Obv.: MARIA.⬛.D.G.ANG.FRA.Z.HIB.REGI.
Pellet stops. Large Roman letters.
Rev.: same die as **723**.
North 1958; Seaby 2490. Ex Lord St Oswald (18).

CLASS 4 (with name of Philip)

London mint only

726 Angel			
	5.18	79.9	160°

I.m. lis both sides.
Obv.: ✠PHILIP.Z.MARIA.D:G.REX.Z.REGINA   Pellet stops, double after D.
Rev.: ✠A.DNO.FACTVM.EST.ISTVD:Z.EST.MIRABI.   Pellet stops, double after ISTVD.
North 1965; Seaby 2496. Bt Spink 1967; ex Angers hoard.

727 Angel			
	5.11	78.8	100°

I.m. lis both sides.
Obv.: ✠PHILIP:Z:MARIA:D:G:REX.Z.REGINA.A.   Pellet stops, double after first Z and MARIA.
Rev.: ✠A.DNO'FACTVM:EST:ISTVD.Z:EST.MIRABILE   Pellet stops, double after FACTVM, first EST and Z.
North 1965; Seaby 2496. No provenance.

728 Angel			
	5.09	78.6	350°

I.m. lis both sides.
Obv.: ✠PHILIP:Z.MARIA D:G:REX.Z.REGIN: Pellet stops. Beaded inner circle.
Rev.: ✠A:DNO:FACTVM.EST.ISTVD.Z.EST.MIRABI: Pellet stops. Beaded inner circle.
North 1965; Seaby 2496B. Bt Spink 1956.

[*continued overleaf*]

PLATE 67

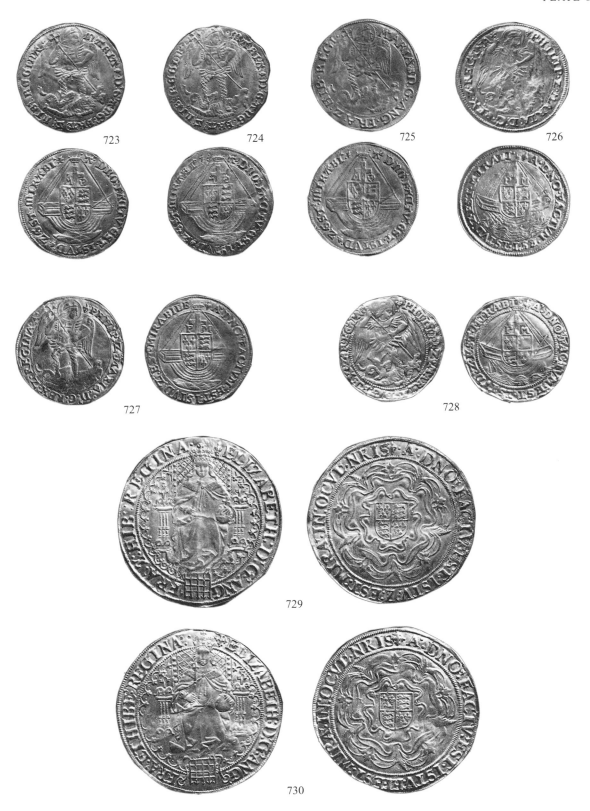

723

724

725

726

727

728

729

730

Plate 67 (*cont.*)

ELIZABETH I (17 November 1558–24 March 1603)

FIRST ISSUE (31 December 1558–19 April 1572)

Gold coinage issued at two standards of fineness:

A. Fine gold of 23 ct 3½ gr. (0.995 fine)[358]. Nominal weights 240 gr. (15.552 g) to the sovereign of 30s 0d and 80 gr. (5.184 g) to the angel of 10s 0d. Denominations struck were sovereign, angel and half-angel.

B. Crown gold of 22 ct (0.917 fine). Nominal weight 87.3 gr. (5.657 g) to the half-pound of 10s 0d. Denominations struck were half-pound, crown and half-crown.

The classification used is that set out in Brown and Comber 1989 (BC 2). References are also made to Brown and Comber 1988 (BC 1). For milled coinage struck to the same standards as the First Issue see Plate 70.

Initial marks:

	Lis	1 Jan. 1559–31 July 1560
	Cross crosslet	1 Jan. 1561–31 Aug. 1565
	Rose	1 Oct. 1565–31 March 1566
	Portcullis	1 May 1566–31 Jan. 1567
	Lion	1 Feb. 1567–30 June 1567
	Coronet	1 July 1567–28 Feb. 1570
	Castle	1 March 1570–15 Dec. 1571

A. FINE GOLD COINAGE

Characteristics: conventional types; Roman letters.

London mint only

729 Sovereign
  15.49   239.1   110°

I.m. lis both sides.
Obv.: ✠ELIZABETH:D:G:ANG'/.FRA:Z:HIB·:REGINA.
    Pellet stops, double after ELIZABETH and Z, treble after HIB. Garnishing interrupted by back of throne. No chains on portcullis below throne.
Rev.: ✠.A:DNO:FACTV:EST.ISTV:Z:EST:MIRA:IN:OCVL:NRIS
    Pellet stops, double after A, Z, second EST and IN. Same die as next coin, **730**, before alterations.
BC 2, A1 (different obverse die, same reverse); North 1978; Seaby 2511. Ex Hird (private sale); ex Raynes (114).

730 Sovereign
  15.30   236.1   280°

I.m. cross-crosslet/cross-crosslet over lis.
Obv.: ✠ELIZABETH:D:G:ANG:/FRA:ET HIBE:REGINA·:
    Pellet stops, double after ELIZABETH, inverted triangle of pellets after REGINA. Garnishing interrupted by back of throne. No stop between ET and HIBE.
Rev.: ✠A:DNO:FACTV:EST.ISTV:ET.EST:MIRA:IN:OCVL:NRIS
    Pellet stops, double after A, second EST and IN ET struck over Z:. Same die as last coin, **729**, with the i.m. altered and ET added.
BC 2, A4, same reverse die; North 1978; Seaby 2512. No provenance.

---

[358] See n. 275.

FIRST ISSUE (*cont.*)

A. FINE GOLD COINAGE (*cont.*)

London mint (cont.)

731 Angel

	Weight		
	g	*gr.*	*Die-axis*
	5.12	79.0	330°

I.m. lis both sides.
Obv.: ✠ELIZABETH.D:G:ANG:FRAN:Z.HIB:REGI:
    Pellet stops. Wire-line inner circle.
Rev.: ✠.A.DNO.FACTVM.EST.ISTVD.Z.EST.MIRABILE:.
    Pellet stops, triple after MIRABILE.
BC 2, C1; North 1979; Seaby 2513. Ex Ryan (278).

732 Angel

5.36	82.7	100°

I.m. lis both sides.
Obv.: ✠ELIZABETH:D:G:ANG:FRA:Z.HIB:REG'
    Small square pellet stops, double after ELIZABETH. Wire-line inner circle.
Rev.: ✠A:DNO:FACTVM EST.ISTVD Z.EST:MIRABI:
    Small square pellet stops, double after A and second EST.
BC 2, C3; North 1979; Seaby 2513. Bt Spink 1967; ex Angers hoard.

733 Angel

5.00	77.2	120°

I.m. cross crosslet both sides.
Obv.: ✠ELIZABETH.D:G:ANG:FRA:ET.HIB:REGINA.
    Pellet stops.
Rev.: ✠A.DNO:FACTVM.EST.ISTVD:ET EST.MIRABI:
    Pellet stops, double after ISTVD. E and rose by ship's mast over rose and E.
BC 2, C7 (same reverse die); North 1979; Seaby 2514. Ex Herentals hoard(no. 246 in Naster 1956).

734 Angel

5.13	79.1	270°

I.m. coronet both sides.
Obv.: ⚓ELIZABETH:D:G:ANG:FR:ET:HIB:REGINA∵
    Pellet stops, double after ELIZABETH and ET, a triangle of pellets after REGINA.
Rev.: ⚓A:DNO:FACTVM:EST ISTVD:ET:EST MIRABI':
    Double pellet stops, single after DNO.
BC 2, C9; North 1991/1; Seaby 2514. Ex Hird (35); ex Ryan (281); ex P. W. P. Carlyon-Britton.

735 Half-angel

2.48	38.3	350°

I.m. lis both sides.
Obv.: ✠ELIZABETH.D:G:ANG:FRA:Z.HIB: Pellet stops. Beaded inner circle.
Rev.: ✠.A:DNO:FACTVM.EST.ISTVD.Z.EST.M'   Pellet stops, double after A.
BC 2, D1; North 1980; Seaby 2517. Ex Galerie des Monnaies sale, Olten, 4.2.1969 (43).

B. CROWN GOLD COINAGE

Characteristics: crowned bust to right, normally within beaded inner circle. Reverse crowned shield with E–R beside.

London mint only

736 Half-pound

5.59	86.2	150°

I.m. lis both sides.
Obv.: ✠ELIZABET.D:G:ANG:FRA:Z.HIB:REGINA.   Square pellet stops. BC 1, bust 1B. Reads ELIZABET. Wire-line inner circle.
Rev.: ✠SCVTVM:FIDEI:PROTEGET.EAM.   Square pellet stops, double after SCVTVM and FIDEI. Large crown with frosted interior. Wire-line inner circle.
BC 2, G1 (same dies); North 1982; Seaby 2519. Ex Hylton (7).

[*continued overleaf*]

PLATE 68

731   732   733   734

735   736   737   738

739   740   741   742

Plate 68 (*cont.*)

737 Half-pound
5.11   78.8   300°

I.m. lis both sides.
Obv.: ✠ ELIZABETH:D:G:ANG:FRA:Z.HIB:REGIN: Square pellet stops, double after ELIZABETH. BC 1, bust 1B. Wire-line inner circle.
Rev.: ✠ SCVTVM:FIDEI:PROTEGE:EAM Square pellet stops, double after SCVTVM and FIDEI. Wire-line inner circle.
BC 2, G2; North 1982; Seaby 2519. Ex Ryan (320).

738 Half-pound
5.56   85.7   10°

I.m. cross crosslet both sides.
Obv.: ✠ ELIZABETH:D:G:ANG:FRA·ET.HI:REGINA Pellet stops, triple after ELIZABETH. BC 1, bust 3C.
Rev.: ✠ SCVTVM:FIDEI:PROTEGET:EAM Double pellet stops, triple after SCVTVM.
BC 2, G5/G6; North 1982; Seaby 2520. No provenance.

739 Half-pound
5.52   85.2   220°

I.m. rose/rose over cross crosslet.
Obv.: ◉ ELIZABETH:D:G:ANG:FRA:ET.HI:REGINA Pellet stops, double after ELIZABETH. BC 1, bust 3C.
Rev.: ◉ SCVTVM:FIDEI:PROTEGET:EAM Double pellet stops.
BC 2, G8; this is the coin referred to in Schneider 1983 which elicited the response, Comber 1983; North 1994; Seaby 2520. Bt Spink 1983.

740 Half-pound
5.61   86.5   110°

I.m. rose both sides.
Obv.: ◉ ELIZABETH:D:G:ANG:FRA:ET.HI:REGINA Pellet stops, double after ELIZABETH and ET. BC 1, bust 3C.
Rev.: ◉ SCVTVM.FIDEI:PROTEGET.EAM. Pellet stops, double after FIDEI.
BC 2, G9; North 1994; Seaby 2520. Ex Glendining sale 18.5.1960 (12).

741 Half-pound
5.52   85.2   100°

I.m. rose both sides.
Obv.: ◉ ELIZABETH:D:G:ANG:FRA:ET.HI:REGINA Pellet stops, double after ELIZABETH and ET. BC 1, bust 3C.
Rev.: ◉ SCVTVM:FIDEI:PROTEGET:EAM Double pellet stops.
BC 2, G9 (this coin cited); North 1994; Seaby 2520. Ex Lockett (3292).

742 Half-pound
5.58   86.1   120°

I.m. portcullis both sides.
Obv.: ▦ ELIZABETH:D:G:ANG:FR:ET:HI:REGINA Pellet stops, double after ELIZABETH and ET. BC 1, bust 3C.
Rev.: ▦ SCVTVM:FIDEI:PROTEGET:EAM Double pellet stops.
BC 2, G11; North 1994; Seaby 2520. Ex Glendining sale 9.12.1964 (17); ex Carter.

ELIZABETH I (*cont.*)

FIRST ISSUE (*cont.*)

B. CROWN GOLD COINAGE (*cont.*)

London mint only (cont.)

743 Half-pound

	Weight	
g	*gr.*	*Die-axis*
5.52	85.2	270°

I.m. lion both sides.
Obv.: 🦁ELIZABETH:D:G:ANG:FR:ET:HI:REGINA
Pellet stops, double after ELIZABETH and ET. BC 1, bust 3E.
Rev.: 🦁SCVTVM:FIDEI:PROTEGET:EAM   Double pellet stops.
BC 2, G14; North 1994; Seaby 2520. Bt Baldwin 1964.

744 Half-pound
| 5.60 | 86.4 | 20° |

I.m. lion both sides.
Obv.: 🦁ELIZABETH:D:G:ANG:FR:ET:HI:REGINA   Pellet stops, double after
ELIZABETH and ET. BC 1, bust 4A.
Rev.: 🦁SCVTVM:FIDEI:PROTEGET:EAM   Double pellet stops.
BC 2, G15 (this coin illustrated); North 1994; Seaby 2520. Ex Hird (49); ex Ryan (325).

745 Half-pound
| 5.58 | 86.1 | 30° |

I.m. coronet both sides.
Obv.: 👑ELIZABETH:D:G:ANG:FR:ET:HI:REGINA   Pellet stops, double after
ELIZABETH and ET. BC 1, bust 4A.
Rev.: 👑SCVTVM:FIDEI:PROTEGET:EAM   Double pellet stops.
BC 2, G16; North 1994; Seaby 2520. Ex Lockett (4393).

746 Half-pound
| 4.44 | 68.5 | 40° |
| (clipped) | | |

I.m. coronet both sides.
Obv.: 👑ELIZABETH꞉D꞉G꞉ANG꞉FR꞉ET꞉HI꞉REGINA
Stops in the form of small fat crescents, double after ELIZABETH and,
probably, ET. BC 1, bust 4A.
Rev.: 👑SCVTV꞉FIDEI꞉PROTEGET꞉EAM   Stops in the form of small fat
crescents, double after FIDEI and PROTEGET.
BC 2, G17; North 1994; Seaby 2520. No provenance.

747 Half-pound
| 5.55 | 85.6 | 20° |

I.m. castle both sides.
Obv.: 🏰ELIZABETH:D:G:ANG:FR:ET:HI:REGINA   Pellet stops, double after
ELIZABETH and ET. BC 1, bust 4A.
Rev.: 🏰SCVTVM:FIDEI:PROTEGET:EAM   Double pellet stops.
BC 2, G18; North 1994; Seaby 2520. Bt Baldwin 1953; ex Carter.

748 Crown
| 2.78 | 42.9 | 100° |

I.m. cross crosslet both sides.
Obv.: ✠ELIZABETH:D:G:AN:FR ET.HI:REGINA
Pellet stops, double after ELIZABETH. BC 1, bust 1F.
Rev.: ✠SCVTVM:FIDEI:PROTEGET:EAM'   Double pellet stops, treble after
PROTEGET.
BC 2, H5; North 1983; Seaby 2522. Bt Baldwin 1953; ex Carter

749 Crown
| 2.71 | 41.8 | 260° |

I.m. rose over cross crosslet both sides.
Obv.: ◉ELIZABETH:D:G:ANG:FR:ET:HI:REGINA
Pellet stops, double after ELIZABETH and ET. BC 1, bust 1F.
Rev.: ◉SCVTVM:FIDEI:PROTEGET:EAM.   Double pellet stops, single after
EAM.
BC 2, H7/- (reverse altered i.m. not confirmed by them); North 1995; Seaby 2522. Bt
Baldwin 1977.

[*continued overleaf*]

PLATE 69

743   744   745   746

747   748   749   750   751

752   753   754   755

Plate 69 (*cont.*)

750 Crown
2.79   43.1   270°

I.m. portcullis both sides.
Obv.: ⊞ELIZABETH:D:G:AN:FR:ET:HI:REGINA   Pellet stops, double after
    ELIZABETH and ET. BC 1, bust 1F.
Rev.: ⊞SCVTVM:FIDEI:PROTEGET.EAM   Double pellet stops, single after
    PROTEGET.
BC 2, H8; North 1995; Seaby 2522. Bt Spink 1965; ex Thompson; ex Hird (55); ex
Ryan (337).

751 Crown
2.80   43.2   50°

I.m. coronet both sides.
Obv.: ⚜ELIZABETH:D:G:AN:FR:ET:HI:REGINA   Pellet stops, double after
    ELIZABETH and ET. BC 1, bust 4C.
Rev.: ⚜SCVTVM:FIDEI:PROTEGET:EAM   Double pellet stops.
BC 2, H11; North 1995; Seaby 2522. No provenance.

752 Half-crown
1.48   22.9   130°

I.m. lis both sides.
Obv.: ✚ELIZABETH:D:G:ANG:FRA:Z HIB.RE.   Small square pellet stops,
    double after ELIZABETH. Wire-line inner circle. BC 1, bust 1G
Rev.: ✚SCVTVM:FIDEI:PROTEG:EAM.   Pellet stops, double after SCVTVM
    and FIDEI.
BC 2, J1, apparently the third known specimen; North 1984; Seaby 2523. Bt Spink
1993 and reported to be an isolated find made in 1981 near to Loughborough, Leics.

753 Half-crown
1.41   21.8   50°

I.m. cross crosslet both sides.
Obv.: ✠ELIZABETH:D:G:AN:FR:ET:HI:REGINA
    Pellet stops, double after ELIZABETH and ET. BC 1, bust 3F.
Rev.: ✠ SCVTVM.FIDEI.PROTEGET.EAM   Pellet stops.
BC 2, J5; North 1984; Seaby 2524. No provenance.

754 Half-crown
1.39   21.5   70°

I.m. portcullis both sides.
Obv.: ⊞ELIZABETH:D:G:ANG:FR:ET:HI:REGINA   Pellet stops, double after
    ELIZABETH and ET. BC 1, bust 1G.
Rev.: ⊞SCVTVM:FIDEI:PROTEGET:EAM   Double pellet stops.
BC 2, J8; North 1996; Seaby 2524. Ex Hird (60); ex Raynes (161);
ex Clarke-Thornhill.

755 Half-crown
1.42   22.0   0°

I.m. castle both sides.
Obv.: ⚏ELIZABETH:D:G:ANG:FR:ET:HI:REGINA   Pellet stops, double after
    ELIZABETH. BC 1, bust 4D.
Rev.: ⚏SCVTVM:FIDEI:PROTEGET.EAM   Double pellet stops, single after
    PROTEGET.
BC 2, J11; North 1996; Seaby 2524. No provenance.

FIRST ISSUE (*cont.*)

B. CROWN GOLD COINAGE (*cont.*)

Milled Coinage (1561–68)

Struck in crown gold to the weights of the first issue at a mint set up in the Tower of London. Classified according to Brown and Comber 1989 (BC 2) and Borden and Brown 1983 (BB).

Characteristics: No inner circles. Superior quality of striking. Later issues (i.m. lis) with serrated edges.

Initial marks:	Star	1 Jan. 1561–*c.*1564
	Lis	15 Feb. 1564–1 Sept. 1568

London mint only

756 Pattern half-pound

Weight			
g	*gr.*	*Die-axis*
6.09	94.0	170°

I.m. star both sides.
Obv.: ✶ ELIZABETH.D.G.ANG.FRA.ET.HIB.REGINA   Pellet stops. BB, bust A.
Rev.: ✶ SCVTVM.FIDEI.PROTEGET.EAM.   Pellet stops.
BC 2, L1 (BB 1), dies 1.01/1.R1, described as a pattern in BC 2 and BB which seems to be confirmed by the irregular weight and the use of bust and letter punches from the intermediate size shilling; North 2019/1; Seaby 2543. Ex Hird (private sale); ex Lockett (2038); ex Sir John Evans.

757 Half-pound

5.55	85.6	160°

I.m. star both sides.
Obv.: ✶ ELIZABETH.D.G.ANG.FR.ET.HIB.REGINA   Pellet stops. BB, bust C.
Rev.: .✶ SCVTVM.FIDEI.PROTEGET.EAM.   Pellet stops.
BC 2, L2 (BB 2), dies 2.01/1.R1; North 2019/2; Seaby 2543. No provenance.

758 Half-pound

5.70	87.9	180°

I.m. star both sides.
Obv.: ✶ ELIZABETH.D.G.ANG.FRA.ET.HIB.REGINA   Pellet stops. Plain Z in ELIZABETH. BB, bust D.
Rev.: .✶ SCVTVM.FIDEI.PROTEGET.EAM.   Pellet stops.
BC 2, L3 (BB 3), dies 3.O1/1.R1; North 2019/3; Seaby 2543. No provenance.

759 Half-pound

5.59	86.2	190°

I.m. star both sides.
Obv.: ✶ ELIZABETH.D.G.ANG.FRA.ET.HIB.REGINA   Pellet stops. Curly Z in ELIZABETH. BB, bust D. Pellet outer circle.
Rev.: ✶ SCVTVM.FIDEI.PROTEGET.EAM   Pellet stops. Pellet outer circle.
BC 2, L4 (BB 5), dies 5.O1/5.R1; North 2019/3; Seaby 2543. Ex Vaughan Morgan (40).

760 Half-pound

5.67	87.5	170°

I.m. lis both sides.
Obv.: ⚜ELIZABETH.D:G:ANG:FRA:ET.HIB:REGINA   Pellet stops. BB, bust E.
Rev.: ⚜SCVTVM.FIDEI.PROTEGET.EAM   Pellet stops.
Edge: serrated.
BC 2, L5 (BB 6), dies 6.O1/6.R1; North 2019/4; Seaby 2543. Ex Price (149).

761 Pattern crown

3.45	53.2	170°

I.m. star both sides.
Obv.: ✶ ELIZABETH.D.G.ANG.FRA.ET.HIB.REGINA   Pellet stops. Groat die. BB, bust A.
Rev.: ✶ SCVTVM.FIDEI.PROTEGET.EAM   Pellet stops.
BC 2, M1 (BB 6), dies 7.O1/7.R1, the high weight tends to confirm that this coin is a pattern; North 2020/1; Seaby 2544. Bt Spink 1962.

[*continued overleaf*]

PLATE 70

756   757   758   759

760   761   762   763   764

765   766   767   768

Plate 70 (*cont.*)

762 Crown
    2.83   43.7   190°

I.m. lis both sides.
Obv.: ✚ELIZABETH.D.G.ANG.FRA.ET.HIB.REGINA   Pellet stops. BB, bust E.
Rev.: ✚SCVTVM.FIDIEI.PROTEGET.EAM   Pellet stops. Note reading FIDIEI.
Edge: serrated.
BC 2, M3 (BB 9), dies 9.O1/9.R1; North 2020/3; Seaby 2544. Ex Hird (private sale); ex Carter.

763 Half-crown
    1.27   19.6   20°

I.m. star both sides.
Obv.: ✱ ELIZABETH.D.G.ANG.FRA.ET.HIB.REGINA   Pellet stops. BB, bust D.
Rev.: ✱ SCVTVM.FIDEI.PROTEGET.EAM   Pellet stops.
BC 2, N1 (BB 10), dies 10.O1/10.R1; North 2021/1; Seaby 2545. Ex Burton (7).

764 Half-crown
    1.43   22.1   180°

I.m. lis both sides.
Obv.: ✚ELIZABETH.D.G.ANG.FRA.ET.HIB.REGINA   Pellet stops. Curly Z. BB, bust E. Pellet outer circle.
Rev.: ✚SCVTVM.FIDEI.PROTEGET.EAM   Pellet stops.
Edge: serrated.
BC 2, N2 (BB 11), dies 11.O1/11.R1; North 2021/2; Seaby 2545. Bt Baldwin 1939.

SECOND ISSUE (19 April 1572–10 June 1593)

FIRST PERIOD OF SECOND ISSUE (to 30 January 1583)

Fine gold coinage of 23 ct 3½ gr. (0.995 fine) until 1 October 1578 and 23 ct 3¼ gr. (0.992 fine) thereafter, at a weight of 80 gr. (5.184 g) to the angel of 10s 0d. Denominations struck were angel, half-angel and quarter-angel. The coins are classified according to Brown and Comber 1989 (BC 2).

Characteristics: Conventional angel type. On a few dies the ship is headed to left instead of the usual right. Note that the usual legend has FR and not FRA as indicated in Brown and Comber 1989.

Initial marks:		
	Ermine	19 April 1572–30 Oct. 1573
	Acorn	1 Nov. 1573–25 May 1574
	Eglantine	29 May 1574–30 July 1578
	Cross	1 Oct. 1578–17 May 1580
	Long cross	1 June 1580–31 Dec. 1581
	Sword	23 July 1582–31 Jan. 1583

London mint only

765 Angel
    5.07   78.2   340°

I.m. acorn both sides.
Obv.: ❦ELIZABETH:D:G:ANG:FR:ET:HI:REGINA   Pellet stops, double after ELIZABETH and ET.
Rev.: ❦A:DNO:FACTVM EST ISTVD:ET:EST:MIRABI: Double pellet stops, single after MIRABI'. No stops after FACTVM and EST. Ship headed left.
BC 2, C13; North 1991/2 (but this i.m. not listed); Seaby 2515. Bt Spink 1973 (*NCirc* 6988).

766 Angel
    5.09   78.6   190°

I.m. eglantine both sides.
Obv.: ✿ELIZABETH:D:G:ANG:FR:ET:HI:REGINA   Pellet stops, double after ELIZABETH.
Rev.: ✿A:DNO:FACTVM:EST:ISTVD:ET:EST:MIRABI: Double pellet stops, single after MIRABI'. Ship headed left.
BC 2, C14; North 1991/2; Seaby 2515. No provenance.

Plate 70 (*cont.*)

767 Angel
    5.17   79.8   100°

I.m. cross both sides.

Obv.: ✠ELIZABETH:D:G:ANG:FR:ET:HI:REGINA   Pellet stops, double after ELIZABETH and ET.

Rev.: ✠A:DNO:FACTVM:EST:ISTVD:ET:EST:MIRABI: Double pellet stops, single after MIRABI'.

BC 2, C17; North 1991/1; Seaby 2525. No provenance.

768 Angel
    5.09   78.6   10°

I.m. long cross over cross/long cross.

Obv.: ✝ELIZABETH D:G:ANG:FR:ET:HI:REGINA   Pellet stops, double after ET.

Rev.: ✝A:DNO:FACTVM.EST.ISTVD:ET.EST.MIRABI'.   Pellet stops, double after A, DNO and ISTVD.

BC 2, C18; North 1991/1; Seaby 2525. Ex Hird (private sale).

769 Angel

	Weight		
	g	*gr.*	*Die-axis*
	5.17	79.8	200°

I.m. sword both sides.
Obv.: ✚ELIZABETH:D:G:ANG:FR:ET:HI:REGINA
Pellet stops, double after ELIZABETH and ET.
Rev.: ✚A:DNO:FACTVM:EST:ISTVD:ET:EST:MIRABI:
Double pellet stops, single after MIRABI'.
BC 2, C20; North 1991/1; Seaby 2525. No provenance.

770 Half-angel
2.48 38.3 110°

I.m. acorn both sides.
Obv.: ♥ELIZABETH:D:G:ANG:FR:ET HI:REGINA   Pellet stops, double after
ELIZABETH. Punctuation after ET, if any, not visible.
Rev.: ♥A:DNO:FACTVM:EST:ISTVD:ET:EST:MIRA   Double pellet stops, tre-
ble after DNO.
BC 2, D6; North 1992/1; Seaby 2517. Ex Noble (565).

771 Half-angel
2.59 39.9 170°

I.m. eglantine both sides.
Obv.: ✽ELIZABETH:D:G:ANG꙳FR:ET HI REGINA   Double pellet stops in
the form of fat crescents, single after ANG and FR'. Large letters E, I and A.
Rev.: ✽A:DNO'FACTVM:EST ISTVD ET.EST:MIRA   Double pellet stops,
single after ET. Large letters A, F, I and V. No bowsprit.
BC 2, D7; North 1992/1; Seaby 2517. Ex Hird (private sale).

772 Half-angel
2.61 40.3 0°

I.m. cross both sides.
Obv.: ✚ELIZABETH:D:G:ANG:FR:ET:HI:REGINA   Double pellet stops.
Rev.: ✚A:DNO:FACTVM:EST ISTVD:ET:EST:MIRA   Double pellet stops.
BC 2, D8; North 1992/1; Seaby 2526. Ex Ryan (301).

773 Half-angel
2.62 40.5 60°

I.m. long cross both sides.
Obv.: ✝ELIZABETH:D:G:ANG:FR:ET:HI:REGINA   Pellet stops, double after
ELIZABETH and ET.
Rev.: ✝A:DNO:FACTVM:EST:ISTVD:ET:EST:MIRA.   Double pellet stops,
single after MIRA. Letter E and rose omitted from beside cross on mast.
BC 2, D9, this coin cited; North 1992/1 (this i.m. not listed); Seaby 2527. Ex Ryan
(302); ex Bruun (658 part, where incorrectly called 'plain cross').

774 Half-angel
2.49 38.5 230°

I.m. sword both sides.
Obv.: ✚ELIZABETH:D:G:ANG:FR:ET HI:REGINA   Pellet stops, double after
ELIZABETH and ET.
Rev.: ✚A:DNO:FACTVM:EST:ISTVD:ET:EST:MIRA: Double pellet stops,
single after MIRA'.
BC 2, D10; North 1992/1; Seaby 2526. No provenance.

775 Quarter-angel
1.28 19.8 20°

I.m. eglantine both sides.
Obv.: ✽ELIZABETH꙳D꙳G ANG꙳FRANCIE   Double pellet stops in the form of
fat crescents.
Rev.: ✽ET:HIBERNIE:REGINA:FIDEI: Double pellet stops.
BC 2, E5; North 1993; Seaby 2518. Bt Spink 1955.

776 Quarter-angel
1.28 19.7 220°

I.m. long cross both sides.
Obv.: ✝ELIZABETH:D.G.ANG.FRANCIE   Pellet stops, double after
ELIZABETH.
Rev.: ✝ET.HIBERNIE.REGINA.FIDEI.   Pellet stops.
BC 2, E8, this coin cited; North 1993; Seaby 2528. Ex Lockett (4096).

[*continued overleaf*]

PLATE 71

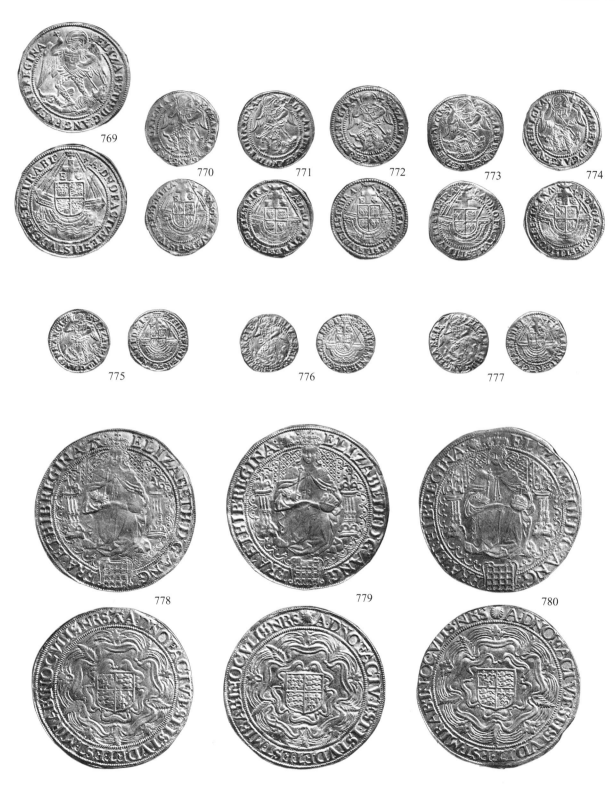

769

770   771   772   773   774

775   776   777

778   779   780

Plate 71 (*cont.*)

777 Quarter-angel

    1.30   20.0   190°

I.m. sword over (long?) cross/sword.

Obv.: ✠ELIZABETH D·G·ANG·FRANCIE   Pellet stops, double after **G**.

Rev.: ✠ET·HIBERNIE·REGINA·FIDEI.   Pellet stops.

BC 2, E9, but not recorded by them with the altered initial mark; North 1993; Seaby 2528. No provenance.

SECOND PERIOD OF SECOND ISSUE (1 February 1583–10 June 1593)

Fine gold coinage of fineness restored to 23 ct 3½ gr. (0.995 fine) at 240 gr. (15.552 g) to the sovereign of 30s 0d. Denominations issued were sovereign, ryal of 15s 0d, angel of 10s 0d, half-angel and quarter-angel. The classification used continues to be that set out in Brown and Comber 1989 (BC 2).

Characteristics: conventional types.

Initial marks:	Bell	1 Feb. 1583–29 Nov. 1583
	Gothic Ⴀ	1 Dec. 1583–13 Feb. 1585
	Scallop	14 Feb. 1585–30 May 1587
	Crescent	1 June 1587–31 Jan. 1590(?)
	Hand	1 Feb. 1590(?)–31 Jan. 1592(?)
	Tun	1 Feb. 1592(?)–(10 June 1593)
		(i.m. tun continued to be used into the third issue)

London mint only

778 Sovereign

    15.36   237.1   310°

I.m. Gothic Ⴀ both sides.

Obv.: Ⴀ:/ELIZABETH:D:G:ANG:/FRA:ET:HIB:REGINA: Pellet stops, double after i.m., **ELIZABETH**, **ET** and **REGINA**. Tressure divided by queen's head only. This die used on the next coin, **779**, with the i.m. altered.

Rev.: Ⴀ·A·DNO:FACTV:EST·ISTVD·ET·EST·MIRAB:IN·OCVLIS·NRS. Pellet stops. This die used on the next coin, **779**, with the i.m. altered.

BC 2, A9, this coin cited; North 2003; Seaby 2529. Ex Lockett (4088).

779 Sovereign

    15.07   232.5   330°

I.m. scallop over Gothic Ⴀ both sides.

Obv.: ❀:/ELIZABETH:D:G:ANG:/FRA:ET:HIB:REGINA: Pellet stops, double after i.m., **ELIZABETH**, **ET** and **REGINA**. Tressure divided by queen's head only. Pellets on pillars at back of throne. Same die as last coin, **778**, after alteration of the i.m.

Rev.: ❀·A·DNO:FACTV:EST·ISTVD·ET·EST·MIRAB:IN·OCVLIS·NRS Pellet stops. Same die as last coin, **778**, after alteration of the i.m.

BC 2, A10; North 2003; Seaby 2529. Ex Schulman sale 6.3.1958 (2703); ex Menso.

780 Sovereign

    15.14   233.7   180°

I.m. scallop both sides.

Obv.: ❀:/ELIZABETH:D:G:ANG:/FRA:ET:HIB:REGINA: Pellet stops, double after i.m., **ELIZABETH**, **ET** and **REGINA**. Tressure divided by queen's head only. Pellets on pillars and back of throne.

Rev.: ❀·A·DNO:FACTV:EST·ISTVD·ET·EST·MIRAB:IN·OCVLIS·NRS Pellet stops.

Similar to BC 2, A10 but without any evidence of the scallop mark being struck over Gothic Ⴀ; North 2003; Seaby 2529. Ex Hird (30).

781 Sovereign

	Weight	
g	*gr.*	*Die-axis*
15.38	237.3	20°

I.m. scallop both sides.
Obv.: ❀./ELIZABETH.D:G:ANG:/FRA:ET.HIB:REGINA.
Pellet stops. Tressure divided by queen's head. Pellets on pillars and pellets in annulets on back of throne.
Rev.: ❀A.DNO:FACTV:EST.ISTVD ET.EST.MIRAB:IN.OCVLIS.NRS:
Pellet stops.
Similar to BC 2, A18 but with pellets in annulets on back of throne; North 2003; Seaby 2529. No provenance.

782 Sovereign
15.46   238.6   120°

I.m. hand/hand over crescent.
Obv.: ➥/ELIZABETH.D:G:ANG:/FRA:ET.HIB:REGINA Pellet stops. tressure divided by queen's head. Pillars of throne plain and pellets in hatching on back of throne.
Rev.: ➥A.DNO:FACTV:EST.ISTVD:ET.EST.MIRAB:IN.OCVLIS.NRS'
Pellet stops.
BC 2, A25/A23, pl. 8, same die; North 2003; Seaby 2529. Ex Hird (31).

783 Sovereign
15.55   239.9   150°

I.m. tun both sides.
Obv.: ⬬/ELIZABETH.D:G:ANG:/FRA:ET.HIB:REGINA.   Pellet stops. Tressure divided by queen's head. Pellets in pillars of throne and pellets in hatching on back.
Rev.: ⬬A'.DNO:FACTV:EST.ISTVD ET.EST.MIRAB:IN.OCVL:NRS:
Pellet stops.
BC 2, A26; North 2003; Seaby 2529. Bt Baldwin; ex Carter.

784 Ryal
7.66   118.2   260°

I.m. Gothic Λ on reverse only.
Obv.: ELI/ZΛB:D:G:ΛNG:FR:ET.h/IB'/REGINΛ.   Pellet stops. Sail furls: 2 left, 3 right. Gothic lettering.
Rev.: Λ.IhS:ΛVT:TRΛNSIENS.PER.MEDIV:ILLORVM.IBΛT.   Pellet stops. Gothic lettering.
BC 2, B2, T(O1/R2,R3); North 2004; Seaby 2530. Bt Baldwin 1959; ex Carter. See **889** and **890** for Continental copies of this issue.

785 Ryal
7.60   117.3   290°

I.m. scallop on reverse only.
Obv.: ELI/ZΛB:D:G:ΛNG:FR:ET.h/IB'/REGINΛ.   Pellet stops. Sail furls: 2 left, 3 right. Gothic lettering.
Rev.: ❀IhS:ΛVT:TRΛNSIENS.PER.MEDIV:ILLORVM.IBΛT.   Pellet stops. Gothic lettering.
BC 2, B6, T(O1/R2,R3); North 2004; Seaby 2530.

786 Angel
5.17   79.8   110°

I.m. bell/bell over sword.
Obv.: ⚲ELIZABETH:D:G:ANG:FR:ET:HI:REGINA   Pellet stops, double after ELIZABETH and ET.
Rev.: ⚲A:DNO:FACTVM.EST.ISTVD:ET.EST.MIRABI: Pellet stops, double after A, DNO and ISTVD.
BC 2, C24/C21; North 2005; Seaby 2531. No provenance.

787 Angel
5.18   79.9   80°

I.m. Gothic Λ both sides.
Obv.: Λ ELIZABETH:D:G:ANG:FR:ET:HI:REGINA   Pellet stops, double after ELIZABETH and ET.
Rev.: Λ.A:DNO:FACTVM:EST:ISTVD:ET:EST:MIRABI: Double pellet stops, single after i.m. and MIRABI'.
BC 2, C29; North 2005; Seaby 2531. Ex Lockett (1964).

PLATE 72

781   782   783

784   785   786   787

788 Angel

	Weight		
	g	*gr.*	*Die-axis*
	5.10	78.7	200°

I.m. scallop both sides.
Obv.: ❋ELIZABETH:D:G:ANG:FR:ET:HI:REGINA.
    Pellet stops, double after ELIZABETH and ET.
Rev.: ❋A.DNO:FACTVM:EST:ISTVD:ET:EST:MIRABI:
    Double pellet stops, single after A and MIRABI'.
BC 2, C33; North 2005; Seaby 2531. Ex Hird (37); ex Lockett (1965).

789 Angel

	5.11	78.9	150°

I.m. crescent over scallop/crescent.
Obv.: ☽ ELIZABETH.D:G:ANG:FR:ET.HI:REGINA
    Pellet stops.
Rev.: ☽ A.DNO:FACTVM:EST.ISTVD:ET:EST:MIRABI:
    Double pellet stops, single after A, first EST and MIRABI'.
BC 2, C34; North 2005; Seaby 2531. Ex Lockett (4092).

790 Angel

	4.93	76.1	70°

I.m. hand both sides.
Obv.: ☛ELIZABETH:D:G:ANG:FR:ET:HI:REGINA.
    Pellet stops, double after ELIZABETH and ET.
Rev.: ☛A.DNO:FACTVM:EST ISTVD:ET:EST:MIRABI:
    Double pellet stops, single after A and MIRABI'. BC 2, C39; North 2005;
    Seaby 2531. Ex Christie sale 10.10.1967 (166).

791 Half-angel

	2.55	39.3	0°

I.m. bell both sides.
Obv.: 🔔ELIZABETH:D:G:ANG:FR:ET.HI:REGINA
    Pellet stops, double after ELIZABETH.
Rev.: 🔔A:DNO:FACTVM:EST:ISTVD:ET:EST:MIRA:
    Double pellet stops, single after MIRA'.
BC 2, D13; North 2006; Seaby 2532. Bt Spink 1961.

792 Half-angel

	2.66	41.1	50°

I.m. crescent over scallop both sides.
Obv.: ☽ ELIZABETH:D:G:ANG:FR:ET:HI:REGINA
    Pellet stops, double after ELIZABETH and ET.
Rev.: ☽ A:DNO FACTVM:EST ISTVD ET:EST.MIRA. Struck from a very
    rusty die which may obscure some stops which are possibly double throughout,
    except after MIRA.
BC 2, D17; North 2006; Seaby 2532. Bt Spink 1965.

793 Quarter-angel

	1.22	18.8	90°

I.m. bell both sides.
Obv.: 🔔ELIZABETH D.G:ANG:FRANCIE Double pellet stops, single after D.
Rev.: 🔔ET.HIBERNIE.REGINA.FIDEI. Pellet stops.
BC 2, E11, this coin cited; North 2007; Seaby 2533. Ex Lockett (1979).

794 Quarter-angel

	1.24	19.2	100°

I.m. Gothic A over bell/Gothic A, possibly over bell.
Obv.: Ⱥ ELIZABETH:D:G:ANG:FRANCIE Pellet stops, double after
    ELIZABETH.
Rev.: Ⱥ ET.HIBERNIE REGINA.FIDEI. Pellet stops.
BC 2, E12; North 2007; Seaby 2533. Ex Hird (43); ex Grantley (1535).

795 Quarter-angel

	1.33	10.5	330°

I.m. hand both sides.
Obv.: ☛ELIZABETH.D:G:ANG'FRANCIE Pellet stops.
Rev.: ☛ET.HIBERNIE.REGINA.FIDEI. Pellet stops.
BC 2, E18; North 2007; Seaby 2533. Ex Noble (572).

[*continued overleaf*]

PLATE 73

788

789

790

791

792

793

794

795

796

797

798

799

Plate 73 (*cont.*)

796 Quarter-angel
    1.25   19.2   170°

I.m. tun both sides.
Obv.: ⏻ELIZABETH:D:G:ANG:FRANCIE   Pellet stops, double after ELIZABETH.
Rev.: ⏻ET.HIBERNIE.REGINA.FIDEI   Pellet stops.
BC 2, E19; North 2007; Seaby 2533. Bt Baldwin 1960.

THIRD ISSUE (10 June 1593–24 March 1603)

Gold coinage issued at two standards of fineness:

  A. Crown gold of 22 ct (0.917 fine) at a nominal weight of 174.5 gr. (11.31 g) to the pound of 20s 0d. After 29 July 1601 this weight was reduced to 171.9 gr. (11.14 g). Denominations struck were pound, half-pound, crown and half-crown.
  B. Fine gold of 23 ct 3½ gr. (0.995 fine) at a nominal weight of 80 gr. (5.18 g) to the angel of 10s 0d. After 29 July 1601 this weight was reduced to 78.9 gr. (5.11 g). Denominations struck were angel, half-angel and quarter-angel (the fractions were not made after 29 July 1601).

The classification used continues to be that put forward in Brown and Comber 1989 (BC 2).

Initial marks:

Tun	(10 June 1593)–8 May 1594	
Woolpack	9 May 1594–13 Feb. 1596	
Key	14 Feb. 1596–7 Feb. 1599	
Anchor	8 Feb. 1599–30 April 1600	
0 (cypher)	1 May 1600–20 May 1601	
1	29 July 1601–14 May 1602	
2	15 May 1602–24 March 1603	

A. CROWN GOLD COINAGE

Characteristics: Similar to the crown gold coinage of the First Issue but now with a bust with long hair and a highly ornamented dress.

London mint only

797 Pound
    11.18   172.6   180°

I.m. tun, with lion at the end of the legend/tun.
Obv.: ⏻ELIZABETH⸱D⸱G⸱ANG⸱FRA⸱ET⸱HIB⸱REGINA⸱🦁.
    Annulet stops, double after ELIZABETH and ET. BC 1, bust 7A. Pellet after lion.
Rev.: ⏻SCVTVM⸱FIDEI⸱PROTEGET⸱EAM⸱   Double annulet stops, single after EAM.
BC 2, F3; North 2008; Seaby 2534. Bt Spink 1952.

798 Pound
    11.05   170.5   330°

I.m. tun both sides.
Obv.: ⏻ELIZABETH:D:G:ANG:FRA:ET:HIB:REGINA.
    Pellet stops, double after ELIZABETH and ET. BC 1, bust 7A.
Rev.: ⏻SCVTVM⸱FIDEI⸱PROTEGET⸱EAM⸱   Double annulet stops, single after EAM.
BC 2, F4; North 2008; Seaby 2534. Ex Beresford-Jones (73).

799 Pound
    11.22   173.1   100°

I.m. woolpack both sides.
Obv.: ✠ELIZABETH:D:G:ANG:FRA:ET⸱HIB:REGINA⸱
    Annulet stops. BC 1, bust 8A.
Rev.: ✠SCVTVM⸱FIDEI⸱PROTEGET⸱EAM⸱   Annulet stops. Same die as next coin, **800**, before i.m. altered.
BC 2, F6; North 2008; Seaby 2534. Ex O'Byrne (36).

THIRD ISSUE (*cont.*)

A. CROWN GOLD COINAGE (*cont.*)

London mint (cont.)

800 Pound

	Weight	
g	*gr.*	*Die-axis*
11.22	173.2	190°

I.m. key over woolpack both sides.
Obv.: ⚓ELIZABETH:D:G:ANG:FRA:ET:HIB:REGINA.
  Pellet stops, double after ELIZABETH and ET. BC 1, bust 8A.
Rev.: ⚓SCVTVM•FIDEI•PROTEGET•EAM• Annulet stops. Same die as last
  coin, **799**, after the i.m. has been altered.
BC 2, F12; North 2008; Seaby 2534. Bt Baldwin 1953; ex Carter.

801 Pound
  11.16 172.3 180°

I.m. key over woolpack to left of crown/key over woolpack.
Obv.: ⚓/ELIZABETH:D:G:ANG:FRA:ET:HIBER:REGINA
  Pellet stops, double after ELIZABETH and ET. BC 1, bust 8A. Reads HIBER.
Rev.: ⚓SCVTVM.FIDEI.PROTEGET.EAM. Pellet stops.
BC 2, F14; North 2008; Seaby 2534. Bt Spink 1978; ex Bernstein; ex Hird (not in
sale).

802 Pound
  11.11 171.5 310°

I.m. long key/key over woolpack.
Obv.: ⚓ELIZABETH.D:G:ANG:FR:ET.HIB:REGINA.
  Pellet stops. BC 1, bust 8A. Reads FR'
Rev.: ⚓SCVTVM.FIDEI.PROTEGET.EAM. Pellet stops.
BC 2, F18; North 2008; Seaby 2534. Bt Spink.

803 Pound
  11.17 172.4 10°

I.m. anchor over key both sides.
Obv.: ⚓ELIZABETH:D:G:ANG:FRA:ET:HIB:REGINA.
  Pellet stops, double after ELIZABETH and ET. BC 1, bust 8A.
Rev.: ⚓SCVTVM:FIDEI:PROTEGET:EAM. Double pellet stops, single after
  EAM.
BC 2, F21, this coin cited; North 2008; Seaby 2534. Ex Lockett (3290); ex Bliss (295);
ex Murdoch (585).

804 Pound
  11.26 173.7 50°

I.m. O (cypher) to left of crown/O (cypher).
Obv.: O/ELIZABETH.D:G:ANG:FRA:ET.HIB:REGINA.
  Pellet stops. BC 1, bust 8A.
Rev.: O SCVTVM.FIDEI.PROTEGET.EAM. Pellet stops.
BC 2, F22; North 2008; Seaby 2534. Ex Hird (48); ex Lockett (1984).

805 Pound
  11.05 170.5 260°

I.m. 1 both sides.
Obv.: 1:ELIZABETH.D:G:ANG:FRA:ET.HIB:REGINA.
  Pellet stops, double after i.m. BC 1, bust 8A.
Rev.: 1:SCVTVM.FIDEI.PROTEGET.EAM. Pellet stops, double after i.m.
BC 2, F23; North 2008; Seaby 2539. Bt Baldwin; ex Carter.

806 Pound
  11.14 171.9 180°

I.m. 2 both sides.
Obv.: 2:ELIZABETH.D:G:ANG:FRA:ET.HIB:REGINA.
  Pellet stops, double after i.m. BC 1, bust 8A.
Rev.: 2:SCVTVM.FIDEI.PROTEGET.EAM. Pellet stops, double after i.m.
BC 2, F24; North 2008; Seaby 2539. Ex Hird (private sale).

PLATE 74

800

801

802

803

804

805

806

THIRD ISSUE (*cont.*)

A. CROWN GOLD COINAGE (*cont.*)

London mint (cont.)

807 Pattern half-pound

Weight		
g	*gr.*	*Die-axis*
5.62	86.7	310°

I.m. tun both sides.
Obv.: ⏣.ELIZABETH.D:G:ANG:FRA:ET.HI:REGINA.
   Pellet stops. Small bust wholly within inner circle (BC 1, bust P3).
Rev.: .⏣SCVTVM.FIDEI.PROTEGET.EAM.   Pellet stops. Round crown and
   large shield which differ from the crown and shield normally used on the Third
   Issue.
BC 2, G20, 'usually described as a pattern'; North 2040; Seaby –. Bt Baldwin 1953; ex
Carter; ex Roth (281); ex Montagu (46); ex Brice; ex Bergne (601).

808 Half-pound

5.61	86.6	60°

I.m. tun both sides.
Obv.: ⏣ELIZAB:D:G:ANG:FRA:ET:HIB:REGINA.
   Pellet stops, double after ET. BC 1, bust 7B.
Rev.: ⏣.SCVTVM.FIDEI.PROTEGET.EAM.   Pellet stops.
BC 2, G21; North 2009; Seaby 2535. No provenance.

809 Half-pound

5.61	86.5	20°

I.m. tun both sides.
Obv.: ⏣ELIZAB:D:G:ANG:FRA ET:HIB:REGINA
   Pellet stops, none after FRA double after ET. BC 1, bust 7D.
Rev.: ⏣SCVTVM:FIDEI:PROTEGET:EAM.   Double pellet stops, single after
   EAM.
BC 2, G22; North 2009; Seaby 2535. Bt Baldwin 1953; ex Carter.

810 Half-pound

5.69	87.8	300°

I.m. woolpack both sides.
Obv.: ✂ELIZABETH.D:G:ANG.FRA:ET:HI:REGINA.
   Pellet stops, double after ET. BC 1, bust 8B.
Rev.: ✂SCVTVM.FIDEI.PROTEGET.EAM.   Pellet stops.
BC 2, G26, but unlike the variety described this one does not have the R of REGINA
over B of HIB; North 2009; Seaby 2535. Bt Spink; ex Birchmore; ex Hird (52); ex
Sangorski.

811 Half-pound

5.64	87.0	200°

I.m. key both sides.
Obv.: ⚷oELIZAB:D:G:ANG:FRA:ET.HIB:REGINA.
   Pellet stops. BC 1, bust 8B.
Rev.: ⚷oSCVTVM.FIDEI.PROTEGET.EAM.   Pellet stops.
BC 2, G28, this coin cited; North 2009; Seaby 2535. Ex Ryan (331).

812 Half-pound

5.51	85.1	100°

I.m. 2 both sides.
Obv.: 2:ELIZAB:D:G:ANG:FRA:ET.HIB:REGINA.
   Pellet stops, double after i.m. BC 1, bust 8B.
Rev.: 2:SCVTVM.FIDEI.PROTEGET.EAM.   Pellet stops, double after i.m.
BC 2, G32, this coin cited; North 2009; Seaby 2540. Ex Lockett (4100).

813 Crown

2.82	43.5	80°

I.m. tun both sides.
Obv.: ⏣ELIZAB:D:G:ANG:FRA:ET.HIB:REGI:
   Pellet stops. BC 1, bust 7C.
Rev.: ⏣SCVTVM:FIDEI:PROTEGET:EAM   Double pellet stops.
BC 2, H13; North 2010; Seaby 2536. No provenance.

814 Crown

2.79	43.1	200°

I.m. woolpack to left of crown/woolpack.
Obv.: ✂/ELIZAB:D:G:ANG:FRA:ET.HIB:REGI:
   Pellet stops. BC 1, bust 7C.
Rev.: ✂SCVTVM:FIDEI:PROTEGET:EAM.   Double pellet stops, single after
   EAM.
BC 2, H15; North 2010; Seaby 2536. Ex J. C. S. Rashleigh (35).

PLATE 75

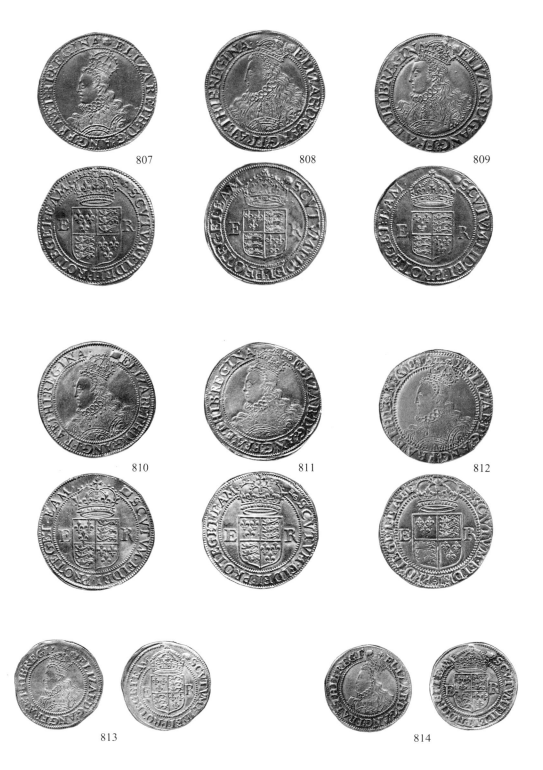

807   808   809

810   811   812

813   814

THIRD ISSUE (*cont.*)

London mint (cont.)

815 Crown

	Weight	
g	*gr.*	*Die-axis*
2.80	43.2	110°

I.m. O (cypher) both sides.
Obv.: O ELIZAB:D:G:ANG:FR:ET.HI:REGINA
 Pellet stops. BC 1, bust 8C.
Rev.: O SCVTVM.FIDEI.PROTEGET.EA: Pellet stops.
BC 2, H22; North 2010; Seaby 2536. Ex Ryan (342); ex Powell (32).

816 Crown
 2.53 39.1 250°

I.m. 1 both sides.
Obv.: 1:ELIZAB:D:G:ANG:FRA:ET.HIB:REGI:
 Pellet stops, double after i.m. BC 1, bust 8C.
Rev.: 1:SCVTVM.FIDEI.PROTEGET.EA: Pellet stops, double after i.m.
BC 2, H23, this coin cited; North 2010; Seaby 2541. Ex Glendining sale 9.12.1964
(18); ex Lockett (1995).

817 Crown
 2.69 41.5 210°

I.m. 2 both sides.
Obv.: 2:ELIZAB:D:G:ANG:FRA:ET.HIB:REGI:
 Pellet stops, double after i.m. BC 1, bust 8C.
Rev.: 2SCVTVM.FIDEI.PROTEGET.EA: Pellet stops.
BC 2, H24; North 2010; Seaby 2541. Ex Hird (private sale); ex Ryan (343); ex
Vaughan-Morgan (52 part).

818 Half-crown
 1.43 22.1 0°

I.m. tun both sides.
Obv.: ⬓ELIZAB:D:G:ANG:FR:ET.HIB:REGI.
 Pellet stops. BC 1, bust 7D.
Rev.: ⬓ SCVTVM FIDEI:PROTEGET.EAM. Pellet stops, none after SCVTVM,
 double after FIDEI.
BC 2, J13; North 2011; Seaby 2537. No provenance.

819 Half-crown
 1.20 18.5 210°

I.m. none/tun.
Obv.: ELIZAB:D:G:ANG:FR:ET:HIB:REGI:
 Pellet stops, double after ET. BC 1, bust 7D.
Rev.: ⬓SCVTVM:FIDEI:PROTEGET:EAM. Double pellet stops, single after
 EAM.
BC 2, J14; North 2011; Seaby 2537. Ex Reynolds (34).

820 Half-crown
 1.41 21.8 200°

I.m. key over woolpack to left of crown/key over woolpack.
Obv.: ⚷o/ELIZAB:D:G:ANG:FR:ET.HIB:REGI
 Pellet stops. BC 1, bust 7D.
Rev.: ⚷oSCVTVM.FIDEI.PROTEGET.EAM. Pellet stops.
BC 2, J17, same dies; North 2011; Seaby 2537. Ex Glendining sale 24.11.1976 (117).

821 Half-crown
 1.42 21.9 200°

I.m. O (cypher) both sides.
Obv.: O ELIZAB:D:G:ANG:FR:ET.HI:REGI:
 Pellet stops. BC 1, bust 7D.
Rev.: O SCVTVM.FIDEI.PROTEGET.EAM. Pellet stops.
BC 2, J21; North 2011; Seaby 2537. Ex Hird (private sale); ex Napier (23 part).

[*continued overleaf*]

PLATE 76

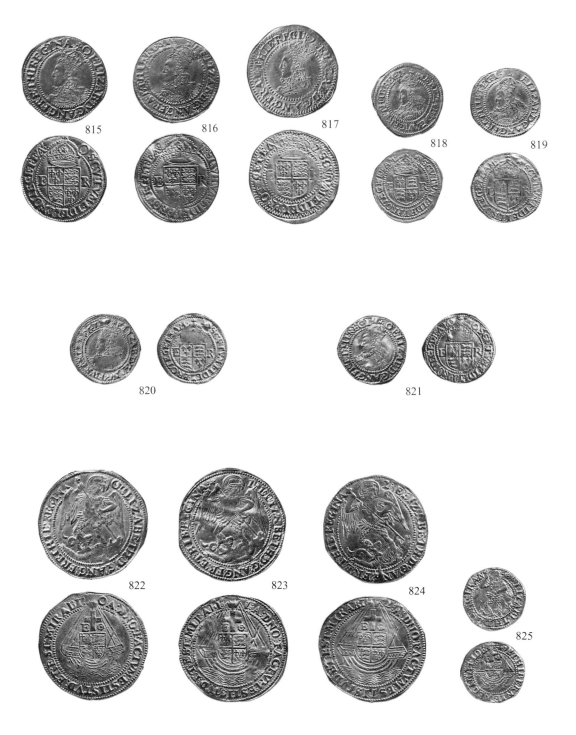

815   816   817   818   819

820   821

822   823   824   825

Plate 76 (*cont.*)

Characteristics: these continue to be of the conventional angel type.

London mint only

822 Angel
5.15   79.4   0°
    I.m. O (cypher) both sides.
    Obv.: O ELIZABETH:D:G:ANG:FR˙ET HIB˙REGINA
        Pellet stops, none after FR˙, ET, HIB˙ and REGINA, double after
        ELIZABETH.
    Rev.: O A:DNO:FACTVM:EST ISTVD:ET:EST:MIRABI:
        Double pellet stops, none after first EST, single after MIRABI'.
    BC 2, C48; North 2005; Seaby 2531. Ex Lockett (4093).

823 Angel
5.06   78.1   80°
    I.m. 1 both sides.
    Obv.: 1ELIZABETH:D:G:ANG:FR˙ET:HIB:REGINA.
        Pellet stops, double after ELIZABETH and ET.
    Rev.: 1:A:DNO:FACTVM:EST.ISTVD:ET:EST:MIRABI:
        Double pellet stops, single after the first EST and MIRABI'.
    BC 2, C49 and pl. 9, this coin; North 2005; Seaby 2538. Ex Doubleday (123).

824 Angel
5.12   79.0   280°
    I.m. 2 both sides.
    Obv.: 2:ELIZABETH:D:G:ANG:FR˙ET:HIB:REGINA.
        Pellet stops, double after i.m., ELIZABETH and ET.
    Rev.: 2:A:DNO:FACTVM:EST.ISTVD:ET:EST:MIRABI:
        Double pellet stops, single after the first EST and MIRABI'.
    BC 2, C50, this coin cited; North 2005; Seaby 2538. Ex Lockett (3282).

825 Quarter-angel
1.36   21.0   270°
    I.m. key (over woolpack?) both sides.
    Obv.: ⚷O ELIZABETH.D˙G˙ANG˙FRAN: Pellet stops.
    Rev.: ⚷O ET HIBERNIE.REGINA FIDE   Pellet stop.
    BC 2, E20 and pl. 9, this coin cited; North 2007; Seaby 2533. Ex Lockett (3288).

CONTINENTAL IMITATIONS

IMITATIONS OF NOBLES OF HENRY VI

For classification see p. 85 and Table 15 above.

GROUP 1

Characteristics: Imitating annulet nobles. Two large pellets on side of ship. Usually read Ihℰ. Trefoil stops on obverse, annulet stops on reverse.

826 Noble

	Weight		
	g	gr.	Die-axis
	6.79	104.8	50°

Obv.: h/ℰNRIℭ✠DI·GRℲ·RℰX·ℲNGL·S·FRℲN·DNS·hY·
Ornaments, 1–1–1. Ropes, 2/1. Lis after hℰNRIℭ. Annulet by wrist.
Rev.: ✠Ihℰ✳ℲVT⋮TRℲNSIℰNS°PℰR°MℰDIVM°ILLOR⋮IBℲT
Cinquefoil after Ihℰ. Annulet in first spandrel of second quarter. Same die as next coin, **827**.
Group 1a. Ex Dee (87).

827 Noble
6.55   101.1   230°

Obv.: h/ℰNRIℭ[   ]RℰX·ℲNGL·S·FRℲN⋮DNS·hY·
Ornaments, 1–1–1. Ropes, 2/1. Quatrefoils, 3/3. No annulet by wrist.
Rev.: same die as last coin, **826**.
Group 1a. Bt Spink 1970.

828 Noble
6.58   101.6   80°

Obv.: h/ℰNRIℭ✠DI·GRℲ·RℰX·ℲNGL·S·FRℲN⋮DNS·hY·
Ornaments, 1–1–1. Ropes, 2/1. Lis after hℰNRIℭ. Annulet by wrist.
Rev.: ✠Ihℰ✳ℲVT⋮TRℲNSIℰNS°PℰR°MℰDIVM°ILLOR⋮IBℲ
Cinquefoil after Ihℰ. Annulet in first spandrel of second quarter. Pellet in central h.
Group 1a. No provenance.

829 Noble
6.75   104.2   180°

Obv.: h/ℰNRIℭ✠DI·GRℲ⋮RℰX·ℲNGL·S·FRℲN⋮DNS⋮hY·
Ornaments, 1–1–1. Ropes, 2/1. Lis after hℰNRIℭ. Annulet by wrist.
Rev.: ✠Ihℰ✳ℲVT⋮TRℲNSIℰNS°PℰR°MℰDIVM°ILLORV⋮IBℲT
Cinquefoil after Ihℰ. Annulet in first spandrel of second quarter.
Group 1a. Bt Spink 1962.

830 Noble
6.60   101.9   250°

Obv.: h/ℰNRIℭ·DI·GRℲ·RℰX ℲNG[   ]ℲN⋮DNS·hY·
Ornaments, 1–1–1. Ropes, 2/1. Trefoil after hℰNRIℭ. Nothing by wrist.
Rev.: ✠Ihℰ·[ ]VT⋮TRℲNSIℰNS°P[   ]DIVM°ILLORV⋮IBℲT
Trefoil after Ihℰ. Annulet in first spandrel of second quarter.
Group 1b. No provenance.

GROUP 2

Characteristics: Similar to Group 1 but without the two large pellets on the side of the ship.

831 Noble
6.80   104.9   80°

Obv.: h/ℰNRIℭ✠DI⋮GRℲ⋮RℰX⋮ℲNGL·S·FRℲN⋮DNS·hYB
Ornaments, 1–1–1. Ropes, 2/1. Lis after hℰNRIℭ. Annulet by wrist.
Rev.: ✠Ih'ℭ·ℲVT⋮TRℲNSIℰNS°PℰR°MℰDIVM°ILLOR⋮IBℲT
Reads Ih'ℭ. Trefoil after Ih'ℭ. Annulet in first spandrel of second quarter.
Group 2a. No provenance.

832 Noble
6.65   102.7   100°

Obv.: h/ℰNRIℭ⋮DI⋮GRℲ⋮RℰX·ℲNGL·S·FRℲN⋮DNS·hY·
Ornaments, 1–1–1. Ropes, 2/1. Trefoil after hℰNRIℭ.
Rev.: ✠Ihℰ✳ℲVT⋮TRℲNSIℰNS°PℰR°MℰDIVM°ILLOR⋮IBℲ
Cinquefoil after Ihℰ. Annulet in first spandrel of second quarter.
Group 2b. No provenance.

833 Noble
6.58   101.5   170°

Obv.: h/ℰNRIℭ·DI·GRℲ⋮RℰX·ℲNGL·S·FRℲN⋮DNS⋮hY·
Ornaments, 1–1–1. Ropes, 2/1. Trefoil after h/ℰNRIℭ. Annulet by wrist.
Rev.: ✠Ihℰ ℲVT⋮TRℲNSIℰNS°PℰR°MℰDIVM°ILLORV⋮IBℲT
Trefoil after Ihℰ. Annulet in first spandrel of second quarter.
Group 2c. Bt Spink 1959 (*NCirc* no. 17447).

[*continued overleaf*]

PLATE 77

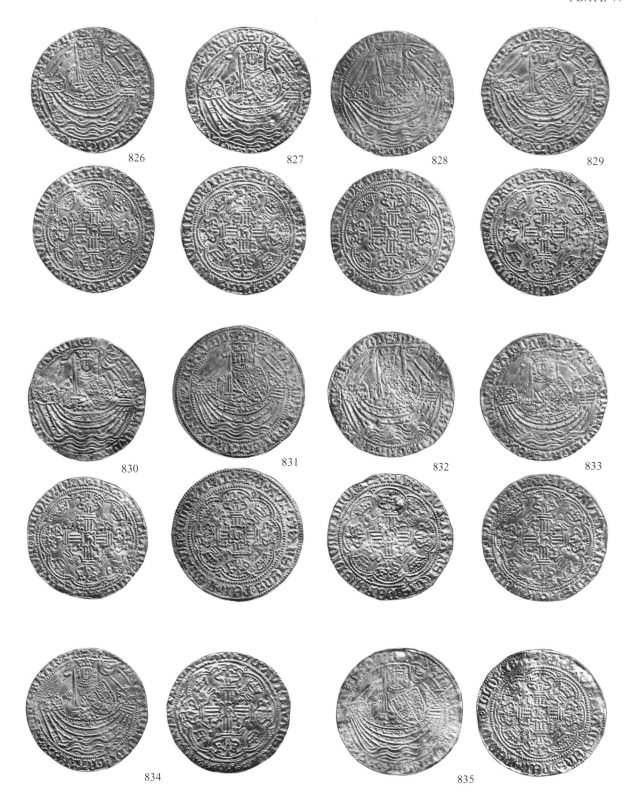

826 827 828 829

830 831 832 833

834 835

Plate 77 (*cont.*)

834 Noble
    6.68   103.1   140°

Obv.: h/ЄΠRIႢ⠆DI⠆GRꓥ⠆RЄX·ꓥΠGL⠆S·FRꓥΠ⠆DΠS·hY'
Ornaments, 1–1–1. Ropes, 2/1. Trefoil after hЄΠRIႢ. Annulet by wrist.

Rev.: ✚IhႢ·ꓥVT⠆TRꓥΠSIЄΠS°PЄR°MЄDIVM°ILLOR°IBꓥT
Reads IhႢ. Trefoil after IhႢ. Annulet in first spandrel of second quarter.

Group 2d; same dies as Serooskerke hoard 61a(4), lot 650. No provenance.

835 Noble
    6.64   98.0   10°

Obv.: h/ЄΠRI[   ]RЄX·ꓥΠG[   ]FRꓥΠ⠆DΠS hYB
Ornaments, 1–1–1. Ropes, 2/1. Probably trefoil after h/ЄΠRIႢ. Annulet by wrist.

Rev.: ✚Ih'Ⴀ·ꓥVT⠆TRꓥΠSIЄΠS°PЄR°MЄDIVM°ILLOR⠆IBꓥT
Reads IhႢ. Trefoil after IhႢ. Annulet in first spandrel of second quarter.

Group 2d. Ex Lockett Continental (257).

IMITATIONS OF NOBLES OF HENRY VI (*cont.*)

GROUP 3

Characteristics: Annulet on ship. Trefoil stops now both sides.

836 Noble

	Weight		Die-axis
	g	gr.	
	6.62	102.1	60°

Obv.: Һ/ЄΝRIΛ·DЄI·GRΛ·RЄX·ΛΝGL·S·FRΛΝɑ·DΝS·IBЄ'
Ornaments, 1–11–1. Ropes, 3/2. Trefoil after Һ/ЄΝRIɑ. Annulet by wrist.
Rev.: ✠IҺЄ·ΛVT·TRΛΝSIЄΝS·PЄR·MЄDIVM·ILLORVM·IBΛT
Trefoil after IҺЄ. No annulet in spandrels.
Group 3a. No provenance.

GROUP 4

Characteristics: Types inspired by other than annulet issues.

837 Noble

6.66	102.8	240°

Obv.: Һ/ЄΝRIɑ·'DЄI·'GRΛ·'RЄX·'ΛΝGL·S·FRΛΝɑ·DΝS·'IBЄ·'.
Ornaments, 1–11–1. Ropes, 3/2. Trefoil after ҺЄΝRIɑ. Nothing by wrist.
Trefoil stops. Nothing on ship.
Rev.: ✠IҺЄ·'ΛVT·'TRΛΝSIЄΝS·'PЄR·'MЄDIVM·'ILLORV·'IBΛT
I.m. cross. Reads IҺЄ. Trefoil stops. No annulet in spandrels.
Group 4a. Ex Lockett Continental (258).

838 Noble

6.72	103.7	350°

Obv.: Һ/ЄΝRIɑ·DI·GRΛ·RЄX·ΛΝGL·S·FRΛΝɑ·DΝS·IBΛ
Ornaments, –11–11. Ropes, 3/2. Trefoil after ҺЄΝRIɑ. Lis by wrist. Trefoil
stops. Nothing on ship.
Rev.: ✠IҺɑ·ΛVT·'TRΛΝSIЄΝS·'PЄR·'MЄDIVM·'ILLORVM·IBΛT[?]
I.m. cross. Reads IҺɑ. Trefoil stops. No annulet in spandrels. Central Һ (which
has the appearance of a Gothic Ν) is inverted.
Group 4b. No provenance.

IMITATIONS OF RYALS OF EDWARD IV

Classified according to Thompson 1945–8, extended as indicated on pp. 87–9 above.

GROUP I, EARLY STYLE

839 Ryal

7.60	117.3	80°

I.m. sun with all rays intact both sides.
Obv.: ✴Є/DWΛRD·DI·'GRΛ·'RЄX·'ΛΝGL·'S·FRΛΝɑ/·DΝS·'I·B·'
Same die as next coin, **840**, and Thompson pl. A, 5, though in an earlier state
than the latter, since it shows all eight of the sun's rays unbroken and the ship's
mast is visible.
Rev.: ✴IҺ·ɑ·ΛVT·'TRΛΝSIЄΝS·PЄR·MЄDIVM·ILLORVM·IBΛT.
Different die from Thompson pl. A, 7 (8).[359]
Thompson group I. Ex von Thielau (1537).

840 Ryal

7.58	116.9	30°

I.m. sun with all rays intact/crown with stops either side.
Obv.: same die as last coin, **839**, and Thompson pl. A, 5, though in an earlier state
than the latter, with all eight of the sun's rays unbroken and the ship's mast
visible.
Rev.: .♔.IҺ·ɑ·ΛVT·'TRΛΝSIЄΝS·PЄR·MЄDIV·'ILLORVM·IBΛT
Same die as Thompson pl. A, 6.
Thompson group I. No provenance.

---

[359] See Introduction, p. 87.

[*continued overleaf*]

PLATE 78

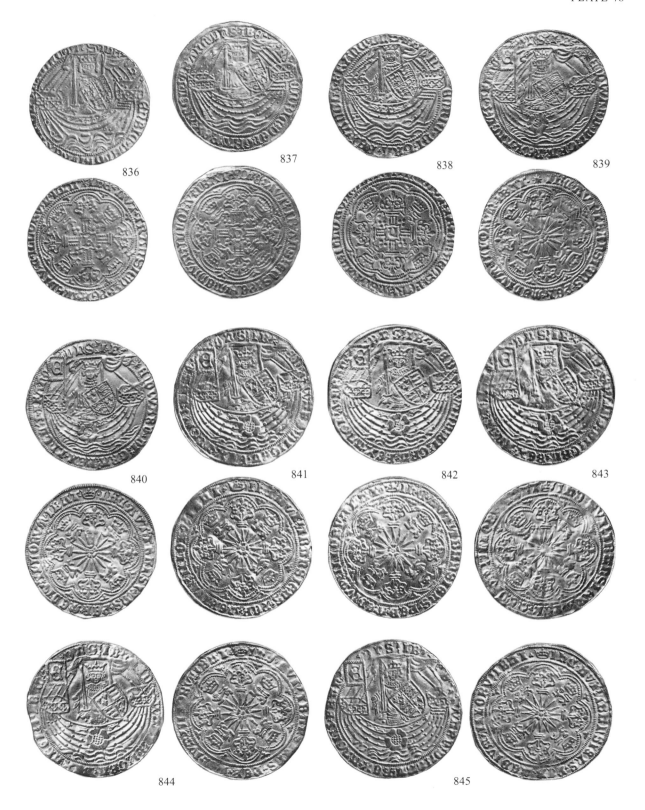

836

837

838

839

840

841

842

843

844

845

Plate 78 (*cont.*)

Class 1

841 Ryal
    7.52   116.1   220°
                          I.m. none/crown.
Obv.: ED·/·WARD·DI·GRA·REX·ANGL·S·FRAN·/·DNS·IB·
         Same die as next three coins, **842**, **843** and **844**, and as Thompson pl. B, 4–6.
Rev.: IhC AVT·TRANSIENS·PER·MEDIVM·ILLORV·IBAT·
         Same die as Thompson pl. B, 5.
Thompson Group II, Class 1. No provenance.

842 Ryal
    7.57   116.9   170°
                          I.m. none/crown.
Obv.: same die as last and next two coins, **841**, **843** and **844**, and as Thompson pl. B, 4–6.
Rev.: IhC·AVT·TRANSIENS·PER·MEDIVM·ILLORV·IBAT·
Thompson Group II, Class 1. Ex Goulburn (241); ex Carter.

843 Ryal
    7.47   115.3   270°
                          I.m. none/crown.
Obv.: same die as last two and next coins, **841**, **842** and **844**, and as Thompson pl. B, 4–6.
Rev.: IhƷ·AVT·TRANSIENS·PER·MEDIVM·ILLORV·IBAT
         Thompson Group II, Class 1. Ex Glendining sale 21.9.1960 (814).

844 Ryal
    7.53   116.3   40°
                          I.m. none/crown.
Obv.: same die as last three coins, **841**, **842** and **843**, and as Thompson pl. B, 4–6.
Rev.: IhƷ·AVT·TRANSIENS·PER·MEDIVM·ILLORV·IBAT·
Thompson Group II, Class 1. Ex Burton (158).

Class 2

845 Ryal
    7.61   117.5   110°
                          I.m. none/crown.
Obv.: ED/·WARD·DI·GRA·REX·ANGL·S·FRAN·/·DNS·IB·
         Same die as next two coins, **846** and **847**, and as Thompson pl. B, 7.
Rev.: IhC·AVT·TRANSIENS·PER·MEDIVM·ILLORV·IBAT·
Thompson Group II, Class 2. Bt Spink 1966.

IMITATIONS OF RYALS OF EDWARD IV (*cont.*)

GROUP II (*mint of Gorinchem*) (*cont.*)

Class 2 (*cont.*)

846 Ryal

Weight		
g	*gr.*	*Die-axis*
7.55	116.5	350°

I.m. none/crown.
Obv.: same die as last and next coins, **845** and **847**, and as Thompson pl. B, 7.
Rev.: ⚓ IhႠ·ႨVT·:TRႨNSIENS·PER·MEDIVM·:ILLORV·:IBႨT·:
  Same die as Thompson pl. B, 7.
Thompson Group II, Class 2. Bt Spink 1961.

847 Ryal
7.57 116.9 60°

I.m. none/crown.
Obv.: same die as last two coins, **845** and **846**, and as Thompson pl. B, 7.
Rev.: ⚓ IhႠ·ႨVT·:TRႨNSIENS·PER·MEDIVM·:ILLORV·:IBႨT·
  Thompson Group II, Class 2. Bt Spink 1992; ex Bourgey, Paris.

848 Ryal
7.57 116.8 110°

I.m. none/crown.
Obv.: ED/··WႨRD·:DI·:GRႨ·REX·ႨNGL·:S·FRႨN·/DNS·:IB·:
Rev.: ⚓ IhD·ႨVT·:TRႨNSIENS·PER·MEDIVM·:ILLORV·:IBႨT·
Thompson Group II, Class 2. Ex Vassallo (571).

849 Ryal
7.48 115.4 170°

I.m. none/crown.
Obv.: ED/··WႨRD·:DI·:GRႨ·REX·ႨNGL·:S·FRႨN·/·DNS·:IB·:
Rev.: ⚓ IhႠ·ႨVT·:TRႨNSIENS·PER·MEDIVM·:ILLORV·:IBႨT·
Thompson Group II, Class 2. Ex an unidentified Schulman sale (670).

850 Ryal
7.52 116.1 290°

I.m. none/crown.
Obv.: ED/··WႨRD·:DI·:GRႨ·REX·ႨNGL·:S·FRႨN/DNS·IB·:
Rev.: ⚓ IhD·:ႨVT·:TRႨNSIENS·:PER·MEDIVM·:ILLORVM·:IBႨT
Thompson Group II, Class 2. Bt Spink 1992; ex Bourgey, Paris.

851 Ryal
7.62 117.6 180°

I.m. none/crown.
Obv.: ED··WႨRD·:DI·:GRႨ·REX·ႨNGL·:S·FRႨN·:/DNS·:IB·:
  Arms of Arkel instead of a quatrefoil as the central decoration of the forecastle.
  Same die as next three coins, **852**, **853** and **854**, and as Thompson pl. C, 1.
Rev.: ⚓ IhD·ႨVT·TRႨNSIENS·PER·MEDIVM·:ILLORV·:IBႨT
  Same die as Thompson pl. C, 1.
Thompson Group II, Class 2. Bt Seaby 1957.

852 Ryal
7.48 115.5 280°

I.m. none/crown.
Obv.: same die as last and next two coins, **851**, **853** and **854**, and as Thompson pl. C, 1.
Rev.: ⚓ IhD·ႨVT·TRႨNSIENS·PER·MEDIVM·:ILLORV·":IBႨT
  Double abbreviation mark after ILLORV.
Thompson Group II, Class 2. No provenance.

853 Ryal
7.56 116.7 80°

I.m. none/crown.
Obv.: same die as last two and next coins, **851**, **852** and **854**, and as Thompson pl. C, 1.
Rev.: ⚓ IhD·ႨV.T[ ]TRႨNSIENS·PER·MEDIVM·:ILLORV·:IBႨT
  Apparent annulet between V and T of ႨVT; however, the coin is very thin at that point and this could be a spurious effect due to 'ghosting'.
Thompson Group II, Class 2. No provenance.

[*continued overleaf*]

PLATE 79

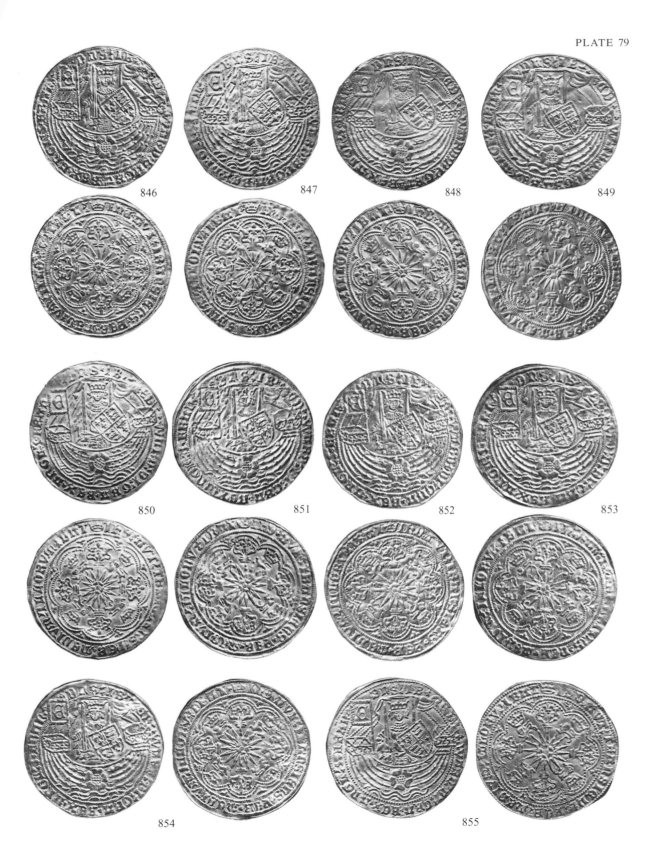

846   847   848   849

850   851   852   853

854   855

Plate 79 (*cont.*)

854 Ryal
    7.46   115.1   170°

I.m. none/crown.
Obv.: same die as last three coins, **851**, **852** and **853**, and as Thompson pl. C, 1.
Rev.: ⚓ IhD·ΛVT⫶TRΛNSIENS·PER·MEDIVM⫶ILLORV⫶IBΛT·
Thompson Group II, Class 2. Bt Spink 1971; ex Thompson; ex Hall.

855 Ryal
    7.56   116.7   50°

I.m. none/crown.
Obv.: ED/·⫶WΛRD⫶DI⫶GRΛ·REX·ΛNGL⫶S·FRΛN'/DNS⫶IB⫶
Rev.: ⚓ IhD·ΛVT⫶TRΛNSIENS·PER·MEDIVM⫶ILLORV⫶IBΛT
    The ornaments in the spandrels are strawberry leaves, quite different from the normal trefoils.
Thompson Group II, Class 2 but this variety not recorded by him. However, as all other characteristics are normal for Group II, Class 2, it seems safe to place the coin here. Ex O'Byrne (13).

IMITATIONS OF RYALS OF EDWARD IV (*cont.*)

GROUP II (*mint of Gorinchem*) (*cont.*)

Class 3a

	Weight			
	g	*gr.*	*Die-axis*	

856 Ryal

7.57	116.8	130°

I.m. none/crown.
Obv.: ЄD/··WᴧRD˸DI˸GRᴧ˸RƆX˸ᴧNGL˸S·FRᴧN'/·DNS˸IB˸
Reversed Ɑ for Є in RЄX.
Rev.: ⚓IhD·ᴧVT˸TRᴧNSIЄNS·PЄR·MЄDIVM˸ILLORV˸IBᴧT·
Same die as next coin, **857**.
Thompson Group II, Class 3a. Bt Spink 1960.

857 Ryal

7.59	117.2	10°

I.m. none/crown.
Obv.: ЄD/··WᴧRD˸DI˸GRᴧ·RЄX˸ᴧNGL˸S·FRᴧN'/·DNS˸IB˸
Rev.: same die as last coin, **856**.
Thompson Group II, Class 3a. Ex Münzen and Medaillen sale, Basel, 27.11.1964 (967).

858 Ryal

7.53	116.3	260°

I.m. none/crown.
Obv.: ЄD/··WᴧRD˸DI˸GRᴧ·RЄX˸ᴧNGL˸S·FRᴧN'/·DNS˸IB˸
Rev.: ⚓IhD·ᴧVT˸TRᴧNSIЄNS·PЄR·MЄDIVM˸ILLORV˸IBᴧT·
Same die as next four coins, **859**, **860**, **861** and **862**.
Thompson Group II, Class 3a. Ex Brauner (46).

859 Ryal

7.57	116.8	310°

I.m. none/crown.
Obv.: ЄD/··WᴧRD˸DI˸GRᴧ·RЄX·ᴧNGL˸S·FRᴧ'/·DNS˸IB˸   No N in
FRᴧN'.
Rev.: same die as last and next three coins, **858**, **860**, **861** and **862**.
Thompson Group II, Class 3a. Bt Spink 1961.

860 Ryal

7.52	116.1	190°

I.m. none/crown.
Obv.: ЄD/··WᴧRD˸DI˸GRᴧ·RЄX·ᴧNGL˸S·FRᴧN'/·DNS˸IB˸
Rev.: same die as last two and next two coins, **858**, **859**, **861** and **862**.
Thompson Group II, Class 3a. Bt Spink 1965; ex Thompson.

861 Ryal

7.57	116.8	50°

I.m. none/crown.
Obv.: ЄD/··WᴧRD˸DI˸GRᴧ·RЄX·ᴧNGL˸S·FRᴧN/·DNS˸IB˸
Rev.: same die as last three and next coins, **858**, **859**, **860** and **862**.
Thompson Group II, Class 3a. Bt Spink 1961.

862 Ryal

7.51	116.0	190°

I.m. none/crown.
Obv.: ЄD/··WᴧRD˸DI˸GRᴧ·RЄX·ᴧNGL˸S·FRᴧN'/·DNS˸IB˸
ᴧ in GRᴧ broken.
Rev.: same die as last four coins, **858**, **859**, **860** and **861**.
Thompson Group II, Class 3a. Bt Seaby 1966.

863 Ryal

7.65	116.7	20°

I.m. none/crown.
Obv.: ɑD/··WᴧRD˸DI˸GRᴧ·RɑX·ᴧNGL˸S·FRᴧN'/·DNS˸IB˸
Rev.: ⚓IhD·ᴧVT˸TRᴧNSIЄNS·PЄR·MЄDIVM˸ILLORV˸IBᴧT·
ᴧ in IBᴧT broken.
Thompson Group II, Class 3a. Bt Spink 1959.

864 Ryal

7.53	116.3	230°

I.m. none/crown.
Obv.: ЄD/··WᴧRD˸DI˸GRᴧ·RЄX·ᴧNGL˸S·FRᴧN'/·DNS˸IB˸
Rev.: ⚓IhD·ᴧVT˸TRᴧNSIɑNS·PɑR·MɑDIVM˸ILLORV˸IBᴧT·
Thompson Group II, Class 3a. Bt Spink 1958.

[*continued overleaf*]

PLATE 80

856   857   858   859

860   861   862   863

864   865

Plate 80 (*cont.*)

Group II, Mule of Class 3a/3b–c

865 Ryal
   7.54   116.4   190°

I.m. none/crown.
Obv.: ЄD/·· W ᴧR ⁝ DI ⁝ GR ᴧ · RЄX · ᴧNGL ⁝ S · FR ᴧN'/· DNS ⁝ IB ⁝
          Reads ЄD/W ᴧR' and FR ᴧN'. Early form of letter I.
Rev.: ⚓ IhD · ᴧ V T ⁝ TR ᴧNSIЄNS · PЄR · mЄDIVm ⁝ ILLOR V ⁝ IB ᴧ T
          Same die as **868** and Thompson pl. C, 6.
     Thompson Group II, Class 3a/3b. Bt Baldwin 1957.

IMITATIONS OF RYALS OF EDWARD IV *(cont.)*

GROUP II *(mint of Gorinchem)* *(cont.)*

Class 3b

866 Ryal				
	Weight			I.m. none/crown.
	g	*gr.*	*Die-axis*	*Obv.*: ED/··WARD·DI·GRA·REX·ANGL·S·FRAN/·DNS IB·
	7.52	116.1	160°	Same die as next coin, **867**.

Rev.: IhD·AVT·TRANSICNS·PCR·MCDIVM·ILLORV·IBAT

Thompson Group II, Class 3b. No provenance.

867 Ryal			
7.43	114.7	350°	I.m. none/crown.

Obv.: same die as last coin, **866**.

Rev.: IhD·AVT·TRANSICNS·PER·MCDIVM·ILLORVM·IBAT
A of IBAT with cross bar.

Thompson Group II, Class 3b. Bt Spink 1961.

Class 3c

868 Ryal			
7.51	116.0	240°	I.m. none/crown.

Obv.: ED/··WARD·DI·GRA·REX·ANGL·S·FRAN/·DNS·IB·

Rev.: same die as **865** and Thompson pl. C, 6.

Thompson Group II, Class 3c. No provenance.

869 Ryal			
7.51	115.9	200°	I.m. none/crown.

Obv.: CD/··WARD·DI·GRA·RCX·ANGL·S·FRAN/·DNS·IB·
Same die as next coin, **870**, and Thompson pl. C, 5.

Rev.: IhD·AVT·TRANSICNS·PCR·MCDIVM·ILLORV·IBAT

Thompson Group II, Class 3c. Bt Spink 1969.

870 Ryal			
7.56	116.6	310°	I.m. none/crown.

Obv.: same die as last coin, **869**, and Thompson pl. C, 5.

Rev.: IhD·AVT·TRANSICNS·PER·MCDIVM·ILLORVM·IBAT
Same die as next coin, **871**.

Thompson Group II, Class 3c. Ex Serooskerke hoard (675).

871 Ryal			
7.53	116.2	320°	I.m. none/crown.

Obv.: ED/·WARD·DI·GRA·REX·ANGL·S·FRA·/·DNS·IB·

Rev.: same die as last coin, **870**.

Thompson Group II, Class 3c. Bt Spink 1962.

872 Ryal			
7.55	116.5	340°	i.m. none/crown.

Obv.: ED/··WARD·DI·GRA·REX·ANGL·S·FRAN/·DNS·IB·
Same die as next coin, **873**.

Rev.: IhD·AVT·TRANSICNS·PER·MCDIVM·ILLORVM·IBAT

Thompson Group II, Class 3c. Ex Glendining sale 17.7.1962 (10).

873 Ryal			
7.55	116.5	30°	I.m. none/crown.

Obv.: same die as last coin, **872**.

Rev.: IhD·AVT·TRANSICNS·PER·MCDIVM·ILLORVM·IBAT

Thompson Group II, Class 3c. Bt Spink 1968.

874 Ryal			
7.56	116.6	240°	I.m. none/crown.

Obv.: CD/··WARD·DI·GRA·REX·ANGL·S·FRAN/·DNS·IB·

Rev.: IhD·AVT·TRANSICNS·PER·MCDIVM·ILLORVM·IBAT
Same die as next coin, **875**.

Thompson Group II, Class 3c. Ex Schulman sale 9.3.1959 (1782).

PLATE 81

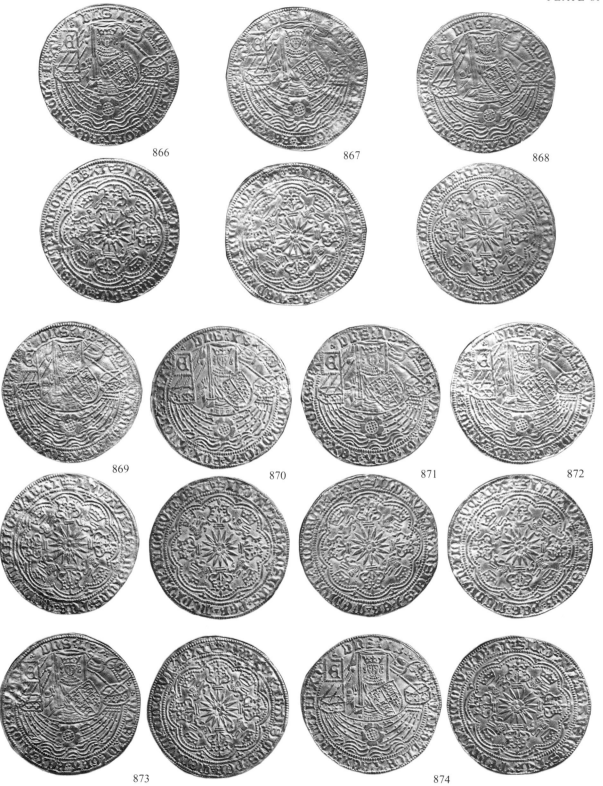

866

867

868

869

870

871

872

873

874

IMITATIONS OF RYALS OF EDWARD IV (*cont.*)

GROUP II (*mint of Gorinchem*) (*cont.*)

Class 3c (*cont.*)

875 Ryal

	Weight		
	g	*gr.*	*Die-axis*
	7.42	114.5	310°

I.m. none/crown.
Obv.: ED/·WΛRD·DI·GRΛ·REX·ΛNGL·S·FRΛN·/·DNS·IB·
Rev.:   same die as last coin, **874**.
Thompson Group II, Class 3c. Bt Baldwin 1964.

876 Ryal

	7.50	115.7	120°

I.m. none/crown.
Obv.: ED/WΛRD:DI·GRΛ·REX·ΛNGL·S·FRΛNΛ·/·DNS·I·B·
Letter **B** in waves below ship.
Rev.: IhΛ·ΛVT·TRΛNSIENS·PER·MEDIVM:ILLORVM·IBΛT
Probably Thompson Group II, Class 3c, but he knew of no coin of this type with **B** in the waves, and this attribution must, for the present, remain tentative. No provenance.

GROUP III (*mint of Culemborg*)

There are no specimens of this group in the Schneider collection.

GROUP IV (*the Ornate* Ɛ) (see p. 88 and Figure 1).

Class 1 (Ɛ without cross bar)

877 Ryal

	7.55	116.5	260°

I.m. none/crown.
Obv.: ΛD·/·WΛRD·DI·GRΛ·RΛX·ΛNGL·S·FRΛ·/·DNS·I·B·
Ɛs are Λs.
Rev.: IhΛ·ΛVT·TRΛNSIΛNS·PΛR·MΛDIVM:ILLORVM·IBΛT
Group IV, Class 1. Bt Spink 1971.

878 Ryal

	7.58	117.0	110°

I.m. none/crown.
Obv.: ΛD/WΛRD·DI·GRΛ·RΛX·ΛNGL Z·FRNΛ·/·DNS·IB·
Ɛs are Λs.
Rev.: IhΛ·ΛVT·TRΛNS·P·ΛR·MΛDIVM·ILLORVM·IBΛT·
Ɛs are Λs. This is Thompson's reverse die no. 19 (pl. A, 9) before the i.m. was altered to boar's head.
Group IV, Class 1. Bt Spink 1967.

Class 2

879 Ryal

	7.49	115.6	20°

I.m. none/crown.
Obv.: ED/WΛRD·DI·GRΛ·REX·ΛNGL·FRΛN/·DNS·IB·
Same die as next coin, **880**.
Rev.: IhƐ·ΛVT·TRΛNSIENS·PER·MEDIVM·ILLORV·IBΛT
Group IV, Class 2. Bt Baldwin 1968.

880 Ryal

	7.47	116.9	50°

I.m. none/crown.
Obv.: same die as last coin, **879**.
Rev.: IhƐ·ΛVT·TRΛNSIENS·PER·MEDIVM·ILLORV·IBΛT
Group IV, Class 2. Bt Spink 1958.

881 Ryal

	7.59	117.1	330°

I.m. none/crown.
Obv.: EDW/ΛRD DI·GRΛ·REX·ΛNGL S FRΛN·Ɛ·/·DNS·IB·
Note division of EDWΛRD after **W**.
Rev.: IhƐ·ΛVT·TRΛNSIENS·PER·MEDIVM·ILLORVM·IBΛT
Group IV, Class 2. Bt Spink 1964.

PLATE 82

875   876   877   878

879   880   881   882

883   884

Plate 82 (*cont.*)

Class 3 (Roman G)

882 Ryal
    7.57   116.9   170°

I.m. none/crown.
Obv.: 'ƐDW/ᛒRD·DI·GRᛒ·REX·ᛒNG.FRᛒ·/Ɛ·DNS·IB
        ƐDWᛒRD divided after W.
Rev.: ⚓IhƐ·ᛒVT·TRᛒNSIƐNS·PƐR·MƐDIVM·ILLORVM·IBᛒT
Group IV, Class 3; similar to Thompson pl. C, 9. No provenance.

883 Ryal
    7.44   114.8   270°

I.m. none/crown.
Obv.: ƐD/·VᛒRD·DI·GRᛒ·REX·ᛒNG·ET·FRᛒN·/·DNS·IB·
Rev.: ⚓IhƐ·ᛒVT·TRNSIƐNS·PƐR·MƐDIVM·ILLORVM·IBᛒT·
Group IV, Class 3; similar to Thompson pl. C, 9. Bt Baldwin 1967.

884 Ryal
    7.35   113.4   20°

I.m. none/crown.
Obv.: ƐD/WᛒRD·DI·GRᛒ·REX·ᛒNGL·S·FRᛒN·/·DNS·IB·
Rev.: ⚓IhƐ·ᛒVT·TRᛒNSIƐNS·PƐR·MƐDIVM·ILLORVM·IBᛒT
Group IV, Class 3; similar to Thompson pl. C, 9. Bt Spink 1965.

IMITATIONS OF RYALS OF EDWARD IV (*cont.*)

GROUP IV (*cont.*)

Class 3 (*cont.*)

885 Ryal				I.m. none/crown.
Weight				*Obv.*: ED/WARD:DI:GRA'IREX:ANGL':S:FRAN·/:DNS:IB:
g	*gr.*	*Die-axis*		*Rev.*: ✠IhꝐ·AVT:TRANSIENS:PER:MEDIVM:ILLORV:IBAT
7.48	115.5	220°		Group IV, Class 3; similar to Thompson pl. C, 9. Bt Spink 1967.

INFERIOR IMITATIONS OR FORGERIES

| 886 Ryal | | | | I.m. none/crown. |
| 6.84 | 105.6 | 210° | | *Obv.*: ED/WARD:·D:GRA:REX:ANGII Z FRAꝐ/:·DNS·I·K·: |

Ropes, 6/2. Ornaments on forecastle reduced to cross-hatching. Rose small and irregular. Face and other features generally crude.

Rev.: ✠INꝐ·AVT:TRASIE:NS:PER·:MEDIVM:ILORVM:IBAT

Sun has pellet in centre with rays. Nothing in the spandrels.
Bt Münzen und Medaillen, Basel, 1957.

887 Ryal				I.m. none/crown.
5.99	92.5	240°		*Obv.*: ED/WARD:DI·GRA·REX·ANGL:Z·FRANꝐ:/·DNS·I·B·
				Rev.: ✠IhꝐ·AVT·TRANSIENS·PER·MEDIVM·ILLORVM·IBAT

The dies are quite neatly made but the punches employed do not correspond with any regular fount. The gold has a very base appearance and corrosion on the high points suggests that the coin may have a core of base metal. Bt Spink 1967; ex Angers hoard.

888 Ryal				I.m. none/rose.
7.01	108.2	110°		*Obv.*: ƎD/VVARD:DI:GA[ ]REX:ANGL[?]:FRANꝐ·/·NS·I·B·
				Rev.: ☉IhS:AVTEM:TRANSIENS:PER·MEDIVM·ILORVM·IB:

Rather cruder than the last coin and the metal looks very base indeed. Bt Spink 1967; ex Angers hoard.

IMITATIONS OF RYALS OF ELIZABETH I (for prototype cf. **784**)

The first (**889**) is attributed to Marie of Brimeu, Princess of Chimay, striking at the mint of Gorinchem, see pp. 89–90.

| 889 Ryal | | | | I.m. Gothic A on reverse only. |
| 7.56 | 116.6 | 300° | | *Obv.*: ELIZABET:ANGL.MA:D:G/.P/Ꝑ.A.L./REGINA. |

ER monogram in flag.

Rev.: A.IhS:AVT.TRANSIENS.PER.MEDIV:ILLORVM.IBAT.N.

Additional N at end of legend.
Thompson 1941, no. 12, 08/ R7. Ex Lockett (English pt II) (1955).

| 890 Ryal | | | | I.m. Gothic A on reverse only. |
| 7.46 | 115.2 | 180° | | *Obv.*: ELIZAB:D:G:ANG:FR:ET.hI/B/REGINA· |

Trefoil after REGINA.

Rev.: .A.IhS:AVT:TRANSIENS.PER.MEDIV:ILLORVM.IBAT

Thompson 1941, foreign dies, no. 11, O7/R6. No provenance.

PLATE 83

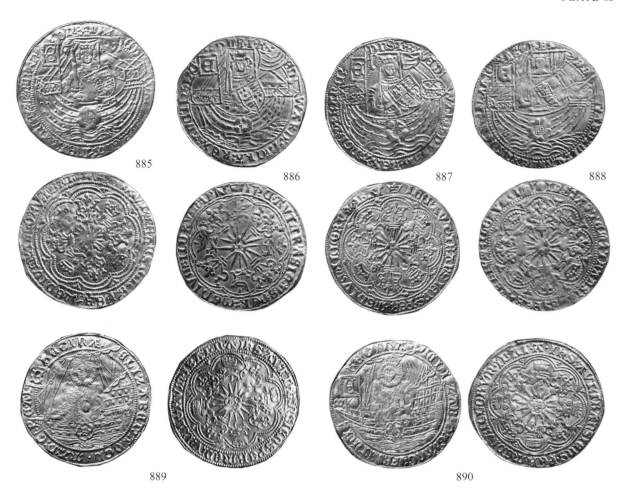

885

886

887

888

889

890

INDEX

This is primarily an index to the introductory chapters of this book. However, where appropriate, it includes references to coins in the catalogue section. In the case of coins relating to rulers, mints, or groupings other than denominations, this is done by indicating the serial number, or range of numbers, of the coins. In the case of denominations, the reference is to the number of first appearance, followed by a hyphen if it appears more than once. This index does not include references to hoards and finds, since those are listed alphabetically at the end of the Hoards and Finds chapter; nor does it include provenances noted in the catalogue or works of reference cited in the text, since those are listed alphabetically in the Provenances and Bibliography chapters respectively.

References to pages are in normal type; references to coin numbers in the catalogue are in bold type.

SYLLOGE OF COINS OF THE BRITISH ISLES

Published by the British Academy, except Nos. 8 and 34 published by the Trustees of the British Museum, and Nos. 16, 31, 33, 38, 43, 44, 46 and 47 published by Spink & Son Ltd.